The Old Testament

An Introduction to Its Literary, Historical, and Religious Traditions

The Old Testament

H. Keith Beebe
Occidental College

Dickenson Publishing Company, Inc.
Belmont, California

Library of Congress Catalog Card
Number: 77–121024
Printed in the United States of America

1 2 3 4 5 6 7 8 9 10 – 73 72 71 70

The Scripture quotations in this
publication are from the Revised Standard
Version of the Bible, copyrighted 1946
and 1952 by the Division of Christian
Education of the National Council of the
Churches of Christ in the U.S.A., and
used by permission.

Designed by Dale Smith

Contents

The Old Testament is more like a small library than a unified book. It contains the thoughts of men whose lives were separated by centuries, and who wrote under cultural conditions ranging from nomadic and agrarian simplicity to cosmopolitan complexity.

Since the Old Testament is like a library, the reader can achieve best results by using it as he would a library: he does not read from A to Z; he reads selectively. This magnificent collection must be used so that the reader earns the greatest comprehension with the most economical use of time and energy.

There are some quite boring passages in the Old Testament. Upon arriving at the genealogies in Genesis 5 and 10, for instance, one might be led to ask, "Where is this getting me?" And trying to read through the description of the Tabernacle in Exodus 35–40 might be so frustrating that the reader would be tempted to skip the important Holiness Code in Leviticus.

**A Chronological
Approach**

If a reader begins the Old Testament with Chapter I of Genesis he will be exposed to a sophisticated artistic style and religious thinking which in later chapters gives way to untutored literary form and simple thought. Considering the rule of science that forms are usually simple in their beginnings, becoming complex as they grow, a careful reader might well be puzzled by this reversal.

Reading the Old Testament can be confusing unless one comes to it with a clearly defined plan. One of the purposes of this book is to offer such a plan. The method followed in this study will be to explore the literary growth of the Old Testament documents in the order in which they were written, from their earliest expressions through to their final stages. We will not begin with Genesis 1, for example, inasmuch as that chapter was written near the midpoint of the Old Testament's growth. Careful use of this method will dispel confusion, even though most persons are not in the habit of skipping about in a book. The whole panorama of Israel's literature, history, and religion through its 1,200 years will become clear.

The Old Testament as Literature, as History, and as Religion

As we approach units of the Old Testament—for example, the book of Amos, or individual parts within the books of Samuel and Kings—our introduction to each unit will be an exposition of its literary characteristics and qualities. This means the reader will be familiarized with the organizing principles of each unit, its literary peculiarities and difficulties, and the way in which modern scholars have reconstructed the original plan when necessary.

Next the reader will be given a reconstruction of the historical conditions under which the literary unit was composed. Then, a discussion of religious implications will set forth the inevitable link between literary expression, historical conditions, and religious affirmation.

Psalms

Where possible, psalms typifying those of particular historical periods are described. Hebrew psalms are expressions of living religion, and they give in unadorned fashion a "feeling" for the religious attitudes of the communities from which they arose. The precision achieved in dating most literary units of the Old Testament is impossible with the psalms because the historical allusion in them is scanty. Some interpreters place the composition of the majority of psalms late in Israel's history; others put most of them in the period of the monarchies of Israel and Judah.

Since dating the psalms has been difficult, some scholars have forsaken that task for the simpler one of classifying the psalms according to types. This technique is helpful, but it does not substitute for the honest effort of putting these expressions of religious experience and practice into historical perspective. Wherever literary form, psalm type, vocabulary, and religious terms permit, we estimate the particular age in which a psalm was composed. Such dating is tentative, so the reader must be prepared to make his own evaluations.

Following the three-stepped method of literary inspection, understanding historical conditions, and observing religious beliefs and practices, the reader will be enabled to conduct his own study founded on empirical evidence. This procedure may provide the experience of a full appreciation of the literary and historical significance, and the religious grandeur, of these truly great books.

The Chapters of This Book The Old Testament's influence on many literary, artistic, musical, historical, and religious works in Western civilization is discussed in Chapter I. In Chapter II archaeology, geography, and climate in Palestine show how important empirical data are in making accurate interpretations of the Old Testament.

Composition of the Old Testament, as the reader will soon become aware, was not evenly distributed over the 1,200 years it was being formed. Writings cluster about cultural crises in the life of the Hebrew people. At the founding of the nation poetry, history, law, and epic dominated the literary field. These literary forms, the historical conditions out of which they arose, and the religious affirmations expressed in them are reported in Chapters III through VIII. These chapters cover the years between the Age of the Patriarchs and 922 B.C.

Chapter IX describes the historical events from the dissolution of the United Monarchy to the fall of Jerusalem. It deals with the years between 922 and 587 B.C.

The literary and religious movement known as prophecy engaged some of the finest minds among the Israelites, and the story unfolds in Chapter X. That movement spans the years 850 to about 700 B.C.

The years from 640 to 540 B.C. were marked by critical social, political, and religious upheavals. The nation of Judah ceased to exist. Prophecy, the writing of history, and juridical processes went through such changes that entirely new understanding of the nature of Israel as a community emerged. This story is reported in Chapters XI and XII.

Chapter XIII attempts to reconstruct the blurred picture of the Babylonian Jews' return to Palestine and their efforts to reconstitute themselves a nation. These are the years between 540 and 400 B.C.

Writings of the sages of Israel engage our attention in Chapter XIV. In that chapter we discover the form and content of wisdom and related literature. Exact years cannot be assigned to the growth of this literary movement, but most of it occurred between 600 and 150 B.C.

Chapter XV rounds out our literary, historical, and religious study as the Old Testament age comes to a close. These are the years between 350 and 63 B.C.

The Core Readings   Suggestions for use of the Core Readings are in order at this point. These may be used in either of two ways. Readers who like to explore the terrain on their own may wish to study the Core Readings assigned in each chapter before reading the chapter itself. Those who want the author's interpretations before reading the Old Testament may do the core reading after having studied the chapter. Either approach is acceptable, although the author believes that the former is the better. One must not expect to profit from reading this book without reading the Old Testament. Copious references are given so that readers have ample directions for becoming personally involved in the great Book itself.

Twenty years teaching the Bible — some of which were spent living in the Near East, excavating its venerable cities, and traveling through that ancient land — have been the stimulation for preparing this book. The wise counsel and critical suggestions of several colleagues, however, have stretched my imagination and sharpened my eye in writing this introduction to Old Testament traditions. Outstandingly helpful have been Professors John L. Anderson of Lewis and Clark College, William A. Beardslee of Emory University, C. Milo Connick of Whittier College, Ronald Hamowy of Stanford University, E. Willard Hamrick of Wake Forest College, A. Leland Jamison of Syracuse University, J. Kenneth Kuntz of the University of Iowa, and Gene M. Tucker of Duke University.

Mrs. Nancy Farris typed the manuscript and revisions of the typescript. Mr. Robert Wells rescued many sentences and paragraphs from the doldrums. Mr. Jack Reid's hawk-eyes relentlessly spotted flaws in format, structure, and makeup. Mr. Basil C. Wood has executed maps, time charts, and drawings with sensitive care. Mr. Richard Trudgen, Editor-in-Chief of Dickenson Publishing Company, has been patience personified and a perennial source of enthusiasm. To these many persons, and especially to my long-suffering and vacationless family, I offer my gratitude.

Los Angeles, California H. Keith Beebe

The Old Testament

An Introduction to Its Literary, Historical, and Religious Traditions

**Abiding Uses
of an Ancient
Book**

Many parts of the Old Testament were ancient when Rome was founded and when Socrates wandered over the cobbled paths of Athens. When Jesus of Nazareth lived the entire book as we know it had been written, and most of it had been accepted as supremely authoritative.

In an age of spacecraft and computers one might suspect that so old a book, a book which describes people living in tents or mud-brick houses and believing the earth was flat under an arched canopy, would be of antiquarian interest only—hardly worth one's serious study in this sophisticated time. And certainly one will be disappointed if he looks to the Old Testament for accuracy in astronomy, geology, or anthropology. But one who takes the humanistic approach to the Old Testament will find religious qualities and ethical insight which are strikingly applicable to the modern world.

**The Old Testament
and the Arts**

Besides its religious impact, the Old Testament has been the inspiration for some of the finest literary achievements of Western civilization. Many masters of poetry and prose have drawn deeply from the well of Old Testament themes and stories. John Keats, for instance, penned his *Ode to a Nightingale* likening the mysterious song of the philomel to the beating in the heart of Ruth who abandoned her Moabite homeland to abide with her mother-in-law in a new land.

> *The self-same song that found a path*
> *Through the sad heart of Ruth, when,*
> *sick for home,*
> *She stood in tears amid the alien corn.*

Milton plunged into Old Testament lore for themes and allusions in his famous *Paradise Lost*. In five short lines he mentions Israel's plundering of Egyptians on their last night in captivity, Aaron's golden calf at Mt. Sinai, rebellious king Jeroboam, that king's defiant cult shrines, and idols placed in those shrines.

> *. . . Nor did Israel scape*
> *Th' infection when thir borrowed Gold compos'd*
> *The Calf in Oreb: and the Rebel King*
> *Doubl'd that sin in Bethel and in Dan,*
> *Lik'ning his Maker to the Grazed Ox. . . .*

Thomas Mann wrote his monumental *Joseph and His Brothers, Joseph in Egypt,* and *Joseph the Provider* inspired by the legend of Joseph in the book of Genesis. Contemporary men of letters have found the Old Testament a reservoir of literary themes and symbols too. One of the themes of William Faulkner's *Absalom, Absalom!,* for instance, is the story of the relationship between father and son from 2 Samuel 13–18. Through his choice of title, Faulkner conveys to his reader that his serious social concerns are related to, and perhaps based upon, the convictions of an Old Testament writer.

In his novel *East of Eden,* John Steinbeck, like Faulkner a recipient of the Nobel Prize for literature, drew significant thematic material from the Old Testament story of Cain and Abel. A reader who has more than a casual acquaintance with the Old Testament will find explicit biblical allusions in *East of Eden* which undergird the moral implications of the author's story.

Pulitzer Prize winner Robert Penn Warren draws upon several Old Testament passages in his novel *All The King's Men.* A surface reading of this work may miss these biblical references, but a reader who knows the Old Testament can see how Warren has used this ancient source in imaginative and creative ways.[1]

Michelangelo and the Vulgate

Much of the great art of Western civilization cannot be appreciated fully without a knowledge of the Old Testament. Michelangelo's sculpture of Moses, for example, can produce powerful emotions in the viewer. The artist has portrayed a man whose leadership is

[1]For a treatment of Robert Penn Warren's use of the Bible see H. Keith Beebe, "Biblical Motifs in *All The King's Men,*" Journal of Bible and Religion, XXX, No. 2 (1962), pp. 123–30.

Michelangelo's "Moses" in the Church of San Pietro in Vincoli, Rome.

indisputable, but whose wrath may burst out in terrifying suddenness; the seated Moses is at once attentive and introspective; he appears to be gazing across vast spaces as though looking into Canaan from Mt. Nebo, or staring fascinated by the horizon of his own imagination. The impact of this dramatic marble is so profound that the sensitive person may not focus his attention on the two curious horns on Moses' head. These horns can be understood only in the context of Old Testament literature. St. Jerome, in translating Exodus 34:29–30 into Latin (the Vulgate), rendered the Hebrew word *qaran* as "horned." It is not surprising that Jerome made this mistake, since this was the ordinary meaning of the word (cf. Psalm 69:31). Of course, *qaran* as used in the story of Moses really means "to shine," or "to emit rays," and thus the proper understanding of the text is "that the skin of his face [Moses'] shone because he had been talking to God" (Exod. 34:29). Michelangelo and other Renaissance artists knew the Bible through the Vulgate, and consequently in their painting and sculpture represented Moses with horns.

Mendelssohn's oratorio *Elijah* carries a special quality and significance for him who knows the story of conflict, suffering, and triumph in that prophet's life. Ernest Bloch's magnificent setting of the Jewish *Sacred Service* moves a listener profoundly when he understands and appreciates the Temple service described in the Old Testament's narratives and memorialized in the Psalms.

Old Testament Comparisons With Classical Literature

The serious reader may make fascinating comparisons and contrasts between the Old Testament and classical literature. The world of Homer's Odyssey, of gods and heroes, tribes and chieftans, personal valor and cunning deceit, is illuminated when read in contrast with Old Testament literature. Even though it has not been fully established that the people of the Old Testament and the people of Homer's epic had a common background, there are good reasons why the two great works should be read conjunctively.

Odysseus and Abraham. Erich Auerbach's essay "Odysseus' Scar" contrasts the Old Testament's and the Odyssey's representation of reality.[2] Auerbach contrasts two scenes, the one of Odysseus' return home after his years away at the Trojan War, and the other of Abraham's attempted sacrifice of his son Isaac. Odysseus, who kept his identity secret when he arrived at his home island, was received hospitably by his wife Penelope, and was accorded the rights of any weary traveler as the aged servingwoman Euryclea washed his feet. This entire scene in the Odyssey is narrated in leisurely fashion; Homer leaves out no detail, even telling the reader that it was with his right hand that Odysseus took the old woman by the throat to keep her from speaking when she recognized him from the scar on his thigh. This intensely dramatic scene is interrupted by more than seventy verses describing the hunt in which Odysseus received his wound from a boar. While reading about the boar hunt, one is thoroughly engrossed in the idyllic picture with its wealth of detail. Homer leaves nothing to imagination: even the characters' psychological processes are described in detail.

[2] Erich Auerbach, *Mimesis: The Representation of Reality in Western Literature*, trans. W. Trask (Garden City, N.Y.: Doubleday & Co., Anchor 107, 1957), ch. 1.

In contrast is the style of the writer describing Abraham's attempted sacrifice of Isaac (Gen. 22:1–14). He begins, "After these things God tested Abraham, and said to him, 'Abraham!' And he said, 'Here am I.'" After reading Homer, this opening is startling. We are not told where the two speakers are. The reader knows they are not usually found together, and that God has entered the human domain from some unknown height or depth. In contrast with mentions of the god Zeus, who may be described by the writer as returning from a feast with the Ethiopians, or as just concluding a council with the gods, we are told nothing of God's whereabouts. We are not informed of God's reasons for testing Abraham. This God has no fixed form, no local habitation, no cohorts as did the more visible gods of the neighboring peoples. When we look at the other person in the dialogue we learn no more of Abraham's whereabouts than we do of God's. Whether he is in a house, in a tent, out of doors, or riding on a donkey, remains unexpressed. Abraham's answer means, in Hebrew, "Behold me," and indicates no geographic orientation but rather a moral position in respect to God. The physical relation of the two speakers is left to the imagination. God appears, but not in bodily form. Abraham may be standing erect, or he may be prostrate, or kneeling, or bowing with outstretched arms. Details are omitted, but may be supplied by the reader. Abraham's answer, "Behold me," is a response implying obedience and readiness, not physical condition.

The story unfolds without recourse to episodes or detailed description of landscape. A journey is being made, but there is no account of it. Members of Abraham's party, the age, stature, and attitude of Isaac, and the object of the journey, are left in darkness. As with the description of physical details, so is it with the thoughts of the characters. What speech takes place between God and Abraham, and between Abraham and Isaac, does more to indicate thoughts which remain unexpressed than to clarify the thought and feelings of the participants.

In Homer a full description of conditions and events is given with time and place and persons fully described. In Genesis only enough information is given to carry the narrative. Decisive points are emphasized, but that which falls between these points is obscure. Homer's characters are always "the foreground" where the present is stressed. The Old Testament's characters possess a "background" in which depth of time, fate, and consciousness envelop them. Despite the complex grammatical structure of Homer's poems the human beings depicted through his medium are comparatively simple. They take great pleasure in their physical existence: hunts, banquets, athletic contests, battles, passionate arguments, adventures, and perils. Homer's poem conceals nothing, and contains no mysterious teachings or double meaning. Attempts to allegorize it have ended in utter failure. The Old Testament writer, on the other hand, presents his characters less distinctly as to detail, but they are infinitely more complex. The absence of detail allows far wider and deeper interpretation of the moral demands placed upon them. Whereas the effect of Homer's style is to guide the reader in forgetting his own reality for a while in favor of the adventures of his heroes, that of the Old Testament writer "seeks to overcome our reality: we are to fit our own life into its world, feel ourselves to be elements in its structure of universal history."[3]

The Old Testament and History

The Old Testament deals with nations and peoples from Egypt eastward to Persia and northward to Anatolia, who were ancient before the classical period began. The United Hebrew Monarchy flourished between 1000 and 922 B.C., when Greece was still undeveloped and dominated by small cities and tribal groups. When Greece achieved her brilliant successes in tragic literature, architecture, and philosophy, Israel had already passed into her decline.

"The Father of History"

The Greek Herodotus stands traditionally as the "father of history." He wrote his splendid books in those fateful years between 480 and 425 B.C. when Persian dominance of the eastern Mediterranean was crumbling and Greek power was mounting. A reading of the historical sections of the Old Testament, however, shows that Herodotus came relatively late, and that the title "father of history" may more rightfully belong to the unnamed but brilliant interpreter of national events who lived during the reign of Solomon (960–922 B.C.). It is amazing how much history is packed into the short document 2 Samuel 9–20. The basic ingredients of the writing of history are there: attention to factual detail, relation of cause to effect, the concatenation of events stemming from a single cause, the power of individuals to affect the destiny of nations, and penetrating suggestions as to motivation in human lives.

Although Israel was one of the smallest nations in that part of the Mediterranean, she produced historical literature superior to that of any of her neighbors! The Old Testament, reporting conditions and events older than those we know as classical history, is an historical document around which one may organize the complex histories of the Near Eastern nations from the Persian Gulf to the

[3]*Ibid.*, p. 12.

Nile River, during the centuries from about 2000 B.C. to the conquests by Alexander the Great.

The Old Testament and Religion

Besides being a sourcebook of ancient history and a work of art in itself, the Old Testament is, of course, a book of religion, and it most definitely has religious applications to the modern world. Despite theoretical reconstructions of the beginnings of the world, most persons are still concerned about creation, if not in terms of natural explanation, at least in terms of its significance for themselves and their place in things. The Old Testament treats this question with artistic subtlety.[4]

Amos' insistence that Israel's God was God equally of the Ethiopians, the Philistines, and the Syrians is an emphasis needed in this world so beset by nationalistic pride, religious divisions, and economic differences. The questions of a man's relationship to the Power or powers which he conceives as having control over his destiny were asked and commented on by Job and Ecclesiastes in such a manner as to be provocative today. The poetic responses of psalmists to crises in personal and national experience have been appreciated for longer than two thousand years. Not every psalm is applicable to modern life, but many evoke a response in readers which no other literature has done as well.

Some Outdated Concepts. Needless to say, not all the ideas of the Old Testament have a twentieth century applicability. The view of the earth as the center of the cosmos, the image of the heavens as a vast canopy through which the lights of heaven glow, the image of God as dwelling in regal splendor above this canopy, the earth as set upon pillars with roaring waters tossing about beneath, have all been rendered false by science. Religious and civil laws applicable to semi-nomadic, agrarian, and simple commercial societies can only by the grossest perversions of logic be made applicable to a technological civilization. Images of God in men's minds based on patterns of tribal chieftains or kingships are no longer as useful to the everyday world as they may have been several centuries ago.

The Old Testament and Modern Scholars. Nevertheless, the true insights of the Bible have challenged some of the finest scholars of the twentieth century to treat the religious affirmations of that book

[4] See Claus Westermann, "God and His Creation," *Union Seminary Quarterly Review,* XVIII (1963), pp. 197–210.

as the starting point of their own appraisals of the human condition. Such scholars may not always agree in their interpretations of Old Testament religion, but their comments are never trivial. Walther Eichrodt finds the Old Testament illuminated best when interpreted in the light of the ancient understanding of covenant. He has expressed the viewpoint that this central concept formed the basis of community among the Israelites and defined the basis of their relationship to God.[5] H. H. Rowley finds a fundamental unity in the books of the Bible even though they express cultural conditions and religious beliefs separated by over a thousand years. The Bible, in his opinion, is a record of the progressive revelation of God to and through the people of Israel.[6] Robert H. Pfeiffer makes yet another emphasis, holding that the Old Testament, being "the record of man's groping after God," provides varied and multiple ways of dealing with this basic human aspiration. He claims that it is correct to imagine the Bible as a library of books all devoted to the same theme but handling that theme in different ways.[7]

It can be seen that religious problems in the Old Testament are usually more difficult to solve than are literary or historical problems. But it is doubtful that satisfactory solutions to religious problems can be proposed without sufficient basic work in the literature and history of the Old Testament.

Language, Text, and Canon   Some comments about the original language, the text, and how the Old Testament became sacred will help to establish additional modern perspectives on this ancient book.

The Old Testament was written originally in Hebrew except for a few passages in Aramaic.[8] Some of the directness, vitality, and simplicity of the Hebrew language is lost in translation. Translators' attempts to render Hebrew idioms in English seldom have been entirely successful, although Moffatt's translation is a splendid achievement.[9] Professor Moffatt tried to improve the Hebrew. When Samson's Philistine companions at his marriage gave him the answer to the riddle "From the eater came something to eat, / from the strong came something sweet" (Judg. 14:14), he accused

---

[5] Walther Eichrodt, *Theology of the Old Testament*, trans. J. A. Baker (Philadelphia: The Westminster Press, 1961).
[6] H. H. Rowley, *The Unity of the Bible* (Philadelphia: The Westminster Press, 1953).
[7] Robert H. Pfeiffer, *Religion in the Old Testament*, ed. Charles Conrad Forman (New York: Harper & Brothers, 1961).
[8] Ezra 4:8–6:18, 7:12–26, Jeremiah 10:11, Daniel 2:4–7:28.
[9] James Moffatt, *The Bible: A New Translation* (New York: Harper & Brothers, 1922).

them, "Had you not used my heifer for your plough / you never would have guessed my riddle now" (Judg. 14:18). The closest approximation to the Hebrew is, perhaps, "If you had not plowed with my heifer, / you would not have found out my riddle."[10] Yet, Professor Moffatt's rendition is his effort to show the rhyme of the doublet, an *unusual* device in Hebrew poetry.

Biblical Hebrew

Biblical Hebrew has several characteristics shared by most Semitic languages. First, words are usually formed of three consonants, whose general meaning is indicated by this "root." Second, there are no written vowels: vowel sounds have to be supplied by the speaker in order to indicate the precise meaning of the word in the speaker's mind. KTB means "writing" in the general sense, KaTaB means "he wrote," KoTeB means "writer," KaTuB means "written," and so forth. Third, biblical Hebrew avoided forming compound words. Fourth, sentence structure is amazingly simple.

Three Types of Words. Biblical Hebrew has three types of words which when put together provide a meaningful sentence: nouns, verbs, and particles which indicate the relationship between nouns and verbs. The verb is the dominant element in Hebrew, so that action infuses the language. Sentence order is normally predicate, subject, object, and other words employed to give more specific meaning. Adjectives usually follow nouns. Adverbs are rare in Hebrew.

The Massoretic Vowel System

Since there were no vowels in the Hebrew alphabet, the vowels being supplied by the speaker or the reader, some system of denoting them had to be developed once Hebrew was no longer a living language. Aramaic replaced Hebrew as the language of Palestine after 586 B.C., and classical Hebrew served as the language of religious learning and cult, somewhat like Latin in the Roman Catholic Church today. The Massoretes, a group of medieval Jewish scholars, developed a system of vowel signs to preserve the pronunciation of Old Testament Hebrew. Their work was probably completed around 800 A.D., and the Old Testament used by modern scholars is called the Massoretic Text. The Massoretic vowel system is responsible for many difficult readings in the original Hebrew because by the time the Massoretes had completed their work many words had lost their original sounds and their meaning changed. Nevertheless, textual critics of the Old Testament usually commend the Massoretic scholars for their amazing accuracy in the preparation of the Massoretic Text.

[10] Revised Standard Version (New York: Thomas Nelson and Sons, 1952). All quotations are from this version unless otherwise specified.

This brief reference to the Hebrew language may help one appreciate some linguistic aspects of the Old Testament which are profoundly different from our own language. The Old Testament often provides a general impression of an object without supplying precise data. After reading the story of Noah's ark (Gen. 6:14–16) it might dawn on one that he is unable to draw a picture of the ark from the description of it. In fact, it is not a description at all. It is a report on the construction of the ark. What interested the Israelites was how the ark came to be made. The overall dimensions and the materials are given, but not a single word tells the color, the texture, the paneling, or where the rooms were placed. The reader of Genesis makes the acquaintance of Adam and Cain and Abel and Noah, but one cannot sketch these men from what one has been told. Hebrew writers recounted their impression of the human figure: Joseph, Saul, David, and Absalom were handsome, but the narrators did not attempt elaborate descriptions of their heroes. The Hebrew language lent itself to giving quick impressions of an object.[11]

No original text of the Old Testament exists. Since this is the case one may rightly question the accuracy of the Hebrew text from which translations are made. Before the invention of the printing press all copies of the Old Testament were made by hand, and errors crept onto the page because of a scribe's carelessness, or his inability to read a word in a worn manuscript, or because he deliberately changed a word or phrase if he failed to agree with it or to understand the text. The Massoretes were scholars who did their best to keep the text from scribal corruption and their name derives from the word *massorah,* which means "tradition." One of their duties was to add clarifying notes to the text so that errors would be reduced. In addition to inventing the scheme for sounding vowels in the consonantal text of the Old Testament, they standardized the spelling of words and divided the Old Testament into convenient units for public reading.

Textual Criticism.   Despite such precautions scribes made errors, and one of the scholarly tasks of modern Old Testament study is called *textual criticism.* In this work men who know Hebrew and many other ancient languages perfectly spend their professional lives seeking to recover a more accurate text of the Hebrew Old Testament. This work is possible because there existed in ancient times several copies of the Old Testament in Hebrew, as well as

[11] See "Hebrew Language," in George A. Buttrick, ed. *The Interpreter's Dictionary of the Bible,* E–J (New York: Abingdon Press, 1962), p. 558. Cited as *IDB* henceforth. An interesting introduction to Hebrew is given in Edward Horowitz, *How the Hebrew Language Grew* (New York: Jewish Education Committee Press, 1960).

in Greek, Syriac, and Latin. Discoveries of scrolls in caves at Wadi Qumran and in other caves near the Dead Sea since 1947 have given scholars large amounts of material for making accurate comparisons with the Massoretic Text of the Old Testament. Jews who lived in Alexandria, Egypt, translated the Old Testament into Greek for those Jews who had lost their use of Hebrew. The work of translation probably began about 250 B.C. and continued for several generations. This version of the Old Testament is the *Septuagint,* a name derived from an historical romance recorded by a certain Aristeas. Ptolemy II Philadelphus, who ruled Egypt from 285 to 246 B.C., wished to complete his famous Alexandrian library by including the Jewish Torah. His appeal to the high priest in Jerusalem for wise men who would translate the Hebrew Bible into Greek brought to Egypt seventy-two elders. They worked without interruption for seventy-two days. At the end of this time the whole of the Old Testament had been translated. When the scribes read it to Ptolemy II, he was so greatly moved that he ordered reverent care of the book, and sent the seventy-two elders home to Jerusalem with rich presents.

Despite the fanciful story of the Septuagint's origins, its use in scholarly study of the Old Testament is inestimable. It preserves a translation of the Old Testament which is at least eight centuries older than the Hebrew text standardized by the Massoretes. This provides an excellent check upon the Massoretic Text, and many scribal errors have been corrected by comparison with the LXX.[12] The following passage gives an example of the way in which textual comparison is made in order to discover the most accurate Old Testament reading. The text is 1 Samuel 1:22–23.

MT	LXX	Qumran Cave 4
But Hannah did not go up, for she said to her husband, "As soon as the child is weaned, I will bring him, that he may appear in the presence of the Lord, and abide there forever." Elkanah her husband said to her, "Do what seems best to you. . . ."	But Hannah did not go up *with him,* for she said unto her husband, "I will not go up until the child goes up when I have weaned him and he shall appear before the Lord and abide there forever." *And* Elkanah her husband said unto her, "Do what seems best to you. . . ."	But Hannah did not go up with him, for she said to her husband, "I will not go up until the child goes up when I have weaned him that he may appear before the Lord forever. *And I shall give him for a Nazirite forever, all the days of his life."* And Elkanah her husband said unto her, "Do what seems best to you. . . ."[13]

[12] This is the usual abbreviation for Septuagint. MT is the abbreviation for the Massoretic Text.

[13] Frank M. Cross, Jr., "The Scrolls and the Old Testament," *The Christian Century* (August 10, 1955), p. 921. Reprinted by permission of the publisher. See Numbers 6 for description of a Nazirite.

The Samuel Manuscript from Qumran Cave 4 seems to be the most accurate text here. Samuel throughout his career did seem to live as a Nazirite. Close comparison, such as this, indicates that sometimes the MT gives the most accurate reading, sometimes the LXX does, and sometimes the Qumran Scrolls do.

There are other versions of the Old Testament which scholars use in order to restore the text's accuracy. The Samaritan Pentateuch is a copy of the first five books of the Old Testament which may be as old as the LXX. Some scholars have estimated that there are six thousand variants from the MT in the Abisha Scroll of the Samaritan Pentateuch which is in possession of the Samaritan community in Nablus today.[14] There are also Aramaic Targumim which were oral paraphrases of the Old Testament rendered by scribes to synagogue congregations whose language was Aramaic rather than Hebrew. These oral recitations were often elaborate and became fixed by their frequent repetition. They were then put into writing and now serve as a basis for comparative study of the Old Testament text. Another excellent source for studying the text of the Old Testament is the Latin Vulgate. St. Jerome completed his great translation in 384 A.D., after learning Hebrew from scribes in Jerusalem. Thus, his work depended upon manuscripts older by four hundred years than the ones finally formalized by the Massoretes. Modern students of the Old Testament are recipients of the dedicated labor of brilliant linguists whose patient collation of ancient manuscripts has provided the most accurate Old Testament text available.

From these corrected Hebrew texts many English translations have been made, and comparison of the translations becomes profitable labor. *The Revised Standard Version*[15] is a fine translation prepared by a committee of American scholars. The word "version" indicates that a group of scholars joined together under the auspices of an authoritative body to do the work of translation. The great *King James Version* of 1611 was done under an appointment by James I.[16] "Translations" are usually the work of one person as in the case of James Moffatt's *The Bible: A New Translation*,[17] or of a small group, as in the case of Smith and Goodspeed, *The Complete Bible, An American Translation*.[18] *The Holy Scriptures:*

[14] "Samaritan Pentateuch," *IDB*, R–Z, p. 190.
[15] New York: Thomas Nelson & Sons, 1952, or *Oxford Annotated Bible*, (New York: Oxford University Press, 1962).
[16] See the preface to the Revised Standard Version.
[17] New York: Harper & Brothers, 1922.
[18] J. M. Powis Smith and Edgar J. Goodspeed. Chicago: University of Chicago Press, 1939.

A New Translation[19] is an excellent work by Jewish scholars. Roman Catholics may find the Douay Version of 1610 to their liking although *The Jerusalem Bible* is a modern version.[20]

Ancient religions taught that gods communicated intelligibly with men. The Old Testament cites the usual methods by which such contact took place: by dreams or visions, by Urim and Thummim (priestly oracles), and by prophets (1 Sam. 28:6). It is probable that the idea of sacred scripture had its roots in prophetic utterances because what the prophet spoke constituted the words of God. But several centuries passed before any *prophetic writings* were believed to be literally the word of God. The idea of divine revelation as given through certain special men was formulated into doctrine, however, when the book of Deuteronomy was canonized. The discovery of "the book of the law" is related in 2 Kings 22 and 23, and there is no question that the prophetess Hulda, King Josiah, and the people regarded the book as sacred. "The book of the law" was probably chapters 12 through 26 of Deuteronomy, and this was the first document to be canonized as sacred scripture.

"Canonization."   What does canonized mean? "Canon," derived from the Greek word *kanon,* was originally a Semitic word *qanu* meaning "reed." It was a unit of measurement in the construction trade, and through usage the word came to mean in a figurative sense something firm and straight like a reed. Metaphorically the word means a rule or standard. Thus, the book of Deuteronomy was the standard for religious and social behavior.

The Torah.   In subsequent generations, Judaism gave sacred status to the first five books of the Old Testament when the three epic narratives[21] and the ancient laws had been formulated into a single work and the scroll of Deuteronomy associated with them. The scrolls with the names Genesis, Exodus, Leviticus, Numbers, and Deuteronomy, namely the *Torah,* meaning "law," "teaching," or "guidance," became "canon" about 400 B.C. After canonization the Torah was read regularly in synagogues, and successfully resisted any efforts to add to or to detract from its contents.

The Prophets.   Since the Torah had become sacred, there was no difficulty in crediting the historical books with the same status two

[19] New York: Jewish Publication Society of America, 1917, reprinted 1958.
[20] General Edition, Alexander Jones (Garden City, N.Y.: Doubleday & Co., 1966).
[21] J, E, and P, which will be studied later.

hundred years later. The Jews honored the books of Samuel and Kings for their historical value, and additions of old traditions and reinterpretations were constantly made to the historical books, including Joshua and Judges. The connections of these historical books with prophetic figures such as Samuel, Elijah and Elisha gave them additional authority. It was an easy step to canonize them by 250 B.C. Probably the most popular books among post-exilic Jews were those of the prophets. The number of glosses and additions to these books between 500 and 200 B.C. attest this popularity, and by 200 B.C. the prophetic writings were considered sacred.

The Writings. The final group of scrolls to be canonized was the Writings. Most scholars believe this occurred at the Council of Jamnia, under the leadership of Rabbi ben Zakkai about 90 A.D. The three major groupings of Hebrew sacred scripture, the Torah, the Prophets, and the Writings, were fixed forever, and no change has been made from that day to this.[22]

[22]Torah: Genesis, Exodus, Leviticus, Numbers, Deuteronomy; Prophets: former prophets are Joshua, Judges, Samuel, and Kings; latter prophets are Isaiah, Jeremiah, Ezekiel, and the Twelve (Hosea, Joel, Amos, Obabiah, Jonah, Micah, Nahum, Habakkuk, Zephaniah, Haggai, Zechariah, Malachi); Writings: Ruth, Chronicles, Ezra, Nehemiah, Esther, Job, Psalms, Proverbs, Ecclesiastes, Song of Solomon, Lamentations, and Daniel. Judaism refers to the Old Testament as TaNaK, a word created to refer to the whole of the Old Testament in its three major divisions: T = Torah or Law, N = Neviim or Prophets and K = Kethuviim or Writings; the vowel "a" makes it a pronounceable word. For further reading see "Canon of the Old Testament," *IDB*, A–D, 498–520.

▌▌

**Perspective on
Palestine**

The intellectual tools for solving religious problems found in the
Old Testament have been forged of deep curiosity, systematic
literary and historical study, and respect for human reason. More
recently scientific investigation of human artifacts has been successfully applied to the Old Testament so that scholars in the last
fifty years have produced volumes of factual information related to
the Bible. The study of ancient languages, such as Ugaritic, Akkadian, and Hittite, has produced fascinating insights into the
language of the Old Testament. Historical evidence long hidden in
the earth has been uncovered so that fuller and more accurate interpretations of the people of the Bible is possible.

**Archaeology in
Palestine**

The discovery of clay tablets at ancient Ugarit, present day Ras
Shamrah near Latakia in Syria, has shown that many biblical poems
were borrowed from Canaanite literature. In a long poem about
Baal and Anath, god and goddess in the Canaanite pantheon,
appears the stanza

> *Now thine enemy, O Baal*
> *Now thine enemy wilt thou smite,*
> *Now wilt thou cut off thine adversary.*[1]

The author of Psalm 92:9 borrowed the thought and style of the
earlier poem, using it as follows:

> *For, lo, thy enemies, O Lord*
> *for, lo, they enemies shall perish;*
> *all evildoers shall be scattered.*

[1] James B. Pritchard, ed., *Ancient Near Eastern Texts Relating to the Old Testament*
(rev. ed.; Princeton, N.J.: Princeton University Press, 1955), p. 136. Reprinted by
permission of Princeton University Press.

Recent excavations in Jerusalem have shown conclusively that buildings in that ancient city, constructed by a Canaanite clan known as Jebusites between 1500 and 1000 B.C., were far larger and heavier than those subsequently built during the reign of David (1000–962 B.C.) on the same site.[2]

The Mesha Stone further illustrates how archaeological discoveries have clarified history in the Old Testament. Mesha, King of Moab, was mentioned in 2 Kings 3:4 on the occasion of an Israelite-Judean-Edomite coalition in a war waged against Moab. Mesha had been a vassal of Omri and Ahab, kings of Israel, paying annually a tax in sheep and wool. When Jehoram, Ahab's son, became king of Israel in 849 B.C., Mesha rebelled against Jehoram, and Israel's king set out to bring his vassal into line. The account in 1 Kings 3 implies that Jehoram was successful in his efforts to subdue Mesha, but the Mesha Stone gives a different impression. In it Moab's king reported that he captured the territory of Ataroth and Nebo, both under Israelite political and military control. He also drove Israel's army from Jahaz and subsequently used Israelite captives to build a highway in the Arnon Valley. Although the biblical text reported that "there came a great wrath upon Israel; and they withdrew from him [Mesha] and returned to their own land" (2 Kings 3:27), it does not report that Mesha's rebellion was successful. But Mesha wrote, "I reigned [*in peace*] over the hundred towns which I had added to the land."[3] On the other hand, the report in 2 Kings 3 and the report on the Mesha Stone may not refer to the same historical event. If that is the case, the Mesha Stone gives evidence of another war between Israel and Moab and thus supplements the incomplete biblical narrative.

In some cases archaeological discoveries confirm biblical reports. In Jerusalem excavations demonstrate that a terrific destruction of city walls took place about 600 B.C., and the report in 2 Kings 25:10 that the Babylonian armies "broke down the walls around Jerusalem" shows that the historical narrative was accurate, even though subdued.[4] In other cases archaeologists have corrected inaccurate information for a clearer understanding of biblical history. Joshua 8 reports the capture of Ai by Israelite troops in an attack which followed the fall of Jericho. Excavations by Judith Marquet-Krause at Et-Tell, a mound not far from ancient Bethel, shows no

[2] Kathleen M. Kenyon, "Excavations in Jerusalem, 1962," *Palestine Exploration Quarterly* (January–June 1963), p. 10.
[3] Pritchard, *Ancient Near Eastern Texts,* p. 321.
[4] Kathleen M. Kenyon, "Excavations in Jerusalem, 1961," *Palestine Exploration Quarterly* (January–June 1962), pp. 89 ff.

occupation of that site between 2200 and about 1200 B.C. Therefore the site known as Ai was in ruins when the Israelite forces, according to historical deductions from the biblical narrative, were involved in the conquest of Canaanite cities. Excavations in 1964, 1966, and 1968 at Et-Tell confirmed the earlier expedition's conclusions.[5]

The previous examples make it clear that archaeology has provided readers of the Old Testament with material for making secure historical interpretations. Such security rests in part upon the careful and systematic manner in which modern archaeology is conducted. Although some information is obtained from surface exploration, such as that done in Transjordan, most excavations are carried out on mounds which jut from the valley floor or cap a hill. Such a mound or cap is called *tell*, the Arabic word for a man-made hill, which was created by sucessive generations of occupation which left their debris behind them. This debris was incorporated into the growing *tell* when a new generation built on the site. Thus, after hundreds of years of occupation a low hill may have grown into a sizable one. There were several factors which determined the location of a city and the subsequent formation of a *tell*. *First*, a sufficient and steady supply of water was essential both for domestic consumption and for some types of irrigation. If a spring or well dried up, the city died. *Second*, the terrain needed to be easily defensible. Most ancient cities were built on low hills where the foundation work of fortification was provided by the natural surroundings. On top of the hill a wall could be constructed about the city which thwarted raiders, and sometimes was capable of repelling major invasions. *Third*, the *tell* developed because the surrounding territory was capable of intensive farming. The surplus produce would supply the needs of those in the city who did not cultivate the land. *Fourth*, the city usually survived over centuries if it was located at a point where trade routes converged. There it served as a clearing station or a storage depot for goods exchanged in international barter. Some cities were built where not all four of the preceding conditions coincided. Sometimes a single factor was of such compelling importance that it took precedence over all others. Samaria was founded by Omri about 870 B.C. even though its water had to be brought from a distance, and it was not located at the junction of major trade routes. The terrain was excellent for defense, and international political pressures made the building of Samaria necessary without the other requirements of easy water and trade.

[5]Joseph A. Callaway, "The 1964 Ai (Et-Tell) Excavations," *Bulletin of the American School of Oriental Research*, No. 178 (April 1965), pp. 13–40.

Tell Dothan, in central Palestine, jutting up from the valley.

Identification of a *tell* with a biblical city is often possible because the modern Arabic name is similar to the biblical name. Examples are Jbeil, the modern name for the ancient city of Gebal (the Greeks called it Byblos), Tell Tinnik, a village on the eastern slope of ancient Taanach, and El Jib, a village at the site of Old Testament Gibeon. Excavating these and other sites has supplied precise factual information about the cities which, when corrollated with the literary record in the Bible, fills out our historical understanding.

Tombs   Tombs provide another source of information for archaeologists. If a tomb has never been plundered it can provide amazingly accurate and extensive information on the kind of life and beliefs the ancients had. Often the finest implements and household goods were buried with the body, and these provide a substantial clue to the material achievements of a civilization over a fairly long period of time. Tombs often were hewn into the face of a rock cliff or chiseled out of a flat rock surface, and then generation after generation deposited bodies in these graves with their tools and precious objects. By an exceedingly careful clearance of a tomb a cross section of cultural change can be obtained. The careful work re-

An Early Bronze Age Canaanite tomb. Excavated in Jericho, it was reassembled, exactly as found, in the Palestine Archaeological Museum, Jerusalem.

quired in clearing a tomb and in recording every detail is illustrated in the photograph which shows the precision with which the excavated tomb was reassembled. Thus, it is seen that surface exploration, digging on *tells,* and clearing tombs have been a boon to students of the Old Testament.

Archaeological Dating

Archaeology's biggest boon has been its provision of a factual framework into which the Old Testament writings can be set. A few examples will illustrate. Whereas fifty years ago the only code of laws from the ancient Near East was found in the Old Testament, today there are seven codes, or their fragments, known to scholars, the earliest dating from about 2050 B.C. The discovery of these ancient codes has vastly increased our understanding of law in the Old Testament. Furthermore, discoveries in Egypt and Babylon of lists of kings have made possible an accurate dating of significant events and important persons in the Old Testament.

Archaeological explorations east of the Jordan River have provided some historical controls for dating Israel's infiltration into Canaan. It has been possible to date mounds in Transjordan which show that there was no extensive sedentary occupation in the regions of Edom,

Moab and Ammon before the Iron Age, about 1200 B.C.[6] Yet the Old Testament states unequivocally that at the time of the Israelite infiltration Edom was settled with "field (and) vineyard" (Num. 20:17), and that cities flourished with smaller villages clustered about them in all of these regions (Num. 21:25). There were well defined boundaries between Moabites and Amorites (Num. 21:13). If the biblical record has reported accurately at this point, the Israelites' penetration of those regions must have occurred during the Iron Age. In this way archaeology provides some tests for the dating of significant historical events reported in the Bible.

Table of Archaelogical Periods of Palestine

Mesolithic (Natufian) through Chalcolithic	ca. 8000–3000 B.C.
Early Bronze (EB)	ca. 3000–2100 B.C.
Middle Bronze (MB)	ca. 2100–1550 B.C.
Late Bronze (LB)	ca. 1550–1200 B.C.
Iron I or Early Iron (EI)	ca. 1200–900 B.C.
Iron II or Middle Iron (MI)	ca. 900–600 B.C.
Iron III, Late Iron, or Persian	ca. 600–300 B.C.
Hellenistic	ca. 300–63 B.C.
Roman	ca. 63 B.C.–A.D. 323
Byzantine	ca. A.D. 323–636
Islamic	ca. A.D. 636–present

Geography of Palestine

Palestine's importance was not due to its size, but rather to its geographical position in the ancient Near East. Palestine lay between the two major civilizations of the ancient world. The Tigris and Euphrates Rivers provided the conditions for agricultural and trade economies to flourish to the east of Palestine, and the Nile River sustained the same economies to the southwest. Both of these centers of population developed agriculture and industries sufficient to create surpluses, and trade developed between the two areas. The main trade routes lay across Palestine, and this topographical fact made that small part of the ancient Near East a controversial area. The political power that controlled Palestine could protect itself by establishing military and political strongholds there, and could plunder caravans en route or demand a fee for their safe passage.

The Caravan Routes

Three major routes of travel between Egypt and Mesopotamia[7] crossed Palestine. One left Egypt from the Delta region and fol-

[6] Nelson Glueck, *The Other Side of the Jordan,* (New Haven, Conn.: American Schools of Oriental Research, 1940).
[7] The land between the two rivers, Euphrates and Tigris.

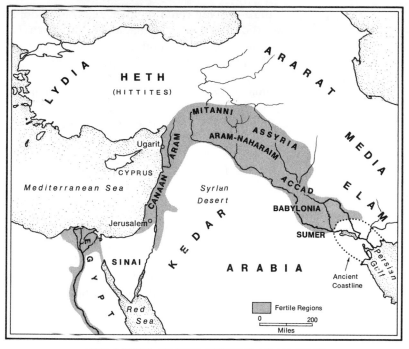

THE LANDS OF THE ANCIENT NEAR EAST
often called "the Fertile Crescent"

lowed the coastal plain northward beginning in Gaza and ending in Ugarit. Coastal cities received products from Cyprus, Crete, and the Aegean regions to be traded inland throughout Palestine, Syria, and Mesopotamia.

A second caravan route left Egypt at Lake Timsah, traversing the wilderness of Shur, and entering Palestine through the Negeb. Wells along this line provided adequate water, but Beersheba was the first major settlement a caravan would come upon after leaving Egypt. From Beersheba the trade route continued via the mountains through Jerusalem to Bethshan. From Bethshan the road turned east of the Sea of Chinnereth heading northeast across the plains for Damascus. This route connected with Tadmor (also known as Palmyra), midpoint between Damascus and the Euphrates River. There in the North Syrian desert this great oasis served to attract travelers not only for commercial purposes but also because of its pleasant climate during winter months. From Tadmor the desert road proceeded due east until it intersected the Euphrates River a few miles north of Mari. The road then pursued the course of the river to Babylon.

A third caravan route handled sea trade from the regions bordering the Red Sea, South Arabia, and East Africa. Commercial products, such as gold, hides, and spices, were carried in single-sail dhows to the port of Ezion-geber. From there the goods were loaded on the backs of donkeys and carried overland across the wilderness regions of Edom to Damascus. The legendary visit of the Queen of Sheba to Solomon gives an impression of the wealth accumulated by commerical enterprises in the second and first millennia B.C. (1 Kings 10:1–10). These three routes of travel placed Palestine at the core of cosmopolitan trading transactions, and during the height of Israel's power one of the major sources of revenue was taxation on caravan travel across Israelite-held territory.

Palestinian Topography

The topography of Palestine is another element which contributed to the unique position that the area held in ancient days. The unusual terrain made it possible for three economies to lie side by side with all of the difficulties their cultural differences brought about. Herding, farming, and trading existed as ways of life in every region of the ancient Near East, but to an unusual degree these occupations existed side by side in Palestine because of the nature of its terrain. Small valleys and terraced hillsides planted to wheat, barley, vegetables, olives, and grapes were hard by rocky hills where only sheep and goats could live nibbling on the sparse grass. Cities such as Hebron, Jerusalem, Megiddo, and Shechem were major trading centers whose immediate neighbors were villages with small farms and shepherds. These three ways of life were vastly different, so that city dwellers looked upon villagers as uncouth boors, nomads spurned the luxurious decadence of city dwellers and despised the attachment of the villagers to their land and houses, and villagers distrusted the promises of wealthy city merchants, and feared the barbarous attitude of the bedouin. In lands where merchant, farmer and shepherd were separated by large distances and only occasional business contacts with one another were normal, conflicts were less prone to germinate into open fighting. In Palestine, all three elbowed one another, and warfare of varying degrees of intensity plagued the land. These conflicts help to explain some of the tensions which characterize many parts of the Old Testament.

Four Regions of Palestine

There are four major regions of Palestine in which the Old Testament stories were enacted. Each is at once a self-contained area, and at the same time flows over into the next region. By studying the topographical map, beginning with that region which Old Testament tradition relates as the direction from which the Israelite conquerors came into the land of Canaan, one will achieve a working knowledge of the land.

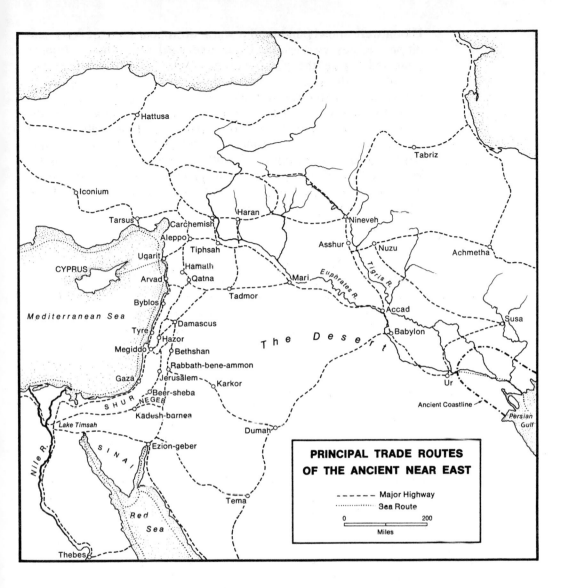

The map image contains the following labels:

Hattusa

Tabriz

Iconium

Haran

Tarsus
Carchemish
Aleppo
Tiphsah

Nineveh

Asshur
Nuzu
Achmetha

Ugarit
Hamath

CYPRUS
Arvad
Qatna

Mari

Euphrates R.

Tigris R.

Byblos
Tadmor

Mediterranean Sea

Accad

Susa

Tyre
Damascus

Babylon

Megiddo
Hazor

The Des e r t

Bethshan

Rabbath-bene-ammon

Gaza
Jerusalem
Karkor

Beer-sheba
Ur

Ancient Coastline

S H U R
NEGEB

Kadesh-barnea

Dumah

Persian Gulf

Lake Timsah

Nile R.

S I N A I

Ezion-geber

**PRINCIPAL TRADE ROUTES
OF THE ANCIENT NEAR EAST**

- - - - - Major Highway
.... Sea Route

0   200

Miles

Tema

*Red
Sea*

Thebes

Transjordan. Region one is located east of the Jordan River. This is often designated as Transjordan, and until 1948 it was, in fact, a kingdom by that name. Its northern limits are the plains region of southern Syria which begin east of the Sea of Chinnereth. Its southern limit is usually considered the Brook Zered at the southern end of the Dead Sea. This is a mountainous region but with wide expanses of open country suitable for growing cereal grains and cattle. It is gashed by deep canyons formed by runoff waters of heavy winter rains. The winter of 1964–65, for example, brought heavy snows to this region and the cities of Kerak and

Dibon were snowbound until a warm downpour brought flood conditions. Roads were washed out, and steel and concrete bridges crumbled before the gigantic force of the swollen streams. The elevation in this region averages about 1,500 feet above sea level, but several mountains top 3,000 feet. The plateau gives way eastward to wilderness where little rain falls during the year. In the area covering approximately 100 miles east of the Jordan River rainfall annually will be from 16 to 24 inches, plenty to supply wells and springs during dry months. Seepage which takes place in the fissures of the limestone hills provides water for the springs in the desert regions further east and south making a large bedouin population of the wilderness possible.

The Jordan River Valley.   Region two is the Jordan River Valley. This great rift lies on a geologic fault running from the Lebanon mountains in the north to modern Tanzania in the south. On this fault lies the lowest point on the earth's surface, the Dead Sea, 1,285 feet below sea level. *Jordan* in Hebrew means "The Descender," and the river drops from 695 feet below sea level at the Sea of Chinnereth to the Dead Sea in about 65 miles. It gives one an impression of the river's sluggish, winding nature to know that in its 65-mile journey its serpentine course is actually 195 miles long. The Jordan River is lined on both sides with lush growth of jungle-like thickness. In Biblical days it sheltered wild animals in large numbers, and lions roamed the valley until about 1300 A.D. The last two in the region were reported killed near Beisan.[8]

Adjacent to the jungle region bordering the river, the Jordan Valley flourished as an agricultural paradise. Three crops a year can be produced where the soil is irrigated, and Jericho is especially well known for its sweet produce. The winter climate is ideal for outdoor living although summer and early fall are so hot that physical activity must be reduced somewhat. Natives of the area have no difficulty working in the heat of summer, however, and shopkeepers carry on their normal business at midsummer, especially during morning and evening hours. Several perennial streams feed the Jordan River. The cold waters of Mount Hermon pour into the Sea of Chinnereth after they pass through Lake Huleh. The Yarmuk and Jabbok empty their flow from the east into the Jordan the year round. Wadi Far'ah and a few lesser streams flow from the western hills. Each of these streams is lined with farms. The Jordan Valley is a patchwork of green and brown.

[8]"Lion," in George A. Buttrick, ed., *The Interpreter's Dictionary of the Bible,* K–Q (New York: Abingdon Press, 1962), p. 136. Hereafter referred to as *IDB.*

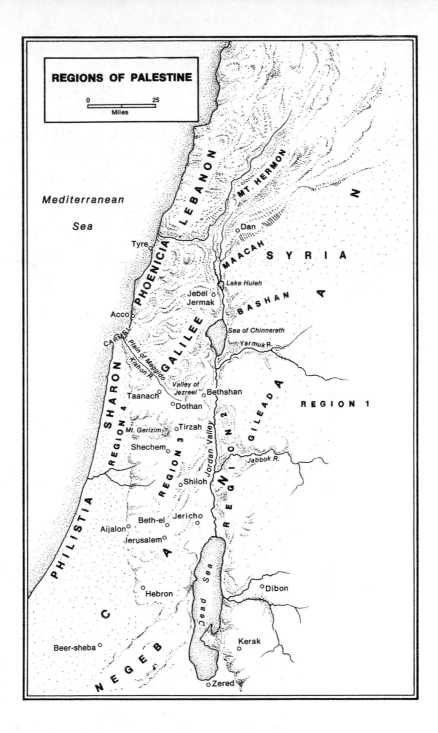

REGIONS OF PALESTINE

0   25
Miles

Mediterranean

Sea

MT HERMON

PHOENICIA

LEBANON

Dan

Tyre

MAACAH

SYRIA

Lake Huleh

Jebel
Jermak

Acco

BASHAN

CARMEL

Plain of Megiddo

Kishon R.

Sea of Chinnereth

Yarmuk R.

GALILEE

Valley of
Jezreel

Bethshan

SHARON

REGION 4

Taanach

Dothan

Tirzah

GILEAD

REGION 1

Mt. Gerizim

Shechem

REGION 2

REGION 3

Jordan Valley

Jabbok R.

Shiloh

PHILISTIA

Beth-el

Jericho

Aijalon

Jerusalem

Dibon

C

Dead Sea

Hebron

Beer-sheba

Kerak

NEGEB

Zered

In country typical of Canaan's mountainous Region 1, Amman,
the capital of the Kingdom of Jordan, is seen from the ruins of a
Byzantine building.

The military significance of this region is as great as the economic.
There are three major valleys which lead into the highlands of Palestine. The southernmost was guarded by Jericho. The central route
had no city at its opening into the hills, but the exceedingly steep
declivity as Wadi Far'ah approaches the highland area makes this
defensible without a fortified city at its mouth. The northernmost
was the Valley of Jezreel. It is the most open of the three, and provided the easiest access into Palestine. This route was guarded by
the fortified city of Bethshan. That city was fortified strongly by
Thutmose III (1490–1435 B.C.) as protection from marauders who
crossed the Jordan River to attack northern Palestine.

The Ridge. Region three is west of the Jordan Valley. It is composed of rugged hills and steep valleys. In some places, such as in
the region of Lebanon a few miles south of Tyre, and at Mount
Carmel, the mountains elbow the sea. In Lebanon the peaks rise
over 6,000 feet, and in Galilee one hill, Jebel Jermak, is nearly
4,000 feet. Jerusalem lies on a plateau at about 2,500 feet, while
Bethel, a few miles to the north, is 3,310 feet above sea level. These
mountains rise rather gradually out of the plains to the west and
descend sharply to the Jordan Valley on the east making this region
appear like a spiny backbone along the north-south length of Pales-

tine. In a sense this metaphor is applicable to the history of the land too, because along this ridge the rulers of major cities exercised hegemony over indigenous tribes and villages on both sides of the spiny ridge. Hebron, Jerusalem, Shiloh, Shechem, Tirzah, and Dothan were situated on this ridge and were major centers of Israelite economic and political activity.

The traditional boundaries of Israel were Dan in the north at the foot of Mount Hermon and Beersheba in the south where the wilderness became accentuated (1 Sam. 3:20). The high mountains of Galilee are broken by the Plains of Megiddo and Jezreel which serve as a sea-level route to the Jordan Valley. These plains provide excellent conditions for farming, with rainfall between 20 and 30 inches annually. The Kishon River floods extensively in winter, as was attested by ancient writers (Judg. 5:21) as well as modern. Professor Ernst Sellin reported that his wagons were bogged down in the mud, and three of his horses drowned when en route to excavate at Taanach in the spring of 1903. The hills to the south of Megiddo and Jezreel rise sharply again and continue without significant interruption to the wilderness south of Beersheba. Small valleys cut these mountains providing sufficient space for planting, and villages are tucked neatly away among these hills so that a larger population than one would suspect on first traveling through the land lives there. The hills are planted with fig and olive trees, and stone terraces enable farmers to plant the hillsides with cereal grains and vegetables. West of Jerusalem four east-west valleys provide fairly easy access to the hill country from the western plains. These are the valleys of Aijalon, Sorek, Elah, and Qubeibah, and one should become familiar with their location in relation to Jerusalem because they were very significant in Old Testament history. These valleys are planted in grains, grapevines, olives, and sycamore.

Although this high, spiny ridge is rainless from May to October, many springs break forth from the limestone to provide water the year round. Where springs are not natural, deep wells are sunk. In places suitable for defense massive cisterns hewn from the stone and plastered with water-resistant mortar were filled by runoff from winter rains, supplying water through the summer. Springs are the most reliable sources of water, however. The limestone hills with fissures and cracks absorb winter rains, which percolate down to be released slowly through springs. Two such perennial springs feed Jerusalem. Jericho too has a constant flow of fresh water. Tirzah was blessed with two fine springs which today send a tumble of water down Wadi Far'ah. Shechem tapped a spring at the base of Mount Gerizim and brought a steady supply of water into the city. To think of Palestine as a desert region with drifting sand and windblown dunes is erroneous, and brought about by inaccurate notions of movie producers and adventure writers. It is rocky and bare in places, but this was not always the case since the Old Testament mentioned thick forests (2 Sam. 18:6). Invaders used the fine timber for their own commercial purposes or else destroyed whole forests as well as crops while besieging cities. One of the finest things happening in Palestine today is the reforestation of the hills, and hardy pines dot the hills promising a stand of firs to the benefit of the water supply, the thin soil, and the beauty of the landscape.

The Plain.   Region four is the plain between the sea and the mountains. The width of this plain varies from a few hundred feet at Mount Carmel and the Lebanon to as much as thirty miles. The Plain of Phoenicia is divided from the Plain of Acco by the steep cliffs of the Ladder of Tyre. South of Mount Carmel the plain broadens and forms a luxuriant flat land suitable for farming and grazing. In ancient times this Plain of Sharon was covered with oak forests. The Plain of Philistia was the most densely populated area in biblical Palestine. The rolling hills were superb for wheat farming, and the Old Testament is well stocked with references to this region. One physical characteristic of this region that contributes to understanding the people of the Old Testament was the absence of harbor facilities from Mount Carmel south. The uneven coast north of Mount Carmel provided suitable harbors, and the Phoenicians developed a magnificent sea trade. But there was no strong tradition of seamanship among the Old Testament people despite Solomon's efforts to establish a maritime trade in the Red Sea (1 Kings 9:26–28). Jehoshaphat, about fifty years after Solomon, attempted to launch a fleet of ships in the Gulf of Aqaba, but his efforts failed, owing probably, to a storm, if not to poor sailors (1 Kings 22:47–48). There is only one Old Testament tradition about trading via lanes of the Mediterranean Sea (1 Kings 10:22). Thus the Israelites developed trade relations along overland routes in a north-south direction.

A clear appraisal of these physical factors in Palestine will help one understand Old Testament history and religion. The proximity of three different cultures, the four major regions, weather conditions, and the natural productivity of the region combined to create cultural conditions which are background to the literature of the Old Testament.

Climate   Striking climatic differences in Palestine are found within short distances.[9] Since the plains of region four are so close to the sea, the temperature changes are less dramatic than in the Jordan Valley where temperatures will rise well above 100 degrees Fahrenheit during the day and may drop forty degrees during the night. The hill country of region three may be hot during the middle of the day in summer, but usually cools to a comfortable level in late afternoon and night. In winter the mountains of both regions one and three are cold.

The mountains of Palestine run north-south, and these present a barrier to the prevailing winds from the Mediterranean Sea. Therefore, Jerusalem will have an average annual rainfall of twenty-six inches whereas the shores of the Dead Sea, only fifteen miles further inland, will receive an average of only three inches. In the north where the mountain barrier is broken by the Plain of Jezreel storm clouds carried on gusty winds ride far inland and deposit heavy rains east of the Jordan. The cool winds of the Mediterranean Sea bring moisture-laden clouds during the winter, but almost as important to agriculture is the heavy evening dew which settles on the land during the summer months (cf. Judg. 6:36–40).

Palestine is, in fact, a land of two seasons. Winter is usually mild although it becomes cold enough to snow. The average minimum temperature in Jerusalem is 44 degrees Fahrenheit, and night frosts are common from December through March. Winter begins with the rains of October and continues through the last rains of April. Then, summer has no rain at all, and all vegetation, sparked to life by the rains, dries up and remains brown during the summer's six months. Summer is the time of year when maximum temperatures average 84 degrees at Tel Aviv and 99 degrees at Beisan in the Jordan Valley. During this weather a child might suffer sunstroke while working in the fields (2 Kings 4:18–25), and men sit in the doorway of their tents "during the heat of the day" (Gen. 18:1). The "cool of the day" (Gen. 3:8) begins when the wind from the Mediterranean Sea pushes beneath the rising hot air mass, and spreads cooling breezes over the land. Jerusalem receives the cool air between twelve noon and two o'clock, and by four in the afternoon men and women are carrying on their normal activities of trading and visiting. Jericho gets some relief from the oppressive heat by about two o'clock, and by late afternoon, citizens of Salt, Amman and other cities in Transjordan are able to resume normal

---

[9] "Palestine, Climate of," *IDB*, K–Q, p. 622.

activity. Summers are usually cloudless, except for a few high-flying cumulus and stratocumulus formations. Most days in winter find clouds scudding across the sky, and Jerusalem is beautiful when an approaching storm forces the clouds over the plateau only a few feet above the buildings.

The Harvests.   In Old Testament times harvesting of crops took place before and after the early and the late rains (Jer. 5:24), although there were unusual cases of "rain in harvest" (Prov. 26:1). Flax was harvested in March and April (Josh. 2:6). Barley harvest was in April and May, while May and June were the months for the wheat harvest. Summer produce such as figs, pomegranates, and grapes, were picked during August and September although grapes often extended into October. Olives were harvested from mid-September through November by beating the trees with long sticks (Deut. 24:20, Isa. 17:6).

Temperate conditions of climate make Palestine a highly desirable land in which to live, and much of the year can be spent out of doors. Occasional desert winds, the terrifying khamsin or sirocco (Hos. 13:15), parch the land and bring fine dust to settle over everything, and winter's cold sometimes brings discomfort to the poor and make the rich move to rooms in their houses especially prepared for such conditions (Jer. 36:22, Amos 3:15). But usually natural conditions favor the inhabitants with sun and rain in good balance, and except under rare conditions of drought, there is enough food to ensure healthful living.

Placing the biblical lands in proper perspective can be accomplished by noting Palestine among the regions of the ancient Near East. Consideration of Palestinian topography and weather are essential, too, if one is to understand the Old Testament. These matters will only be accomplished by careful study of maps. Study the four natural regions of Palestine with the aid of the relief map on page 25. Note the regions where rainfall permits agriculture, and where dry conditions make herding necessary. Observe Palestine in relation to the Sinai Peninsula, the Syrian Desert, Egypt, Mesopotamia, and Asia Minor. Each of these regions had major influences upon Old Testament history. Although the civilizations on the edges of the Mediterranean Sea seem to have had less effect than the peoples of adjacent regions upon the Israelites, so far as economic, social, and political matters were concerned, they still were a major factor in determining the extent to which the Israelites could expand their enterprises.

It is impossible to exaggerate the importance of knowing where events occurred and important sites were for an accurate comprehension of Old Testament literature, history, and religion.

Poetry: The Earliest Traditions

Oral Tradition and Literature

Ancient poems and songs transmitted by word of mouth eventually became Israel's earliest literature. A distinction between oral tradition and literature should be borne in mind because nearly all literature in the Old Testament was preceded by a stage of oral transmission. The literature as it now stands bears the indelible mark of the literary style and the religious convictions of Judaism's men of letters, but with careful scrutiny the traces of original oral traditions can still be observed.

We are more familiar with literature than we are with oral tradition. Our dependence upon the written word is traceable to ages long before the invention of the printing press, but our use of that mechanism has tied us so completely to written forms of learning and knowledge that it is difficult for us to conceive of a culture in which memory was more dependable than written texts. The Old Testament people lived in such a world. There was probably not any distinction between oral tradition and literature among the ancient Old Testament authors but since the distinction is valid to us we should try to distinguish between the two.

In Old Testament days writing was used for the most practical and routine purposes, such as military records, tax and census lists,

Core Readings

Genesis 4:23–24, 9:25–27, 27:27–29, 39–40, 49:1–27
Exodus 15:1 –21
Numbers 10:35–36, 21:14–21, 21:27–30, 23:7–10, 18–24, 24:3–9, 15–24
Deuteronomy 32:1–44, 33:2–5, 6–25, 26–29
Joshua 10:12–13
Judges 5, 14:14–18, 15:16
I Samuel 18:7
2 Samuel 1:17–27, 3:33–34, 20:1
Psalm 29

commercial transactions, and enumeration of court officials (2 Sam. 8:15–18, 20:23–25). These forms are not usually considered literature. Literature is artistic composition, poetry or prose, which relates to or interprets the life of a community. It is material that is consciously created. Oral tradition, on the other hand, is the deposit of "memories" of a community, tribe, or clan which carries the storyteller's style. It reflects the cultural conditions of a relatively small community, simple living conditions, and homogeneity. The stories sprang from the life situations of the people and they were repeated generation after generation because they continued to meet the community's needs. The simple artistry of much of the Old Testament, especially the stories in Genesis, Judges, and Samuel, is due to the fact that its form and style was given by storytellers rather than by "literate" scribes.

The Early Poems

The earliest poems of the Old Testament clearly carry the marks of oral tradition even though as we now find them they have passed through several stages of literary development. They were available to the authors of our present Old Testament in at least two books: the Book of Jashar and the Book of the Wars of Yahweh (2 Sam. 1:18, Num. 21:14).[1] The Old Testament clearly indicates that while some of the oral tradition had been reduced to literature, as in these two writings, oral tradition still flourished both in carrying on old forms and in creating new ones. Reference to ballad singers in Numbers 21:27 and Judges 5:10, whose task it was to report deeds of tribal heroes, shows that while written collections of Israel's songs had been made, oral tradition existed side by side with those collections.

The Oral Tradition

We who have been trained in a literate society wonder how oral tradition continued to exist after writing became fairly widespread. We might ask, did not the efficiency and accuracy of written documents eliminate the less dependable memorized forms? The answer is no! The practice of oral recitation of poems and stories was, and still is, a common matter in the Near East. One requirement for entrance to the theological school of the Islamic University in Cairo, Egypt, is to recite the whole of the Quran from memory. The Talmud was passed on for centuries in oral form by Jewish teachers.[2] Baruch, secretary of the prophet Jeremiah, wrote from memory the oracles that Jeremiah had dictated to him after Jehoiakim, the

[1] Sigmund Mowinckel believes these terms may refer to a single writing by different names. "Literature," in George A. Buttrick, ed., *The Interpreters's Dictionary of the Bible*, K–Q (New York: Abingdon Press, 1962), p. 141.
[2] *Talmud* derives from the Hebrew *lamad*, "to study" or "to learn." It is commentary upon the Old Testament, comprising thirty-six volumes in English translation.

King of Judah, had destroyed the entire scroll upon which Jeremiah's words had been originally recorded. The report indicates that Jeremiah was capable of producing the original words without difficulty.[3] Evidence is conclusive that persons trained in the oral tradition were capable of reproducing accurately and from memory the poems, songs, and narratives of their own communities.

This tenacity of memory among the ancient Semitic storytellers is what assures us that the situations reported in the earliest poetry of the Old Testament reflect accurately the actual conditions. But since any human memory is fallible when large quantities of new and strange material is brought to it, ancient scribes found it advisable to write down the vast store of traditional knowledge that the community possessed. The immediate prompting for this was usually a rapid change of social conditions. When dependable ways of life were suddenly upset and accepted forms of thinking and behavior changed rapidly, the funded knowledge of the community was reduced to writing. The written was not considered preferable to the oral, but it was better to write down the finest oral traditions of the community than to lose them. Thus, it was probably during the development of the United Monarchy, the period of most extensive social and political upheaval in the life of ancient Israel, that many of these early peoms were incorporated into written documents. Naturally, we can no longer call directly upon the oral tradition, but we may reconstruct it from the literature which bore it along, and which was modified somewhat in the very act of preserving it as part of the national culture.

Types of Early Poetry

Poetry was the literary form which developed earliest among the people of the Old Testament, and as such it expressed the deep emotion of that simple culture. Although the powers of sound intellect lie behind the greatest poetry, its appeal is to man's passion rather than to his cold, analytical reason. Poetry, we might say, is the language of the heart, not the mind. John Milton wrote, "Poetry must be simple, sensuous and passionate." A modern poet has said much the same thing: "I always try to share with my readers the immediacy of my own delight and despair of the world as I see it through my window."[4] The early poems of the Old Testament are typified by the strong emotion packed into them. There is little question that the poetic expression of other peoples may be more

[3]See Jeremiah 36.
[4]Bernard Kalb in an interview with Phyllis McGinley. Reprinted by permission of the publisher from *Saturday Review* (September 18, 1954), p. 11.

beautiful in style and form, but few people can claim their poetry to be inspired by richer insight and more fervent emotions.

The Revenge Song

One type of Hebrew poem packed with deep emotion was *the revenge song*. Genesis 4:23–24 recorded the chant of a chieftain whose power enabled him to do more than take "eye for eye, and tooth for tooth." He struck back with a death blow to avenge a slight wound to his person or dignity. Notice that this poem is out of context. The author of the prose materials has enumerated the supposed origins of nomads, musicians, and metalsmiths. This chant probably clung to the editor's memory because of its vigor and fierceness, and he included it as an explanation of the origins of the vendetta. Another example of the revenge song is Exodus 15:21. In this chant the God of Israel has taken his revenge upon the Egyptian chariotry for their threat to the fleeing Israelites. The song was accompanied by women dancing to the sound of percussion instruments. The vengeful quality of this chant has been somewhat reduced by its employment as the theme of a great hymn ascribed to Moses in praise of Israel's God (Exod. 15:1–18).

Blessings and Cursings

Two closely related types of early Hebrew poems were *the blessing and the cursing*. Genesis 9:25–27 depicts Noah cursing Ham, father of the Canaanites, for having viewed him drunk and naked. Shem, father of the Semites, and Japheth, father of the Indo-Europeans, were blessed because they observed the modesty expected of sons in the Israelite culture. Note, too, that the three sons were named Canaan, Shem, and Japheth. In Genesis 9:18 the sons of Noah are called Shem, Ham, and Japheth. This fact demonstrates that the poem and the prose tradition came from different sources. It seems quite likely that this poem commemorated the historical conditions during the reign of David when Canaanites had become subject to Israel and no hostilities existed between Israel and Indo-European peoples to the north. In the poems commemorating Isaac's blessing of Jacob (Gen. 27:27–29), and cursing of Esau (Gen. 27:39–40), the two types are combined. The original poem was disjointed by being placed in a narrative passage originally independent of the poem itself. When one reads Genesis 27 he notices that the type of life depicted is nomadic. Emphasis is upon flocks and wild game. In the poem the setting is agricultural. "The smell of a field" refers to a cultivated, irrigated field. "Fatness of earth, and plenty of grain and wine" are not the conditions of even semi-nomads since grape vines are the results of several years of growth and careful handling. Isaac believed he was blessing his nomadic son, Esau, and would not have wished upon him a settled way of life. Furthermore, Genesis 27:29 reports: "May your mother's sons bow down to you," but, the narrative indicates that Rebekah had only two sons, Esau and Jacob, so that the mention of subservience of plural "sons" to another son indicates that the poem originated in a context different from the one in which it is now placed. It was probably a Canaanite poem used by the Israelite narrator because it made his point better than any Israelite song he knew.

Taunt Songs

Taunt songs such as the one in Numbers 21:27–30 were chanted by the ballad singers at tribal festivals to glorify the clan's achievements. The emphasis in the song in Numbers upon the victories of the Amorite king, Sihon, makes the poem almost certainly Amoritic in origin. It was taken into the repertoire of the Israelite ballad singers after Israel had successfully secured political and military control of Canaan, subduing the last pockets of Amoritic resistance. The Israelites used the song, then, to taunt both the Amorites and

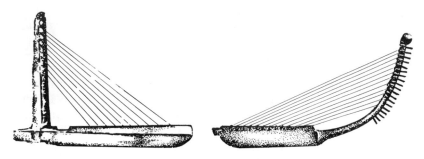

These Egyptian harps typify the kinds of instruments poets used to accompany their songs. Found in tombs between 1550–1000 B.C.

the Moabites who had fallen before the military supremacy of the Israelites. Judges 15:16 is another taunt song, in this instance directed against the Philistines. It is a poem that clearly glorifies the manhood of Israelites as contrasted with the ineffective soldiers of the Philistines. The poet boasted that one lone Hebrew warrior with only a ridiculous bone weapon in his hand was more than a match for a whole contingent of Philistines armed with their iron swords and spears.

Riddles

Riddles were a popular form of village amusement just as they are today. Two ancient Near Eastern riddles were preserved in Judges 14:14 and 18. They have been put into the narratives about Samson, although they were probably independent before placed in this context. The ancient answer to the riddle

> *What is sweeter than honey?*
> *What is stronger than a lion?*

was *love*. The answer to the riddle

> *Out of the eater came something to eat.*
> *Out of the strong came something sweet.*

may be the constellation Leo which appears in the skies of the Near East during the harvest season.

Folk Poems Successful village enterprises, such as bringing in a newly dug well, were subjects of *folk poems*. In some arid regions wells supply copious amounts of water, and striking such a pool was cause for celebration. The poem in Numbers 21:16–18 commemorated that joyous occasion. The thrill the community feels as a well newly dug begins producing precious water is much the same today as it was anciently. Alois Musil, a collector of Arab folklore, reported the following poem sung by residents in the same area referred to in Numbers 21:16, a little north of the Arnon Valley and about fifteen miles east of the Dead Sea:

> *Spring up, O well,*
> > *Flow copiously.*
> *Drink and disdain not.*
> > *With a staff have we dug it.*[5]

Cultic Hymns The remnant of *a hymn* glorifying a cultic object is found in Numbers 10:35–36. When the ancient Israelites went into battle or the campsite removed to a new location, the Ark of Yahweh was addressed because it symbolized the abiding presence of the Israelites' God. The Ark was removed from its tent sanctuary only during critical periods, usually to fight a battle when the tribes moved to fresh grazing territory or to wrest a well from another tribe. This poem demonstrates the primitive view of the Ark held by the Israelites during the Exodus period.

[5]Quoted in Julius A. Bewer, *The Literature of the Old Testament*, rev. by Emil G. Kraeling (3d ed.; New York: Columbia University Press, 1962), p. 4.

A *prayer* before battle is preserved from the ancient Book of Jashar in Joshua 10:12. It reported that Joshua prayed that the day would be long enough for his warriors to defeat the Amorites in the hills around Gibeon. Is it possible that

> *Sun, stand thou still at Gibeon,*
> *and thou Moon in the valley of Aijalon.* (Josh. 10:12b)

is the opening doublet of *a long poem* which commemorated an Israelite victory over the Amorites at Gibeon? Joshua 10:13 could be the closing lines of that poem. The possibility is supported by the existence of a prose version of Joshua's victory in Joshua 10: 6–14. There may have been a poetic version, too, just as there are two versions of another great Hebrew victory recorded in Judges 4 and 5. The prose version of Joshua's battle indicates that a tremendous hailstorm was partially responsible for the victory. Another interpretation may be that after an exhausting night's march from Gilgal, Joshua prayed that his soldiers would be spared a long battle in the heat of the day. As if in answer to his prayer, a great storm rolled in from the northwest and his refreshed and grateful troops were able to fight with surprising vigor. Some pious copyist was convinced that not only an unusual victory had been won but that it was accomplished because of an unusual day. He added to the text, "The sun stayed in the midst of the heaven, and did not hasten to go down for about a whole day. There has been no day like it before or since . . ." (Josh. 10:13b–14).

Poems of National Consciousness   Another type of ancient poem was the recitation about the *growing national consciousness* of Israel. Genesis 49:1–27 is cast in the form of Jacob blessing his twelve sons predicting what will befall them in the years ahead. Of course, the poems are not predictions at all, but reports of tribal conditions as they existed during the height of the United Monarchy (1000–922 B.C.). The two longest poems, about Judah and Joseph, probably reflected the conditions of Judah and Israel (Joseph) after the division of the Monarchy had taken place in 922 B.C. A close reading of these poems gives one an introduction to the social and political conditions during a period of extensive transition for the Israelites. Another poem of the same type is the blessing of Moses recorded in Deuteronomy 33. It is clear that the poem as it now stands was not composed by Moses, since it treats the tribal units so differently from those in Genesis 49. In Deuteronomy 33 Judah deserved only four lines, Simeon had disappeared entirely, Levi had become a priestly figure and teacher of the law, and Joseph (Israel) was given the longest and most favorable notice. It is probable that Deuteronomy 33 originated in the north and was used in cultic ceremonies in the tribal shrine at Shechem. Numbers 23 and 24 are also poetic expressions of the growth of national consciousness in Israel. Although this poem's context places it between Israel's Exodus from Egypt and her entrance into Canaan, it was probably composed to glorify the rise of Israel's power during the Davidic period. Balaam, a foreign prophet, is depicted as having been called upon to curse Israel. He was unable to do so because the spirit of Yahweh had entered him and he could only *bless* Yahweh's people. The poem probably alluded to David's great victories over the bedouin of the southern desert (Num. 24:7), his subjugation of Moab (Num. 24:17), and his capture of Edom (Num. 24:18). It is possible that Numbers 24:23–24 is a guarded reference to the Philistine invasion of the hill country of Canaan which threatened the existence of Israel until David was able to contain their advances after a series of successful battles.[6]

The Victory Song

The *victory song* recorded in Judges 5 is probably the earliest Israelite poem preserved in the Old Testament. It glorified Israel's surprising victory over Canaanite armies. Its impressions of war, its report on social conditions, its violent emotions of hate and glory, and its surprising sympathy for the mother of the defeated general mark it as the finest of Israel's early poems. The importance of this poem will bring us back to it when we look at the historical and religious details contained in these early poems. See also another short chant of victory in 1 Samuel 18:7.

The Dirge

The *dirge* was another type of early Hebrew poem, the most famous being in 2 Samuel 1:17–27. This poem, too, was originally found in the Book of Jashar, and some scholars believe it was actually composed by David. Notice in this poem the respect in which Saul was held. Whereas David might have been expected to sing a song of thanksgiving upon the death of Saul, since Saul had driven him from the court and threatened his life, David lamented over the great warrior's defeat and death. The depth of feeling in this dirge is not artificial, and may indicate one of the finer qualities in David's character: a profound admiration for the truly great men of his nation.

The major types of early Hebrew poetry have been identified, and organizing them this way will help to distinguish them clearly in

[6]W. F. Albright, "The Oracles of Balaam," *Journal of Biblical Literature* LXIII, (1944), pp. 207–33, assigns the poems to the 12th century B.C. as authentic utterances of a North Syrian seer who was converted to Yahwism while at the court of Balak, king of Moab.

one's mind. Another aid to appreciation of these poems will be an understanding of their literary structure.

Understanding Hebrew Poetry

Early Hebrew poetry was related to singing. It was also closely related to the dance. Miriam danced as she sang of Yahweh's victory over the Egyptians at the Red Sea (Exod. 15:20), and certainly the opening of a new well (Num. 21:16–18) was accompanied by dancing as is the case among Arabs today. There was spontaneity in Hebrew poetry, as in most primitive song and dance, but there was formal structure as well. The ancient poet was more than a creator of ditties. He followed a pattern which made the poems easy to remember and at the same time permitted spontaneity of expression.

Parallelism

The basic pattern of Hebrew poetry is parallelism. The poet balanced thoughts, so that the first line of a poem was paralleled in the second line by the same thought but using different words and phrases. Furthermore, Hebrew poetry did not depend upon rhyme. Rhythm was a more important feature. Naturally the rhythms became complex as expertness in poetic facility developed. There are three prevailing rhythms. One is a three, three beat—that is, the first line has three accents and the second line three. A second rhythm is two, two, two, where the first line has two accents, a second line two, and a third line two. A third is three and two, where the first line has three beats and the second line two. This last is sometimes called *qinah* ("lament") meter because it gives a kind of mournful sound. It is the dominant beat in the book of Lamentations.

Parallelism was first described as the principal characteristic of Hebrew poetry by Robert Lowth in 1753. Since that date, intensive study of this subject has developed and expanded his insights, but has not significantly changed them.

Synonymous Parallelism. One form of parallelism is called "synonymous." In this form there are two lines, the first giving the thought followed by the same thought in different but equivalent terms. The first stanza of David's dirge on Saul's death is made up of three doublets of synonymous parallelism:

> *Thy glory, O Israel, is slain upon thy high places!*
> *How are the mighty fallen!*

> *Tell it not in Gath,*
> *publish it not in the streets of Ashkelon;*

> *lest the daughters of the Philistines rejoice,*
> > *lest the daughters of the uncircumcised exult.*
> (2 Sam. 1:19–20)

Antithetic Parallelism. There are no uses of antithetic parallelism in David's dirge, so we turn to Psalms and Proverbs where examples abound. In antithetic parallelism the first line states a theme and the second line states the opposite idea:

> *He who walks in uprightness fears the Lord,*
> > *but he who is devious in his ways despises him.*
> (Prov. 14:2)

> *A faithful witness does not lie,*
> > *but a false witness breathes out lies.* (Prov. 14:5)

> *For the Lord knows the way of the righteous,*
> > *but the way of the wicked will perish* (Ps. 1:6)

Synthetic Parallelism. Synthetic parallelism, the third type, is well illustrated in David's dirge. In this form the first line states a theme, a second line adds another dimension to the theme, and a third line completes the idea.

> *Jonathan lies slain upon thy high places.*
> *I am distressed for you, my brother Jonathan;*
> *very pleasant have you been to me.* (2 Sam. 1:25b–26a)

> *Ye daughters of Israel, weep over Saul,*
> *Who clothed you daintily in scarlet,*
> *Who put ornaments of gold upon your apparel.* (2 Sam. 1:24)

Notice that this last tristich is inverted. The concluding idea is placed first and the two synonymous lines support the concluding idea.

A third example of synthetic parallelism, from the Israelite victory song at the Red Sea, will be sufficient.

> *At the blast of thy nostrils the waters piled up,*
> *the floods stood up in a heap;*
> *the deeps congealed in the heart of the sea.* (Exod. 15:8)

Sometimes synonymous and synthetic parallelism are used so that a stanza of mixed type results:

> *Ye mountains of Gilboa,*
> > *let there be no dew or rain upon you,*
> > *nor upsurging of the deep!*
> *For there the shield of the mighty was defiled,*
> > *the shield of Saul, not anointed with oil.* (2 Sam. 1:21)

Hebrew poetry may appear repetitious upon first reading, but parallelism may be clearly distinguished from repetition as a literary device, by noting that the *idea* is repeated, not the words or phrases. There are many cases of repetition in Hebrew prose, usually for the sake of stressing a point. Avoiding this confusion of literary devices is essential in appreciating the beauty and emotional strength of Hebrew poetry. Much of the Old Testament is in poetry, and a firm understanding of parallelism will make clear a great deal that is otherwise obscure.

Even writers closer to the original poetic works of the Old Testament than we misunderstood parallelism. The author of the book of Matthew quoted a passage from Zechariah which is clearly synonymous parallelism:

> *Tell the daughter of Zion,*
> *Behold, your king is coming to you,*
> *humble, and mounted on an ass,*
> *and on a colt, the foal of an ass.* (Matt. 21:5)

Matthew quoted Zechariah 9:9 and thought Jesus rode on the backs of two donkeys when he entered Jerusalem. He wrote: " . . . they brought the *ass and the colt* and put their garments on *them*, and he sat thereon" (Matt. 21:7).

History in Early Poetry

The earliest Hebrew poetry was lyric. It expressed the feelings and experiences of the poet in response to events rather than giving a descriptive account of the events. Even though the poet did not recount events in precise fashion he often employed factual information that is valuable to us as we strive to learn the historical conditions which gave rise to the poetry. Such unconscious recording of history may even be more dependable than later attempts when some authors made historical conditions conform with theological presuppositions. Therefore, it is helpful to analyze some of these early poems for their historical content as well as for their literary type and structure.

Judges 5 is usually referred to as the Song of Deborah. Whether it was her composition or some unknown poet's will not likely be known for sure, but the vitality of this war song practically assures its composition contemporaneously with the events. It is datable to about 1125 B.C.[7] The Song of Deborah can, therefore, provide historical information that is essential to understanding conditions among the Israelites in the last half of the 12th century B.C.

The persons involved in this fateful battle were Deborah, a prophetess; Barak, a military commander; Jael, a bedouin woman; and Siscra, general of the Canaanite troops. Sisera's mother appears in the poem in a secondary scene as the Hebrew poet expressed either a cruel taunt over the death of the general or a poignant and heartfelt sympathy for a bereaved mother.

The situation for the Israelites was desperate. Plundering of caravans and robbing of travelers was common practice. Whether the Canaanite city-states were systematically afflicting the Israelites or whether the plundering and robbing was conducted by the Peoples of the Sea, the Philistines, is not clear. Some of the Peoples of the Sea had invaded the southern coast of Canaan about 1188 B.C. by ship, and some had come overland along the coast from the north. Normal trade seems to have come to a standstill. Raiding villages for the sake of taking prisoners to be sold into slavery may account for the phrase "The peasantry ceased in Israel" (Judg. 5:7). Israel seems to have been weaponless (Judg. 5:8b), although it is more probable that the superior weaponry of either the Canaanites or the Philistines with their chariots and iron-pointed weapons made the foot soldiers and bronze weapons of the Israelites ineffective.

A desperate situation and the courageous leadership of Deborah and Barak brought response from some of the tribes. They forgot their tribal differences for a while to rally behind the leadership of Barak. However not all of the tribes responded to the war call. Reuben and Gilead,[8] both from east of the Jordan River, did not join the fight. Dan and Asher, coastal tribes to the north, avoided

---

[7] W. F. Albright, *The Archaeology of Palestine* (London: Penguin Books, 1956), pp. 117–18.
[8] Gad, see Genesis 49:19.

the war because of their profitable sea trade, perhaps with the people who were harassing the Israelites. Six tribes, Ephraim, Benjamin, Machir,[9] Zebulun, Issachar, and Naphtali, all located in the central section of Canaan, were those which joined the battle. Three tribes, Judah, Simeon, and Levi (Gen. 49:5, 8) were not even mentioned. These facts make it necessary to ask, why did not all the tribes join the battle if they had all sworn allegiance to Yahweh as the stories in Exodus 19 and 20 and Joshua 24 report? Is it possible that Judah, Simeon, and Levi were not considered part of Israel at that time? It seems probable that these historical facts supply us with information that considerably modifies the traditional view of tribal unity supposedly originating at Mt. Sinai.

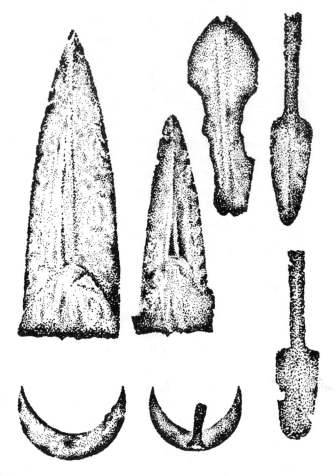

Bronze spearheads and daggers used by Canaanites in the 15th–14th centuries B.C.

[9] Manasseh, see Joshua 17:1.

The battle was fought in the Plain of Megiddo, a region where massed chariots would be effective against mountain-raised foot soldiers. But, Sisera did not anticipate a mighty cloudburst. The poet recounted that all the heavens joined to fight against Sisera (Judg. 5:20), but this poetic expression probably means that the downpour was unusually heavy. Soggy soil bogged down the chariots. Flood waters drowned heavily mailed charioteers. Israel's lightly armed infantry struck effectively at the immobilized chariot army.[10] This battle may have changed history considerably. The plight of the Israelites seemed intolerable, and they might have lost their tribal identities had the practices of village raiding and curtailment of trade been maintained long. This victory gave them a start which over a century later resulted in freedom from both Canaanite and Philistine domination and an independent nation under David.

Other Historical Songs Genesis 49 is another poem that provides some helpful historical information and also permits a fairly accurate dating for the composition of the poem as it now stands. The separate stanzas about the fortunes of the twelve tribes may originally have been longer recitals characterizing each tribe. Only a basic quality of each tribe has been recited in order to permit the poems to fit into the narrative structure where they now appear. The song about Reuben reported some event which brought punishment upon that tribe (Gen. 49:3–4). Genesis 35:22 carries a brief prose tradition which corresponds to the one in the poem about a serious violation of a sexual taboo. The poem represents Reuben as losing his leadership in a tribal confederation. Levi and Simeon were wild, undisciplined tribes small enough that they dwelt together. Compare the treatment of Levi in 49:5–7 with that in Deuteronomy 33:8–11, and notice that over the years the qualities of the tribe of Levi change. First, Simeon separates completely from association with Levi. Second, the violent and war-minded Levi becomes the priest and teacher in Israel. Third, in Genesis 49, Levi's lawlessness is so great that he will be disbanded as a tribe and scattered among the several Israelite tribes, whereas in Deuteronomy anyone that offends Levi shall be cursed with sexual impotence.

Thus, the poet who compiled these songs allowed a single characterization of each tribe to stand. The Judah and Joseph tribes were given much longer treatment.[11] Judah was described as suc-

---

[10] Exodus 14:24–25 reports a similar tactical situation. Joshua 10:9–11 reports a hailstorm as responsible for an Israelite victory.

[11] Joseph, so the narrative reports, had two sons, Ephraim and Manasseh (Gen. 48:8–20).

cessful in war, fierce as a lion, and the recipient of economic benefits from its successful wars (Gen. 49:8, 9, 11–12). Joseph's agricultural bounty was extolled by the poet (Gen. 49:22, 25, 26) as well as his ability to protect himself from attack (Gen. 49:22–26).[12] The poem thus informs us that two units among the Israelites predominated, that they were equal in military strength, and that they both accumulated great wealth. The historical period when Judah dominated the other tribes of Palestine was during the United Monarchy. The wealth of the country during that period overflowed into public buildings and a large military establishment controlled from Jerusalem. David originated from the Judah tribe. It seems reasonable to conculde that Genesis 49 actually represents a glorification of the reigns of David and Solomon, with some materials respecting the lesser tribes drawn from earlier tribal poems. The poem took its present form during the 10th century B.C. The man who edited Genesis took it from a source book, perhaps from the Book of Jashar, and used it as a blessing of the twelve sons of Jacob.

Exodus 15
Exodus 15, a song of praise to Yahweh, shows signs of composition during the United Monarchy, too. The author of this victory hymn used the ancient chant

Sing to the Lord, for he has triumphed gloriously;
the horse and his rider he has thrown into the sea. (Exod. 15:21)

as his theme, and developed a hymn proclaiming national greatness under Yahweh. Historical allusions provide almost certain evidence that most of the poem was composed in the 10th century B.C. (Exod. 15:13–16). Although the song was attributed to Moses, reference to Philistia indicates he could not have been the author. Moses did not live when the Philistines trembled before Israel's power. No Old Testament historian places Moses later than 1200 B.C., and the Philistines (Peoples of the Sea) did not invade Canaan until 1188 B.C., the eighth year of Ramses III. Moses had contact with Edom and Moab no doubt, but that the phrase "the inhabitants of Canaan have melted away" (Exod. 15:15) could refer to the time of Moses is impossible. The biblical record reports that Moses died before entering Canaan (Deut. 34:1–6), and the successful infiltration of that land by Hebrew tribes took as much as two hundred years before most Canaanite resistence had bowed to Israelite power. It seems, though, that this hymn to Yahweh was composed

[12] For a completely different understanding of 49:22 see E. A. Speiser, *Genesis, The Anchor Bible* (Garden City, N.Y.: Doubleday & Co., 1964), p. 363.

when David had successfully subdued Philistine aggression, made Moab a vassal state, and occupied Edom with troops (2 Sam. 8:1, 2, 13).

There are in Exodus 15 some older fragments, however, as verse 1 indicates. Professor Albright has shown that the lines

> *Thou wilt bring them in, and plant them on thy own mountain,*
> *the place, O Lord, which thou has made for thy abode*
> (Exod. 15:17)

may have been drawn from a Canaanite poem from the time of Moses since almost identical lines are found in a 14th century Canaanite epic which depicted Baal's home on a mountain.[13]

David's dirge over Saul and Jonathan (2 Sam. 1:17–27) is a poem which without doubt was composed contemporaneously with the events described. There are no anachronisms. What is known about military and political conditions among the Philistines in the 11th century B.C. is not controverted. The important station in Israelite life attributed to Saul and Jonathan in the poem is supported by historical narrative (1 Sam. 11, 13, 14).

Thus, it is possible to glean historical information from these poems even though no attempt has been made to compose history. This type of information may be more accurate than some Old Testament narratives which relate events but do, in fact, seriously distort situations because of the writer's theological presuppositions. Each poem should be studied with the historical conditions in mind both for information obtainable on the events themselves and for placement of the poem in the development of Old Testament literature.

Religion as Reflected in Israel's Early Poetry

As Israel's earliest poems may be studied for their literary qualities and the historical information contained in them, so too, most yield important details of Israel's religious beliefs and the forms the people used to express their beliefs. Not all the earliest Hebrew poems were religious, however, and some of them contain no reference to Yahweh or religious practices (Gen. 4:23–24, Num. 21:14–18, 27–30). Since most of Israel's early poems were expressions of spontaneous feelings, they provide a rich source of informa-

[13] Albright, *The Archaeology of Palestine*, p. 233.

tion on religious beliefs and practices. It is possible that the poets' beliefs were expressed relatively free of sanctions, and that there was less adjustment of the text by later editors than in the case of prose literature. Therefore, these early poems may give us a quite accurate representation of religion at the time they were composed.

The Hebrew Image of God Judges 5 provides one of the earliest sources for learning what the Hebrews believed about God. They called their God Yahweh. The Revised Standard Version of the Old Testament translates the Hebrew word YHWH as LORD. This word in its anglicized form, Yahweh, has been used already in referring to the God of the Israelites, and it renders the Hebrew idea about their God better than the English word Lord. Yahweh was the personal name of the Israelite God. Many scholars have suggested meanings for the name YHWH. Some believe that it is a form of the verb "to be," and thus gives the meaning of "the one who is." Such an interpretation emphasizes a static view of Israel's God. The activities reported in the Old Testament into which Yahweh entered with the Israelites makes this meaning unlikely. Others believe that the Arabic word HWY, which may have meant origianlly "to show passion," lies behind the word Yahweh. He is the one who acts with passion. Others would have Yahweh mean "he who speaks," that is, one who reveals himself. A few scholars insist that Yahweh, or its short form Yah or Yahu, was originally a cry of emotion as some cultic rite was performed and has, therefore, no intelligible meaning. With more credibility some scholars have found Yahweh derived from a verb meaning "to cause to fall" so that lightning, rain, and hail were caused by Yahweh. Closely allied to this meaning is that in which the name Yahweh derived from the verb "to blow." The Old Testament often depicts Israel's God revealing Himself during storms in mountains.[14] Another theory explains Yahweh as a form of the verb "to come to pass, to come into being." Yahweh was the Being who causes whatever is; who brings to pass whatever happens. This meaning reflects the liturgical patterns found in Egypt in which the deity was called Creator and Sustainer of Existence. Moses knew this idea, so the theory claims, and organized Israelite beliefs about it. The Old Testament explanation in Exodus 3:13–15 is that Yahweh means "I Am Who I Am" and connects the divine name with *hayah*, in Hebrew the verb "to be." This meaning, however, also presents a rather static view of Yahweh.

The character of Yahweh in the Song of Deborah was certainly not static. He traveled from his abode in the south,[15] and caused the

[14] See Exodus 19; 1 Kings 19:1–18; Job 38:1.
[15] Seir, which means "south" in Hebrew, is in parallelism with Edom (Judg. 5:4).

cloudburst which swamped the Plain of Megiddo (Judg. 5:20–21). The violence of Yahweh's storm was likened to those which shook Mount Sinai where He lived in terrifying splendor. It is tempting to interpret Judges 5:8 as showing the jealous character of Yahweh, but the Hebrew text is unclear at this point, and the reading

> *When new gods were chosen,*
> *then war was in the gates*

is conjectural. The refrain in Judges 5:31 shows that Yahweh was understood to be the God of Israel who fought for his people and their friends, defeating their enemies.

Other Names for Israel's God   Upon reading Genesis 49 one discovers that other names were used for Israel's God. Rather than Yahweh as the divine name,[16] Mighty One, Shepherd, Rock, Almighty, and God were names for the deity. "Almighty" is a translation of the Hebrew *Shaddai,* probably designating a mountain god (cf Exod. 6:3). "Shepherd" and "Rock" were names employed from ancient images where gods were likened to protecting personages such as shepherds or kings, or to topographical features such as protection from sun or storm afforded by a great rock. The Hebrew word *'abir* is translated "Mighty One," and it may be derived from a verb which means "to fly, to soar" like a great bird (see Job 39:26). *Elohim* is the Hebrew word which is usually rendered in English translations as "God." *Elohim* is a plural form, and there may be a remainder of polytheism in the word. It is used, however, most of the time in the Old Testament in a singular sense. It is related to the general term *El* which appears in ancient Semitic literature as the designation for God in Babylon, in Canaan, and in South Arabia. It probably meant originally "that which is powerful," and it may have designated the divine, mysterious power in the world which filled ancient men with dread and awe. Sacred places, such as special mountains, springs, streams, wells, and trees, often manifested the power of El.

In Genesis 49:25 God was clearly depicted as the power which brought fruitfulness to the earth. Such a depiction would certainly emerge from a time when the tribe was engaged in agricultural pursuits. The contrast between Elohim in Genesis 49 and Yahweh in Judges 5 is quite clear. It is well that a distinction be made between Yahweh and Elohim in their translations as Lord and God

---

[16] Genesis 49:18 is an editorial addition.

respectively because they will be referred to when discussing other types of Old Testament literature.

Both Hebrew words for deity were employed in Exodus 15; however, Yahweh was clearly the name preferred by the poet. Yahweh was a god of war, and as such he was capable of defeating the armies of rival gods. In Egyptian religious thought Pharaoh was not a representative of Egyptian gods but was divine himself. Thus, the contest was between Pharaoh and Yahweh (Exod. 15:4). Obviously the Pharaoh was not in the battle, but "Pharaoh's chariots" refers to the patrol or task force which pursued the fleeing Hebrew slaves. The poet contrasted Yahweh with the gods of other nations surrounding Israel and each, Philistine, Moabite, and Edomite, showed badly in contrast with the power of Yahweh (Exod. 15:11-12, 14-15). Yahweh exercised awesome capability in war but he treated his own people with special care. He led them in "steadfast love," a phrase which translates the Hebrew word *hesed,* and carries the sense of kindness and mercy as a companion to Yahweh's power.[17] The poem refers to a special abode of Yahweh (Exod. 15:13, 17), and if those portions of the poem originated in the days of Moses, as Professor Albright believes, the abode was Mount Sinai. On the other hand, if the poem originated in the period of the United Monarchy the Temple in Jerusalem may have been what was meant by "thy abode." A contractual relationship between Yahweh and his special people is suggested by the words "redeemed" (Exod. 15:13) and "purchased" (Exod. 15:16). Yahweh defeated Israel's enemies in war, was ever so much more powerful than foreign gods, protected his own people with kindness and mercy, and was bound to them in a contractual relationship, according to the Song of Moses.

A peculiar characteristic of David's dirge over Saul and Jonathan (2 Sam. 1:19-27) is its omission of any reference to Israel's God. If David was the devoted follower of Yahweh that usual Old Testament tradition made him out to be, it seems odd that he would make no reference to Yahweh. This may signify that David's personal regard for Yahweh was something subsequent writers incorporated into traditions about him. Or it may mean that since Yahweh's forces were defeated on the battlefield, reference to Yahweh would infer his weakness, so that at this point his name was not used. This lament, in fact, asserts directly that Saul and Jonathan were Israel's instruments of warfare. The poem then indicates that defeat is always man's failure whereas victory is inevitably Yahweh's.

[17] Notice the parallelism in Exodus 15:13.

These poems may be studied to discover the earliest religious beliefs and practices of the Hebrews. These lyrical utterances were direct and spontaneous, rather than elaborate constructions created to communicate an official version of Israel's history and religion.

An Early Hebrew Psalm Psalm 29 may be the earliest Hebrew psalm. Some of its literary characteristics show that it was typical of hymnody before the period of the United Monarchy. Canaanite literary characteristics abound in this hymn. Mitchell Dahood has written, "Virtually every word in the text can now be duplicated in older Canaanite texts."[18] It synonymous parallelism

> *The voice of the Lord is powerful*
> *the voice of the Lord is full of majesty* (Ps. 29:4)

and its synthetic parallelism

> *The voice of the Lord is upon the waters;*
> *the God of glory thunders,*
> *the Lord, upon many waters* (Ps. 29:3)

are borrowings from Canaanite poetic style. The images of Yahweh speaking in thunder, striking down the cedar forests with lightning, and enthroned above the waters, relate the psalm to Canaanite literary themes. Its basic simplicity as a vehicle for expressing the singer's reaction to what he observes about him places it in an age which had not reached literary sophistication. Its religious thought represents its early origins, since Yahweh's power is depicted in terms of a mighty storm breaking about the tops of mountains, a description of Yahweh consistent with that in Judges 5. Yahweh's presence is felt in two regions, Lebanon and Kadesh. The storm crashing into Lebanon's mountains, swirls over them eastward into the Orontes River valley where at Kadesh its violence subsides.

The earliest poems of the Old Testament were simple and lyrical. They dealt with significant events concerning tribal and national

[18] From Psalms I, 1–50 by Mitchell Dahood, S.J., in *The Anchor Bible*, p. 175. Copyright © 1965, 1966 by Doubleday & Company, Inc. Reprinted by permission of the publisher.

origins and survival. Because of their simplicity they resisted major modifications of their literary structure, historical allusions, and religious affirmations. They have, therefore, given readers of the Old Testament a fine source for investigating the actual conditions among the first literate Hebrews without extensive influence from official beliefs about the history and religion of the Israelite tribes.

IV

A Nation Springs
to Life

The years just before and after 1000 B.C. rate special attention in Old Testament lore. During those years enduring literary forms were cast, historical precedents were set, and religious expressions were formalized.

Literary Inspection of Historical Sources

Narratives of the United Monarchy sprang from sources at times duplicative, and at others contradictory, displaying different literary styles and religious beliefs. One version of how Saul became king in Israel is treated in 1 Samuel 11. Ammonite troops laid siege to Jabesh on the slopes overlooking the Jordan Valley. Saul responded rapidly to the Ammonite threat, and mustered an army to defeat the besiegers. After the battle, the army elevated him to kingship at Gilgal (1 Sam. 11:15). Except for the exaggeration of the number of men mustered to arms, 330,000 (1 Sam. 11:8), and loss of part of the narrative between 11:11 and 11:12, this is a sound historical version of how Saul became king.

Accounts of Saul's Ascendancy

Another version was a popular folk story (1 Sam. 9:1–10:16). In it Saul, a big handsome man, went out to hunt for strayed asses, and returned to Gibeah king of Israel. In this version Samuel, a prophet, anointed Saul king and he did it somewhere in "the land of Zuph" (1 Sam. 9:5). Samuel, not Saul, was the chief figure in a third story describing Saul's selection as king (1 Sam. 8:4–22,

---

Core Readings

1 Samuel 4–16
2 Samuel 1–6, 9–20, 24
1 Kings 1–6, 9–12
Psalms 2, 16, 60
Reading all of 1 Samuel, 2 Samuel, and 1 Kings 1–12 and Psalms 18, 68,
    82, 108 is recommended

10:17–27). In this story the coronation was at Mizpah. Further duplications can be found by reading the accounts of the origin of the proverb "Is Saul also among the prophets?" (1 Sam. 10:9–13 and 19:18–24), and the stories of why Saul lost favor with the prophetic party (1 Sam. 13:8–15 and 15:4–31).

Accounts of David's Ascendancy

Three accounts are given of how David rose to a position of influence in Saul's court. One tells that David was a skillful musician called upon to soothe Saul's troubled spirits (1 Sam. 16:14–23). Another reports how David was recognized for his bravery and skill in weaponry (1 Sam. 17). In the third he was anointed by Samuel (1 Sam. 16:1–13). Two stories report Saul's marriage of his daughter to David (Merab in 1 Sam. 18:17 ff; Michal in 1 Sam. 18:20 ff). Three stories report David's flight to safety (1 Sam. 19:1–7, 11–17; 19:8–10, 18; and 20:1–21:6). Two versions of David's treason are told (1 Sam. 21:11–16; 27:1–12).

Some of the stories, furthermore, are actually contradictory. A folk story looks favorably upon Saul's anointment as king because he led Israel successfully against the Philistines (1 Sam. 9:1–10:16). Another looks upon the monarchy as a calamity in Israel (1 Sam. 8:4–22, 10:17–27).

Radical differences of style also draw attention to the composite nature of these narratives. The sermonic style of 1 Samuel 8:4–18 is different from the simple conversational style of 1 Samuel 9:5–27. Contrast, too, the styles of 2 Samuel 7 and 9.

These are a few instances of duplications and contradictions, as well as religious and stylistic differences in the narratives which point to the sources used in these historical books.

Early Historical Narratives

Before any of Israel's history was written, popular war stories such as the tales of king Saul's victory over the Ammonites (1 Sam. 11) and David's conquest of the Arameans (2 Sam. 8:3–12) were circulated orally. An early written history, however, is the story of David's court in 2 Samuel 9–20. This is a study of conditions existing after David's personal military leadership was ended (2 Sam. 10:7, 11:1, 18:1–4). Perceptively, the author of this court history interweaves stories of David's magnanimity, his sensuality, his failure as a father, the loyalty of Joab, Hushai, Zadok, and Abiathar, the instability of David's rule in his last years, and his fear of Yahweh's prophet into a superb narrative. His report of David's impact upon events carries such penetrating psychological insight that few sections in the Old Testament are its equal. The unitary character of 2 Samuel 9–20 is demonstrated by the summarizing lists of administrative officials found at the end of this unit (2 Sam. 20:23–25; cf. 1 Kings 11:41–43, 1 Kings 2:10–12). A section reporting David's securing the kingship and extending his territory is found in 2 Samuel 1–8. Here, too, the section ends with a list of administrative officials (2 Sam. 8:15–18).

Another literary unit which may be nearly as old as the recital of court life during David's later years is the story of the Ark of Yahweh (1 Sam. 4:lb–7:2, 2 Sam. 6). Style, vocabulary, and the conspicuous absence of the prophet Samuel clearly mark the story off from its context. Jerusalem's priests told the story of the Ark intent upon defending the cult of the Ark against those who questioned its authenticity. These priests conveniently overlooked the failures of the Ark to bring victory against the Philistines while noting that it brought death to Israelites who were curious about its contents (1 Sam. 6:19–7:2). Written during the United Monarchy, the history of the Ark may have been written to defend the Ark's inclusion among the furnishings of the new Temple (1 Kings 8:1–9).

Stories of Saul's kingship (1 Sam. 9:1–10:16, Chapters 11, 13, and 14) and tales of David's military and political exploits (1 Sam. 16:14–2 Sam. 5:10) formed another scroll. The tales about Saul do not endeavor to enhance his moral and religious stature, but those about David make him into a virtuous follower of Yahweh. Stories about a youthful David killing the seasoned warrior Goliath (1 Sam. 17), his intimate friendship with the king's son (1 Sam. 20), and his magnanimous sparing of Saul's life (1 Sam. 24 and 26), bear the marks of legends told to glorify a beloved personality. Threads of history run through these legends, however. Saul did conduct a difficult war against the Philistines. David did spark a rebellion. He did enter an alliance with the Philistines. He did wait shrewdly for Saul to fall in war before making his play for kingship. He did venture energetically to please the religious leaders of Israel.

The report on David's court, the story of the Ark, and popular tales about Saul's and David's leadership were the earliest historical narratives in Israel's collection. The editors of this material drew upon both oral and written sources, retained the basic form of the narratives, and deleted or added as editing demanded to cement together the several sources.

These early narratives do not, of course, exhaust the accounts of the United Monarchy. Documents composed much later were added to the original narratives as time passed. There was an official record book of Solomon's reign (1 Kings 11:41–43). Using this and modeling his story on the earlier tales of Saul and David, someone wrote a scenario of how Solomon became king (1 Kings 1:1 – 2:46). Other stories about Saul and David were created by the prophetic circle in Israel who pronounced their convictions that the monarchy was a decided evil in Israel. They contended that Samuel the prophet had been the true leader of Israel; this attitude is emphasized in stories about the cult's center at Shiloh (1 Sam. 1–3), in the report on Saul's election as king (1 Sam. 8:4–22), 10:17–27, 16:1–25), in the account of Samuel's judgment of Saul's rule (1 Sam. 15 and 16), and in the tale of Saul's association with the witch of Endor (1 Sam. 28).

There may be a Canaanite myth neatly couched in these narratives. There is a story that Samuel anointed David king over Israel. In that story seven of Jesse's sons passed before Samuel, and he rejected each. The eighth son, David, was called from the fields, and when he appeared before the prophet, Samuel anointed him as leader of the people. This sketch closely parallels part of the Ugaritic poem of Kret, a mythical king who feared that his line would die out. He prayed to El that his wife would be restored to him. He had, then, eight sons, the youngest of whom was suckled at the breasts of a goddess so that he would qualify to rule.[1]

These narratives were edited in a final step by writers known to scholars as the Deuteronomists.[2]

Preparation for David

One of the basics of a critical examination of Old Testament history is the principle that the narrative closest to the events reported gives the most accurate recital of those events.

Having traced the order in which the narratives of the United Monarchy came into existence, one is now able to select events from the narratives in order to establish reliable history.

The early narratives in 1 Samuel reflect a stage in Hebrew history when a transition of major proportions was in progress.

[1] Cyrus H. Gordon, *The World of the Old Testament* (Garden City, N.Y.: Doubleday & Co., Inc., 1958), p. 96.
[2] A discussion of the Deuteronomists' work is in chapter XI.

They are silent, for instance, about Egypt, Assyria, and the Hittites, and this suggests a great deal. Canaan was no longer dominated politically and militarily by these peoples as it had been before the 12th century B.C. The eclipse of these major powers for about three centuries resulted in the establishment of many small independent states in Canaan and its bordering territories. Philistines landed on the southwest coast of Canaan about 1188 B.C., and migrated into Syria overland from the north.

Israel in the Wake of the Major Powers

Several small Aramaean states were created around Damascus. Ammon, Moab, and Edom flourished east and south. Israel caught a foothold in the mountains of Canaan and clung to its precarious existence until David gave it solid footing. Samuel was depicted in these stories as the last of the Judges who led Israelite forces against Philistine attacks upon Israelite territory, but he seems to have been unsuccessful.[3] Saul was presented, especially in chapters 11, 13, and 14, as the warrior who momentarily contained both Philistine and Ammonite expansion. Although the narratives about Samuel's domination of Saul are full of legend, enough historical facts come through to show that Saul was consistently opposed by Israel's religious leader. Samuel was a prophet (1 Sam. 9:9), and Israelite historians recorded several times that prophets were makers and breakers of kings (1 Kings 16:7, 21:20–24, 22:5–12, 2 Kings 9:4–10). Perhaps Samuel's antagonism was provoked because he was not consulted in the crowning of Saul at Gilgal (1 Sam. 11).[4]

The Rise of Saul

Saul came to power as a result of his personal qualities as well as his military success. Legend affirmed that Saul was handsome, big, and wealthy (1 Sam. 9:1–2, 10:23) as fitted a king. When he was told about the siege at Jabesh in Gilead "the spirit of God came mightily upon Saul . . . and his anger was greatly kindled" (1 Sam. 11:6). Butchering his oxen betokened a charismatic spirit at work. Legend added its share, and told how Saul had ecstasy like the prophets whose seizures were induced by music (1 Sam. 10:3–13) or by exposure to the elements (1 Sam. 19:21–24). Before Elisha could prophesy about weather conditions, a minstrel had to play him into a state of prophecy (2 Kings 3:13–20). Present-day instances of prophecy among primitive tribes of Turkey, Hindustan,

[3] See 1 Samuel 4:10–11, 7:5–17 where both defeat and a semblance of victory were reported. But chapter 13 reported that the Philistines attacked Israel in force, which contradicts 7:13.
[4] 1 Samuel 15 gives the reason as Saul's failure to sacrifice to Yahweh all the booty taken in battle. This story has qualities identical with the prophetic ideals of the 8th century B.C.

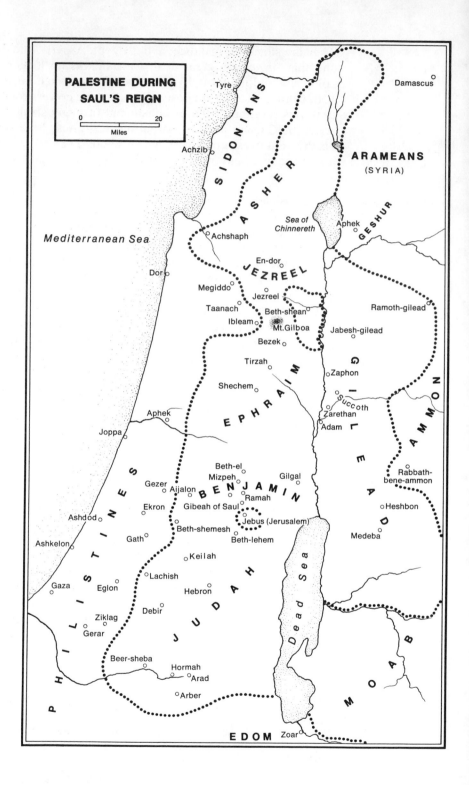

PALESTINE DURING
SAUL'S REIGN

0   20
Miles

Tyre

Damascus

Achzib

S
I
D
O
N
I
A
N
S

A
S
H
E
R

ARAMEANS
(SYRIA)

Mediterranean Sea

Achshaph

Sea of
Chinnereth

Aphek

G
E
S
H
U
R

Dor

En-dor

JEZREEL

Megiddo

Jezreel

Ramoth-gilead

Taanach

Beth-shean

Ibleam

Mt.Gilboa

Jabesh-gilead

Bezek

Tirzah

Zaphon

Shechem

G
I
L
E
A
D

Succoth

Zarethan

Adam

Aphek

Joppa

E
P
H
R
A
I
M

A
M
M
O
N

Beth-el

Gilgal

Mizpeh

Gezer

Rabbath-
bene-ammon

Aijalon

BENJAMIN

Ramah

Ekron

Gibeah of Saul

Heshbon

Ashdod

Jebus (Jerusalem)

Beth-shemesh

Ashkelon

Gath

Beth-lehem

Medeba

Keilah

P
H
I
L
I
S
T
I
N
E
S

Lachish

Gaza

Eglon

Hebron

J
U
D
A
H

Debir

Ziklag

Gerar

D
e
a
d

S
e
a

Beer-sheba

Hormah

Arad

M
O
A
B

Arber

EDOM   Zoar

and Siberia demonstrate the influence of music in bringing a prophet to his full strength.[5]

That part of Saul's kingly power depended upon these peculiar seizures was attested by his need for music. One legend twists Saul's need for music by reporting that David was brought to his court to play the lyre whenever the king needed relief from an evil spirit (1 Sam. 16:23). But Saul's ecstatic moments were brought on by music, according to another story (1 Sam. 10:1–13). Evidence points to Saul's employment of David as a musician for the purpose of helping him to achieve those states of mantic experience in which his fullest powers of body and personality once had thrived. When David's music failed to induce ecstasy in Saul, he became angry and attempted to kill him (1 Sam. 19:8–10).

Saul's leadership of Israel was exercised by means of his charismatic gifts and military prowess rather than by political power. The surge of the Philistines' power about 1050 B.C., and their attempt to dominate all of Palestine threatened the independence of Israelites in the mountains. Ammonite penetration of territory held by Israel east of the Jordan River erupted into open conflict. Elevating Saul to kingship represented the tribes' effort to preserve their territory even while losing some of their freedom.

Few details of the administrative structure of Saul's kingship have survived, but it is probable that he ruled from his home in Gibeah. Excavations at Tell el Ful, ancient Gibeah, have uncovered the remains of a fortress that fits the conditions of the days of Saul. It is estimated that the building was about 170 feet long by 114 feet wide, with walls about seven feet thick made of roughly shaped stones, the chinks filled with small field stones and chips.[6]

The Extent of Saul's Power. It is likely that Saul held a loose control over tribes and villages, but there is no record that he had power to levy taxes or to conscript an army. He had a personal army of three thousand men at one time, but only when a crisis threatened did a larger corps rally to his call (1 Sam. 13:1–4). His rule was tolerated by Israelites because of his charismatic gifts and his popularity among the soldiers. There was probably no provision, when Saul was first made king, that his son should succeed

[5] See Nora Chadwick, *Poetry and Prophecy* (New York: Cambridge University Press, 1942), pp. 1–9, 14, 45.
[6] Paul W. Lapp, "Tell el-Ful," *The Biblical Archaeologist,* XXVIII, No. 1 (1965), p. 2.

him. As pressures from the Philistines and Ammonites continued and a feud between Samuel's prophetic party and Saul's military party developed, it became apparent that a member of Saul's family should continue to rule. The longer Saul was in power the more he encouraged this point of view. On the other hand, David may have expected to succeed Saul because he was his son-in-law, and a custom existed among southern tribes, such as Edom and Judah, that the mightiest warrior was married to the chief's daughter, thus binding him to the chief whom he would eventually succeed. That Jonathan acted upon this premise is suggested by 1 Samuel 20:13–17.[7] Other reasons for enmity between Saul and David may have been Saul's jealousy over David's brilliant military exploits as well as the failure of David's music to stimulate Saul to renewed vigor through ecstasy (1 Sam. 18:6–9).

Saul, despite his deficiencies as a political leader and his incapacity to control effectively all domestic and international situations, may be credited with competence in containing Philistine aggression. Editors of these historical accounts favored the Davidic dynasty, but they could not completely excise the material which showed Saul as an honorable, dependable, and capable king of Israel.

David's Rule

David was a member of the powerful tribe of Judah, whose principal trading centers were Hebron and Bethlehem. His fame as a warrior was widespread before he was enticed into Saul's army (1 Sam. 16:14–23). But David was not content to be only a soldier. With his powerful tribe behind him, his capacity for aligning himself with diverse groups, and his political sagacity, David was destined for a mission larger than sheikh of a powerful tribe. Under David the Judah tribe mustered military power sufficient to wage war against Saul's son Ishbosheth.[8] Elders of the Israelite tribes rightly foresaw the outcome of David's and Ishbosheth's war, and sued for peace with David (2 Sam. 5:1–5). They assessed the power of the Judah tribe, and correctly anticipated David's ambitions.

David's Early Political Alignments

Early in his career David aligned himself politically and economically with a number of different groups which broadened his political opportunities. *First,* there was the band of "discontented" who made him its captain (1 Sam. 22:2). With this army of four hundred (six hundred in 1 Sam. 30:9) he threatened sheep raisers (1 Sam. 25),

---

[7] Julian Morgenstern, "David and Jonathan," *Journal of Biblical Literature,* LXXVIII (1959), pp. 322–5.
[8] Eshbaal was his real name (1 Chron. 9:39). Ishbosheth means "man of shame," a term substituted for Eshbaal by pious editors. Eshbaal means "Baal's man."

and raided bedouin in the Negeb (1 Sam. 30). This group formed the core of his standing army when later he faced internal enemies and conquered other nations (2 Sam. 23:8–38). *Second,* his marriage to Saul's daughter Michal (1 Sam. 18:20–29) provided a connection with Israel's royal family, approved by Saul's eldest son Jonathan and by the people of Israel. This marriage was his claim to Israel's throne, sanctioned by custom among the semi-nomadic population of Judah. David, *thirdly,* secured wealth by marrying Abigail, whose dowry was her deceased husband's sheep and goat herds (1 Sam. 25). She owned large tracts of land in the hills south of Hebron. Marriage to Ahinoam, daughter of an influential Judean family, brought him additional support from a clan that opposed Saul's rule (1 Sam. 25:43). Thus it is clear that David carefully nurtured support for himself in Judah south of Saul's boundaries. His *fourth* alignment was with the Philistine Achish of Gath. The Philistines, therefore, certainly considered David an ally in their war against Saul. The *fifth,* and probably the most important alignment was with the priests and prophets in Israel, particularly those with whom Saul had quarreled. No ruler could be successful long without the full support of these religious leaders. Surely David noted Saul's alienation of them, and he took steps to ingratiate himself with all whom Saul had injured (1 Sam. 21:1–9). Records of David's court indicate the important spot that priests and prophets held in his government (2 Sam. 8:17, 12:1–15, 20:25).

The Death of Saul   After David had consolidated his position as a sure contender for Israel's throne by aligning himself with such diverse groups, he waited for events that would clear the road to his goal. The first of these events came in the form of a Philistine military campaign against Israel. The Philistine armies mustered at Aphek (1 Sam. 29:1). Rather than risk ambush when attacking Israel's mountain fortresses, they marched north to Megiddo and Jezreel. Their chariots would be effective in the broad valley, and the successful control of the Plain of Megiddo and the valley of Jezreel would separate from Saul the Israelites to the north and those east of the Jordan River. Philistine strategy worked, and Saul, separated from reinforcements, faced a superior army. Saul and three of his sons died in the battle of Mount Gilboa (1 Sam. 31:1–7). The Philistines once again threatened to annihilate Israel, much as they had threatened twenty years earlier when the tribe had been saved by Saul.

David Made King of Judah   David reacted promptly. He moved to Hebron in Judah, and there the tribe of Judah made him king. The people realized, no doubt, that it would be only a matter of time before Philistine armies would overrun Judah as they had Israel unless there was unity behind a single qualified leader. While Philistine attention was directed toward expansion of their holdings in the north, David began building his state in the south. The war which broke out between Judah under David and Israel under Ishbosheth (Eshbaal) probably pleased the Philistines, who considered Israel utterly defeated inasmuch as Ishbosheth had moved his feeble government east of the Jordan River to Mahanaim. From there he attempted to rule the kingdom of Saul with Abner, general of his army, in charge of relations with Judah (2 Sam. 2:8–11).

The Incident at Gibeon

Apparently David and Ishbosheth tried to reach some agreement before the civil war became too widespread. They sent their respective commanders, Joab and Abner, to conduct talks at Gibeon (2 Sam. 2:12–17). What happened at the Pool of Gibeon is obscure, but there seems to have been a cultic ceremony sealing the treaty, which got out of hand. The discovery in 1957 of an immense shaft carved through the rock at Gibeon helps to interpret the biblical account.[9] This shaft, thirty-seven feet in diameter, thirty-five feet deep with a five-foot-wide staircase winding around the edge of it, was an awesome sight to the ancients. The shaft continued into a stepped tunnel which descended another forty-five feet through solid rock, opening into a chamber eighty feet below street level. This was Gibeon's source of water, and as was often the case among the ancients, important sources of water were also likely spots for making treaties. Its importance is signalized further by Solomon's use of the site for religious ceremonies (1 Kings 3:4–5). Some evidence suggests that Joab's and Abner's "young men" were, in fact, "cadets" (2 Sam. 2:14) and this is the translation Roland de Vaux makes of the Hebrew word ne'arim.[10] There may have been a display of military techniques which became so competitive that combat broke out on the spot. A battle followed, and Joab's "cadets" defeated Abner's. There was no hope of reconciling Israel and Judah after this shameful affair, and "there was a long war between the house of Saul and the house of David" (2 Sam. 3:1).

David Becomes King of Israel

The Fall of Ishbosheth. A quarrel between Ishbosheth and Abner worked to David's benefit (1 Sam. 3:6–11). Abner was angered by Ishbosheth and sought to make a treaty with David without consent of his king. David's political sagacity brought him success in these negotiations. He demanded that his wife Michal, whom Saul had

[9]James B. Pritchard, *Gibeon Where the Sun Stood Still* (Princeton, N.J.: Princeton University Press, 1962), pp. 64–73.
[10]Roland de Vaux, *Ancient Israel: Its Life and Institutions,* trans. John McHugh (New York: McGraw-Hill Book Co., 1961), p. 220.

given to Palti when David had aligned himself with the Philistines, be returned to him (1 Sam. 25:44). This shrewd move guaranteed him the popular support of his own tribesmen in his claim to Saul's throne. Abner's negotiations with David were supported by the leading men of Israel because Ishbosheth probably had proved himself incapable of strong leadership. Abner travelled to Hebron, where David treated him with respect. Joab knew nothing of the negotiations for a treaty until his return from a military campaign. Why he distrusted Abner is not reported, but it may have been because Abner had ordered his cadets to attack Joab's at Gibeon. At any rate he assassinated Abner on the excuse that there was a blood feud between their families (2 Sam. 3:27). David turned this event to his benefit by mourning Abner's death publicly, and he himself composed the dirge (2 Sam. 3:33–34) used in the funeral ceremony. Without a strong general Ishbosheth was doomed. He was assassinated in his bed (2 Sam. 4:5–12). The elders of Israel came to David, and crowned him king of Israel.

The Capture of Jerusalem

David's next move was another brilliant political and military achievement. A powerful enclave of Canaanites in the city of Jerusalem separated Judah from Israel. Jerusalem had never been subdued by Israelites, and its massive walls and perennial flow of water provided the means of resisting attempts to take it by force or by siege. David foresaw that his leadership of Israel would never be fully effective until Jerusalem was in his possession. Its location upon a major route between north and south cut off communications between Israel and Judah. It could easily cast its lot with the Philistines, and thus provide the Philistines with a major point of assault against Israel's strongholds in the mountains. With the conclusion of the concordat between Abner and David the Philistines may have recognized that David was no longer a dutiful vassal of Achish, and that he must be controlled. David's conquest of Jerusalem anticipated this Philistine move.

The story of the capture of the city reported in 2 Samuel 5:6–10 is not clear. Some interpreters believe that Joab got into the Jebusites' city by going through the tunnel through which the citizens carried their water from the spring into the city. Others believe that Joab successfully blocked the entrance to the spring, and eventually the city submitted to David because of thirst. The archaeology of ancient Jerusalem has made clear that the Gihon Spring was outside the city walls. A shaft cut through the solid rock beneath the city's eastern wall provided citizens access to the spring. Excavations have shown that a heavy wall dating from about 1800 B.C. lay about 120 feet up the steep slope from the spring. The tunnel was stepped, and two curious niches in the wall, with natural stone pedestals, have been interpreted as sentry posts. The shaft is so narrow that two soldiers could easily protect it from any attack by way of the spring.[11] This evidence, added to 2 Samuel 5:8 which can be translated "let him cut off the water shaft," supports the second theory.

The capture of Jerusalem gave David a source of wealth in addition to his possessions of land and flocks through marriages to Abigail, Ahinoam, and Michal. It became the capital of Judah and Israel, now united for the first time geographically as well as politically. But, the city remained David's private possession. As booty of war he had all rights to it, and his construction of a palace probably was paid for by income derived from possession of the city. David allowed the Jebusite residents to remain in their homes, and no dislocation other than bringing the royal entourage into the city occurred.

David's Rapprochement with the Religious Leaders

After Jerusalem became David's prize city he began to centralize the government. He had wisely begun this process by recognizing his debt to the religious leaders of Israel. Saul had alienated the prophetic party in Israel, and David had become king of Judah without religious sanction (2 Sam. 2:1–4). David rectified these past errors by receiving coronation at Hebron in a religious ceremony, in which David and the elders of Israel agreed to a covenant The celebration probably took place at the sacred site called Mamre (Gen. 13:18, 18:1, 23:17). The content of the covenant was not given in the report of the coronation, but a later tradition, probably dependent upon early Israelite legal sanctions, listed the following stipulations: that the king may not be a foreigner; that he may not gain wealth by selling his subjects as slaves; and that he may not marry wives of foreign nations (Deut. 17:14–17; 1 Sam. 8:10–18). The right of hereditary succession was not agreed to, and the difficulties which resulted from this omission in the covenant are fully treated in 1 Kings 1, 2, and 12. The elders of Israel probably expected to choose a king upon David's death, and David probably expected one of his sons to succeed him. The crowning of David in an acceptable religious ceremony secured him the support of Israel's religious leaders.

David and The Army

David consolidated his government by expanding his army. Saul's defensive system had depended upon a small standing army which

[11] Kathleen M. Kenyon, "Excavations in Jerusalem, 1962," *Palestine Exploration Quarterly* (January–June 1963), p. 10.

provided internal security and repelled Philistine and Ammonite forays into Israelite territory. When major wars threatened, Saul had to call upon a civilian militia. This was probably one cause of his tragic defeat at Mount Gilboa. He was too slow in mobilizing an army to meet the surprise attack mounted by the Philistines. David recognized this deficiency. Experience with his small army of outlaws had taught him the advantages of a disciplined corps, and he applied this lesson on a grand scale in operations against the Philistines. He hired an army of mercenaries who were his body-guards and palace troops. These were the Gittites, Cherethites, and Pelethites (2 Sam. 8:18) who proved loyal to David when rebellion broke out in his palace (2 Sam. 15:18). These soldiers were probably Philistines who had been under his command when he was a vassal of Achish. In addition he conscripted a large army from native Judeans and Israelites. The story in 2 Samuel 24 reported the conscription under Joab.[12] This conscription policy provided David with sufficient troops to garrison Israel's borders while he fought the Philistines with his efficient band of mercenaries. The Philistines mounted two campaigns against him, using tactics which attempted to divide the country by capturing Jerusalem. It is likely that these two campaigns decided the fate of Canaan. It was either Philistine or Israelite control: David was the victor (2 Sam. 5: 17–25).

How is it possible that David was highly successful against Philistine armies while Saul had succeeded only in limiting their spread into the hill country? David was the better strategist. He was also more alert politically. But equally important, no doubt, was David's equipping his army with iron-tipped weapons. The Philistines had knowledge of ironworking during Saul's reign, and had managed to protect the secret until David wrested it from them. The Hittites seem to have been the first to use iron in the 14th century B.C., and the Philistines had learned it from them while migrating to Canaan. The Israelites supplied themselves with iron tools and weapons only slowly, since the Philistines monopolized the source of the metal as well as the secret of its manufacture (1 Sam 13:19–23).

Mobilization of a large army for Israel's defense was one of David's decisive moves. Once the Philistine menace had been destroyed, defensive troops had to be given something to do. They were given the task of creating an empire. Waging wars against Moab, Syria, and Edom, demanded wealth, complex logistics, and organization. David heavily taxed the citizens of Israel.

[12] The tale belongs between chapters 6 and 7 of 2 Samuel in order to place it historically in the account of David's rule.

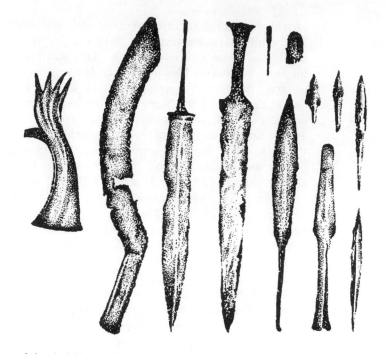

Axhead, sickle sword, spearheads, dagger, and arrowheads used
by armies in Palestine.

Canaanite Taxation

Canaanites had lived for generations under two systems of taxation. One was employed by the Egyptians when they controlled Canaan with collection of taxes by military commanders. The other was payment to the rulers of city states whose authority extended over the agricultural and grazing regions adjacent to the city. In the first system no questions arose about who collected the taxes. In the second, boundaries of city-states were ill-defined, and collectors of revenue from competing city-states made life for villagers and shepherds miserable. David's centralization of the tax system was probably a relief from the tax competition of rulers of city-states, and in that respect was appreciated by the people. The imposition of forced labor (2 Sam. 20:24), on the other hand, was deeply resented. It violated the covenant respecting taking no slaves from among Israelites which David probably had agreed to at Hebron.

Cultural Changes in a Cosmopolitan Empire

David's combined Judean and Israelite nation rapidly grew into a complex empire as a result of his wars of expansion. As Canaanite cities were incorporated into the nation their residents rubbed shoulders with Syrian, Moabite, and Edomite merchants and soldiers who frequented Jerusalem. Transactions for timber and for maritime shipment of trade goods also brought the Israelites into touch with Phoenician merchants. The Davidic Empire did not remain long a Judean-Israelite confederation, but rapidly emerged as a Canaanite-Syrian empire with David as sole ruler in Jerusalem. Such tremendous cultural changes brought new ways of thinking and living, and these changes are illustrated in several ways.

Changes in the Legal System. Tribal justice had been administered by the chief of the clan when he sat at the gate of the city or in the entrance of his tent. Those who needed cases adjudicated appeared before the chief and presented their grievances. Precedents guided the leader in his decisions, but there was no written code by which cases could be settled. Two stories of the Hebrew monarchy report how simple justice was administered. David received a woman from the village of Tekoa who set forth a case of fratricide (2 Sam. 14:1–20), and Solomon heard the case of two harlots who claimed the same child (1 Kings 3:16–28). These stories indicate that David and Solomon both tried to maintain the unsophisticated system which had been practiced before centralization of government in Jerusalem. Another story of the administration of justice shows clearly that the legal system adopted major changes when David's empire expanded. The story of Absalom's administration of justice indicates that David found himself too busy to handle the problems of humble people. Absalom ingratiated himself with them by sitting at the gate of Jerusalem settling their grievances (2 Sam. 15:1–6). As David's duties governing an empire grew he devoted less time to preserving justice at home. This was one source of disaffection among those Israelites who rose in rebellion against him, and tried to make Absalom their king.

Development of Court Life. David's long reign in Jerusalem saw the growth of a complex imperial court life laced with intrigue. The author of 2 Samuel 9–20 wrote a revealing report of what went on behind the walls of the palace. He told how David added to his entourage even those who were physically defective, simply for sentimental reasons (2 Sam. 9:1–13), how David seduced the wife of one of his best field commanders (2 Sam. 11:1–27), and how his sexual indulgence blinded him to the intrigue behind his back. This report included the story of how Absalom's hatred for Amnon mounted to murder after Amnon's rape of Tamar (2 Sam. 13:1–29), how David's neglect of traditional legal procedures prepared the way for Absalom's rebellion (2 Sam. 15:1–37), and how the king's uncontrolled grief over the death of the rebellious Absalom lessened the political benefits of crushing the revolt (2 Sam. 18:31 – 19:8). These pitiful conditions verified that ancient practices of personal

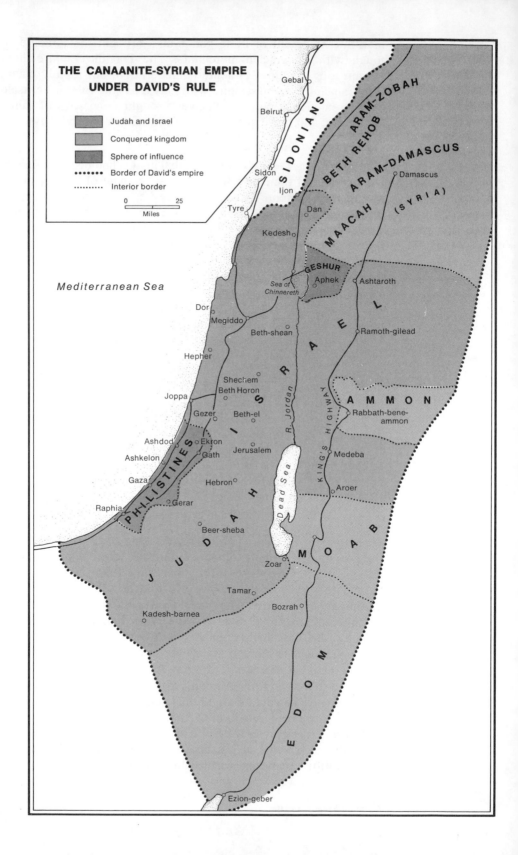

THE CANAANITE-SYRIAN EMPIRE
UNDER DAVID'S RULE

- Judah and Israel
- Conquered kingdom
- Sphere of influence
- •••••• Border of David's empire
- ·········· Interior border

0   25
Miles

Mediterranean Sea

Gebal

Beirut

SIDONIANS

ARAM-ZOBAH

BETH REHOB

Sidon

Ijon

ARAM-DAMASCUS

Damascus

Tyre

Dan

(SYRIA)

Kedesh

MAACAH

GESHUR

Sea of
Chinnereth

Aphek

Ashtaroth

Dor

Megiddo

Beth-shean

I
S
R
A
E
L

Ramoth-gilead

Hepher

Shechem

Beth Horon

Joppa

Beth-el

A M M O N

Gezer

Rabbath-bene-
ammon

Ashdod

Ekron

Jerusalem

Ashkelon

Gath

Medeba

Gaza

Hebron

Aroer

Raphia

Gerar

Dead Sea

KING'S HIGHWAY

R. Jordan

Beer-sheba

J
U
D
A
H

Zoar

M
O
A
B

Tamar

Bozrah

Kadesh-barnea

E
D
O
M

PHILISTINES

Ezion-geber

integrity were disappearing while the court embraced corrupt manners.

Loss of Tribal Identity.   Tribal identities began to break down as power was concentrated in Jerusalem. David's army, drawn from his captured territories, Philistia, Edom, Moab, Ammon, and Syria, as well as his own Israelite tribes, owed their allegiance to the king instead of tribal chiefs. In order to control an empire stretching from the Gulf of Aqaba to Damascus communications and rapid travel had to be improved, thereby obscuring tribal territories. Foreigners in Jerusalem naturally looked to the king for protection rather than to tribal justice, and a law to protect them commanded that "You shall not oppress a stranger" (Exod. 23:9).

Growth of a City Elite.   Court officials drawn from all over David's realm created a class of favored functionaries. Whereas grazing and property rights were held by families among the Israelite tribes, the Canaanite practice was for the king of a city-state to own all the property and to lease it out to his most faithful supporters. Since David was unable to manage all lands himself, a group of landed citizens loyal to the king rose to power in Israel. By tradition the king held all rights to trade. But here again the task of administering such a large enterprise forced him to divide his businesses among his favorites, who grew wealthy and powerful as a result of this patronage.

In spite of cultural upheaval, ideals such as tribal independence, possession of land and grazing rights, voluntary military service, control of trade routes passing through their territory, and suspicion of foreigners persisted among the semi-nomads in Israel. These people were the main source for stirring up rebellions. So long as David could control or appease these dissidents he had stable conditions in his empire.

David and the Priests   Other persons David needed to appease were the religious leaders. Whereas Saul had alienated the party under Samuel's leadership, David did all in his power to keep on good terms with it. One tradition reported that priests at Nob supplied David with food and weapons when Saul outlawed him (1 Sam. 21:1–9). Because of this favor Saul's swordsmen massacred the priestly village. Abiathar alone escaped from Saul's massacre at Nob (1 Sam. 22:20), and served as David's oracle-giver during his days as an outlaw (1 Sam. 23:6–14). Later David rewarded Abiathar with a chief place among the monarchy's priests. A priest closely associated with Abiathar was Zadok, whose name first appeared in the records of David's chief officials (2 Sam. 20:25). Although the early history of Zadok is not known, it is possible that he was priest of the shrine at Jerusalem when David captured the city. The name Zadok had a special association with Jerusalem before David captured it, according to traditions about the city (Josh. 10:1 and Gen. 14:17–20).

Ira, otherwise unknown, was also listed as a priest in David's court (2 Sam. 20:26), although in a similar list of officials (2 Sam. 8:15–18) David's sons were given that designation. This position may not have been a specifically religious one since one interpretation of the phrase "and David's sons were priests" (2 Sam. 8:18) is that "David's sons were the chief officials in the service of the king" (1 Chron. 18:17). On the other hand David may have designated some of his sons who did not stand in line of succession to the throne as religious officials, so as to keep that distinctive party closely allied to the throne. There is no evidence from literary sources of the United Monarchy indicating that priestly positions were hereditary in David's monarchy. With Solomon's accession to the throne it is likely that the family of Zadok established itself so firmly as the priestly party in Jerusalem that it held that position for four hundred years.

David's real or calculated respect for the prophetic and priestly groups in his empire vividly illustrates how astute he was as a political strategist. He had a keen sense of the traditional and the publicly acceptable, at the same time that he made significant modifications of the old ways. He showed, for instance, high respect for Saul as a chieftain who had received his power from Yahweh. Saul's power had been consecrated by Samuel the prophet, so that violation of this divine authority would bring a curse upon the offender. When David could have assassinated Saul and received the adulation of his fellow tribesmen, he did not. A terrifying guilt would have settled upon David for having done such a deed (1 Sam. 26:6–12). In addition, one story about Saul's death in battle related how an Amalekite warrior claimed to have killed Saul when the end was near. He expected David to reward him for his deed but instead David ordered his execution for having "slain the Lord's anointed" (2 Sam. 1:1–16). In these and other ways David observed the sanctity of custom, but in many instances he instituted new ways in Israel which changed Israelite religion significantly.

David's achievements in politics and religion were won by shrewd calculations. Unlike Saul, who acquired power by physical and psychic prowess, David acquired power by adept maneuvers conducted within the conventions of his people. He aligned himself with the ruling family by his marriage to Saul's daughter and his intense friendship with Jonathan. Even when Saul attempted to assassinate him he never disavowed his loyalty to Saul nor advocated retaliatory action against Israel's king. He made friends with the Philistines, and used his vassalage to Achish to camouflage his intentions of driving the Philistines back to their coastal cities. David did not attack Saul's successor, Ishbosheth, when he had been severely weakened by Philistine victories, but rather fostered Abner's defection from the weak Ishbosheth (2 Sam. 3:12–21). David publicly mourned Abner's murder by Joab, and composed a funeral dirge for him, but Abner's death conveniently removed the last strong leader in Israel.

The Elements of David's Success

The Old Testament records indirectly how powerful in their several spheres of influence men like Saul, Samuel, Joab, and Abner really were. What accounts for a leader of David's caliber rising to political supremacy in competition with men like these? There are several explanations:

1. David's policy of waiting for events to work favorably toward his political advancement paid handsomely. The deaths of Saul and Abner, the political uncertainty in Israel, and tense international conditions combined to lift David to the position of foremost leader of the people of Israel and Judah.

2. David was able to view the entire cultural scene in Canaan, with its complex units, Canaanites and Israelites, nomads and farmers, merchants and military, Syrians and Phoenicians, priests and prophets, chieftains and people, with a vision that eluded other men in positions of power. Whereas the other men may have seen one special group as the source of order and stability in the land, David looked upon himself as that source.

3. David was unique in his capacity to weave the traditional and the new into a single pattern. Raised in Judah, a border tribe between the settled regions of Canaan and the bedouin of the south where calculating compromise was essential to survival, David put that art to use in weaving diverse cultural units into an empire.

4. David used the fanatical religion of Yahwism around which to organize the diverse cultures which became parts of his empire.

No detailed account of Solomon's reign over Israel has been preserved. The combination of historical and legendary accounts of
David's rule, even though inadequate and incomplete by modern
standards, give recital of a full-blooded person. Why Solomon did
not inspire some scribe to record the details of his court life and
popular stories about his early years is not known. Perhaps, it was
because he was not a popular king, or because some records were
destroyed. What did remain for the editors was a Book of the Acts
of Solomon, now of course no longer in existence, from which editors of the books of the Kings of Israel and Judah drew a few
excerpts to show how the monarchy was managed in his hands
(1 Kings 11:41).

The strongest traditions of Solomon concern his wisdom, his wealth,
and his construction of the Temple. A legend telling of his judgment in deciding the fate of a baby claimed by two harlots (1 Kings
3:16–28), his fame as a learned man (1 Kings 4:29–34), and the
connecting of his name with the book of Proverbs, speak for his
wisdom. Tales about his exceptional wealth are found throughout
1 Kings 3–11, but the most famous is the story of the visit of the
Queen of Sheba (1 Kings 10:1–13). His responsibility for construction of a temple to Yahweh on the pattern of Phoenician temples (1 Kings 5–9) represents Solomon as using his immense wealth
in the cause of religion. In addition to these popular tales there is
much information tucked away in the details of his rule which permits a reliable reconstruction of events and conditions during his
reign.

**The Accession
of Solomon**

It was with difficulty that Solomon succeeded his father David,
although the records indicate that his way was prepared by Bathsheba, his mother, by Zadok, the priest, and by Nathan, the prophet.
Adonijah, David's son next in line of succession after Absalom
(1 Kings 1:6), was supported by Abiathar and Joab. Adonijah made
an active bid for kingship by public fanfare (1 Kings 1:5, 9–10), but
Solomon seems to have played a waiting game, and he let others in
the palace conduct the political maneuvering for him. The narrative depicted the confusion of two coronation banquets held
simultaneously within a half mile of each other. Adonijah held one
at the spring En-rogel (1 Kings 1:9); Solomon at the spring Gihon
(1 Kings 1:33). This narrative may be an accurate report of the confusion which resulted since no one really knew whom David had
appointed as his successor.

Ruthless Consolidation of Power. Once Solomon had been
crowned he acted promptly to secure his authority in Jerusalem and

throughout Israel. He had Adonijah assassinated on the pretext that in asking for Abishag, David's latest concubine, Adonijah had committed a serious breach of political etiquette (1 Kings 2:13–25). Joab was slain even while he took sanctuary at Yahweh's altar (1 Kings 2:23–35). Shimei, who had consistently supported Saul's heirs as the legitimate ruling house in Israel (2 Sam. 16:5–14), was confined to the city of Jerusalem, and upon violation of his confinement he was put to death (1 Kings 2:36–46). Abiathar the priest was allowed to live, but his banishment from Jerusalem to Anathoth killed him politically (1 Kings 2:26–27). All opposition was ruthlessly put down, and Solomon's extermination of his opponents was accepted without rebellion by citizens in the villages and cities of Israel. This acceptance may reflect the general support that Solomon had among the people. Or, perhaps the swiftness and ruthlessness of his actions did not permit opposition to form outside Jerusalem before he had complete political and military control throughout the land. The records report no uprising in Israel. Edom and Syria, on the other hand, revolted from Israel's domination when Solomon ascended the throne in Jerusalem (1 Kings 11:14–25), indicating that garrison troops used to control those states may have been recalled to Israel's soil in order to preserve civil obedience. On the other hand it is possible that records of an uprising in Israel at that time against Solomon were excluded from the Old Testament. A serious rebellion in Israel did occur in Solomon's reign, but it was long after he had become king (1 Kings 11:26–40).

Emphasis on Trade

Although Solomon lost territory to Edom and Syria, he made excellent treaties with Egypt and Phoenicia. These relationships indicated that Solomon placed his confidence for maintenance and growth of his empire in trade relations rather than in conquest by war. David had enriched Israel by conquest of farm lands and major caravan routes. Solomon, although he supported a large army, made no attempt at military expansion. His expansion was through treaty obligations and trade relations. The Israelite-Egyptian treaty (1 Kings 3:1) was solemnized by Solomon's marriage to the daughter of a Pharaoh of the Twenty-first or Tanite Dynasty. A note about this marriage is tucked away at 1 Kings 9:16, reporting that Pharaoh captured Gezer, a walled Canaanite city, and gave it to Solomon. Two conditions lay behind this alliance by marriage and the gift of Gezer to Solomon which were not mentioned directly in the text. *First*, some Canaanite cities were independent of Israel's control. It may be that David had been unable to bring every fortified Canaanite city under his control, or perhaps during the change in kingship in Jerusalem Gezer had proclaimed its independence. *Second,* Egypt had become again economically and militarily strong enough to send armies beyond her borders. Solomon's treaty with Egypt was probably essential to preserve his independence in the face of revived Egyptian power.

The Israelite-Phoenician treaty involved furnishing timber and workmen for construction of Solomon's palace and the temple of Yahweh (1 Kings 5:1–12). Payment for these materials and services was accomplished by Solomon's agreement allowing Hiram of Tyre to tax mercilessly twenty cities in Solomon's northern territories (1 Kings 9:10–14). Phoenician capability in architecture, metal working, and shipbuilding was far superior to anything Israel had produced. In order for Solomon to bring Israel's cultural attainments up to the level of those in Egypt, Phoenicia, and Mesopotamia he had to employ craftsmen from those other states. It was necessary, too, for Solomon to employ Phoenician shipbuilders and sailors in order to carry on profitable maritime trade with Arabia and East Africa. Solomon's loss of territory to Hadad of Edom did not stop Israel's trade far to the south. But for some unknown reason building a fleet of ships to sail from Ezion-geber through the Gulf of Aqaba into the Red Sea and beyond was cheaper and more efficient than bringing goods by the overland trade routes (1 Kings 9:26–28, 10:11–12).[13] Solomon's prosperity depended upon his treaties rather than upon military exploitation, but this policy did not eliminate the need for military preparedness.

Solomon's Military Policies According to the Old Testament, Solomon conducted no major wars as had his father. This does not mean, however, that he was militarily weak. In fact, he strengthened Israel's defenses. At the heart of his empire he fortified Jerusalem by expanding the habitable area inside the city walls. Some archaeologists believe that the Millo constituted a series of stone platforms built on the steep eastern slope of ancient Jerusalem so that the restricted residential area could be expanded. A rock scarp runs north-south, and a series of rocky ribs were built parallel to the scarp, filled with rubble, and packed with soil. Buildings were then erected on these platforms. The wall was also repaired and improved (1 Kings 9:15).[14] On the northern perimeter of his territory he fortified Hazor, which faced the Aramaean states clustered about the Lebanon mountains. At Megiddo, which controlled the pass from the Carmel range and the

---

[13] It is tempting to make a biographical conclusion about Solomon based on the lack of Old Testament reports. There were no stories about Solomon's early years in the biblical accounts. Those that record his years as king dwell on his love of ostentatious display. Attach these to the reports of his capability as a trader and one could almost conclude that he spent much of his life before becoming king of Israel among the Phoenicians.

[14] See Kenyon, "Excavations in Jerusalem, 1962," p. 14.

entrance into the highlands from the Jordan Valley through Jezreel, he built another major fortification. The threat from revived Philistine power was met by building fortified cities at Baalath, Gezer, and Bethhoron to control the principal ascents to Jerusalem from the west. A major fort was built south of the Dead Sea at Tamar to protect Israel's southern regions from attack by Hadad the Edomite and to supply a mobile force to guard the trade road to Ezion-geber (1 Kings 9:15–18). So long as Moab and Ammon remained docile no major fortifications were required on the east. Thus, Solomon was prepared for invasion from the north, west, and south, and his troops were garrisoned so as to provide rapid mobilization in case of internal revolt or rebellion from vassal states to the east.

Solomon also improved Israel's offensive capability. Neither Saul nor David had employed the chariot because it was of little use in the mountainous terrain at the heart of Israel. Furthermore, its use was based upon a military élite which had wealth enough to own horses and to buy expensive chariots. Solomon's economic policies brought into existence an aristocratic class which could affort such weapons. Furthermore, wealthy Canaanite princes whose loyalty to David was suspect, with the passage of time and a new generation developed loyalty to Solomon and could be trusted with this formidable weapon in their possession. There is no archaeological confirmation of the biblical statement that Solomon built "cities for his chariots, and the cities for his horsemen" (1 Kings 9:19), but there is little question that if Solomon carried on an extensive import-export trade in horses and chariots, and if a military aristocracy similar to that in pre-Israelite Canaan had been revived, he would have employed the chariot for his own army.[15]

Solomon's Economic Policies

Solomon's military policy was closely allied with his economic policies. With a standing army of great mobility at his disposal, he was able to effect economic policies which would have been resisted by a population less intimidated by an effective army. Solomon probably deserved the resentment which eventually destroyed his empire. His extensive building projects in Jerusalem, such as the Millo, his palace, and the temple to Yahweh, his fortification of cities, and his maritime trade, all caused him financial strain. In addition to accepting twenty cities in exchange for labor and materials (1 Kings 9:11), Hiram of Tyre loaned Solomon 120 talents of gold (1 Kings 9:14). Since there were two standards of weight, common and royal, and the Bible does not specify which was meant,

---

[15] See Yigael Yadin, *The Art of Warfare in Biblical Lands in the Light of Archaeological Discoveries* (New York: McGraw-Hill Book Co., 1963), p. 288 f.

this loan may have amounted to 9,660 pounds of gold, or it may have been as much as 16,560 pounds. In either case these figures show how indebted Solomon was to Hiram.[16]

The Use of Forced Labor. Probably because of this and other debts Solomon used forced labor to get his ambitious projects done. Records of Solomon's labor were so complete that reference to them is made four times in his short biography (1 Kings 4:6, 5:13, 9:15–23, 11:28). One account tried to modify the implications of these records by claiming that Israelites were not enslaved; only remnants of the Canaanite population were so treated (1 Kings 9:2–22). This effort was unsuccessful in view of the clear assertion that Solomon enslaved the people of Israel (1 Kings 5:13 and 12:1–5).

Taxation. Solomon placed a heavy hand on his nation through taxation. Although David may have organized Judah into administrative districts while he ruled at Hebron, Solomon so thoroughly reorganized and taxed Israel that his policy completely destroyed tribal identities in the north. This obliteration of ancient loyalties was part of his plan, no doubt, since tribes might have bred revolt. Each district was responsible for supplying the needs of the central government for one month in twelve. This plan also broke down Canaanite and Israelite distinctions in the population so that control was centralized effectively in the hands of the twelve governors of the districts. These men were personally loyal to Solomon, and two of them were his sons-in-law (1 Kings 4:11, 14). It is easy to see, then, why a strong army was necessary to patrol the country when such serious social and economic measures were in force.

Another source of income for satisfaction of Solomon's expensive tastes was extractions from caravans passing through his territory. The three routes running through Canaan, the coastal, the central, and the King's Highway east of the Jordan River, carried tremendous quantities of goods during peaceful times from Egypt and Arabia to Anatolia and Mesopotamia. By controlling Ezion-geber, too, he was able to tax the overland trade between Arabia and Egypt. Each caravan had to pay for safe passage through Israel, and such income was available with little investment other than strong military checkpoints.

[16] See "Weights and Measures," in George A. Buttrick, ed., *The Interpreter's Dictionary of the Bible,* R–Z (New York: Abingdon Press, 1962), pp. 828–39. Hereafter referred to as *IDB*.

Solomon's Commercial Investments. Solomon's economy was bolstered by commercial investments which may have increased his personal wealth. He received the Queen of Sheba, who made her trip from southern Arabia to Jerusalem for more serious reasons than simply to meet a wise and rich man. Solomon controlled the northern outlet for rare spices and jewels which sparked south Arabian trade. Furthermore, the Sabeans, who had developed a small empire in the region known today as Yemen, had expanded into Ethiopia where rich minerals were easily mined. Solomon's marriage to an Egyptian princess had probably given him trade rights in Ethiopia, long a region exploited by Egypt. Solomon's maritime trade had cut into the Queen of Sheba's own business. Thus, her journey to Jerusalem may have been to discuss trade relations with Solomon. She was received royally, and she and Solomon came to a satisfactory compromise. At any rate, a lucrative trade with Arabia continued to put wealth into Solomon's hands (1 Kings 10:14–15, see map, p. 23).

Solomon's fleet of ships on the Red Sea was an enterprise which exploited his friendship with Egypt, and it may have captured some trade from the resourceful Queen of Sheba (1 Kings 9:26–28). Archaeological evidence has made clear that major construction took place at Ezion-geber between 1200 and 900 B.C. Solomon's pact with Hiram of Tyre put Phoenician shipbuilders to work constructing a merchant fleet manned by mixed Israelite and Phoenician crews. These ships sailed to Ophir for gold, wood, and jewels. The location of Ophir is problematic, and some scholars think that it was located in India, some in southwest Arabia, a region near the Queen of Sheba's territory, and some think that Ophir was in East Africa. This last designation seems most likely since Egyptian records referring to Punt claim the same imports.[17]

Competent archaeologists no longer believe that Solomon's large and prosperous copper smelting industry was located at Tell el-Kheleifeh, midway between the modern towns of Aqaba and Eilat on the north shore of the Gulf of Aqaba.[18]

If this area was not the location of Solomon's bronze industry, where was it? It may have been at Succoth and Zarethan in the

[17] See "Ophir," *IDB*, K–Q, p. 605.
[18] This theory was put forth by Nelson Glueck in the *Bulletin of the American School of Oriental Research*, LXXI (October 1938), pp. 3–18, and was followed by a popular treatment in *Rivers in the Desert—A History of the Negev* (New York: Grove Press, 1960), pp. 153–68. He has subsequently revised his interpretations in "Ezion-geber," *The Biblical Archaeologist*, XXVIII, No. 3 (1965), pp. 70–87.

Jordan Valley (1 Kings 7:45–47).[19] Solomon probably obtained his copper from trade with ports on the Mediterranean Sea, since he "had a fleet of ships of Tarshish at sea with the fleet of Hiram" (1 Kings 10:22). This passage is usually interpreted as an expansion of the report of Solomon's Red Sea fleet. However, Tarshish originally meant "refinery."[20] Since a refinery of major proportions did not exist at Ezion-geber, as previously supposed, it is likely that the ships of Tarshish should be associated with shipments of copper from Mediterranean ports. It is likely that Solomon engaged a Mediterranean fleet which sailed to Cyprus, Sicily, and even to Spain where he traded Israel's chief exports, grain and olive oil, for metals which the land of Canaan did not have. The ore, once landed at Phoenician ports, was then sent overland to the Jordan Valley where a plentiful supply of wood for making charcoal was available in the heavily wooded valley. The trip from the port of Tyre by way of Megiddo and Jezreel would have been simple and economical.

The Slave Trade. Another source of revenue which swelled Solomon's personal treasury was his trade in slaves. Solomon made slaves of the Canaanite population which continued to live side by side with Israelites (1 Kings 9:21). It is possible that Solomon enslaved Israelites also. One of the limitations placed upon the kings of Israel was that they should not "cause the people to return to Egypt in order to multiply horses" (Deut. 17:14–17). The phrase "cause the people to return to Egypt," where the Hebrews had been slaves, is a literary expression for slavery. The phrase "to multiply horses" probably was a direct reference to Solomon's trade with Egypt whereby he purchased Egyptian horses for human beings enslaved within his own empire. It is entirely possible that this prohibition, although formulated during the reign of Manasseh (687–642 B.C.) whose reign saw greater evils even than Solomon's, was a reaction to what Solomon had done when he traded horses and chariots to Kue and Syria (1 Kings 10:28–29) using enslaved human beings as his collateral.

The Beginnings of Revolt

Solomon's wealth and glory came at a high cost. The cost was rebellion by those people in Israel upon whom the burdens of excessive taxation, imposition of strict administrative governors, and slavery had fallen. Jeroboam, who was Solomon's administrator of

[19] See James B. Pritchard, "The First Excavations at Tell es-Sa'idiyeh," *The Biblical Archaeologist,* XXXIII, No. 1 (1965), pp. 10–17, and "Two Tombs and a Tunnel in the Jordan Valley: Discoveries at Biblical Zarethan," *Expedition,* VI, No. 4 (1964), pp. 2–9.

[20] John Bright, *A History of Israel* (Philadelphia: Westminster Press, 1959), p. 192.

forced labor, revolted after having received assurances from Israel's prophetic party that he would have their support (1 Kings 11:29–37). The revolt failed. Jeroboam fled from Solomon's reprisals, and received sanctuary in Egypt from Shishak, founder of the Twenty-second Egyptian Dynasty and usurper of the Tanite Dynasty which had been friendly with Solomon. Solomon's policies prepared the way for tearing the monarchy into two small and struggling nations (1 Kings 12).

Religious Conditions During the United Monarchy

The men responsible for preserving and editing the Old Testament were sophisticated literary and religious critics. They edited their sources with an eye to excising those crudities which in no way had offended their less sensitive predecessors. In studying this period it is necessary to use only those literary sources traceable to Israel's United Monarchy, but this ideal is often hard to achieve. It is possible with these precautions to relate what the religious situation was during this period. Information from other cultures in the ancient Near East supplies valuable help in interpreting the religious conditions of the Israelites during the United Monarchy. Even this material, however, is not always reliable because Israel's religion was in many respects distinct from that of nearby cultures — drawing exact parallels with Egyptian, Canaanite, Aramaean, or Mesopotamian religious beliefs and practices is thus impossible. Scholarly opinion on these matters differs radically, so that one cannot simply depend upon experts to explain what the conditions were.[21] Special care must be taken in reading the earliest sources, and in drawing conclusions from them about the religion of the United Monarchy.

Religious Leaders

The Forms of Priesthood

Priesthood was a common form of religious leadership in Israel. Priests served in three capacities during the period of the United Monarchy, and as a result of Solomon's construction of the Temple a fourth was added before the end of his reign. *First*, priests were custodians of shrines. Such religious centers usually had existed from the most ancient times, and a specialized leadership developed in connection with them. For the most part priesthood was hereditary, and the privilege of holding the position was jealously maintained. The custodian of the Hebrew shrine at Shiloh was Eli, and even though according to later tradition his sons were evil, there is no suggestion that they were not entitled to serve as priests at Shiloh. As custodians of the shrine they collected fees from worshippers

---

[21] For different interpretations of the same basic material see Robert H. Pfeiffer, *Religion in the Old Testament*, ed. Charles Conrad Forman (New York: Harper & Brothers, 1961) and Walther Eichrodt, *Theology of the Old Testament*, trans. J. A. Baker (Philadelphia: The Westminster Press, 1961).

THE RULE OF ISRAEL UNDER SAUL, DAVID, AND SOLOMON

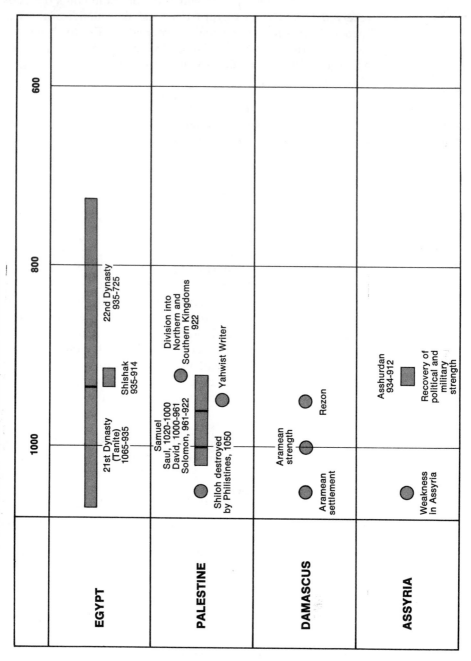

to keep the holy place in operation. They also were guardians of the sacred symbol of Yahweh's presence, in this case the Ark, a symbol of Yahweh's military quality (1 Sam. 1–4).

Second, priests manipulated the means of divination. One means of divination was a box, or garment called an *ephod*. It was carried or worn by the priest who when consulted for a decision plunged his hands into the instrument and brought forth the stones or objects which gave a yes or no decision (1 Sam. 14:3, 19, 23:9–12). Sometimes no answer was brought forth (1 Sam. 14:37), and this was considered cause for alarm because a sin committed by someone had kept the divine voice from answering (1 Sam. 14:38).

Third, priests were the dignitaries responsible for the preservation and transmission of religious traditions. The traditions would be the beliefs and practices of a particular shrine, but might include as well the stories and legends, both oral and written, of the people who visited the site.[22] There is no doubt that priests were, if not the only literate persons in antiquity, certainly among the most influential, and some were listed among the highest officials in David's and Solomon's governments (2 Sam. 20:23–25, 1 Kings 4:1–6).

A *fourth* function delegated to priests during the reign of Solomon was the administering of the king's sacrifices. From the emphasis upon the function of priests as sacrificers in much of the Old Testament, especially in Leviticus and Deuteronomy, one might think this had always been a priestly responsibility. Early sources indicate, however, that in ancient Israel the head of each family offered sacrifices at special seasons of the year and during times of crisis. Saul and David offered sacrifice whenever it was expedient; Saul just before going into battle (1 Sam. 13:8–10) and David at the auspicious occasion of bringing the Ark to Jerusalem (2 Sam. 6:17–20). A brief text indicates that Solomon gave up the ritual of sacrifice except for three times a year. He delegated that duty to priests whose influence probably expanded rapidly once the temple of Yahweh, as the royal chapel, had been completed (1 Kings 9:25).

The Prophets Prophets were also important as religious leaders during the monarchy. These were persons who believed they were possessed by the spirit of a deity and thus especially qualified to carry the deity's message either through speech or physical activity. Saul was considered a prophet (1 Sam. 10:12), and Samuel was associated with

[22] See Edward Nielsen, *Oral Tradition* (London: SCM Press, 1954), p. 18–38.

prophets in a way not clearly defined (1 Sam. 10:1–8). Prophetic behavior often was kindled by music and dancing, and a frenzied state of mind led some prophets to tear their clothing and to expose themselves to the weather (1 Sam. 19:24). The threat to Israel's existence posed by the Philistine invasion in the west and the Ammonite incursions in the east incited especially sensitive men to vigorous faith in Yahweh and a patriotic fervor to preserve His people from annihilation.

Prophets were also consultants of the kings, and in that capacity seemed to have an official position, although prophets were not cited in the official lists of administrative posts. The story of Nathan's reproach of David for stealing Uriah's wife (2 Sam. 12:1–15) indicates that Nathan was a favored official. He had ready access to the king, and he could denounce the king without danger of being put to death. (Compare, for example, two views of Nathan the prophet. One source contemporary with David depicts Nathan as going straight into the king's presence [2 Sam. 12:1], while a later source depicts an intermediary announcing him, and obsequious bowing before the monarch [1 Kings 1:22–24].) Prophets were special advisors to the kings, and that position was secured by their intelligent counsel as well as by their unique physical behavior.

The Seers

Another type of religious leader was the seer. This English word is used to translate two different Hebrew words, *ro'eh* and *khozeh*. Although it is difficult to identify their precise functions as distinct from priests and prophets, both looked into the future; the *ro'eh* by means of clairvoyance and occultism (1 Sam. 9:9), the *khozeh* by observations of omens such as the planets, the flight of birds, the livers of sheep, or the movement of animals (2 Sam. 24:10–14). They did not occupy a major place in Hebrew religion, and probably came into Yahwism from Canaanite religion.

The King as a Religious Official

The king, too, was a religious official. Saul was a devotee of ecstatic prophecy and conducted ceremonies at an altar to Yahweh (1 Sam. 14:35). Although Saul had no special associations with the Ark of Yahweh, David signified his personal relationship with it by dancing vigorously in its procession. One story shows clearly that there was a close connection between the Ark, the king, and the fertility of Israelite women who participated in the ceremony of the Ark (2 Sam. 6:17–7:2). David wore a garment called an ephod, which exposed his genitals when he cavorted before the Ark (2 Sam. 6:14). Looking upon the reproductive organs of the great king in the presence of the deity that had given him such power would produce children in the wombs of the women whose sons would achieve greatness similar to David's. His wife Michal rebuked him for thus exposing himself before "his servants' maids," and because of her criticism she remained to her death childless (2 Sam. 6:20–23).

The Ark   The chief religious object cited in these early historical sources was the Ark of Yahweh. It was so important that a whole history was written about it, which served as one source for the final edition of the history of the United Monarchy. Even with a history of the Ark there is still confusion about its origins and function. Some scholars think that every religious sanctuary had an ark which contained the lots used by priests in giving divine oracles. It may have been a receptacle for storing the most important cult objects associated with a shrine. Confusion about the nature of the Ark arose because religious dogma would not accept historical fact. One scholar advanced the theory that Jewish dogma held there was only one Ark, since Moses made the Ark to house the sacred stones upon which the Ten Commandments were written. Jewish scribes substituted the word *ephod* for the word *'aron*, meaning ark, whenever reference to an ark could not mean the one located at Shiloh.[23] This demanded a slight change of only two Hebrew letters. Some scholars believe it was a religious object borrowed from Canaanite practice, and that through misunderstanding of the function of ark and ephod these terms became confused.[24] Others are quite sure that it originated with Moses in the wilderness, having a uniquely Israelite origin and use.[25]

Whatever its origins, it is clear that David brought the Ark to Jerusalem, and that Solomon later placed it in his newly constructed temple to Yahweh, where it remained (1 Kings 8:1–9). From that point on there is no reference to the Ark in Israel's early historical writings, and no one knows what eventually became of it. It has been suggested that its ceremonial use was lost through neglect when it was placed in the Temple. It may have remained an object of veneration until the temple was destroyed in the Babylonian war of 588–587 B.C. During the monarchy it served as a visual reminder of the presence of Yahweh (1 Sam. 6:3, 5, 8, 20), but it was chiefly a guardian in time of war. When Israel suffered defeat by the Philistines, it was thought that the absence of the Ark was responsible. The Ark was brought from Shiloh and carried into battle among Israel's warriors; its awesome quality caused the Philistine god

[23] See W. R. Arnold, *Ark and Ephod* (New York: Cambridge University Press, 1917).
[24] Pfeiffer, *Religion in the Old Testament*, p. 81. Also see 1 Samuel 14:18–19 where *ephod* should certainly be read for *ark*.
[25] See Julian Morgenstern, *The Ark, the Ephod, and the Tent of Meeting* (Cincinnati: Hebrew Union College, 1945), and "Ark of the Covenant," *IDB*, A–D, p. 222–6.

Dagon to fall down before it (1 Sam. 4:1–4, 5:1–5). It caused the bubonic plague among Israel's enemies (1 Sam. 5:1–12). It forced cows with calves to forsake their young in carrying it back to Israelite territory (1 Sam. 6:1–16). It struck dead those who through curiosity looked into it (1 Sam. 6:19–20). Even those who touched it when an accident almost threw it to the ground were killed (2 Sam. 6:6–8). Although a fearful thing, in some instances it brought blessing to those who cared for it. It made Obed-edom prosperous (1 Sam. 6:11), and gave fertility to women who looked upon the genitals of those who guarded it (1 Sam. 6:16–23). Although the importance of the Ark may have declined after the Temple to Yahweh was built, during the high point of the monarchy it was the most important religious object in Israel.

Other Religious Objects

The *cherubim* (1 Sam. 4:4) were religious objects connected in some way with the Ark. It appears they were attached to the top of the Ark, images upon which the invisible Yahweh rode. Perhaps the cherubim were like the winged figures which flanked the throne of King Hiram of Byblos or the winged bulls and human-headed lions which guarded the entrances to Assyrian palaces. The connection between cherubim and Ark is further shown by the carving of such images for the room in Solomon's temple in which the Ark was kept (1 Kings 6:19–28). The early accounts in Samuel and Kings do not attribute divine power to these images, but Psalm 18:10 recites that Yahweh "rode on a cherub, and flew," and an early story reports that cherubim guarded the Garden of Eden when Yahweh drove Adam and Eve from it (Gen. 3:24).

The *teraphim* doubtlessly were idols, and in one instance they appeared to be about the size and shape of a man (1 Sam. 19:13, 16). These images were mentioned only once in Samuel and Kings, but other passages show that they were common objects of veneration prior to the monarchy (Judg. 17:5, 18:14, Gen. 31:19, 34:35). These idols were household gods, and could be as large as a man or small enough to be portable and easily concealed. Possession of teraphim may have given a person the power of inheriting the property which the teraphim guarded. This possibility is likely in view of the presence of one in David's home.

Temple Paraphernalia

Jachin and Boaz were two pillars of bronze standing on each side of the entrance to the Temple to Yahweh (1 Kings 7:15–22, 41–42). Their function is not made clear precisely in the text, although they were definitely freestanding, decorative, and symbolic. Several theories have been proposed for their symbolism. They may have been sacred obelisks with phallic associations. Some scholars think they represented cosmic pillars similar to the pillars of Hercules which held up the heavens. Some believe they were stylized sacred trees which recalled the Israelites' worship of nature. Others regard them as gigantic fire-altars. Archaeological evidence from Tyre, Marisa in southern Palestine, Cyprus, and Khorsabad supports the last of these interpretations.[26] The pillars may have borne inscriptions which commemorated the king's dependence upon Yahweh. *Jachin* means "he will establish" and *Boaz* means "in strength of." The full inscriptions may have been "He will establish the throne of David forever" and "In the strength of Yahweh shall the king rejoice."[27]

Limestone altar in the Palestine Archaeological Museum. Upon it incense was burned and blood was sprinkled on the "horns of the altar" at each corner.

The *altar* of the Temple to Yahweh was a major religious object. It is interesting that it was not mentioned in a description of the Temple's paraphernalia in 1 Kings 6–7. This was probably an error for which no satisfactory explanation has been made. That there

[26] See W. F. Albright, *Archaeology and the Religion of Israel* (4th ed., Baltimore, The Johns Hopkins Press, 1956), pp. 144–8.
[27] "Jachin and Boaz," *IDB*, E–J, p. 780–1.

was an altar is certain because parallel passages from the Chronicles, a document from the late 4th century B.C., mentions an altar (2 Chron. 4:1), and the books of Kings supplied most of the information for the author of the Chronicles. Furthermore, archaeological data from Megiddo, Beth-shan, Lachish, and Hazor indicate that stone altars similar to the dimensions of the one listed in 2 Chronicles were part of temple furnishings in those cities. The altar to which Joab fled for safety had horns, and supposedly anyone clinging to the altar was safe from assassination (1 Kings 2:28). These horns were probably abutments of some sort which had symbolic and functional value, but there is no description in early Old Testament sources on how they were used. The altar as a whole was the spot where animals were sacrificed in efforts to appease and to commune with Yahweh. The horns of the altar may have functioned originally as hooks to tie the sacrificial animal. In time these became obsolete, but they continued as decorative elements. The altar, before the Temple to Yahweh was built, stood in front of "the tent of the Lord" (1 Kings 2:28). The tent was the dwelling of Yahweh, and housed the furniture used in cultic ceremonies for him (1 Kings 1:39). It had been used in the period when some of the Hebrews were semi-nomads, and continued to serve as the main shrine in Jerusalem from the time David captured the city until Solomon had finished the Temple. Probably it was then placed with the Ark within the Temple itself as a sacred object but having no function anymore. Jewish writers idealized this object many centuries later and described it as a complex and ornate tabernacle (Ex. 25–31, 35–40).

Another object associated with the Temple to Yahweh was the *molten sea* (1 Kings 7:25–26). The exact function of this giant bronze bowl is not given in Kings, although a late source claims that "it was for the priests to wash in" (2 Chron. 4:6). It was about fifteen feet in diameter, about seven feet high, and about forty-five feet in circumference. It was capable of holding about 11,000 gallons of water. It probably had some cosmic meaning since both Phoenician and Babylonian stories treat the sea as the source of life and fertility. Whether the Israelite molten sea signified a freshwater lake as the source of life or the Mediterranean Sea from which direction always came the life-giving rain is not known. This massive bowl stood upon the backs of twelve bronze oxen, a common symbol of fertility in the ancient Near East, three facing in each direction. This arrangement probably represented the four seasons of the year pointing in the four directions.[28] It is possible too that such

[28] See Albright, *Archaeology and the Religion of Israel*, pp. 148–150.

a large supply of water was necessary for washing down the sacrificial altar in order to clean up the filth. This practical function and its cosmic symbolism would not be incompatible.

Divination and Sacrifice Divination and sacrifice were religious acts performed for chiefs of state and for a few private individuals during the United Monarchy. In the case of divination priests and prophets were specialized in using the ephod or Urim and Thummim for answering critical questions. The *ephod* may have been a garment worn by a priest as he performed his divination. Some scholars think that the ephod was a box which held the sacred lots.[29] On the other hand, Samuel wore a linen ephod as a young priest, and David wore an ephod when he danced before the Ark (1 Sam. 2:18 and 2 Sam. 6:14). The ephod was used by the priest when a crisis called for divine information. Ahijah wore an ephod (1 Sam. 14:3), and Saul demanded that Ahijah give a reading from the ephod whether or not to attack the Philistines (1 Sam. 14:18–19, reading "ephod" for "ark"). David consulted the ephod worn by Abiathar when he wanted to know if the residents of Keilah would hand him over to Saul (1 Sam. 23:9–12). The ephod could give only a yes or no answer, as in the case when David asked if he should pursue the Amalakites (1 Sam. 30:7–8). *Urim and Thummim* were connected with the ephod in some way. They may have been the oracle received from the ephod[30] or the objects manipulated by the priests in order to get an oracle (1 Sam. 14:41–42). There was only one recorded instance where the Urim refused to supply an answer to a crucial question (1 Sam. 28:5–7).

Necromancy, or conjuring the spirits of the dead, was another form of divination used during the United Monarchy. It was either not in widespread use or the pious editors of the early historical documents eliminated all references to it except in the case of Saul who sought information from a female sorcerer (1 Sam. 28). Divination by use of arrows was also practiced, as the story of Jonathan's shooting arrows over the hidden David suggests (1 Sam. 20). Although direct allusions to divination have been eliminated from this account, a similar tale reported how arrows were used to decide whether or not to war against Syria (2 Kings 13:14–19).

Sacrifices of several kinds were made by kings and citizens during the United Monarchy. Some quite primitive elements existed in

[29] See Pfeiffer, *Religion in the Old Testament*, p. 81.
[30] *Ibid.*

practices of sacrifice in that period, and must be contrasted with the late and sophisticated idea of sacrifice as depicted in 1 Samuel 15:22–26. One idea associated with sacrificial rites was that Yahweh needed nourishment, and so the priests ministering for him took a specified amount of food from the worshippers to give to the deity (1 Sam. 2:12–17). This was a common practice at ancient shrines like Shiloh where dues for support of priests and their implements was exacted from the people.

Another type of sacrifice was a gift to the deity. In the case of Hannah (1 Sam. 1:9–11) a vow was part of her gift to Yahweh. When it came time to fulfill her vow, that if blessed with the birth of a son she would devote him to the service of Yahweh, she took a bull, flour, and wine as presents for Yahweh (1 Sam. 1:24–25). Trophies of war also were given to Yahweh and hung in His shrines. Goliath's sword was housed at the shrine at Nob (1 Sam. 21:9), and David devoted the war emblems of his enemies to decorate the tent of Yahweh in Jerusalem (2 Sam. 8:7). The offerings David made to Yahweh upon the transfer of the Ark from the house of Obed-edom to Jerusalem were gifts to Yahweh in appreciation of success (2 Sam. 6:17).

Most accounts of sacrifice in these early narratives reported it as a form of communion with Yahweh. Saul offered sacrifices when he was named king, in order to bring himself into special relationship with divine power. This was a high moment in affairs of state, and a meal with the deity conveyed upon the king and his associates some of the power which they believed the deity to possess (1 Sam. 11:15). On another occasion a communion meal was held before Saul went into battle against the Philistines. It was stated explicitly that such a meal would bring him Yahweh's favor (1 Sam. 13:8–12). After victory in war sacrifices of booty were made to Yahweh. One story shows that war, abstention from food, and proper sacrificial procedures were all related (1 Sam. 14:31–35). Before battle with the Philistines, Saul took an oath that neither he nor his troops would eat food before victory was assured. After the victory his warriors fell upon the booty of sheep and cows killing them without proper sacrificial rites. This constituted a flagrant violation of Saul's oath, and before calamity struck from on high Saul hastily built an altar. There he performed the proper rites draining the blood of the animals into the ground. After this, the soldiers settled down to a meal in communion with Yahweh who had given them victory.

Sacrifice served yet another purpose. In some cases it served to expiate a crime or guilt which some disaster caused people to believe had been committed. The Philistines believed that the presence of the Ark of Yahweh among them had brought a plague. Consequently they made sacrifices of gold to it (1 Sam. 6:4). When the Ark was returned to Israelite territory, the Israelites at Bethshemesh sacrificed cows as an expiation for any guilt they might have incurred in handling a sacred object (1 Sam. 6:14). David offered an expiatory sacrifice at the threshing floor of Araunah in order to arrest the plague he thought had come from ordering a census of men for military service (2 Sam. 24:18–25). In these examples it is clear that sacrifices were conducted by political leaders as well as by priests at designated shrines during the 11th and 10th centuries B.C. Solomon probably began the practice of designating to priests only the responsibility of animal sacrifice in the Jerusalem Temple.

Sacred Places The people of Israel during the monarchy believed that special places revealed the power of deity in unique ways. Places set aside by Israelites as special locations for the appearance of Yahweh were ancient Canaanite shrines, springs, and high places.

Canaanite Shrines Sites that served the Canaanites' worship were annexed by Israel, and with little modification continued as special sanctuaries. *Shiloh,* where Samuel took his training as a priest, was a sanctuary to which pilgrimage was made yearly (1 Sam. 1:3). Although Shiloh's importance was due in part to the Ark's presence, it is likely that the original deity worshipped there was Sabaoth, depicted as borne by cherubim.[31] When the Israelites came to use Shiloh as their shrine the two deities were merged into a single one creating the formula "the Lord of hosts (Yahweh Sabaoth) who is enthroned on the cherubim" (1 Sam. 4:4). Excavations at the modern village of Seilun indicate that Shiloh was destroyed about the middle of the 11th century B.C. The temple of Yahweh Sabaoth was destroyed at that time and never rebuilt.

Gilgal, in the Jordan Valley east of Jericho, where Saul was crowned king (1 Sam. 11:15), was another sacred place. David received representatives of Judah and Israel there when Absalom's rebellion had been put down (2 Sam. 19:15–18). It was marked by a circle of stones,[32] and a shrine from which oracles and judgments were dispensed stood there (1 Sam. 7:16). *Mizpah* was an important shrine since it, too, had tradition that Saul was selected to be king at its sanctuary (1 Sam. 10:17–24). The shrine at *Hebron* was a

---

[31] De Vaux, *Ancient Israel: Its Life and Institutions,* p. 304.
[32] Gilgal is derived from the Hebrew word meaning "to roll," such as stones.

sacred spot, and Absalom offered sacrifices there before he began his rebellion against David. At Hebron the presence of the mosque Haram al-Khalil where the veneration of Abraham and Sarah continues today, indicates how sacred these areas were thought to be.

Some springs were believed to be sacred. Canaanite religions emphasized female fertility, and since gardens, trees, and flocks were sustained by the water flowing from springs, they were often treated with special reverence. The ancients believed that the god of life-giving forces resides in or near the spring. Two springs at Jerusalem seemed to be especially sacred spots during the monarchy. Rival sons of David undertook their struggles for power at them. Adonijah chose En-rogel for making his sacrifices before his contest for the throne. Its association with the Serpent's Stone indicated the life-giving and healing qualities of the spring (1 Kings 1:9–10).[33] Solomon chose the Gihon spring from which to make his bid for power (1 Kings 1:32–40). It is possible that the Ark was housed near Gihon, for Zadok in anointing Solomon took oil from the shrine of the Ark (1 Kings 1:39).

High Places

High places were also sacred to Israelites during the United Monarchy. The high place at Gibeon seems to have been the most famous. A grisly rite was performed at Gibeon to bring an end to a famine (2 Sam. 21:1–14). The famine occurred, so the Israelites believed, because Saul had massacred some residents of Gibeon in violation of an ancient pact between Israel and its citizens. There, in order to end the plague, seven of Saul's sons were put to death in a religious ceremony (2 Sam. 21:9). In later years Solomon offered sacrifices at Gibeon because it was a high place. A high place, the Hebrew word *bamah* meaning something which stands out in relief from its background, usually has been interpreted as a high hill, but several Old Testament passages indicate that *bamoth* (the plural of bamah) were also located in towns (1 Kings 13:32) and in valleys (Jer. 7:31). Archaeology has provided helpful information about this term. Oval platforms about 24 by 30 feet and 6 feet above the surrounding ground, with steps leading to the top, were uncovered at Megiddo and Hazor. At Malhah, southeast of Jerusalem, a mound 75 feet in diameter made of stones and earth held together by a wall with steps leading to the top was excavated. It seems certain that these man-made structures were *bamoth*.[34] Solomon remained through the night at Gibeon's *bamah* in order to absorb the power emanating from Yahweh in that place. It was there in the presence of Yahweh that he set his mind, so the tradition reads, on becoming rich, powerful, and wise (1 Kings 3:3–14).

[33] See Numbers 21:9 for serpents as the symbol of healing.
[34] De Vaux, *Ancient Israel: Its Life and Institutions*, p. 284f.

The threshing floor of Araunah was another important elevation referred in these early narratives (2 Sam. 24:18–25). A threshing floor was any flat surface, usually on a great rock, where grain was gathered, threshed, and winnowed. The best site for a threshing floor was on a hill where the wind blew unobstructed and without currents. Such a place became the site of an altar where David offered sacrifice to Yahweh when a plague stopped short of decimating the population of Jerusalem. Scholars are in unanimous agreement that upon this spot the Temple to Yahweh was constructed by Solomon, where another temple was built in 516 B.C. which Herod the Great expanded and beautified beginning in 19 B.C., and where the Muslims' Dome of the Rock stands today.

Beliefs Concerning Yahweh

What did Israelites believe about Yahweh during the United Monarchy? It is actually impossible to note all the characteristics of Yahweh since so many are implied in the narratives of the monarchy. It is necessary to distinguish carefully between the views of Yahweh depicted in narratives contemporary with the monarchy and those in narratives written centuries later. Israelite understanding of Yahweh's nature changed significantly as revolutionary ideas were incorporated into the religion of Israel.

National God of the Israelites

Israelites believed Yahweh was a national god. He was identified strictly with Israel, just as Chemosh was with Moab, Dagon with Philistia, Hadad with Syria. What happened when victors carried the physical presence of Israel's god into foreign territory is reported in the story of the Philistine's capture of the Ark (1 Sam. 5 and 6). Vows made to Yahweh could be fulfilled only on Israel's territory and at a shrine where Yahweh's name was called on (2 Sam. 15:7–8). As the national deity he waged war against Israel's enemies. His presence could be identified by the wind when it blew the tree tops as Israel prepared to fight the Philistines. He was extolled by the people of Israel because he gave victory to David in his campaigns against Syria and Edom (2 Sam. 8:6, 14). In bringing victory to Israelite troops he sometimes manifested himself in frightening thunder storms (1 Sam. 7:10), and earthquakes which threw the enemy into panic (1 Sam. 14:15). Yahweh acted through nature in other ways: according to the Israelites, he brought famine upon the nation for a crime committed by Saul (2 Sam. 21), and pestilence because David had conducted a conscription (2 Sam. 24).

Yahweh as a Personal God

It was believed, too, that Yahweh was a personal god. He had a personal name so that this people could address him. He was influenced by the worship that men gave him, and he responded with emotions that were human. He repented of evil and blessed those who pleased him. He commanded obedience and rewarded those who were faithful to him. He entered the inner lives of some men by means of a spirit and prompted those men to unusual behavior (1 Sam. 10:9–13). He had spokesmen for him in priests and prophets, and to special persons he appeared in dreams (1 Kings 3:5) or by means of a voice (1 Sam. 3:10). Above all he made contracts with kings so that they acted on his behalf (1 Sam. 10:1, 16:13). David, for instance, considered the covenant between Yahweh and Saul so sacred that he would not kill Saul when he had an ideal opportunity (1 Sam. 24:1–15). The covenant between Yahweh and king was so strong that even when Shimei, a member of Saul's family, cursed David during Absalom's revolt, David restrained his soldiers' desire to kill Shimei: he might still have had some of the blessing of Yahweh which had been imparted to Saul when he was anointed king (1 Sam. 16:5–14). David's contractual relationship with Yahweh was in some respects unique in that he understood Yahweh to be his God. David made Yahweh *his* God, so that the paraphernalia of Yahweh's worship, ark, tent, and priests, came directly under his control. Thus, national destiny was bound up precisely with David's destiny. This conception of Yahweh was carried into Solomon's rule but was contested by the Yahwist writer who understood Yahweh as being the God who had brought Israel from slavery in Egypt to prosperity in Canaan. Solomon's prosperity, so he believed, came as a gift from Yahweh. Yahweh blessed the king and the king in turn brought blessing upon the people. This idea of monarchy persisted throughout the life of Judah as a nation, although the great prophets, agreeing with the Yahwist writer, violently condemned monarchs as coming between Yahweh and the people of Israel.

Israel's religion underwent changes rapidly during the period of the United Monarchy. This was due in part to the assimilation of Canaanite forms of governmental administration, the absorption of Canaanite population, and the incorporation of Canaanite shrines and forms of worship into the religion of Yahweh. But probably as important as these was the impact of a single man, David of Judah, who made Yahwism into the religion of the monarchy whose benefits flowed to the people only because of their loyalty to the king and his family.

Psalms of the United Monarchy

Excavations at Ras Shamra on the coast of Syria have given scholars new understandings of Old Testament psalms. This was the location of a major Canaanite city known as Ugarit. Destroyed about a hundred years before David, it preserved thousands of clay tablets with economic, political, and religious texts written on them.

It is not surprising that some of the religious texts should parallel verses in the Hebrew psalms. After all, there was a rich literary and religious tradition among the Canaanites before the Hebrews came to possess the land.

Two Understandings of the Psalms

Two different understandings of the book of Psalms have been held by scholars. The traditional understanding has been that David composed all seventy-three of the psalms which bear his name. Many modern scholars have rejected this, pointing out that probably none of the psalms was composed by David, and that in all probability the earliest came from a period in Israelite history several generations after David. Moses Buttenwieser attempted to organize the psalms in chronological order.[35] He did this by finding in them all of the historical allusions which could be identified with Israel's history and by citing literary parallels from other historically datable writings, especially the prophets of the 8th century B.C. and later. Sigmund Mowinckel has shown that often what Buttenwieser thought were historical allusions are actually cultic expressions which can in no way be accurately dated.[36] Although many of the psalms use Aramaic expressions, which led some interpreters to give a late dating to them, recent studies of Aramaic indicate that it was a literary language as early as the 10th century B.C.[37] It is possible that Aramaic expressions had drifted into use in Canaanitic speech as early as the 10th century B.C. [38]

The translation of religious texts from ancient Ugarit has changed some interpretations of the psalms. It is believed that several of them were composed in the 10th century B.C. Traditions that David was a musician (1 Sam. 16:17–23, 2 Sam. 1:17–27), that he organized the musical part of Israel's religious rites (Ezra 3:10, Neh. 12:24, 36–46), and the fact that seventy-three psalms give titles connected with David, combined with the discoveries at Ugarit suggest that it may be safe to credit several psalms (see p. 51) to the 10th century B.C. A study of the vocabulary of these psalms shows that many of their words, images, and parallelisms are found in texts from Late Bronze Age Canaanite literature.[39]

[35] Moses Buttenwieser, *The Psalms Chronologically Treated with a new Translation* (Chicago: University of Chicago Press, 1938).
[36] Sigmund Mowinckel, *The Psalms in Israel's Worship*, 2 Vols., trans. and rev. D. R. Ap-Thomas (London: Oxford University Press, 1963).
[37] Aramaic was a Semitic language related to Hebrew spoken by the people of Aram, a territory northeast of Syria. It was the official language of the Assyrians between 1100 and 605 B.C., and became the language of Palestine after the 7th century B.C. See William R. Taylor, "The Book of Psalms, Exegesis," *The Interpreter's Bible*, Vol. IV, p. 23.
[38] "Aramaic," *IDB*, A–D, p. 185–90.
[39] Mitchell Dahood, S.J., "Psalms I, 1–50," *The Anchor Bible*, (Garden City, N.Y.: Doubleday & Co., 1964), pp. xxix–xxx.

Psalm 2 was written, perhaps to accompany the coronation of a king. Since its vocabulary and phraseology are similar to Ugaritic poems it may have been composed by a Canaanite in David's court to honor David at an anniversary celebration of his accession to the throne. The elements of anointing (Ps. 2:2), the holiness of Zion (Ps. 2:6), the idea of covenant (Ps. 2:7), military successes (Ps. 2:9), and fanatical devotion to Yahwism (Ps. 2:11–12) reflect conditions which were found in David's monarchy.

Psalm 16 may be the composition of a Canaanite who had become a devotee of Yahweh. There are several things in this psalm besides the grammar which suggest such a possibility. *First,* the author used the Phoenician form of the word for God, El, rather than the Hebrew Elohim (Ps. 16:1). *Second,* he makes his profession of faith, "O Yahweh, thou art my Lord," and uses in parallelism a phrase familiar in Ugaritic literature, "there is none above you" (Ps. 16:2). The text of the Revised Standard Version seems to be clarified by this Ugaritic phrase. *Third,* the translation "As for the saints" may be rendered "As for the holy ones," the name for Canaanite deities in a Byblos inscription and in Ugaritic texts. *Fourth,* the translation of verse 5 may be "O Yahweh, you have portioned out my cup of smooth wine." Ugaritic texts refer to "sweet wine," "wine that is not sweet," and "smooth wine." "The smooth wine symbolizes a tranquil and happy existence. . . ."[40] In 1960 a pitcher with an engraving showing El seated with a goblet in his right hand was discovered at Ras Shamra. In texts found nearby El was described as the banquet-giver who invited his seventy children to eat and drink. *Fifth,* the reference to eternal life, exceedingly rare in the earliest portions of the Old Testament, was an idea well-known to Canaanites. This verse might be translated

You will make me know the path of eternal life,
filling me with pleasures at your right hand forever (Ps. 16:11).

The tale of Aqhat expresses the same idea: "Ask for eternal life and I will give it to you, immortality and I will bestow it upon you. I will make you number years with Baal, with the gods you will number months."[41]

Psalm 18 may have been composed as early as the Davidic period, according to its diction and subject matter, although some scholars

---

[40] *Ibid.,* pp. 87, 89.
[41] *Ibid.,* p. 91.

place it late in Israel's history. The psalm has two parts: verses 1–30 and 31–50. The poet chanted praise to God in verses 1–3, described his terrifying distress in verses 4–6 in language similar to Canaanite mythology, then proclaimed Yahweh's revelation as mighty power in nature, verses 7–19. Part one concludes by proclaiming God's justice (Ps. 18:20–30). As in Ugaritic literature, the ideal ruler judged fairly the cases of the weak and oppressed. The gods, too, were called upon to administer justice. Yamm, god of the sea, bore the epithet 'Judge River,' while the regencies of Baal and Mot (Death) were defined by the word 'jurisdiction.' At different times each was threatened with punishment by the father of the gods: "Will he not overthrow the throne of your rule? Will he not break the scepter of your jurisdiction?"[42] In the second part, the poet praised God for having prepared him as a warrior and given him "a bow of bronze" or a miraculous bow (Ps. 18:31–50). God gave him victory both military and political over his enemies at home, and caused foreign nations to submit to him. This psalm may have been a poetic summary of David's political experiences.

Psalms 60 and 68   Psalm 60 may be a poetic expression of the anxiety David felt when his troops were pinned down in a war with Syria in the north (2 Sam. 8:3–8) while the Edomites attacked Judah from the south. In Psalm 68 many passages show that it had parallels in other 10th century B.C. literature. Psalm 68:1 is a parallel to the song of the Ark in Numbers 10:35. Baal in Ugaritic texts is spoken of as "one who rides upon the clouds" (Ps. 68:4). Baal and Mot were protectors of orphans and widows, as was the God of Israel (Ps. 68:5). Yahweh marched through the wilderness with his people (Ps. 68:7–9) just as a poem earlier than the United Monarchy proclaims (Judg. 5:4–5). Psalm 68 may have been sung when the ark was transferred from the sacred tent into the completed Solomonic Temple. All of these psalms convey attitudes corresponding to the religious mood of Israel in the 10th century B.C. as communicated in Israel's earliest historical narratives.

[42] A. F. Rainey, "The Kingdom of Ugarit," *The Biblical Archaeologist,* XXVIII, No. 4 (1965), p. 115.

V

**Codifying The
Laws**

Like the poetry of the pre-monarchical period, and the legends about Samuel, Saul, and David, Israel's laws were communicated to each generation orally by elders, priests, and judges (2 Sam. 7:15–16). As in the case of poetry and legends, laws at one time passed on by word of mouth were eventually written down, and by that act became literature.

Israel's earliest laws were formalized soon after the first narratives of the United Monarchy had been written. Three codes of laws, the Decalogue, the Covenant Code, and the Ritual Code, became monuments of Israel's new political status, contributing everlastingly to its legal tradition. Adding to the nation's growing literary tradition, they memorialized in precise forms some of Israel's unique characteristics.

Literary Inspection

The laws in Exodus 20–24 and 34 were codified long before they were set within their narrative contexts. The people in the narrative of Exodus 19 lived in a wilderness. They were camped at the foot of a mountain which they considered sacred, and unauthorized persons who touched the mountain were put to death. These people were bedouin preparing for some exceptional event. They expected Yahweh to appear in a thick cloud, and they had washed their clothes in preparation for an act of consecration. Trumpet blast, thunder and lightning, fire and smoke, and an earthquake accompanied Moses' departure from the camp to meet God. These descriptions portray a religious ceremony of massive proportions,

Core Readings

Exodus 19:1 – 20:17, the Decalogue
Exodus 20:18 – 24:8, the Covenant Code
Exodus 34:1–28, the Ritual Decalogue

and one is prepared by all this for proclamations concerning cultic practices.

Textual Anachronisms But expectations are not fulfilled. When God spoke (in Hebrew the word Elohim is used, Exod. 20:1), He uttered only three statements about Himself and the remaining seven were about social relations. After all the preparation, the words which God spoke were rather practical and earthy and not at all in keeping with the fiery introduction. It appears, then, that Exodus 20:1–17 was inserted into a narrative context describing cultic rites, but the mood of cult was broken by the laws themselves.

If that was the case, what happened to the statements concerning cult which belonged to this ceremonial introduction? It is possible that they are found in Exodus 34:1–28 where, after fire, smoke, earthquake, and dire warnings of death for approaching the holy mountain, requirements were given for Israel's worship before Yahweh.

Other Insertions It is obvious that Exodus 20:1–17 is not the only insertion into the narrative context. At Exodus 20:18 a description of cultic procedures begins again with instructions for building an altar of earth, low enough so that steps are unnecessary. Upon that altar sacrifices of sheep and oxen shall be made. But, following the cultic description, a series of legal statements are offered which deal with a wide range of social and economic matters. Only a few cultic requirements are scattered (Exod. 22:20–30, 23:15–19) among the numerous social and economic ones. It is clear that the laws in Exodus 20:1–17 and 21:1–23:33 are out of context, and that only the code found in Exodus 34:1–28 is consistent with a description of cultic duties.

Inconsistencies With Nomadic Culture There is yet another problem. A careful reading of the cultic requirements in Exodus 34:1–28 shows that not all these laws fit a nomadic culture where sheep, goats, asses, and camels can survive in an arid terrain but cattle cannot (Exod. 34:19). Three harvests shall be observed with religious rites (Exod. 34:22). But when nomads do plant and harvest, which is possible with seasonal rains, it is only one crop of barley or wheat that is taken, not three harvests. Two laws were without doubt Canaanitic in origin (Exod. 34:26). The offering of first fruits assumes the harvesting of fruit such as grapes, figs, almonds, and apricots that are gathered over a period of one or two months. Also, "You shall not boil a kid in its mother's milk" is the prohibition of a Canaanite religious practice.

The laws in Exodus 21–23 show the same characteristics.[1] Most of these laws were applicable to a simple agricultural and trading society. Many of them could in no specific way apply to nomads living in Sinai. An ox was an agricultural beast of burden (Exod. 21:28–32, 35–36). Lending of money suggests economic practices more complex than those needed by bedouin (Exod. 22:25–27). Cultivating land for six years and letting it lie fallow one, suggests an advanced form of agriculture (Exod. 23:10–11). One concludes that these laws were compiled in their present form for farmers. It is probably correct, then, that the three sets of laws did not originate with the narratives in which they are found, nor do they accurately represent the cultural conditions implied in those narratives.

Literary Form

Each of the sets of laws under discussion has the same general literary form. There is a prologue, the body of laws, and an epilogue. The prologues and epilogues are not complete in each instance, probably because they were adjusted to fit the narrative into which they were placed. The prologue in each identifies the author of the laws and describes the historical circumstances. The prologue of the Ten Commandments states that God spoke the laws and that the occasion was His victory in bringing Israel out of Egypt (Exod. 20:1–2). The prologue of the laws in Exodus 21–23 identifies the author as Moses who had been instructed in legal matters by Yahweh (Exod. 20:21–21:1). Its historical setting has been lost unless sections of Exodus 19:7–20 were once part of that prologue. The laws in Exodus 34 depict Yahweh as the author of those laws, and places the historical setting just prior to Israel's wars against the inhabitants of Canaan (Exod. 34:10–16). Following the prologue come stipulations in precise form with occasional comments about the reasons for or applications of the laws. Finally, the epilogue recites the punishment for disobedience of the laws and the fear which the people feel. They will be blessed or cursed in proportion to their obedience (Exod. 20:18–20, 23:20–21).

Similarities in Ancient Near East Codes

This literary form corresponded closely with that of other codes of law from the ancient Near East. The famous Code of Hammurabi (1728–1686 B.C.) has this same threefold form. In it the laws originated by action of the god Shamash, who appointed Hammurabi to administer the laws wisely and justly. The body of laws deals with the affairs of a complex society, and are oriented toward ownership of property. The epilogue states that the king should uphold

---

[1] The designation given these chapters by biblical scholars is the Covenant Code or Book of the Covenant.

these laws faithfully, and that curses will fall upon those who violate them or damage the stele upon which they are written.[2]

Some scholars have found a careful structuring of form in the Covenant Code, so that they see all of the laws arranged into five decads each divided into two pentads.[3] But such an order demands a great deal of rearrangement of the text which a western mind trained in orderly scientific procedures might demand. There may have been some arrangement by decads at one time, but it is now difficult to find it.[4] Like other codes of law from the ancient Near East, they show little formal arrangement because the laws were added to and amended over a long period of time before they achieved their final written form.

The Decalogue

The term *Decalogue* has been given to the laws found in Exodus 20:1–17.[5] In literary and historical usage, this term is preferred over "Ten Commandments" because it more accurately describes the original form of the laws. The laws in Exodus 20 were of the simplest order. Word formation in ancient Hebrew was much simpler than in English, so that "You shall not kill" was rendered by only two words in Hebrew, *lo tirtsah*. The tradition that they were written on stone may be accurate (Exod. 34:1–4). Other ancient Near Eastern codes were written on stone, such as that of Hammurabi, and deposited in a temple where from time to time they were brought out and read before the public assembled for that purpose. Therefore, the simple form of the language and the custom of writing on stone combined to render the Decalogue in its earliest form as the following:

1. You shall have no other gods.[6]
2. You shall make no graven images.
3. You shall not take the name of Yahweh in vain (worthlessly).

[2] For the text of the Code of Hammurabi see James B. Pritchard, ed., *Ancient Near Eastern Texts Relating to the Old Testament* (rev. ed.; Princeton, N.J.: Princeton University Press, 1955), pp. 163–80. Hereafter referred to as *ANET*.
[3] J. M. Powis Smith, *The Origin and History of Hebrew Law* (Chicago: University of Chicago Press, 1931), p. 17.
[4] See Aage Bentzen, *Introduction to the Old Testament*, (2d ed.; Copenhagen: G. E. C. Gadd, 1952), pp. 213–31.
[5] Another version of the same Decalogue is in Deuteronomy 5:6–21.
[6] Some interpreters list the first law as "I am Yahweh your God" and omit "you shall make no graven images." They argue that image worship was practiced in Moses' time and into the monarchy. Therefore, "you shall make no graven images" is a late addition to elaborate the first command. However, if this interpretation is adopted, it eliminates the prologue typical of other Hebrew and ancient Near Eastern sets of laws.

4. Remember the sabbath day.
5. Honor your father and mother.
6. You shall not murder.
7. You shall not commit adultery.[7]
8. You shall not steal.
9. You shall not bear false witness.
10. You shall not covet your neighbor's household.

Commentary attached to commandments 2, 3, 4, 5, and 10 represent *halakah*, the interpretation of Old Testament legal texts to make ancient precepts apply to conditions long after the original law was formulated.

It is interesting that so little explanatory material accompanies the laws of the *Covenant Code*. This may indicate that they were actively in use for many generations after being compiled. Furthermore, the scarcity of commentary may indicate that they were chiefly guidelines or precepts which elders, priests, and judges used to decide how to treat a case. Except for those laws in which the penalty for violation was death, the judge exercised a good deal of discretion regarding the penalty.

The Ritual Decalogue
The cultic laws in Exodus 34, sometimes designated the *Ritual Decalogue,* have been buried amidst a good deal of explanation. Listing them will help one compare them with the two other sets of laws.

1. *34:14* You shall worship no other god (cf. Exod. 20:3, 22:20, 23:13).
2. *34:17* You shall make no molten gods (cf. Exod. 20:4).
3. *34:18* You shall keep the feast of unleavened bread (cf. Exod. 23:14).
4. *34:19* All that opens the womb is mine (cf. Exod. 22:30).
5. *34:20b* You shall redeem your first born sons (cf. Exod. 22:29).
6. *34:21* You shall rest on the seventh day (cf. 20:8, 23:12).
7. *34:22* You shall observe the feast of weeks, the feast of first fruits, and the feast of ingathering (cf. Exod. 23:15–16).

[7]One argument, that this law was not part of the Ten Commandments during the Mosaic Age nor even during David's reign, and consequently that the Decalogue was organized after the United Monarchy, is found in 2 Samuel 11 and 12. David stole Uriah's wife. Nathan, the prophet, accused David of theft by telling a parable about a man who stole a poor man's sheep even though he had plenty of his own. Neither the parable nor Nathan's denunciation mentioned adultery as the crime. If it had been forbidden formally and specifically in Israel would not Nathan have used it in his charge against David?

8. *34:25*   You shall not offer the blood of my sacrifice with leavened bread (cf. Exod. 23:18).
9. *34:25b*   You shall not permit the sacrifice of the feast of passover to remain overnight (cf. Exod. 23:18).
10. *34:26*   You shall bring your first fruits to the house of Yahweh (cf. Exod. 23:19).
11. *34:26b*   You shall not boil a kid in its mother's milk (cf. Exod. 23:19).

These laws may originally have formed a decalogue, and some scholars pare down the eleven to ten, omitting either numbers 4 or 5 to make them fit. In whatever way these laws may be reconstructed, it is generally agreed that the first two and the last four belonged to the original set. The original form is now hidden from sight. In fact, those ancient editors who incorporated them into the narratives may have purposely obscured its character as a decalogue because religious tradition held that there was only one set of laws (Exod. 20:1–17) given to Moses.

Casuistic and Apodictic Laws: "If or When . . . Then" and "Thou Shalt Not . . ."

Two legal forms were available to the Israelites when they codified their laws. The "thou shalt not" form is probably more familiar, since that is the form used in the Ten Commandments, than the "if or when . . . then" form. Scholars have tried to distinguish which of the two forms was distinctively Hebraic and which Canaanitic. Special names were given these two forms by Albrecht Alt, and it has been convenient to call the "thou shalt not" laws *apodictic* and the "if . . . then" laws *casuistic*.[8]

The Covenant Code

Apodictic and casuistic laws were mixed together in the *Covenant Code*. Casuistic laws were always introduced by "if" or "supposing that" followed by one or several conditional clauses in which the persons involved in the case were referred to in the third person. Then followed in detail penalties resulting from the unlawful act. Invariably casuistic laws dealt with social situations as distinct from ceremonial acts. The body of "if . . . then" laws served as reminders to judges of what the community had practiced in past cases. In all likelihood casuistic laws were derived mainly from Canaanite civilization.

Apodictic laws, on the other hand, dealt with absolute certainty. There were no ifs, ands, or buts in the punishment of certain crimes.

[8]"The Origins of Israelite Law," in *Essays on Old Testament History and Religion*, trans., R. A. Wilson (Garden City, N.Y.: Doubleday & Co., Anchor Books edition, 1968, pp. 101–71.

In these laws there was an intensity of form and content that set them off from Canaanitic casuistic laws. The language of apodictic law was weighted in such manner that the recital of consequences produced a feeling of slow motion. The last five words of the line, "shall be put to death," (Exod. 21:15, 16, 17) were spoken in Hebrew in slow rhythm so as to emphasize the dire consequences of the acts. Furthermore, casuistic laws used the second person familiar "thou" (Exod. 22:18, 21, 28, 29). In contrast with casuistic laws, apodictic laws did not consider the intent of the crime. They dealt solely with the outward consequences of an act and the punishment was exact retribution. Whereas casuistic laws handled social violations without reference to God or cultic ceremonies, apodictic laws handled man's special relations with deity which did not specify differences in religion, morality, and law. All of life was viewed as under the jurisdiction of Yahweh. The forms in which the "thou shalt not . . ." laws were expressed imply that they were used in religious ceremonies which implicated the community as a whole in the divine economy. It is likely that the occasion for reciting aloud the apodictic laws to an assembly was when the ceremony of covenant-renewal of the nation's existence under Yahweh was performed at Shiloh or Shechem or Hebron. The unequivocal quality of apodictic laws places them as part of the Israelite conception that Yahweh was the author and sustainer of community life in Israel. It is noteworthy that civil laws were mostly casuistic while cultic laws were mostly apodictic. Although these forms may not reveal the historical period in which these codes originated, an educated guess is possible in the light of historical conditions in Israel.

Mosaic or Solomonic?

Jewish and Christian traditions have taught that Moses was the author of the Torah. This belief has had a venerable history, and only in the last 100 years has widespread doubt been raised about it. The modern study of ancient Israelite law has disrupted a dogma that had been accepted generally since about 550 B.C.: the belief that on Mount Sinai, Yahweh gave Moses the laws in Genesis through Deuteronomy. If it can be shown that Moses did not codify the laws in Exodus, who did?

Evidence that Moses Did Not Write the Laws

It is easier to demonstrate that Moses did not write down the laws than it is to show who did. Law rests upon the generally accepted opinion that some acts are wrong and must be punished or compensated for by the collective power of a community. The historical study of the laws that regulate modern society has shown that laws develop out of customs. Customs solidify into accepted usage, and eventually receive the approval of the governing powers. It is rare that a single man, even though inspired by God, formulates laws that are accepted by the entire community. It is possible to apply what is known about the development of modern law to ancient codes. Furthermore, social conditions are never static: practice that was once accepted changes, and new laws become necessary to apply to changed conditions. This observation is illustrated in Exodus where three sets of laws give a different reason for resting on the seventh day: in the *Decalogue* because Yahweh rested on the seventh day (Exod. 20:11), in the *Covenant Code* so that animals and slaves may be refreshed (Exod. 23:12), in the *Ritual Code* no reason is given and the command applied only to seasons of plowing and harvesting (Exod. 34:21). The explanation given in Deuteronomy for the necessity of rest on the seventh day and to whom it applies is different again (Deut. 5:12–15).

Inconsistencies in the Torah also indicate that Moses did not write it. A Hebrew slave who has served for six years shall be freed in the seventh year, according to the *Covenant Code* (Exod. 21:2). In Deuteronomy a Hebrew slave when freed at the end of six years of indentureship shall be given grain, sheep, and wine as a departing present (Deut. 15:12–14). Again in the *Covenant Code,* a man guilty of seducing a virgin shall pay the marriage price and marry her. The father, however, may refuse to give the girl to the seducer (Exod. 22:16–17). In Deuteronomy a man guilty of seducing a virgin shall pay the father fifty shekels of silver, and he must marry her (Deut. 22:28–29). Such modifications in the same laws *prove* that they served generations over a long period.

Moses may have been responsible for some of the laws found in Exodus, but he couldn't have given those which dealt specifically with an agricultural or urban society. He and his tribes were consistently portrayed in the Pentateuch as bedouin, living in the wilderness at least a full generation, if one follows the biblical account exactly. Yet, laws which dealt with fields (Exod. 22:5), loans (Exod. 22:25), stacked grain (Exod. 22:6), and first fruits (Exod. 34:26) can only have been applicable to a sedentary community.

Comparisons With Other Near Eastern Codes

A hundred years ago it was still possible to believe that all the laws in the Pentateuch originated with Moses, but archaeology has disrupted that belief. At that time the laws in the Bible were the only ones known to have originated in the ancient Near East. Now, however, there are six codes of Near Eastern law known to have existed before the earliest Israelite code. Although most of these have survived only partially on clay tablets, enough has remained to indicate clearly that a millennium before the earliest Israelite code existed there were laws similar to it in use. An historical review of these ancient codes will illustrate this. The oldest goes back to about 2050 B.C., and is called the *Ur-Nammu Code*. It is the oldest law code yet known to man. Ur-Nammu was king of the Third Dynasty of Ur. The tablet on which the laws were found had eight columns, four on each side. The prologue told of Ur-Nammu's defeat of Lagash, a neighboring city, and of domestic reforms respecting sheep stealers and weights and measures. Three of the laws were identical with three in the *Covenant Code:* orphans shall not fall prey to the wealthy, widows shall not fall prey to the powerful (Exod. 22:22), and "eye for eye, and tooth for tooth" (Exod. 21:24).[9]

Another code dates from about 1930 B.C., and it has been named the *Code of Bilalama* after the name of the king of Eshnunna. Only about sixty laws were preserved from a longer list, and its prologue is mutilated, too. The *Code of Lipit-Ishtar* has been dated to a hundred years before Hammurabi. His code had more than a hundred laws, according to estimates made on the basis of the thirty-eight which still exist. It had a prologue and an epilogue. The *Code of Hammurabi* was discovered by French archaeologists in the winter of 1902–3 and they took it to the Louvre in Paris where it is now on display. Hammurabi was king of the Old Babylonian Dynasty from 1728 to 1686 B.C., according to Professor Albright's chronology. Hammurabi "enacted the law of the land," that is, he codified the existing laws in the second year of his reign. A bas-relief at the top of the diorite stele depicts Shamash, the sun-god, giving the commission for codification of the laws to Hammurabi with the usual prologue and epilogue. There are many laws in the *Code of Hammurabi* that parallel those in the *Covenant Code,* and such parallels are listed in the margins of Pritchard's *Ancient Near Eastern Texts* (pages 163–80). Professor Hugo Winckler found several clay tablets in his excavations at Boghaz-köy in modern Turkey in 1906–7. The laws on these clay tablets were written in an unknown cuneiform script but the language was finally deciphered by Professor F. Hrozný of Prague in 1915, and translation and publication continued for the next thirty years. This *Hittite Code* dates from about 1450 to 1200 B.C. Another set of laws known now as the *Middle Assyrian Code* dating from about 1350 B.C. was discovered at ancient Ashur by German archaeologists just before 1914. The state of preservation of the clay tablets was so poor that the code is only fragmentary, and no other tablets have been discovered to fill the gaps.[10]

[9] See Samuel Noah Kramer, "The Oldest Laws," *Scientific American*, Vols. 188–9 (1953), pp. 27–8.
[10] See Pritchard, *ANET* pp. 159–97 for translations of all but the Code of Ur-Nammu.

Codification as the
Province of Priests and
Prophets

These facts demonstrate conclusively that Moses did not originate the Israelite Torah. But the task of placing the laws in Exodus 20, 21–23, and 34 in their proper historical setting is still to be done. The task would be easier if the Old Testament carried even a small tradition that one of the kings of Israel had codified the laws. But there is no such tradition. David and Solomon were both cited as judges in cases calling for decisons based on typical disputes (2 Sam. 14:4–20, 1 Kings 3:16–28), but nowhere does the Old Testament claim their hands in drawing up the laws. Is it possible that a private individual codified Israel's earliest law, as was the case with the *Middle Assyrian Code?* After all, the Old Testament does say that Moses was the responsible individual, even though it is impossible that Moses was that man. But, the tradition which attached Israelite law to Moses grew up because priests and prophets were responsible for the codification of law in Israel. This does not mean, of course, that kings had no jurisdiction in the process. A king could forbid the collections of precedents into a code by force of arms, or he could appoint men who would do his bidding in organizing a common legal system. But it does mean that a strong tradition existed that gave priests and prophets special jurisdiction in that area of society. What cultural factors made a new code necessary?

1. A community must have law to exist. Before the monarchy in Israel basic communities were units such as the clan, the tribe, the village, and the city. Legal transactions were handled by elders, priests, and judges at the city gate (2 Sam. 15:2). There was then no central political authority to which Israelites owed allegiance or which forced its power over them. The establishment of the monarchy broadened the legal community and citizens' object of loyalty. The struggle to remain free of foreign domination resulted in domestic control in the person of a king. The rule of David generated drastic changes in the lives of the people, although he did a masterful job in preserving the customary at the same time new ways were being incorporated into national life. Cultural changes under Solomon proceeded at a faster rate than under David, and with less regard for established ways.

2. As the size of Israel's political unit expanded and social structures fluctuated a code of laws applicable to the enlarged nation was required to stabilize the legal system. At least three other ancient Near Eastern codes originated under such revolutionary conditions: the founder of a new state gave the *Ur-Nammu Code;* *Hammurabi's Code* originated during a period of expansion of the Babylonian Empire; and the *Hittite Code* marked the transition

between the Old and New Empires. In order to be acceptable to Israel's citizens the central authority in Jerusalem under David and Solomon had to resemble the old and customary. Codification of tribal, village, and city law to serve as the new nation's legal precedent demonstrated to the people that the old supported the new. As David had brought the Ark to Jerusalem as a sign of his affection for ancient religious customs, so Solomon may have provided for the inclusion of Canaanite and Israelite laws in the new code to prove his appreciation of both esteemed legal practices.

3. Incorporating Canaanite, Philistine, Aramaean, Edomite, Ammonite, and Moabite populations under a single political head increased the number of government officials. No doubt local legal precedents continued in use where there was no conflict with the central government. But wherever the government's influence was felt new officials had to be appointed to further the interests of Jerusalem's authority. Solomon organized twelve new districts (1 Kings 4:7–19), and this new system required officials who would do the bidding of their king and at the same time keep local citizens satisfied. The new code served as a handbook for officials who administered justice. Where a conflict of interest arose between local citizens and the government's representative, the code served as the principal reference for judicial procedure.

4. David's military successes and Solomon's trading ventures put Israelites in touch with foreign communities. Dealing with legal traditions different from Israel's demanded a common standard. So long as citizens of the same village were in dispute there was no need of an Israelite code. But when citizens from two widely separated cities with no common legal tradition clashed, or a citizen and an officer of Solomon's court were in dispute, a common legal standard had to be invoked. A knowledge of the law of the central government was necessary for any official who had contacts with the diverse social and national groups in the Israelite empire.

Since the level of jurisprudence in the *Covenant Code* reflected conditions in which elders, priests, and judges administered justice at the city gate or at the entrance to the chief's tent, and since the greatest alterations in Israelite society took place during the United Monarchy, it is probable that the *Covenant Code* was created during the early years of Solomon's reign. The tradition that Solomon was a wise man does not directly support the belief that codification of Israelite law took place under his patronage, but it does suggest that a king who was interested in collecting proverbs, and poems, and who knew zoology and biology, would also be interested in jurisprudence (1 Kings 4:29–34).[11]

The Covenant Basis of Israel's Law

The Old Testament depicted law as given to Israel through Moses in a covenant agreement with Yahweh (Exod. 34:10, 23:22–33). In the political realm David established a covenant with the elders of Israel in a solemn ceremony in which the name of Yahweh was invoked (2 Sam. 5:3). The idea of covenant relationship bound together religious and political practices so that the new nation under David and Solomon was a religious as well as a political community in which religious leaders were prominent. With these traditions Solomon could place legal authority in the hands of priests and prophets.

Examples of Secular Covenants

The world of the Old Testament had covenant relationships of various orders. There were covenant treaties between superior powers and vassal kings, and numerous examples from the Hittite Empire (1400–1200 B.C.) are available.[12] In this type of covenant the vassal owed allegiance to the king who promised protection from attack and who secured the military resources of the vassal state. This covenant had the purpose of maintaining peace in the empire, and protecting the vassal from any arbitrary action by his lord. There were also parity covenants in which two parties of about equal power bound each other by oaths. This was, perhaps, the kind of covenant between David and Jonathan (1 Sam. 18:3), although the precise stipulations of the oath were not reported. David and Abner may have made a covenant of this type, in which Abner promised to deliver Israel and Michal over to David, and David may have promised no unnecessary bloodshed (2 Sam. 3:12–21). Another type of covenant was that drawn up among several small powers in a promise to fight the advance of an empire. The Amarna letters of the 14th century B.C. reported a coalition of Syrian and Palestinian kings gathered to form a covenant in which they promised to drive out the Egyptian overlords. The Assyrian king Shalmaneser III (858–824 B.C.) reported that a coalition of small nations covenanted together to face his great army at Qarqar in 853 B.C.[13] With covenant-making a common practice throughout the ancient Near East, it is not surprising that religious thinkers should employ that form to depict the relationship between Israel and its God.

[11] See George E. Mendenhall, *Law and Covenant in Israel and the Ancient Near East* (Pittsburgh: The Biblical Colloquium, 1955), pp. 9–11.
[12] See O. R. Gurney, *The Hittites* (Baltimore: Pelican, 1952), ch. IV; also Pritchard, *ANET*, pp. 109–206.
[13] Pritchard, *ANET*, p. 278.

Thus, the covenant idea provided the setting for the earliest codes in the Old Testament. Even though they did not originate in their present forms under Moses, the practice of covenant-making is traceable to experiences common to the Mosaic Age. A religious tradition so lengthy as that was precisely the instrument to give authority to the Solomonic law. As the new code was deposited in the royal temple in Jerusalem, a ceremony of covenant relationship undoubtedly was celebrated.

Contrasts Between the Covenant Code and the Code of Hammurabi

There is little question that the idea of a covenant with Yahweh modified Canaanite law as it was incorporated into the Israelite code. The *Code Of Hammurabi* serves well for comparison and contrast because, having been transmitted through Amoritic influences, it was probably the basis for Canaanite laws found in the Old Testament. Some examples of how the covenant idea modified Canaanite law will clarify this point. *First,* one of the important concerns of the political covenant was protection. The covenant between Yahweh and Israel provided protection for each party. The law was responsible for the safety of each member of the community, regardless of social and economic position, even a thief. Whereas the *Code of Hammurabi* demanded death for theft (Laws 6, 8, 22), the *Covenant Code* required only restitution (Exod. 22:1, 4). *Second,* the covenant idea gave Israelite law a concern for the rights of common people. Babylonian lawmakers were rich merchants and political leaders. Their motives in establishing a code were to maintain economic prosperity and to promote the status quo. The *Code of Hammurabi* (Laws 49–52, 88–102) legislated high interest rates, but the *Covenant Code* prohibited them (Exod. 22:25–27). The *Code of Hammurabi* required that escaped slaves be returned to their owners (Laws 15–20), but the *Covenant Code* legislated respecting slavery in an atmosphere implying that slaves should be treated decently (Exod. 21:1–10).[14] *Third,* life and death were in Yahweh's hands. In the case of an ox that gored, the *Code of Hammurabi* (Laws 250–52) required no payment for a man killed in the open street, one-half mina of silver for goring a member of the aristocracy, and one-third mina of silver for goring a slave. But the *Covenant Code* demanded that an ox that gored a man be stoned to death. If the ox habitually gored and its owner was negligent, ox and owner were both stoned (Exod. 21:28–32). Since in the Israelite idea of covenant only Yahweh could give and take life, an ox and a negligent owner who had taken

---

[14] A later revision of the law legislated that escaped slaves should be given sanctuary (Deut. 23:15–16).

life must be punished by death. The penalty was carried out by stoning (in which many people took part) so that it was the covenant *community* that served the interest of Yahweh: no individual was responsible for the death of the guilty. In a day when corporal punishment was handled by the relatives of the offended person rather than by agents of the state, death by stoning absolved any single person of a violation against Yahweh's decree that Israelites should not kill their fellows.

Fourth, even though Israelite law demanded the death penalty for some crimes that the *Code of Hammurabi* did not, the offenses in such cases were considered crimes against Yahweh. But on the whole there is a kind and humane character in Israelite law, owing to its foundation in covenant, which other ancient Near East codes did not have. Slaves could become part of an Israelite family (Exod. 21:5–6). Men were charged with the duty of returning strayed animals even to an enemy (Exod. 23:4). Men should render help to an animal that had fallen beneath its load and was unable to regain its footing (Exod. 23:5). Creditors who took the heavy outer cloak of poor men as collateral for a loan must return the garment before sunset (Exod. 22:26–27). None of these provisions is found in the *Code of Hammurabi.* Not laws in the strict sense, they admonished people in covenant with a righteous and merciful God to conduct themselves accordingly. Such humane recommendations give a clue to the purpose and use of the *Covenant Code.* It was compiled to serve as a general standard for judges throughout the Israelite empire. These laws were in no sense exact stipulations for regulation of all possible cases. They were really precedents from many parts of Israelite society, and they were in force over longer or shorter periods which served to guide judicial authorities.

Since religious leaders had in their hands the business of collecting local laws into an imperial code, and since covenant-making was given religious coloring, and since Israel's king was *not* represented as lawgiver, two insights into the relation between law and religion become clear. (1) Yahweh was King, delegating his authority to a political king who administered Yahweh's justice through religious leaders. This provided for a *division of power,* so that ideally absolute authority never rested in a single person. (2) The combination of political practice and religious belief created a social revolution. This revolution fostered rebellion against the feudalistic system practiced by Canaanite princes, and it spearheaded a fight for freedom from Philistine and Ammonite political exploitation. Thus, a new state was created in which religious values had precedence over political and economic interests. Israel did not in fact operate long at that level, but the whole history of the Old Testament was an effort to identify and maintain these two principles, and to live in accordance with them.[15]

[15] See "Covenant," in George A. Buttrick, ed., *The Interpreters' Dictionary of the Bible*, A–D (New York: Abingdon Press, 1962), p. 718.

VI

**Ecology of
Israel's Epic**

Because we are studying the books of the Old Testament chronologically *according to their time of writing,* we find ourselves dealing with the earliest days of the *Hebrews after* studying about the United Monarchy. The stories of creation, of Abraham and his descendants, and of Moses are among the best known in biblical lore, and yet they do not weary one by repeated readings. These narratives deserve special attention because they are instructive about the life, the history, and the religion of the Hebrews in the time before the United Monarchy. They are also lovely showpieces of the growth of biblical literature. Some of these stories were written down in the last years of the United Monarchy. Others joined the parade of literary forms many generations after Solomon's death. The earliest of the narrative accounts in Genesis, Exodus, and Numbers were added to Israel's literary achievements subsequent to the earliest poems, early historical writings, and codes of laws. Our treatment of these splendid narratives begins with an inspection of the literature.

**Literary Inspection
of the Pentateuch**

The tradition that Moses wrote the first five books of the Old Testament, the Pentateuch, has great antiquity, but nowhere do these books state that he was their author. One passage reports that Moses wrote a story of Israel's victory over the Amalakites (Exod. 17:14). Another claims that he wrote the book of the covenant (Exod. 24:4, 7). According to another he wrote down the itinerary of the wandering Hebrews (Num. 33:2). Deuteronomy states that Moses wrote "this law in a book, to the very end" (Deut. 31:9, 24). Jewish scribes in the 4th century B.C. believed that Moses was the author of the laws in the Old Testament (Ezra 3:2, 7:6), and passages in the New Testament assume that he authored all of the Penta-

---

Core Readings

Genesis 1–3, 7, 8, 12–25, 27–35, 37–50
Exodus 1–19, 24, 32, 33
Numbers 10:11–14:45, 16, 20–24

teuch (Mark 12:26, John 5:46, Acts 15:21, Rom. 10:5). It is natural that a tradition with such antiquity originating from such authoritative sources would be generally accepted among Jews and Christians.

The Unreliability of the Tradition of Moses' Authorship

Four characteristics of narratives in the Pentateuch indicate the unreliability of the tradition of Moses' authorship. There are inconsistencies within some of the stories, duplications of some stories, interruptions of the narratives, and chronological inaccuracies. Each of these can be illustrated briefly. An outline indicates a few of the inconsistencies:

THE STORY OF CREATION
  Genesis 1:26−2:4 Man was Elohim's last act of creation.
  Genesis 2:4b–7 Man was Yahweh Elohim's first act.[1]
  Genesis 1:1–2 Elohim created order from a watery chaos.
  Genesis 2:4b–5 Yahweh Elohim planted a garden in a desert.

THE BIRTH OF SETH
  Genesis 4:1, 2, 25 The third son of Adam.
  Genesis 5:1–3 The first son of Adam.

THE FLOOD
  Genesis 6:19 Two of each kind of animal taken into the ark.
  Genesis 7:2 Seven pairs of clean animals and two of each unclean animal taken into the ark.

JACOB'S NAME
  Genesis 32:24–28 Jacob's name changed to Israel at Peniel.
  Genesis 35:9 Jacob's name changed to Israel at Paddan-aram.

ISRAEL IN EGYPT
  Genesis 41:34 One-fifth of the produce collected to avoid famine.
  Genesis 41:35 "All the food of these good years" was stored.

YAHWEH'S NAME
  Genesis 4:26 Enosh was the first to know Yahweh by name.
  Exodus 6:3 Moses was the first to know Yahweh by name.

MOSES' SPIES
  Numbers 13:17 Spies went into the Negeb, southern Canaan.
  Numbers 13:21 Spies went to Rehob in Syria.

These narratives also reveal that some stories were told two or three times. Such repetitions indicate that different sources carried stories about Israel's early heroes with similar plots but with different details. Repetition of narratives is illustrated as follows:

---

[1]"Elohim" is the Hebrew word for God. "Yahweh Elohim" (Lord God) is the compound use of the two most common Hebrew words for the deity.

Genesis 12:10–16   Abraham lies to Pharaoh.

Genesis 20:1–7   Abraham lies to Abimelech.

Genesis 26:6–11   Isaac lies about his wife to Abimelech.

ABRAHAM'S HEIR

Genesis 15:4   Yahweh promised Abraham an heir.

Genesis 17:16   Elohim promised Sarah a son.

Genesis 18:10   Yahweh promised Sarah a son.

HAGAR

Genesis 16:4–14   Sarah drove Hagar away.

Genesis 21:9–21   Abraham sent Hagar away.

Genesis 28:19 and 35:6, 15   Jacob named Bethel twice.

Exodus 3:14–15 and 6:2–3   Yahweh revealed His name two times to Moses.

Exodus 17:1–7 and Numbers 20:1–13   Moses twice struck a rock to secure water.

Several interruptions make smooth reading of these narratives difficult. At Genesis 13:18 Abraham is in Hebron where he had built an altar. At Genesis 14 he goes off to war, and ends up feasting with the king of Salem. Genesis 15 resumes the narrative of sacrifice, presumably upon the altar at Hebron. Stories of Jacob's construction of altars and shrines are recorded at Genesis 33:18–20 and 35:1–21. These exploits, however, are interrupted by an independent story about a war between Jacob's sons and the inhabitants of Shechem (Gen. 34). At Exodus 19:10–23 washing, abstention from sex, music, and the presence of God in thunder, fire, and earthquake indicate preparation for a great ritual, but the story of ritual is interrupted by a long set of civil laws (Exod. 20–23). The ceremony was resumed at Exodus 24:1.

Chronological inaccuracies appear when one compares some passages. Genesis 12:11 records that Sarah was a beautiful woman. At Genesis 17:17 the reader learns that she was ten years younger than Abraham, who was one hundred years old. When Abraham came to Canaan, he was seventy-five years old (Gen. 12:4). Soon he went to Egypt where Sarah's beauty attracted the Pharaoh's attention. Therefore she was at least sixty-five years old when the flirtation took place; rather old for a bedouin woman still to be attractive!

Isaac's old age presents even more difficulty. Genesis 25:26 records that Isaac was sixty years old when Rebekah bore Esau and Jacob. Esau was forty years old when he married two Hittite girls (Gen. 26:34). Chapter 27 tells how Jacob tricked Isaac into blessing him as

Isaac lay on his bed blind and dying at age one hundred. Eight chapters later Isaac dies at a hundred and eighty years (Gen. 35:28–29). Thus, he was eighty years lying on his death bed.

The past two hundred years have witnessed a revolution in our knowledge of the ancient Near East so that several anachronisms in the Pentateuch are now apparent. Certain historical conditions are recorded in these narratives which Moses could not have known about. Genesis 26:1, 14, 15 report that Isaac lived among the Philistines during a famine in Canaan. Exodus 13:17 records that Elohim did not lead the Hebrews to Canaan by the short route because the Philistines were there. Both these accounts probably are inaccurate. Reliable historians have set the Hebrew Exodus from Egypt in the 13th century, and the Philistines first landed in Canaan in 1188 B.C. Moses had died before that date.[2] The person who recorded those stories was fully aware of the existence of Philistines in Canaan but he did not know that his ancestors had no contact with them.

Abraham was reported as having become wealthy in Egypt in sheep, oxen, asses, *and camels* (Gen. 12:16). The person who told this tale knew about camels, and assumed they had been domesticated in the age of Abraham. But historical investigation makes it doubtful that the Egyptians had camels so early. They were not mentioned in early Egyptian texts even though they were crudely pictorialized before the Iron Age. Their bones have not been found in Bronze Age deposits in Palestine although bones of asses have. Although excavations at Mari on the Euphrates River had produced immense amounts of information about life on the edge of the Syrian desert during the Middle Bronze Age (2100–1500 B.C.), no historical account of camels has come to light. It is probably that camels were not domesticated until the end of the Late Bronze Age (1500–1200 B.C.).[3] The first accurate historical reference to camels is in Judges 6:1–6, at least a generation after Moses' death.[4]

[2] Cyrus H. Gordon contends that Philistines were settled in Canaan before 1500 B.C., and that the invasion that occupied southwest Canaan around 1200 B.C. was a late wave of their migrations. *The Ancient Near East* (3d ed., New York: W. W. Norton & Co., 1965), pp. 121 f.

[3] William F. Albright, *From the Stone Age to Christianity*, (Garden City, New York: Doubleday & Co., 1957), p. 165.

[4] For a different point of view see "Camel," in George A. Buttrick, ed., *The Interpreter's Dictionary of the Bible*, A–D (New York: Abingdon Press, 1962), pp. 490–492. Cyrus H. Gordon presents some evidence for the domestication of the camel in the Amarna Age, 14th century B.C. However, his source material is drawn from northern Mesopotamia, not Egypt and Canaan. *The Ancient Near East*, p. 124. John Van Seters advises caution in drawing conclusions about dating the Patriarchal Age based on information excavated at Mari. See "The Problem of Childlessness in Near Eastern Law and the Patriarchs of Israel," *Journal of Biblical Literature*, Vol. LXXXVII (December 1968), pt. IV, 401–8.

With such literary and historical difficulties in the Pentateuch, biblical scholars have not been content to let them remain unresolved. Therefore several theories have been set forth to replace the traditional belief that Moses wrote the Pentateuch. The story of critical study of the Pentateuch is complicated, but a few of its contributions over the past three hundred years may be given.

Early Theories of the Literary Origins of the Pentateuch

Pastor Witter of Hildesheim, Germany, suggested in 1711 that the use of two names for God, Yahweh and Elohim, and the narratives in Genesis indicate that Moses had collected older written sources into a single narrative.[5] About forty years later Jean Astruc, a French physician, claimed that two main sources, one using Yahweh and the other using Elohim, plus ten other sources, had been used by Moses in his composition of Genesis. These independent critical studies stimulated Old Testament scholars to abundant investigation.

Eichhorn's Scientific Study of the Origins

By 1778 Johann Eichhorn had put the literary study of Genesis on a scientific footing. Eichhorn's main contribution was to show that the sections which used Yahweh and Elohim had, in fact, distinctive literary styles.[6] Later two German scholars were responsible for developing the theory of the origin of the Pentateuch which still holds considerable influence among Old Testament scholars.

Graf's Study of the Development of the Laws

In 1865 Karl H. Graf published the results of his study on Old Testament law. He accepted an earlier proposal that the "book of the law" discovered while the Temple in Jerusalem was under repair was Deuteronomy (2 Kings 22:3–10). King Josiah, who had ordered the repairs on the Temple, ruled from 639 to 609 B.C. There was little doubt, therefore, that the book of Deuteronomy was compiled in the 7th century B.C. The laws in the Covenant Code were obviously earlier than those in Deuteronomy. A third body of laws was preserved in Exodus 25–31, 35–40, the book of Leviticus, and Numbers 1–10. These laws were later than Deuteronomy, and showed that they had been created by social conditions and religious beliefs considerably different from those affecting either Deuteronomy or the Covenant Code. The theory that all laws develop from simple to more complex forms was applied to the codes of laws in the Pentateuch. Thus, Graf suggested that stages of growth were observable in the legal portions of the Pentateuch.

[5] Artur Weiser, *The Old Testament: Its Formation and Development,* trans. Dorothea M. Barton (New York: Association Press, 1961), p. 75.
[6] This is noticeable even in English. Cf. Genesis 17 and 18 for names of deity and for style of composition.

Julius Wellhausen offered a useful theory of the origins of the narrative portions of the Pentateuch in a series of monographs published between 1876 and 1885. He applied the same theoretical considerations to the development of narrative as Graf had applied to codes of laws. The theoretical assumption that growing forms become progressively more complex permitted Wellhausen to use the literary studies of his predecessors with ingenuity and creativity. He concluded that the Yahwist strand of narrative about Hebrew origins from creation to the conquest of Canaan was the earliest, because it represented the simplest attitude toward religious practices, because the social customs described in it were simple, and because its view of the deity was decidedly anthropomorphic. He detected a special interest in the geography of southern Canaan, particularly Hebron and Beersheba.

Wellhausen thought that the J document[7] showed an author whose attitude had been nurtured in a period of social equilibrium. Thus he dated its composition from earlier oral traditions and fragments of documents to the reign of Jehoshaphat (873–849 B.C.). This king had brought an end to the constant warfare between Judah and Israel, and Wellhausen thought that peaceful conditions had been especially conducive to literary activity in the kingdom of Judah.

Wellhausen proposed that a second strand of narrative in the Pentateuch again traced the history of the Hebrew people from their forefather Abraham to the conquest of Canaan. This account, called the Elohist document because of its consistent use of Elohim as the name for the Hebrew God, revealed social conditions more advanced than those in the Yahwist narrative. Furthermore the Elohist's view of God was more elevated in that Elohim appeared to his Israelite heroes in visions and by angelic messenger (Gen. 28: 12) rather than, as in the Yahwist's stories, by walking on earth in the cool of the day (Gen. 3:8) or by eating with Abraham (Gen. 18:1–8). Since the concentration of interest in the Elohist's stories centered about the shrines at Shechem and Bethel, Wellhausen concluded that the E narrative originated in Israel during the reign of Jeroboam II (786–746 B.C.).[8]

According to Wellhausen, a Priestly account was the last of the three narratives of Israel's origins, its place in the growth of epic literature determined by its complex style and legal demands. Wellhausen labeled this the P document. Its author was interested in

[7] *J* for Yahwist: the German *J* is pronounced like an English *Y*.
[8] E for Elohist.

detail, so that usually, when precise numbers are given in the text, the presence of the P document is indicated (Gen. 5, 12:4b–6a, 16:15–17:27). The author of P was guided by the principle that Israel's history should be understood in the light of cultic ceremony: covenant-making, sacrifice, circumcision, sabbath day observance, and other priestly acts. His literary style was governed by his interest in cultic themes, and therefore it is dry and detailed, cluttered with annoying repetitions. Wellhausen proposed that this document was written in the 5th century B.C. when Israel was reestablished in Canaan following the Exile. During this period a priestly hierarchy virtually controlled all aspects of Israelite life.

Deuteronomy The book of Deuteronomy always existed independently of the J, E, and P strands of narrative. Composed by priests in Jerusalem about 650 B.C., it prompted a major social and religious revolution during the reign of Josiah (639–609 B.C.).

Wellhausen hypothesized *redactors* from the Deuteronomic school in Jerusalem who, finding themselves with two accounts of Israel's origins after the defeat of Israel by the Assyrians in 722 B.C., undertook to combine them into a single narrative. Therefore J and E were woven together to create JE. This was accomplished by 650 B.C. Some of the work was done so skillfully that it is difficult to find the two separate strands of narrative (cf. Num. 10:29–11:35), while some was treated so that lengthy sections retained the individuality of their originals (cf. Gen. 30:24–43, J, with 31:4–16, E). The P document was composed independently of JE. It is not known how long P existed separately from JE, but eventually JE was woven into the frame work of P and the final result was JEP. By 350 B.C. the four major documents which lay behind the Pentateuch were fully brought together to make JEDP, the Pentateuch as it stands today.

Wellhausen's Theory Modified Wellhausen's theory did not go uncontested. Many persons reject all the evidence piled up since the first efforts of Pastor Witter in

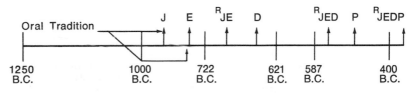

Wellhausen's hypothesis in diagram, showing the redactor's (R) combination of existing written sources.

1711, and maintain that Moses was the sole author. Some Old Testament scholars, dissatisfied with Wellhausen's work, separate each strand into more precise units. Some find, for instance, that the story of the Tower of Babel (Gen. 11:1–9) was actually two stories, one about building a tower and the other about the confusion of tongues, joined into one, and so throughout there were two J strands.[9] Pfeiffer claims there is a fifth source in the Pentateuch which he calls the S source. S, originally an Edomitic document, stands for *Seir* which means "south" in Hebrew. Pfeiffer believes the S document was woven together with the Priestly narratives in Genesis 1–11, but that Genesis 14, 19, 34, 36:9–39, and 38 are large blocks of S material which were left relatively intact by the redactor. The S document was incorporated into the Pentateuch about 400 B.C.[10] Eissfeldt asserts that there is a strand of narrative representing an even earlier tradition than J. This is called the "Lay Source," L, because it has the least concern of all the strands for priestly or cultic interests. This source is traceable as distinct from J, E, and P throughout the narratives of the Pentateuch, but differs from Pfeiffer's S source. It may have been written as early as the end of David's reign, and if so it was contemporary with the composition of the history of David's court (see p. 55), perhaps by that same author.[11]

Other Explanations of the Origins of the Pentateuch

Julius Wellhausen's work roused some scholars to refine the JEDP hypothesis and others to give different explanations for the Pentateuch as it now stands. Hermann Gunkel, whose work is called "form criticism," concentrated his attention on the origin and growth of the oral tradition which lay behind the Pentateuch. He found the supposed historical periods in Israel's history, such as the reign of Jehoshaphat for J, the reign of Jeroboam II for E, and the post-Exilic period for P, to be less important considerations than Wellhausen had supposed. Gunkel believed that the sources of the Pentateuch were not literary compositions at all, but rather collections of oral and written traditions: fragments culled from an extensive tradition by the demands of religious practices. Gunkel admitted with Wellhausen the existence of writers who collected these traditions, but he differed from Wellhausen in how accurately the traditions represented actual historical conditions. Gunkel claimed much more accuracy for the traditions than did Wellhausen.[12]

[9] See Cuthbert A. Simpson, *The Early Traditions of Israel* (London: Oxford University Press, 1948), pp. 47–8.
[10] Robert S. Pfeiffer, *Introduction to the Old Testament* (New York: Harper & Brothers, 1948), pp. 159–67.
[11] Otto Eissfeldt, *The Old Testament: An Introduction,* trans. Peter R. Ackroyd (New York: Harper & Row, 1965), pp. 191–9. The word "lay" refers to a nonclerical, nonpriestly person.
[12] See Hermann Gunkel, *The Legends of Genesis,* trans. W. H. Arruth (New York: Schocken Books, 1964).

Some scholars lay even greater emphasis upon the strength and vitality of the oral process in communicating Israel's traditions than did Gunkel. The narratives in the Pentateuch, these scholars claim, were passed on orally, and those who trace documents through the Pentateuch are relying on Western notions of literature rather than upon ancient Near Eastern literary practices. These scholars belong to the Oral Tradition school of interpretation, and although they accept the helpfulness of Wellhausen's analytical work, they reject the idea of documents datable to exact periods in Israel's history. They claim, rather, that there were no *documents* of the sort proposed by Wellhausen before the establishment of the post-Exilic Jewish community. The existence of a redactor who drew together documents of the Pentateuch is a pleasant fiction, which does not accord with the oral character of ancient Semitic literature. The whole idea of documents and redactors underestimates the force of oral tradition in the Old Testament. The bulk of Old Testament material existed in oral forms until the Jews of the Exilic period fixed these forms by writing them down. Before that time Israel's national traditions were recited at her great religious festivals by men specially prepared for that exalted task. Even the laws were expository: the opening words of each set of laws show that they were originally spoken rather than written (Exod. 20:1, Lev. 1:1, Deut. 1:1). The only condition radical enough to force Israel's oral traditions into written form was a culture threatened at its basic roots. This grave threat occurred when Babylonian armies invaded Judah, destroyed Jerusalem, took the leaders captive, deported them to Babylon, and almost exterminated Israel's national life. Under such dire threats to national existence it was necessary to commit Israel's epic stories to writing.[13]

The problem of how the Pentateuch came to be written is treated in yet another way. Samuel Sandmel argues that neither were there documents of the sort imagined by Wellhausen, nor were oral sources reduced to writing during the Exilic period. Sandmel rejects two suppositions of the document theory: that a redactor existed who took J and E and made them JE, and that the redactor of the material was blind to the obvious contradictions and duplications of the supposed documents.[14] These obvious problems are explained, however, by reference to a popular Jewish literary device used for keeping ancient stories alive and fresh. This is called *haggada. Haggada* is narration based on older stories which makes the ancient story applicable to contemporary conditions even though the retelling becomes somewhat fanciful. An example will clarify

[13] See Edward Nielsen, *Oral Tradition* (London: S C M Press, 1954).
[14] "The Haggada Within Scripture," *Journal of Biblical Literature*, LXXX (1961), p. 107.

this. The Document Theory claims that Genesis 12:10–20 is from J and that Genesis 20:1–17 is from E. The basic elements of the tale in Genesis 12:10–20 are: Abraham took Sarah to Egypt. She was taken into the Pharaoh's harem. Abraham prospered because of that relationship. Then, Yahweh brought a plague on Pharaoh. Pharaoh expelled Abraham, with Sarah, from Egypt. In the story in Genesis 20: 1–17 Abraham sojourned in Gerar. Abimelech took Sarah to live with him. Elohim warned Abimelech in a dream that he might die because of the married woman he had taken. Abimelech had not consorted with her, and protested his innocence. Elohim attested to Abimelech's purity, and advised him to send Sarah back to Abraham. Elohim said that Abraham would pray for Abimelech. Abraham was given great wealth. Abraham prayed that the sterility of the Philistine women be cancelled, for Elohim had caused it.

What typical haggadic embellishments are found in the second tale? First, the random plague in Genesis 12:10–20 became a plague of sterility on the Philistine women. Second, deity intervened, and Sarah's virtue remained unspotted. Third, Abraham was depicted as a prophet. Fourth, Abraham did not really lie; Sarah was actually his half sister. This story also went through other haggadic hands. Philo, the Jewish philosopher, retold the story so as to describe the king of Gerar as a base fellow who was guilty of the grossest disrespect of eastern hospitality. Josephus (37–95 A.D.), the Jewish historian, embellished the narrative by relating that Abraham went to Egypt to convert the Egyptian priests or to be converted by them. While there he taught the Egyptians mathematics which they in turn taught the Greeks.[15] Rabbis further elaborated the tale by having an angel present in the bedroom to administer beatings to Pharaoh whenever his lust prompted him to make advances toward Sarah.

These haggadic embellishments from the Pentateuch and later Jewish literature bring Sandmel to the following conclusions: (1) there never was an E document, but only *haggada* on the original source. (2) J, the original source, was no long, continuous recital of Israel's history from creation to conquest. (3) the redactor in Wellhausen's theory was a fictitious figure of the scholar's imagination.

Improvements on the Documentary Tradition

Criticisms, like the foregoing, have been instrumental in modifying Wellhausen's Documentary Hypothesis. Gunkel made clear the tenacious quality of literary forms, and it has become clear that much which Wellhausen thought was created in the imagination of the J writer was, in fact, an accurate account of early Israelite cul-

[15]*Antiquities of the Jews*, bk. I, ch. VIII.

ture. The study of oral tradition has shown how rigorously ancient bards clung to stories of Israel's past and how those recitations controlled what went into the written stories. The way in which *haggada* kept contemporary the ancient heroic tales has increased scholarly appreciation of the Hebrew literary genius. Thus, the Documentary Hypothesis has been improved upon in the following ways: First, it is recognized that oral tradition continued to flow even after literary works were composed. Second, the creative genius of authorship is clearly visible in the three documents. It is no longer possible to think of the authors of J, E, and P as mere collectors of Israelite traditions. J, at least, put the seal on Hebrew literature so as to influence all subsequent narrative styles.

The literary growth of the Pentateuch has a complicated history, and it is no longer possible to think of its development along a single line as Wellhausen and his successors did. Today scholars grasp the idea of the Pentateuch's growth in broader perspective, represented in the following chart.

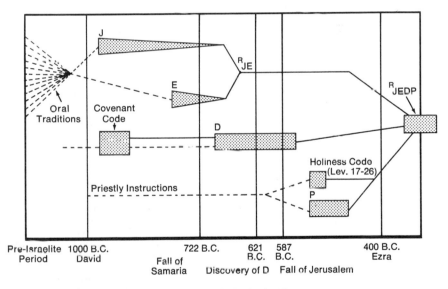

Growth of the Pentateuch, (Adapted from C. R. North, "Pentateuchal Criticism," in H. H. Rowley, ed., *The Old Testament and Modern Study,* London: Oxford University Press, 1961.)

Broken lines indicate oral tradition stemming from Israel's earliest memories. Solid figures represent the continuing, yet diminishing vitality of the oral tradition. Solid lines show the presence of documents, combined finally in the full Pentateuch.

Even though some scholars have questioned the accuracy of the Documentary Hypothesis, it still functions as an effective tool in discovering the origins of Israel. Ability in spotting inconsistencies and duplications, differences in style of composition, earlier and later ideas, and different religious points of view, make one's reading of Israel's epic narratives more enjoyable and intelligible.

The following chart sets J, E, and P in columns so that one may compare and contrast the original strands woven together by the redactor. The famous story of crossing the Red Sea (Exod. 13: 17 – 14:31) serves this purpose excellently. Note especially the coherent stories in J and P. There is no way to know why the redactor eliminated so much of the Elohist narrative. Probably that narrative was quite similar to the Priestly so that it was redundant to tie those two together. The Yahwist and Priestly were sufficiently unique so as to demand their inclusion in the combination. These columns reveal the wide differences of detail in reporting the event, especially the different views of God's activity.

Yahwist	*Elohist*	*Priestly*
Exodus 13:21 And the Lord went before them by day in a pillar of cloud to lead them along the way, and by night in a pillar of fire to give them light, that they might travel by day and by night; ²²the pillar of cloud by day and the pillar of fire by night did not depart from before the people. 14:5 When the king of Egypt was told that the people had fled, the mind of Pharaoh and his servants was changed toward the people, and they said, "What is this we have done, that we have let Israel go from serving us?" ⁶So he made ready his chariot and took his army with him, ⁷and took six hundred picked chariots and all the other chariots of Egypt with officers over all of them. ¹⁰When Pharaoh drew near, the people	*Exodus 13:17* When Pharaoh let the people go, God did not lead them by way of the land of the Philistines, although that was near; for God said, "Lest the people repent when they see war, and return to Egypt." ¹⁸But God led the people round by the way of the wilderness toward the Red Sea. And the people of Israel went up out of the land of Egypt equipped for battle. ¹⁹And Moses took the bones of Joseph with him; for Joseph had solemnly sworn the people of Israel, saying, "God will visit you; then you must carry my bones with you from here."	*Exodus 13:21* And they moved on from Succoth, and encamped at Etham, on the edge of the wilderness. 14:1 Then the Lord said to Moses, ²"Tell the people of Israel to turn back and encamp in front of Pihahiroth, between Migdol and the sea, in front of Baalzephon; you shall encamp over against it, by the sea. ³For Pharaoh will say of the people of Israel, 'They are entangled in the land; the wilderness has shut them in.' ⁴And I will harden Pharaoh's heart, and he will pursue them and I will get glory over Pharaoh and all his host; and the Egyptians shall know that I am the Lord." And they did so. ⁸And the Lord hardened the heart of Pharaoh king of Egypt and he pursued the people of Israel as

of Israel lifted up
their eyes, and behold,
the Egyptians were
marching after them;
and they were in
great fear.
¹¹ And they said to
Moses, "Is it because
there are no graves in
Egypt that you
have taken us away to
die in the wilderness?
What have you done
to us, in bringing us
out of Egypt? ¹² Is not
this what we said to
you in Egypt, 'Let us
alone and let us serve
the Egyptians?' For it
would have been better
for us to serve the
Egyptians than to die
in the wilderness."
¹³ And Moses said to
the people, "Fear not,
stand firm, and see the
salvation of the Lord,
which he will work for
you today; for the
Egyptians whom you
see today you shall
never see again. ¹⁴ The
Lord will fight for
you, and you have
only to be still."
^{19b} and the pillar of
cloud moved from be-
fore them and stood
behind them, coming
between the host of
Egypt and the host of
Israel. And there was
the cloud and the dark-
ness; and the night
passed without one
coming near the other
all night.
²¹ And the Lord drove
the sea back by a
strong east wind all
night, and made the
sea dry land. ²⁴ And
in the morning
watch the Lord in the
pillar of fire and of
cloud looked down up-
on the host of the
Egyptians, ²⁵ clogging
their chariot wheels
so that they drove
heavily; and the

14:10c   And the
people of Israel cried
out to the Lord;

¹⁶ Lift up your rod,

^{19a} Then the angel of
God who went before
the host of Israel
moved and went
behind them;

they went forth de-
fiantly. ⁹ The Egyptians
pursued them, all
Pharaoh's horses and
chariots and his horse-
men and his army, and
overtook them en-
camped at the sea by
Pihahiroth, in front
of Baalzephon.
¹⁵ The Lord said to
Moses, "Why do you
cry to me? Tell the
people of Israel to go
forward. Stretch out
your hand over the
sea and divide it, that
the people of Israel
may go on dry ground
through the sea. ¹⁷ And
I will harden the
hearts of the Egyp-
tians, so that they
shall go in after them
and I will get glory
over Pharaoh and all
his host, his chariots,
and his horsemen.
¹⁸ And the Egyptians
shall know that I am
the Lord, when I
have gotten glory
over Pharaoh, his
chariots, and his
horsemen."
²¹ Then Moses
stretched out his hand
over the sea; and the
waters were divided.
²² And the people of
Israel went into the
midst of the sea on
dry ground, the waters
being a wall to them
on their right hand
and on their left. ²³ The
Egyptians pursued,
and went in after them
into the midst of the
sea, all Pharaoh's
horses, his chariots,
and his horsemen.
²⁶ Then the Lord said
to Moses, "Stretch
out your hand over
the sea, that the water
may come back upon
the Egyptians, upon
their chariots, and
upon their horsemen."
^{27a} So Moses stretched

Yahwist	*Elohist*	*Priestly*
Egyptians said, "Let us flee from before Israel; for the Lord fights for them against the Egyptians." ^{27b} And the sea returned to its wonted flow when the morning appeared; and the Egyptians fled into it, and the Lord routed the Egyptians in the midst of the sea. ³⁰ Thus the Lord saved Israel that day from the hand of the Egyptians; and Israel saw the Egyptians dead upon the seashore. ³¹ And Israel saw the great work which the Lord did against the Egyptians, and the people feared the Lord; and they believed in the Lord and in his servant Moses.		forth his hand over the sea, ²⁸ The waters returned and covered the horsemen and all the host of Pharaoh that had followed them into the sea; not so much as one of them remained. ²⁹ But the people of Israel walked on dry ground through the sea, the waters being a wall to them on their right hand and on their left.

Another technique for spotting sources is contrasting J, E, and P materials for their styles, vocabulary, mood, and religious emphases. Three sufficiently long and unbroken passages are selected to provide contrasts. Read the Yahwist at Genesis 18:1–33, the Elohist at Genesis 22:1–19, and the Priestly at Genesis 17:1–27.

J	*E*	*P*
1. Story unfolds by use of dialogue.	1. Narrative with some use of dialogue.	1. Monologue.
2. Use of Yahweh for name of deity.	2. Elohim used in the narrative; Yahweh used to designate geographic locations.	2. Use of El Shaddai (Gen. 17:1) for name of deity as well as Yahweh and Elohim. Abram for Abraham. Sarai for Sarah. Covenant, descendants, generations are favorite words.
3. Simple, pastoral mood.	3. Intensely dramatic.	3. Detailed and repetitious.
4. Yahweh acts directly with Abraham and Sarah.	4. Elohim speaks through an angel (messenger in Hebrew).	4. Elohim speaks to Abraham, but no account of his presence is given.

The J narrator recites a story in four parts. The first part tells of events and conditions from the act of creation to Abraham. Building upon myths and legends known throughout the ancient Near East, the author creates a prologue to the story of Israel's origins that satisfies certain curiosities about man in general. He explaines why man is both body and soul (Gen. 2:7), why men and women are different and yet join in marriage (Gen. 2:20–24), why snakes have no legs (Gen. 3:14), why women have pains in childbirth (Gen. 3:16), why the soil is so stubborn (Gen. 3:17–19), why man is mortal (Gen. 3:22–24), why farmers and bedouin are enemies (Gen. 4:1–16), who invented various crafts (Gen. 4:17–24), how giants were born (Gen. 6:1–4), who originated sacrifice (Gen. 8:20–22), and why there are different languages (Gen. 11:1–9). This first part of J can be rather easily identified.[16]

Abraham, Isaac, and Jacob The second part of J's narrative recounts the intriguing story of Abraham, Isaac, and Jacob. Abraham, a man with no son, is destined to be the father of the Hebrew people. He comes from the north, travels the length of Canaan, and settles in Hebron. One day Yahweh visits Abraham in his tent, and promises that Sarah, beyond the normal age of child bearing, will become a mother. She gives birth to Isaac who, when it comes time to marry, journeys back to Mesopotamia to take a bride from his father's people. Isaac and Rebekah have two sons, Esau, who was the father of the Edomites, and Jacob, to whom Israel traced its origins. Jacob's trip to Haran to escape Esau's anger for being tricked out of his inheritance brings him a turbulent career. He serves his uncle Laban, takes four wives, and has twelve sons. In a wrestling match with God his strength and stamina so impress the deity that He changes his name from Jacob to Israel, that is, "he who strives with God." After this Jacob settles in the Jordan Valley at Succoth. The second part of J's narrative can be separated from E and P without much difficulty.[17]

Joseph in Egypt The third part of J's story of Hebrew origins takes place in Egypt. To that land Joseph had been sold as a slave by his jealous brothers. The ability of Joseph as an interpreter of dreams and administrator of lands and harvests saves Jacob (Israel) and his family, as well as Egypt, from starvation. Jacob dies in Egypt during the seven-year

---

[16] The following passages are from J: Genesis 2:4b – 4:26; 5:29; 6:1–8; 7:1–5, 7–10, 12, 22–23; 8:6–12, 13b, 20–22; 9:18–27, 10:8–19, 21, 24–30; 11:1–9.

[17] The following passages are from J: Genesis 11:28–30; 12:1–4a, 6b–20, 13:1–5, 7–11a, 12b–18; 16:1–2, 4–14; 18:1 – 19:38; 21:1a, 2a, 7, 33; 22:15–18, 20–24; 24:1–67; 25:1–6, 11, 21–26a, 27–34; 26:1–33; 27:1–27a, 30–38, 41–45; 28:10, 13–16, 19a; 29:2–14, 31–35; 30:1–8 is a confusion of J and E, 9–16, 24–43; 31:1, 3, 3, 46–50; 32:3–13, 22, 24–32; 33:1–17.

famine. Joseph takes his body back to Canaan and buries it. Joseph and his brothers continue to dwell in Egypt. J can be separated from E and P in the passages listed below.[18]

The fourth part of J's superb story is the longest. It recounts Israel's escape from Egypt, the years in the desert, and triumph in the land of Canaan. Moses, Israel's greatest hero, is portrayed in brilliant colors. The shadowy years of Israel's residence in Egypt are quickly passed over, and the story of Moses begins. He is a fugitive from Pharaoh's justice, but he escapes to live in Midian. While there he experiences a theophany of Yahweh. The object of his return to Egypt is to secure the release of the Hebrew slaves. After several failures in convincing Pharaoh that his best interest lie in allowing the Israelites freedom, Moses finally begins the flight. At the Red Sea Yahweh saves the fugitives from annihilation by an Egyptian chariot patrol, and He leads them deeper into the wilderness. At Sinai, the sacred mountain, Yahweh and Israel make a covenant of protection and service. After a generation of nomadism, Israel begins its trek toward Canaan. Moses dies before the conquest of Canaan starts, and Joshua succeeds him to lead a successful campaign into "the land of milk and honey."

Most scholars are agreed that J had a story of the conquest of Canaan, but that it survived only in snatches and fragments since it was superceded by the Elohist's story. This predominantly E account is found in the book of Joshua. The Yahwist's story of Israel in Egypt, Sinai, and the march to Canaan is found below in the following passages separated from E and P.[19]

At this point in the narrative scholarly views differ widely. Some believe J was almost entirely suppressed in favor of E. Others think J is found in the following: Exodus 19:9b, 11b–13, 18, 20–23; 24:1–2, 9–11; 32:9–14, 25–34; 33:1–4, 12–23; 34:1–28. Between Exodus 34:28 and Numbers 10:29 is a large body of Priestly material dealing with religious ceremonies, cultic paraphernalia, and laws administered by priests. When the narrative resumes at Numbers 10:29 it is still difficult to distinguish between J and E. Most

---

[18] Genesis 37:12–16, 21, 25–27, 28b, 31–35; 39:1–23; at this point much of J was eliminated in favor of E; 42:38; 43:1–34; 44:1–34; 46:28–34; 47:1–27, 29–31; 49: 33; 50:1–11, 14.

[19] Exodus 1:6, 8–12, 20b; 2:11–23a; 3:2–4a, 5, 7–8, 16–18; 4:1–16, 19–20a, 22–26, 29–31; 5:3, 5–23; 6:1; 7:14–15a, 16–18, 20b–21, 23–25; 8:1–4, 8–15a, 20–32; 9:1–7, 13–21, 23c, 24b, 25b–34; 10:1–11, 13b, 14b–15a, 15c–19, 24–26, 28–29; 11:4–8; 12:21–27, 29–30; 13:3–16, 21–22; 14:5–7, 10a, 11–14, 19b–20, 21b, 24–25, 27b, 30–31; 15:22–27; 16:4–5, 25–30; 17:1b–2, 7, 14–16; 18:7–11.

Egyptian chariots were light and maneuverable. Tut-ankh-Amon
stands in his chariot charging into a herd of gazelles. Painting
found in the king's tomb at Thebes.

scholars admit that the redactor was so efficient in combining J and
E in the book of Numbers that only JE can be distinguished from P.
The passages below are attributed to JE.[20]

Any serious effort at reconstructing Israel's early history and the
religious beliefs and practices of the Israelites before their life in
Canaan must reckon with the Yahwist tradition as a distinct unit.[21]
A diligent study of Yahwist passages affords one a feeling for the
quality of writing so distinctively different from E and P.

[20] Numbers 10:29–36; 11:1–35; 12:1–16; 13:17b–20, 22–24, 26b–31, 32c–33; 14:
3–4, 8–9, 11–25, 31–33, 39–45; 16:1b–2a, 12–15, 25–26, 27b–34; 20:1b, 3a, 5,
14–21; 21:1–3, 4b–9, 12–13, 16a, 18b–26, 31–35; 22:2–41; 23:1–6, 11–17, 25–30;
24:1–2, 10–14, 25; 25:1–5; 32:1–17, 20–27, 34–42; Deuteronomy 31:14–15, 23;
34:1–6, 10.
[21] James Moffatt, in his *The Bible: A New Translation* (New York: Harper &
Brothers, 1922), has put the J narrative in italics, the E narrative in brackets, and
P narrative in normal type. This is a very convenient edition for use by beginning
readers.

What are a few characteristics of the J narrative? Obviously, the use of Yahweh for the name of God is one. Another is J's fondness for explaining the origins of the names of places and people (Gen. 11:9, 16:14, 25:30, 26:33, 31:48–49, 32:28, 33:17). The J narrative uses Sinai for the name of the sacred mountain, and Canaanites for the inhabitants of Canaan. The Patriarchs lived in southern Canaan, at Hebron (Gen. 13:18), at Beerlahairoi (Gen. 25:11), and in the Jordan Valley (Gen. 33:17). Scenes and characters are pictured with extraordinary charm, such as his depiction of women drawing water at a well (Gen. 24:15–20, 29:2–12, Exod. 2:15–21). Each male character had a distinctive quality: Abraham was magnanimous (Gen. 13:8–18), Isaac was serene (Gen. 24:62–67), Jacob was deceptive (Gen. 30:25–43), Moses was courageous.

Individual stories used by J were drawn from the legends and folk tales of humble people and molded into a masterpiece of noble thoughts and aspirations expressed through the events and lives of Israel's heroes. Their consciousness of living by the promises made to them by Yahweh their God was the motivating theme throughout the narrative. Its overall tone was nationalistic, and the author looked upon David's successes as the end of a series of events that started with Abraham and which were brought to fulfillment by Yahweh's trustworthy promises.

Pride in Israelite accomplishments under David and Solomon was accompanied by contempt for Israel's neighbors. There was a decided bias against Canaanites (Gen. 24:3, 37). Edomites were so simple they could be duped (Gen. 25:27–34). The bedouin were feared (Gen. 16:12). The Arameans were tricky and to be handled by equally deceptive tactics (Gen. 30:25–43). Egyptians were despoilers (Gen. 12:17–20) and enslavers (Exod. 1:8–12), and Yahweh had to deal with them by use of His great power (Exod. 14:14–25). Yahweh's partiality for Israel was stated at the beginning of Abraham's story: "I will bless those who bless you, and him who curses you I will curse; and by you all the families of the earth will bless themselves" (Gen. 12:3). In all this there lay an implicit warning that unless strict adherence to Israelite ways, as nurtured by the heroes of the past, was followed, grievous judgment from Yahweh would fall upon the new nation of Israel. Solomon's foreign tastes in religion, in architecture, in trade, in women, and in tax and labor policies, may have been the social disintegration prompting the Yahwist writer to create this narrative. It served, with the story of the rise of the United Monarchy and its weaknesses during the latter years of David's reign (1 Sam. 1–14 and 2 Sam. 9–20), as warning of the fate of the empire unless the ancient customs and tested manners of Israel were still embraced, and Yahweh accorded all the honors the forefathers had bestowed upon him. With these considerations in mind it is conceivable that the Yahwist wrote his superb story about 950 B.C.

Narratives written by the Elohist and Priestly writers will be discussed as literature in the sections of this book which deal with the times when they took literary form.

VII

Israel's Origins: Fact or Fiction?

The books of Joshua and Judges continue the story of Israel's origins begun in the Pentateuch. They show how Yahweh's promises to the patriarchs and to Moses were fulfilled in the land of Canaan. Inconsistencies and duplication of narratives are observable in these two books as they are in the Pentateuch (cf. Josh. 8:9 with 8:12; 11:21–22 with 15:13–15; 16:68 with 18:21–28), so that some scholars have traced J, E, P, and D's redactorial hand through both Joshua and Judges. The strands, however, were woven together in a way different from that in Genesis and Exodus. Whereas large portions of J and E were identifiable in those books, in Joshua J and E have been so tightly bound together that they are almost inseparable. The romantic attitude of the Elohist author almost eliminated the J narrative in Joshua so that an unrealistic view of the conquest was presented. The Yahwist admitted that some Israelite tribes were incapable of capturing Canaanite towns (Josh. 17:17–18, Judg. 1:27–36) but the Elohist believed that Joshua captured all of Canaan in three swift military campaigns. Furthermore, much of Joshua is identical with the style of writing and religious thought in Deuteronomy. The author of Joshua used J and E sources almost exclusively in chapters 1–12 and 24, but he depended upon P for chapters 13–23.

The Book of Judges

The book of Judges cannot be reconstructed along the lines of J, E, and P with any assurance. There are repetitions such as both a narrative and poem about Israel's victory over Sisera (Judg. 4 and 5), and duplicative accounts of Gideon's exploits (Judg. 6) with qualities similar to J and E, but the literary organization of Judges is unique to that book.

Core Readings

Joshua 1–11, 24
Judges 1–8, 11, 14–21

The Three Parts of Judges

There are three parts to Judges. The first part (Judg. 1:1 – 2:5) is an account of two invasions of Canaan, one south of Jerusalem (Judg. 1:1–21), the other in central and north Canaan (Judg. 1:22 – 2:5). The southern invasion was successful, but in the north the Israelites were too weak to dislodge the Canaanites from their cities. The terse presentation of facts indicates that this section was selected from a longer tradition. Its flattering account of southern victories contrasted with the northern tribes' limited success suggests that these details were excerpted from a southern source. In its present position in Judges it is a foreign element because the opening of the second section at 2:6 follows naturally after Joshua 24:28.

The second part (Judg. 2:6 – 16:31) is a collection of stories of tribal leaders. The editor bound them in a fabric that ties those stories together. The fabric was a philosophy of history that explained Israel's military weakness as the result of the people's neglect of Yahweh. When Israel worshipped Canaanite gods, Yahweh abandoned the nation to foreign invasion which was punishment for their evil. Then, Yahweh raised up "judges," twelve in all, who drove off the enemy and restored Israel to religious purity. In each tale the number of years that Israel was oppressed by the enemy (Judg. 3:8, 14, 4:3, etc.), the events by which freedom was won, and the length of time that Israel faithfully worshipped Yahweh (Judg. 3:11, 30, 5:31, etc.) is stated. In this way the author of the book of Judges drew up a didactic narrative to explain Israel's history, at the same time he accounted for the years between Israel's entrance into Canaan and the establishment of the monarchy.

These stories were handed down by oral tradition over a long period of time so that heroic tales often were combined with cultic traditions. A renowned warrior also was given the reputation of defender of the cult. The story of Gideon is an example of this combination. Judges 6:11–32, 8:22–27 is a cult story in which Gideon transformed a Canaanite shrine into an Israelite one. The remainder of the story recites his success as a tribal warrior.

The Samson Story: A Combination

The story of Samson is an example of the combination of several tales into a single story. His dedication as a Nazirite was part of the saga of a cultic shrine (Judg. 2:2–23). Tales of his superior strength, of his expertise in war, and of his pranks were common of those told about renowned persons. The story of Delilah was a folk tale combined with historical memories of the grave danger Israel faced from the Philistines. The placement of the story of Samson at the end of Judges was probably done in the original edition of the scroll because it related the "judges" to the events of 1 Samuel, where Israel's dealings with the Philistines is continued.

The third part of Judges (chs. 17–21) interrupts the flow of narrative between Judges 16:31 and 1 Samuel 1. A distinct literary unit, it was added at this point to prepare the way for stories about the monarchy. It reports anarchy in Israel (Judg. 17:6), and the inference was that anarchy existed because there was no king (Judg. 18:1, 19:1, 21:25). Another possible explanation of placing the story of Micah the Levite after the Samson tales was the author's attempt to put an uncomplimentary tag upon the tribe of Dan in whose territory Jeroboam I had established a cult shrine (1 Kings 12:25–30). The story probably originated in religious circles which were antagonistic toward the religious pilgrimages made to the shrine at Dan.

The second story (Judg. 19–21) is the tale of a nasty crime committed by the tribe of Benjamin against a Levite's concubine which brought war among the tribes. Although the story originally recounted the origins of the Benjamin tribe (especially Judg. 21:13–23), in its present form, it probably circulated as a story to besmirch Saul's descendants, since it belittled that tribe. David's political henchmen probably circulated the tale, when Saul's family still claimed David's throne.

Knowing something of the literary growth of Joshua and Judges makes it possible to use those books in distinguishing fact from fiction in Israel's history before the United Monarchy.

The Simplified Biblical Version of Israel's Origins

The Old Testament's version of Israel's origins is a simplified account as it now appears in the Pentateuch, Joshua, and Judges. Abraham traveled from Ur in Chaldea[1] to Haran in Mesopotamia. While in Haran Abraham received a call from Yahweh to travel to another land. He arrived in Shechem where he built an altar. His next stop was Bethel where he built another altar. He continued to traverse the length of Canaan, and ended in the Negeb. Famine drove him to Egypt, and after he grew wealthy there, he returned to Bethel. He lived in Canaan where many adventures with invaders, with his nephew Lot, and with Yahweh, kept him well occupied.

In his old age he had a son, whom he named Isaac. Isaac took a wife from his relatives in the city of Nahor in Mesopotamia, and

[1] The name Chaldea was first mentioned in Assyrian records in the 9th century B.C. This is an anachronism, since biblical and archaeological evidence would place Abraham in Middle Bronze Age II (1800–1500 B.C.). Abraham lived in the Late Bronze Age (1500–1200 B.C.) according to Cyrus H. Gordon, *The Ancient Near East* (3d ed. rev.; New York: W. W. Norton & Co., 1965), ch. VIII.

returned to live in Beersheba in the Negeb. From his union with Rebekah two children were born. Esau and Jacob were twins, with Esau only minutes older, but therefore the rightful heir of Isaac's property and tribal leadership. Jacob tricked Esau and Isaac so that he received the privileges of the elder son. Then, he traveled to Mesopotamia for his bride. His return with Rachel and Leah as wives and Bilhah and Zilpah as concubines showed how prosperous his sojourn had been. From these four women he had twelve sons. Joseph, a son by Rachel, was sold into slavery by ten of his jealous brothers. While in Egypt as a slave he rose to power in Pharaoh's court. Famine sent Jacob and his eleven remaining sons into Egypt where by the wisdom of Joseph all Egypt and the nucleus of the Israelite people were saved from starvation.

Israelite Slavery and the Appearance of Moses

Jacob died in Egypt, and his twelve sons with their families lived on there. But as time passed, the Egyptian pharaohs forgot about Joseph's wisdom, and the Israelites were made slaves. From this slave group, whose burdens were worsened by Egyptian cruelty, Moses appeared as a deliverer. His murder of an Egyptian overseer caused him to flee to Midian where he married the daughter of a Midianite priest. While there he had a visitation from Yahweh who commanded that he return to Egypt, lead the suffering Israelites from slavery to serve Yahweh at the holy mountain, and eventually guide them to the land of Canaan where Abraham had once lived. After many failures, ten plagues, and a final celebration of Passover, Moses was able to deliver Israel from bondage. However, Pharaoh was unhappy with the turn of affairs, and he sent a chariot army in pursuit of his escaping slaves. At the Red Sea the Israelites were trapped between the chariots and the sea, but God parted the sea, and Israel escaped even as the Egyptian pursuers were drowned. But this event only introduced a series of hardships, hunger and thirst, attack from Amalekites, and legal problems, before they arrived at the holy mountain in Sinai. At the holy mountain the twelve tribes made a covenant with Yahweh in which they promised to observe the laws that Yahweh gave them since he had saved them from annihilation and had given His promise to lead them on to Canaan.

The Worship of Yahweh; Joshua's Campaign into Canaan

Aaron's golden calf led to more trouble, and Moses broke the stone tablets upon which the laws were written. He had to write out another copy. After completing this task, Moses turned his attention to building the tabernacle, the ark, and all the articles necessary for a detailed and complex liturgical system. Precise regulations were laid down detailing how Yahweh should be worshipped and how the Israelites should conduct themselves. Two years, two months, and twenty days after the escape from Egypt, Israel began its trek to-

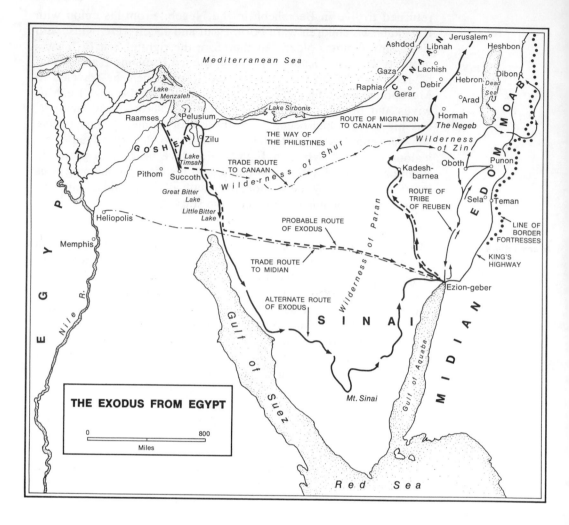

THE EXODUS FROM EGYPT

0   800
Miles

ward Canaan with the Ark at the head of the procession. Hunger, dissension, and a report from spies sent to Canaan drove them to try an attack on Canaan from the south. They were soundly defeated at Hormah. More rebellions, the death of Aaron, thirst, hunger, serpents, and warfare made wilderness existence intolerable. Their journey was extended because Edom refused Israel permission to pass over its territory. Israel suffered a religious breakdown in Moab, but severe punishment saved them from total infidelity. Territory east of the Jordan River was captured from Amorites and Ammonites, and preparations for the invasion of Canaan were undertaken. The death of Moses put Joshua in command. He led his people over the Jordan River, and began his assault on the land by subduing Jericho. From Jericho Joshua led his warriors into the highlands striking deadly blows first to the southern, then to the central, and finally to the northern parts of Canaan. His victory was total and decisive.

Samuel, Saul, and the Monarchy   As the Israelites settled among the Canaanites they again lost their zeal for Yahweh and began to follow Canaanite gods. Due to this weakness Yahweh sent invaders who subjected Israel to foreign domination until a judge faithful to Yahweh arose to lead them back to the worship of Yahweh alone. After several generations of this rhythm of apostasy, defeat, victory through the powers of a judge, and recovery of faith, Samuel, a judge and prophet, arose. His efforts to save Israel from Philistine attacks were fruitless. In desperation the elders of Israel called upon Samuel, and demanded a king. Saul was crowned king, and the monarchy which was to last, with various degrees of success and failure, for over four hundred years was launched.

Passover   The story of how Israel came into existence drew upon diverse traditions, as was seen in the literary analysis of the Pentateuch, Joshua, and Judges. Large and small remnants of varied traditions prove that this simplified story was originally complex. Why were the complex elements reduced to an elementary pattern? The answer to this question is found in Exodus 13:14–16. "And when in time to come your son asks you, 'What does this mean?' you shall say to him, 'By strength of hand Yahweh brought us out of Egypt, from the house of bondage. For when Pharaoh stubbornly refused to let us go, the Lord slew all the first born in the land of Egypt, both the firstborn of man and the firstborn of cattle. Therefore I sacrifice to the Lord all the males that first open the womb; but all the firstborn of my sons I redeem.' " The occasion of telling this story of the origins of Israel was the celebration of the Passover festival. The purpose of telling the story was to explain to the young and to new members of the Israelite community why such a festival was conducted.

It was impractical to permit varied bits of tradition and history about Israel's origins to protrude in this cultic recitation when its main purpose was to celebrate in rite and in story the mighty works of Yahweh in making Israel a nation. *The story as told in the Old Testament is not history in the modern sense, but "salvation-history": the account of how Yahweh dealt with a people with whom he had made a covenant.* "Salvation-history" drew upon ordinary human events in order to tell about the work of Yahweh. But, trustworthy historical facts are found in this religious explanation. By a judicious use of early sources, traditions controlled by known historical facts, and critical imagination, a reconstruction of Israel's origins may be put forth.

There are nearly as many attempts to re-create the factual history of Israel's pre-monarchical period as there are Old Testament scholars. Some reject the historical accuracy of the patriarchal tales and still retain the story of Exodus and covenant-making at Sinai as based on sound facts. Others find the total biblical account basically accurate, and need only to eliminate the number of years that Israel spent in Egypt (Exod. 12:40) in order to have every detail work out so that patriarchs, Moses, and Joshua fit together just as the Old Testament reports. Others see the stories of patriarchs, covenant-making at Sinai, and conquest of Canaan as the imaginative product of Judah and Israel in their late monarchical periods. Some scholars find historical accuracy in the traditions, but believe that they have been used artificially to conform to a religious scheme dictated by the demands of cult practices. Several examples of interpretations will indicate how diversified the approaches to this subject have been.

Some scholars believe the legends and traditions of Israel's origins are so complex that it is impossible to rearrange them so as to obtain any clear historical picture.[2] But even with this caution they consider that the patriarchs were real people who lived in Middle Bronze Age II (1800–1500 B.C.). They see them as part of the Amorites' migration into Western Syria and Canaan. Some Hebrews then entered Egypt with the Hyksos conquerors (ca.1700 B.C.), but not all were expelled when Egypt gained strength enough to wrest power from those foreign rulers about 1550 B.C. Those who were not expelled remained in Egypt and became slaves. Other Hebrews were brought into Egypt as slaves to join their kin when pharaohs raided Canaan. Amenophis II (1435–1414 B.C.) claimed that he took thirty-six hundred 'Apiru to Egypt as prisoners of war. Others may have wandered as landless freebooters who sold their services to the highest bidder as mercenaries. These wanderers were known elsewhere as Khabiru, and ancient records reported them in many parts of the ancient Near East. Not all of the twelve Hebrew tribes were in Egypt, and it is impossible to name for sure the ones that were there. Old Testament traditions emphasize the presence of Joseph in Egypt, so that Ephraim and Manasseh should be considered as having been enslaved, and Moses of the Levi tribe had such a central place in the story that the Levi tribe must have been

[2]John Bright, *A History of Israel* (Philadelphia: Westminister Press, 1959), pp. 60–160; George Ernest Wright, *Biblical Archaeology* (Philadelphia: Westminister Press, 1957), pp. 40–97.

slaves, too. But beyond that it is impossible to be clear. The formation of the covenant was the central event of the Exodus, and Moses was the towering personality in bringing it to pass, although the formal twelve-tribe confederation cannot be traced to Sinai. Traditions and archaeology both support the conclusion that a single onslaught broke the back of Canaanite resistance. This occurred in the middle of the 13th century B.C. Israel's twelve-tribe confederation was formed in Canaan under Joshua at Shechem.

Deemphasis of the Pre-Canaanite Period

Yet another interpretation begins neither with the patriarchs nor with Moses, but with the tribes in Canaan.[3] The tribes which came to compose the twelve-tribe confederation entered Canaan peacefully without disturbing the inhabitants. They settled in the unoccupied mountain regions, and cleared the forests to pursue modest agriculture. Gradual settlement took a long time. Although the Old Testament tells a story of all the tribes working in concert, the traditions originally were gathered from many tribal stories of their ancestors, their migrations, and their settlements in Canaan. For example, the Benjaminite tradition preserved the story of their occupation of the land by telling of victories over Jericho, Bethel, and Gibeon. This important tradition became standard for all the tribes during the period of the twelve-tribe confederation. In reality, the Reuben tribe was content to settle west of the Jordan River, and the Judah tribe originally entered Canaan from the south. Since no strong tradition was preserved about the tribes in the extreme north it is doubtful that they had well defined stories of their origins and their settlements. No exact dates can be given for the Hebrew occupation of Canaan but its beginning probably was during the Amarna Age, about 1350 B.C., and its completion about 1100 B.C.

The Tribes Confederate Around a Religious Shrine: The "Amphictyony"

After several tribes had secured territory in Canaan, they banded together around a religious object at a central shrine. The reason for a twelve-tribe organization was the practical purpose of supporting the shrine on a monthly rotation system. A similar organization was characteristic of Greek tribes during the same period of history. The Greek tribal confederation was called an "amphictyony," a sacred society which dwelt around a particular shrine. The Hebrew shrines were from time to time at Shechem, Bethel, Gilgal, and Shiloh where annual renewal of the tribal covenant took place. Old Testament traditions show clearly that the tribes in the amphictyony were not always the same.

[3] Martin Noth, *The History of Israel* (2d ed., New York: Harper & Row, 1960), pp. 53–163.

Only certain spots could serve as sacred places for the renewal of the covenant of confederation. Since they were originally Canaanite holy places, Israelite storytellers developed traditions to hallow them as Israelite shrines. This necessity created the oral traditions of patriarchs and tribal movements, wanderings, and enslavements which were preserved in the Pentateuch. Traditions of the patriarchs, enslavement in Egypt, the covenant at Sinai, and wilderness wandering, are devoid of "facts," and therefore it is exceedingly dangerous to reconstruct the origins of Israel for any period prior to the fully historical period when Israel was situated in Canaan.

Economic conflict between Canaanites and Israelites flared up, since Israel farmed less favorable ground. Moral conflicts broke out as the strict practices of the tribes conflicted with the looser ones of the Canaanites. The event of an Israelite girl raped by a Canaanite prince brought war (Gen. 34). The desecration of a Canaanite shrine by a fanatical Israelite demanded retaliation (Judg. 6:25–32). Although Israelites absorbed Canaanite ways, and Canaanites married into Israelite clans, there were some things which cultural exchange could not bridge. War broke out. Some Canaanite cities suffered massive destruction, and these ruins are the ones reported by archaeologists. Scholars who take this approach feel this evidence should be used to support the theory that Canaanites and Israelites really were engaged in civil war rather than war of conquest and defense. This interpretation regards the book of Judges as more reliable history than the Pentateuch.

No Conquest of Canaan

There was no conquest of Canaan either peacefully or violently by alien Israelite tribes—so argues another scholar.[4] Most Old Testament scholars explain Israel's origins on the model of the Islamic conquest of the Near East. They were restless and overcrowded bedouin looking for plunder and a place to live. This is, however, a false model based on falsely treating tribe and nomad as synonymous. All people of the ancient Near East were identified with a tribe even if they lived in villages. The formative quality of a tribe was loyalty to a group which guaranteed food and provided protection and pleasures. Tribalism was a subjective attitude rather than a genealogical identification.

Yahwism as a Focus for Social Revolution

The Hebrews belonged to established villages and cities, but they formed tribes of persons who protested the authoritarian power of the Canaanite feudal lords. They organized groups which withdrew

[4]George E. Mendenhall, "The Hebrew Conquest of Palestine," *The Biblical Archaeologist*, XXV, No. 3 (1962), pp. 66–87.

from the society they hated. One sees this characteristic in the Khabiru of the Amarna Letters and the Hebrews of the Old Testament. Instead of an invasion of Canaan by Khabiru or Hebrews, large groups revolted from the parties in power. There was no invasion of Canaan. There was no displacement of the native population. There was no genocide. Only lords and royal administrators were put to death or driven from the land. There was a peasants' revolt against the network of interlocking Canaanite city states.

A single Hebrew tribe was incapable of resisting the injustices of Canaanite rule, but bound together they presented a formidable threat to the existing power structure. Some slaves escaped from Egypt, and under Moses' inspiration they established a community around Yahweh. Yahweh, they believed, manifested Himself to human beings in protective acts and in righteous behavior. The novelty of this religion transcended all other tribal affiliations, and created a loyalty above the tribal level. This new community spread its beliefs. Those oppressed in Canaan adopted the image of a repressed slave group fleeing from Egypt to explain their condition of servitude. Thus identified, these tribes formed themselves into a confederation around the belief in and worship of Yahweh.

The beliefs and practices of these tribes were a deliberate contrast to those of Canaan's city-states. For one thing, there was a genuine concern for slaves, whereas Canaanite lords bought and sold whole villages without regard for personal feelings. For another, Canaanite politics fomented intercity warfare, so that peasants suffered incredible hardships. The Hebrew ideology called for a "promised" land which Yahweh had given them forever.

Traditions of "exodus" and "conquest" bear the following similarity with fact. Fugitive slaves fled from Egypt to the desert where they were saved "miraculously" by Yahweh. In their wanderings they found sanctuary east of the Jordan River (Num. 21:25–35). The Khabiru revolts in Canaan so disrupted normal existence that many of those rebels fled to the fringes of civilization east of the Jordan River. There they joined the Hebrew tribe in its loyalty to Yahweh. Yahwism spread by word of mouth rather than military conquest, and its revolutionary proposals so frightened the Canaanite kings that they formed coalitions in an effort to prevent any more of the peasantry from joining this religious movement. This conflict of ideologies meant war! Some of the city-states were defeated and burned, and although the new leaders from the peasantry rebuilt some of them, many lay abandoned for generations.

The twelve tribes of Israel were neither geneological nor nomadic. They were disaffected individuals who formed bonds of loyalty with similar persons. In a short time several tribes banded together at Shechem where Joshua proposed an entente of twelve tribes whose religious affections were given to Yahweh. Such loyalty lay the groundwork for David's empire. Under Solomon, though, the original ideology dwindled away as Israelites accommodated their beliefs and practices to Canaanite ways.

Infiltration into Canaan

Even though all traditions in the Pentateuch, Joshua and Judges cannot be taken as fact, there are some reliable details among them. These details coupled with archaeological finds and Near Eastern history provide one with information for yet another view of Israel's origins.[5]

The Eastern Route

Canaan in the Middle Bronze Age (2100–1500 B.C.) was a turbulent land. It witnessed the amalgamation of several Semitic groups who migrated from Mesopotamia and the Caucasus Mountains. The Hyksos flooded Syria and Palestine, and conquered Egypt. There, from about 1730 B.C., they held control for about two hundred years. Josephus, the Jewish historian of the 1st century A.D., wrongly identified the Hyksos with the Hebrews in Egypt. But as the Hyksos wave inundated Canaan it swept with it some of the Hebrews. Abraham's visit to Egypt (Gen. 12:10–20), Isaac's sojourn in Gerar (Gen. 26:1–16), and Joseph's life in Egypt (Gen. 37–50) dimly recall the successive waves of Hyksos into the Valley of the Nile. At that period, "Hebrew" did not denote an ethnic group. It was a descriptive term meaning a nomad, a transient, or one who crosses borders. It may be that the Khabiru, a name found in records from ten different regions in the ancient Near East, like the Hebrews, were freebooters, adventurers, soldiers of fortune, and aliens, who thrived during periods of war and social dislocation.

When the Hyksos were expelled from Egypt, its troops marched into Canaan. Egyptian power prevented wandering tribes from entering that land for over a hundred years. But under Amenophis III (1406–1370 B.C.) and Amenophis IV (1370–1353 B.C.) Egyptian power dwindled. Internal religious reform was more important to Amenophis IV (Akhenaton) than ruling an empire, and threats to Egypt's power gathered quickly. Native governors charged one another with disloyalty to Egypt. Hittite and Mitanni princes in Syria, and Khabiru, who sold their services to rebel Canaanite gover-

---

[5] This interpretation follows that in Theophile J. Meek, *Hebrew Origins* (New York: Harper & Brothers, 1960), pp. 1–48.

nors, dreamed of independence from Egypt. The Amarna letters were written from loyal governors in Canaan and Syria appealing for military and economic support from Amenophis IV's government.[6] Soldiers were not sent, and the Khabiru got control of the cities of Jericho, Shechem, Gibeon, Mizpah, and Shiloh. The Amarna letters reported conditions in Canaan so similar to those in the Old Testament's story of Israel's infiltration of the land, that the two probably refer to the same period. Both reported petty kings at war and craftily changing allies. The Gibeonites outwitted Joshua (Josh. 9) to gain his protection much as Labaya, Milkili, and Tagi of the Amarna letters allied themselves with Khabiru. The infiltration of Canaan by the Hebrews probably took over a century. The Amarna letters may have reported the beginning of the movement, and the Old Testament may have reported the end.

Looking east of the Jordan River one finds archaeological evidence lacking for a sedentary population between 1800 and 1200 B.C. Nomads roamed that land. Deterioration of political conditions during the Amarna Age in Syria thrust thousands of wanderers into the Transjordan region. Excavations at Bethel and Schechem point to a change of culture about 1375 B.C., and the stele of Seti I (1309–1290 B.C.), discovered at Bethshan, refers to an invasion from east of the Jordan River by the 'Apiru. Recent excavations at Jericho indicate that people less cultured than its former residents occupied the city between 1400 and 1325 B.C.

'Apiru in Egyptian records, Khabiru in other Near Eastern annals, and Hebrews in the Old Testament, were related by time and circumstances. Appearing in the 14th century B.C. they were rootless vagabonds. Tribes without protection and pasturage infiltrated the hills west of the Jordan normally barred to them by powerful Egyptian troops and high-walled cities. But a weakened Egypt and discontented Canaanite princes opened the doors to invasion. Forced to defend themselves from frightened Canaanites, they banded together into a confederation of tribes at Shechem.

Shechem, the Covenant Place At Shechem Joshua became the chief of this new federation of tribes. The Old Testament preserves a strong tradition of covenant-making at Shechem, where religious and legal traditions were recited, preserved, and renewed. The Canaanite god was Baal-berith, "Lord of the Covenant" (Judg. 8:33), but the Israelites called him El-berith "God of the covenant" (Judg. 9:46). Canaanites had

---

[6] Letters written on clay tablets found at modern Tell el-Amarna two hundred miles south of Cairo have been called the Amarna letters.

revered this shrine for generations, but Israelite traditions gradually laid claim to it. Stories recalled that Jacob had dedicated an altar to El-Elohe-Israel there (Gen. 33:20). Shechemites and Israelites had concluded a treaty there generations earlier (Gen. 34). Joshua wrote "the book of the law of God" which symbolized the covenant between the people and Elohim (Josh. 8:30–35, 24:1–28). Thus, the first traditions of covenant-making and lawgiving preserved in Israel originated at Shechem.

The Infiltration of the Tribes into Canaan

One may summarize the several steps of infiltration of Joshua's tribes into Canaan. (1) Rootless clans driven from Egypt by the expulsion of the Hyksos, and tribes deprived of land by political dislocations in Syria during the Amarna Age overloaded the regions east of the Jordan River. (2) Streams of migrants flowed into Canaan during the 14th century B.C. (3) Entrance to prosperous Canaan was through the pass defended by Jericho, which had cast off Egyptian domination; Bethshan, guarding the easier access to Canaan, was still garrisoned by Egyptian troops. (4) Jericho's destruction left the way open for increased migrations to the highlands, where Israelite tribesmen appropriated property. (5) A tribal federation was created at Shechem where Joshua made a covenant with El, God of that region, and prepared laws by which the federated tribes lived. (6) Thereafter Israel lived in the mountains of Canaan and only gradually occupied land in the valleys. War with Canaanite city states was inevitable (Judg. 4 and 5), but Israel's place was secure until Ammonite and Philistine invasion threatened it.

The Southern Route

Some tribes failed to force their way across the Jordan, and were refused grazing rights east of the river. They migrated south. Attempts to assault Canaan from the south were unsuccessful (Num. 14:39–45; Deut. 1:41–44). These stories, placed after the Exodus, are pointless there, and fanciful explanations of failures were invented (Num. 14:44; Deut. 1:43). Failure to penetrate Canaan forced these migrants to settle among the nomads of the Negeb's grasslands: the Kenites, Calebites, and Kenizzites. Some overflowed into Egypt where benevolent officials allowed them to settle in Goshen (Exod. 8:22, 9:26). Egyptian records reported frontier officials of the Nineteenth Dynasty permitting passage of bedouin tribes through customs at the eastern entrance to Goshen. "We have finished passing the bedouin tribes of Edom by the fortress of Merneptah, belonging to Tjeku, towards the pools of Pithom of Merneptah, belonging to Tjeku, in order to feed themselves and to feed their flocks."[7]

[7]James B. Pritchard, ed., *Ancient Near Eastern Texts Relating to the Old Testament* (rev. ed.; Princeton, N.J.: Princeton University Press, 1955), p. 259.

Some traditions imply that not all the tribes that merged in Canaan were in Egypt. Exodus 1:10 implies a small number of Hebrews in Egypt, and two midwives could take care of all the births (Exod. 1:15). It is true that Exodus 12:37 reported "six hundred thousand men on foot, besides women and children" who escaped from Egypt. This is so obvious a mistake that no scholar takes it seriously. So large a number of men would mean at least two million persons taking part in the Exodus. It would be impossible for that number to survive in Sinai and the Negeb.[8] One tradition revealed that the Judah tribe settled among Canaanites and intermarried with them (Gen. 38). Another affirmed that Hebrews had dwelt continuously east of the Jordan River for three hundred years before the days of Jephthah (Judg. 11:26). Seti I (1309–1290 B.C.) and Ramses II (1290–1224 B.C.), mentioned a tribe named Asher dwelling in northern Canaan during their reigns.[9] The book of Numbers infers that the oasis of Kadesh was controlled by tribes friendly to those in the Exodus (Num. 13:26b, 20:1b). Both biblical and nonbiblical evidence indicates that while some Hebrews lived in Egypt and made their escape from there, other Hebrews lived in the Negeb, and Israelite tribes had settled firmly in Canaan. One tradition clearly affirms that the invasion of Canaan was by individual tribes (Judg. 1).

The Tribes in Egypt Historians cannot be sure which tribes were in Egypt. Surely though, the Levite tribe was since a number of individuals in that tribe bore Egyptian names. Moses himself was from the tribe of Levi.[10] It is remarkable that Egyptian names are found among no other Israelite tribe. The Hebrews prospered during Egypt's Eighteenth Dynasty, but when Seti I came to the throne conditions changed. Egyptian records show that Ramses II, III, and IV used 'Apiru as slaves on their public buildings at Pithom and Raamses (Exod. 1:11). It is almost positive that Ramses II was the king who oppressed the Hebrews, therefore the Exodus could not have taken place earlier than his reign (1290–1224 B.C.). The Exodus from Egypt may have occurred during the period of anarchy that followed Merneptah's reign (1224–1216 B.C.) and the establishment of the Twentieth Dynasty under Ramses III (1175–1144 B.C.). It has already been demonstrated that the conquest of Canaan via the pass at Jericho took place early in the 14th century B.C. under Joshua. Therefore Moses and Joshua cannot have been contemporaries. Judean

---

[8] It is possible that the figure "six hundred thousand" was derived from the census David ordered in 2 Samuel 24, details of which were placed incorrectly in Numbers 1–4 and 26.
[9] This tribe was adopted into the Joshua amphictyony although it was clearly Canaanitic in origin.
[10] See Exodus 2:1, 6:19–20, Numbers 26:59; Assir (Exod. 6:24), Pashhur (Ezra 2:38), Hophni, and Phinehas (1 Sam. 1:3), and Merari (Exod. 6:16).

editors fused the two traditions giving Moses chronological priority so as to place on his shoulders the glory of making the covenant and giving the law for the first time. One needs to remember that the Old Testament was preserved through the work of Judeans, who viewed their traditions of covenant and law as prior to Israelite traditions. Several places show Judean prejudices against Israel's claims. They placed, for example, Mount Gerizim in the district of Jericho, closer to traditional Judean territory than was Shechem (Deut. 11:29–30), and Mount Ebal, the mountain of curses, was substituted for Mount Gerizim by a Judean scribe where Mount Gerizim is clearly demanded by the circumstances (Deut. 27:4, Josh. 8:30).

The Hebrews escaped from Egypt's tyranny when the Nineteenth Dynasty folded. They settled at the oasis of Kadesh. There they coalesced with tribes in that region, and Moses, whose reputation as victor over the Egyptians at the Red Sea gave him right of command, became chief of all the tribes. He organized the amphictyony with Yahweh as God, and structured tribal law as part of the covenant with Yahweh. It is impossible to know precisely what the relation of Kadesh and Mount Sinai was, but it is most improbable that Mount Sinai was located at the southern end of the Sinai peninsula. It seems more likely that it was somewhere near the northern end of the Gulf of Aqaba. The amphictyony formed at Kadesh probably was composed of the tribes of Levi, Judah, Reuben, Kenites, Calebites, and Kenizzites. Gradually these tribes pushed north, moving from Kadesh to Beersheba to Bethlehem where they were dominated by Judah the largest tribe. The Levites remained somewhat independent since they constituted the priestly element in the Judah tribe responsible for heralding the religion of Yahweh. Egyptian control of Canaan vanished as the dissolution of the Nineteenth Dynasty took place, and these southern tribes moved northward to fill the vacuum left by Egypt.

Archaeological Evidence of Southern Invasion

Archaeology partially supports the idea of a southern invasion taking place at the beginning of Iron Age I. Excavations at Debir and Bethzur show a cultural change in those towns about 1200 B.C. The Canaanite city of Arad in the Negeb was destroyed at the beginning of Iron Age I.[11] The biblical narrative carries a story of Arad's destruction (after which the site was renamed Hormah because it means "destruction," — Num. 21:1–3), as it does a story of the destruction of Debir by the Calebites (Josh. 15:14–19). The in-

[11] See Johanan Aharoni, "Arad," *Archaeology* (Spring 1964); also "Arad: Its Inscriptions and Temple," *The Biblical Archaeologist*, XXXI, No. 1 (1968).

vasion was from south to north, according to Judges 1:1–21. The attack was mounted from "the city of palms." This must refer to Tamar ("palm"), a city in the Arabah south of the Dead Sea (Judg. 1:16). If this is an acceptable date for a southern invasion by Moses' tribes, the tradition of Philistines being in Canaan is not anachronistic (Exod. 13:17).

The Wandering of the Tribe of Reuben

If invasions of Canaan by Israelites from the east under Joshua and Hebrews from the south under Moses was the order of events, how does one account for the story of the Israelites' itinerary through Edom and Moab? Reuben was the oldest tribe but it never rose beyond a semi-nomadic stage. Both poetic and narrative traditions recite that because of a violation of custom the southern amphictyony held Reuben in contempt (Gen. 49:3–4 and 35:22). They were generally troublemakers, and the rebellion against Moses was organized by Dathan and Abiram of the Reubenites (Num. 16:1–35). Were the Reubenites, expelled from the confederation at Kadesh, so badly weakened that they wandered directionless barely escaping war with more powerful groups? If so, the tribe's route of travel is preserved in Numbers 21:4–25:17. How else can one account for asking permission to pass through Edom and Moab but being forced to travel around those regions? Before 1200 B.C., according to archaeology, there was no large sedentary population there. After 1200 B.C. small border fortresses were built in Edom and Moab.[12] Would a people powerful enough to capture fortified cities such as Jericho, Bethel, Shechem, and Hazor ask permission to pass through Edom and Moab? The answer is obviously no. Reuben finally settled northeast of the Dead Sea (Num. 32:37). The story of a journey from Kadesh to Gilead was a single tribe's history which became part of all Israel's traditions.

Local Converts to the Invading Amphictyony

Some tribes carried no traditions of invasion and conquest. These tribes, Zebulun and Naphtali, dwelt west and north of the Sea of Chinnereth. Their entrance into Canaan was less dramatic than either the Israelite group under Joshua or the Hebrew group under Moses. They were offshoots of Aramaean settlers who established small states at the foot of Mount Hermon, in the Valley of the Beqa between the Lebanon mountains, and in Damascus. Native to the land when the coalition of Canaanite city-states under Sisera went to war against the Israelites (Judg. 4 and 5), they joined the Israelite confederacy when that war broke out.

[12] Nelson Glueck, *The Other Side of the Jordan* (New Haven, Conn.: American Schools of Oriental Research, 1940). Also, Fred W. Winnett and William L. Reed, *The Excavations at Dibon* [Dhiban] *in Moab* (New Haven, Conn.: American Schools of Oriental Research, 1964).

In summary, then, it is likely that three tribal groups entered Canaan at different times and different points. The first, a group under Joshua, entered Canaan from the east beginning about 1400 B.C. The second infiltrated the land from the south under Moses about 1200 B.C., and eventually was absorbed into the powerful Judah tribe. The third habited the north, and when threatened by wars attached themselves to the Israelite amphictyony at Shechem. Covenant-making and lawgiving characterized both Joshua and Moses, and their achievements were woven into the fabric of Israel's national traditions. Since Judeans were the ones finally responsible for preserving Israel's traditions, it was normal that they present Moses as the dominant historical and religious figure. The amalgamation of these traditions began under the impetus of the Davidic empire, when politics dictated the priority of Moses and the gift of the law at Sinai rather than at Shechem. Tribal traditions were difficult to erase, however, so that minute stories have been retained, even those that came from the weak and disobedient Reubenite tribe.

**Separate Origins of
Israel and Judah**

Not only do traditions about Israel's origins and conquest of Canaan support such an interpretation, but the history of Israel from a hundred years before the United Monarchy to the end of Israel and Judah as national entities supports that conclusion. The evidence is plentiful.

Judges 5 memorialized Israel's victory over a Canaanite coalition under Sisera. Six Israelite tribes federated in this war: Ephraim, Manasseh (Machir, Judg. 5:14), Zebulun, Issachar, Benjamin, Naphtali. Four tribes did not fight: Reuben and Gad (Gilead, Judg. 5:17), east of the Jordan River, and Dan and Asher along the seashore in the north. Three tribes were not mentioned: Judah, Simeon, and Levi. When this poem was chanted (1125 B.C.) there was no twelve-tribe amphictyony. There was a six-tribe confederation and four loosely related tribes, but southern tribes had no part in the amphictyony at Shechem and the war against Sisera.

Differences between tribes west and east of the Jordan River were so great that war between them was commonplace (Judg. 12). Language differences were significant enough so that a test of pronunciation determined to which tribal group a soldier belonged. Inaccurate pronunciation brought death (Judg. 12:5–6). It is clear that cultural differences among tribes due to their separate origins persisted in Canaan for generations.

Absalom's rebellion (2 Sam. 15–18) was localized in Hebron. Hebron had been the center of the Calebite tribe (Judg. 1:20), and David's first seven years as a monarch over Judah was with Hebron as his chief city. One of the reasons the potentially rebellious tribesmen followed Absalom was that he represented a simpler tradition respecting administration of the law (2 Sam. 15:1–6) as against the more advanced legal tradition borrowed from Israel (Exod. 21–23). Furthermore, Absalom's chief support was supplied by bedouin leaders who were contemptuous of the effete ways of the agricultural Israelites (2 Sam. 17:25). Even though descendants of Saul were happy to see David in flight (2 Sam. 16:5–14) Saul's family did not support Absalom in his revolt. Absalom's rebellion was not Judah *and Israel* against the king. Only Judah revolted. On the other hand, a revolt led by Sheba (2 Sam. 20:1–2) was confined solely to Israel, and Judah held steadfastly to David. These two rebellions illustrate that even during the monarchy the tribes in the northern and southern regions were distinct units and expressed their loyalties to the Davidic monarchy differently.

Different practices maintained for generations account for the friction over Solomon's successor. None of the first three kings had been crowned at Shechem. Yet, when Rehoboam succeeded his father he went to Shechem for confirmation of his kingship. An assembly was called to demand that Rehoboam accede to the demands of reduction in taxes and forced labor (1 Kings 12:1–11). When Rehoboam exerted his arrogance, Israel revolted and drove him from the land. That Rehoboam went to Shechem indicates that the ancient northern shrine had not been replaced fully by Jerusalem, and the most serious political and religious matters in Israel were still handled at the site of the ancient amphictyony.

The official establishment of royal shrines at Dan and Bethel, the appointment of priests for those shrines, and the creation of festivals competitive with Judean rites (1 Kings 12:25–33) indicate the practice of separate religious traditions. Jeroboam's appointment, for example, of an Israelite feast to compete with Judah's Passover festival was calculated from the agricultural New Year, and put in the spring. This shows plainly that Israel's calendar was based on the agricultural year beginning in the early fall, while Judah's calendar was based upon nomadic customs.

War continued between Israel and Judah through most of their existence as separate nations (1 Kings 15:16). This would have been

THE PATRIARCHAL AGE

THE HEBREWS IN EGYPT

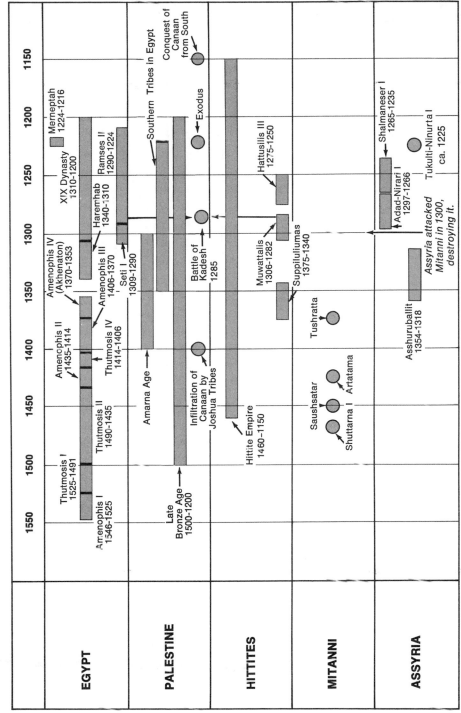

HEBREW INDEPENDENCE IN CANAAN

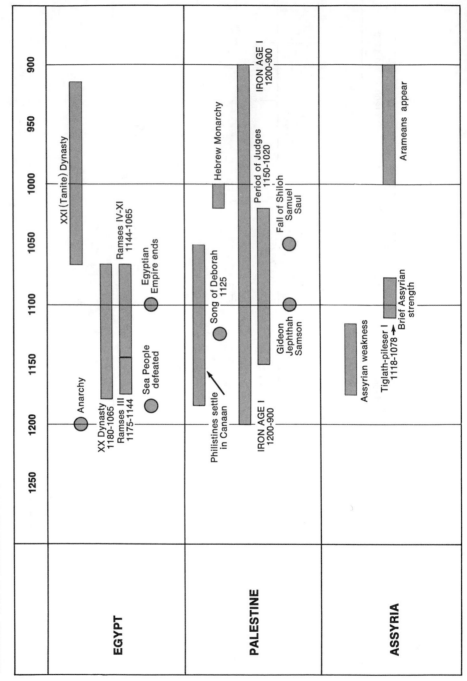

a peculiar condition if they had been a nation formed at Sinai, solidified by wandering in the wilderness, united in a common crusade against Canaanite city-states, and rededicated at Mount Gerizim under Joshua. The separate origins of the people of north and south in Israel contributed greatly to the continuation of their separation following the dissolution of the monarchy.

Even a late prophetic tradition refers to the separate origins of Israel and Judah. Ezekiel called Samaria an elder sister and Jerusalem a younger sister of the same mother (Ezek. 23:1–4). This probably refers to Israel's greater age as compared with Judah. Historical reconstruction shows that Israelite tribes entered Canaan about two hundred years prior to those which combined to form Judah.

Israel's Origins: Fact or Fiction?   Israel put its stories of origins in the context of religion. They excited interest and satisfied curiosity in young and old alike, but primarily they stimulated praise of Yahweh. Children asked, why do we celebrate Passover? (Exod. 13:14); Why do we pray over these stones? (Josh. 4:6); How do we ward off evil? (Judg. 4:1). Then stories of Yahweh's salvation wrought through pillars of fire and smoke, chaotic waters serving His purposes, and warriors fighting His battles, answered the inquirer.

VIII

**Rites and
Affirmations in
Early Israel**

High in the mountains of Lebanon, at the source of the Nahr Ibrahim (Abraham River), are the ruins of an ancient temple. This
temple was built near the falls that issue from a mammoth cave in
the limestone mountain. A beautiful stream of silvery water pours
into the valley, where it collects the red earth and swirls it toward
the Mediterranean Sea. The Arabs named the river after Abraham,
but it was called the Adonis River in classical times. The myth of
Adonis, who was slain by the wild boar, and of Aphrodite, whose
grief was so great that the gods required Adonis to spend only half
the year in Hades, had its setting there. Each year, according to the
myth, Adonis bled from his wound and filled the river with his
blood. Each spring the ferruginous soil of the mountains, flushed
into the river by runoff from snow and spring rains, turns the water
a muddy vermilion. The discoloration of the usually clear stream
extends into the Mediterranean for hundreds of feet. It is a fabulous
sight where blue sea and rust-red river meet.

From days so ancient that no memory recalls exactly, men have
worshipped at the headwaters of this river. Candles burn in a grotto
and rags hang from branches of nearby trees left there by men and
women who have recently prayed at the ruins of the temple. These
men and women are Christians and Muslims, and it makes no
difference that they pray at a site that had originally been a pagan
temple. The awesome beauty of the place and the ageless tradition
that it was proper to worship there, call the humble still to this
ground.

A similarly tenacious quality characterized the religious rites and
convictions of Israel's ancestors. Despite changes in religion which

Core Readings

Review of the Yahwist narrative in the Pentateuch
Review of Joshua and Judges

Headswaters of the Nahr Ibrahim (Abraham River; also Adonis River of Greek mythology), Lebanon. This awesome place received worshippers 5000 years ago and still does so today.

inevitably took place between the days of the Patriarchs and when the Yahwist and Elohist memorialized their traditions in the nation's epic, much of what they believed and practiced survived in the Old Testament. Languages, too, change slowly, so that the meanings of words long forgotten or applied in a new way are often retained even though their original usage no longer is known. Jews, in telling the story of Esther and Mordecai (The Book of Esther), for instance, have long forgotten that the sound of Ishtar and Marduk, Babylonian deities, is still in those names. Christians forget that "Wednesday" and "Saturday" preserve the memory of Teutonic Wotan and Roman Saturn. People usually are unaware that jewelry was originally worn to keep away demons.

Careful attention to archaic shrines, words from ancient sources, and religious rites and convictions whose origins long ago were forgotten enable us to recover some idea of religion among the Old Testament people before the United Monarchy.

The places where men practiced their beliefs, such as sacred stones, springs, trees, and mountains, often endured over centuries. The ancients sometimes worshipped at peculiar rock formations, such as those that looked like a human being (Gen. 19:26). Stones that protected one from enemies or weather or served as resting spots upon one's journey often became sacred. The great stone at Bethel, where Jacob experienced a theophany, was such a spot (Gen. 28:11–22). Some springs were hallowed. The legend of the El of Beerlahai-roi portrayed a visible and friendly spirit. One could see him and still live (Gen. 16:7–14). At Kadesh, also called Enmishpat, lived an El who gave legal decisions (Num. 13:26, Gen. 14:7). Trees also were favorite places for worship. Oak trees near Shechem (Gen. 12:6) and Hebron (Gen. 13:18) served Abraham as places of worship. The oak at Shechem harbored a guardian god to whom Jacob entrusted his precious jewels and idols when he went off to settle his vow to the El at Bethel (Gen. 35:4). Special mountains attracted worshippers. Stories about Abraham found him serving Yahweh at a mountain east of Bethel (Gen. 12:8), and sacrificing Isaac on Mount Moriah (Gen. 22). Mountains on the border between the territory of two peoples were favorite places to sacrifice as treaties were made (Gen. 31:51–54).[1]

Precisely what forms worship took at ancient shrines is not known. It was a matter of bringing gifts for the support of a temple (Gen. 35:7) and praying before the local deity (Gen. 21:33). Jacob sacrificed to Pakkad, Fear (Gen. 31:53), but sacrifices were made only under critical circumstances.[2] Jacob, for instance, sacrificed upon sealing a border agreement. Abraham offered sacrifice, so one story relates, when God promised that he would father a great nation (Gen. 15). Abraham cut a heifer, a goat, and a ram in halves, and laid two birds opposite each other. In a trance he waited for God to make his appearance. Vultures tried to steal the flesh, but Abraham drove them away. As darkness settled God, as a flaming torch, danced between the halved animals in a rite symbolizing what would happen to Abraham's descendants if they failed Abraham's

[1] Mount Hermon, 9,100 feet, is the highest mountain in Canaan. It has always been a sacred place. The root HRM means "to devote to God."
[2] W. F. Albright renders Fear as the "Kinsman of Isaac," since Aramaic and Arabic cognates show this meaning for *pakhid. From the Stone Age to Christianity: Monotheism and the Historical Process* (2d ed.; Garden City, N.Y.: Doubleday & Co., Anchor Books, 1957), p. 248.

God. This type of rite may have been typical of those practiced by the patriarchs.

Although temples were commonplace for worshipping, some of the patriarchs carried images of gods about so that worship needed not be confined to established shrines. Nuzu texts of the 16th century B.C. show that possession of images of gods bestowed tribal leadership, spiritual power and property rights upon the possessor (Gen. 31:33–35).

The Patriarchs performed the rite of circumcision (Gen. 17:9–27). Although the account in Genesis is from the late Priestly source, it is probably an accurate historical notation about the antiquity of the rite among the Israelites' forefathers. Long before the days of Abraham it was a rite of initiation into a community conferring upon a boy responsibility for making war and procreating. Some scholars believe that the rite was introduced in Israel by Moses (Exod. 4:24–26), others by Joshua (Josh. 5:2–7), but its widespread practice in the ancient Near East, except among Babylonians and Assyrians, would argue for its antiquity.

Passover is not mentioned in the book of Genesis, and it first appears as a rite associated with the Exodus from Egypt (Exod. 12:1–36). Yet, *pesakh,* the Hebrew word for Passover, has great antiquity. The language of the Old Testament was really the speech of Canaan, but the antiquity of the word *pesakh,* and some customs attached to the rite, indicate that it was as old as sheepherding itself. Shepherds sacrificed a lamb during the lambing season in hopes of warding off epidemics. Smearing lamb's blood on the tent poles protected the shepherd's family and his flocks. Other features, such as the lamb's meat being roasted, not boiled, leftovers from the meal being destroyed by fire, and no one leaving the dwelling before morning (Exod. 12:7–14, 21–28) show archaic forms. It is possible that reference to Passover before Moses was eliminated from the texts for the reason that Passover was believed instituted by Moses.

A few modern scholars believe that Abraham, Isaac, Jacob, and Joseph were monotheists.[3] This interpretation is hard to accept when the Old Testament itself preserves the names of so many

[3] Among them are W. F. Albright, *From the Stone Age to Christianity,* pp. 243–9, and John Bright, *A History of Israel* (Philadelphia: Westminster Press, 1959), pp. 86–93.

different gods worshipped by those venerable forefathers. When Abraham and Joseph used the name El Shaddai (Gen. 17:1, 43:14), they were calling upon a mountain god that was renowned for frightful power. When Abraham devoted a tenth of his war booty to El Elyon (Gen. 14:18–23), he worshipped the High God of Jerusalem. At Beersheba Abraham prayed to El 'Olam (Gen. 21:33). Jacob's god at Bethel was El Bethel (Gen. 35:7) and at Shechem El-Elohe (Gen. 33:20). Thus, it seems that wherever the patriarchs went they worshipped a local god.

Joshua and Moses

The religion of Joshua is truly difficult to characterize, because the narrative about him was subjected to such thorough editing by the Deuteronomists seven hundred years after he lived. But some reliable details may be gleaned by careful study of JE material.

The Shrines of Joshua

Joshua's Israelites had three important shrines. One was located at Gilgal, near the Jordan River, where giant stones stood. Israel thought of these as commemorating the crossing of the Jordan, although the shrine may have been devoted originally to the rite of circumcision (Josh. 4:20, 5:2–3, 8–9). It is likely that these dolmens had been erected in the Neolithic age.[4] Shiloh and Shechem were other important shrines. Shiloh stood, from time immemorial, as a place where property litigation was conducted. Land surveys were attested for their accuracy and honesty before the god of the shrine (Josh. 18:8–10). At Shechem the covenant between Israel's federated tribes and Elohim was concluded, a code of laws propounded, and a sacred stone erected to recall the event (Josh. 24:1–28, Judg. 9:1–6).

Stories about Joshua do not provide full accounts of how his tribes worshipped, but circumcision, altar-building, and oath-taking were described. Covenant-making, too, was serious business, and demanded a traditional ritual. Although the book of Joshua carries no account of the ritual of covenant-making, a later source, which may have genuine antiquity, does (Deut. 27:11–26). In that ritual Mount Gerizim and Mount Ebal served as stations for antiphonal choirs which chanted the blessings and cursings of covenant responsibility. This ancient litany was known to Joshua and his people.

Moses at Sinai

Stories about Moses stress Mount Sinai as the one sacred site where he and his people worshipped. Although Kadesh, where the Hebrews

---

[4]Such stone structures may still be seen in the hills east of the Jordan today. See James L. Swauger, "Dolmen Studies in Palestine," *The Biblical Archaeologist,* XXIX, No. 4 (1966), pp. 106–14.

encamped for nearly a generation, was a sacred spring, none of the narratives gives it special attention as a center of worship. In contrast with traditions about the patriarchs and Joshua who travelled from shrine to shrine, Moses revered one hallowed spot. At Sinai unauthorized persons were denied access to the mountain (Exod. 19:12–13), while within its holy precincts rituals were performed. Purification of garments, animal sacrifice, and a communion meal with Yahweh constituted proper ritual (Exod. 19:19, 24:9–11). As at Shechem with Joshua, the rite of covenant-making had special significance for Moses' tribes. Veneration of reptiles formed part of Hebrew ritual. Serpents symbolized healing and images of them were carried on poles to ward off misfortune (Num. 21:4b–9). The image of a bull was worshipped, according to one tradition, but Moses stamped out this practice in anger (Exod. 32).

Circumcision

The rite of circumcision originated, so the Yahwist believed, with Moses (Exod. 4:22–26). Its origins remain obscure because two stories were woven together. In one, Zipporah saved the lives of Moses and her son by observing the proper ritual. In the other story Zipporah circumcised her husband on their wedding day as a sign of his engrafting into the Midianite tribe.

The Ark

The Ark appeared in Hebrew history, according to the biblical story, only after the experience at Sinai. It then continued as part of the story into the monarchy.[5] An idealized account of the Ark came from the pen of the Priestly writer, but the cult object venerated by Moses was probably unadorned (Exod. 26). The tent in which the Ark was housed was a simple structure (Exod. 33:7–11, Num. 11:16–17, 24, 26). Ark and tabernacle together served as the holy place where Moses received divine guidance. There, too, the Hebrew's leaders met and judgements were meted out (Exod. 18:1–27). Since it was a place of mystery, only one person was needed to guard it (Exod. 33:11).

[5] It is possible that the ark was a cult instrument associated only with the Israelite tribes which settled central Canaan. Its location at Shiloh, an Israelite shrine, and its use in the Philistine war by Israelite troops under Samuel's leadership (1 Sam. 4:1–4) indicates that it may have been identified only with the El religion of Israel. On the other hand, Julian Morgenstern, *The Ark, the Ephod, and the Tent of Meeting* (Cincinnati: Hebrew Union College, 1945), has shown that a portable religious symbol used by Arabs in the Islamic period may be like the Old Testament Ark of Yahweh. Each Arab tribe had some such sacred symbol, and it may be that such was the case with Israelite and Hebrew tribes. As in the case of tribal traditions which were amalgamated into a single national story, so religious objects of similar design and function may have been reduced to a single object in the literature. The tradition of a probable cult object associated with Moses' amphictyony is very strong (Num. 10:35–36).

Moses and Yahwism

Moses and the religion of Yahweh were linked inseparably. The sources of Moses' inspiration about Yahweh have been questioned, but none has eliminated Moses completely from the origins of Yahwism. The J tradition taught, of course, that Yahweh had been worshipped from early times by the patriarchs. The Elohist and Priestly writers, on the other hand, believed that Yahweh revealed Himself for the first time to Moses. Biblical scholarship on the whole supports the E and P position while disclaiming suggestions that we know precisely the origins of Yahwism. Several expansions on the biblical accounts have been set forth. (1) Some scholars believe that Yahwism was an entirely new religion inspired by Moses' awesome experience when, as a shepherd in Midian, he saw the burning bush (Exod. 3:1-6). This moment so changed him that he devoted his life to disseminating his beliefs, in which his tribesmen supported him fully. (2) Others hold that Moses took from Egypt convictions about a single, powerful God to whom he owed personal allegiance. The world's first monotheism, some claim, was the worship of Aton, the sundisk, by Amenophis IV, or Akhenaton (1369–1353 B.C.). This Pharaoh disavowed the age-old, ram-headed god Amon, and put in its place Aton. Moses' Egyptian training prepared him for belief in one god to which he added the rigorous moral demands of Yahweh. (3) Other scholars claim that Moses learned of Yahweh from the Kenites. These nomadic metalworkers wandered from place to place forging weapons and utensils.[6] Moses' flight from Egypt took him to the grazing lands of Midian, where the Kenites had rootage. In addition to the Elohist's tradition that Jethro, the priest of Midian, was Moses' father-in-law, several other sources associated Kenites and Hebrews (Exod. 3:1). One tradition cited Hobab the Kenite as Moses' father-in-law (Judg. 4:11). Saul would not fight them (1 Sam. 15:4-7), and Kenites lived in the territory of Judah (1 Sam. 30:29). Whatever the origins of Yahwism before Moses, he gave it the content and imagination that made it a religion whose dynamism carried the Hebrew tribes to the heights of empire under David.

Similarities Between Yahweh and Other Gods

In many respects Yahweh was not much different from other gods. Some passages show Yahweh as a God who rescued His followers from misfortune and relieved their suffering (Exod. 3:7-8). He demanded obedience from His followers under pain of severe punishment (Exod. 5:3). He manipulated nature as in the case of plagues

---

[6] For an excellent discussion of the blacksmith tribe among bedouin in the modern Near East see Raphael Patai, *The Kingdom of Jordan* (Princeton, N.J.: Princeton University Press, 1958), pp. 161-2.

in Egypt, wind and tides at the Reed Sea,[7] and fire and thunder on Mount Sinai. He was, as well, a war god, a wilderness guide, and provisioner of food and water (Exod. 17:8–13), Num. 10:35–36, Exod. 16). He was most powerful among the gods, proof being His destruction of the army of Pharaoh, himself a god (Exod. 14:5–7, 30:31, 15:10–11).[8]

The unique characteristic of Yahweh, however, was His willingness to form a covenant with the Hebrews. They believed that He had joined them to Him because they were His special people. The covenant relationship was on the order of king and vassal, to be sure, but the unique aspect of the covenant was that Yahweh had already saved them from slavery in Egypt and annihilation at the Sea of Reeds, and now he promised them a homeland if they would abide by His laws. Some scholars have felt that the idea of a God who made a covenant with a particular people was really too sophisticated a religious idea for the Hebrews under Moses. There is no question that refinements were added to this original idea, but that people in the late 13th century B.C. were incapable of producing such an idea has been disproved by the number of political covenants known between kings and vassals during this very period. Moses took a common historical event, the practice of covenant-making, and raised it to the level of a religious idea. This idea gave direction to the Hebrew's action, and motivated them to concerted efforts. A covenant between God and people became the dominating motif of Yahwism, and was contributory to the creation of the Israelite empire. It also served as the guidelines for an ethical monotheism that was one of Israel's unique contributions to western civilization.

Early Beliefs About Yahweh

Did Moses believe that Yahweh was the only God? One answer affirms that Moses taught that Yahweh was the sole cause of all existence, that He had no wife, no children, no concubines, no family of any sort, and that He had no regular abode, dwelling in the heavens and coming to visit when and as He chose. Moses

---

[7]The Hebrew *yam suph* is rendered Reed Sea rather than Red Sea, and should so be read wherever Red Sea appears in Exodus. *Yam* means "sea" and *suph* means "reed." The King James Version wrongly translates the Hebrew as Red Sea, and that error has been perpetuated in many modern translations. See Jonah 2:5 where *suph* is rendered properly as "weeds." See Exodus 23:31, Numbers 21:4, 1 Kings 9:26, Deuteronomy 1:40 and 2:1 which show that the northern end of the Gulf of Aqaba is the intended site when *yam suph* is used.

[8]These passages claim that Pharaoh led the chariot patrol himself. This may be a historical fact. On the other hand, it is likely a *legendary device* by which to put Pharaoh into the field where Yahweh showed His superior power.

affirmed that Yahweh was the sole source of justice, that His power extended equally over Egypt, Canaan, and the wilderness, and that although He was in human form He could not be seen.[9]

Another answer states that Yahweh was originally the God of a single tribe. The Hebrews, like the Israelites, thought of gods as members of tribes. Some of the tribal gods originated in totemism. Leah, for example, means "wild cow," Rachel means "ewe," and Caleb means "dog." Dan, Gad, and Asher were the names of gods. Issachar means "men of Sakar," and Sakar appears as a god in the Ras Shamra texts. It is likely, then, that all the tribes which formed Israel and Judah had individual tribal gods. Therefore, Yahweh was originally the god of *one of the tribes* that eventually made up the Davidic empire. Which one was it?

Both Old Testament traditions and modern scholarship affirm that Yahwism came originally from south of Canaan. What tribe was strong enough to impose its deity upon all others? It would be a tribe established for a long time in its territory, one whose personal names were compounded with Yahweh, and one whose leadership in a confederation was unquestioned. The tribe that meets these characteristics is Judah. Judah dwelt in the south (Gen. 38). Names compounded with Yahweh are found in greatest number among Judeans. Levites, Kenites, Simeonites, Calebites, Jerahmeelites, and Reubenites, all southern clans, merged with Judah. The Levite tribe only, from which Moses came, remained at all distinct, serving as priests in the confederation. Only under Judah's domination did all of the southern tribes embrace Yahweh as their God. This happened during David's reign, not during Moses' lifetime.

It seems clear enough, from this evidence, that Moses was not a monotheist. Yet, to call him a polytheist seems inaccurate too. We can conclude that Moses stood somewhere between totemism and monotheism. A term to describe this position is *henotheism*. Moses certainly believed in Yahweh, but not to the exclusion of the existence of other gods for other people. The study of religion in the ancient Near East supports such a view of the earliest beliefs about Yahweh.

Religion of the Judges

The Old Testament deprecated the Canaanites. They are presented as blood-thirsty, lustful, and degenerate people, and readers of the

[9] See Albright, *From the Stone Age to Christianity*, pp. 257–72 for the complete argument.

The Canaanite People   Old Testament usually accept uncritically those charges. It is easily forgotten that from the Canaanites came an alphabetic system and literary models borrowed by the Israelites. Canaanites were accomplished people with charted shipping routes on the Mediterranean Sea, a brilliant trade in dyed garments and pottery, and sophisticated forms of city-state government. They had a complex social structure humanized by respect for slaves and the poor.[10] It is easy to skip also the evidence that Israel borrowed extensively from the Canaanites' rites and convictions.

Canaanite Religion   Yahwism was a fanatical religion which spread its convictions as tribes with priests of Yahweh among them wandered over the land. The Danites, for example, migrated north, and the benefits from having a Levite in their midst were felt to be so great that they kidnapped one (Judg. 18). But the missionary zeal of Yahwists could not stamp out entirely Canaanite religion. The Canaanites were polytheists, so that gods and goddesses abounded which served the cause of rainfall, productive fields and herds, and successful commerce. Baal was the general name for lord of a city-state, but each locality had its own special gods. Asherah was the goddess, and she accompanied Baal in fertility rites. Worship of these deities was conducted at high places, and a large upright stone often symbolized the Baal while a wooden pole signified the presence of Asherah. Fertility rites made available both male and female sacred prostitutes attached to temples. The purpose of sacred prostitution was to ensure magically the fertility of land, herds, and people. Figurines of the mother goddess carried by women to insure pregnancy have been found in large numbers at most archaeological excavations in Palestine. Human sacrifice was offered to placate the Baalim.[11] Often the first son was sacrificed to the deity to win divine favor. Sometimes a small child was placed in a pottery bowl and buried beneath the foundations of a new house to assure blessings on the house and family. Canaanite influences upon Israel's rites was rather pronounced. Gideon's father was a worshipper of Baal and Asherah, until Gideon, under inspiration of his new Yahwism, destroyed the clan's altar. Gideon was named first Jerubbaal, because he fought for Baal (Judg. 6:12); only when he became a Yahwist did he take the name Gideon, that is, "a slasher" for Yahweh (Judg. 6:34–35). Even then he followed the Canaanite practice of making an image of deity which the people of Ophrah worshipped (Judg. 8:27). At Shechem Israelites worshipped a Canaanite god named Baal-berith (Judg. 8:33, 9:4, 46). Israelites sometimes

[10] See A. F. Rainey, "The Kingdom of Ugarit," *The Biblical Archaeologist*, XXVIII, No. 4, (1965), pp. 102–24.
[11] Plural of Baal.

Figurines of Asherah, the goddess of fertility, were carried by Canaanite and Israelite women to insure fecundity. Figurines like these dating from 2000 to 600 B.C. have been found in abundance in archaeological excavations.

borrowed the Canaanite rite of human sacrifice. Jephthah vowed to Yahweh that if he were victorious over the Ammonites, he would sacrifice whomever met him first (Judg. 11:30–31). His vow demanded that he offer his daughter since she met him on his return from war.

A Canaanite rite of fertility of vineyards was adopted by Israelites (Judg. 21:16–24). When the fresh shoots of the grape vine were showing, women danced in the vineyards in hopes that their own fertility would be sympathetically communicated to the vines and the vines' fertility to them. At the conclusion of the ceremonial dance the unmarried women were seized by the onlooking men, and copulation took place in the fields. These women were taken to the homes of their new husbands to establish a family. The story is an attempt to explain the origins of a custom which Yahwism could not eliminate from village life. Using it to explain the survival of an Israelite tribe gave it acceptable status among Yahwists.

Yahwism did not borrow, of course, all of the religious practices of Canaan. Many were rejected and were prohibited by official Yahwism. Image-making was prohibited (Exod. 20:4), although Yahwists continued to manufacture images for generations (Num. 21:9, Judg. 8:27, 18:14, 1 Sam. 19:13, 2 Kings 18:4). Eating animals that had been strangled rather than having their throats cut and the blood drained from their veins was forbidden (Gen. 9:4, Lev. 17:10–13), because among the Canaanites eating meat with the blood in it was considered a delicacy due only to nobles and kings. Prohibition of eating a goat boiled in its mother's milk (Exod. 23:19) was leveled against a Canaanite custom that for some reason, as yet unclear, shocked Yahwists. Eating the meat of some animals was considered unclean (Deut. 14:7–8), and singled out from a list for special notice were swine. Why the camel, rabbit, badger, and pig were forbidden is really not known. Some historians have suggested that danger to health in a climate that hurried spoilage of meat was the reason. Yet bedouin Arabs eat camels today and they have no refrigeration. Tracing illness to trichinosis derived from pork was, of course, far too sophisticated for the ancients. Prohibition of eating swine was probably a rejection of a Canaanite religious rite. Yahwists had to stop the assimilative process somewhere, but there seems to be no consistent rationale behind Yahwism's assimilation of some and rejection of other Canaanite religious practices.

The Meaning of Myth

An elaborate mythology was attached to Canaanite religious rites. Several poems have been pieced together from hundreds of clay tablets discovered at Ugarit. One tells how *Baal,* rain and fertility god, and *Anath,* warrior-goddess, perform heroically their tasks of ruling as a whole parade of gods come and go. *Yamm,* the Sea, *Judge Nahar,* the River, *Kathar wa-Khasis,* Skillful and Clever, and *Mot,* Death, pass across the divine stage. *El,* who dwells at the "Source of the Two Floods, in the midst of the headwaters of the Two Oceans," receives maiden *Anath* into his presence while he sits with his feet on a stool and twiddles his thumbs. *El* instructs *Kathar wa-Khasis,* the craftsman god, to build a palace on his grounds. He announces that *Yamm* is his beloved son and shall be Master of the palace. He authorizes *Yamm* to banish *Baal* from his throne.[12]

The Ancient Use of Myths

As in other matters of religion, the Israelites borrowed myths from the Canaanites. Myths served not only as explanations of the nature of reality but also as tools to control reality. It was not enough to personify almost all of nature and human behavior in gods and goddesses. Men tried to control forces of nature and human actions by reciting and dramatizing the myths. Myth was, in fact, the vehicle which carried philosophy, science, religion, and ethics to ancient man. On this vehicle imagination roamed over explanations of nature, human nature, and divine nature.

Ancient men invented myths because they had a persistent desire to know the world in which they lived. They wanted to know *why* the buried seed sprang to life each year, why one field produced an abundant harvest and another a small yield, why the Nile flooded each year to benefit the land, and why the Tigris and Euphrates poured such murderous destruction over their banks. Men needed to control food production and to harness water power, and so they recited myths and accompanied them with sacred actions to influence the Powers that gave life to the seed and let loose the rampaging rivers. In Babylon myth and sacred ritual accompanied spring planting. A twelve-day festival opened the New Year, and mythic ritual accompanied the festival daily. At first the king was humiliated ritually before Marduk, the patron deity of Babylon. Later, as priests recited portents for the coming year stressing fertility of land, the king and a priestess enacted the sacred marriage of Marduk and Ishtar. A procession of gods then paraded through city streets to a shrine outside the wall. There king and priestess consumated their marriage, while the myth of Marduk's conquest of Tiamat was dramatized and chanted. Words and actions ensured the prosperity of the community for another year.

Fertility was only one theme of many that fascinated imaginations of Near Eastern men. The conflict between man and nature also had its explanation in a myth in which all was chaos with monsters loose in the sea. Man and nature were reconciled only when God's creative will intervened (Gen. 1). The Akkadian myth of creation portrayed a gruesome conflict between Marduk and Tiamat.

[12] See James B. Pritchard, ed., *Ancient Near Eastern Texts Relating to the Old Testament* (rev. ed.; Princeton, N.J.: Princeton University Press, 1955), pp. 129–42.

Thy weapons shall not fail; they shall smash thy foes! . . .
He released the arrow, it tore her belly,
It cut through her insides, splitting the heart.
Having thus subdued her, he extinguished her life.
He cast down her carcass to stand upon it. . . .
He split her like a shellfish into two parts:
Half of her he set up and ceiled it as sky.[13]

The Gilgamesh Epic Man's conflict with the gods over immortality was told brilliantly in Babylon's Gilgamesh myth. Enkidu, shaggy and coarse like a beast, was enticed away from his primitive state by the charms of a "harlot-lass." Enkidu was not satisfied only with leaving the fields and becoming a man. Enkidu wanted to be like the gods.

Gilgamesh opened his mouth, Saying to [Enkidu]:
"Who, my friend, can scale heaven?
Only the gods live forever under the sun.
As for mankind, numbered are their days:
Whatever they achieve is but the wind."

Enkidu and Gilgamesh set out upon the quest of killing the Bull of Heaven. Success in this venture so angers the gods Anu, Enlil, Ea, and Shamash, that in their council they order the death of Enkidu.[14] Mankind could not trespass the barrier between himself and the gods and live. Behind the biblical version of man's failure to achieve immortality lay the myth of Gilgamesh (See Gen. 3).

Other themes excited mythic imagination in the ancients: the marriage of gods with women (Gen. 6:1-4); the terrifying experience of a flood (Gen. 6-9); the gods' jealousy of man's creative powers (Gen. 11:1-9). Each found its way into biblical lore through the mediating agency of Canaanite literature.

The Canaanite Myths The biblical writers borrowed these myths, looked at the problems
and Yahwism they tried to solve, cleansed the stories of their crudities, and converted them to conform pretty well with Yahwism. Some of the myths explained the cause of conditions (etiology). Man's limited

[13] James B. Pritchard, ed., *Ancient Near Eastern Texts Relating to the Old Testament* (rev. ed.; Princeton, N.J.: Princeton University Press, 1955), p. 67. Reprinted by permission of Princeton University Press.
[14] *Ibid.*, p. 79.

lifespan, his feebleness in the face of nature, women's suffering in childbirth, and why men and women have different dispositions, were mythically explained (Gen. 3). At one point two etiological myths were combined into a single story (Gen. 11:1–9). One story explained the existence of ziggurats in Babylon. These half-destroyed towers led the curious to conclude that men had tried to build a tower to the gate of heaven. *Babel* means "gate of god" (Gen. 11:9). The story of the ziggurat explained how God had scattered people over the face of the earth because they presumed to enter His domain. The other story dealt with building a city. It tried to explain why there were so many languages. The Hebrew word meaning to confuse is *balal*. When these two myths were combined, the editor lost the key work, *balal*, and *babel*, with a sound like Babylon where ziggurats were found, was substituted.

Sometimes myths were recited to explain the origin of an institution or a name. Woman was so named because she originated from man: *ishah*, "woman," from *ish*, "man" (Gen. 2:23). Long myths reported the origins of arts and crafts, like the myth of Prometheus' theft of fire from the gods, but in the Old Testament they were curtailed. Jabal was the first bedouin, Jubal the first musician, Tubal-cain the first smith. Lamech started blood revenge. Naamah, whose vocation was not reported, may have been the first prostitute or dancer. A pious editor cut out that part (Gen. 4:17–22). Myths also explained cultic rites. Why pour blood on the ground (Gen. 9:1–7)? Why pour oil over the stone at Bethel (Gen. 28:11–12, 17–18, 20–22)? Why swear an oath in making a contract at Beersheba (Gen. 21:25–32)? These are useful in understanding how ancient mankind understood his world and himself.

We are right in treating some myths, such as those about the origins of language and explanations of Israel's superiority over Ammonites and Moabites, as merely interesting and quaint. Scientific philology explains variations in language, and distinctions among Ammonites, Moabites, and Israelites no longer disturb us. But myths did not signify tales devoid of truth to the ancients, and we would be unwise to treat all of them that way ourselves. Myths were the ancients' way of giving imaginative expression to thoughts and convictions about human experiences. Some myths make us ponder still some fundamental questions men ask: what is the meaning of existence? what does it mean to be *healthy, rational,* and *spiritual?* who is fully a human being? why is there evil in the world? Answers to these questions are offered by many voices, but perhaps none so profoundly as those offered in the myths in Genesis 1–11. Some of them have not yet outlived their time.

The literary, historical, and religious study of the Pentateuch has been extensive because of its significance for understanding subsequent portions of the Old Testament. It is necessary, however, to move to the literature that developed in Israel and Judah following the division of the monarchy in 922 B.C.

IX

**From Grandeur
to Humiliation**

This chapter recites the melancholy story of how Israel's grandeur faded. Oral traditions and written records, based on literary themes and styles produced during Israel's grander days, were formalized in the books of 1 and 2 Kings. This effort came to fruition at the end of the 7th century B.C. marking the close of an era. This chapter would not be placed here, were we rigorously to pursue the study of Israel's literary development. The books of 1 and 2 Kings did not take formal structure until about 600 B.C., but the material in them dates from earlier days. Much of 1 and 2 Kings may be treated as reliable witness to the events described.

**Literary Inspection
of the Books of Kings**

The author of 1 and 2 Kings drew selectively from many documents in writing his story of Israel and Judah under the rule of Yahweh.

**Earlier Sources of
1 and 2 Kings**

Three Early Histories. He had three histories from which he chose certain sections. They were a book of the acts of Solomon (1 Kings 11:41), a book of the chronicles of the kings of Israel (1 Kings 14:19), and a book of the chronicles of the kings of Judah (1 Kings 14:29). The book about Solomon was a biography. At least, the stories are samplings of the achievements that a biographer would use to glorify his monarch (1 Kings 3–11). The books about the kings of Israel and Judah carried official court records, and stories of personal and family achievements such as building projects and wars. It is possible that these histories used the same objective style as did the author of David's court life. That objectivity has been lost, however, since the author had in mind a particular interpretation of the nations' destinies when he chose his material.

Core Readings

1 Kings 13–22
2 Kings 1–11, 17–18, 21–25
Psalms 20, 21, 45, 72, 106, 110, 132
1 and 2 Kings are worth reading in full

When 1 and 2 Kings were written, the chronicles of the kings of Israel and Judah were still in existence and might have been consulted.

Stories of the Prophets. The author of 1 and 2 Kings also drew upon stories about prophets who were, on the whole, critics of Israel's kings. Four traditions were drawn upon: stories about Elijah, stories about Elisha, a collection of tales about less important prophets, and some legends about the great Isaiah.

Originally the Elijah stories were independent units by which the prophet's disciples extolled the divine power vested in their leader. Wild birds fed him (1 Kings 17:2–7). A widow's supply of flour and oil was limitless because she obeyed Elijah (1 Kings 17:8–16). His influence over supernatural forces was greater than four hundred priests of Baal (1 Kings 18:17–40). Elijah was more powerful than a company of fifty warriors (2 Kings 1:5–16). Such legends about the great man were sewn together by the thread of narrative about a famine (1 Kings 17:1, 17:14) before the author of the books of Kings took them. Elijah on Mount Horeb (1 Kings 19:1–18), restoring a dead boy to life (1 Kings 17:17–24), and cursing Ahab and Jezebel for murdering Naboth (1 Kings 21) circulated in another series among the prophet's disciples. These narratives have a literary excellence comparable to the legends about Saul and David. They were, of course, oral accounts originally, which is attested by the transference to Elisha of themes of unfailing jars of oil and flour and restoring life to the dead (2 Kings 4:1–37). The author of 1 and 2 Kings selected only some of the Elijah stories in circulation. For instance, Yahweh named Elijah to anoint Hazael king in Damascus and Jehu king in Samaria, but the story of Elijah's completion of that commission was omitted (1 Kings 19:15–18). A story of Elisha's fulfillment of Elijah's commissions was the author's way of showing the continued political influence of the prophetic party (2 Kings 8:7–15).

Stories about Elisha have inferior literary and historical qualities, but they were selected by the author of 1 and 2 Kings because Elisha inspired Jehu's rebellion against the Omride dynasty (2 Kings 2:1 – 13:21). These legends endowed Elisha with magical powers outdoing the tales of Elijah, so that Elisha worked magic for the sake of magic. He cursed little boys so that bears ate them up (2 Kings 2:23–25), decontaminated food (2 Kings 4:38–41), doomed the Syrian army with magic arrows (2 Kings 13:14–19), and resurrected a dead man when he touched the prophet's bones (2 Kings 13:20–21). One story of Elisha that matches the quality of tales about Elijah is the healing of Naaman's leprosy (2 Kings 5). This tale was recited to glorify Yahweh more than Elisha, although the narrator could not resist contrasting the magnificent Elisha with Gehazi, the greedy little servant.

A collection of tales about less important prophets also was fused into the narratives of 1 and 2 Kings. These were stories about men who never reached the popularity of Elijah and Elisha. Stories about Shemaiah (1 Kings 12:21–24), Ahijah (1 Kings 14:1–16) and Jehu (1 Kings 16:1–4, 12) appear now as partial reports from once longer narratives. Those about the unnamed prophet (1 Kings 13:1–34), the disguised prophet (1 Kings 20:35–43), and Micaiah (1 Kings 22:1–28) appear to be complete as they stand. The author of 1 and 2 Kings wove into his original history stories such as Shemaiah's warning to Rehoboam not to war against Jeroboam (1 Kings 12:21–24). The long story about the unnamed prophet, however, was inserted into the original text (1 Kings 13).

A mixture of history and legend about Isaiah rounded out prophetic traditions incorporated into the books of Kings (2 Kings 18:13–20:19). The prophet's disciples told how Isaiah predicted Sennacherib's death, how he cured Hezekiah's illness with a poultice of figs, and how the shadow on the sundial moved backward at Isaiah's command.

A History of Ahab's Reign.   The author of 1 and 2 Kings also had available a special history of Ahab's reign. Perhaps Ahab's significant years were recorded as David's had been, but only those sections which met the author's special purposes were kept. The "Monolith Inscriptions" of Shalmaneser III (858–824 B.C.) indicate what kinds of historical events the author chose to eliminate. On a stone stele Shalmaneser III had his scribe report campaigns in western Syria and his war against the Aramaean coalition. This inscription listed the twelve kings who combined their military resources to stop Shalmaneser's advances into Syria at the battle of Qarqar in 853 B.C. Ahab of Israel supplied 2,000 chariots and 10,000 infantry.[1] Such a large investment would probably not go unrecorded in an account of Ahab's reign, and a battle so important as Qarqar for the political welfare of Syria and Canaan would have been a big item in a list of Ahab's accomplishments.

[1] See James B. Pritchard, ed., *Ancient Near Eastern Texts Relating to the Old Testament* (rev. ed.; Princeton N.J.: Princeton University Press, 1955), p. 278. Hereafter referred to as *Anet*.

Tales of Common People. Stories about common people in un- usual situations give 1 and 2 Kings a popular quality. Tales about cannibalism during the Syrian wars (2 Kings 6:24–31) and how food supplies became available during a seige (2 Kings 7:3–20) are typical.

Annals of the Temple. Annals of the Jerusalem Temple were also available as a source. Explanation for the presence of bronze plaques instead of gold ones (1 Kings 14:25–28), reports of repairs on the Temple (2 Kings 12:4–16, 15:35f, 16:10–18), accounting records noting the money owed by King Hezekiah to the Temple (2 Kings 18:14–16), and the priests' support of a palace revolt (2 Kings 11:1–20) were some Temple records woven into 1 and 2 Kings.

The Theme of 1 and 2 Kings The author himself provided the theme under which these various sources were combined. The theme put the stamp of uniformity upon the whole. He wished to show that Israel and Judah had pros- pered or suffered according to their devotion to, or rejection of, purity of worship as instituted by Josiah's regime (638–609 B.C.). Josiah's rebellion against Assyria won political freedom and un- restricted worship of Yahweh in Jerusalem. The author condemned every king of Israel for his adherence to the "sin of Jeroboam," that is, the worship of idols (1 Kings 12:26–30). Judah's kings were censored for their failure to destory all cult centers other than the Temple. Only Hezekiah and Josiah met the author's full specifica- tions for a good king (2 Kings 18:1, 22:2). The emphasis on purity of worship has reduced the value of the books as historical docu- ments, but it has revealed the religious theme which motivated the political and religious revolution under Josiah between 621 and 609 B.C. One scholar has called it "theological pragmatism."[2] The author of 1 and 2 Kings believed that Judah's welfare as a nation was di- rectly proportional to the diligence of the king in providing for and demanding pure worship in the Jerusalem Temple as prescribed by Deuteronomy 12.

This religious standard controlled the author's methods and con- clusions. According to him, Jeroboam I (922–901 B.C.) was the king of Israel who first fell short of the standard, and every king after him likewise failed. That Omri (876–869 B.C.) and Ahab (869– 850 B.C.) were kings of sufficient stature so that Assyria took serious account of them did not impress the author. He overlooked, too,

[2] Artur Weiser, *The Old Testament: Its Formation and Development,* trans. Dorothea M. Barton (New York: Association Press, 1961), p. 173.

the economic success of Jeroboam II (786–746 B.C.), which made land-hungry Assyria eager to incorporate that territory within its domain (2 Kings 14:23–27, Amos 1:1, 5:10–12, 21–22, 6:4–6). In Judah David was romanticized as the example of purity and consistency of worship although the Temple did not exist in his lifetime. Guided by this theme the author put every king of Israel and Judah under scrutiny.

The following chart shows, by way of example, the sources upon which the author of 1 and 2 Kings drew in composing his story of

Literary Sources of 2 Kings 1–11

Chronicles of the Kings of Israel	Chronicles of the Kings of Judah	Elijah and Elisha Stories
2 Kings 1:1 Moab rebels	2 Kings 8:20–22 Judah's territorial losses	2 Kings 1:2–17a Elijah and Ahaziah's death
1:17a Jehoram rules	8:29 Ahaziah's league with Israel	2:1–25 Elisha succeeds Elijah
3:4–9, 21–27 Israel's war with Moab	11:21 the boy king	4:1–6:23, 6:32–7:2 Stories about Elisha
9:14a, 15b–24 Jehu assassinates Joram		8:7–15 Elisha in Syria
9:27–28 Jehu assassinates Ahaziah		9:25–26, 36–37 Elisha's words fulfilled
9:30–35 Jehu assassinates Jezebel		10:18–27 Yahwists massacre Baal prophets
10:32b–35 Israel's territorial losses		

Stories of Independent Prophets	Popular Stories	Temple Annals
2 Kings 9:1–13 a young prophet anoints Jehu	2 Kings 6:24–31 a story of famine	2 Kings 11:1–20 a temple coup d'etat
10:1–17a a Rechabite story	7:2–20 a story of famine and Syrian war combined	

Deuteronomic Framework and Commentary
2 Kings 1:18
3:1–3
8:16–19
8:23–24
8:25–27
9:14b–15a
9:29
10:10b, 17b
10:28–32a
10:34–36
11:21

the kings of Israel and Judah. This section furnishes blocks of material large enough to isolate. Style, mood, and emphases of the sources reveal their original independence.

Rebellion The author of 1 and 2 Kings tried by his system of synchronism to maintain that Israel and Judah were always one nation under Yahweh. In fact, Israel and Judah were two nations often at war, occasionally in league, usually fighting for their separate existences. Judah had a more stable dynastic tradition than did Israel, and maintained a member of the Davidic family upon the throne throughout its history. Short-lived dynasties came and went in Israel, and kingship there was dotted with frequent usurpations of the throne. The strength of the Davidic family in Judah derived from the unified state David bequeathed to Solomon, from Judah's geographical location apart from the principal routes over which armies marched, and from a homogeneous population which looked upon their early traditions with pride. Israel, on the other hand, had a diverse population, was crossed by important trade routes, had been a subject people under David and Solomon, and had no strong king at the beginning of its independence.

War Between Israel and Judah The war between Israel and Judah was bred during Solomon's reign. His beautification of Jerusalem with great buildings on the Phoenician plan, his heavy taxation of Israel, his disruption of traditional tribal identities and boundaries by establishment of his administrative districts, his use of slave labor taken from Israel, and his disrespect for Israel's religious shrines and strong prophetic tradition, alienated that section of the empire from the monarch. Upon the death of Solomon, Israel waited to see how Rehoboam would handle the dissatisfaction that was abroad in the land.

Rehoboam's Accession. Rehoboam (922–915 B.C.) successfully assumed control in Jerusalem. No incidents were recorded which may have marred a peaceful transition. The most significant event for Rehoboam was his journey to Shechem to receive the assurance of Israel's representatives that he was king there too. Rehoboam's journey to Shechem was probably his attempt to placate the aroused tempers of elders who had for two generations felt the suffocation of Jerusalem's economic and political domination of the north. The elders of Israel acted reasonably when they asked Rehoboam if he intended to maintain the heavy-handed control over the north that had characterized Solomon's rule. The north had not prepared for war, expecting that a change of policy would come from Rehoboam's accession to the throne. When Rehoboam asserted his intention of bringing strict control and increased labor gangs by sending Adoram to round up recruits, the long bitterness of Israel burst out in the assassination of Adoram. Rehoboam's life was endangered, too.

Jeroboam's Return. Jeroboam's second try at rulership in Israel was successful. His first try had been against Solomon (1 Kings 11:26–40). Exiled to Egypt after his strike against Solomon, he found a welcome in the court of Shishak (935–914 B.C.). There he waited until the elders of Israel recalled him to lead the new nation in its bid for independence from Judah. It is most unlikely that a rebel as able and popular as was Jeroboam would be permitted to return to his home and to participate in the negotiations with Rehoboam (1 Kings 11:28). References to his part in the elders' appeal to Rehoboam are probably the author's view of things rather than events as they actually occurred. His return to Israel came after the rebellion had started, when both popular acclaim and his own qualities of leadership had prompted the elders to recall him. It is easy to see why the author of 1 and 2 Kings would wish to have Jeroboam's name associated with the civil disruption from the very beginning: he traced all of the sins of Israel's kings directly to Jeroboam (1 Kings 15:25–26, 34).

Disaffection of the Prophetic Party. Rebellion against centralization of authority in Jerusalem was one of the reasons for Israel's secession from Judah. Two other reasons are less obvious but quite important. First, the prophets were an opposition party to the kings of Israel and Judah. From Shiloh, Ahijah inspired Jeroboam to make his first thrust for power against Solomon (1 Kings 11:26–40). He prompted Jeroboam in this undertaking because Solomon had opened a national shrine in Jerusalem which competed with the ancient cult center at Shiloh where Ahijah ministered. Shemaiah spoke hotly against Rehoboam's attack upon Israel (1 Kings 12:21–24). The prophets tried to maintain the ancient way of doing things. Solomon's dissolution of the confederation of tribes under the rule of Yahweh in which prophets were chiefly influential was met by their determined and bitter opposition.

Dislike of Hereditary Monarchy. A second reason for Israel's secession from Judah was widespread negativity in Israel toward hereditary monarchy. Solomon's monarchy had only confirmed the tradition that leadership in Israel should be by popular acclaim, not by inheritance. Saul, by popular acclaim, was made king in Israel (1 Sam. 11). Jeroboam was selected in the same way. The subsequent history of kingship in Israel shows that efforts to establish dynastic succession ended in intrigue, murder, and a king without royal credentials.

Shechem and Tirzah: Two Capitals

Narratives in 1 and 2 Kings mention two capitals of Israel, Shechem and Tirzah, within a span of fifty years, before Samaria was built in 869 B.C.

Jeroboam began to fortify Shechem, but he abandoned the city before fortifications were finished. Archaeological evidence indicates that Shechem was without walls from 1100 to 900 B.C. A casemate wall was built after 900, but it was insignificant compared with those at Megiddo, Hazor, and Ain Gev. Excavators of Shechem have attributed a layer of ashes to an Egyptian attack upon the city in 918 B.C., but there is insufficient evidence to conclude without doubt that the conflagration was caused by Pharaoh Shishak's army. The cities in Canaan which he attacked were listed in his Karnak inscription, but Shechem does not appear, and Tirzah, only seven miles away, does.[3]

Egyptian Support of Jeroboam

The difficulties of fortifying Shechem were, in part, due to the pressure put upon Israel by Judah's superior forces (1 Kings 14:30). Rehoboam nibbled away at Jeroboam's outlying defenses for five years until he was sure that full war with Jeroboam would be successful. Egypt had not attacked in that five years, but suddenly Shishak sprang to action, launching a campaign against Rehoboam. The recital in 1 Kings 14:25–28 and Shishak's Karnak inscription leave little doubt that Shishak took a hand in Israel's affairs in order to extricate Jeroboam from a hopeless situation.

Rehoboam's Tactical Position

Rehoboam did not lose every square yard of territory in Israel to his rival. Loyal troops still garrisoned Israelite cities such as Hazor and Megiddo north of Shechem, and Gezer, Bethhoron, and Baalath southwest of Shechem (1 Kings 9:15–19). Rehoboam also controlled the region north of Jerusalem where the tribe of Benjamin had traditionally lived, and Gibeon and Mizpah were under his control (1 Kings 12:21). A "no man's land" may have extended

[3] Professor J. H. Breasted believed that about fifty cities in Israel and about one hundred cities in Judah were in the original list. Only seventeen can be located with any degree of certainty. Besides Tirzah the following appeared in the Karnak inscription: Rabbith, Shunem, Bethshan, Rehob, Hapharaim, Machanaim, Gibeon, Bethhoron, Ajalon, Pernoual, Megiddo, Taanach, Aruna, Soccoh, Yeraza, Field of Abram, Arad, Beth Anoth, Sharuhen. *Ancient Records of Egypt,* Vol. IV (Chicago: University of Chicago Press, 1906), pp. 348–55.

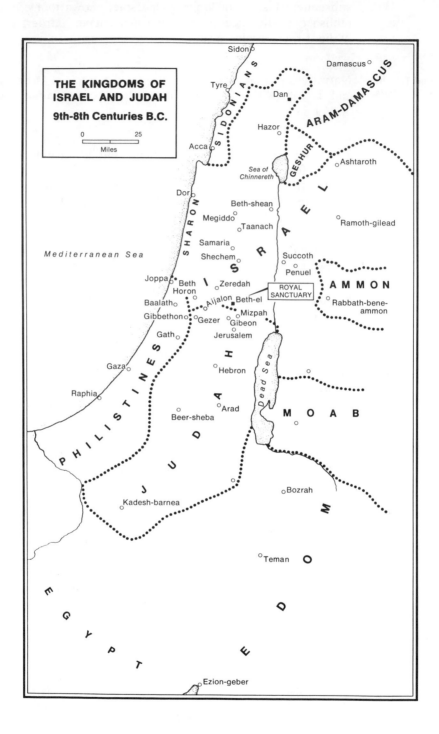

THE KINGDOMS OF
ISRAEL AND JUDAH

9th-8th Centuries B.C.

0   25

Miles

Sidon

Damascus

Tyre

Dan

ARAM-DAMASCUS

SIDONIANS

Hazor

Acca

GESHUR

Sea of
Chinnereth

Ashtaroth

Dor

Beth-shean

Ramoth-gilead

Megiddo

Taanach

I
S
R
A
E
L

Samaria

Shechem

Succoth

Penuel

AMMON

Mediterranean Sea

Joppa

Beth
Horon

Zeredah

Baalath

Aijalon

Beth-el

ROYAL
SANCTUARY

Rabbath-bene-
ammon

Gibbethon

Gezer

Mizpah

Gibeon

Gath

Jerusalem

Dead Sea

Gaza

Hebron

MOAB

Raphia

Arad

J
U
D
A
H

Beer-sheba

J

Kadesh-barnea

Bozrah

M

Teman

O

E
G
Y
P
T

D
O
M

Ezion-geber

between Bethel and Mizpah. One explanation for Rehoboam's failure to attack Jeroboam depicted Rehoboam as obedient to a prophet's oracle (1 Kings 12:21–24). But the historical reason was probably the threat of Egyptian attack from the south if he used his Judean and Benjaminite troops in a full-scale assault on Shechem. Furthermore, Rehoboam may have considered a delayed military operation against Jeroboam better strategy. His troops at Megiddo and Hazor controlled the northern routes to Shechem. His line of fortresses across the plains at Baalath, Gezer, and Bethhoron made direct help from Egypt impossible. Rehoboam's descent from an Ammonite princess made relations with Ammon cordial, and that exposed Jeroboam's eastern flank to Ammonite attack (1 Kings 14:31). In every tactical respect Rehoboam had the advantage. Jeroboam needed help in the face of Rehoboam's continuous incursions into the north.

Shishak's Campaign Shishak's strategy was soundly conceived. He attacked first south of Jerusalem taking cities that controlled the route of supplies to Rehoboam from the port of Ezion-geber and the southern tribesmen.[4] Then he launched an attack against Gezer, Aijalon, and Bethhoron whose garrisons were still faithful to Rehoboam. He moved unmolested into the hills, crossed over at Gibeon, descended into the Jordan Valley, and raided cities there. He moved again into the hill country north of Shechem, hitting Tirzah and Rehob before moving to Bethshan, Megiddo, and Taanach to smash those walled towns into submission. A stone stele commemorating his achievement was left at Megiddo.[5] When he attacked Jerusalem he was on his way home with spoils of war so that it was necessary only to force Rehoboam to pay tribute money by stripping the Temple and palace of their ornamental riches. The walls of Jerusalem were not breached.[6]

Not all Israelites supported Jeroboam (1 Kings 12:26–29), and so Shishak attacked those cities in the north which sheltered troops loyal to Jerusalem. Pharaoh's attack saved Jeroboam from almost certain annihilation at the hands of Rehoboam, and gave Israel's new monarch time to consolidate his kingdom and to build a fortified capital. Shechem was incapable of first class defense, and Shishak's

---

[4] Excavations at Arad, a city mentioned in Shishak's Karnak inscription, show a destruction of that trading center in the late 10th century B.C. See Johanan Aharoni and Ruth Amiran, "Arad," *Archaeology* (Spring 1964), p. 47. See also Johanan Aharoni, "Arad: Its Inscriptions and Temples," *The Biblical Archaeologist*, XXXI, No. 1 (1968), pp. 2–32.

[5] See Pritchard, *ANET*, p. 264.

[6] For Shishak's route see Yigael Yadin, *The Art of Warfare in Biblical Lands*, Vol. II (New York: McGraw-Hill Book Co., 1963), p. 375.

campaign opened Jeroboam's eyes to the need for a stronger capital. Shishak's threat of attack upon Judah protected Jeroboam from Rehoboam, but the death of Shishak in 914 B.C. changed strategic and political factors. Jeroboam's protection vanished when Osorkon I (914–874 B.C.) became Pharaoh in Egypt. He had to find a defensible capital. He chose Tirzah with its strategic superiority over Shechem.

Jeroboam's New Capital

Tirzah was located at the site of modern Tell el Far'ah.[7] Two perennial springs afforded it an unfailing supply of water. It lay a short distance from the head of Wadi el Far'ah, which offered the quickest but steepest route into the hill country from the Jordan Valley. It controlled the direct road from Shechem to Bethshan and on to Damascus as well as the one from central Canaan into Ammon. The natural area for construction of the city was large enough to expand without excessive outlay of physical energy and wealth. The northwest, west, and south portions of the site were ably defended by the deeply-cut stream beds, and another valley isolated northeast and east sides. Information about Tirzah from the Bible is less than one might expect for a capital city, but its destruction by Zimri may have destroyed its official records (1 Kings 16:15–20).

Shrinkage of Judah

Turning again to Rehoboam, one learns that he lost other portions of the Davidic empire. Aramaean states declared their independence and within twenty-five years they had consolidated behind Damascus into a formidable nation (1 Kings 15:16–20). Philistine cities declared their independence, and deprived Judah of large tracts of its best agricultural land (1 Kings 15:27). Although the Old Testament narratives do not mention Ammon, it is unlikely that Jerusalem was able to control that wide territory east of the Jordan River. Moab broke with Jerusalem only to lose its independence to Omri (876–869 B.C.), according to the Moabite Stone.[8]

David's political power and Solomon's wealth were gone forever. The empire was reduced to two small states whose existence was possible so long as Egypt and Assyria were quiet. A balance of power existed in the region until about 750 B.C. The small states in Canaan and Syria attacked one another from time to time, but none conquered the territory of the Davidic empire after Rehoboam's failures at Shechem.

[7]W. F. Albright, "The Site of Tirzah and the Topography of Western Manasseh," *Journal of the Palestine Oriental Society,* Vol. XI (1931), pp. 241–50; and Roland de Vaux, "The Excavations at Tell el Far'ah and the Site of Ancient Tirzah," *Palestine Exploration Quarterly* (1956–1957), pp. 125–40.
[8]See Pritchard, *ANET,* pp. 320–1.

Judah's military power diminished after 922 B.C. but was still formidable, and Rehoboam's son, Asa, continued his father's efforts to reconquer Israel (1 Kings 15:16–22). But an Egyptian garrison at Gerar threatened Asa's southern border, and his defense of that frontier permitted Baasha (900–877 B.C.) of Israel to construct fortresses on Judah's north without harassment. After Asa had secured his southern border, he turned his attention to Baasha. He made a mutual defense pact with Syria's Benhadad, who attacked Baasha's northeastern border. Asa was able then to dismantle Israel's southern forts, and to use the materials for construction of his own.

Judah was not disturbed by internal discord to the extent that Israel was. Abijah ruled in Judah for a scant three years with no domestic or international problem worth mentioning in the eyes of the author of these narratives. Asa (913–873 B.C.) fought wars with Israel and Egypt, tried to eliminate cult prostitution, and reduced the power of the queen mother, Maacah, who practiced the worship of Asherah. The quaint notation about Asa's diseased feet may be a disguised reference to a disease of Asa's genitals (1 Kings 15:23). The Hebrew word *reglayim* was used in some places as a euphemism for the reproductive organs.[9] The notation may be also the author's disguise for stating that Asa ceased to be king in his old age. A king or priest afflicted with a disease could not officiate.[10]

Israel's first fifty years were marred by assassinations of two kings and the suicide of a third. There was no strong tradition of hereditary succession in Israel and the people, influenced by prophets, preferred kingship by popular acclaim to orderly succession by one trained to lead (1 Kings 11:26–40, 14:1–16, 16:1–7, 15–18). Such leadership almost proved fatal to Israel. Elah died by the hand of Zimri, prompted to his bloody deed by the prophet Jehu (1 Kings 16:7–10). Zimri had a mere seven days in command before Omri attacked him at Tirzah. Tibni, as well as Omri, bid for kingship as the elders of Israel supported him. Tibni was a member of an influential family in Israel (1 Kings 16:22). But Omri had the army's backing. Since his father's name was not mentioned, he may have been a foreigner whose leadership of Israel's army had been won by sheer ability. His victory at Tirzah gave Omri rule for eight years, and within that time he stabilized the government, built a

[9] See 1 Samuel 24:3, for example, where Saul relieved himself. The Hebrew verb is *ragal*. Also Ruth 3:1–9 may represent a solemn rite in which the woman exposed and then covered a man's genitals during the harvest season in symbolic hopes of achieving fertility for herself.
[10] See 2 Kings 15:1–7 where Azariah was deprived of rule due to a skin disease. Also, see Leviticus 21:21, a late document, but representing an ancient practice.

new capital, formulated treaties with Judah and Phoenicia, and began a conquest of Moab preparatory to attacking Aramaean holdings in Syria. Despite a short and negative notice of his rule by the author of 1 and 2 Kings, Omri was one of the greatest kings of Israel.

The Omride Dynasty

Jeroboam had chosen Tirzah as Israel's capital because it provided a strategic location superior to Shechem's. From Tirzah Baasha directed a successful blockade against Judah only eight miles north of Jerusalem, and besieged the Philistine garrison at Gibbethon in the coastal plain (1 Kings 15:17, 27, 16:15). The drunken Zimri burned the palace to the ground, but Omri still conducted the government there for six years. Then, Tirzah was abandoned for Samaria. The text does not give reasons for the move, but a crisis must have confronted Israel.

Evacuation of Tirzah

Excavations at Tell el Far'ah indicate that Tirzah was abandoned suddenly. A "brutal destruction" of the city occurred in the 10th century B.C. This was undoubtedly Shishak's attack. New buildings were constructed upon the ruins of the destroyed city. Houses were well built and "grouped with their backs to each other along parallel streets . . . all the houses follow more or less the same arrangement and have roughly the same dimensions."[11] This rebuilding was Jeroboam's construction of the new capital after 914 B.C. The city was planned, rather than being a haphazard development of individual residences. Father de Vaux discovered also that there was a destruction of the level which contained the uniformly designed houses. This may have been the ruin brought by Zimri's arson. This level was in process of being rebuilt but it was never completed. A building, for example, of impressive proportions had been started with its foundations laid and its chiselled stones prepared, but the structure was abandoned. "There are several indications that work was interrupted. Near the north east corner a great dressed stone stands on a ground level belonging to an earlier era. . . . It was made to be set on the corner but never put in place. Outside the building several large blocks of stone still untrimmed stand in line and beside them was a heap of lime."[12] The archaeological evidence shows that Omri's action was abrupt.

Omri's Reasons for Leaving Tirzah

Domestic Political Considerations. Strategic and political forces combined to bring Omri to his decision to evacuate Tirzah. These

[11] Roland de Vaux, "Excavations at Tell el Far'ah and the site of Ancient Tirzah." Reprinted by permission of the publisher from the *Palestine Exploration Quarterly* (1956–57), p. 132.
[12] *Ibid.*, p. 133.

Tools used in Palestinian archaeology. The rubber basket is used
to carry dirt and the woven basket to carry pottery and artifacts.
All records are kept in the field book at the right. Trowel, broom,
and brush are used for close work and keeping one's work area
clean.

forces were not mentioned by the author of 1 and 2 Kings, and so
they must be deduced from conditions known from other sources.
A few Old Testament scholars have offered some explanations.
One believed that Tirzah was abandoned because of domestic
political issues. Omri ruled a kingdom where Israelities and Canaanites dwelt side by side, and he had to provide a special capital
for his Canaanite subjects. He fortified Samaria for this purpose.
He wished also to break with the Israelite past, and to that end he
established an Israelite capital in Jezreel.[13] One problem with that
suggestion is its failure to consider military matters. Another is
that the archaeological evidence shows that Omri did not make a
complete break with his Israelite past by building at Samaria. Tell
el Far'ah shows almost total abandonment in the 9th century B.C.,
which means that nearly the entire population moved to Samaria.
Another scholar believed that the move to Samaria aimed to secur-

---

[13] See 1 Kings 21:1 for slight evidence of an Israelite capital in Jezreel. Also John
Bright, *A History of Israel* (Philadelphia: Westminster Press, 1959), p. 224, n. 49.

ing a political relationship with Phoenicia in orienting the capital to the west instead of to the east.

Omri's son Ahab married a Phoenician princess (1 Kings 16:31). Fortified Samaria would also be a staging center for defense of the Plain of Sharon from Philistine raids.[14] Roland de Vaux believes that by establishing a dynasty on neutral ground, Omri minimized tension among Israel's political parties. Communications with the southern and western parts of the nation were difficult from Tirzah, and Samaria relieved that problem. Samaria was nearer the geographical center of the kingdom than was Tirzah. Trade and political alignments with Phoenicia were more desirable than dealing with Rabbah and Damascus. Since the region around Tell el Far'ah today has a high incidence of malaria, so in early times the recurrence of that disease may have made it necessary to vacate Tirzah for a more healthful location.[15]

Interregional Politics and Military Strategy. Two factors have been overlooked by these previous conclusions. One factor was interregional politics, the other military strategy. When the Davidic empire ruptured, Israel's secession so weakened Rehoboam that he lost vast territories in Syria. Rezon established a small Aramaean empire with Damascus as its heart. The Aramaean empire expanded until it threatened Israel's independence. Moving the capital from Shechem to Tirzah was partial response to Aramaean threats to Israel's territory east of the Jordan Valley.

The Advance of Asshurnasirpal

Farther to the northeast Assyria's revival of political and economic aspirations under Asshurnasirpal II (883–859 B.C.) was hedged by the powerful Aramaean states of Bit-Khalupe and Bit-Adini on the upper Euphrates River. Control of commercial centers on the Euphrates and roads to markets on the Mediterranean Sea were Asshurnasirpal's major objectives. In 878 B.C. he invaded states on the upper Euphrates, subdued them with frightful ruthlessness, and struck west to the Sea. This was the year that Omri became king over Israel *at Tirzah*. Asshurnasirpal's armies established garrisons at Hamath, Emessa, and Tripolis. He "washed his weapons in the Sea," and called on the kings of Arvad, Tyre, and Sidon to pay him tribute.[16] Assyrian control in western Syria alerted Omri to his danger. For a year or two he watched interregional politics, then he put his confidence in Phoenician stability. He married his son to the Phoenician princess, Jezebel. As Assyrian strength in

[14] Albright, "The Site of Tirzah," p. 242.
[15] De Vaux, "The Excavations at Tell el Far'ah," pp. 139–40.
[16] Pritchard, *ANET*, pp. 275–6.

western Syria did not diminish, he abandoned his eastern perimeter with its core at Tirzah and moved to Samaria. Damascus' Benhadad (880–842 B.C.) was so busy protecting his northern frontier from Assyrian agitation that he had neither time nor materials for threatening Israelite territory.

The New Assyrian Ram. The strategic factor was probably more important than the political. When Omri heard how Asshurnasirpal had accomplished his march to the Sea, he knew that Tirzah's days were numbered. Asshurnasirpal's engineers had developed an offensive weapon that made two types of city defenses vulnerable: the city on a plain, and the city with casemate walls. This weapon was a battering ram operating on the principle of twisting the horizontal leverage of stone walls rather than butting them head on. The battering ram was mounted on a body about nineteen feet long, about ten feet wide, and with six wheels. A turret protected the operators from the missiles of the defenders. The operational head of the battering ram was shaped like the blade of an ax. The head was driven between the stones of the walls and levered to right and to left, displacing stones and collapsing a section of wall.[17] A city on level ground received the full thrust of the ax-headed battering ram, and cleavage was easily made. Casemate walls situated on a hill were even vulnerable because ramps could be built across a fosse and up a glacis. Then the relatively thin walls could be dislodged easily. Defense against this new weapon was thicker walls built of hewn stones tightly fitted together, construction of salients so that defenders could shoot at the battering ram's operators from the side, and a corbeled parapet so that stones could be dropped on top of the battering ram. Casemate city walls gave way to solid walls in many Israelite cities during the 9th century B.C., as excavations at Megiddo, Hazor, and Ain Gev have shown. At Samaria the height of the hill, the excellence of the masonry, and the demands for rapid completion combined to permit construction of a casemate wall.

It seems probable that Omri moved the captial of Israel from Tirzah to Samaria because Asshurnasirpal's advance into western Syria in 876 B.C. had changed international politics radically. Israel's eastern holdings could survive without the protection afforded by wary observers at Tirzah because Aramaean energy was directed toward the threat from the north. In addition, he saw that the new battering ram made Tirzah vulnerable. A capital on a high hill was the only safe location for the most important city in the nation.

[17] See Yadin, *The Art of Warfare in Biblical Lands*, p. 314.

Foreign powers recognized Omri's ability, even though the author of 1 and 2 Kings gave him only five sentences. Omri and his son Ahab made such impressions upon Assyrian kings that Israel's monarchy was known as the "house of Omri" even after the last of his line had been assassinated by the usurper Jehu.[18] His policy was to secure peace with his neighbors wherever possible. He made a treaty with Ittobaal of Tyre and sealed it by marriage of Ahab to Ittobaal's daughter Jezebel. This treaty gave Israel an outlet for its surplus olive oil and grain. Ittobaal benefitted as commercial carrier for Israel's exports and imports. These combined powers deterred the expansion of the Aramaeans in Syria. Omri also settled differences with Judah by marriage treaty. He gave his daughter Athaliah in marriage to Judah's king Jehoram (2 Kings 8:16–18).[19]

Peace at home and commercial and political ties with Tyre and Judah gave Omri time to reestablish Israelite hegemony over territory east of the Jordan Valley. He made Moab a vassal state and assured Israel of a steady supply of cereal grain and sheep (2 Kings 3:4–8). Control there also gave him a strategic position from which to contain Aramaean expansion southward. No war between Omri and Benhadad was recorded in either Old Testament or extrabiblical sources. His son Ahab, however, had to repel Aramaean attacks several times.

Ahab (869–850 B.C.) stepped into Omri's big shoes and in most respects he filled them admirably. But his years in power were loaded with problems which were not his own doing. His father's military and diplomatic skills had brought peace and increased prosperity to Israel. The capital at Samaria was a model of workmanship and defensive engineering. Excavations at ancient Samaria reveal one of the finest construction jobs ever done in Israel. But four problems made Ahab's task difficult. First, the area suffered a serious drought. Second, religious revolution kept the people in turmoil. Third, Assyria's aggression brought war. Fourth, intermittent warfare with the Aramaean state retarded Israel's growth.

Drought in Israel.   Legends of Elijah were filled with stories about a serious drought (1 Kings 17:1, 18:1–6, 41–46). Israel's prosperity

---

[18]See Pritchard, *ANET*, p. 280

[19]2 Kings 8:18 calls Athaliah the daughter of Ahab. 2 Kings 8:26 refers to her as the daughter of Omri. (The RSV reads granddaughter in order to harmonize with 2 Kings 8:18.) But since her son Ahaziah was 22 years old when he became king in Judah he was born about 846 B.C. Ahab and Jezebel had been married only ten years so that it seems unlikely that their daughter, Athaliah, gave birth to a son when she was less than ten years old.

Stone carving at Nimrud glorifies Asshurnasirpal in a lion hunt.

suffered from this condition. Small farmers lost their lands when crops failed, and they sold their property and themselves to large landlords. The story of Naboth's vineyard (1 Kings 21:1–19) reflects this condition, although its present form stresses personal ethics rather than social disintegration.

Religious Revolution.   The religious revolution will be treated in the section on religious matters.

The Threat of Assyria.   Assyria again threatened the small nations in western Syria and Canaan when Shalmaneser III (859–824 B.C.) became king. No single state could successfully counter Assyria's massive armies. The author of 1 and 2 Kings left out the story of Ahab's part in a coalition of small states which combined their military units to stop the onslaught of those dreadful armies. Ahab contributed 2,000 chariots and 10,000 infantry, and probably led those forces personally. Ahab combined his forces with troops from Damascus, Hamath, Kue, and eight other small nations to check Shalmaneser's aggression at the battle of Qarqar in 853 B.C. It was another five years before he could mount the attack upon Damascus which brought the Aramaeans to heel.

Wars with Benhadad the Aramaean

The most devitalizing matter in Ahab's Israel was his wars with Benhadad of Damascus. Ahab's father died in his second year of kingship in Samaria. Apparently his death was sudden and unexpected. Ahab was not more than twenty-two or twenty-three years old when he became king. Benhadad undoubtedly knew about the confusion that existed on the death of the strong Omri, and that the construction work on the new capital was not completed. He undertook a hastily prepared campaign against Ahab at Samaria hoping to strike before Ahab had consolidated his power. A common interpretation of this war with Syria is that Samaria was actually under siege.[20] The story in 1 Kings 20:1–21 actually presents a different situation. The word translated "besieged" in the Revised Standard Version means "to disturb" or "to distress." The description of Benhadad's tactics indicates a campaign of harassment. Probably Benhadad had marched south from Damascus, if he had not already been on a raid when news of Omri's death reached him, to the site of modern Jerash. There he turned west following the course of the Jabbok River (the Wadi Zerqa) to the Jordan Valley. With plenty of grass and fresh water at the confluence of the Jabbok and Jordan Rivers he rested his troops and animals at Succoth. The translation again obscures the historical situation. Benhadad was relaxing riotously in Succoth, not "in the booths" (1 Kings 20:16). *Succoth* means "booths" in Hebrew, but it was also the name of a city in the Jordan Valley where harvest festivals were celebrated. The capture of the harvest had given Benhadad and his officers reasons for celebrating.

A Raid Rather than War.   Benhadad's behavior indicated that he believed his campaign was more a raid than a serious war. His first message to Ahab demanded immediate delivery of silver, gold, and women. He countermanded this by an ultimatum demanding right of search and seizure (1 Kings 20:2–6). Ahab appeared willing to accede to the first order, but he refused the indignity and devastation that the second would bring upon Samaria. After an exchange of boastful notes, the armies prepared for war, something which both kings had hoped to avoid (1 Kings 20:10–11).

Samaria Not Besieged.   Four facts indicate that Benhadad was not besieging Samaria. First, it would have been unnecessary for him "to send" messengers if he had surrounded Samaria (1 Kings 20:2, 10). Ahab could have heard Benhadad's demands from the top of the city wall and seen the size of his army.[21] Second, that Ahab would have been able to contact his 232 district governors in an appeal for troops while he and his staff were encircled by Aramaean troops seems incredible. Third, the procurement of 7,000 troops took place after Ahab had contacted his district governors. How could they have gotten into Samaria? Fourth, 7,000 soldiers

[20] For example, George A. Buttrick, ed., *The Interpreter's Bible*, Vol. III (New York: Abingdon Press, 1955), p. 165.
[21] See 2 Kings 18:13–27 for an example of diplomatic negotiations conducted from a wall when Jerusalem was under siege.

could not march out of the gates of besieged Samaria and be deployed for action before being mauled by missiles and cavalry attacks (1 Kings 20:15).

The engagement may have taken place in something of the following way. Benhadad was stationed at Succoth from where he sent his scouts to study Ahab's defenses. That Ahab's defensive perimeter was concentrated about Samaria gave Benhadad confidence. He tried to bluff Ahab into giving him the spoils of war without a fight. Ahab's consultation with his advisers convinced him to make a fight and a hasty muster of militia produced 7,000 soldiers. When Benhadad's scouts reported that Ahab had moved his troops out of Samaria, he decided to meet Israel's relatively small force in the field (1 Kings 20:17).

Into an Ambush. The Aramaean army took the road up the Wadi Far'ah, either not knowing about the rugged terrain at the head of the valley or being led by overconfident commanders. Ahab's army allowed the main body of Aramaeans to enter the steepest and roughest part of the gorge where Wadi Far'ah and Wadi Beisan join, and then they struck. The element of surprise, and fighting from an elevated position, gave Ahab's troops advantages over an army already tired from marching during midday up a steep valley.[22]

Benhadad's Second Campaign

Benhadad directed a second campaign in the spring of the next year (1 Kings 20:26). Having been beaten in the mountains, the Aramaeans decided to entice Ahab into battle in the open country (1 Kings 20:23). Ahab was better prepared for the spring war than he had been for the one the previous fall. His losses then had been small, and he was willing to risk a battle against superior chariotry. Benhadad reorganized his army by putting his own commanders in charge, replacing the chieftains who had been responsible for Benhadad's defeat in the previous campaign (1 Kings 20:24). He marched on Israel hoping to rest at Bethshan. From there he could easily reach the Plain of Jezreel where his superior chariotry would annihilate Ahab's smaller army. Ahab reacted more quickly than was expected. He met the Aramaeans in terrain that would limit the mobility of Benhadad's chariotry. He waited for the Damascan army at Aphek east of the Sea of Chinnereth (1 Kings 20:26–30). The Israelites routed the Aramaeans, and Benhadad surrendered

---

[22] Field Marshal Wavell reported in *Allenby: A Study in Greatness* (London: G. G. Harrap and Co., 1940–1943), p. 279, that the British defeated the Turkish army in 1917 at Wadi Far'ah when the Turks allowed themselves to be trapped there. Air bombardment and artillery smashed their columns of troops and materials. Thousands of prisoners were taken as they attempted to climb the steep gorge to safety.

after he had fled into the city of Aphek. Ahab's generosity in permitting a defeated king to live was politically motivated. It was better to have trade concessions in Damascus and a buffer state between Israel and Assyrian spheres of influence than the glory of unconditional surrender.

Death of Ahab Ahab's defense of Israel was successful, but offensive warfare brought him defeat and death. Ahab persuaded Judah's Jehoshaphat to join him in a war to wrest Ramoth in Gilead from Aramaean control (1 Kings 22:1-3, 29). It is not clear why Ahab attempted that campaign. He may have anticipated Assyria's eventual success against the Aramaean state, and hoped to establish control over disputed territory before it fell into Assyrian hands.[23] On the other hand, Benhadad may have defaulted on his treaty obligations, in which case Ahab would have mounted his campaign as a punitive attack (1 Kings 20:34, 22:3). At any rate, he met death in an insignificant part of the battle for Ramoth.

Israel suffered an economic and political blow soon after Ahaziah (850-849 B.C.) succeeded his father Ahab. Moab successfully rebelled. Under Jehoram (849-842 B.C.), another of Ahab's sons, Israel's efforts to win back territory from Moab were futile (2 Kings 3:4-27). Jehoram succeeded in taking Ramoth in Gilead where Ahab had failed, but he was constantly pressed by Aramaean forages (2 Kings 9:14). While he was convalescing at his home in Jezreel from wounds received in war with the Aramaeans, he was killed by Jehu (2 Kings 9:14-24). Jehu's *coup d'etat* ended Omri's dynasty which had lasted a mere thirty-four years.

Two Centuries of Conflict Judah and Israel fought with each other and their neighbors for nearly the next two hundred years, seriously depleting their wealth in men and material. Judah's Jehoshaphat (873-849 B.C.) tried to revive Solomon's lucrative trade in regions bordering the Red Sea but a South Arabian navy destroyed his entire fleet (1 Kings 22: 47-48).[24] Jehu's bloody *coup d'etat* in Israel returned the religion of Yahweh to its former position of dominance, but Israel was nearly swept to oblivion before political and military powers that the usurper Jehu had blithely ignored. Jeroboam II (786-746 B.C.) revived Israel for a generation, but upon his death disintegration proceeded at a rapid pace (2 Kings 15:8-31). Hezekiah (715-

---

[23] See Pritchard, *ANET*, p. 280, in which records of Shalmaneser's campaign in his eighteenth year reported his sack of Damascus.

[24] Psalm 48:7 mentions the east wind that shattered the ships of Tarshish, but other passages indicate that the Hebrew word *shobar* means breakage by human agents, too. See Exodus 32:10, 2 Kings 18:4.

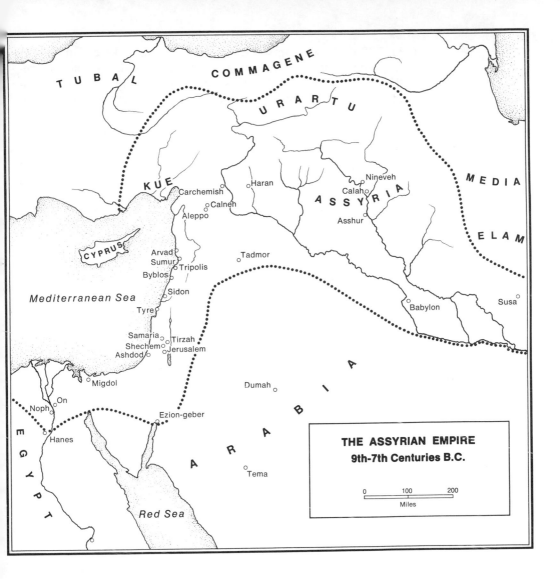

THE ASSYRIAN EMPIRE
9th-7th Centuries B.C.

0   100   200
Miles

687 B.C.) tried to reestablish Judah's independence of Assyrian control but his road to freedom was barricaded by Assyrian occupation troops in Damascus, Israel, and on the Philistine plains.

Israel's Last Twenty Years: The Assyrians Enter Canaan

Quarreling among Syria's and Canaan's small nations was an invitation to Assyria to take command there.

The Israelite-Aramaean coalition against Judah brought Assyria's armies under Tiglath-pileser III (745–727 B.C.) into Canaan to stay (2 Kings 16). They devastated Israel's northern cities, and Hoshea

(732–722 B.C.) gave himself to Assyria as a vassal king. But as soon as Assyrian armies were engaged elsewhere he began plotting rebellion. Tiglath-pileser's death seemed like his chance. He negotiated with So, a general in charge of Egypt's Delta troops.[25] When agents of Shalmaneser V (727–722 B.C.) heard of Hoshea's duplicity and reported it to Nineveh, Shalmaneser sent a huge army against Israel to settle accounts. Hoshea appeared before his vassal lord, excusing his actions and appealing for mercy, but he was taken prisoner. Shalmaneser destroyed more cities in Israel, and besieged Samaria. Sargon II (722–705 B.C.) completed the task Shalmaneser had started.

The Seige of Samaria

Samaria's defenses were supurb. The attack began in 724 B.C. and lasted for three years. General So of Egypt tried to honor his commitments to Hoshea, and attacked the Assyrian army, but there was not much of a battle. Sargon II boasted that So ran away upon hearing the noise of his army, and "has not been seen again."[26] The city had occasional relief from constant siege, but one can imagine the suffering and horror within the walls. In the end 27,290 prisoners were taken from Israel to be sold as slaves among the Assyrians in Mesopotamia. All identity as Israelites was lost. Citizens left around Samaria were soon indistinguishable from those people whom Sargon brought from widely separated parts of his empire to settle in Samaria (2 Kings 17:24–25). This exchange of populations was a deliberate policy aimed at reducing rebellions. People without common language and culture were less capable of conniving together. With Samaria's leadership deported to Mesopotamia, the territory was organized as a province with an Assyrian governor. Israel as a nation no longer existed.

Judah's Last Years

Cooperation With Assyria. When Manasseh (687–642 B.C.) succeeded Hezekiah as king in Judah, he abandoned his father's nationalism. Hezekiah's policy had brought Assyrian punitive expeditions into Judah three times; in 713–711 B.C., in 703–701 B.C., and in 688 B.C.[27] Manasseh suspended nationalistic schemes, and rather than struggle along against a huge empire Manasseh rolled with the punch. The author of 1 and 2 Kings despised Manasseh for his cooperation with Assyria. The Old Testament mentioned only

---

[25] At 2 Kings 17:4 he was called "king of Egypt." It is unlikely that So (Sib'e) was more than a general for one of the rival kings, during a period of political confusion between 759 and 715 B.C.

[26] Pritchard, *ANET*, p. 285.

[27] Bright, *A History of Israel*, pp. 282–287, presents a cogent argument for a campaign against Hezekiah in 688 B.C.

his cooperation in religious matters,[28] but Esarhaddon, king of Assyria (681–669 B.C.), listed Manasseh as one of several kings who supplied logs, beams, boards, stone, and slabs of limestone for his construction work in Nineveh. Manasseh also supplied troops for Esarhaddon's military operations in Egypt.[29]

Judah Turns Against Assyria

Assyrian fortunes continued to affect events in Judah following the death of Manasseh in 642 B.C. Revolts in Babylon and Elam occupied Asshurbanapal (669–633 B.C.) for several years. Subduing those rebellions so weakened Assyria in the west that Pharaoh Psammetichus I (663–609 B.C.) was able to reunite Egypt, and withheld tribute to Assyria. Syrian bedouin tribes overran the regions east of the Jordan Valley. The Medes north of Elam threatened Assyria's borders. In Judah a palace *coup* put an end to cooperation with Assyria by assassinating Amon, Manasseh's son. The Assyrian empire had fallen on difficult days. Josiah, the eight-year-old son of Amon, was elevated to kingship. The first information given about Josiah's rule (639–609 B.C.) reports what happened in his eighteenth year (2 Kings 22). The high priest found "the book of the law" while repairs to the Temple were being made.

Josiah's Cautious Detachment of Judah From Assyria

The author of 1 and 2 Kings recorded that the discovery of "the book of the law" stimulated religious reform in Judah. It is likely that reform was already under way before the discovery of the book, since the Temple had received funds and materials to begin repairs. Judah's nationalist leaders were plotting revolt, and waiting for the right moment to declare their independence. The death of Asshurbanapal in 633 B.C. would have been the signal for resuming a Judean way of doing things in Jerusalem.[30] Discovery of the "book of the law" was Judah's proclamation of independence from an Assyrian Empire which was staggering from blows on every side. Temple repairs symbolized to Judeans that a change was forthcoming, since worship of Assyrian gods in local shrines demonstrated subservience to the Assyrian king. Repairing the Temple also tested how tightly Assyrian regulations would be enforced. Josiah's advisors had learned lessons from Hezekiah's blundering tactics in

[28] 2 Chronicles 33:11–17 reports that Manasseh rebelled, was taken prisoner, and was tried before the king of Assyria. Acquitted, he was returned to his throne. This story, coupled with an account of his religious reforms, appears to be fictitious.
[29] See Pritchard, *ANET*, p. 291.
[30] This is W. F. Albright's date. Other scholars suggest 629 and 626 B.C. See "Ashurbanapal," in George A. Buttrick, ed., *Interpreter's Dictionary of the Bible*, A–D (New York: Abingdon Press, 1962), p. 256 (hereafter referred to as *IDB*), and Norman K. Gottwald, *All the Kingdoms of the Earth* (New York: Harper and Row, 1964), p. 240.

rebelling against Assyria, and they followed a cautious course. They tried the Temple repairs first; these were not stopped. Then, they brought forth the new constitution contained in the book of Deuteronomy. Then, they risked everything by a ceremony in the Temple area which bound Josiah to the new constitution rather than to the Assyrian king. Assyrian armies did not retaliate! Reform of Judah's political and religious life then continued in Jerusalem and extended into the villages and towns (2 Kings 23:4–14; Jer. 11).

The author of 1 and 2 Kings was so enamored with Josiah's religious reformation that he left out Josiah's political accomplishments. He told us only the sad story of his death at Megiddo (2 Kings 23: 28–30). Events leading to Josiah's death developed in an international context. Asshurbanapal's two sons struggled for their father's throne. This domestic fight further weakened Assyria's control over its farther provinces. Sin-sharishkun (629–612 B.C.) came off victor, but by that time the Medes under Cyaxares (625–585 B.C.) were ready to attack Assyria's eastern border. Nabopolassar (626–605 B.C.) declared himself king in Babylon after defeating an army sent to restore Babylon to vassalage. Psammetichus in Egypt sent troops to help Assyria against the Babylonian army which by 616 B.C. had taken territory far up the Euphrates River. The Medes and the Babylonians allied themselves in the common cause of destroying Assyria, and this they succeeded in doing. Nineveh was destroyed in 612 B.C. The remnants of government and army fled west to Haran. That city capitulated in 610 B.C., and although Asshur-ubalit II (612–609 B.C.) made a try at recapturing Haran in 609 B.C., the Assyrian Empire was finished.

Judah Between Babylon and Egypt

Psammethichus wanted a buffer region between Egypt and the growing power of Babylon, so he moved his troops into Canaan and western Syria. While the Medes and Babylonians consolidated their newly won territories in the east, Psammetichus dominated the west. Judah's nationalists had not foreseen this squeeze of forces when they had proclaimed freedom in 621 B.C. Josiah had annexed Assyrian provinces to his state, forcing his rule on the region that had once been Israel. Josiah met death at Megiddo, either trying to defend his new territories, or trying to negotiate with Neco II (609–593 B.C.) of Egypt for some distribution of territory and influence in Canaan. Neither the Bible nor other ancient records give clear reasons for Josiah's conflict with Neco at Megiddo (2 Kings 23:28–30). Jehoahaz took his father's place in Jerusalem, but Neco fixed his rule over Judah, and demanded Jehoahaz's appearance at Hamath (2 Kings 23:31–37). Jehoahaz was exiled to Egypt, and Jehoiakim seated as vassal king over Judah. Neco imposed a heavy tax on Judah, and Jehoiakim (609–598 B.C.) was permitted precious little freedom in the government of his kingdom.

Once Nabopolassar had made good his conquest of the Tigris-Euphrates valley, he turned his energies toward the west. Egyptian troops under Neco were routed at Carchemish in 605 B.C., and pursued to Hamath on the Orontes River where they were given another thrashing by Babylon's aroused army. Nabopolassar's death in the fall of 605 B.C. slowed the advance southward, but once Nebuchadnezzar (605–562 B.C.) had matters in hand at home, the conquest of the west continued rapidly. With Egypt driven out of Syria and Canaan, Jehoiakim switched allegiance to Nebuchadnezzar. Jehoiakim was edgy under Babylonian control, however, and when Nebuchadnezzar had to retire from the west to reorganize his army after Neco mauled his troops on the Egyptian border, Jehoiakim rebelled. Nebuchadnezzar could not attend to that little matter immediately, so he paid mercenary troops from Syria, Moab, and Ammon to harass Jehoiakim (2 Kings 24:2) until he could return to punish Judah with a sizable army. In 598 B.C. he descended on Jerusalem. Jehoiakim was probably assassinated by Judeans who hoped to escape violent retaliation if they cooperated with Babylon. Jehoiachin, at eighteen years, faced a man's task in the defense of Jerusalem. Within three months the city had capitualted. The royal family, leading citizens, and Temple and palace treasure were carried away to Babylon. Zedekiah ruled in place of Jehoiachin, but he was not accepted as king by Judeans themselves. In fact, Jehoiachin was still recognized as king even while a hostage in Nebuchadnezzar's court. He probably collected income from his land under cultivation in Judah.

Judah Destroyed by Babylon   Zedekiah ruled in Jerusalem from 597 to 587 B.C. As vassal of Nebuchadnezzar and unlawful king, since Jehoiachin was still alive in Babylon, he was despised by Judeans. Unfortunately he listened to the counsel of opportunists in Jerusalem. His advisors were excited by news from Babylon that a rebellion amongst dissident elements of the army had weakened Nebuchadnezzar's control. Representatives from Edom, Moab, Ammon, Tyre, and Sidon met in Jerusalem to consider what steps they could take to foster the revolt (Jer. 27:3). Even though this plot never materialized, rebellious seeds were planted. They sprang to full fruit in 589. Urged on by Egypt, both Judah and Tyre withheld tribute money and declared open hostility. This time Nebuchadnezzar spared nothing. He attacked Jerusalem in 588, and despite the heroic resistance of its army and citizens, the city fell before siege weapons, battering rams, and a blockade of supplies in the summer of 587. Walls were bat-

THE KINGDOMS OF ISRAEL AND JUDAH

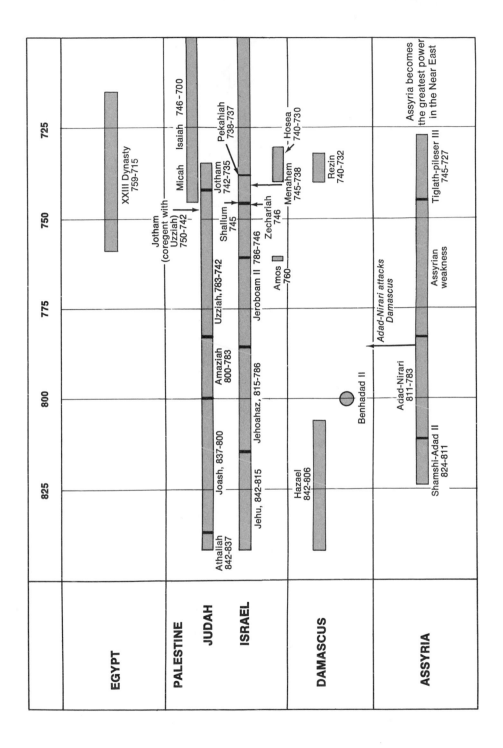

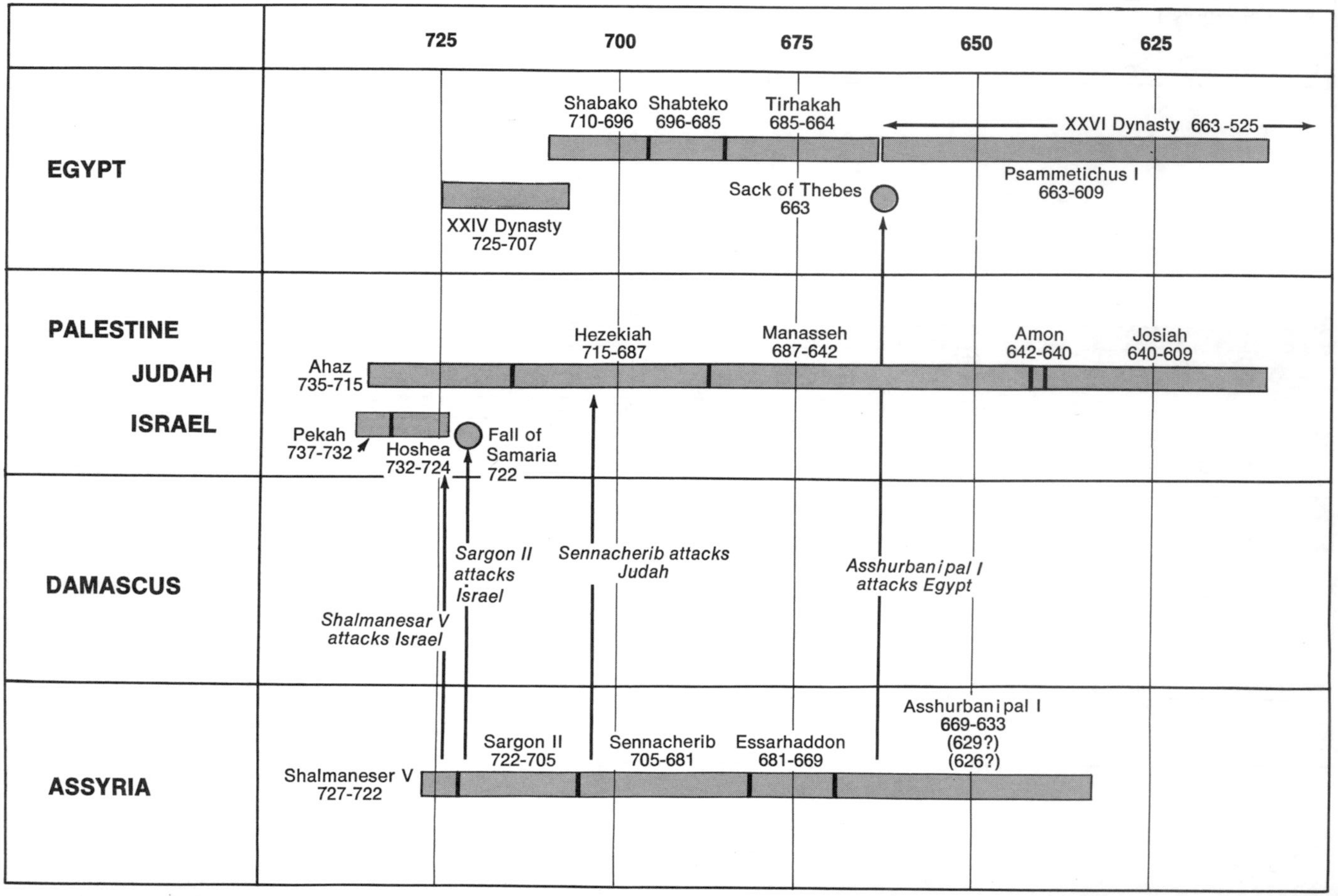

Timeline chart (rotated). Time axis (top): 725 · 700 · 675 · 650 · 625

EGYPT

Shabako 710-696 Shabteko 696-685
XXIV Dynasty 725-707
Tirhakah 685-664
Sack of Thebes 663
Psammetichus I 663-609
XXVI Dynasty 663-525

PALESTINE

JUDAH

Ahaz 735-715
Hezekiah 715-687
Manasseh 687-642
Amon 642-640
Josiah 640-609

ISRAEL

Pekah 737-732
Hoshea 732-724
Fall of Samaria 722

DAMASCUS

Shalmanesar V attacks Israel
Sargon II attacks Israel
Sennacherib attacks Judah
Asshurbanipal I attacks Egypt

ASSYRIA

Shalmaneser V 727-722
Sargon II 722-705
Sennacherib 705-681
Essarhaddon 681-669
Asshurbanipal I 669-633 (629?) (626?)

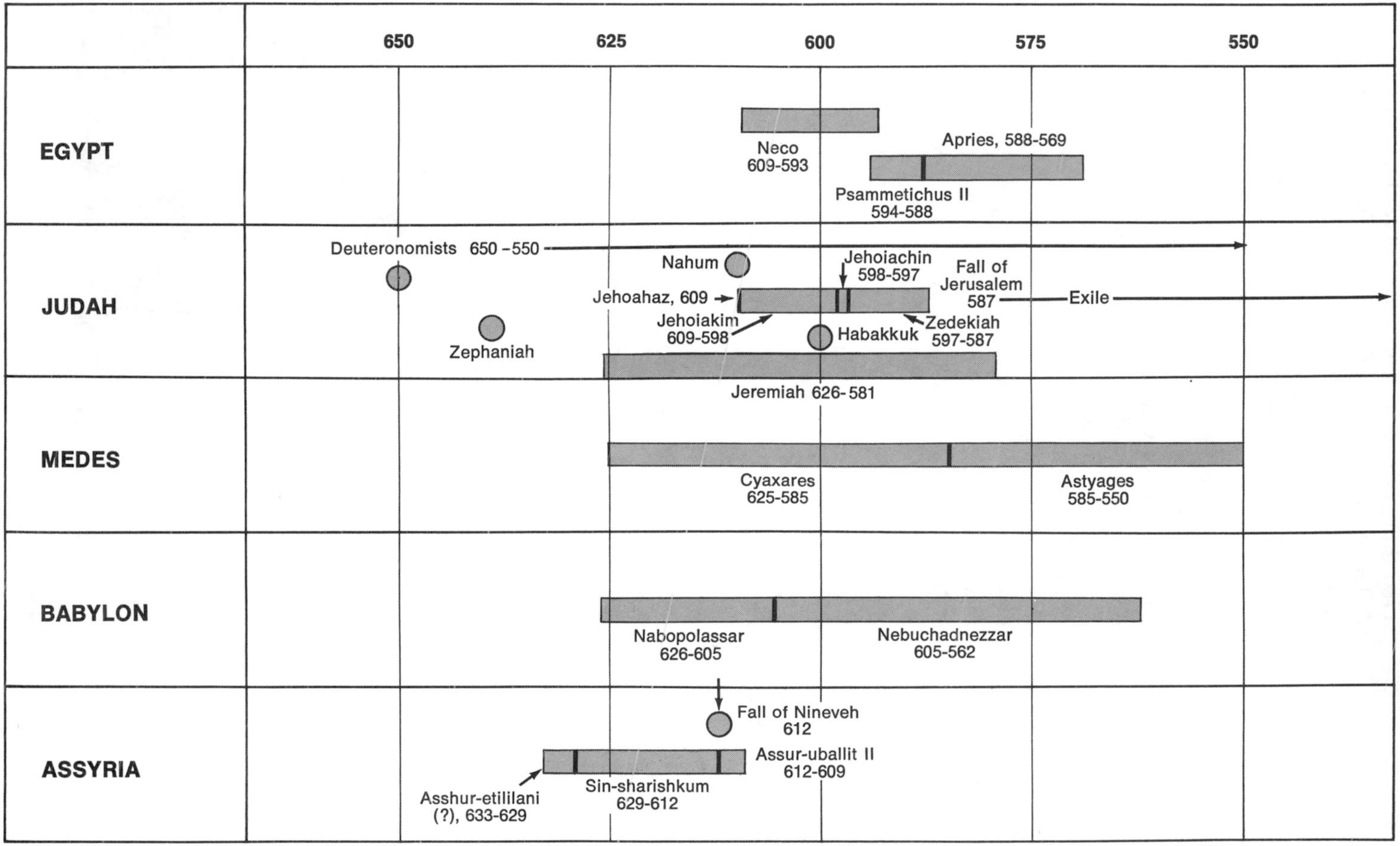

650
625
600
575
550
EGYPT
Neco 609-593
Apries, 588-569
Psammetichus II 594-588
JUDAH
Deuteronomists 650 –550
Nahum
Jehoiachin 598-597
Fall of Jerusalem 587
Exile
Jehoahaz, 609
Jehoiakim 609-598
Zedekiah 597-587
Habakkuk
Zephaniah
Jeremiah 626-581
MEDES
Cyaxares 625-585
Astyages 585-550
BABYLON
Nabopolassar 626-605
Nebuchadnezzar 605-562
ASSYRIA
Fall of Nineveh 612
Assur-uballit II 612-609
Asshur-etililani (?), 633-629
Sin-sharishkum 629-612

tered down, the city was fired, and leading citizens made captives. Zedekiah was taken before Nebuchadnezzar to stand trial. There he saw his sons executed, his own eyes were put out, and he was hauled away in chains to Babylon (2 Kings 25:1–7). Judah as a political unit was finished.

Cultural Characteristics of the Period

A study of the people of the Old Testament leaves one disappointed if he is looking for aesthetic accomplishments comparable to Egypt, Mesopotamia or Greece. Israel produced no mammoth statues and wall carvings, as did the Egyptians and Assyrians. Nothing comparable to Greek achievements in free-standing sculpture and architecture has been found in excavations or on hilltops in Palestine. In the areas principally of literature and religion, however, ancient Israel triumphed. Although little of Israel's artistic creativity has survived, the externals of Israelite culture, passed over so lightly in the Old Testament or known only through archaeological research, assist in appreciating the people of the Bible.

Ceramics

Most excavations in Palestine have demonstrated that a degeneration in ceramic craftsmanship accompanied the Hebrew occupation

Potter in Hebron.

These specimens of pottery typify the potter's ability to create utilitarian articles in aesthetic forms. *Top:* Late Bronze Age juglet, pixis, and bilbil. *Center:* Iron Age II lamp and pitcher. *Bottom:* Iron Age I decanter.

of Late Bronze Age Canaan.[31] The Israelites learned well, however, and ceramic craftsmanship after the 10th century B.C. achieved distinctive qualities of form and materials. So usable were the pottery forms and so high the quality of materials that the ware continued unchanged in basic design for about three hundred years.

Native clay was mixed with water and trod upon until thoroughly malleable. In order to keep the clay from being too sticky the potter mixed in fine sand or quartz. The finer the sand or quartz the better the final product. The clay was placed on a potter's wheel, a moveable disc turned by hand or foot, and molded by the potter to the shape he desired. The potter's wheel enabled the craftsman to make his product rapidly. A mass of clay was put on the wheel and formed into a cone. As the wheel turned rapidly, the potter formed his article at the top of the cone. Upon completion he "pinched" it off or cut it from the mass of clay by a string in order to ensure a flat bottom. The clay bowl or decanter was set out in the sun to harden to the consistency of leather. Common houseware and storage pots usually were fired without a finishing process, but finer pieces were covered with a slip. This was a coating of cream-thick clay with a high amount of iron in it. When fired below 970 degrees centigrade the finish would turn red, and various hues could be achieved by differing amounts of red ochre added to the slip. Another process for getting a high finish was burnishing. After the pot had dried to leather toughness, a stone, bone, or wooden tool was rubbed over the outer surface sealing the pores. After firing, the pottery gave off a shine that is aesthetically pleasing. The addition of a slip or burnishing reduced porosity of the ware so that oil could be stored efficiently.[32] Some of the most common pottery jars were beautifully designed, and they compete successfully for a place among the fine artistic creations of the ancient world. A good example of this is the common "water decanter" from the 8th and 7th centuries B.C. It was carefully made, highly burnished so that it appears to be glazed, and has pleasing artistic quality to it.

Metallurgy   Discovery of furnaces in ancient Canaan indicates that metallurgy was an advanced craft in Israel. The working of gold, silver, and copper in their native states was practiced long before smelting ore was undertaken. With the discovery of smelting, the construction of furnaces, and the mixing of metals the art of metallurgy passed

[31]See William F. Albright, *The Archaeology of Palestine* (London: Pelican Book, 1956), pp. 112–28.
[32]Today in the Near East water is often stored in large jars placed in the ground. The porous wall of the jars allows water to seep through so that the earth is damp. This keeps the water pleasantly cool at all times.

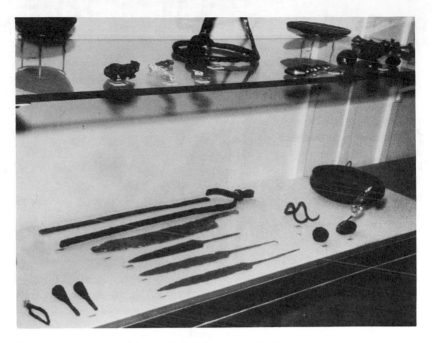

Metal weapons, tools, and ornaments in daily use in ancient Israel.

from creation of ornaments to the manufacture of tools and weapons. Few tools and weapons have survived in a sufficiently preserved condition to show the artistry that went into their making, but the assortment of artifacts speaks for the vitality of metalcraft. Arrowheads spear tips, daggers, and battle axes show fine workmanship. Household tools and ornaments included chisels, awls, bowls, double-bladed axes, adzes, needles, safety pins, tweezers, spatulas, bracelets and anklets. A listing of Israelite personal ornaments and clothing is found in Isaiah 3:18–24, and although many of the Hebrew words are obscure, this list shows that wealthy women commonly wore metal ornaments. Weapons, too, were artistically treated, as may be inferred by the tradition of Goliath's sword (1 Sam. 21:8–9). It was kept in Yahweh's sanctuary as a memorial of a significant Israelite victory. It was also wrapped in cloth, presumably to keep its beauty from being spoiled by exposure and disuse.

Skill in Writing   The art of writing in the ancient Near East was limited to a few literate men whose livelihood depended upon that skill. Writing flourished in Israel, too, and it is probably true that Israel produced great amounts of written material which have been lost. Whereas Babylonian, Assyrian, and Phoenician records, stories, business transactions, and so forth were kept on clay tablets, and Egyptian

Left: Reed pen, ink pots, and water jar used by Egyptian scribes. Israelite scribes probably had similar equipment.   *Right:* Scribes, seated at their work and holding wooden writing palettes, record their lord's words with reed pens. Note the similarity of the center scribe's ink pots to those in the photo at left.

literature, carved in stone and written on papyrus, was preserved in the dry climate of that land, Israelite literature was written on papyrus that deteriorated in the wetter climate of Palestine. Furthermore, Palestine suffered more than its share of war, pillage, and burning so that official and business records were probably destroyed when conquerors wrecked the major buildings. The Old Testament is the only significant literature that has been preserved from the culture that was Israel's. However, writing as a social necessity flourished among Israelites. David had secretaries in his government (2 Sam. 8:17, 20:25), and Solomon's far-flung business enterprises and administrative procedures demanded a larger staff than his father's (1 Kings 4:3). Other passages show that when officials counted money or went to conferences, they took secretaries with them to record the procedures (2 Kings 12:10, 18:18).

Importance of Scribes. Although most scribes found work in business and in government handling corresponsence, contracts, receipts, deeds, and official records, they were also employed in writing down the histories and legends of Israel during times of cultural crisis. Since these forms of literature were passed from generation to generation orally, there was commonly no necessity to write them. But when crucial times threatened to change conditions so radically that the ancient stories might be lost forever, scribes reduced the spoken word to written form. Scribes also engraved seals by which businessmen and government officials affixed their "signatures" to documents. Scribes dealt with weights and measures, marking them so that weighing gold and silver and other media of exchange was standardized. In a sense, the guild of scribes constituted a "bureau of standards" whose integrity and accuracy determined business efficiency.

Scribes carried reed pens and ink with a supply of papyrus or parchment in a case. But broken pieces of pottery and even wood were used as writing materials. The scribe often dressed in linen, which indicated that his occupation provided him the means of buying the better garments (Ezek. 9:2). The word translated "book" in the Old Testament means a scroll of papyrus or parchment formed by pasting or sewing pieces together. On these scrolls the text was inscribed in columns. If the scroll was a business document or diplomatic correspondence, it was rolled up, sealed with wax, and the seal of the author was impressed upon the soft wax before it hardened. The authenticity of the scroll was attested by the seal. A messenger was dispatched with the scroll, and in some cases the messenger was informed of the details recorded on the scroll so that he could report orally the contents of the correspondence (2 Kings 20:12–14). If the scroll was a state document or stories of national heroes, it was deposited in the sacred precincts of a shrine where the best protection was afforded.[33]

Art Objects and Ornamentation

Creation of art objects of a purely ornamental and aesthetic nature did not flourish in Israel. Ceramic work, although skillfully developed, did not produce artistic forms other than those used in daily life. Metalworking, too, was carefully executed, but for the sake of utility rather than aesthetic pleasure. Since Israelites had a strong revulsion to depicting their God in material form one of the main impulses for creative work was denied them. The chief memorial to the Israelites' artistic temperament was the Bible.

Architecture

Little architecture above foundations has survived from ancient Israel, and it is impossible to determine how much artistic capacity flowed into that medium of expression. The only building that received much attention in Old Testament writings was the Temple in Jerusalem. The description of it in 1 Kings 6–7 provides sufficient dimensions so that a floor plan can be drawn, but nothing stands today as a precise check against imaginistic reconstructions. Ar-

[33] See 2 Kings 22:3–10; Edward Nielsen, *Oral Tradition* (London: S C M Press, 1954), ch. II.

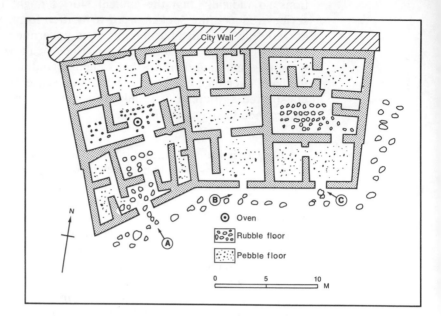

Ground plans of three houses built against the north wall of the city of Megiddo. Courtyards are in the center with rooms on two sides. There is a single entrance to each house from the street. The houses are separated by common walls. (Adapted from Gordon Loud, *Megiddo II, Seasons of 1935–1939*, Chicago: University of Chicago Press, 1948).

chaeologists have uncovered at Megiddo ruins of buildings which served as administrative headquarters during Solomon's reign (1 Kings 9:15–19). Humbler buildings received slight attention from the biblical writers, and archaeologists have been able to furnish only limited information. There was an ordinance in Israel that required newly constructed homes to have a parapet on the roof to prevent people from falling off (Deut. 22:8). Some buildings had a "cool roof chamber" (Judg. 3:20). Windows were latticed (Judg. 5:28), and those on the second floor were large enough so that Jezebel could be thrown out of one at the command of Jehu (2 Kings 9:30–33). Mud-brick walls were daubed with whitewash, and unless carefully repaired could be washed away by a hailstorm (Ezek. 13:10–16). There are frequent allusions to roofs, doors, bedrooms, courtyards, walls, rafters, upper rooms, and cellars but it is difficult to visualize a house of ancient Israel. Palestinian archaeologists have reconstructed the floor plans of several types of Houses in Israel so that it is possible to get an image of what Israelite homes were like.[34]

[34] H. Keith Beebe, "Ancient Palestinian Dwellings," *The Biblical Archaeologist,* xxxi, No. 2 (May 1968), pp. 38, 49–58.

Israelite Houses. The simplest house was a single room on one side of a courtyard. In more elaborate dwellings as many as six rooms composed the building at the side of the court. Some houses had a courtyard with rooms on two sides of the court. Sometimes the buildings were on adjoining sides, at other times they were on opposite sides. There were also homes with rooms on three sides of a courtyard. This was the type common in Israel during the period of the divided monarchies. Excavators have uncovered several of these homes with courtyard and rooms on three sides built next to one another. It appears they were based on identical plans and constructed at the same time.

Most homes were constructed so that the courtyard was usually on the east side of the building. Cooking was done in ovens in the courtyard. The prevailing winds in Palestine are from the west, so that smoke would be blown over the walls rather than into the living quarters. The better homes were located on the western side of the village where they got the fresh breezes. Homes in Israel often doubled as industrial and commerical shops. A water system and large open hearth were found in the courtyard of a house at Shechem. This may have been a lime-baking plant.[35] At biblical Debir dye vats in courtyards and rooms attest dyeing industries in homes.[36] Many pottery bowls in small rooms facing a street at Hazor may indicate that food was sold from them.[37]

Other conclusions might be drawn from the limited information on architecture supplied by archaeology. For one thing, during the United Monarchy large houses at Debir, Megiddo, and Hazor stood side by side with small, poorly built houses. Houses belonging to 8th century B.C. Tirzah and Shechem show that a sharp distinction between rich and poor had grown up. A wall separating well-built houses from poorly-built houses at Tirzah may indicate a deliberate effort to accentuate economic distinctions.[38] Houses built on a uniform plan with identical methods of construction dating from 10th century B.C. Israel found at Tirzah, Tell Qasile, and Megiddo may mean that a strong, centralized authority under Omri and Ahab was responsible for building those homes. On the other hand, such facts may imply that favorable economic conditions during the 9th century B.C. enabled householders to have a

[35] G. Ernest Wright, *Shechem: Biography of a Biblical City* (New York: McGraw-Hill Book Co., 1965), pp. 159–62.
[36] William F. Albright, "Tell Beit Mirsim" in Vol. III, *The Iron Age,* Annual of the American Schools of Oriental Research, New Haven, Conn., 1943, p. 55.
[37] Yigael Yadin, *Hazor II* (Jerusalem: Hebrew University, 1960), p. 17.
[38] See de Vaux, "The Excavations at Tell el Far'ah," pp. 133 ff.

contractor build their homes rather than each owner building his house with his own hands.

The ordinary house was limited by the length and strength of roofing timbers available, so that rooms were small. Since probably the home owner built his own house, he was limited by his own technical ability, and by the quality of stone and mud-brick available to him. The technique of vaulting, long used in Mesopotamia and Egypt, whereby a large gap could be spanned by using small units dependent upon resistance to compression, was not used in Israel before the Persian period.[39] Except for the Temple and palace of Solomon at Jerusalem, his headquarters at Megiddo, the royal quarters at Samaria, and a few buildings at Hazor, most of Israel's architecture was modest in proportion and built of uncut stone foundations with mud-brick superstructures. Domestic architecture met the basic needs of shelter and a center for family life, where the courtyard was accentuated, but it is doubtful that much artistry went into the construction of houses.[40]

Dress Citizens of ancient Israel are often pictured as wearing clothes like those of modern Arabs. Drawings and stone reliefs show us

Reconstruction of a typical home of Old Testament times. There are rooms on three sides of a court. (Redrawn from E. W. Heaton, *Everyday Life in Old Testament Times,* New York: Charles Scribner's Sons, 1956).

[39] See "Architecture," *IDB,* A–D, p. 120.
[40] See Beebe, "Ancient Palestinian Dwellings," pp. 38–58.

however, an entirely different dress. Men wore a short skirt extending midway between hip and knee wrapped around the waist. A waistband held the skirt in place and served also as a deposit for valuables, for a dagger, or for instruments used by a worker. These waistbands were decorated, and were probably the supreme work of the weaver's art. Joab was willing to pay ten pieces of silver and a girdle to the man who killed Absalom (2 Sam. 18:11). The waistcloth was made of linen for the wealthy and of leather for the poor. A cloak was worn over one's shoulders. It was made of linen or wool, although Elijah wore one made of camel or goat hair (2 Kings 1:8). The cloak was decorated with fringes or tassels, which were probably colored. The art of dyeing was highly developed in Israel, and purple dye was imported from Phoenicia. Tiglath-pileser III reported that he received "linen garments with multicolored trimmings, blue-dyed wool, purple-dyed wool" as tribute during one of his campaigns in Israel.[41] Headgear was a skullcap or cloth wound about the head. The wealthy wore richly-ornamented turbans. In the Lachish relief depicting Sennacherib's defeat of that city, the elders are shown wearing ankle-length robes. Sleeves cover the upper arms. Other drawings of this type of garment show that it was elaborately decorated. Footwear was sandals on special occasions, but usually the Israelite went barefoot. Women dressed in garments similar to those of men, but with longer skirts and fuller upper garments.

Hair Styles Men wore their hair and chin beards long, but shaved the upper lip. Women's hair arrangements were quite elaborate. Drawings and clay representations of goddesses show hair falling below the shoulders, neatly combed. One fashion was to comb the hair from the middle of the lady's head so that it framed her face. Sometimes the ends were curled up. Other coiffures were tightly braided hair falling over the breasts, and trimmed hair with bangs on the forehead and tightly curled style around the lady's crown. The quantity of cosmetic bowls found in excavations show that Israelite women delighted in the use of face paint. Perhaps Jezebel intended to divert Jehu from his goal of assassinating her by her attractive eye shadow and fancy hair-do (2 Kings 9:30).

Between 1000 and 600 B.C. Israel developed artistic proficiency in ceramics and metal working, but the remnants of architecture indicate modest achievements in that line. Israel did not reach superior levels of artistic development as did her neighbors in Egypt and Mesopotamia. The prohibition against image making, the con-

---

[41] See Pritchard, *ANET*, p. 283.

Drawings made from ivory carvings.   *Left:* This carving of a nude woman shows how carefully braided some Canaanites wore their long hair.   *Right:* The long robe worn by this woman possibly typifies the linen garments Israelites gave in tribute to Tiglath-pileser III.

stant warfare that disturbed the people, and the physical energy necessary to force a living from Canaan's stubborn soil, combined to limit artistic achievement in Israel.

Religious Practices

Israel and Judah were politically independent after the revolt in 922 B.C., but the religious situation did not conform to political boundaries. Yahwists in Israel considered the Temple in Jerusalem as Yahweh's special abode, and made pilgrimages to worship there.

Jeroboam's Religious Competition with Jerusalem

Such loyalty to Yahweh among Jeroboam's subjects was politically dangerous. Therefore he commissioned centers for the official cult at two ancient holy places: Bethel and Dan. He commissioned a national festival to be celebrated at the cult centers in competition with the one in Jerusalem (1 Kings 12:26–33). It seems unlikely that he completely blocked pilgrimages to shrines outside Israel, because Amos mentions worshippers going to Beersheba in Judah as well as to Bethel (Amos 5:5). The chief symbol at the Israelite shrines was a golden calf. Some historians have interpreted this golden calf as Jeroboam's return to a cult practiced in Israel before Yahwism became the national religion under David. This is, in

Ivory carving of a woman's head framed in a window illustrates the elaborate coiffures of women of antiquity.

fact, the interpretation of the author of 1 and 2 Kings as well as Hosea, who observed that "men kiss calves" (Hos. 13:2). Others believe that the golden calf was a pedestal upon which the invisible Yahweh stood. This interpretation makes Jeroboam into a good Yahwist.[42]

Whether Jeroboam supported Yahwism or turned these shrines into syncretistic cult centers, he tried to compete with the Jerusalem Temple. There the great seraphim (Isa. 6:1–8) and the sacred serpent (2 Kings 18:4) attracted pilgrims. Israel's secession did not manifestly change the religious ceremonial in the Temple, but its rich ornamentation was reduced when Shishak's tribute was paid him from interior decorations (1 Kings 14:25–28). The Temple was a focal point for political as well as cultic activity. There a revolt against Queen Athaliah was initiated and completed (2 Kings 11). During Ahaz's reign (735–715 B.C.) Assyria forced Judah to stage Assyrian rites in Jerusalem. In the ancient Near East political vassalage always included recognition of the more powerful state's

[42] See William Foxwell Albright, *Archaeology and the Religion of Israel* (Baltimore: The Johns Hopkins Press, 1942), pp. 155–6.

gods. When Ahaz appeared before Tiglath-pileser in Damascus to receive his orders as a vassal king, he visited a temple that had an ornate altar. Ahaz ordered a duplicate of it built for the Jerusalem Temple (2 Kings 16:10–16). Before that altar Ahaz celebrated rites that demonstrated obedience before both Assyrian king and gods. Under Josiah the Temple became the principal symbol of independence as Judah struggled to cast off Assyrian domination in the 7th century B.C.

Popular beliefs about the nature of Yahweh changed radically after David's direct influence diminished in Israel and Judah. Under David Yahweh had been a God of war who led Israel's armies successfully. He was the God of hosts.[43] He was the God who saved the nation. In the Mosaic age Yahweh had been the God of a sacred mountain, but in Canaan He had to serve as God of the land. Thus, He was in competition with the Baalim of Canaan, and in actual danger of being lost among the many Canaanite deities. Yahweh survived the syncretistic process, however, and under Elijah's prophetic movement Yahweh defeated the Phoenician god Melkart's bid, supported by Queen Jezebel, to become dominant lord of the

The *bamah* (high place) at Megiddo, dating from about 2300 B.C.
Prophets of Israel condemned the Canaanite high places.

[43] *Sabaoth* in Hebrew means "army" or "those who serve." See 1 Samuel 14:50 and 15:2 where the same Hebrew word is translated "army" and "hosts."

land. After Yahweh won the battle with Melkart, beliefs about His nature went through a metamorphosis. Stress on His character as God of a nation, as leader in war, and as champion of kings subsided as He became the God who sent rain and granted fertility to the herds (1 Kings 18). Yahweh became identified with the function of Canaanite gods to the extent that the 8th century B.C. prophets reacted strenuously against the movement. As these changes were taking place Yahweh remained local, with no jurisdiction over neighboring lands. Absalom, for example, could not worship Yahweh in Geshur (2 Sam. 15:8), and Elijah, when fleeing Jezebel's assassins, received an oracle from Yahweh on Mount Horeb (Sinai), His original abode (1 Kings 19:9–18). Yahweh manifested Himself in local shrines and temples which the Israelites had taken over from Canaanite religion, and usually qualities of the local god and Yahweh merged.

The Prophets

Priestly ceremonies at local shrines were important in Israel and Judah, but priestly rites were overshadowed in 1 and 2 Kings by stories of the prophets. The prophetic movement was rooted deeply in Israel but it was not unique to Israel. Prophets were common in north Syria along the Euphrates River. Balaam, hired to curse Israel, was from the upper Euphrates region (Num. 22:5, 23:7, 24:3–4). Prophecy was practiced in Phoenicia. An Egyptian papyrus tells the story of Wen-Amon, an official at the Temple of Amon at Karnak, who was sent to Byblos to buy lumber for the god's ceremonial river boat. Wen-Amon's treasure was stolen, and he was stranded in the harbor of Byblos. Each day he appealed to the Prince of Byblos to help him recover his treasure. On the last day of Wen-Amon's enforced stay at Byblos he went to the Prince of Byblos, and while there he witnessed an amazing event. "Now while he (the Prince of Byblos) was making offering to his gods, the god seized one of his youths and made him possessed. And he said to him: 'Bring up[the] god! Bring the messenger who is carrying him! Amon is the one who sent him out! He is the one who made him come!' And while the possessed [youth] was having his frenzy on this night, I had [already] found a ship headed for Egypt. . . ."[44] Both Balaam and the Phoenician youth displayed ecstasy as part of prophetic ardour.

The ecstatic quality in prophecy may be revealed in the Hebrew word itself. The word *na'bi* may have meant originally a person who made incoherent sounds, as was the case with Saul (1 Sam.

[44]James B. Pritchard, ed., *Ancient Near Eastern Texts Relating to The Old Testament* (rev. ed.; Princeton, N.J.: Princeton University Press), p. 26. Reprinted by permission of Princeton University Press.

10:5–6). With the passage of time it came to mean one who speaks out, proclaims, or challenges as Elijah did (1 Kings 18:21). On the whole, the prophets spoke forth the will of Yahweh in *a particular situation*. There is little in their work that was predictive of the distant future. The prophet was a "forth-teller" rather than a "fore-teller," that is, a spokesman for Yahweh.

There seemed to be no sharp difference between prophets and priests in the earlier years of the monarchies. Samuel, for example, served as a priest under Eli at Shiloh, and yet he was called a prophet. He both administered cultic rites and spoke Yahweh's will to Saul. Elijah offered sacrifice on Mount Carmel yet he proclaimed judgment on Ahab and Jezebel. Zedekiah ben Chenanah was a prophet and also performed a ritual dance to symbolize Ahab's victory in battle (1 Kings 22:11).

Nazirites and Rechabites Although "true" prophets opposed incorporating Canaanite religious rites into Yahwism, there were other persons who reacted radically to syncretism of Yahwism and Baalism. Nazirites and Rechabites expressed their opposition in specific behavior. Nazirites devoted themselves to Yahweh through special gifts, such as superior physical strength as in the case of Samson (Judg. 13:5, 14:5–9). In the early years of Yahwism being a Nazirite was a spontaneous vocation, but it became routinized by tradition. In the case of Samuel, his mother's vow dedicated him to the Nazirite vocation.[45] Some Nazirites abstained from wine, grew long hair, and refused to touch a corpse (Num. 6:1–8), and thus protested the absorption of Canaanite religious practices into Yahwism. The Rechabites strictly followed nomadic ways, and in that way avoided contact with Canaanite culture (see Jer. 35).

Prophets flourished in Israel during times of crisis. The testimony of Israelite traditions shows vigorous prophetic activity when existence or precious customs were threatened. Deborah, a prophetess, roused Israelite tribes to defend themselves when Canaanites threatened their independence (Judg. 4 and 5). Two prophets, Samuel and Saul, appeared when Israel was overrun by Ammonite raiders and Philistine armies. Nathan rose when David's theft of Uriah's wife menaced the stability of Israelite family life. Elijah's chief duty as prophet was to reverse the spread of Phoenician religious practices in Israel. Omri's treaty with Ittobaal, king of Tyre,

[45]See p. 11.

had been solemnized by the marriage of Ahab to Ittobaal's daughter, Jezebel. That treaty guaranteed Jezebel's right to import rites of the Phoenician god Melkart to Samaria. Jezebel was a zealous supporter of Melkart, however, and she promoted her religion in Israel while she suppressed Yahwism. Elijah arose during this political and religious crisis to preserve Yahwism from subordination to Phoenician Baalism.

Prophetic Frenzy   How prophets looked and behaved is reported in the narratives of 1 and 2 Kings. For one thing, sometimes the ecstatic condition of the prophet was induced by artificial stimulants. Music was one means of exciting a prophet to frenzy. "Harp, tambourine, flute, and lyre" stimulated Saul to ecstacy (1 Sam. 10:5, 9–13). He brought a musician into his court, according to one tradition, in order to sooth him when tormented by an evil Spirit (1 Sam. 16:14–23). It is probable that Saul by this means tried to revive the ecstatic experience that had once placed him "among the prophets" (1 Sam. 10:12). Scribes deliberately substituted the story of Saul's tormented spirit after frenzied prophecy had become unacceptable behavior in Israel. Elisha needed a minstrel to induce prophecy in him. When "the power of the Lord came upon him," he pronounced doom upon Moab (2 Kings 3:13–20).

Exposure to weather also brought on prophetic frenzy. Saul stripped himself and lay naked all day and night, a story indicating that among prophets this was normal conduct (1 Sam. 19:18–24). It is likely that prolonged periods of silence also worked on Israelite prophets to bring about ecstasy. Shamans in Siberian tribes have been observed sitting in the center of a circle of their fellows in utter silence for hours at a time. After hours of deep concentration the shaman chants lengthy extempore poems which, in terms of the literary production of the tribe, is recognized as the quality of genius.[46] Elijah traveled to Mount Horeb where he sat in silence amidst the overwhelming experiences of the sacred mountain, and then received the prophetic commission to anoint revolutionary kings over Syria and Israel (1 Kings 19:9–16). Such experiences often promoted frenzied behavior, and prophets were called "mad fellows," as the story of the young prophet who anointed the bloodthirsty Jehu demonstrates (2 Kings 9:4–13). Wine also stimulated prophets in their tasks. This practice probably was widespread, and it was condemned by Isaiah.

[46]See Nora Chadwick, *Poetry and Prophecy* (New York: Cambridge University Press, 1942), pp. 59, 60, 63, 72.

> The priest and the prophet reel with strong drink,
>   they are confused with wine,
>   they stagger with strong drink;
> they err in vision,
>   they stumble in giving judgment.
> For all tables are full of vomit,
>   no place is without filthiness (Isa. 28:7–8).

Zedekiah ben Chenanah danced himself into a prophetic state in the presence of the kings of Judah and Israel before he gave his prophetic utterances (1 Kings 22:10–12).

The Guild of Prophets   Some of Israel's prophets lived together in a guild. When Ahab planned war against the Aramaeans, he called into counsel four hundred prophets led by Zedekiah (1 Kings 22:6). A band of prophets at Bethel were called "sons of the prophets," meaning, of course, a prophetic guild rather than filial relationship (2 Kings 2:3). A similar group lived at Jericho, and that guild had fifty men in its company (2 Kings 2:5, 7). When Elisha's guild overflowed its buildings, the members enlarged their quarters by cutting logs by the Jordan River. This was the occasion for the famous incident of the floating ax head (2 Kings 6:1–7).

These prophetic guilds charged fees for their services, or received presents from patrons. In his capacity as prophet Samuel was paid for his services (1 Sam. 9:5–10). Upon inquiring after her child's health King Jeroboam's wife took "ten loaves, cakes, and a jar of honey" for payment of the prophet Ahijah (1 Kings 14:1–3). Elijah's fee for bringing continual good luck to the woman at Zarephath was a little food (1 Kings 17:13), but Elisha took a good meal and a private room from the wealthy woman at Shunem (2 Kings 4:8–10). A prophet could become rich if he accepted all the payments offered him. At least, that was the belief held by the folklorist who told stories about Elisha's cure of Naaman's leprosy and the prophet's announcement that Benhadad of Damascus would recover from his sickness. Naaman offered 750 pounds of silver, 150 pounds of gold, and ten changes of clothing, and Benhadad sent forty camel loads of Damascus' riches to Elisha (2 Kings 5:5, 8:9).

Some prophets wore identifying marks. The narrative does not report what identified Elijah, but he was recognized even by those who had not seen him (1 Kings 18:1–8). One story cited cuts on the face of an unnamed prophet as marks by which Ahab recognized him as a prophet (1 Kings 20:35–43). Elisha's baldness may have been natural, but in the light of the story about his cursing the forty-two boys, it seems more likely that a shaved head was mark of a prophet. The boys jeered at him because his bald head identified him as an odd person (2 Kings 2:23–25).

A few prophets were not attached to guilds, however, and these stood out as rare individualists. Elijah may have been part of a guild of prophets since the narratives in 1 and 2 Kings depict him as Elisha's master. He appears most often, however, as standing alone against the monarchy and the religious guilds of Baalism. Ahijah prompted Jeroboam's revolt against Solomon in a private conference, and was described as living alone at Shiloh when he announced the death of Jeroboam's child (1 Kings 11:29–30, 14: 1–5). Micaiah ben Imlah mocked the four hundred prophets who proclaimed Ahab's victory over the Aramaeans, and stood alone against the wrath of the chief prophet and Ahab (1 Kings 22:13– 28). One tale taught that a true prophet was loyal to his personal experience of the voice of God, even though other prophets attempted to dissuade him from his call (1 Kings 13).

Ecstatic vs. Ethical Prophesy

Most narratives about prophets in Israel and Judah from the 11th to the 9th centuries B.C. show that ecstasy, frenzy, and physical strength were signs of a prophet. These men were also political and religious leaders who spoke for Yahweh to the whole community. Kings especially came under prophetic judgment because the king's beliefs and practices were normative for the entire nation. Prophecy wrestled for two centuries over the stress within the movement. Should the ecstatic or the ethical predominate? The emergence of ethical prophecy in the 8th century B.C. tells the results of that great struggle. Such matters will be the subject of our study in Chapter X, but before turning to them let us see how psalms were used in the Temple cult in Jerusalem.

Psalms of the Temple Cult

Psalm 20

The book of Psalms has preserved some songs reflecting the relationship between Yahwism and the nation's political life. One group of psalms speaks about a crisis faced by a king. A prayer on his behalf as he faced adversity is found in Psalm 20. King and nation faced a crisis in war, and a solemn assembly gathered to petition Yahweh for the safety and success of the king. The crisis was probably a siege. The translation of the Revised Standard Version, with its "the day of trouble," suggests a general problem, whereas the military language indicates more specifically "a time of siege."[47] The words "plans," "victory," "banners," "chariots and horses,"

[47] Mitchell Dahood, S.J., "Psalms I, 1–50." *The Anchor Bible*, p. 127.

represent a king's military action. The priest in calling upon the "name of the God of Jacob" revealed the terror of the situation. The ancients believed that invoking the name of deity released hitherto untapped divine power. A force more formidable than horses and chariots thus joined the fray (Ps. 20:7). Besides seeking to release divine power, exceptionally generous rituals sought to *appease* the divine power (Ps. 20:3). When these things had been accomplished, the priestly chant assured the nation that victory was nigh. Invoking the name of Yahweh Elohim had brought the enemy's collapse. No one really knows what king or what crisis prompted this prayer for victory. It is possible, however, that it was a prayer on Hezekiah's behalf when beseiged Jerusalem felt the Assyrian army's full power in 701 B.C. The legend of the collapse of this siege also put the cause directly with Yahweh (2 Kings 18–19). He had sent his angel in the night to annihilate the army, according to the legend.

Psalm 21

Psalm 21 represents a king's success in a military engagement. It was a chant of praise to Yahweh at the conclusion of the siege referred to in Psalm 20. The psalmist praised Yahweh for bringing glory to the king. The victory rightfully belonged to Yahweh, however, and the priest chanted how He destroyed the enemy like fuel cast into a blazing oven (Ps. 21:9). The psalm affirmed that splendor and majesty were due the king because he trusted in Yahweh. Either the king's anniversary of coronation or birthday was celebrated within the Temple.

Psalms 110 and 144

Psalm 110 is another song that depicted a political crisis. Perhaps it was the coronation of a Judean king whose first task was the defense of the nation. The officiating priest chanted the prospects for the king's victory over Judah's enemies. It is likely that the king in turn responded with the battle cry of Psalm 144. In order to appreciate fully Psalm 110, one should read its companion, Psalm 144:1–2, 5–11. Unfortunately there is no clue to the historical situation from which Psalm 110 arose. It may have been a traditional chant when kings were crowned in Judah. Each hoped to send forth his scepter from Jerusalem and to rule in the midst of his enemies (Ps. 110:2).

Psalm 72

Psalm 72 was a prayer spoken on behalf of the king during crucial days. In this instance the crisis was domestic rather than international. An oppressor crushed the poor and the needy in Judah. The prayer spoke of redress of injustice, a plan to recover prosperity, and the recovery of national dignity. No historical facts were mentioned, but the general condition may reflect the age of Josiah. The Assyrian yoke had been cast off, and expectation of a new national destiny was high. The ceremony in which Josiah promised to rule by the constitution called "the book of the covenant" may have been the formal occasion for this prayer (2 Kings 23:1–3).

Psalm 45

Psalm 45 was chanted during the processional of a king's wedding. The poem divides easily into two parts. Verses 2–9 extolled the king for his beauty and charm, his military skill, and his defense of righteousness against the wicked. Verses 10–15 admonished the bride to turn her back upon her home and family, and to submit to her husband. The queen's wedding garments were the subject of wonder and exultation as she walked in stately procession to meet her groom in the palace. This wedding chorale is secular in its theme, and reference to God is incidental to the king's glory and the expense involved in outfitting the bride. Therefore, it was probably composed quite early in the period of the separated monarchies since such a decidedly secular song would need the authority of antiquity and allegorical interpretation to make it usable in Judaism's hymn book. Scholars have speculated that members of the wedding were Solomon and Pharaoh's daughter, or Ahab and Jezebel, or Joram and Athaliah whose marriages concluded treaties, but nothing in Psalm 45 gives a clue to the identity of the marriage partners.

Psalms 106 and 132

Psalms 106 and 132 reflect liturgies in use during the divided monarchies. Psalm 106 is, on the whole, a sorrowful recital of Israel's religious history. It recounted the traditional story of Hebrew origins in Egyptian slavery, Yahweh's victory at the Red Sea, Israel's apostasy in the years of wandering, and its failure to resist cultic temptations in Canaan. The liturgical setting suggests that this psalm was chanted in a ceremony that commemorated placing the Ark of Yahweh in the Jerusalem Temple. Psalm 132 refers specifically to that occasion (2 Sam. 6:1–19). These two psalms may have been sung as the procession formed at the traditional site of Baaljudah, where the Ark had been kept during the Philistine wars. There the sorrowful chant of Israel's failure to keep trust with Yahweh was sung. Then the procession visited the various places where the Ark had been kept (2 Sam. 6:8, 10, 17), and the last stop was at the sacred Gihon Spring where David had placed it in the tabernacle, and where Solomon had been crowned king of Israel (1 Kings 1:32–35). The mood of the procession then changed to one of joy as it wound its way up the steep hill to the Temple area. There the king, as successor to the great David, was extolled for his service in preserving Yahweh's habitation in the Temple (Ps. 132:13–18).

These two psalms disclose how unified the kingly function and the priestly function were in ancient Israel. Yahwism was the official cult of Israel, and the king was responsible for its preservation. Although his political and military responsibilities prevented personal administration of the complex Temple procedures day by day, as Yahweh's representative he served as the symbol of Israel's allegiance to Yahweh in historic ceremonies and at times of national crisis.

**Crisis and the
Prophetic
Challenge**

The writings of Amos, Hosea, Isaiah and Micah contain some of the finest poems and most elevated thoughts of the ancient world. Brilliant imagery, analogy, and similitude flowered in their hands. Religious concepts worn by time were revitalized, and new insights planted which still yield fruit.

Prophets of the 8th Century B.C.

What manner of men were these prophets? Some interpreters claim they were far removed from the frenzied contagion of earlier Canaanite and Israelite prophets.[1] Their pronouncements, they say, came from perfectly clear minds. Others argue that the 8th century B.C. prophets were similar to ecstatic types, like Balaam and Elijah, throughout the ancient Near East.[2] The evidence is ambiguous, and scholars debate both sides vigorously. Whichever position is more acceptable, both sides affirm that Israel's prophets were among the intellectual élite of their day. Their literary achievements and insights into society's ills were unmatched among their contemporaries.

When one reads Amos 5:21–24 and Isaiah 1:12–20 he finds a bitter criticism of cultic rites and an appeal for ethical integrity.

Core Readings

Amos
Hosea
Isaiah 1–12, 14:4b–32, chs. 17–20, 28–33
Micah
2 Kings 14:23 – 20:21
Psalms 75, 76, 78, 80, 81, 110

[1] "Prophet," in George A. Buttrick, ed., *The Interpreter's Dictionary of the Bible,* K–Q (New York: Abingdon Press, 1962), pp. 897–900.
[2] Alfred Haldar, *Associations of Cultic Prophets Among the Ancient Semites,* trans. H. S. Harvey (Uppsala, Sweden: Almquist and Wiksells, 1945), pp. 118 ff.

These and other passages make the prophets appear opposed to traditional cultic practices in Israel. Some scholars believe that "ethical prophecy" was opposed to the cult of Yahweh. Others, after careful studies of prophets and psalms, argue that prophetic utterances were traditional aspects of cultic ceremonies.

Written vs. Oral Works

Precise study of the "writing prophets" is possible because their ideas are available in "original" works. But here also scholarship offers different opinions. Some scholars insist that the prophets wrote down their words. Other believe that the prophets' disciples remembered their master's words, preserved them in their "schools," and supplemented their original utterances as changed conditions required. The written prophetic word was far wide of the original oral recitation. Other scholars modify those views and recognize that Isaiah, for example, asked reliable witnesses to write down his words (Isa. 8:1–4). He also had disciples who continued his teachings after him (Isa. 8:16). It is likely, therefore, that in some cases oral tradition carried the prophets' words for a long period after the prophets' deaths, and in other cases they were written down soon after the original pronouncement.

Two Contradictory Motifs

The problems of how ecstatic were the prophets, how they related to the cult of Yahweh, and how their words were transmitted, are still unresolved issues. It is accepted generally, though, that two contradictory motifs run through the prophetic books.

Apprehension of Judgment. One motif deals with the prophets' apprehension of judgment. Israel was under Yahweh's judgment because it had violated the covenant relationship. A way of life reflected in Israel's laws—such as "you shall not exact interest" (Exod. 22:25), or "you shall not utter a false report" (Exod. 23:1)—had been corrupted. Some prophets excoriated the people for disregarding the rituals so essential to wholesome community life. They condemned Israel for "whoring" with the gods and goddesses of Canaan. Yahweh enacted judgment, so the prophets believed, through calamitous events such as plagues, earthquakes, and devastations left by invading armies.

Yahweh as Savior. A second motif was the prophets' belief that Yahweh would save Israel from destruction. If the wicked changed, He would suspend natural disasters and preserve the faithful from the rampaging armies. In some prophets both motifs are equally noticeable, whereas in others the element of judgment predominates so that little room remains for the expectation of deliverance.

In the book of Amos the motif of judgment predominates. Since it is a short book, it serves as an excellent introduction to the study of the prophets of the 8th century B.C.

The Book of Amos

The book of Amos is a homogeneous literary unit. The book is divided into three sections, identifiable by their repetitious phrases. The first section (1:3 – 2:16) is identified by the phrase "For three transgressions of . . . , and for four, I will not revoke the punishment" (1:3, 6, 9, 11, 13, 2:1, 6). The second section (3:1 – 6:14) is introduced by the phrase "Hear this word," which is repeated three times (3:1, 4:1, 5:1), and continues with the words "woe to you" three times (5:18, 6:1, 6:4). The third section (7:1 – 9:10) uses the phrase "Thus the Lord God showed me" (7:1, 4, 7, 8:1, 9:1), or a slight variant of those words, to tie that section together. The closing verses probably were editorial additions (9:11–15).

Literary Analysis of the Book of Amos

One might argue that Amos looked forward to the deliverance of Israel from the bitter experience of vassalage and captivity which he anticipated. He knew that empires do not last forever, and announced that Yahweh's people would be independent and prosperous in Canaan at some future date. It is more likely that the reference to the destruction of Jerusalem (9:11–12) dates this small poem from a period after 587 B.C. The image of unlimited prosperity is typical of apocalyptic literature which flourished in Judah's post-exilic days. Probably 9:11–15 was added editorially to bring Amos into line with other prophets whose expectations of deliverance were more pronounced than his. The biographical information at 1:1–2 and 7:10–17 is, of course, editorial. A few other passages show the marks of editorial additions. The verse at 1:2 serves as an introduction to the oracles. The use of the same formula elsewhere shows that it was a standard literary expression (Joel 3:16, Jer. 25:30, Ps. 76:1–3). The oracle against Judah is editorial (2:4–5). Its charges were so general as to contrast sharply with the specific judgments leveled against Damascus, Ammon, and Israel. It was added to Amos' oracles during the Exilic period after Jerusalem had been devastated by Babylon's army.

Several psalm-like passages were additions to the Amos scroll during the Exilic period when the prophetic books were read as part of the synagogue liturgy (4:13, 5:8–9, 9:5–6). They were inserted into the scroll to define the conclusion of a section of reading much as the response "Glory be to the Father and to the Son and to the Holy Ghost as it was in the beginning, is now, and ever shall be" indicates the conclusion of a section in Christian liturgy. A short passage breaks the rhythm and thought of the poem in 3:3–8

(3:7). Whereas the poem uses analogies to declare the salient signs of authentic prophecy, the disputed tristich emphasizes the secret character of Yahweh's work. The passage at 5:13 is a gloss by a pious reader who failed to understand that Amos was neither silent nor prudent in his excoriation of Israel's covenant-breaking. Another editorial addition puts moral behavior in the general categories of evil and good in contrast to Amos' specific charges against the people of Israel (5:14–15). Its tone of gracious favor to the remnant, those who had survived military defeat, reflects the attitude of a scribe strongly influenced by Isaiah's ideas.

Amos' Skill as a Speaker

Amos was a skilled speaker. He cunningly laid a trap for his hearers when he proclaimed Yahweh's implacable judgment on Damascus, Gaza, Ammon, and Moab. He began by condemning Israel's more remote neighbors, then he moved to those closer at hand. These were Israel's bitterest enemies, and one can imagine the heads nodding in agreement. But such agreement led the Israelites to condemn themselves as Amos proclaimed judgment on Israel's breach of covenant with Yahweh. Greed had displaced justice (2:6–7). Fertility rituals were performed upon poor men's garments held as collateral for short-term loans (2:7–8). Belief in Yahweh's guidance of Israel in history was obscured in favor of convictions that Yahweh was able only to provide food and drink (2:8b–10). The prophets had spoken only to be muzzled, and Nazirites were treated contemptuously (2:11–12).

Literary Balancing. Amos' style and diction are as notable as his rhetoric. His use of the ancient and honored poetic form of balanced lines indicates his facility with Hebrew literary art. Balance is registered also in the repeated phrases which serve as introductions for new stanzas (1:3, 6, 9, 11 and 3:1, 4:1, 5:1). Refrains relate stanzas within a long poem (4:6, 8, 9, 10, 11). His use of images is vivid, so that pictures describing the prophetic compulsion are unforgettable (3:3–8), and the gruesome spectacle of dragging captives over the ground with fishhooks as a boy drags a fish from a lake is terrifying (4:2). "Cleanness of teeth" is the image of famine (4:6), and fleeing from a lion is like trying to escape Yahweh's anger (5:19). The prophet also used irony. Those who boasted that Israel could not be destroyed were assured that some parts of furniture may be left as a lion leaves a couple of bones (3:12). Amos bid the people to worship at Bethel and Gilgal with sacrifices and bread, but again he spoke with bitter irony (4:4–5). Capable of creating artistic balance, vivid imagery, and biting irony, he also sensitively composed a beautiful elegy of the simplest form (5:2). A poet inflamed by the misuse of affluence and the degradation of the poor, he used his rich vocabulary, his shrewd insight into Israel's degeneration, and his violent passion to condemn the nation's unrighteous. But he spoke also a tragic word as he, in quiet mood, wept over the fall of virgin Israel.

The Historical Situation in Amos

Biographical notations report that Amos lived during the reign of Jeroboam II of Israel (786–746 B.C.). He was a shepherd and caretaker of fig trees. He denied that he belonged to the guild of prophets, asserting that Yahweh alone drew him into the business of prophesying. His habitation was at Tekoa, one of Rehoboam's fortified sites in Judah (2 Chron. 11:6). This was probably in the vicinity of modern Tequ about ten miles south of Jerusalem. At an elevation of 2,800 feet it was a defensible position with two springs to provide sufficient water. The terrain today is rough and bleak overlooking the Dead Sea, probably suitable in Amos' day, as it is today, for little more than meager farming and extensive grazing.

There were no political difficulties between Israel and Judah during the reigns of Jeroboam II and Uzziah (783–742 B.C.), so that Amos cannot be guilty of partisanship in calling doom upon Israel and not upon Judah. The editor's note at 1:1 placing Amos' career during the reigns of Jeroboam and Uzziah shows that he thought of Amos' pronouncements as applicable to both states. Yahwists had never accepted Israel and Judah as two independent political units. Their understanding was that Israel and Judah were a single people under Yahweh. His jurisdiction extended over all the land once ruled by mighty David. Therefore, Amos felt responsible for the people of Israel under Yahweh without regard to political affiliation. Furthermore, the prophet referred to Israel as the whole people of Yahweh and not only to the northern nation (2:6–16, 3:1–2). There is no reason to believe that Amos thought that Judah was righteous. In fact, the introductory stanza indicates that the oracles were first delivered in Judah and then pronounced under similar circumstances in Israel (1:2).[3]

Historical Conditions of Amos' Time

Palestinian Prosperity. In mid-eighth century B.C. Israel and Judah were strong nations militarily and economically. Jeroboam II and Uzziah had kept the peace, allowing each to prosper domestically and to expand territorial holdings. Jeroboam II pushed Israel's border northward so far as Hamath in northwest Syria, and wrested lands from Damascus (6:13). Uzziah extended control over Edom

[3] See Norman K. Gottwald, *All the Kingdoms of the Earth* (New York: Harper & Row, 1964), p. 108.

so that he once again opened the port of Elath for Judean trade (2 Kings 14:22), and captured Philistine cities (2 Chron. 26:6). Between the two kings David's empire was nearly realized again. General prosperity among the western states of the ancient Near East continued so long as Egypt and Assyria were dormant. Egypt had not bothered Judah since 918 B.C., and Assyrian power had been stymied at the battle of Qarqar in 853 B.C. Most Israelites looked upon these conditions as indicative of Yahweh's favor. Amos pictured the noble advisors to Israel's king as saying among themselves, "Go to Calneh, Hamath, and Gath. Observe how great those states are! Then look at Judah and Israel and note that those kingdoms are no greater than our own" (6:1–2). Amos alluded to the opulence in Israel (4:1, 6:4–6), and excavations at Samaria have confirmed the wealth concentrated at the capital during Jeroboam's reign.

Amos' Oracular Accusations

Attempts to find historical substantiation for the charges made by Amos against nations clustered about Israel and Judah have not been particularly successful. His charge against Damascus that its armies had ruthlessly slaughtered Israel's citizens in Gilead is not compatible with Jeroboam's victories at Lo-debar and Karnaim east of the Jordan Valley (1:3). Although he accuses Gaza of having sold slaves to Edom, this would have been unlikely during a time when Uzziah had subjugated Edom to Judah. He indicts Ammon, that its armies had "ripped up women with child in Gilead," but this would have been unlikely during Israel's control over that region in mid-eighth century B.C. (1:13). Therefore, it is possible that Amos was using traditional prophetic pronouncements which referred to historical events that had happened fifty to seventy-five years earlier.[4] He used them as evidence to support his beliefs that violations of common decency would be punished even though the punishment came years later. The oracles against nations as they now appear in Amos 1:3 − 2:16 state only one charge. The formula "For three transgressions of Damascus, and for four, I will not revoke the punishment" (1:3, 6, 9, 13, 2:1), for example, presupposes that four transgressions were stated in the original charge. A parallel form is found at Proverbs 6:16–19.

There are six things which the Lord hates,
Seven which are an abomination to him:
> *haughty eyes, a lying tongue,*
> *and hands that shed innocent blood,*
> *a heart that devises wicked plans,*
> *feet that make haste to run to evil,*
> *a false witness who breathes out lies,*
> *and a man who sows discord among his brothers.*[5]

[4] See Gottwald, *All the Kingdoms of the Earth,* p. 104.
[5] See also Proverbs 30:15–19, 21–31.

Amos modified the oracles to fit his specific purposes: an introduction to charges against Israel. He probably left out, too, indictments against specific persons, a practice typical of Egyptian execration texts in which foreign nations were condemned along with Egyptian individuals.[6] In his oracles against Israel he charged crimes against merchants (2:6), the rich (4:1, 6:4-6), the king's councelors (6:2), the judges (6:12), and King Jeroboam (7:9, 11), as well as leveling charges against the nation as a whole.

Amos' Emphasis on Exile

The political and military rebirth of Assyria after a full generation of quiescence brought into play a terrifying technique of exploitation. Conquered populations were deported to far corners of the empire to work in mines, to serve in the army, and to man the industries required for a military nation. The word "exile" resounds in the book of Amos, and some interpreters believe that he knew firsthand about Assyrian practices. There is no way, however, to reconcile the historical notation in Amos 1:1 with the fact that Tiglath-pileser III came to his throne after the death of Jeroboam II. Furthermore, the chaos in Israel which followed Jeroboam's death is nowhere mentioned in Amos, as it is so often in Hosea. Therefore, it is correct to infer that Amos worked only during Jeroboam's lifetime. How then does the emphasis on exile come about in Amos?

The practice of taking prisoners of war to serve as slaves was common throughout the ancient Near East. Gaza, for instance, in the 9th century, had raided defenseless villages and sold the captives to Edom to work the mines of the Arabah (1:6). Tyre provided the outlet for slave trade from the interior of Syria (1:9). Egypt and Assyria punished leaders of rebellious nations by carrying them off to their respective capitals where they "reeducated" them. Amos raised the specter of an exile so severe that Israel would be destroyed completely (5:3, 5). He demonstrated no knowledge, however, of Tiglath-pileser's policy of transplanting whole populations from one end of his empire to another. His expectations of judgment by exile were predicated upon practices carried on in Phoenicia and Philistia, exaggerated by the terrifying judgment of Yahweh's righteous anger. It is clear from the historical conditions mentioned in 2 Kings 14:23 − 15:7 and from allusions in the book of Amos that the farthest thing from the minds of Israel's leaders was Assyria's rise to power, threatening Israel's existence.

[6]James B. Pritchard, ed., *Ancient Near Eastern Texts Relating to the Old Testament* (rev. ed.; Princeton, N.J.: Princeton University Press, 1955), p. 329. Hereafter referred to as *ANET*.

Amos' Concern for Justice. Amos had a passionate concern for justice (5:21–24). He condemned ceremonies that permitted ritual prostitution, especially when the ritual was performed in crude disregard of the personal feelings of unfortunate debtors (2:7–8). In Israel small loans secured by collateral of personal property were interest-free, and the poor man's cloak was not to be held overnight (Exod. 22:25–27. But the rich held the poor in contempt by violating the law, and by performing the ritual sex act on the poor man's clothing. Amos condemned such religious rites when they violated legal precedent and human dignity. He condemned also the traditional shrines at Bethel, Gilgal, and Beersheba (5:4–5), to which religious pilgrimages were made. They were no more acceptable than offering sacrifices on any altar. On the whole Amos appeared to set justice and ritual in opposition. Scholars have shown, however, that prophets were attached to cult centers and often offered their oracles from there (9:1). Amos' condemnation of official Yahwism should be understood as relative to the ethical behaviour of those who participated in the cult. Those who thought that Yahweh was gratified by ostentatious display of rich offerings, Amos condemned. For the many poor in Israel who appeared before Yahweh with simple sacrifices respectful of their obligations to their neighbor, Amos had no charge. Unfortunately, it seems that the prevailing custom among the rich was to parade their piety and simultaneously to defraud and victimize the poor (2:6–8).

The Confusion of Prosperity. The road to prosperity in Israel and Judah had left confusion and error strewn along the way. Conquest of territory, abundant trade, the containing of Egypt and Assyria within their borders, vulgar display of wealth among royalty and nobility, all gave the impression that Israel's God had shown his favor overwhelmingly. Despite past warnings of famine (4:6), drought (4:7–8), agricultural problems (4:9), war and its terrible aftermath of plague (4:10), and a severe earthquake (4:11), all signs of Yahweh's anger, the people of Israel had failed to read history correctly. Whereas the people were convinced that those disasters would never fall on Israel again, Amos counseled that prosperity was no assurance of divine favor. Prosperity had, in fact, caused confusion and error so great that the Day of Yahweh would only bring destruction.

The Day of Yahweh (5:18–20, 8:9–10) was a popular expression for the celebration of Israel's ultimate victory over enemies. It signified the final phase of restoration of the Davidic empire toward which nationalistic aspirations pointed. Prosperity, victory, and dominance may have been the thoughts behind the catch-word

"Day of the Lord." Amos reversed the meanings attached so glibly to that slogan. He proclaimed the Day as darkness, destruction, and stinging pain as when a serpent bites. In this inversion of meaning he tried to draw attention to the way in which this nationalistic cliché had obscured the issues of moral duties and ethical responsibility within the state (5:10–12, 8:4–6).

Amos looked upon the Yahwism of a former age as more authentic than the religion in his own day. He believed that Yahweh had worked in Israel's history by rescuing the people from Egypt, by giving them the Amorites' land, and by raising up prophets among them. The experiences of nomadic Israel forged Amos' ideals of moral responsibility and political leadership (2:9–12). This was made explicit in his belief that the Nazirite ideal was superior to all others. In contrast to the Nazirites were Israel's rich, whose frivolous manner of life had been foisted upon the nation by King David (6:4–7). Israel's wilderness period had been devoid of ostentatious sacrifice. The violation of that rigor had brought Israel to national disaster (5:25–27). Amos' insistence that he had no official ties with the prophetic guild, that he followed the simple shepherd life, lent authority to his proclamation that Israel had been untrue to its original life under Yahweh (7:14–15).

The False Optimism of Prosperity

Prosperity had so astigmatized Israel's vision that its citizens actually believed that history could teach it no lessons. Egypt had battered cities in Israel and in Judah in 918 B.C. Assyria had barely been turned back in 853 B.C. Wars with Damascus had drained Israel's vitality. But popular imagination fancied the two nations so strong as to be invincible. Military strength was one thing; internal vitality another. Amos related the visceral sickness of Israel to its capability of defense, declaring that military preparedness was no substitute for moral order. Justice took precedence over the latest weapons manned by crack troops, and without righteousness Israel's armies were a mirage (2:6–8, 13, 14–16). Without moral order Israel's fall would be so complete that a "corner of a couch and part of a bed" is all that would remain (3:12). Moral earnestness guaranteed Israel's life, and Amos, or perhaps one of his interpreters, asserted that a remnant of the nation would survive *if* love and justice were reestablished (5:14–15).

Moral Responsibilities of Nations Under Yahweh

Amos linked Yahweh with a universal morality. Not only was Israel under His moral judgment, but Damascus and Ammon as well were condemned because they had disregarded the *minimal requirements* of humaneness in wars against Israel. Phoenicia, Edom, and Philistia were judged not for crimes against Israel, but for breach of treaties and an inhuman slave trade. Judgment against Moab was for a particularly heinous crime. It had desecrated the body of the king of Edom by calcinating his bones for their lime content (2:1). These oracles infer that Amos understood Yahweh as controller of human affairs. The moral order applied to all nations. Israel, on the other hand, was not only under the demands of these minimal moral requirements, but it had additional responsibility. Yahweh "has known" Israel (3:1–2), so that Israel was "chosen" for the responsibility of a higher righteousness (3:1–2). Yahweh did not expect so much of Tyre and Moab, for example, but His guidance of Israel throughout its history required of that nation a higher righteousness.

Amos' understanding of moral order was expressed in a vivid image. He imagined the trial of Israel at Samaria in which Assyria and Egypt sat as juries. The record of rebellion and oppression in Israel was reviewed, and Yahweh had to hand down the sentence of guilty. If Assyria and Egypt were part of the jury, then Israel had not, in Amos' understanding, lived up to the minimal moral law (3:9–10). Punishment was due by the hands of Israel's enemies. Moral judgment and historical event were integrally related.

Amos saw Yahweh as a God whose jurisdiction extended from Ethiopia in the south, to the islands of the Mediterranean, to the lower basin of the Tigris-Euphrates Valley. The Yahwist narrator had planted two centuries before a seed of universalism in Israel's religion when he depicted Yahweh directing Abraham in his migratory movements (Gen. 12:1–3, 7–16). But he had not specified other people as dependent upon Yahweh as was Israel. In Amos for the first time particular nations were described as being involved equally with Israel in historic processes under Yahweh's guidance (9:7–8). His belief that Ethiopian migration into Egypt, the Philistine conquest of Canaan, and the Aramaean movements into western Syria resulted from the will of a single God culminates the slow growth through two centuries of this unique thought. Yahweh alone was Lord of history, ruler of nations, judge of the world, executor of punishment through agency of national powers. Israel, whose injustice and social rottenness was beyond hope of change, must feel the hand of Yahweh, God of history.

The Book of Hosea

The book of Hosea is a literary confusion, but it contains some gems of poetry. The first of its two parts is somewhat biographical (1:1 – 3:5). The second is a collection of prophetic oracles on varied problems (4:1 – 14:9). The literary confusion exists at several levels.

The biographical part is so unclear that no convincing theory of Hosea's domestic life has been accepted generally. The text at other places is so corrupt that accurate understanding at many points has eluded Old Testament scholars. The structure of the oracles does not develop ideas into a unified whole, but are diverse poems anthologized by an unskilled collector. Despite these literary defects the book of Hosea has poetic insight, artful imagery, and poignant thoughts that place its author among the most gifted of Hebrew poets. Any literary reconstruction is a guess, but some clarification may be achieved from the following suggestions.

Literary Reconstruction of the Book of Hosea

Hosea experienced a call to prophetic vocation as did Amos. The recollection of Hosea's call was not so clear as were Amos' five visions, and it was connected in an obscurely reported way with Hosea's wife Gomer (1:2–3). His marriage to Gomer and the birth of three children, each named to symbolize Israel's defection from Yahweh, testified to his prophetic mission.[7] After his prophetic vocation had been fully established, he lamented Israel's religious and moral defects. These oracles are found at 4:1 through 10:15, with some scattered through chapters 11–14. Probably 2:1–15 belongs to this collection, and could find a place in the context of 9:1–14.

Hosea's Condemnatory Oracles

Against Priestly Corruption. These condemnatory oracles were introduced by a general charge against the people of Israel (4:1–3). Hosea's style in that passage typifies his concise diction throughout. His principal theme of Israel's moral corruption and consequent death was also suggested in that opening stanza. The first oracle was against the priests and prophets (4:4 – 5:7). Priests and prophets, he charged, failed to provide knowledge of Yahweh, and made their livelihood by fostering cult prostitution (4:4–10). Proclamation of oracles under influence of wine, and sponsorship of fertility worship at rural shrines, were denounced (4:11–19). The monarchy encouraged such priestly corruption, and thus the whole nation was guilty (5:1–7).

Against War Between Judah and Israel. A second oracle denounced the attack that the combined armies of Israel's Pekah (737–732 B.C.) and Damascus' Rezin (740–732 B.C.) made against Judah (5:8 – 6:10). Likewise Hosea condemned Ahaz for annexing Israel's territory when he counterattacked during Tiglath-pileser's devastating foray into Israel's northern territory (5:10).

[7] Isaiah had three symbolically named children, too, (Isa. 7:3, 14, 8:3).

The war left the rural districts unpatrolled, and near-anarchy prevailed (6:7–10).

Against Kings and Idols. A third oracle condemned the monarchy because it permitted treason and conducted its foreign policy senselessly (7:1–8:3, 8:7–10). During the celebration of the king's birthday or his anniversary of accession to the throne, the young princes intrigued to overthrow the government (7:3–7). No sooner, it seems, had King Hoshea (732–724 B.C.) accepted vassalage to Assyria than he foolishly began courting Egypt as supporter of his designs to rebel against Tiglath-pileser III (7:11–16), 8:7–10). A fourth oracle was delivered against Israel's idols and multitudinous shrines (8:4–6, 11–14, 13:1–8).

Judgment at Harvest Time. Hosea proclaimed judgment on Israel during a harvest festival (9:1–10:15; perhaps 2:2–13 belongs to that oracle). The harvest was a particularly happy season because another year's supply of food was assured, but Hosea appeared at threshing floors and winepresses proclaiming death instead of life. No wonder the people called him foolish and mad (9:7). The prophet claimed that two sins had brought Israel to its present stage of disintegration: first, its worship of Canaanite gods; second, Israel's confidence in kings and princes instead of in Yahweh, a practice begun when Saul was crowned king at Gilgal (9:15). Instead of fertility, Hosea promised barrenness. Instead of prosperity and peace there would be exile. Israel's citizens, like the sacred calf at Bethel, would be carried away to Assyria as trophies of war (10:5–6). The imagery of plowing and reaping served Hosea well in depicting Israel's plight.

> *You have plowed iniquity,*
> *you have reaped injustice,*
> *you have eaten the fruit of lies.* (10:13)

A few oracles scattered throughout chapters 11–14 proclaimed Israel's desperate plight: the prophets had not been heeded (12:10–14), so exile was inevitable (11:5–7, 12a, 12:7–9, 13:9–16).

Possible Effect on Hosea of Gomer's Infidelity Hosea's pronouncements on the whole were doom-filled. Only in a few places did he express a different mood. In these passages he expressed the expectation of deliverance in stark contrast to the pronouncements of doom. One should notice that Yahweh's second command for Hosea, to love a woman, is attached to a long passage dealing with Yahweh's tender feeling of allurement toward His people (3:1–5, 2:14–23). It has been suggested that the force of "Go again, love a woman. . . ." (3:1) means continue to love your wife despite all that has happened.[8] Is it possible Hosea's discovery that he truly loved Gomer despite her adultery changed his understanding of Israel's relationship to Yahweh? After this revelation he pictured Yahweh teaching Israel as a gentle father teaches his child (11:1–4), and Yahweh loving Israel as a husband loves his wife (2:14–23). Israel, like Gomer, would be redeemed after it had passed through the purging experience of punishment (11:8–11, 14:1–8, 3:2–5).

A few places reveal signs of editorial additions. Except in the oracle on war at 5:8—6:10, it is clear that all other references to Judah are additions to the text (1:7a, 10–11, 4:15a, 5:5c, 6:11, 8:14b, 10:11b, 11:12b, 12:2–6). The concluding proverb at 14:9 was appended by a scribe.

Hosea's Literary Style   Hosea's literary style is characterized by short, almost staccato, lines.

> *There is no faithfulness or kindness,*
>   *and no knowledge of God in the land;*
> *there is swearing, lying, killing, stealing*
>   *and committing adultery;*
> *they break all bounds and murder follows murder.* (4:1–2)

Even where he describes Yahweh's feelings of love he uses the same short expressions (6:4), but in these he implants a tender, warm tone. Hosea passes from one idea to another with little regard for transitions of thought and mood, and few of his oracles are longer than ten or twelve doublets. The one exception to this is a long poem depicting sexual lewdness as analogous to Israel's submission to Canaanite religious practices (2:2–13). Hosea uses imagery from agriculture, and one can suppose that his hearers were primarily peasants and farmers. His intense mood overflows in his censure of Israel's religious and political harlotry. This same intensity is expressed as keenly in his image of Yahweh as as indulgent father (11:3), a farmer who cares for his stock (11:4), and a faithful and kindly husband (2:19–20).

[8] See John Mauchline, "Hosea," in George A. Buttrick, ed., *The Interpreter's Bible,* Vol. VI (New York: Abingdon Press, 1955), p. 595.

Prosperity under Jeroboam II brought false confidence to Israel's monarchy when cautious political planning would have been wise. One should read the pitiful story of Israel's monarchy in turmoil and confusion (2 Kings 15:8 – 17:18). It is doubtful that any king could have forestalled the penetration of Assyria's political agents and war machine into Israelite territory, but the evidence is unanimous that greed for personal power motivated Israel's ruling families in the last two decades of the nation's existence. Hosea's political interpretations suggest that Israel's treaties with Damascus, Egypt, and Assyria were formulated primarily to bring personal gain to the ruler rather than peace and growth to Israel.

Zechariah lived only six months after he had inherited the throne on the death of Jeroboam in 746 B.C. Shallum assassinated Zechariah and himself lasted only one month before Menahem of Tirzah murdered him. Certain Israelite cities resisted Menahem's claim to the throne, and as a result the self-proclaimed king attacked Tappuah and its dependent villages and "ripped up all the women in it who were with child" (2 Kings 15:16). Menahem was able to rule for ten years by such terrorist tactics, and in addition he imposed a fifty-shekel silver tax on landowners who were eligible for military service. With this money he bought, probably in 738 B.C., a treaty of non-invasion from Tiglath-pileser III (2 Kings 15:19–20).[9] The Assyrian king recorded that he collected from Menahem gold and linen garments in addition to silver.[10] Menahem's son tried to perpetuate the family's rule in Samaria, but the captain of his bodyguard murdered him in the palace, and proclaimed himself king (2 Kings 15:23–25). It is possible that the landowners who had been so heavily taxed by Menahem encouraged Pekah to turn against his chief.

Revolt Against Assyria. Tiglath-pileser withdrew his armies from Syria and Israel between 737 and 734 B.C., and Pekah was able to consolidate his rule in Israel during those years. Pekah took an anti-Assyrian stance, and in alliance with Rezin of Damascus he engineered an area-wide revolt against Assyria. Philistine city states and Edom joined Israel and Damascus, but Judah refused to join this western alliance. In attempting to force Judah into the alliance Pekah and Rezin joined forces to attack Jerusalem. Ahaz (735–715 B.C.), who had recently become king of Judah, retreated before attacks against his northern border until his armies were beseiged in Jerusalem. Pekah's and Rezin's strategy was designed

---

[9] It has been calculated that the 1,000 talents paid to Tiglath-pileser III equalled about 2 million dollars.
[10] Pritchard, *ANET*. p. 283.

to force the citizens of Judah to overthrow Ahaz, rather than to destroy his armies, so that a successor favorable to the coalition would replace the recalcitrant king (Isa. 7:1-6). While Pekah and Rezin were making their demands on Ahaz, he sent envoys to Tiglath-pileser with a large supply of gold and silver asking for military assistance. The king of Assyria responded quickly, sending armies in a pincher movement to cut Samaria off from both Damascus and the Philistine states. The Assyrian occupied regions in Transjordan and in Galilee, especially the plain of Esdraelon. Then he turned upon Damascus in 732 B.C., besieging the city until it surrendered. He executed Rezin and deported thousands of Aramaeans to Assyria. Although he permitted Pekah to rule in Samaria, he reduced Israel's northern and eastern territories to Assyrian provinces, obliterated the Aramaean state, and divided all of Damascus' territories into four provinces.

Hosea's Reaction against Pekah and Rezin's War

Hosea reacted to the Israelite-Syrian war against Judah with a "plague on both your houses" (5:8 — 6:10). Judah's attempt to occupy Israelite territory and Israel's unnatural alliance with Damascus were both condemned (5:9-12). Hosea cited the unstable monarchy in Samaria, which could control neither sedition nor intrigue, and its "half-baked" designs in foreign policy as reasons for destruction of the nation (7:1-13). Hosea's keen sense of political and moral responsibility strikes one repeatedly in his oracles, but none more strongly than that attached to the naming of his son Jezreel. In 842 B.C. Jehu had assassinated Jehoram, king of Israel (2 Kings 9:14-24), and Ahaziah, king of Judah (2 Kings 9:27-28), in a massive bid for kingship, supported by Elisha and the prophetic party. Jehu assured the longevity of his kingship by having Jezebel and all of Ahab's relatives who had any claim to royalty murdered. This act was barbarously carried through, and the heads of Ahab's seventy slain kin stacked at the gate of the city of Jezreel for all to see who thought that Jehu might be an easy target for retaliation (2 Kings 10:1-11). This horrible deed was remembered through the years of Jehu's dynasty, and Hosea dramatized Yahweh's judgment upon the monarchy by giving his son the dreadful name Jezreel (1:3-5). In doing so, he issued his conviction that the long reign of Jeroboam II would end disastrously and that military defeat in the plain of Jezreel would seal the doom of the nation. Vengeance in blood was inevitable since the original crime had been a sanguine bath.[11]

Oracles about Menahem also illustrate Hosea's keen political

---

[11] It is possible to ask: Did Hosea instigate Shallum's murder of Zechariah as Elisha had fomented Jehu's murder of Jehoram? In view of his vehement claim that Jeroboam's house would end in disaster, it is possible to answer yes.

insight. The repressive measures Menahem employed to maintain himself in power brought condemnation from Hosea. At 10: 3–8 an oracle declares that the rulers no longer acknowledge Yahweh as king (10:3, where king and Yahweh are in parallelism). As a result their treaties are vain documents and the administration of justice is profaned. Hosea expected that Tiglath-pileser would react to Menahem's perfidy by stripping the treasury (13:15) and by ravaging Israel's citizens as Menahem himself had done at Tappuah (13:16). When Israel's treasury was found empty, the Assyrians would march off with the golden calf in the Bethel shrine as their prize of war (10:5–6). The prophet expected obliteration of Israel's nationhood as a result of Menahem's repressive rule (10:7–8).

The Prophet's Condemnation of Religious Leaders

The monarchy, however, was not the only official party to come under Hosea's condemnation. The religious officials also raised Hosea's ire. The Yahwish prophet understood himself to be the "watchman of Ephraim" (9:8), but policy-makers in Israel no longer listened to the prophet's visions and inspirations. Hosea was derided as a fool and mad (9:7). Most prophets were intent upon personal gain, and like the priests, had turned their vocation into a religious farce for economic advantage (4:8–10). Rather than giving clear visions of Yahweh's will in terms of the covenant relationship, and interpreting those old truths through parables (12:10), they stumbled in their judgments (4:4–5). Hosea's reaction to religious officials in Israel was extremely negative, and he appeared as a second Elijah who felt that he alone stood with Yahweh (1 Kings 19:10). As Hosea pronounced judgment upon Israel and official religious leaders, he used the image of a second Egyptian captivity to make his point clear. Since Israel's exodus from Egyptian enslavement was the commanding example of Yahweh's love for Israel (11:1–3), Hosea also used a new Egyptian enslavement as an example of Yahweh's judgment on Israel for its violent rejection of the covenant (8:13, 9:3, 6, 11:5). Hosea did not mean literally that Israel would be enslaved by Egypt: Egypt did not figure in Israel's political fortunes from 918 B.C. until that country again became active in Israel's politics as an ally against Assyria (2 Kings 17:1–5). Therefore, it is unlikely that Hosea would have meant the "return to Egypt" as anything but a political experience of the *type* suffered by Israel in the past. He thought of Assyria as the instrument of that captivity. The ensuing captivity would be just punishment for the corruption of Israel's religious practices encouraged by priests and prophets.

Hosea's Religious Affirmations

Reading the book of Hosea leaves one with the conviction that Israel's situation was not hopeless. Coming on the heels of Amos, whose condemnation was unrelieved by any word of hope, Hosea gives one a feeling that Yahweh looks with deep affection on Israel. Although a few passages report Hosea expecting a full political restoration of Israel and Judah, these can safely be set aside as glosses added to the original text. Hosea's own attitude was that Yahweh loved Israel and that his love demanded purgation of the corrupted nation before the love relationship could be reestablished. The story of Hosea's relationship with Gomer is the clue to his understanding of Israel and its God.

The Story of Hosea and Gomer

That story is not clear. Various interpretations have been made of it in efforts to clarify Hosea's stand on how Yahweh and Israel were related. One interpreter claimed that the story of Gomer as an unfaithful wife and prostitute was an allegory used by Hosea to prepare his hearers for the message he delivered about Israel. Others hold that the story should be understood literally. Hosea married a temple prostitute, and in this way attracted attention to his oracles. Other scholars think that the account of the birth and naming of Hosea's children was originally part of the story of Hosea's *purchase* of a prostitute and her purification (3:1–4). That part of the story was lost, and only a fragment remains at 2:2 and 2:4–5a.[12] A view widely accepted understands "a wife of harlotry" as reference to the condition which later developed in Gomer's life (1:2). She was Hosea's legitimate wife who gave birth to Jezreel. Hosea named the child symbolically, as prophets so often did. But, the next two children were symbolically named "Not pitied" and "Not my people," because Hosea was uncertain as to their father. If this interpretation is correct, it means that Hosea discovered his wife's adultery, and drove her from his home. She subsequently turned to temple prostitution as a means of livelihood. Hosea's anguish over his action was so great, when he discovered that he still loved her, that he bought her, and isolated her until her purification was completed. The tragedy of unfaithfulness and the experience of enduring love caused him to completely reevaluate his conception of Yahweh's relationship to Israel. Thus, he came, after bitter experience, to understand that Yahweh still loved Israel despite its adulterous political and religious relationships.

The Effect on Hosea's Religion of his Domestic Life

Hosea's view of God may have been altered significantly by his domestic relationships. It is certain that he expressed two radically different views about Yahweh. The predominant view in chapters

[12] See Mauchline, "Hosea," *The Interpreter's Bible*, Vol. VI, p. 562. For a convenient summary of interpretations, see Ernst Sellin, *Introduction to the Old Testament*, completely revised and rewritten by Georg Fohrer, trans. David E. Green, (New York: Abingdon Press, 1968), pp. 419–21.

4–14 is that Yahweh will inexorably crush Israel by means of foreign invasion. In other places (11:1–4, 8–9) Yahweh is depicted as a father who teaches his child to walk, as a farmer who gently looks after his animals, and as a Being with a warm and tender heart. In 14:1–8 Yahweh is likened to the dew that settles on plants during the summer nights in Palestine giving them moisture enough to survive the hot day. He is also likened to a tree whose branches provide soothing shade in a lovely garden. It is essential to explain these two radically different attitudes. It is unusual for a man to have ideas so opposed to one another. In some cases departure from a book's major theme can be explained as additions by a scribe, and it is quite clear that such passages have a different style or break the thought of the passages in which they are located (1:7, 1:10 − 2:1, 3:5). But those in chapters 11 and 14 show the same poetic style and can be understood best in the light of Hosea's biographical information. It is entirely possible that his sad domestic life gave him a new religious perspective. If he could still love Gomer, *how much more* must Yahweh still be able to love a wayward nation!

The concept of a loving God did not devitalize, for Hosea, His righteousness. Yahweh will punish Israel for its political, religious, and moral sins, just as Gomer needed to be punished and purified for her adultery. But a new dimension in the character of God had been discovered. Whereas Israelites had come before Yahweh as slaves before their master, or as subjects before their king, Hosea's concept of Yahweh as a loving father and a forgiving husband established a new relationship between Israelites and their God. Whereas the fear of God had been one of the major motifs of Yahwism, Hosea introduced the knowledge of God as another (4:1, 2:20). This idea is associated in parallelism with steadfast love or loyalty, and Hosea made it perfectly clear that love or loyalty in covenant with Yahweh was infinitely more important than sacrifices (6:6). Israel, like Gomer, had been disloyal, and Israel's love once expressed in meticulous respect for the covenant was now "like a morning cloud, like the dew that goes early away" (6:4).

Hosea enriched the husband-wife simile by expressing his idea of Israel's knowledge of Yahweh through a word with a double meaning. When he chanted "I will betroth you to me in faithfulness; and you shall know the Lord" (2:20), he used the word *yada'*, "to know," which has also the meaning of "sexual intimacy." *Yada'* means sexual intercourse between husband and wife (Gen. 4:1) or between any man and a woman (Judg. 19:25, 21:12). The significance, therefore, of Hosea's use of *yada'* is that a nation which "knows" Yahweh is deeply aware of its intimate relationship with God. Such intimacy with the Source of loyalty, steadfast love, and righteousness should condition the nation's political and social behavior.

Hosea used the metaphor of faithful husband to declare another conviction. He looked upon the years following the Exodus as the days of Israel's deepest loyalty and purest religion. Yahweh's husbandly love will bring Israel again to that virginal condition as he whispers alluring words and entices Israel once again as in the "days of her youth" (2:15). When the nation once again knows Yahweh as her husband, Canaanite rituals will be abolished, hostile nature will return to its original friendly state, war's terrors will be abolished from the land (2:16–18), Jezreel's curse will be removed, and the land will once again produce in abundance (2:22).

Hosea believed that Israel's faithlessness breached the marriage contract with Yahweh in three ways. *First*, Israel was faithless to Yahweh in religious rituals. Worried lest rites performed for Yahweh as a tribal God did not apply to an agricultural economy, Israelites regularly practiced ritual prostitution. Men and women consecrated as prostitutes at special shrines performed so as to assure magically fertility to a farmer's fields and pregnancy to his wife (4:13–14). As Israelites offered gifts to idols, they asked from them forecasts of the future (4:11–13). These shrines, supposedly converted many generations before to the worship of Yahweh, still promoted the worship of Canaanite gods.

Second, Israel was faithless to Yahweh through her moral degeneracy. Religious prostitution had an honorable motive behind it, but Hosea recognized in it a facade for revolting orgies of physical satisfaction. Even more seriously, as men violated the code of personal decency, the fabric of society rotted away so that murder, theft, perjury, and highjacking became commonplace (4:2, 6:9).

Third, Israel was faithless to Yahweh in politics. The institution of monarchy had become a plaything used by ruthless opportunists for their own advantage. Its position had become so dishonored that every petty prince tried his hand at treason (7:1–7). Hosea also understood Israel's political alliances with nations near and far as acts of adultery (7:8–11, 8:8–10). If Israel made alliances with Egypt or Assyria, they would dominate Israel by demanding military bases on its soil, trade concessions, and a voice in domestic politics. Hosea looked upon Israel's history, and believed that he saw in the monarchy under Saul the first foreign contamination of pure devotion to Yahweh (10:9, 9:15, 13:10–11).

Hosea's Harvest Oracle

Hosea's longest oracle was delivered during the harvest season (9:1–14, 2:2–13, 9:15–10:15). The Feast of Ingathering commemorated the harvest, when grapes were brought in, wine was pressed, and a joyous mood of well-being prevailed (Deut. 16:13–15). The old Canaanite New Year festival and the Feast of Ingathering coincided, and Israelites permitted themselves the same sexual abandon that their Canaanite neighbors did. Hosea looked on these scenes with disgust, and proclaimed that what appeared to be prosperity and happiness would soon become "mourner's bread" (9:4). He saw infertility, dry breasts, and miscarriage as the result of Israelites' addiction to sexual license (9:14). Promiscuity will yield sterility and death (2:9–13). Israel also celebrated the anniversary of the king's accession to the throne at the New Year.[13] Hosea directed his oracles to that ceremony, as well as to the harvest festival, since it had degenerated into a farcical exhibition (10:3–4, 7–8, 13–15). Because Israel dishonored this ancient ceremony, Israel's monarchy was doomed to defeat greater even than the worst massacre in recent memory, when Salamanu (Shalman) of Moab indiscriminately killed women and children in his attack on Beth-arbel (10:14).

Hosea stood on the brink of his nation's fall into oblivion. He beheld religious syncretism devitalizing Israel's beliefs and practices, moral degeneracy infecting the peasants, the backbone of the nation, and political ineptitude in domestic and international affairs rendering a once powerful nation helpless. It is to Hosea's lasting credit that he looked upon Yahweh as a God who could still love a people so utterly repulsive. Justice, tempered with compassion, would be administered so that after punishment Israel could be restored as Yahweh's beloved (11:8–9, 14:1–8).

The Elohist's Story

The Elohist writer was another who stood on the brink of Israel's fall into oblivion (see p. 116). This author narrated his story of Israel as crisis after crisis confronted the nation. As Assyrian imperial power began to throttle Samaria's freedom, he composed his majestic warning of Israel's doom if the nation failed to observe the traditions of its famous founders.

Abraham, Joseph, and Moses

Abraham and Isaac. The Elohist composed his narrative along lines similar to those of the Yahwist. The three parts to the story dealt in turn with Abraham, Joseph, and Moses. There was probably a pre-Abrahamic section to E's narrative, but it has been lost. Abraham's story begins at Genesis 15 which has been largely mixed

[13] See Psalms 24:7–10, 48:2, 93:1–2, 95:3 for examples of enthronement poems.

with J. There was probably a call to Abraham as in J's account (Gen. 12:1–2), but it no longer exists (Gen. 20:13). Elohim promised a glorious future to Abraham's heirs through his own son rather than through an adopted heir (Gen. 15:1–3). The birth of Isaac seemed the fulfillment of Elohim's promise, but this was jeopardized by the call to sacrifice Isaac on the mountain in Moriah. Elohim intervened there to save Isaac. In redaction the story of Isaac's betrothal was dropped, and only the Yahwist's story was used. Jacob's journey to the Syrian desert in search of a bride, however, was fully reported.[14] This narrative connects Abraham with the bedouin of the Syrian desert, where Qedem was located, rather than with the city of Haran between the Tigris and Euphrates Rivers. Jacob earned great wealth while with Laban, a desert chief, and his success was attributed to Elohim's intervention. Jacob returned to Canaan and built shrines at Bethel and Shechem. This section can be separated from J and P in the passages listed below.[15]

The Story of Joseph. The second section of the Elohist narrative told about Joseph. Elohim's hand showed itself so clearly in the adventures of this hero that Joseph's rise to power was predicted in his dreams. These dreams drew his brothers' envy, and they sold him to Midianite traders who in turn sold him to Pharaoh's household in Egypt. All these transactions were part of Elohim's plan, however. Joseph's brothers went to Egypt for food, and appeared before Joseph who recognized them. He kept Simeon as hostage and sent the others to fetch Benjamin. Jacob went to Egypt with his sons, having been instructed to do so in a vision. He blessed the Pharaoh, and died in Egypt. Joseph, too, died in Egypt and was buried after the Egyptian manner. The passages of E in this section are easily recognizable.[16]

The Narrative of Moses. The Elohist's third section deals with Moses. Pharaoh ordered the Hebrews' midwives to dispose of all male babies, but they contrived to let the boys live. Because of their humaneness Moses was found in a basket on the bank of the Nile River, and Pharaoh's daughter raised him in Egyptian court life. After killing an Egyptian, Moses fled, finding sanctuary with Jethro in Midian. While keeping his father-in-law's sheep he had a theophany at Horeb, the sacred mountain. He returned to Egypt to

---

[14]*Qedem* in Hebrew means "east" (Gen. 29:1. Qedem was a region between modern Palmyra and the Euphrates River.
[15]Genesis 15:1–21 (mixed with J); 20:1–18, 21:6, 8–32; 22:1–14, 19; 28:11–12, 17–18, 20–22; 29:1, 15–23, 25–28, 30; 30:1–3a, 6, 8, 17–20a, 21, 22b–23; 31:2, 4–45, 47, 51–55; 32:1–2, 13–21, 23; 33:18–20; 35:1–4, 6b–8, 16–20.
[16]Genesis 37:2b–11, 17–20, 22–24, 28ac–30, 36; 40:1–23; 41:1–45, 46b–57;

plead for the Israelites' freedom where he brought five plagues on Egypt by use of his magic staff, convincing the Pharaoh to permit the Israelites to leave. At the Red Sea Pharaoh's troops were drowned in the Sea, and the Israelites continued to Horeb. There Aaron's golden calf brought disaster, and they were driven from the sacred mountain. The passages below can be separated from J and P.[17] The narrative resumes again at Numbers 10:29 after the long section of P material in Exodus, Leviticus, and Numbers. The J and E narratives are so closely woven together from this point on that it is impossible to separate them.[18]

A Possible Fourth Section. A fourth section of the E narrative may have told the story of Israel's conquest of Canaan. If so, it is found in Joshua bound together with J where the Elohist's emphasis on Elohim's divine intervention in Israel's affairs predominates.

Literary Characteristics of Elohist Narrative

The Elohist narrative has well defined literary characteristics. The name for God is Elohim, and even after E told of Yahweh's revelation of His name to Moses, the author continued to use Elohim often (Exod. 3:13–15). The sacred mountain in E was named Horeb (Exod. 3:1). The inhabitants of Canaan were usually called Amorites (Gen. 15:16). The Elohist omitted stories of Abraham living at Hebron (typical of J's tales), and had him dwell at Beersheba, a shrine common to both northern and southern Israelites (Gen. 21: 14, 31, 22:19, Amos 5:5). E identified Abimelech as king of Gerar rather than king of the Philistines as J had identified him (Gen. 26:1, 20:2). The patriarchs originated among the bedouin of the Syrian desert rather than among the Aramaeans in Mesopotamia as J believed (Gen. 29:1). The important religious shrines for the E writer were Shechem and Bethel (Gen. 33:18–20, 28:11–12, 17–22, 35:1, 7–8). God revealed his will to the heroes by dreams and messengers. Ritual acts were more completely described than in J. Moses was depicted as a priest (Exod. 19:14, 24:6–8), and his rod was sign of his special relation to God (Exod. 7:15b, 20b, 17:3–6). No physical appearances of God to human beings other than Moses were permitted in E's story, and the appearance to Moses was permitted in order to set Moses above all other men. Idealization of Israel's heroes received its highest expression in the character of Moses, but other personalities came through with high respect. Abraham did

42:1–37; 45:1–28; 46:1–5; 47:7–12; 48:1–2, 8–22; 50:15–26.
[17] Exodus 1:15–22; 2:1–14; 3:1, 4b, 6, 9–15, 19–22; 4:17–18, 20b–21, 27–28; 5:1–2, 4; 7:15b, 20b; 9:22–23a, 24a, 25a, 35; 10:12–13, 14a, 15b, 20–23, 27; 11:1–3; 12:31–36, 38–39, 42a; 13:17–19; 14:19a; 15:20–21; 17:3–6, 8–13; 18:1–27; 19:2b–3a, 14–17, 19, 24–25; 20:1–23:33; 24:1–8, 12–14, 18b; 32:1–8, 15–24, 35; 33:5–11.
[18] See page 127, note 20 for the JE passages in Numbers and Deuteronomy.

not lie and did not drive Hagar from his encampment (Gen. 20:12, 21:12). Jacob did not cheat Laban; God gave him his riches (Gen. 31:4–13). The Elohist's silence on the Hebron traditions of Abraham, his emphasis on cult shrines at Shechem and Bethel, his citing of the ancestral graves of Deborah, Rachel, and Joseph as being in northern territory, indicate that the Elohist epic originated in Israel (Gen. 35:8, 16–20, Josh. 24:32). The Elohist was a superb story-teller, and the tales of Joseph in Egypt are unmatched anywhere for their artistic quality.

The Elohist's Appraisal of His Times

This writer studied the signs of his times, and concluded, with the prophet Hosea, that a deep rot lay beneath the polished exterior of Israel's prosperity. He used narrative form rather than prophetic pronouncements, demanding a reappraisal of Israel's basic beliefs and practices. Whereas Amos demanded moral integrity and Hosea loyalty and steadfastness, the Elohist demanded cultic purity of the style of Israel's heroes Abraham and Moses. Revival of pure worship and insight from special revelations were the best hopes for Israel's recovery from its social cancer and safety from powerful Assyria's hands.

The Book of Isaiah

The book of Isaiah is an anthology covering a span of about four hundred years. Scholars usually divide the book into three sections: chapters 1–39, 40–55, 56–66. This division is only a starting point, however, because each of these three sections must be analyzed into subsections. Only chapters 1–39 contain the work of Isaiah of Jerusalem.

These chapters were organized around three themes: chapters 1–12 are oracles about Judah; chapters 13–23 are oracles against foreign nations; chapters 24–39 are, on the whole, songs and narratives of salvation.

The Complexity of Chapters 1 through 12

The collection of poems and narratives in chapters 1–12 poses a complex literary problem. An outline will simplify the complexities of this literary unit.

1:1–31 Several independent oracles joined under an introductory title (1:1).

2:6 – 4:1 Authentic oracles denouncing Jerusalem's leaders and arrogant women. (Verses 2:1–5 and 4:2–6 are oracles of promise inconsistent with Isaiah's harsh denunciations. They were editorial additions.)

5:1–30, 9:8 – 10:4 A collection of poems (the insertion of 6:1 – 9:7 mutilated the symmetry of the collection).

5:1-7 The Song of the Vineyard.

5:8-24, 10:1-2 A seven-fold judgment against the inhabitants of Jerusalem.

5:24-30, 9:8-21 Judgment on Judah. The refrain
"For all this his anger is not turned away and his hand is stretched out still" (5:25, 9:12, 17, 21)
shows that these poems stood together originally.

10:5-34 Oracles against Assyria.

11:1-9 A song of salvation. (The authenticity of this song is disputed.)

6:1-13 Isaiah's call to be a prophet.

7:1-8:22 Isaiah's dealings with Ahaz during the Israel-Aramaean war against Judah.

9:2-7 Coronation hymn, probably for King Hezekiah in 715 B.C.

12:1-9 A Psalm. This psalm ended the first anthology. It is not authentic, but the phrase "God is my salvation," the meaning of the name Isaiah, and "the Holy One of Israel," a term originally used by Isaiah, caught the eye of the editor as a hymn of thanksgiving to close the collection.

The collection of oracles in chapters 13-23 are against foreign nations, except for those against Jerusalem and Shebna (ch. 22). The following oracles were delivered by Isaiah himself:

14:4b-21, 24-27 A taunt song on the death of Sargon II (705 B.C.). The introduction and conclusion of this song refer to the king of Babylon, but these were editorial additions when the poem was reused by the exilic Jewish community in Babylon. Evidence that the dirge referred originally to Assyria is found in the words "staff" and "scepter" since they were used at Isaiah 10:5 as well and in reference to the unburied body of the king (14:18-20). This was the fate of Sargon II when he died in battle in Elam, and his body was not returned to Assryia for burial.[19]

14:28-32 An oracle against Philistia, the year King Ahaz died (715 B.C.)

17:1-11 An oracle against Damascus, probably given during the Israel-Damascus war against Judah in 734 B.C.

17:12-14 An oracle against the Assyrian army. It may have been part of the war poetry found in 5:26-30. This poem may have stimulated the growth of the legend of the massacre of the Assyrian army (cf. 17:14 and 37:36).

19:1-15 An oracle against Egypt during the civil wars which racked Egypt's domestic life before Shabako, the Ethiopian, conquered Egypt and established the Twenty-fifth Dynasty (710-663 B.C.).

18:1-7 An oracle against the Ethiopian ambassadors who came to Jerusalem to promise aid to Judah in its rebellion against Assyria.

Ch. 20 A narrative about Isaiah as he warned of political alignment with Egypt.

[19] See Gottwald, *All the Kingdoms of the Earth*, p. 176.

22:1–14 An oracle against Jerusalem's excessive joy when Assyrian armies withdrew the siege. Suffering and death should have brought bitter tears rather than gluttony.

22:15–25 An oracle against a government official.

23:1–12 Possibly an authentic oracle against Tyre. It was a *mock lament* over the Phoenician cities whose dominance in political and commercial affairs of western Syria had made them proud and luxurious. This oracle was probably given as Sennacherib began his western campaign in 703 B.C.

The remainder of the material in chapters 13–23 originated either before or after Isaiah.

Chs. 15 and 16 Oracles against Moab. The editor of the book of Jeremiah also used this oracle (Jer. 48)

Ch. 13 An oracle against Babylon while the Jews were in exile.

The material in chapters 24–39 was added to the end of the Isaiah scroll from several different sources.

28:1–4 A woe against Samaria chanted by Isaiah before the city surrendered to Sargon II (722 B.C.).

28:5–32:20 Oracles and woes against Judah during its revolt against Assyria (703–701 B.C.). Isaiah wrote many of these oracles on a scroll as witness of the message he had proclaimed (30:8).

Chs. 24–27 A collection of apocalyptic songs from post-exilic Judah.

Ch. 33 A song of salvation from the Persian or Greek period.

Chs. 34–35 Songs from post-exilic Judah.

Chs. 36–39 Narratives copied from 2 Kings 18–20.

Poetry and Politics Isaiah was a master of Hebrew poetic style. The lyric quality of the song of the vineyard with its sudden descent to ridicule shows a master of Hebrew verse at work (5:1–7). His woes describe complex scenes in few words (5:8–23, 10:1–4, 28:1–4). His ability to describe tersely yet completely is found also in his war poems (5:26–30, 10:28–32). His use of imagery is unrivalled. Beautiful Samaria was as a fading flower (28:4), Yahweh like hovering birds in His protective care of Jerusalem (31:5), and Assyrian military might like a rampaging river overflowing its banks (8:7–8). Isaiah's literary imagination, his tumultuous political career, and his exalted understanding of Yahweh, mark him as the greatest of Israel's 8th century B.C. prophets.

Isaiah's name means "Yahweh is salvation," and his career was involved in repeated attempts to represent that aspect of Yahweh's character to the rulers of Jerusalem. His call to serve Yahweh as a prophet came in 742 B.C., "the year that King Uzziah died." His career extended over forty years, and during political crises in Jerusalem he played an active role in the city's affairs. A few biographical notations provide more information about Isaiah than is available for Amos and Hosea. He was a resident of Jerusalem, and his imagery is drawn from street scenes and country life near the city. He strolled through the vineyards and gardens near Jerusalem, and he knew the nobility clad in their scarlet robes (1:18). He saw the daily promenade of women as they shopped in the market place (3:16–17). He knew well the vulnerable spots in Jerusalem's defenses where he would find the king inspecting before an attack (7:3–6).

Isaiah may have been of noble birth, since he advised kings Ahaz and Hezekiah during their days of stress (7:1–25; 37:1–7, 21–35; 38:1–6), and sharply criticized high government officials with impunity (22:15–25). Isaiah's wife was designated a prophetess (8:3), not because she had visions and gave signs but because she was married to a prophet. By her he had at least two sons to whom he gave symbolic names (7:3, 8:3). It is possible that he had a third son named Immanuel (7:10–17). He had a group of disciples to whom he committed his oracles, and they preserved his work (8:16; 30:8).

The prophet's career centered on national issues and three international crises.

Isaiah originally decried the decay of moral fiber in the internal life of Judah. Between 742 and 735 B.C. he proclaimed that the nation would be devastated because of its social and religious corruption. A son named Shear-jashub, "a remnant shall return," was born to the prophetess shortly after Isaiah's call to prophesy, and the boy's symbolic name attested the authenticity of Isaiah's oracles. Imminent destruction threatened Judah because of its misuse of wealth and armies (2:6–22). Social decay had gone so far that official leaders could not arrest its progress (3:1–8). Elders and princes crushed the poor (3:14–15). Judah's leaders were incompetent (3:12). Women were haughty and shameless in their actions and dress (3:16–17).

Isaiah specified social problems in Jerusalem itself. He called down woe upon the real estate agents (5:8–10), the party-goers (5:11–

12, 22), the godless cynics (5:18–19), the relativists (5:20), the conceited (5:21), judges who take bribes (5:23), and lawmakers whose laws oppress the poor (10:1–2). Jerusalem's moral roots had withered, and there was no hope for revival of the once beautiful city (5:24). Isaiah promised a day of judgment upon Jerusalem because of these monstrous wrongs, and Yahweh's agent was to be the powerful armies of Tiglath-pileser III (5:26–30). Isaiah was especially angry because neither earthquake nor Assyria's attack on Israel had arrested the downward spiral of the people's conduct (5:25, 9:8–21). The day of Yahweh promised to be a fearful time.

The First Crisis

In the year 735 B.C. Isaiah got involved in international politics. Under King Jotham (742–735 B.C.) Judah followed an anti-Assyrian policy. Israel and Damascus spearheaded an anti-Assyrian coalition including Philistine cities and Edom. When Ahaz took the throne, he changed Judah's foreign policy to nonalignment. Pekah of Israel and Rezin of Damascus believed that a nonaligned nation at their backs would be disastrous militarily.[20] They attacked Ahaz hoping to force him into their coalition or to cause a rebellion that would elevate the anti-Assyrian son of Tabeel to the throne (7:6).

The Prophet Takes a Stand Against the Anti-Assryian Coalition

When attack on Jerusalem seemed inevitable, Ahaz inspected Jerusalem's water supply. Isaiah went to meet Ahaz hopeful of forestalling precipitous action. All Jerusalem was jumpy about the intentions of Pekah and Rezin. By the upper pool the prophet reminded Ahaz that two years before he had pronounced an oracle on Samaria and Damascus by writing his son's name, Maher-shalal-hashbaz, "The spoil speeds, the prey hastes," on a slate, witnessed by two trustworthy officials, and publicly displayed it (8:1–4). The action recounted in those verses is out of place, and it should appear before Isaiah's confrontation with Ahaz at the upper pool. Maher-shalal-hashbaz was born early in the last year of Jotham's reign when his strong anti-Assyrian policy had nearly produced an alliance with Pekah and Rezin. By this sign Isaiah declared his conviction that within two or three years, that is, following the period of pregnancy and infancy until the child first began to speak, both Damascus and Samaria would be captured by Tiglath-pileser. His counsel had been to stay out of the alliance. Now with Shear-jashub, "A Remnant (only) Shall Return," in hand he reminded Ahaz of Jotham's policy.

[20]Gottwald believes that Ahaz assumed a pro-Assyrian stance when he became king in Judah, and that his bid for Assyrian vassalage brought attacks from Israel, Damascus, Edom, and Philistia. See *All the Kingdoms of the Earth*, p. 150.

The oracles in 17:1–6 probably were registered during this same crisis since they, too, spoke of Damascus "as a heap of ruins" and Israel as the gleanings of a field at harvest (17:1, 5).

In an oracle given directly to Ahaz, Isaiah again threatened the destruction of the northern coalition, but he spoke no word against Judah (7:3–9). The next sign, however, issued a portentous threat. One must imagine a period of time between Isaiah 7:9 and 7:10 sufficient for Ahaz to organize a diplomatic mission to Assyria and for the attack of Rezin and Pekah to develop against Jerusalem. Ahaz had refused Isaiah's counsel, had sent envoys to Tiglath-pileser, and had promised vassalage to Assyria for protection from his attackers (2 Kings 16:7–8). Isaiah considered Ahaz's move exceedingly unwise, and gave the sign of Immanuel (7:10–17). He stated that a son would be born to a young woman. By the time the boy was capable of choosing what he liked to eat, that is, good meaning palatable and evil meaning bitter,[21] about a year and a half counting the time of pregnancy, Assyria's armies would fall upon attacker and attacked alike. Because Ahaz had tried God's patience as well as his people's, Yahweh would send so many Assyrian soldiers that they will appear like insects settled on all the vegetation (7:18–19). After the Assyrians were finished with Judah, it would be shaved clean (7:20). The mode of life will be reduced to nomadism, and the remnant will eat only cheese and honey (7:21). The vineyard will be thorn patches, and herds will trample over the once valuable vines (7:23–25). Ahaz's foolish foreign policy could only result in Judah's complete subjection to Assyria.

The Sign of Immanuel

The sign of Immanuel needs further explication. The author of the Gospel according to Matthew thought of the sign as a portent of the birth of Jesus (Matt. 1:23). It is quite clear, however, that Isaiah had no intention of predicting Immanuel's birth by a virgin. Had he so intended, he would have used the Hebrew word *bethulah* rather than *'almah. Bethulah* means a virgin, but *'almah* means a young woman of marriagable age, with no reference to her virginity. Matthew derived his use of the Greek word *parthenos* from the Septuagint version of the Old Testament, but the Greek translators were inaccurate in using *parthenos* for *'almah.* Since Christian writers of the 1st century A.D. saw in Jesus the fulfillment of messianic expectations in Israel it is not surprising that Matthew, too, used a collection of Old Testament passages which supported those convictions about Jesus.

If the mother of Immanuel cannot be identified with Mary of the New Testament, who was she? It is possible that the sign of Im-

---

[21] The same idea is expressed in Deuteronomy 1:39.

A view of Jerusalem from the south. Somewhere in this area Isaiah met King Ahaz when he was inspecting Jerusalem's water supply.

manuel referred to the popular Near Eastern myth that a divine mother should bear a son who would replace the evil king, and who would rule his subjects righteously. On the other hand, the young woman may have been Ahaz's wife. It is most likely that Isaiah referred to the birth of his third child. The sign of Immanuel ("God is with us") was similar to the signs of Shear-jashub and Maher-shalal-hashbaz. Naming his children thus was the prophet's dramatic way of authenticating his message.

Isaiah's Estimate of Assyria Isaiah had estimated the political and military forces in the Near East accurately. Whereas Ahaz thought of Israel and Damascus as the threat to his kingship, Isaiah saw that the real threat was Assyria. He perceived with Hosea that the internal corruption of Israel had so weakened the nation that even with the help of Damascus' chariots it could not stop the powerful Tiglath-pileser. Submission either to the warlords of Israel and Damascus or Assyria were steps toward national calamity. Isaiah claimed that Ahaz had put his trust in a false power, and that Yahweh was the only power that could maintain him upon the throne.

During this crisis Isaiah spoke another oracle, this time to the people of Jerusalem implicating them in Ahaz's decision to submit to Assyrian domination (8:5–15). Their refusal to look to Yahweh and their unreasoned fear of Rezin and Pekah had brought them to the brink of disaster. Isaiah made it quite clear that what the people called his conspiracy and his fear were entirely different things from what he had in mind. He conspired with and feared only Yahweh of hosts (8:11–15). It is possible that Isaiah's failure to influence Ahaz's foreign policy and his conviction that Judah's end was at hand caused him to leave public life. He had testified before king and people. Now he asked his disciples to write down what he had said and keep the scrolls as witness of his integrity (8:16). He and his children had been given as signs to warn Jerusalem, but the leaders preferred to consult mediums and wizards. For this there would be only "distress and darkness . . . gloom . . . and thick darkness" (8:18–22).

The Coming of the Assyrians

In 732 B.C. Damascus fell to the Assyrians after an extended siege. It was sacked, its citizens were deported, and the Aramaean state was divided into four Assyrian provinces. Israel was cut off from any effective Egyptian aid because Tiglath-pileser sent his army down the coast to destroy Gaza and to establish an outpost on Egypt's northern perimeter. Then he struck at the regions of Galilee and Transjordan effectively reducing Israel's holdings to regions adjacent to Samaria. From these captured lands Tiglath-pileser formed three Assyrian provinces, and left Hoshea, Israel's last king, bottled up in the highlands of north-central Canaan. Hoshea finally professed allegiance to Assyria's king.

The death of Tiglath-pileser III brought hope of independence to Hoshea, and he connived with Egypt to revolt against Shalmaneser V. It was probably during those fateful days that Isaiah came out of retirement to utter an oracle against Israel (28:1–4). Drunkenness and lavish living still characterized Hoshea's court despite the poverty of the economy and the threat of Assyrian annexation. Isaiah mused also on Judah's priests and prophets who had abetted Ahaz in his ridiculous blindness to the danger of Assyria's annexation of Judah (28:7–10). Yahweh will speak to his people through an alien tongue, that is, through the scourge of Assyrian armies (28:11–22).

Hoshea's revolt brought immediate retaliation, and Samaria fell to Assyrian attack in 722 B.C. after a prolonged siege. Isaiah's direful oracles had their vindication.

The Second Crisis

Assyria's control of western Syria and Palestine was not easily maintained, despite great armies and ruthless tactics. The destruc-

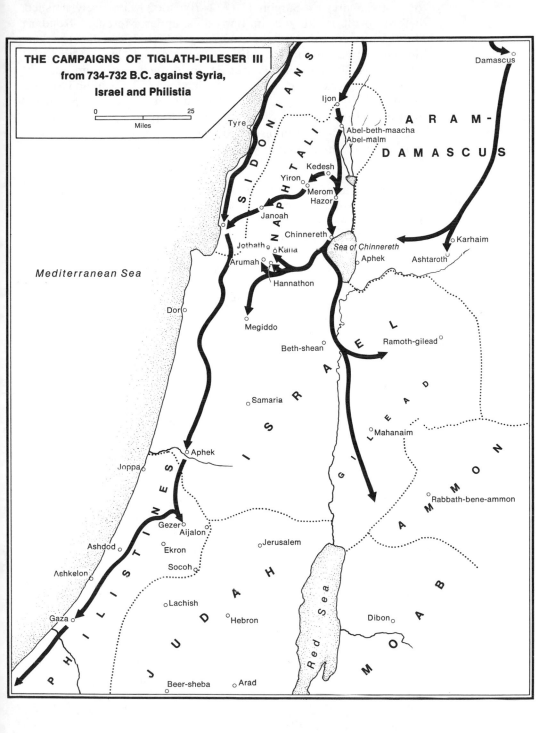

THE CAMPAIGNS OF TIGLATH-PILESER III
from 734-732 B.C. against Syria,
Israel and Philistia

0   25
Miles

Damascus

A R A M -

D A M A S C U S

Ijon

Tyre

Abel-beth-maacha
Abel-malm

Kedesh

Yiron
Merom
Hazor

Janoah

Chinnereth

Karhaim

Jothath   Kana

Sea of Chinnereth

Aphek

Ashtaroth

Arumah

Hannathon

Mediterranean Sea

Dor

Megiddo

Beth-shean

Ramoth-gilead

Samaria

Mahanaim

Aphek

Joppa

Rabbath-bene-ammon

Gezer
Aijalon

Ashdod

Ekron

Jerusalem

Socoh

Ashkelon

Lachish

Hebron

Dibon

Gaza

Beer-sheba   Arad

S I D O N I A N S

N A P H T A L I

I S R A E L

G I L E A D

A M M O N

P H I L I S T I N E S

J U D A H

M O A B

Red Sea

tion of Samaria by Sargon II (722–705 B.C.) was barely finished before revolt broke out in Babylonia under Merodach-baladan. Sargon lost control of Babylonia for a full twelve years. He conducted campaigns in Asia Minor against Midas, king of Phrygia, and against the city of Carchemish in Syria. Indo-Aryan nomads from the Caucasus poured into the kingdom of Urartu, and Sargon seized this opportunity to attack Urartu from the south. (See map, p. 189.) These military operations gave Sargon little time for the western end of his empire. Unhappy politicians and militarists chafed under the Assyrian yoke.

Insurrection in Palestine

Such conditions inspired Egypt's Sibe and Hamath's Iaubidi to foment insurrection among the small states and provinces of Palestine. A delegation of Egyptian ambassadors appeared in Ahaz's court (18:1–2). Egypt was eager to establish a buffer zone of independent states between itself and the massive Assyrian armies. In typical diplomatic language Isaiah flattered the envoys by extolling their physical appearance and their alacrity in sizing up the international scene (18:2), but he proclaimed in a cryptic message that Egypt would eventually meet defeat (18:3–7). That Isaiah was ultimately influential in Ahaz's refusal to be involved in any revolt is not certain, but the king did reject the Egyptian ambassadors' diplomatic gestures.

Isaiah Counsels Against Revolt

Another dangerous situation faced Judah in these same years. The Philistine cities verged on a revolt that could implicate Ahaz. The prophet spoke an oracle against Philistia (14:28–32). It implies that an Assyrian king, "the rod which smote you is broken," had died. This was the most favorable time for vassal nations to revolt. The superscription dates this oracle in 715 B.C., "the year that King Ahaz died," but that seems an improbable year since it does not coincide with the death of an Assyrian monarch. The more probable date is 722 B.C., the year that Shalmaneser V (727–722 B.C.) died while the siege of Samaria was on. Assyria's western armies were deployed against Samaria, and the consolidation of Sargon's leadership would take some time. These factors made revolt seem favorable. Isaiah issued a warning to Philistia that although retaliation might not be immediate,

> *and the first born of the poor will feed,*
> *and the needy lie down in safety*

it would inevitably fall,

> *For smoke comes out of the north,*
> *and there is no straggler in his ranks.*

The new king would "be a flying serpent," swift to strike and deadly in his attack.

When Ahaz died in 715 B.C., Judah entered upon a foreign policy destined to bring reprisals from the strongest nation on the face of the earth. As might be expected, Philistia did not heed Isaiah's warning, and entertained schemes for throwing off Assyria's yoke. In 714 B.C. Ashdod withheld its tribute money. Sargon's annals report that "Azuri, king of Ashdod, had schemes not to deliver tribute [any more] and sent messengers [full] of hostilities against Assyria to the kings [living] in his neighborhood."[22] Sargon deposed Azuri, put his younger brother on the throne, and withdrew expecting acquiescence. Instead, the citizens revolted, threw the youngster out, and selected a certain Iamani, who, without any royal credentials, promised freedom. The revolt was successful for about three years, but the Philistines knew that without support from their neighbors the rebellion would crumble.

Isaiah Warns King Hezekiah

Hezekiah (715–686 B.C.) succeeded Ahaz in Judah. He was a traditionalist in religion, and his Yahwism guaranteed his nationalism. He looked jealously toward Ashdod whose revolt had appeared successful, taking his cue from that city as he connived to weasel out of the commitments his father had made to Tiglath-pileser. Apparently Isaiah anticipated Hezekiah's policies, because he appeared in the streets of Jerusalem shockingly naked except for a loincloth. This dramatic action depicted Judah's future as a captive if it joined Iamani's revolt (20:2-6). It is hard to correlate Isaiah's report of Egypt's deep implication in the plot with Sargon's own annals. Sargon reported that Iamani took the lead, sending bribes to Egypt and spreading rumors in Judah, Edom, and Moab to get those nations to join him in rebellion.[23] We need not think of Isaiah going daily about Jerusalem looking like a prisoner of war. He probably did so, however, when Philistine officials appeared in Hezekiah's court and when the anti-Assyrian party in Jerusalem propagandized to support Hezekiah's nationalism.

The Oracle Against Moab. Isaiah's oracle against Moab was also given during the critical years of 713–711 B.C. (16:1-5). These

---

[22]James B. Pritchard, ed., *Ancient Near Eastern Texts Relating to the Old Testament* (rev. ed., Princeton, N.J.: Princeton University Press, 1955), p. 286. Reprinted by permission of Princeton University Press.
[23]*Ibid.*, p. 287.

words depicted envoys from Moab sending sheep to Judah's ruler in hopes that some assistance would be given to Moab's scattered fugitives (16:2–4). During the revolt of 713–711 B.C. Moab and Judah equally were beguiled by Iamani's promises although neither committed itself irrevocably to the rebellion. The remainder of the oracle against Moab derived from a traditional taunt song (16: 6–12) probably of Ammonite or Edomitic origins, which Isaiah appended to his own proclamation of doom if Moab enticed Judah into revolt (16:13). Fortunately for Moab as well as for Judah they did not overtly join Iamani, and their lands were saved from spoliation. But Ashdod was not so fortunate. Probably to the surprise of the rebels, according to Sargon's report, he mobilized his troops in the early spring and "led my army over the Tigris and Euphrates, at the peak of their flood,"[24] to deal with the treacherous Iamani. The adventurer fled long before the troops reached Ashdod, and although he expected sanctuary in Egypt, Pharaoh Piankhi bound him hand and foot and delivered him to Sargon. It is likely that Isaiah's consistent depiction of such a fate befalling Hezekiah and his little country deterred that nationalist from committing the same error. Judah dwelt in comparative peace for about ten years.

The Third Crisis

Isaiah unquestionably approved of Hezekiah's reforms which consisted of regulating religious practices in the villages and in the Temple itself. He destroyed cult centers where Yahwism and fertility goddesses were worshipped side by side. He stripped the sacred serpent, reputedly made by Moses himself, from the Temple (2 Kings 18:1–8; cf. Num. 21:5–9). These reforms were undertaken guardedly at first in order to see what reaction Assyrian political agents in Jerusalem might have. Since no reaction set in, Hezekiah continually pushed the nationalization of religion and politics until at the death of Sargon II in 705 B.C., he was ready to announce his independence. He refused tribute money to Assyria and simultaneously attacked her Philistine provinces in a bid to expand his territory and to collect revenue from the rich harvests in the Shephelah.

Isaiah's Taunt at the Death of Sargon

One might suspect Isaiah's vigorous disapproval of such overt hostility toward Assyria. On the contrary Isaiah took an approach different from the one he'd taken a decade earlier, and proclaimed that Yahweh had broken Assyria's leadership. The oppressive domination of Sargon II had finally gone further than the limits Yahweh would permit. Assyria would be punished. Isaiah chanted a song (14:4b–27) in which he pictured the reception of the dead

---

[24]James B. Pritchard, ed., *Ancient Near Eastern Texts Relating to the Old Testament* (rev. ed.; Princeton, N.J.: Princeton University Press, 1955), p. 287. Reprinted by permission of Princeton University Press.

ruler in Sheol where all the "kings of the nations" were gathered, and they gloated over the fate of the magnificent and terrible Sargon.

> *You too have become as weak as we are!*
> *you have become like us!*
> *maggots are the bed beneath you,*
> *and worms are for your covering.* (14:10–11)

Isaiah believed that Sargon's arrogance in ruling his subject people with unscrupulous cruelty and his aspiration to be elevated to the status of a god had brought his ultimate collapse. Isaiah used a Canaanite myth which told about the struggle of the Day Star (Helel ben Shohar) to overpower the sun in order to become chief of all gods, and applied it to Sargon.

> *You said in your heart,*
> *"I will ascend to heaven;*
> *above the stars of God*
> *I will set my throne on high;*
> *I will sit on the mount of assembly*
> *in the far north;*
> *I will ascend above the heights of the clouds,*
> *I will make myself like the most High."* (14:13–14)

The taunt song as it now stands refers to the king of Babylon (14:3, 4a, 22–23), but it is likely that this song was appropriated by Jewish exiles a hundred and fifty years later and applied by them to their situation. It is almost certain that the chant applied to Sargon II because of the specific reference to his burial "away from your sepulchre" (14:19–20). Sargon was killed in an expedition in Elam, and his body had not been given an honorable burial in the capital.[25]

The Prophet Still Opposes Open Revolt

Yet, we look in vain for any assertion from Isaiah that the empire will crumble. He rejoiced over the death of the monarch, while he opposed open revolt. With Sennacherib's accession to the throne there were many rebellions in the empire. Babylon recovered its independence under Merodach-baladan.[26] He sent envoys to Hezekiah, and they were shown the whole of Hezekiah's armaments

[25] See André Parrot, *Nineveh and the Old Testament* (New York: Philosophical Library, 1955), pp. 49–50.
[26] Marduk-apal-iddina in the cuneiform texts.

and treasury which he had stockpiled secretly (Isa. 39). This act constituted a tacit agreement to conspire against Sennacherib, for Hezekiah had revealed Judah's intentions. Isaiah's anger blazed against Hezekiah for having been so simple. He now expected Assyria's punitive campaign (39:5–7).

Merodach-baladan's agents had stirred up trouble throughout the west. Sidon, Ashkelon, and Ekron joined the empire-wide revolt, although Ashdod and Gaza remained faithful. Apparently Egypt was in the revolt, too, because Isaiah pronounced woe upon Judah for seeking refuge in Egypt's promises of aid (30:1–7; 31:1–3). In these oracles Egypt was described as militarily powerful, but Hezekiah had put too much confidence in that nation's ability to send aid. Isaiah said,

> *The Egyptians are men, and not God;*
> *and their horses are flesh, and not spirit.* (31:3)

Hezekiah's caravan of asses and camels is pictured struggling toward Egypt through the Negeb loaded down with the silver, gold, spices, and oil that Hezekiah had stored up in anticipation of buying Egypt's military aid (30:6–7). But Isaiah claimed "Egypt's help is worthless and empty" (30:7), and he derided Egypt's claim of being as violent as the sea monster Rahab. Isaiah made his point before Judah's military strategists in a powerful statement about Yahweh's utter contempt for Judah's boasts of victory over Assyria. He asked, "Hasn't history proven to you that Assyrian warfare is so terrible that our beautiful Jerusalem will reap only devastation?"

> *Oh, Assyria, the rod of my anger,*
> > *the staff of my fury!*
> *Against a godless nation I send him,*
> > *and against the people of my wrath I command him,*
> *to take spoil and seize plunder,*
> > *and to tread them down like the mice of the streets.*
> *But he does not so intend,*
> > *and his mind does not so think;*
> *but it is in his mind to destroy,*
> > *and to cut off nations not a few;*
> *for he says:*
> > *"Are not my commanders all kings?*
> > *Is not Calno like Carchemish?*
> > *Is not Hamath like Arpad?*
> > *Is not Samaria like Damascus?*

> *As my hand has reached to the kingdom of the idols*
> > *whose graven images were greater than those*
> > *of Jerusalem and Samaria,*
> *shall I not do to Jerusalem and her idols*
> > *as I have done to Samaria and her images?"* (10:5–11)

Isaiah was convinced that Yahweh used Assyrian force to punish offenders against His moral and cultic requirements. The tragedy was that Assyrian kings believed themselves independent of any responsibility to divine requirements (10:7). Even Judah, under the righteous Hezekiah, seemed oblivious to the moral and religious causes behind the coming devastation (10:10–11). Assyria will do the bidding of Yahweh in punishing Judah, but then its loud boasting will have to be swallowed (10:12–15). Isaiah was contemptuous toward Sennacherib's claims that "the awe-inspiring splendor of the *weapon* of Asshur, my lord" were behind Assyria's successful military campaigns. He claimed that Yahweh was the agent truly behind international events. Neither Judah nor Assyria would triumph in the long run because both had failed to accept guilt for the tragedies brought by war. In the jungle of international intrigue and violence every nation, small and great, had its share of guilt, and all would eventually come under Yahweh's judgment.[27]

Sennacherib Strikes Sennacherib's campaign against Merodach-baladan was conducted with surprising rapidity. That Chaldean prince had expected the outbreak of hostilities in Syria and Palestine to draw Sennacherib's best military units to quell that uprising. After the Assyrian king had committed himself to stamping out the brush fire in the west, Merodach-baladan planned attack in force from the east. (See map of Assyrian Empire, p. 189.) Sennacherib's strategy was to strike hard against rebels one at a time. He hit Merodach-baladan with full force, and drove the rebel into hiding in the swamps of the lower Tigris-Euphrates valley. When Sennacherib's cavalry appeared in the west in 701 B.C., most of the nations which had quivered between revolt and loyalty rushed to pay tribute. Byblos, Arvad, Ashdod, Moab, Edom, Ammon, each sent delegates to kiss the feet of the king while sumptuous gifts were deposited in his mobile pavilion.

But Ashkelon, Ekron, and Judah had gone too far to retreat. Their appeals to Egypt for military backing were fully known to Sennacherib's agents, and he would make them reckon with his wrath.

[27] See Gottwald, *All the Kingdoms of the Earth,* pp. 175–83.

Egypt sent a token army to support the Philistine cities, and that was promptly defeated at Eltekeh. Then, rather leisurely Sennacherib reduced the walled cities one by one deporting or executing the leaders. When he turned his attention to Judah, he began the systematic destruction of its cities as he worked his way toward Jerusalem.

Isaiah's Lamentations

Isaiah chanted oracles during the Assyrian's devastation of Canaan's cities. He wailed over the destruction of Phoenicia which had had close commercial and political ties with Judah for three hundred years (23:1–12). Phoenicia's destruction as a result of her excessive pride in her colonies (23:2, 7) and in her traders (23:3, 8) was consistent with Isaiah's belief that prideful nations would eventually come to grief (10:5–19). Isaiah lamented Sennacherib's devastating attack upon Judah (1:4–9). Jerusalem's pitiful plight was likened tearfully to a booth in a vineyard. During the harvest season owners of vineyards and melon patches built, and do so today, pole and brush huts, sleeping in them at night so as to protect their crops from thieves. After the harvest these structures are grotesquely dilapidated reminders that the productive season has passed. Isaiah sang

> *Your country lies desolate,*
> > *your cities are burned with fire;*
> *in your presence*
> > *aliens devour your land;*
> > *it is desolate, as overthrown by aliens.*
> *And the daughter of Zion is left*
> > *like a booth in a vineyard,*
> > *like a lodge in a cucumber field.* (1:7–8)

Sennacherib's Campaign in Judah

Sennacherib's campaign wreaked havoc on Judah. He claimed that forty-six walled cities were destroyed, and that 200,150 persons were deported.[28] Jerusalem did not fall to the invaders, and why not is a disputed historical problem.

The Assyrian Withdrawal From Jerusalem

Why did Sennacherib not besiege Jerusalem until it surrendered to him? One answer may be that Hezekiah released Padi, king of Ekron, into custody of the Assyrians. When Ekron began its rebellion, Padi had tried to remain loyal to his Assyrian lord. But the citizens of Ekron took him prisoner, and delivered him to Hezekiah in Jerusalem where he was kept a prisoner. Then Ekron proceeded

[28] The figure is probably more like 2,150.

to foment rebellion. Sennacherib forced Hezekiah to release Padi, and he was returned to power and given several Judean towns as his feudal reward for having remained loyal to Assyria.

The biblical narrative suggests other answers (37:33–38). Perhaps a devastating plague was responsible for Sennacherib's withdrawal of his army (37:36). Perhaps a court intrigue in Nineveh sent Sennacherib scurrying home with his army. Herodotus reported that Sethos of Egypt[29] rounded up a citizen's army to attack Sennacherib. During the night, as the two armies faced each other, a multitude of field mice devoured the quivers, bowstrings, and leather strappings of the Assyrian army. At dawn the Assyrians beat a rapid retreat, and the Egyptians overtook them to cut down the weaponless soldiers in a mighty massacre.[30]

Whatever the historical reason, it is certain that Sennacherib withdrew from Palestine before he had completed his plans. Normally the Assyrians replaced a disloyal vassal with one who could be trusted, or else organized the captured territory into a province with an Assyrian governor. That this did not take place with Jerusalem is sufficient reason to support the belief that Sennacherib withdrew his troops under unusual pressure.

Isaiah's Reaction to Sennacherib's Withdrawal

Jerusalem's residents as well as Hezekiah's advisors saw the Assyrian's departure as a vindication of the king's foreign policy. Isaiah was of a different mind. Whereas the citizens raised a tumultuous outburst on the roofs of the houses as the troops were withdrawn, Isaiah grieved over those whose deaths came from famine and plague (22:1–2). Although Hezekiah's rule seemed stable, Isaiah recalled to mind those who had fled from the city and were captured by the Assyrians (22:3). Sennacherib referred precisely to those troops which Hezekiah had put in defense of Jerusalem but who had deserted to the Assyrians.[31] Furthermore, the people too quickly forgot that the troops from Elam and Kir which had battered down the houses in the valleys beyond Jerusalem's protective walls were mercenaries and not the crack Assyrian regiments used in other campaigns (22:5–7). Judeans should not be so proud of their defense after all. Hezekiah had done a good job of logistics: the pool of Siloam had been built in time, houses had been torn down to reinforce and elevate the city's walls, and defensive weapons had been stockpiled (22:8–11). But Isaiah's complaint was that

[29] The Egyptian name is Shabako, 710–696 B.C. (See chart, p. 196.)
[30] See *The History of Herodotus,* Bk. II.
[31] Pritchard, *ANET,* p. 288.

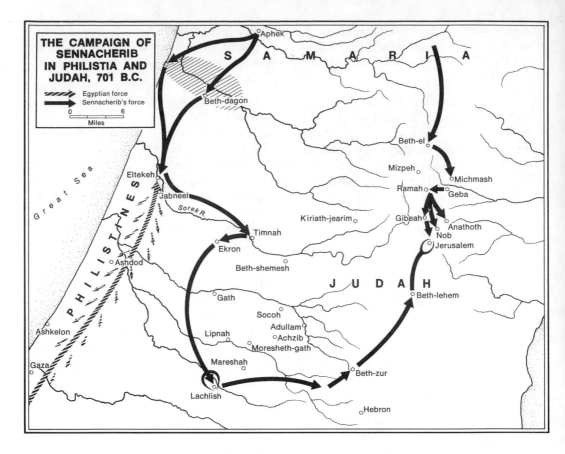

THE CAMPAIGN OF
SENNACHERIB
IN PHILISTIA AND
JUDAH, 701 B.C.

///// Egyptian force
→ Sennacherib's force

0   6
Miles

Yahweh's part in the salvation of Jerusalem had been forgotten.
While the siege was in force, those with ample supplies argued

Let us eat and drink,
for tomorrow we die. (22:13)

Whereas Isaiah would have the truth:

Let us repent, for tomorrow we die.

Isaiah believed that the desperate situation through which Jerusalem
had just passed should be sufficient warning of the rotteness at
the core of its national life, but he saw no sign that many accepted
this truth. Hezekiah's pious cultic reforms had blinded most to the
cancerous disease that affected the moral structure of the whole

society. Judeans were not significantly different from Assyrians: both trusted inordinately in themselves rather than in Yahweh.

The End of Isaiah. This is the last crisis Judah faced in which Isaiah played a part. There is no historical material reporting Isaiah's death, although a Jewish tradition holds that he died a violent death perhaps at the hands of Manasseh (687–642 B.C.), Hezekiah's successor.

Isaiah's Religious Affirmations

Isaiah favored his disciples with a description of how he became a prophet. He had had a religious experience of such magnitude that he felt called to a special task in Yahweh's service (6:1–9). One day "in the year that King Uzziah died," 742 B.C., while he performed his priestly duties at the Temple's altar, he had a vision of the incomparably holy God. He was utterly shocked by what he felt. He, a priest, whose duties prescribed that he be morally and cultically clean, felt himself unworthy of being in the presence of the Holy One. Only after he imagined his lips made clean by the touch of a heated stone from the incense altar was his sin taken away. He was then able to put himself into Yahweh's hands as His agent. This mighty enthusiasm at the beginning of his career when he said, "Here I am! Send me," had turned to bitterness at the people's unreceptivity. It appears that when he informed his disciples of his withdrawal from public life because he had failed in his mission, he told them of his great commission (6:1–13).

The Elements of Isaiah's Faith

Isaiah 6 is one of the greatest passages in the Old Testament. Its influence upon Judeo-Christian traditions of worship has been immense, and its insight into the nature of religious experience is unparalleled. In little more than two hundred words the classic design of worship and spiritual renewal are enunciated.

Grandeur and Mystery. One element in the design of worship is its symbolic language in phrases like "the Lord sitting upon a throne," "the voice of him who called," "flying seraphim," and "burning coal put to unclean lips." These images convey the sense of grandeur, clarity, mystery, and intensity which Isaiah experienced in the presence of spiritual power.

The Vision of God. The vision of God is another element in the design of worship. Isaiah was overwhelmed with the majesty, purity, and universality of Yahweh. Worship is predicated upon an elevated conception of God, which is expressed in images of a kingly throne, in the unleashed forces of the natural world, or in the whisper of moral responsibility (Exod. 19:16–23; 1 Kings 19:9–18).

A Sense of Uncleanness.   A third element was Isaiah's awareness of his uncleanness in the presence of Yahweh and his sensation of guilt. His sin was not in the things which he had done or failed to do, but in the feeling that he stood infinitely inferior to the God of the universe. No blame was attached to his feeling, but a confession of his unworthiness in the presence of the Holy One was necessary to relate himself objectively to Yahweh.

A Sense of Renewal.   A fourth element in the design of worship is a sense of renewal. Isaiah symbolized the burning coal on his lips as purifying that human organ through which pride and arrogance are expressed. Only purified lips could speak of the grandeur, power, and holiness of Yahweh. Isaiah dedicated himself to the task of speaking the word of renewal to the people of Jerusalem.

Personal Dedication.   The fifth element in the design of worship is personal dedication. Isaiah's dedication to a prophetic career was not so simple as it may appear. It meant that he cast himself as a critic of his society, of his national leaders, and of his nation's false aspirations, a task never easy in any generation.

Isaiah's Impact on Affirmations of the Nature of Yahweh

The impact of Isaiah's Temple vision conditioned several affirmations about Yahweh's nature.

1. Yahweh was transcendant. Isaiah understood his God to be above the earth so that he towered over all things terrestial. He was "Yahweh . . . high and lifted up," "the king, Yahweh of hosts." In order to express his conceptions of Yahweh's elevation he borrowed an image from Canaanite literature which depicted "the Lord . . . riding on a swift cloud" (19:1). From this vantage point Yahweh controlled the movements of men and nations. As Lord of heaven and earth Yahweh had at his disposal his "hosts" who did his bidding among the nations.

2. Yahweh's elevation was not only physical; it was also moral. Yahweh was thrice holy. His purity, justice, and righteousness were impeccable and stood in full contrast with man's sin and guilt.

3. Isaiah's understanding of Yahweh was different from other Near Eastern beliefs about gods who were worshipped because they

were found in nature: trees, rocks, mountains, rivers, springs, storms, and the sea, His beliefs also contrasted with those who understood the gods to be the sun, moon, and stars. Even the concept of Yahweh as a tribal or national God was subordinated to that in which Yahweh was Lord of the universe and of all nations. Isaiah was sympathetic with Amos' belief that Yahweh controlled the migratory movements of Ethiopians, Philistines, and Aramaeans (Amos 9:7).

4. Isaiah thought of Yahweh as so powerful that even though Assyrian kings did not believe in Yahweh, they were, nonetheless, doing his bidding. When Assyrian kings, however, became as proud and as cruel as Sargon II and Sennacherib, then Yahweh repudiated them as his agents and destroyed them.

5. Isaiah did not conceive of Yahweh as tribal or national in a narrow sense, but he did understand Him as having a special interest in Jerusalem. Unlike the gods of most Near Eastern nations, Yahweh did not dwell solely in His temple in Jerusalem, but he dwelt in the heavens above. It was in Jerusalem and in the Temple specifically that Yahweh made Himself known and from whence He administered justice. Isaiah's beliefs at this point appear inconsistent, and perhaps they were. But his love of Jerusalem was so great that he could actually understand the powerful and holy Yahweh as having a special concern for that city. It was the one spot in which the transcendant Yahweh could communicate with man. Jerusalem was the symbol of Yahweh's active presence in the affairs of men. Those men who dwelt there were privileged because Assyria, so Isaiah believed, could not destroy the city (10:24–27). In fact, Yahweh hovered like an eagle over the city to protect it, and He would descend with his hosts of heaven to fight for it (31:4–5). There afflicted people could find refuge (14:32).

The Small "Remnant" of Just Men

Although Isaiah thought of Yahweh as hovering over Jerusalem, that special concern did not offer privilege without responsibility. Once a source of righteousness Jerusalem had become a place where currency was degraded, wine diluted and sold for full price, bribes taken, and the unfortunate left to their dismal fates (1:21–23). That such unseemly behavior should go unpunished was unthinkable to Isaiah. He saw Jerusalem's inhabitants purged like dross from molten metal so that rebels and sinners were destroyed and replaced by the just and the righteous (1:24–28). The just and the righteous were a small number, however, compared with the multitudes doing evil, and Isaiah called them the "remnant." He named his first son "A remnant shall return," realizing that the number who responded to his prophetic proclamations would be few indeed (7:3, 10:22). When Yahweh's agents in the guise of Assyria's hordes had finished punishing the rebellious and unrighteous in Judah, only a remnant would travel the roads from Assyrian exile to Judah again (11:16).

Isaiah's Conception of a Messiah

Intimately related to the idea of a remnant was that of a messiah. The messiah was, of course, a person from the ranks of those righteous persons who affirmed Yahweh's demands of justice, but he was of kingly stature. He bore power righteously in his hands. Two brilliant passages, Isaiah 9:2–7 and 11:1–9, reported the birth of Yahweh's anointed and his subsequent righteous rule. Although Christian theology applied these two magnificent poems to Jesus, in their historical context they meant a king in Isaiah's lifetime. No name was given in these eulogies, but it is a fair guess that Isaiah had Hezekiah in mind when he sang these songs. After the disastrous events of Ahaz's career, Hezekiah, in Isaiah's opinion, appeared like one specially anointed to do God's bidding. Perhaps Isaiah 9:2–7 was the accession hymn Isaiah composed for Hezekiah's coronation. Isaiah was close to the royal family, and his personal associations as well as his superb artistry were sufficient to get him this august commission.[32] He composed two hymns of such power and beauty that even though they depicted the rule of a descendant of David, they have been interpreted as meaning a divine person specially designated to do God's work. It is understandable that such magnificent words should be the theme of George Frederick Handel's *Messiah*.

Isaiah's View of Israel's History

Finally, Isaiah's view of Israel's history differed from that of Amos and Hosea. He looked upon the events that had brought Judah to its moment of crisis from the perspective of a monarchist. He was more impressed by the Davidic influence on Israel's history than by the Exodus and wilderness period. He never mentioned Moses, and he cited the Exodus only once (11:16). Compared with the city of David and the Davidic monarchy, the history and beliefs of early Israel were unimportant to him. Both Amos and Hosea looked upon the Exodus period as the ideal age of Israelite religion, but Isaiah saw the Davidic period as ideal (Amos 5:25, Hosea 11:1–2). The throne of David, not the Mosaic covenant, was the source of righteousness (Isa. 9:7, 11:1). The Temple in Jerusalem, not the holy mountain in Sinai, was the place of Yahweh's revelation

[32] See Isaiah 7:3–5, 10–17, 37:1–4, 38:21–22. Psalm 2, 72, 89, 110 are examples of enthronement psalms.

(6:1–8). In a sense, Isaiah's view of history was based more upon historical reality than upon the legendized traditions of the Hebrews.

The Book of Micah Isaiah was the greatest of the 8th century B.C. prophets and as such completely overshadowed his contemporary, Micah. Like Amos and Hosea, Micah was not a prophet of the official guild. He rose from the ranks of the peasants, if his denunciation of the landowners and the principle officials can be taken as an indication of his status (2:1–2, 3:11). He prophesied before Samaria fell to the Assyrians in 721 B.C., and he worked until Sennacherib's advance on Judah in 701 B.C. (1:6, 9–16, 3:12). Moresheth, Micah's home, was a village southwest of Jerusalem, and it felt the full weight of Assyria's heel in its suppression of Hezekiah's revolt.

Although Micah does not have the strength of the other three 8th century B.C. prophets, one passage has a power that rivals any other Old Testament spokesman:

> *"With what shall I come before the Lord,*
> *and bow myself before God on high?*
> *Shall I come before him with burnt offerings,*
> *with calves a year old?*
> *Will the Lord be pleased with thousands of rams,*
> *with ten thousands of rivers of oil?*
> *Shall I give my firstborn for my transgression,*
> *the fruit of my body for the sin of my soul?"*
> *He has showed you, O man, what is good;*
> *and what does the Lord require of you*
> *but to do justice, and to love kindness,*
> *and to walk humbly with your god? (6:6–8)*

Micah, like Isaiah, used the idea of a remnant, but he saw that group as people who had suffered the awful ravages of war and returned to their homes, or those who were refugees in an alien land (4:7, 5:7–8).

Micah's Prophecies Micah differed from Isaiah in three other respects. *First,* he pronounced the destruction of Jerusalem (3:12). From his village six miles north of Lachish he heard about, perhaps even witnessed, the horrendous seige of that city in 701 B.C. This experience prompted his conviction of Assyria's invincible power. *Second,* he announced a king-messiah from the Davidic line whose chief function was to avenge the devastation Assyria had brought to Judah (5:2–9). If Micah 5:3–9 is not editorial addition from the days of the Exile, then Micah understood the Davidic messiah to be an avenging military commander. *Third,* Micah looked back to the Exodus, the leadership under Moses, and the migration into Canaan, as Israel's ideal period (6:3–5). Differences of this magnitude indicate the independence of prophetic minds in interpreting events of their lifetimes within the history of Israel. The prophets did not have the same insights into Yahweh's dealings in history as a result of the events in which they commonly participated.

Prophetic Teachings of the 8th Century

The 8th century B.C. was a tumultuous period in the Near East. Nationalistic fervor burned white hot, and imperial armies rolled over the land from the Persian Gulf to the Nile River. Nation after nation collapsed under the weight of Assyrian political and military superiority. It is not surprising that Israel was snuffed out and that Judah lost its independence. From these political catastrophes some of the most elevated spiritual teachings were proclaimed. One can summarize these achievements by noting eight principles our four prophets had in common.

The Conception of Yahweh as the Lord of Nature

Yahweh was the Lord of nature. This belief was constantly in danger of contamination from Canaanite cults whose main stress was upon the deified reproductive powers of nature. Canaanites worshipped their gods in order to manipulate them. It was utterly essential to satisfy the lord of the land who died after harvest, went to the Nether World, and whose goddess-consort searched him out in winter. Her victory over the natural forces which held him captive explained the coming of spring. The Canaanites thus performed rites symbolizing the subordination of the gods to the forces of nature. The prophets, on the other hand, conceived of Yahweh as master of the natural world who gave the land its fertility or withheld the rain, sent the plagues or supplied honey. Yahweh was not part of nature. He was over, above, beyond. He controlled nature. Yahweh was the Lord of creation. The prophets sometimes chose Canaanite mythic ritual-dramas to emphasize their beliefs, and when they did so, they cleansed them of their obscene elements and reformulated them so as to depict Yahweh as in complete control of the cycles of nature (Hos. 9:1–14; 2:2–23; Isa. 14:12–14). It was apparent to the prophets that Yahweh both managed the earth's resources and punished His people by withholding its beneficence.

The Conception of Yahweh as the Lord of History

Yahweh was the Lord of history. The Yahwist writer, of course, two centuries earlier, understood Yahweh as the push behind Abraham's migration from Haran to Canaan. He saw Israel's flight from Egypt as Yahweh's action in the life of a people. But the 8th century B.C. prophets set the *whole panorama of world history* under Yahweh's scrutiny. Assyria and Egypt were Yahweh's instruments in history. The migrations of the Ethiopians from eastern Africa, the Philistines from Crete, and the Aramaeans from Mesopotamia, were all in Yahweh's hands (Amos 9:7). The prophets believed that social and political sins brought disasters of universal dimensions. Yahweh, Amos claimed, would punish Israel by exile. Isaiah claimed the same, but he believed in addition that Yahweh's strong hand would fall on Assyria too because of its cruelty and pride (Isa. 10:15–16; 14:4b–20). It was clear as crystal to the prophets that Yahweh's hand reached out to grasp all men in their historical associations.

The Conception of Yahweh as a God of Goodness

The prophets identified Yahweh with good. Yahweh had always been known to the Hebrews as a God of power. He was visible in the terrific lightning storms around Sinai (Exod. 19:16–19). He worked his power over Israel's enemies in surprise cloud bursts and hail storms (Judg. 5:19–21, Josh. 10:11). He struck down good men who presumed to touch His sacred objects (2 Sam. 6:6–7). Yahweh's power did not diminish in the eyes of the prophets but it came forth both good and dependable. Good had long been defined in Israel as a man's obligations to his fellows, especially as formalized in the Covenant Code (Exod. 21–23). But Yahweh had not always been understood as subject to the same requirements of human relationships as were men. With the prophets' teachings Yahweh was shown to be goodness, as well as power, and his goodness extended even to pursuing his erring children in compassion and love (Hos. 11:3–4). Since Yahweh was dependable goodness he required of His covenanted people the same (Isa. 10:1–2; Mic. 6:6–8).

The Conception of Yahweh as a God of Law

Yahweh stood behind the law. One of the commonest images of Yahweh in the Old Testament is that of a king. Kings, however, were capricious, and did not always make trustworthy decisions. So too were the gods. After Amos a conception of Yahweh as a capricious tyrant was finished. Yahweh could not be false to his own nature. Since He was good, He had to respond in dependable ways; that is, He was law-abiding. Since He was reliable, the prophets, who spoke for Him, could foresee divine judgment on violations of acceptable human behavior. Obedience to the covenant brought Yahweh's blessing upon the people. Violation of the covenant brought punishment through natural calamity or alien armies. When Israel and Judah pampered foreign governments in seeking military support, it meant acquiescence to foreign gods.

This breach of relations with Yahweh inevitably brought retribution. The prophets knew Yahweh to be governed by His own principles, so to that extent Yahweh's power was limited. He could not violate His principles of righteousness and goodness.

The Conception of Yahweh as a Moral God

Yahweh was the author of universal morality. The prophets were spokesmen of the belief that there exists a minimal moral obligation to which men and nations are bound. Yahweh's moral qualities guided behavior in Israel, and the Covenant Code had been the objective representation of that guidance for generations. Amos universalized this concept so that all nations were answerable to Yahweh for violations of the standard (Amos 1:3 — 2:3). Other prophets boldly declared that cruelty and injustice wherever perpetrated were subject to Yahweh's judgment. The prophets condemned atrocities in war and violations of treaties committed by Israel's neighbors. Those nations must answer to Yahweh in light of their own standards, since they did not have the benefits of a covenant with Yahweh. They, however, would not suffer the severity of punishment that Yahweh imposed on Israel, since only Israel had the high responsibility to the standards of the Covenant Code (Amos 3:1–2).

Yahweh's Special Relationship With Israel

The prophets saw Israel in special relationship with Yahweh. The paradox in this understanding of Yahweh is apparent. How can Yahweh be universal and also treat the people of Israel with special care? The Old Testament on the whole affirms that God has in a special way revealed Himself to men. This conception of special revelation is more personal than that which is set forth in the belief in gods which work only in the processes of nature. Most men, the Old Testament affirms, have the capacity to comprehend God's work in nature, but special revelation must emanate from special men. The prophets were understood as specially endowed persons equipped to set forth Yahweh's particular character and will. These spokesmen seeing themselves as particularly related to Yahweh believed that Yahweh must have chosen all Israel for a designated task, too. That task was to witness to Yahweh's demands for personal and social righteousness, purity in cultic rites, and humility before the awesome power that created and sustains the world. Hosea, for example, understood Yahweh to be like a father who treated Israel like a son. In this special relationship Israel had been privileged, but its obligations were also greater. To the extent that Israel had failed its special position as a son, it was doomed to a harsher punishment than nations that had no privilege. Yahweh was the God of Israel not only because He extended privileges, but as well because he called for responsibility to goodness and righteousness.

The Conception of Yahweh as a Punisher of Nations

The prophets believed in the inevitability of Yahweh's punishment of nations. The prophets rejected, on the other hand, the belief that Yahweh was arbitrarily vindictive. Since He was the Lord of nature, history, law, goodness, and universal morality, His nature determined the extent of His punishment. The cause for punishment lay not with Yahweh Himself but with the transgressions of nations. The moral structure of the world was so ordered that punishment was bound to result from evil. There is evil, therefore the land mourns (Hos. 4:1–3). When nations go to war without reason, then moth and dry rot infect the leaders (Hos. 5:8–12). Evil by man or nation recoils like a spring, flinging punishment upon the doer (Isa. 1:21–23, 2:6–19). Punishment terminates when the people reject evil and turn again to justice and righteousness (Hos. 14:1–7).

The Conception of Yahweh as the Lord of Final Events

Yahweh was the Lord of final events. Each of the prophets spoke with the belief in mind that he was living at the end of an era. Amos expected Israel's complete collapse. Hosea anticipated Samaria's destruction in war (Hos. 13:16). Isaiah announced Assyria's prostration even when Jerusalem was under vicious attacks (Isa. 14:24–27). Micah proclaimed Jerusalem's defeat (Mic. 3:12). The eschatological motif was given specific content in Amos' proclamation of the day of the Lord (Amos 5:18–20; 8:9–14). The day of the Lord in popular belief promised Israel's victory over all her enemies. Amos turned it into a day of darkness, mourning, famine, and death for Israel. The prophets' expectations of final events developed into one of the major ideas among subsequent Old Testament thinkers. The prophets understood it as a day of destruction under specific historical circumstances. Later, however, eschatology became highly speculative, and devoted itself to describing non-human, cosmic forces at work loosing God's anger upon the demonic forces in the world. But this is an aspect of Old Testament literature that shall be studied in proper sequence.

The 8th century B.C. prophets were formidable men. They opposed kings and nobles and championed the causes of the poor and underprivileged. While they backed the cause of the poor they also condemned the easy popularization of Yahwism that the peasantry found desirable. These prophets remain enigmas of history. They were out of step with their times. Somehow, though, they were more alert to the actual course of historical events than were their contemporaries. In a unique way they left their marks upon their own days, but they have challenged subsequent generations to respectful consideration of their claims.

Psalms of the 8th Century

Psalms 76 and 77

Several psalms allude to historical events and conditions reflective of the prophetic period of the 8th century B.C. One song sounded the pride of Jerusalem as it emerged from siege. A stunned cavalry and vast destruction of arrows, shields, and swords have the ring of Sennacherib's withdrawal from Jerusalem (Ps. 76:3, 6). Psalm 76 may have been part of the victory celebration chanted ceremonially in the Temple. Reference to Jacob and Joseph without allusions to Judah in Psalm 77 suggests its origins in Israel. The psalm was composed, perhaps, before Israel fell to Sargon II in 722 B.C. The concepts of steadfast love, graciousness, and compassion have the quality of Hosea's language (Ps. 77:7–10). The psalm possibly was written in the tragic years between 732 and 722 B.C. when Israel repeatedly failed to overthrow Assyrian hegemony.

Psalm 78

Psalm 78 is a didactic song on Yahweh's leadership of Israel from Egyptian slavery to the fall of Samaria. The song recounted the plagues in Egypt, the crossing of the Reed Sea, the wilderness period, the migration into Canaan, the Philistines' destruction of Shiloh where the Ark was kept, and Israel's defeat by Sargon II. But the Temple in Jerusalem still stood (Ps. 78:69). Judah alone remained Yahweh's special people with a Davidic king still on the throne (Ps. 78:68, 70–71). Allusions to the Jerusalem Temple, a Davidic ruler in Jerusalem, and the destruction of Israel, date this psalm between 722 and 686 B.C. It is doubtful that any psalmist would chant the glories of Manasseh (686–642 B.C.), who was a complete vassal of Assyria. The only other king worth such praise was Josiah (638–609 B.C.). The most likely circumstance, however, when Yahweh put his adversaries to rout, was in 701 B.C. (Ps. 78:65–66).

Psalms 75 and 81

Psalms 75 and 81 carry in them pronouncements typical of prophetic speech. Psalm 75:2–5 is a prophetic oracle uttered by some unnamed prophet. This judgment against pride and insolence sounds much like Isaiah. The remainder of the psalm are excerpts from a communal thanksgiving (75:1), a personal hymn (75:9–10), and an eschatogical judgment (75:6–8). A prophetic oracle is embedded in Psalm 81. As Hosea cited Yahweh's saving acts in rescuing Israel from Egypt and preserving the people in the desert, verses 5b–16 of this psalm recount God's salvation history. This oracle has many elements found in Hosea: forsaking Yahweh for alien gods (Hos. 1:2), salvation from Egypt which Israel spurned when secure in Canaan (Hos. 11:1–2), stubborn hearts (Hos. 11:5–7), and the promise that Yahweh will ever be faithful despite Israel's rejection of the Lord (Hos. 14:4–7). The remainder of the psalm commemorates a harvest festival (Ps. 81:1–5a).

Psalm 110   Some psalms honored kings at their coronation. A vigorous nationalistic hymn was sung as a new king of Judah was enthroned (Ps. 110). The opening verse may be confusing to one unfamiliar with Hebrew. "The Lord" in Hebrew is *Yahweh;* "my lord" in Hebrew is *adoni. Adon* was simply a title of respect in addressing a superior. In modern Hebrew it means "mister." Therefore, "Yahweh says to my king" would be a clear translation of the first line. The king's vanquished foes often served as footstools during official audiences in order to symbolize the power of the victor and the humiliation of the defeated. The Judean king, as agent of Yahweh, symbolically was depicted as seated at Yahweh's right hand, but in times of trouble Yahweh was thought to march at the right hand of the king as he went forth to smash his foes (Ps. 110:5–6). The weak ending of this hostility-minded psalm (Ps. 110:7) makes it likely that an account of a battle between the newly-enthroned king and an enemy already defeated formed the concluding stanza of the hymn. This hymn may have been chanted at the coronation of Jotham (742–735 B.C.) whose good reputation among Judah's historians was assured because "He did what was right in the eyes of Yahweh" (2 Kings 15:34). He was an aggressive ruler who improved Jerusalem's defensive posture and soundly defeated the Ammonites (2 Chron. 27:1–8). The author of Psalm 110 had sufficient reason to praise the new king in such manner.

XI

**Revolution:
Anatomy of
Survival**

Few literary achievements are preserved in the Old Testament for the nearly two generations after Isaiah. The books of the prophets of the late 7th century, and Deuteronomy, were the next challenging writings produced. The psalms of this period are particularly important because they reflect the beliefs and practices of the cult of Yahweh just before it was manifestly modified by destruction of its national character.

The books of Zephaniah, Nahum, and Habakkuk stand in the shadow of Deuteronomy. All, however, are important for a complete assessment of Judah's revolutionary effort to survive.

The Book of Zephaniah

The Prophecy of the Day of the Lord. Zephaniah made famous the Day of the Lord as a literary image. Its awesome portents struck the pious of the old world with fear. Among those who read the Bible that image is readily recalled when catastrophy descend on a community. Thomas of Celano, about 1250 A.D., was reminded of Zephaniah's Day of the Lord when events in his life time seemed to foreshadow the end of the world and divine judgment. He wrote

> *Dies irae, dies illa*
> *solvet saeculum in familla.* . . .

Core Readings

Zephaniah
Deuteronomy 5–7, 10:12–22, 12–26
Nahum
Habakkuk
2 Kings 21–25
Psalms 61, 63, 93, 121

> *The day of wrath, that day*
> *Shall dissolve the world in fire. . . .*

and so through nineteen stanzas his hymn described the Last Judgment. The power of Dies Irae was felt by Johann Wolfgang von Goethe. He used a few stanzas of it in that powerful scene in *Faust* where Gretchen stands in the rear of the cathedral after Faust has killed her brother. The evil spirit torments Gretchen's thoughts, and then the choir and organ burst forth in *dies irae, dies illa*.[1] William J. Irons set the Latin hymn to English verse in 1848.

> *Day of wrath, O day of mourning!*
> *See fulfilled the prophets' warning*
> *Heaven and earth in ashes burning!*
>
> *O what fear man's bosom rendeth,*
> *When from heaven the Judge descendeth,*
> *On whose sentence all dependeth!*
>
> *Wondrous sound the trumpet flingeth;*
> *Through earth's sepulchres it ringeth;*
> *All before the throne it bringeth.*
>
> *. . .*

There is, of course, much more in Zephaniah than the concept of the Day of the Lord. An outline will distinguish authentic material from doubtful passages.

1:2–6, 8b–13 The first image of the Day of Yahweh: Destruction of men and nations.
1:7, 14–2:3 The second image of the Day of Yahweh: A sombre picture, ending with a plea for the humble people to turn to righteousness.
3:1–13 An oracle against Jerusalem.
　　3:1–5 Denunciations of princes, judges, priests, and prophets.
　　3:6–8 Jerusalem in the context of world events.
　　3:9–13 The righteous remnant.
2:13–15 An oracle against Nineveh.

Two oracles against foreign nations whose content is very general may be unauthentic.

---

[1] *Faust,* Part I, line 3798.

2:4–12 Judean charges against neighbors. The emphasis upon Judah's eventual domination of them may make an exilic date more preferrable than one in the 7th century B.C.

3:14–19 A promise of Jerusalem's eventual victory. This, too, may be exilic.

Editorial additions: 1:1; 1:8a; 2:7a, c; 2:9a; 3:20.

The Historical Situation in Zephaniah

Zephaniah (642–621 B.C.) lived during the acme of Assyria's empire, when Asshurbanapal (669–633 B.C.) conquered Egypt, and sacked the capital at Thebes, far up the Nile River, in 663 B.C. Everywhere Assyria held a tight rein on vassal kings. In Judah, Manasseh (686–642 B.C.) held his throne only because he was a dutiful subject. According to 2 Kings 21:1–18 Manasseh adopted Assyrian religious practices, encouraged the worship of a pantheon of gods in the Temple, revived human sacrifice, and murdered all who opposed his support of foreign rites (2 Kings 21:6, 16). The author of 1 Kings 21 despised Manasseh, but it is fair to remark that a vassal king who could keep his nobility from rebellion for forty-six years was no weakling.[2] Judah prospered sufficiently during his reign so that fanatic Yahwists were unsuccessful in stirring up trouble among the landed nobility.

Assassination of Manasseh's Successor

For two years Amon held the throne after Manasseh's death, but a palace revolt cut his life short. Amon's rule appeared to be more of Manasseh's type, and yet the report is confusing (2 Kings 21:23–24). Those who put him to death were unnamed and unidentified, and one might suppose they were members of a nationalistic party which despised Assyrian rule. Yet, "the people of the land," Judah's nobility and landowners, apprehended the assassins and promptly put them to death. Those men wielded economic power in Judah, and might have had the most to gain from political independence. Accurate information on Amon's assassination still eludes historians.

Prophet Zephaniah Criticizes the Judean Government

Assyria did not retaliate for Amon's murder, which may have been a sign to the Judeans that Assyria's interests lay elsewhere. Josiah, the son of Amon, was put upon the throne when he was eight years old, and regents held power until he came of age. It is likely that a coalition of priests and prophets took responsibility for governing. Zephaniah, however, did not find such leadership to his liking. He interpreted this coalition government as both "rebellious and

---

[2] 2 Kings 21:1 reports that he ruled for fifty-five years.

defiled," one whose policies were caricatures of Yahweh's law (Zeph. 3:1–5). He may have interpreted the murder and its retaliation as preliminary to the earth-shattering cataclysm that he chanted in the first chapter of his book.

The Scythian Invasion. Some scholars, on the other hand, associate the oracles of the Day of the Lord with an invasion by Scythian nomads from the Caucasus mountains who overran the Near East around 626 B.C. Herodotus reported that hordes of Scythian horsemen descended upon the Medes from the north, and after defeating them became "masters of Asia." They were able to dominate Asia for nearly a generation while their "insolence and oppression spread ruin on every side." When they reached the borders of Egypt Pharaoh Psammetichus I made a treaty and offered them sumptuous gifts. They then returned whence they came, plundering cities, temples, and the countryside before they disappeared into the mountains again.[3]

Dissolution of the Assyrian Empire. Zephaniah may have uttered the oracle against Nineveh on the death of Asshurbanapal in 633 B.C. (Zeph. 2:13–15). When that strong monarch died, Assyrian power began to crumble so that rebellions broke out on the farthest borders of the empire. Scythian raiders rode unchecked against helpless towns and villages. Babylon furiously asserted its independence. On the southwest fringe of the empire the long awaited moment of Assyria's defeat had come. Yahweh had stretched out his hand to destroy Assyria (Zeph. 2:13). Zephaniah's references to Judah's near neighbors as well as to farther lands indicate that his perspective was international in scope. He spoke of "lands of the nations" (Zeph. 2:11), "inhabitants of the earth" (Zeph. 1:18), "nations and kingdoms" (Zeph. 3:8), "speech of the peoples" (Zeph. 3:9). The hope that the "speech of the peoples" will become a pure speech, and that Egypt will be the first to bring offerings to Yahweh in Jerusalem, has historical significance (Zeph. 3:9–10). Zephaniah may have expected a conversion of foreigners to belief in Yahweh when a large colony of Judeans in Egypt had considerable contact with Judah. Asshurbanapal's armies had penetrated far into Egypt. Many Jews served as mercenaries in the Assyrian army and stayed on in Egypt after Assyria had withdrawn its regular troops. Other Judeans served in the Egyptian army of Psammethichus I, and formed a large community on the island of Elephantine at the first cataract on the Nile. Discoveries of papyri at Elephantine

---

[3] *The History of Herodotus,* Book I.

inform us that there was a settlement of Jews there long before the Persians invaded Egypt in 525 B.C. Zephaniah may have used the conversions of some Egyptians to Israelite beliefs and practices as a forecast of what the future held for all nations after the destruction of Nineveh (Zeph. 3:11–13).[4]

Zephaniah's Religious Affirmations

Since Amos had first used the concept, the Day of Yahweh had been a basic idea in prophetic thought. Zephaniah used it as the major emphasis in his short book. Zephaniah's ire rose over the Judeans' moral disintegration and religious defection. Judean nobles dressed and behaved like foreign rulers (Zeph. 1:8). Traders dealt falsely in silver (Zeph. 1:11). Men who should be leaders sprawled in drunken stupor (Zeph. 1:12). Disbelievers said in their hearts that Yahweh does not act any more (Zeph. 1:12). Proud and haughty princes, judges, prophets, and priests oppressed the poor and violated the law (Zeph. 2:1–3, 3:11, 19). Judeans petitioned astral deities, and sacrificed to Milcom, an Ammonite god which craved human sacrifice (Zeph. 1:5). Many practiced a rite borrowed from the Philistines in which worshippers did a hopping dance through the doorway of the temple (Zeph. 1:9).[5]

Three Oracles of Punishment, Repentance, and Renewal

Three oracles present a remarkable image of punishment, repentance, and renewal (Zeph. 3:6–13). The first lamented the disasters which had struck Jerusalem (Zeph. 3:6–7). The Lord tried in this way to teach repentance to Judah. But Judah behaved even more corruptly. The second chanted the failure of chastisement (Zeph. 3:8–10). Yahweh will gather the nations, and judgment shall be given all. Judah will then see that the "speech of the peoples" will become "a pure speech," and foreign nations, like the Ethiopians (Egypt), will bring gifts to Jerusalem. When the nations of the world have repented, they will "serve him with one accord" (Zeph. 3:9). The language is more vivid in Hebrew. It is the image of yoked oxen pulling together "as with one shoulder." A world with "pure speech" means that all men would worship one God. In a third oracle Zephaniah sang of consolation (Zeph. 3:11–13). Zephaniah saw the day of "pure speech" as embarrassing Jerusalem, since its citizens worshipped many gods. But Yahweh will remove from the city those haughty and deceitful persons leaving only "a people lowly and humble" to worship Yahweh on the holy mountain joined by people from all nations.

[4] See D. Winton Thomas, ed., *Documents from Old Testament Times* (New York: Harper & Row, 1965), 256–75.
[5] It is possible that Zephaniah 1:9 referred to thieves and bullies who worked for a "boss" by breaking into houses and threatening householders. Then they brought their loot to "fill their master's house with violence and fraud."

The Book of Deuteronomy

Hilkiah found "the book of the law" in the Jerusalem Temple while repairs were being made there (2 Kings 22). When a secretary read it to King Josiah, he expressed consternation that its precepts were not followed in Judah. Huldah the prophetess promised dire punishment upon the nation if the book were not followed to right the wrongs in Judah. In Jerusalem a convocation of chief men in the nation advocated a covenant by which the king pledged deeds consistent with the demands of the book. Alien religious rites were purged from the Temple's precincts, and cultic centers throughout the country were destroyed (2 Kings 23:1–25).

Literary Inspection

Literary analysis of Deuteronomy is a complex and formidable enterprise.[6] Its repetitious phrases are tiresome. Its attribution to Moses despite its inapplicability to a semi-nomad culture is clearly inconsistent. Its chaotic presentation of legal precedents is confusing (esp. Deut. 19–25). Echoes of the prophetic mood amidst priestly prescriptions reverberate confusedly in one's mind. In contrast with the power of prophetic proclamations Deuteronomy is dull.

Deuteronomy Between Two Eras

On the other hand the book of Deuteronomy stands at the dividing line between two drastically different eras, so that its religious reflections are positively exciting. Behind Deuteronomy stands the vigorous, nationalistic traditions of Yahwism. Those traditions were ringed with tribal memories orally proclaimed, claims of empire under David, and a brilliant struggle to maintain cultural identity as Assyrian armies charged across the land. Ahead loom the beginnings of a religion whose authority was the written word rather than the spoken, whose perspective was international, and whose abiding concerns were humanitarian, born of personal and communal suffering. The book of Deuteronomy was the fountainhead of Judaism.

The name "*Deuteronomy*" was given to the English translation from the Septuagint. "Deuteronomy" means "the second law," or "a copy of the law" (Deut. 17:18, 29:1).[7] Its name in the Hebrew Bible is '*eleh haddebarim*, "these are the words"; that is, the words which Moses spoke.

---

[6] One may put himself in the mood to study Deuteronomy by listening to Ernest Bloch's "The Sacred Service." Although this is modern music, Mr. Bloch used many traditional Jewish melodies, and deep respect for ancient ceremonies comes over the listener as orchestra and chorus perform. A sensitive listener will imagine the magnificent liturgies conducted in the Jerusalem Temple as Josiah's religious revolution took hold throughout the land. *Avodath Hakkodesh*, London, Long-playing 123.

[7] In Greek *deutero nomion*.

The book represents Moses delivering three speeches to the assembled Israelites prior to their crossing the Jordan River to conquer Canaan. An outline will help one read the book.

I. The First Speech
   A. *1:1–5* An introduction to the first speech—establishing the geographical and historical setting.
   B. *1:6—4:40* The first speech—recounting the glorious acts of Yahweh in taking Israel from the sacred mountain to the banks of the Jordan.
      1. *1:6—3:29* Yahweh's guidance en route.
      2. *4:1–40* Yahweh's care demands Israel's positive response.
      3. *4:41–43* Moses sets aside cities of refuge.

II. The Second Speech
   A. *4:44—5:1a* An introduction to the second speech—establishing its geographical and historical setting.
   B. *5:1b—28:68* The second speech presenting the law of Yahweh.
      1. *5:1b—11:32* The covenant and its requirements.
      2. *12:1—26:19* The laws of the covenant.
      3. *27:1–26* The liturgical rites on Mt. Ebal and Mt. Gerizim.
      4. *28:1–68* Blessings and curses in respect of the law.
   C. *29:1* Conclusion.

III. The Third Speech
   A. *29:2—30:20* The third speech exhorting Israel to live by the covenant with Yahweh.
      1. *29:2–15* Moses' plea for Israel to accept the covenant.
      2. *29:16–29* Punishment for disobedience.
      3. *30:1–20* Obedience is life; disobedience is death.

IV. *31:1—34:12* Appendices
   A. *31:1–13* Moses' last words to Joshua and the priests.
   B. *31:14–23* Yahweh commissions Joshua and commends Moses.
   C. *31:24–29* Covenant and ark.
   D. *31:30—32:47* The Song of Moses.
   E. *32:48–52* Moses prepares for death.
   F. *33:1–29* The Blessing of Moses.
   G. *34:1–12* Narrative of Moses' death.

Deuteronomy as First Discovered

The book of the law found in the Temple contained only Moses' second speech. Three facts in the narrative of its discovery appear to confirm this opinion. First, the narrative relates that the book was read twice in one day; once by Shaphan alone and again by Shaphan before the king (2 Kings 22:8–10). Second, the designation "book of the law" indicates a collection of legal precepts without the narrative materials at the beginning and at the end of our book of Deuteronomy. Third, repetitions in the narrative sections indicate that our book passed through several editions before it reached its present form.

Legal Traditions
Behind Deuteronomy The legal documents which lie embedded in Deuteronomy 12–26 are fairly easy to detect. The compilers of this law drew from a variety of traditions.

The Covenant Code. One body of law from which the Deuteronomists drew was the Covenant Code. The laws in this code were out of date, but their antiquity and association with Israel's greatest legendary figure, Moses, gave them status. The Deuteronomists modernized those outmoded laws. Exodus 21:1–11 and Deuteronomy 15:12–18, for example, deal with treatment of a Hebrew slave. Under the Covenant Code a Hebrew male purchased as a slave served for six years, and was granted his freedom in the seventh year. The master initiated the slave's release. The ex-slave left his master's house just as he entered it, but he had the privilege of petitioning for lifelong service. Wives of slaves remained the owner's property (Exod. 21:4, 7–11). Altered economic and social conditions required a change in dealing with slaves. Under the laws in Deuteronomy a Hebrew became a slave by selling himself into slavery. The slave himself initiated the request for his freedom at the end of six years, at which time he was supposed to be given animals, grain, and wine to enable him to make a fresh start. The new law also recognized the independence of women. They could be enslaved and freed just as could men (Deut. 15:17).[8] The Deuteronomic Law emphasized the humanitarian aspects of the new society.

The Covenant Code handled three types of homicide in summary fashion (Exod. 21:12–14). A murder from passion deserved the punishment of immediate death. Involuntary manslaughter permitted the murderer to seek protection at the altar of any temple where the case would be judged by a priest. Premeditated murder did not warrant safety at a temple, and death followed the murderer's detection. In the Deuteronomic Code cities of refuge were provided for the unintentional killer (Deut. 19:1–13), and an example of manslaughter was provided in this code so that a person would know if he were eligible for the protection of the cities of refuge. Premeditated murder deserved expeditious treatment of the killer (cf. Deut. 4:41–43). The incorporation of cities of refuge into the law made explicit what had been customary since Israel had become a nation. A nomadic society gave into the hands of the dead man's relatives

[8] See 2 Kings 8:1–3 for economic conditions which forced slavery upon a woman for seven years.

the duty of avenging the death. In a complexly organized society limitations were placed upon blood revenge. The unintentional killer had, by fleeing to a refuge city, a chance of having his case heard. The Deuteronomic Code had modernized the Covenant Code.[9]

Casuistic Laws. A second body of law from which the Deuteronomist compilers drew is scattered among chapters 21–25. These casuistic laws as they now stand are mixed with apodictic laws, but they were originally an independent body. They deal with matters such as how to proceed in a case of murder when the killer is unknown (Deut. 21:1–9), how to treat the eldest son even though he was not born of the favorite wife (Deut. 21:15–17), how to deal with a man who has falsely accused his new wife of not being a virgin (Deut. 22:13–21), how to perpetuate a man's name who dies before his wife conceives a male heir (Deut. 25:5–10). [10]

"Abomination" Laws. A third small collection of laws has a peculiarity which sets it off from all others. Each law ends with the expression "that is an abomination to the Lord your God." It is abominable to worship a tree or pole beside an altar to Yahweh (Deut. 16:21). This cultic law presupposes the existence of cult centers other than the Temple in Jerusalem thus "proving" that it was formulated before the book of Deuteronomy, which demanded worship only in Jerusalem. Other abomination laws may be found, at 17:1 concerning sacrifice of a blemished animal, at 18:9–12 concerning human sacrifice and magic; at 22:5 concerning exchange of garments by male and female; at 23:17–18 concerning cult prostitution and payment of a vow; and at 25:13–16 concerning honest weights and measures.

Humanitarian Laws. A fourth type of law deals with humanitarian acts. They are at 22:1–4, care of a neighbor's animals and personal

---

[9]The following are examples of how Deuteronomy used the Covenant Code and modified it to meet changed social conditions.

EXODUS	DEUTERONOMY	EXODUS	DEUTERONOMY
21:16	24:7	23:4–5	22:1–4
22:15–16	22:28–29	23:9	24:17–18
22:20–23	24:17–22	23:12	5:14–15
22:24	23:20–21	23:13	6:13
22:25–26	24:10–13	23:9a	26:2–10
22:28–29	26:1–11, 15:19–23	23:9b	14:21b
22:30	14:3–21		
23:1	19:16–21		
23:2–3, 6–8	16:18–20		

[10]Extract 22:1–7, 22:9–12, 23:1–8, 23:14–20, 24:6, 24:8–9, 24:14–22, 25:4, 25:13–19 for the remainder of this collection.

property; at 23:15–16, protection of a runaway slave; at 23:19–20, no interest charges to a fellow Israelite; at 24:6, pledges for a debt; at 24:14–20, concern for a hired hand; at 24:16, a father shall not be put to death for a child's crime; at 24:17–18, care for the unfortunate; at 24:19–22, food for the poor; and at 25:4, care for work animals.

Laws Original With the Deuteronomists — Those laws which prohibited cultic practices outside the Jerusalem Temple were written by the Deuteronomists themselves. The form of these special laws differs from those taken from the earlier codes. The old laws were stated briefly, dealt with specific instances, and permitted some latitude in interpretation by the judge. The new laws proposed by the Deuteronomists were couched in rhetorical phrases and set within a narrative framework. The altar law, for example, is in narrative style in which five regulations are embedded (Deut. 12:1–31). These regulations demanded the destruction of all unauthorized altars, sacrifice solely in Jerusalem, permission to slaughter animals for food without priestly supervision, provision for pouring the animal's blood onto the ground, and purchase of a sacrificial animal in Jerusalem. These laws lacked precision of statement. The law of tithing was stated precisely, but the narrative which followed attempted to foresee all contingencies and to legislate these rather than permit the individual jurist to make his interpretation of specific instances (Deut. 14:22–29).

In several cases the Deuteronomists combined precepts from two older codes to establish a law applicable to new cultic requirements. Regulations respecting the Feast of Unleavened Bread and of Passover, for example, were combined in order to create a single ceremony (Deut. 16:1–8). Other examples of this technique are: Deut. 15:19–23 — sacrifice of unblemished animals and the firstborn; Deut. 17:8–13 — combination of Levitical civil and cultic functions.

Exilic Additions. Two segments were added to the body of Deuteronomy during the Exile. Regulations for mourning rites and diet became part of Jewish ways during the Babylonian Exile (Deut. 14:1–21). Restrictions upon prophets were necessary because some prophets advocated rebellion and nationalism among Jewish exiles in Babylon (Deut. 18:15–22). Leaders of Babylonian Jewish communities had to curb such enthusiasm in order to avoid reprisals from Babylonian soldiers.

Over half of Deuteronomy contains historical summaries, exhortations to loyalty, songs and blessings, and liturgical directions which are not at all juridical. This shows that the book went through several stages of composition before it reached its present form. There are two introductions to the legal portion, placed side by side (Deut. 1: 1–4:43 and 4:44–11:32). Many of the legal statements were elaborated by sermon-like explanations and appeals. Apodictic laws are followed by lengthy explanations of why the law exists and by appeals to observe it faithfully (Deut. 16:1–8).

Additions in Final Editing

Three individual documents were added to Deuteronomy during its final stages of editing. The ceremony of curses, which interrupts Moses' concluding speech, may be a ritual dating from before the United Monarchy (Deut. 27:11–26). The confederation of Israelite tribes gathered annually about a cult center at Shechem to renew their political ties before the God El. The Song of Moses cited episodes from Israel's history recalling the people's apostasy, Yahweh's divine discipline, and the destruction of Israel's enemies in Canaan (Deut. 32:1–43). The Blessing of Moses is divisible into two parts: a hymn (Deut. 33:2–5, 26–29), and collected sayings about Israelite tribes (Deut. 33:6–25). The hymn's similarity to the diction of early songs may entitle it to a place among Israel's oldest literature (Judg. 5, Ps. 18). The blessings were not composed at one time. The blessing of Israel reflects a period of prosperity and gives no hint of the disaster of 722 B.C. (Joseph, Deut. 33:13–17). On the other hand, the blessing of Levi reports that tribe as the teachers and priests of Israel (Deut. 33:8–11). This reflects the same position they are accorded in other parts of Deuteronomy. Therefore, that stanza may date from the late 7th century B.C.[11]

Characteristics of the Deuteronomist' Style

Deuteronomy is a complex document which passed through several editorial hands before it received its final form. The book's style is distinctive. Certain key phrases predominate, so that when they are found elsewhere in the Old Testament one knows that a Deuteronomist editor has been at work. A list of characteristic words and phrases reveals Deuteronomy's distinctive style.

1. To love (Deut. 6:5, 7:9, 10:12. 23:5 expresses God's gracious concern for His people).
2. To go after other gods (Deut. 6:14, 7:4, 8:19).
3. That your days may be long (Deut. 4:26, 4:40, 5:33).
4. The land which the Lord your God gives you (Deut. 4:4d, 15:7, 19:3, 23:2d).

[11] Frank M. Cross and David N. Freedman, "The Blessing of Moses," *Journal of Biblical Literature*, LXVII (1948), pp. 191–210 date the poem to the 10th century B.C.

5. Out of the house of bondage (Deut. 6:12, 7:8, 8:14).
6. You are a people holy to the Lord your God (Deut. 7:6, 14:2, 26:18).
7. These words which I command you this day (Deut. 6:6, 7:11).
8. A mighty hand and an outstretched arm (Deut. 4:34, 5:15, 7:19, 11:2).
9. So you shall purge the evil from the midst of you (Deut. 13:5, 17:7, 12, 19:19).
10. The fatherless, the widow, and the sojourner (Deut. 10:18, 24:17, 27:19).
11. That all may go well with you (Deut. 4:40, 5:16, 6:3, 12:25, 22:7).
12. With all your heart and with all your soul (Deut. 4:29, 6:3, 10:12, 11:13, 13:8).
13. The place which the Lord will choose (Deut. 12:14, 15, 26, 14:25, 16:7, 13, 17:8, 10).
14. To do that which is right in the eyes of the Lord (Deut. 12:25, 13:18, 21:9).[12]

The literary influence of this style upon many books of the Old Testament is unmistakable.

The Deuteronomists' Other Work

The Deuteronomists established a school of religion at Jerusalem. This is, at least, one way to express the influence they had in creating and preserving the Old Testament. The authors of Deuteronomy believed that history was the arena in which God performed. They agreed with the 8th century prophets that Yahweh had used Assyrians, Aramaeans, Scythians, Philistines, and Babylonians as His agents in working out Israel's destiny. The destruction of Samaria in 722 B.C. and Sennacherib's onslaught against Judah in 703–701 B.C. were frightful proofs that the prophets were correct in claiming that apostasy from the pure worship of Yahweh and disobedience to the Covenant Code brought national ruin. Conversely, purity of worship and loyal obedience would bring national salvation.

1 and 2 Kings

Josiah's reforms prompted the Deuteronomists to explain the revival of religion and prosperity under that pious king. They wrote a history of the Israelite people from Solomon to Josiah, now entitled 1 and 2 Kings, that complemented the story of the growth of the monarchy from Samuel to Solomon. Favorite Deuteronomists' phrases are sprinkled throughout 1 and 2 Kings. "What was right in the eyes of the Lord" (1 Kings 15:11), "the city which the Lord had chosen" (1 Kings 14:21), "keeping my statutes and my or-

[12] A list of forty-one expressions characteristic of Deuteronomy is given in S. R. Driver, *An Introduction to the Literature of the Old Testament* (rev. ed. New York: Charles Scribner's Sons, 1942), pp. 98–103.

dinances" (1 Kings 11:33), are typical of their editorial phrases. In addition the formula of judgments against Israel's kings (1 Kings 15:3), and the formula of commendation of Judah's good kings (2 Kings 22:2), reveal the tone of Deuteronomic style.

Deuteronomists' History

Other literary compositions were capably treated by the Deuteronomists. Not only were the Yahwist and Elohist narratives combined by Deuteronomic editing, but stories about Israel's early years in Canaan were worked into a narrative that expressed the sterling principle of Deuteronomic religion. They believed that a nation which did "evil in the sight of the Lord" would suffer grievous calamities from enemies and natural disasters, but that a nation fully obedient to Yahweh would prosper in all respects. This principle was made explicit in the book of Judges. The introduction presents the Deuteronomic theology (Judg. 2:11–23), and the remaining stories through chapter 16 were drawn together to illustrate those points. With the publication of the history of Israel and Judah (1 Kings 3 – 2 Kings 23:25), the combining of Yahwist and Elohist narratives into a single story, and the editing of early tribal tales into the book of Judges, the Deuteronomists had erected a lasting literary monument.

Later Revisions

The original Deuteronomists ended their history of Israel and Judah on a note of praise for Josiah (2 Kings 23:25). This indicates that they had completed their task before the untimely death of that king in 609 B.C. Later Deuteronomists followed in the footsteps of their colleagues and finished the grim work of reporting what befell Judah after Josiah's death. During the exile, perhaps around 550 B.C., a historian took up the unraveled strands of Judah's story and wove them together. He wrote of the fall of Jerusalem and the exile to Babylon (2 Kings 23:26 – 25:30). Deuteronomist spirit and style went into this appendix, but there were certain revisions and additions which he felt the text needed. He inserted at appropriate spots expectations of Judah's fall. He added a paragraph in which Solomon was depicted as looking forward to the exile and imploring Yahweh to forgive the nation if it repented (1 Kings 8:44–51). He inserted a long note about Yahweh's appearance to Solomon warning him of the dreadful plight to come upon the people (1 Kings 9:1–9). Where the original Deuteronomist explained the reasons for Samaria's capitulation to Assyria (2 Kings 17:7–18), the author of the appendix inserted a note about Judah's defection (2 Kings 17:19–20). Following the lists of grievances against Manasseh graphically supplied by the original author, the reviser affixed his thoughts on the matter in the guise of a prediction (2 Kings 21:12–15). The editor even added a grim note to the happy discovery of the law in the Temple by placing a mournful prediction in the prophetess' mouth (2 Kings 22:15–20a). In the light of history even Josiah's goodness held back Yahweh's revenge only for a short time, and the editor added the note that Judah deserved its fate (2 Kings 23: 26–27). The exilic Deuteronomist did his revision thoroughly, and even went through 1 and 2 Samuel in order to bring it into line with his point of view. Traces of his hand may be seen where he predicted Zadok's descendants as the only legitimate priests in Jerusalem by inserting a note in a passage that dealt originally with Samuel's succession of Eli as chief supervisor of the Israelite cult center at Shiloh (1 Sam. 2:27–36). The prediction presumably was fulfilled when he appended a commentary on the report of Abiathar's banishment from Solomon's court, leaving Zadok solely in charge of priestly duties (1 Kings 2:27). The exilic Deutronomist added the woeful note "and the word of the Lord was rare in those days; there was no frequent vision" as he tried to explain the calamities brought upon Israel by the Philistines' defeat of the army under Samuel (1 Sam. 3:1).

When the Deuteronomists had finished their work, they had developed a history that spanned the years from the Exodus to the Babylonian exile. There were several hands at work composing and editing for more than a hundred years, but each wrote from the same religious perspective, with the same purpose, and in similar style. What an amazing school of religion it was! It may be the major literary achievement of the ancient Near East.

The Historical Situation in Deuteronomy

Josiah was only a child when Assyria's power began to decline, and he was about fifteen years old when the last great Assyrian king died. Josiah's accomplishments from 626 B.C. to his death in 609 B.C. show that he was a gifted, versatile, and vigorous person. As king he met the signs of Assyria's decline with prompt responses. He threw out of the Temple all traces of Assyria's state religion (2 Kings 23:4). Assyria did not retaliate. He ceased payment of tribute to his feudal king, and diverted those funds to arming his militia. Assyria did not retaliate. He annexed the southern part of Assyria's province of Samaria by seizing the city of Bethel, demolishing the shrine which had been the royal sanctuary of Israelite kings (2 Kings 23: 15). Assyria did not retaliate. He moved east annexing Jericho and adjacent parts of the Jordan Valley. The expansionist fever then drew him westward, and the young king absorbed Philistine cities into his widening boundaries.[13] If Assyria had been able to retaliate,

King Josiah's Expansionism

[13] The list of boundaries and cities in Joshua 15, 18, 19 reflect conditions in the New Judean state under Josiah at the end of the 7th century B.C. See Martin Noth, *A History of Israel* (2nd ed.; New York: Harper & Row, 1960). p. 273.

it would have done so when Josiah swept that rich grain-producing region under his control. Josiah seized land east of the Jordan River whose rich produce from farms around Medeba, Heshbon, and Dihon had once supplied King David with a vast income.[14] Josiah's intention was clear: extension of his sovereignty over the territory that had been Israel before it fell to Assyria. One can imagine that the governors of those regions resisted Judah's encroachments, but as Assyrian provinces they were unarmed and could not cope with Josiah's aggressiveness.

Once Josiah had annexed these regions to the state of Judah, he turned his attention to the heartland of Samaria. He wiped out the cult centers in Samaria and assassinated their officials (2 Kings 23:19–20). He was able to do this only because he had full military control of that region. Not satisfied with these territories he sent his soldiers to capture Megiddo, the capital of the Assyrian province of Galilee. He had almost completed his goal of regaining the kingdom of Israel when at Megiddo his grandiose plans died with him (2 Kings 23:29).

Rehabilitation of the Temple got under way only after Josiah had captured rich regions previously outside his rule. Glorification of the Temple symbolized political independence and economic prosperity. As foreign rites were rejected at the Temple, Josiah wisely introduced the religious program set forth in the "book of the law." He himself became the chief custodian of its observation. He revived the ancient custom of covenant-making between Yahweh and the people. He stood as executor of the ceremony, and in so doing he joined the religious order to the state in a monopoly on cultic observances. That ceremony must be studied carefully in order to understand the king's central position in that monopoly (2 Kings 23:1–3). Rejection of Assyrian religious observances soon resolved into persecution of those in Judah who opposed centralizing cultic practices in Jerusalem. Thus Josiah seized upon the ambiguous phrase "the place which the Lord will choose" (Deut. 12:14, 18, 26, 14:25, and elsewhere), and made it to mean Jerusalem alone. He smashed all cult centers outside the capital, and forbade the local priests, usually of Levite descent, from administering rites and sacrifices in their home towns (2 Kings 23:8). Such an infringement on the venerable religious life of the people probably sowed grief and anger, but Josiah's centralized power stood. The curtailment of religious observances except at one holy place so changed the customary mode of village religious life that a separation between the

Rehabilitation of the Temple

[14] See Joshua 13:15–23.

common life and religious activity was inevitable. But Josiah was not content to change only the common life of the people: he wanted to change the face of Near Eastern politics.

The collapse of Assyria and the withdrawal of Scythian raiders from western Syria and Palestine created a power vacuum. Into this vacuum Josiah crept at first, but later he sped at a gallop. His bid for control of Canaan after Asshurbanapal's death was but an episode in a much vaster struggle for power in the Near East. The struggle lasted long enough for him to consolidate the central territories of the old Davidic empire, but not long enough for him to secure experience in the dizzy game of power politics. He permitted himself to be dragged into a fight with Egypt. Pharaoh Neco (609–593 B.C.) marched at the head of his army to support Assyrian troops in their war against the combined forces of the Medes under Cyaxeres (625–585 B.C.) and the Babylonians under Nabopolassar (626–605 B.C.). Neco expected, one supposes, to save some aspects of Assyrian power at Haran and Carchemish so that a buffer state would exist between his territorial claims and the rising tide of Medes and Babylonians. By marching to help Sin-shar-ishkun (621–612 B.C.) he also extended his control over Palestine and Syria. By parading his army over Josiah's newly won lands he became an enemy of that Judean king. All Josiah's political activity had been directed toward the defeat of Assyrian control in the west, and Neco's efforts to bolster Josiah's deadliest enemy made of Neco an enemy too. Josiah was forced by his past political and military operations to thwart Neco's march to Sin-shar-ishkun's aid. They met at Megiddo. When Neco saw Josiah he killed him (2 Kings 23:29). The account gives no report of a battle.[15] The death of their king destroyed the Judeans' morale, and they remorsefully watched Neco parade north while they carried their chief in mournful procession to his tomb in Jerusalem (2 Kings 23:30).

The Humbling of Judah by Neco

The landholders of Judah selected Jehoahaz to be king in place of Josiah, believing Neco's threat to their independence had passed when he withdrew his army from Judean territory. Neco's campaign in northern Syria was short-lived. Assyrian collapse was inevitable, and Neco was clever enough to see the end before it came. He

---

[15] Only 2 Chronicles 35:20–23 reported a battle, but it is unlikely that that report was based on any more factual data than the 2 Kings 23:29 report. Flavius Josephus, *Antiquities of the Jews*, Bk. X, V, I reported that as Josiah readied his army, a single Egyptian arrow directed only at him wounded him mortally. There was no battle. Herodotus, *History*, Bk. II, reported that Neco defeated the Syrians (Jews?) "in a pitched battle at Magdolus (Megiddo?)." Despite these ancient authorities, it is likely that Neco killed Josiah while they were involved in negotiations.

marched south leaving Syrian towns garrisoned with Egyptian troops. Upon arrival at Riblah on the Orontes River his agents brought him word that Judean independence had been proclaimed at Jerusalem. He demanded Jehoahaz's appearance before him because evidence had accumulated that the young king had pursued his father's policies of independence. When Jehoahaz appeared he was put in irons and deported to Egypt. Eliakim, another son of Josiah, was put on the throne, and Neco, in order to prove his point, laid a tax on Judea. Neco forced Eliakim to change his name to Jehoiakim, a new name for a vassal king being proof that Neco's sovereignty was total over Palestine. The bold venture of Josiah backed by his cohorts in the Deuteronomist school had come to a tragic end. The frontiers of Judah's territory shrank to the pre-Josiah period. Heavy taxes were imposed to meet the Egyptian's demands. Judah was in the same plight that it had fled so expectantly in 626 B.C. when Assyrian power had crumbled. What had gone wrong? Whose was the fault? Surely Josiah had been a righteous king (2 Kings 22:2). Was it possible that the religion, which claimed that evil brought disaster and death and that goodness brought prosperity and life, was faulty? There were some spokesmen for Yahweh who thought so.

The Deuteronomists' Religion

Had Deuteronomy been published during the rule of Manasseh heads would have rolled right and left, because it is a subversive book. It tolerates no God but Yahweh, and Assyrian politicians would never have agreed that their gods were less believable than the Judeans'. Polytheistic Assyria simply put to death persons who threatened its political-religious stability! The book of Deuteronomy was prepared quietly, its authors waiting for a propititious moment in history for the "discovery" of this book.

The Concept of Nature in Personal Terms

Deuteronomy reaffirmed the myth that Israel's existence was dependent immediately upon Yahweh. Myth, when used in this way, means an expression, usually in story form, of what man believes about reality. Thoughtful men in ancient Israel, like others in nearby cultures, conceived of the world as personal. The forces of nature impressed themselves vividly upon man's consciousness, especially in matters concerning his daily life. The growth of grains and fruit only at certain seasons of the year, the birth of children and the death of old people, the thunderstorm with its beneficent showers and occasional terrifying hail, came from the mysterious powers in nature. Couple these with dreams, hallucinations, and unconscious emotions, and the ancient Israelite was fully convinced that nature was neither passive nor impersonal.

Native curiosity prompted him to explain in stories these external and internal experiences. Creative minds among the ancients authored truly artistic narratives and poems explaining the mysterious world in which they lived. The idea of history was born when a genius in Israel set forth the idea that Yahweh was personally interested in national happenings. He believed that events of national importance could be understood best in the light of Yahweh's powers at work in the world. Stories which were told originally to give meaning to natural events and to personal concerns were restructured so as to give meaning to the existence of the nation.[16]

The Yahwist narrator had believed that Israel's destiny depended upon Yahweh's immediate overseeing of the nation. The prophets struggled to keep alive the belief that Yahweh was director of historic events as well as producer of food. Their struggle to keep alive the idea that God was involved in history was mighty hard while enemies pounded Israel's cities with siege weapons and ransacked her stores of grain.

The Yahwist writer had believed that the Lord revealed Himself personally to the great men of his nation. He had spoken directly to Abraham: "Go from your country and your kindred and your father's house to the land that I will show you" (Gen. 12:1). He knew Moses by name, and even passed before him to the point of allowing Moses to see His back (Exod. 33:17–23). The prophets were convinced that Yahweh spoke directly through them proclaiming woes against the nation and hopeful promises for the future.

The nation had passed through dreadful years so that the grandeur of the Davidic empire was only a memory. How could Yahweh be trusted if He had not come to the rescue of His people in their dire need? Deuteronomy gave the answer to that question. It reaffirmed the myth of Yahweh's immediate concern for Israel. That book proclaimed anew, after two generations of doubt, that Yahweh had spoken. Yahweh had spoken. Moses had heard. Moses spoke for Yahweh. The Deuteronomists claimed that the words Moses spoke were Yahweh's words (Deut. 1:1, 6, 5:1). To these men it was doubtful that Yahweh any longer spoke clearly to His prophets as He had in the past. But, He had spoken clearly to Moses, the

---

[16] See Brevard S. Childs, *Myth and Reality in the Old Testament* (London: S C M Press, 1962), for a fine treatment of Near Eastern myth.

greatest of the prophets, and the authenticity of His speech was preserved in the words of Moses.[17]

Five Major Themes of Deuteronomy

Deuteronomy's religious affirmations are encapsulated in a lovely passage at Deuteronomy 10:12-22. Here one finds the five major themes of the book. 1. It calls for reverence for Yahweh. The idea is expressed by saying "fear the Lord your God" (Deut. 10:12). 2. Reverence is shown by expressions of love and service to Yahweh (Deut. 10:12-13). 3. Heaven and earth are Yahweh's possessions, and these are the riches any potentate would covet, but Yahweh loves Israel more than these (Deut. 10:14-15). 4. A true Israelite responds to Yahweh's love by keeping the commandments and the statutes. Behavior is the surest measure of the believer's loyalty to Yahweh (Deut. 10:13, 16). 5. Yahweh is the supreme God. This is proven not only by His possession of the heavens and the earth, but even more strikingly by His execution of wonders, His demands of justice for the unfortunate, His ethical purity, and His loving concern for the people whom He has called to serve him (Deut. 10:17-22). These principles prepare one for the vast religious terrain which must be traveled in this book. The Deuteronomists drew upon the resources of a lengthy and honorable religious tradition in order to affirm the myth of Yahweh's governance in all of life.

Four Religious Traditions of Deuteronomy

The Deuteronomists wove together four religious traditions which had given meaning to the nation's corporate life at various stages for six centuries.

Patriarchal Traditions. Judah treasured first, its patriarchal traditions. Stories of Abraham's obedience to Yahweh, his magnanimity, his steadfastness in the face of adversities, his observance of cultic practices at shrines, flooded upon the worshipper's memory as he recited the words "A wandering Aramaean was my father; and he went down into Egypt and sojourned there, few in number . . ." (Deut. 26:5). These were the words chanted at various shrines throughout Palestine where Abraham's name had lingered: Bethel (Gen. 12:8), Beersheba (Gen. 21:33), and Mamre (Gen. 18:1).

The Tradition of Moses at Sinai. The Abrahamic tradition was drawn into Deuteronomy to be combined with a second great tradi-

---

[17] See Eric Voegelin, *Israel and Redemption* (Baton Rouge: Louisiana State University Press, 1956), pp. 355-77, for a fuller treatment of Deuteronomy's impact on Israelite political and religious forms.

tion: Moses at Sinai or Horeb.[18] This tradition occupied the attention of the authors of Deuteronomy more than others as they stressed covenant-making and reception of the Ten Words (Deut. 5:1–21).

The Tradition of the Shrine at Jerusalem. The national shrine at Jerusalem was the third tradition the Deuteronomists incorporated into their book. The demand that all shrines outside of Jerusalem be destroyed paid tribute to the Davidic tradition (Deut. 12).

The Prophetic Tradition. The prophetic was the fourth of the sacred traditions carried by Deuteronomy. The central motifs derived from the prophets were enunciated in summary (Deut. 10: 12–22). The authors of this book drew Israel's diverse traditions into a new expression so that vitality infused them again, and gave direction for future generations of Judeans.

The Assertion of Yahweh as the One God

In Deuteronomy religious differences expressed in the four separate traditions were subordinated to the assertion that Yahweh alone is God. Yahweh, totally distinct from the many Assyrian gods, who had been worshipped by Abraham even as Josiah worshipped him, was proclaimed indivisible, and His single shrine in the Temple proved that He was incapable of division into several manifestations.

The mighty call "Hear, O Israel: the Lord is our God, the Lord alone" demonstrates that the Deuteronomists embraced monotheism (Deut. 6:4). This famous verse contains four Hebrew words literally translated: "Yahweh, our God, Yahweh, one." It is perfectly clear that Yahweh is the sole object of worship. No rival gods and sanctuaries are possible. Although they affirm the worship of one God, the authors recognized that certain persons still held allegiance to other gods (Deut. 3:24, 13:2, 6, 13). Old ways die slowly, so traditional terminology is used to describe Yahweh. He is great, strong (Deut. 3:24), terrible (Deut. 7:21), devastating fire, jealous (Deut. 4:24), loving (Deut. 7:7), following the usage of the four sacred traditions. Some of the anthropomorphisms of the earlier traditions were rejected. It is explicitly stated, for example, that Moses saw no form of Yahweh (Deut. 4:12, 15). The Yahwist tradition depicted the Lord in human form walking in the garden (Gen. 3:8), visiting Abraham in his tent (Gen. 18:1), having hands and face, and showing Moses his back (Exod. 33:22–23). At one point in Deuteronomy Yahweh is depicted as walking in the midst

[18] Sinai was the name the J and P writers used for the sacred mountain. Horeb was the name used by the E and D writers.

of the camp, but otherwise anthropomorphisms have been excluded (Deut. 23:14).

The Chosen People Even though Yahweh was conceived as the universal God, Israel was still His special people. The four sacred traditions had affirmed in different ways Yahweh's particular interest in the Hebrews, and Deuteronomy strengthens that belief by emphasizing Yahweh's love of Israel. The Patriarchal tradition had stressed Abraham's obedience to Yahweh's *mysterious and inexplicable call.* The Mosaic tradition had stressed Yahweh's *care of Israel* because they had been cruelly treated by a more powerful nation. The Davidic tradition had stressed Yahweh's *special blessings upon Israel* because the nation preserved the ancient mode of worshipping Him before the Ark in the tabernacle. The prophetic tradition had stressed Yahweh's *salvation* of those Israelites who kept the Covenant Code. To these Deuteronomy adds the belief that Yahweh had chosen Israel neither because of its size, nor because of its righteousness, but simply for the reason that He loved Israel. It would make more sense for Yahweh to express His power and righteousness through nations such as Egypt and Assyria, where might had equalled right. But Yahweh chose Israel "because the Lord loves you, and is keeping the oath which he swore to your fathers" (Deut. 7:8). Unreasonable to be sure, Yahweh loved Israel before the nation had proved itself worthy of Him (Deut. 7:6–11).

The Deuteronomists weave the prophetic belief that Yahweh is the God of history into their religious fabric. He had rescued the Israelites from slavery. He had preserved the nation from the devouring desert (Deut. 8:2), and from its own stubborn people (Deut. 9:6). He had destroyed nations opposed to Israel's infiltration into Canaan (Deut. 9:3). He used Israel's enemies to punish the waywardness of the nation (Deut. 28:25–35). This chastened people was Yahweh's agent in history. They carried on their shoulders a righteousness demanded only of those He had chosen particularly (Deut. 9:1–29).

Deuteronomy reveals Yahweh as a God of law. The Davidic tradition had declared that Yahweh exercised his will through the king's rulership of the nation. The Deuteronomists believed fervently, on the other hand, that in keeping *Torah* (law) every individual obeyed Yahweh. Torah was the full revelation of Yahweh's will. With the Deuteronomic law before Judah, direct experience of Yahweh, such as known by the Patriarchs, Moses, David, and the prophets, was no longer essential. The Judean people could be educated to know Yahweh. What were the elements of this education? *First,* it was a knowledge of Israel's history. The events through which Yahweh had led Israel should be taught to children (Deut. 6:20–25, 11:18–25). *Second,* that these events were worthy of constant meditation (Deut. 11:19, 6:7). *Third,* that obedience to Torah was proof the children's education had been effective. *Fourth,* that properly educated children gave full obedience to Torah, and that they would be rewarded by rulership of the land from the Euphrates River to the wilderness of Palestine (Deut. 11:22–25).

<table>
<tr><td>Feasts and Holidays</td><td>

Deuteronomy describes Yahweh as especially pleased with ceremonial rites. The Lord, so the Deuteronomists believed, gave gracious rewards for proper worship and delivered terrible punishment if observances were mishandled (Deut. 28). Joy typified worship, and festivals three times a year gave the men of the nation respite from their routine (Deut. 16). The seven-day festival of Passover and Unleavened Bread was celebrated in holiday mood, and offered a time for exchange of news on business, of events of the nation, and of one's friends and relatives (Deut. 16:1–8). The Feast of Weeks, fifty days after Passover and Unleavened Bread, was a one-day celebration marking the end of the grain harvest and the beginning of the fruit picking season. A third festival was another seven-day affair. This occurred in the fall at the end of the agricultural year. Originally Canaanite, the Feast of Booths celebrated the beginning of the grape and olive harvests. Owners built booths in the open fields so they could guard their crops while they harvested. The more Israel glorified its wilderness origins the more booths came to symbolize the hardships of nomadic life and its agricultural meaning diminished. The joyous character of the feast was never lost, however, and wine flowed freely from leather bags as the harvest produced a plentiful supply of wine from the presses (Deut. 16:13–15).

</td></tr>
</table>

The Problem of the Levites

The requirement to worship Yahweh solely at the sanctuary in Jerusalem left large numbers of Levitical priests unemployed in the villages and towns. The Levites did not till the soil, but received their livelihood from their share in the sacrificial meat, grains, and fruit presented at the local shrine (Deut. 18:1). When Josiah forcefully closed all parochial shrines, these Levites found themselves without work and subsistence. Torah recommended that fortunate people share the gratuities given to widows, to aliens (who could not own land), and to orphans, with the Levites (Deut. 14:27–29). Josiah tried to employ them in the Jerusalem Temple, but the Zadokite priesthood which had serviced the Temple rites since the days of King David did not receive the outsiders kindly. Their large numbers and disorganization also made their service there nearly impossible. It is possible, of course, that the number of Levites available to serve in the Temple was significantly reduced by the purge Josiah effected among the Levites who had performed foreign rites during the reign of Manasseh (2 Kings 23:20). Other priests were ineligible for some unexplained reason, and deprived of the privilege of serving in the Temple (2 Kings 23:9). Those who escaped assassination and demotion were relegated to minor posts in the Temple cultus — probably such jobs as overseeing the sacrificial supplies, the collection of fees, and cleaning up the blood and gore.

A Royal Monopoly

Before the Deuteronomic reformation the only meat eaten was customarily that from a sacrificial offering properly slain by the village Levite. After the Deuteronomic revolution slaughtering for consumption of meat in the home was permitted, but all animals to be slain for religious purposes were taken to Jerusalem for the proper enactment of the ritual. Only unblemished animals could be used (Deut. 17:1). It was practically impossible to drive an ox or to carry a sheep from a distant village to Jerusalem without marring it. The ox would loose weight on the drive and the carried sheep might be bruised or cut. A rule had to be enacted that permitted the sale of a perfect animal in the home town and the money earned from the sale put to the purchase of an unblemished one in Jerusalem. Obviously the person who owned the herds near Jerusalem from which perfect animals were selected could become wealthy from that business. The only person eligible for such a lucrative business was, of course, King Josiah himself. He operated the monopoly on sacrificial animals. Like Solomon and Jehoshaphat who monopolized the Arabian and East African trade, Josiah found the Temple animal trade a reliable source of private income.

Before the Deuteronomic reformation Passover was celebrated privately in families. The lamb was roasted over an open fire and eaten as the climactic event of the seven-day festival. It was a joyous gathering of family and relatives, similar to America's Thanksgiving, when the clan expressed symbolically its loyalty to Yahweh. Josiah changed all that. Under penalty of fine and perhaps death all males were required to offer the Passover sacrifice in Jerusalem (Deut. 16:5–8). From a delightful family ceremony, Passover was transformed into a formal national celebration. From a simple ceremony of roasted sheep (Exod. 12:8) under a Palestinian spring sky, it was made to fulfill an obligation to a national cultus with boiled meat in the crush of a crowded Temple court (Deut. 16:7).

Josiah had an eye not only for making money but also for controlling his male population. By requiring all men to appear in Jerusalem three times a year Josiah's constabulary could keep an eye on potential rebels. It is doubtful that the law of appearance three times annually in Jerusalem was enforceable, but it was a convenient law to have in case a citizen fell afoul of the establishment.

The Synagogue
The requirement of worshipping Yahweh only in the Temple may have created the synagogue, an institution unexpected and unwished for by the Deuteronomic reformers. Traditional Judaism affirms that the synagogue originated in Moses' day. Some scholars believe, however, that it was a civic organization for the administration of community life, especially jurisprudence, in Israel beyond the walls of Samaria. The institution was carried with the Israelites when they were enslaved by the Assyrian army in 722 B.C. Others claim that the synagogue originated in the Babylonian captivity, when Jews were permitted to live in colonies in the cities of the Tigris-Euphrates Valley. It is possible, on the other hand, that the synagogue grew in reaction to the Deuteronomic requirement of worshipping only in the Jerusalem Temple. It seems reasonable that when ceremonies as important to villagers as Passover and the Feast of Booths were taken from them, and their priests deprived of an ancient and honored rite, something would be substituted. The synagogue compensated for the loss of religious ceremonies without which the ancient Judean village could not survive. In a poetic description of the destruction of the Temple, the line "they burned all the meeting places of God in the land" seems to report the devastation of houses of worship other than the Temple (Ps. 74:8).[19]

Deuteronomy became to exilic Jews their single most important book. But it was not the sole source of religious inspiration during Josiah's rule. Nahum and Habakkuk were prophets whose small scrolls were significant enough to be retained alongside the great Deuteronomy scroll.

The Book of Nahum
Nahum's short lines, vigorous descriptions, and gloating mood can be appreciated best if read aloud. Its literary style and religious affirmations, even though not the finest among prophetic works, should be given serious study.

As the book of Nahum now stands it is composed of several short poems; whether they are all by one author is impossible to decide. In all likelihood they were the work of one man, but the title shows

[19] See "Synagogue," in George A. Buttrick, ed., *The Interpreter's Dictionary of the Bible*, R–Z (New York: Abingdon Press, 1962), pp. 476–91.

Palaces of Nineveh as conceived by an artist accompanying
Austen Layard during his excavations in the 1840's.

that two compositions were united to form the single book. One
contained the oracle against Nineveh. The other held the vision of
Nahum, the Elkoshite. The editor of the book worked rather slop-
pily when he combined the two books. After disentangling the
mixture in Nahum 1:1 – 2:2 the remainder is easily read.

The poet's vision of Yahweh is found at Nahum 1:2, 3b–6, 8. Verses
3a and 7 should be eliminated as marginal glosses that were added
to the text by a scribe copying the manuscript onto a fresh scroll.
These little passages reverse the mood of the whole poem.

An oracle on Judah's salvation is found at Nahum 1:12–13, 2:1–2
(which should follow 1:13), and 1:15. By putting these verses together one has a poem proclaiming the end of Judah's harassment
by foreigners, a call to renewed vigor and defense, the good news
of peace, the festivals celebrated, and the renewal of religious
ceremonies.

Two oracles against Nineveh should be read next. The first is 1:9–
11, 14, in which a plot against Yahweh is punished. This oracle
is so general in tone that it may not have been against Nineveh,
but its placement in the context of a poem describing Nineveh's
fall makes it probable. The second is 3:1–17 in which a woe against
Nineveh is pronounced, and a destruction of that city as great as
the sacking of Thebes in 663 B.C. is expected.

The poem describing the battle of Nineveh should now be read (2:3–13). In this varicolored account of the battle one is on the scene with the poet. One sees the flashing chariots, the dazed defenders, the prisoners hustled away, the flood gates opened, the massive destruction and desolation. This vivid description may have come from the pen of one who had seen the fight in progress.

The final short poem is an ironic dirge sung by Assyria's former vassals over the once haughty city (Nah. 3:18–19).

The Historical Situation in Nahum

The book of Nahum was written during the latter years of Assyria's domination of the ancient Near East. Two historical references give us the earliest and the latest possible dates for its composition: the destruction of Thebes by Asshurbanapal in 663 B.C. and the defeat of Nineveh in 612 B.C. The oracles against Nineveh probably were given about the time that Asshurbanapal died. The destruction of Thebes was still a fresh memory, and perhaps Judean soldiers who had served in the Assyrian army proudly recounted that grim story. The psalm and the oracle of Judah's salvation may have been sung as the vindication of the prophet's previous denunciations.[20]

The psalm and oracles were joined and read at a religious ceremony rejoicing over the destruction of Nineveh (Nah. 1:15). Its pattern of theophany, oracles against a foreign nation, and the song of Judah's salvation, fits the type of cultic hymns found in use during the Deuteronomic reform.[21]

Religious Affirmations of Nahum

Yahweh was pictured as the Lord of nature who used the overwhelming storm, devastating famine, earthquake, and volcano (Nah. 1:6) as instruments of punishment for His enemies. He also destroyed His enemies by war (Nah. 2:3–13). His favorite nation was Israel which he would restore to majesty (Nah. 2:2). Nahum saw history under Yahweh fashioned on a moral base. Assyria had long ravaged the nations of the Near East. The savagery with which it had displaced whole populations, and its rapacious greed in draining the treasuries of vassal nations and provinces, would be ended by one gigantic deathblow to its capital. Cruel treatment of subject nations was inevitably punished. But it wasn't solely the evil against Yahweh's favorite nation that was subject to punish-

[20] Artur Weiser, *The Old Testament: Its Formation and Development*, trans. Dorothea M. Barton (New York: Association Press, 1961), p. 257.
[21] See Psalm 18:31–50.

ment. All the nations had been abused, and so all shared the sense of relief which came with the fall of Nineveh (Nah. 3:19). To this extent Yahweh was Lord of Israel and of all people.

Indirectly, Nahum was a rebuke of all militarism. No other nation of the ancient Near East used its army with such ruthless abandon as did Assyria. Innocent citizens as well as incurable rebels were treated with the same cruel ferocity. The rather objective portrayal of the sack of Nineveh neither gloated on the city's disaster nor diminished the horrors of war. But it vividly recounted what inevitably happened to a nation whose major interest had been imperial domination of weaker people. Nahum's moral sensitivity proclaimed the end of the military state.

Habakkuk's Dialogue With Yahweh The first part of the book of Habakkuk is a literary form seen for the first time in our study of prophetic literature. It is a dialogue between the prophet and Yahweh. A second part presents the typical prophetic woes, and a third a theophany of Yahweh in nature. Literary analysis will clarify their relations to each other and provide a clear historical perspective.

The dialogue part of Habakkuk is 1:1 – 2:4. It opens with the prophet's complaint to Yahweh that violence, wrongs, and injustice have abounded for too long (Hab. 1:2–4). Yahweh replies by commanding Habakkuk to look to the Chaldeans for an answer to his complaints. That dread and terrible nation has mounted an offensive that will sweep "the wicked" before it (Hab. 1:5–11). Habakkuk then asks Yahweh if the cure which He has prescribed is not worse than the sickness. How can Judah survive so terrible an army when it just barely survived under the Assyrians? Habakkuk will watch from his tower although he is not convinced (Hab. 1:12 – 2:1). Yahweh replies that Habakkuk should state his position plainly, so that all can see it. The vindication of Yahweh's promises of relief from Assyrian domination may be slow in coming, but "it will surely come." The righteous may continue to live by his steadfast faith in Yahweh's promises (Hab. 2:2–4).

The second part contains six woes (Hab. 2:5–20). Although only five appear in the present text, just a slight change at 2:5 is needed to make that verse read as a typical prophetic woe. The Hebrew word for wine is spelled יַיִן. The Hebrew word for woe is הוֹי. By lengthening the second letter, a *yodh*, to a *waw*, and dropping the final letter, a *nun*, the word for "woe" is derived.[22]

---

[22] Hebrew reads from right to left.

Thus the first line of verse 5 might have read "woe to the treacherous (the robber)." These six woes were pronounced as judgments upon the neo-Babylonian empire if it became powerful and arrogant as was the Assyrian empire. Some scholars have difficulty in recognizing all these woes as pronounced against a nation when five of them seem individualistic in tone (Hab. 2:5, 2:6–7, 2:9–10, 2:15, 2:19).[23] The prophets, however, were especially adept at personifying nations as individuals, and this seems to be a typical case of personification. The prophet chanted the woes against the neo-Babylonians for Yahweh, and they served to remind both Judah and the new empire that God ruled over all. Two short passages show an editor's hand. Habakkuk 2:6a should be eliminated from the prophet's original woes, as should 2:18. This last verse is redundant, but if it is kept, it should follow verse 19. The woes end with the prophet's assurance that Yahweh keeps His place in the Temple. That is enough to strike the peoples of the world dumb (Hab. 2:20).

The third part of the book is a psalm (ch. 3). Scholars have often counted this passage as a post-exilic addition to the original work.[24] There are three bits of evidence sufficient, perhaps, to prove its origination with Habakkuk. *First,* the theme is the same as that in 1:1–2:4: hope that Yahweh will soon end an alien's oppression of His people. *Second,* the enemy is known uniformly as "the wicked" (Hab. 1:4, 13, 3:13). *Third,* the emphasis upon visual perception is found throughout. The prophet "saw" the oracle of God (Hab. 1:1). Yahweh orders Habakkuk to "Look among the nations, and see" (Hab. 1:5). Habakkuk "looked for" an answer to his complaint (Hab. 2:1), and Yahweh orders the vision written (Hab. 2:2). The entire psalm deals with the visual perception of Yahweh's power, and what happens physically to the prophet for having seen Him (Hab. 3:16).[25] These arguments are not, of course, conclusive. Two notes about the psalm's use with stringed instruments does not prove that the psalm belonged to a temple hymnal and was transferred to the end of the book of Habakkuk (Hab. 3:1, 19). Habakkuk may have been a member of the Temple cultus, and may have composed this psalm in response to his personal encounter with Yahweh as he sought clarity on Judah's role in international events (See Hab. 2:20). Some scholars argue that the psalm was not original to Habakkuk because it is not found in the Habakkuk Scroll from

[23] See Norman K. Gottwald, *All the Kingdoms of the Earth* (New York: Harper & Row, 1964), pp. 234–5.
[24] See Charles L. Taylor, Jr., "Habakkuk," in George A. Buttrick, ed., *The Interpreter's Bible,* Vol. VI, (New York: Abingdon Press, 1955), p. 996.
[25] The reading "and thy work, O Lord, do I see" (Hab. 3:2) is preferable to "and thy work, O Lord, do I fear." See Otto Eissfeldt, *The Old Testament: An Introduction,* trans. Peter R. Ackroyd (New York: Harper & Row, 1965), p. 421.

the library of Qumran.[26] This argument is inconclusive, since the Qumran scribes picked passages from the Old Testament upon which to make their commentaries, using only what was congenial to their theology. If one places 3:2–19 after 2:4, where it fits nicely as a response to the vision vouchsafed to Habakkuk, the psalm becomes a part of the dialogue.

The Historical Situation in Habakkuk

Habakkuk and Nahum were active about the same time: the end of the 7th century B.C. The Assyrian empire was collapsing, and the neo-Babylonian empire had made a bid for world power. The woes were directed against Assyria, therefore they were spoken before Nineveh fell. The Babylonians had shown their muscle upon Assurbanapal's death. Habakkuk, therefore, rode the same stream of history in which Zephaniah, the Deuteronomists and Nahum rode.

Habakkuk's Religious Affirmations

The prophet had a religious experience of such magnitude as to leave him physically weak. He visualized himself in conversation with Yahweh. He heard the woes pronounced upon an arrogant, rising military power. He had a vision of Yahweh's eventual battle with the proud nation. He was reduced to trembling and unsteady step (Hab. 3:16). But, he was not unnerved. His experience with God had given him patience and courage, and he was all the more able to rejoice in the Lord his God. Even though crops failed, and herds were taken away, he would praise God who was his strength, quietly waiting for the "day of trouble" to come upon the invader (3:17–19, 16).

Habakkuk, like other prophets, felt himself personally involved in world politics. His spirit agonized over evils given wings by empires which relentlessly ground helpless peoples underfoot. Habakkuk's vision of evil was narrower than that of Amos and Isaiah, for he saw all evil as coming from enemies outside the nation. His vision convinced him, though, that only when evil is chastised by God Himself will righteousness reign in the world.

Psalms of the Deuteronomic Period

The Deuteronomic rebellion gave Judah some unsettled, exciting, and dangerous days. The Temple symbolized the independence of Judah, as Yahweh alone was worshipped there and figures of alien gods were dumped upon the trash pile. Psalms 61, 63, 93, and 121 typify hymns chanted as the Temple revived its vitality.

[26]The community which produced the so-called Dead Sea Scrolls.

Psalm 61　Psalm 61 represents an occasion when trouble was brewing. It needs one slight adjustment to make it read more evenly. Place verse 8 after verse 5, so that the lines about vows stand together. If this is done the structure of the poem is modified slightly: the first stanza (Ps. 61:1–2a) has four lines; the second stanza (Ps. 61:2b–3) has four lines; the third stanza has only two lines (Ps. 61:4); the fourth stanza has four lines (Ps. 61:5, 8); and the last stanza (Ps. 61:6–7) has four lines. Notice the balance in the poem's structure, created by the image of the tent and wings which, of course, refers to the Temple in Jerusalem (Ps. 61:4). That is the pivotal point of the poem. Does this literary point focus upon a historical fact: that the cult of Yahweh alone was performed in the Temple? Psalm 61 gives no explicit information about the occasion of its composition. The poet felt the difficulties personally as the king was called upon to deal with the trouble. Some scholars see in the line "from the end of the earth I call to thee" (Ps. 61:2), an allusion to a person in exile who prays toward the Temple. That is probably a metaphorical statement, however, by which the psalmist meant the lowest point in human experience where life ends and death begins.[27] What occasion called forth that painful cry while petitioning for extension of the king's life? Was it the day Josiah left Jerusalem to face Pharaoh Neco in diplomatic or military exchange at Megiddo? If so, some perceptive psalmist knew that all was not well behind the facade of religious revival and nationalistic fervor.

Psalm 63　Psalm 63 represents the period of Deuteronomic revival just as Psalm 61 did. The reference to the king appears editorial to many scholars, but if it is seen in the light of Josiah's official Yahwism it should be taken as authentic (Ps. 63:11). This psalm needs major readjustment, however, to render it smooth reading. After the psalm opens with a plea for God's presence (Ps. 63:1–2), the poet too quickly turns to a mood of spiritual satisfaction. It seems that verses 6–8 should follow upon the opening two verses. If the psalm is rearranged as follows, the lines move evenly in thought and mood: verses 1–2, 6–8, 4, 5, 3, 9–10, 11.[28] When the Psalm is read this way the psalmist expresses his desire for God's presence because experiences of Him in the Temple service have given a sense of new confidence. Assurances of praise to God throughout the psalmist's life are promised (Ps. 63:4, 5, 3). Then, the cause of the poet's anguish is revealed as stemming from enemies who seek to destroy his life. God's power will deliver them to the sword. The final verse turns to the king's rejoicing for his utter trust in God's power.

[27] See Psalms 18:5 and 69:2 for metaphors having that meaning.
[28] See W. Steward McCullough, "Psalms," in Buttrick, ed., *The Interpreter's Bible,* Vol. IV, p. 327.

No allusions give a clue to the historical conditions behind this psalm. The reference to the king gives it a pre-exilic dating if those words are not editorial additions. This psalm reflects the Deuteronomic revolution before the death of King Josiah.

Psalm 93

Psalm 93 typifies those psalms which are called enthronement hymns (Ps. 47, 96, 97, 98, and 99). Ancient Near Eastern kings ruled by divine election. Israel, upon settling in Canaan, borrowed extensively from Canaanite literature, legal practices, and social customs, so that Israelite kings customarily were officially enthroned at the New Year. The enthronement symbolized that they served as Yahweh's regents. Ideally they brought success, prosperity, peace, and justice to the nation. Poets were commissioned to chant songs of praise to Yahweh as the ceremony of kingship was underway in the Temple, much as Benjamin Britten was assigned the task of composing the music for the coronation of Queen Elizabeth or Robert Frost was commissioned to read a poem at the inauguration of John F. Kennedy as President of the United States. The image of Yahweh reigning as a monarch would be the proper one for such an occasion.[29]

Psalm 93 leaves no trace of its historical associations. It is likely, though, that this was the type of psalm composed for the celebration commemorating the covenant Josiah made between Yahweh and the people (2 Kings 23:1–3). This was the beginning of a new life for Judah, and as such it received extensive ceremonial treatment.

Psalm 121

Psalm 121 is a beautiful poem familiar to almost everyone. It was a hymn chanted by pilgrims as they wound their way to the top of the most important mountain in Palestine, Mount Zion. Its qualities of rhythm, vitality, and strong emotion assign it a place in the hymns of world literature that shall not be replaced. Note that the vivid language of this psalm makes it a poetic gem: hills, help, foot, sleep, shade, smite, going out, coming in. How vital these words are! These words carried the poet's affirmations in clean, sharp, visual accents. The title of the psalm gives us the only clue to its historical associations. It was named "A Song of Ascents." The Hebrew words, however, might be translated "a song *to* those who ascend." Who was the unnamed poet, and under what conditions did he sing this hymn? Some scholars suggest that he was a Jew of the Babylonian exile looking westward across the flat plains of Babylon toward his beloved Palestine. His spirit ached for the steep and rugged

[29] See Henri Frankfort, *Kingship and the Gods* (Chicago: University of Chicago Press, 1948), pp. 231–48, 313–33.

terrain of his homeland. Such an interpretation disregards the language of travel implicit in the song. Others have thought that the hills were a source of dismay and fear to the poet, because in them lingered robbers, wild animals, and precipitous trails. He looked beyond the hills to Yahweh who could spare him such perilous adventures. The Hebrew expression "to lift up the eyes unto," however, invariably conveyed a mood of pleasure, hope, and expectation, as in other Old Testament passages. Some interpreters think the poet had cast his eyes up to the various hills upon which were situated the polytheistic worship rites of his ancestors. He did not know which hill to ascend because each was the locality of some ancestral cult. He was bewildered by the many religions. Yet, the whole psalm shows no evidence of polytheism or the remnants of Canaanite cultic practices.

The poem is best understood when one pictures in his mind a group of Yahwists pilgrimaging to Jerusalem during Passover or Succoth (Feast of Booths). They have come in sight of the hill upon which that city stood, and the leader burst into this spontaneous song of confidence and hope. There on those craggy, bare hills were the sharp outlines of Jerusalem's buildings. Psalm 121 was no chant of a religious aesthete or one who finds his religious values in a worship of nature. It was the glad response of one who knew that his journey was nearly finished; the goal of the high country of Jerusalem was within sight. God, who had created the everlasting hills and established His Temple upon them, had been and would continue to be his keeper and protector.

The pilgrim may have experienced serious doubt about the value of his journey, but with the sacred hill in sight these doubts withered away. Although at some moments on his journey the pilgrim felt that Yahweh had gone away and left him alone, or had fallen asleep on his job as Eternal Watchman, he was sure now that nothing could have made his foot slip from the pilgrim's path, and that Yahweh had not fallen asleep on the job. The poet turned to another image, the image of a protective covering. Here the language is most graphic as he expressed how Yahweh is a shield or a shade on his right hand. The image is carefully ambiguous in Hebrew. A *shomer* in biblical Hebrew is a guard of the type afforded by a shield. A military shield, however, protected the left side best, the hand in which it was held, and exposed the right side from which the warrior wielded his sword or spear. A *shomer* may also be a protective covering from the heat of the sun. An expressive paraphrase might be "the Lord is a shelter on the south side of the mountain." This is the exposed area where drought strikes first, and the roots of grass and shrubs are withered by the blast of stifling heat and drying winds. In Hebrew the right hand is the "south side," but even in this vulnerable area, Yahweh was like a shade casting His shadow in a dry and thirsty land.

The sun, although generally productive and beneficial, can at times be a destroyer. So, too, the moon in ancient days was believed to be the source of tragedy and evil. Even the English "lunatic" suggests that demonic powers originate in the moon.

Thus, the poet affirmed his confident belief that despite the past experiences of doubt and question when Yahweh seemed asleep, or the route was tortuous on the sun-drenched side of the mountain, or the cool night travel exposed one to the darts of the moon demon, Yahweh would keep all evil at bay and would preserve the life of the faithful pilgrim on his way to the Temple in Jerusalem.

The glories of the Deuteronomic revolution faded overnight. Josiah's death brought to an end the hope that Judah under Yahweh would revive the Davidic empire. Egypt and Babylon faced each other over Judah's land, and that little nation was helpless in the grip of the two great world powers. The prophets of Judah's last years, Jeremiah and Ezekiel, and spokesmen for Yahweh in the exile, too, will illumine in the next chapter changes in belief and practice that took place among Yahweh's people.

**Through
Calamity to
Hope**

The years between 621 and 538 B.C. witnessed radical alterations
of literary and cultural emphasis among the people of the Old Testament. During those years the people of Judah became known as
Jews, and the foundations of Judaism were laid down for half a
millennium.[1] The prophetic movement ran its course and changed
direction. The religion of the book triumphed over the religion of
Yahweh's direct revelation. When Judah was nearly destroyed by
Babylon, Yahwism ceased as a state religion. Responsibility for the
Jewish community in exile was thrust upon prophets and poets. It
was an awesome, tragic, and creative time.

**The Book of
Jeremiah**

The book of Jeremiah is a complex assortment of literary types.
Jeremiah's authentic words are mixed with narratives and oracles
from generations long after he lived. The book went through several
revisions, and those who finally published the book rather care-
lessly permitted repetitions to remain in the text. Notice the passages that receive verbatim coverage twice:

Jeremiah   6:12–15 at 8:10–12
          10:12–16 at 51:15–19
          16:14–15 at 23:7–8
          23:5–6 at 33:15–16
          23:19–20 at 30:23–24
          30:10–11 at 46:27–28.

Core Readings

Jeremiah 1–45
Lamentations
Ezekiel 1–24, 27–28
Leviticus 17–26
Isaiah 40–55
Psalms 73, 74, 87, 89, 102, 132, 137

---

[1]The term "Jew" may correctly be used after the fall of Jerusalem. The term came
into English from Latin which had taken it from Greek. The Hebrew *yehudi* signifies
a person from or living in the Babylonian province of Judah.

This example alerts one to the literary problems which must be solved before a clear picture of Jeremiah's place in history and his special religious affirmations comes through.

The book of Jeremiah divides into four sections:

1. *Chapters 1–25*   Oracles and dramatic actions against Judah;
2. *Chapters 26–45*   Narratives about Jeremiah, except for chapters 30 and 31;
3. *Chapters 46–51*   Oracles against foreign nations;
4. *Chapter 52*   Material copied from 2 Kings 24:18 — 25:30, exclusive of 2 Kings 25:22–26 for which Jeremiah 52:28–30 has been substituted.

Two Scrolls

The study of the book of Jeremiah may begin at chapter 36. It is odd to start study of a book at its middle, but Jeremiah's banishment from the Temple, his dependence upon a secretary, the reaction of people and nobility to his proclamations, and King Jehoiakim's brutal destruction of Jeremiah's scroll, lead to an important literary discovery. The clue is in the statement: "Then Jeremiah took another scroll and gave it to Baruch the scribe, the son of Neriah, who wrote on it at the dictation of Jeremiah all the words of the scroll which Jehoiakim, king of Judah, had burned in the fire; *and many similar words were added to them*" (Jer. 36:32). Can we find the original book which Baruch read to the people in the Temple, to the nobles in the secretary's room, and to the king in his winter quarters? It is probable that we can. Three characteristics of Jeremiah's original scroll are inferred from chapter 36. *First*, that the book was short enough to be read orally three times in one day; *second*, that it dealt with threats to the people of Judah and to the king on account of immorality and their idolatry; and *third*, that it contained pronouncements uttered by Jeremiah before 605 B.C., the fourth year of Jehoiakim (609–598 B.C.). These three characteristics are satisfied only by material found in Jeremiah 1–25, although not all of the oracles from that section can so qualify. Let us analyze those chapters in order to discover the original scroll from which Baruch read.

Jeremiah's Original Scroll

Jeremiah's call to prophethood, with its two visions of almond stem and boiling pot, probably began the scroll (Jer. 1:4–17).[2] He castigated Judah for its worship of nature gods and goddesses with their

[2] Notice the pun on the Hebrew words. *Shaqed* and *shoqed* sound alike but have utterly different meanings. Hebrew poets consciously created such play on words. *Shaqed* means "almond tree" and *shoqed* means "watching."

fertility rites (Jer. 3:6–13). He delivered a sermon which criticized citizens for reliance upon Temple cult rather than justice; for serving the goddess Astarte, Queen of Heaven; and for dependence upon huge sacrifices rather than obeying the word of God delivered by the prophets (Jer. 7:1–8:3). Jeremiah lamented the abandonment of the covenant (Jer. 11:6–17). In parables about a loincloth and a wine jar he exposed the pride of Jerusalem's residents (Jer. 13:1–14). Jeremiah explained his refusal to marry, to go to funerals, or to attend feasts, as signs that in a short time all social life in Jerusalem would be destroyed (Jer. 16:1–13). He lamented desecration of the Sabbath (Jer. 17:19–27). The parable of the misshapen pot was a sign that Judah's morals were bent (Jer. 18:5–12). He threatened Judean kings in the drama of the broken flask (Jer. 19:3–13). He encouraged a Judean king to righteousness, probably Josiah (Jer. 22:1–5). Jeremiah proclaimed destruction of the people of Judah at the hands of Nebuchadnezzar (Jer. 25:1–13). These passages have a prose style similar to the sermons in Deuteronomy. Some scholars assign them to the Deuteronomic editor of the book of Jeremiah, but others persuasively hold that the first person style used consistently in these sections ties them together and accords with the description of the scroll in chapter 36.[3]

Jeremiah's Expanded Scroll

After Jehoiakim had burned Jeremiah's original scroll, Jeremiah dictated the same sermons "and many similar words were added to them." What was the nature of the expanded scroll? In looking for passages with "similar words" but concerned with events after 605 B.C., the following passages can be selected:

Jeremiah 24	The vision of edible figs and rotten figs likened respectively to the deportees of Babylon and the people left in Jerusalem;
27	The drama of the ox yoke which Jeremiah wore to symbolize Nebuchadnezzar's supremacy;
32:6–28	The narrative of Jeremiah's purchase of a field to symbolize Judah's recovery from attack;
35	The contrast of Judah's faithlessness and the Rechabites' loyalty.

This expanded scroll took the form of personal testimonials to events and conditions of national dimensions to which the prophet reacted publicly. The first and second editions of Jeremiah's scroll formed the nucleus around which his other works were collected.

[3] Otto Eissfeldt, *The Old Testament: An Introduction*, trans. Peter R. Ackroyd (New York: Harper & Row, 1965), p. 352.

Poems Jeremiah composed poems as well as memoirs. Poems from his early years were collected according to content and style. Several of these poems alluded to the evil from the north (Jer. 4:6, 5:15, 6:1, 6:22, 13:20). Others contrasted the purity of religion in Israel's wilderness period with the corruption in Judah during Jeremiah's days (Jer. 2:2–19). Some bewailed the absence of justice, and the persistence of idolatry in Jerusalem (Jer. 5:1–9). Judah's pride, typified by the king and queen, was the subject of another (Jer. 13:15–27). It is now impossible to locate every poem historically, but it is probable that the following poems fall between 626 and 605 B.C.:

Jeremiah 2:2 – 3:5	Jeremiah 10:17–22
3:14 – 4:18	13:15–17, 20–27
4:23 – 6:30	15:5–9
8:4–17	16:19–21
9:2–11	18:13–17

One poem concerning a drought is especially interesting (Jer. 14:1 – 15:3). It was a lament used in a liturgical setting as the people prayed to Yahweh for rain. It has the structure of an antiphonal hymn. First Jeremiah describes the conditions resulting from the drought (Jer. 14:2–6). Then the people acknowledge their guilt, recognizing the justness of God's action (Jer. 14:7–9). But Yahweh rejects their confession (Jer. 14:10). After that Yahweh and Jeremiah hold a dialogue about the false promises offered by priests and prophets (Jer. 14:11–18). The people then respond with anguished questions about Yahweh's rejection of Judah (Jer. 14:19–22). Finally, Yahweh replies that His decision is irrevocable; pestilence, sword, famine, and captivity are Judah's lot (Jer. 15:1–3). Unfortunately there is no clue to dating this antiphonal liturgy.

Oracles A group of titled oracles deals with the kings of Judah (Jer. 13:18–19, 21:11 – 23:8). Each oracle is introduced by a title, such as "Say to the king," "To the house of the king of Judah," "concerning the king." Jeremiah speaks encouraging words to Josiah, calling upon him to bring justice to the land and promising destruction if he fails in that task (Jer. 21:11 – 22:9). He consigns Jehoahaz, whom Neco took captive, to perpetual imprisonment in Egypt (Jer. 22:10–12). Other oracles treat Jehoiakim, Jehoiachin, and Zedekiah, and contrast them with the Messiah king (cf. Isa. 11:1–9) who will "execute justice and righteousness in the land" (Jer. 23:5–8).

A second set of oracles with titles concerns the prophets (Jer. 23:9–40). Although there are no precise historical references, it is likely that these oracles were delivered early in Jeremiah's career. Chapters 26–29, however, show Jeremiah in serious conflict with priests and prophets during the reigns of Jehoiakim and Zedekiah, that is, from 608 to 587 B.C. It is not unlikely, therefore, that his whole career was beset by such antagonism.

Confessions Jeremiah's "confessions" constitute a unique element in his work. These exhibit his personal attitudes toward his prophetic vocation, toward his enemies, and toward God. Perhaps these were composed while he was in prison. They probably were not known to anyone before his death, but when Baruch began compiling Jeremiah's work, he came across them. Their exquisite style and sensitive mood strike the modern reader as dramatically as they did Baruch. It is to Baruch's everlasting credit that he preserved the world's first "confessions." One should study these with special care. They are:

Jeremiah 10:23–25	Dependence upon God.
11:18–20	Vengeance on those who plan my death.
12:1–6	Why do the wicked prosper?
15:10–21	All men curse me.
17:12–18	Vindictiveness.
18:19–23	Appeal for vengeance.
20:7–18	Cursed be the day on which I was born.

Laments Jeremiah's laments have a quality marking them as a cross between the prophetic oracle and the funeral song. The danger is future, but the lament depicts the tragedy as having already taken place. The following passages may be so identified:

Jeremiah 4:19–22	I writhe in pain.
8:18 – 9:1	My grief is beyond healing.
9:17–22	Call for the mourners.
12:7–13	Forsaken my house.

The exceptional pathos of these songs gives an insight into Jeremiah's personality. Perhaps no other writer in the Old Testament was capable of such a variety of moods: from personal vindictiveness to poignant grief at the suffering of the Judeans and the anticipated destruction of Jerusalem.

Biography The second major section of the book of Jeremiah is chapters 26–45. This section is composed of narratives about Jeremiah, except for chapters 30–31 and those passages which belong to the first two editions of Jeremiah's scroll (Jer. 24, 27, 32:6–28, 35). These narratives constituted Baruch's abbreviated biography of Jeremiah. They covered the years between 608 and 581 B.C. Unfortunately, as they now stand they are not in chronological order, but a little manipulation gives one a short biography of Jeremiah.

608 B.C.	*Ch. 26*	Jeremiah's life threatened by a mob rallied by priests and prophets.
605 B.C.	*Ch. 36*	Jeremiah's scroll destroyed by Jehoiakim.
597 B.C.	*20:1–6*	Pashur puts Jeremiah in stocks.
	Ch. 29	Jeremiah writes a letter to exiles in Babylon.
593 B.C.	*Ch. 28*	drama of the iron yoke.
587 B.C.	*32:1–5, 29–44, 33:1–26*	Jeremiah put in prison.
	Ch. 34	slaves in Jerusalem set free.
	37:3–21	Jeremiah suspected of desertion to Babylonians.
	39:15–18	the Ethiopian servant saved.
	Ch. 38	the Ethiopian servant rescues Jeremiah from a cistern.
586 B.C.	*40:1–6*	Jeremiah a Babylonian prisoner, but released.
581 B.C.	*40:7–43:7*	Gedaliah assassinated, and Jeremiah taken hostage to Egypt.

Through twenty crucial years leading to Jerusalem's collapse Jeremiah struggled to be heard. Opposed by royalty, priests, prophets, nobility, and common people, his message was seldom heeded. Mobbed, put in stocks, beaten, held prisoner, dumped in a cistern, and hustled off as a hostage to Egypt, his physical stamina must have been magnificent. One must decide for himself whether Jeremiah was stupidly stubborn or gallantly courageous in proclaiming his message of cooperation with Babylonian foreign policy.

The Book of Consolation

A little book embedded in Baruch's biography of Jeremiah is found at chapters 30–31. This is sometimes called *the little book of consolation*. It was originally a collection of sayings with themes of comfort and restoration binding them together. The earliest poem in this collection probably is Jeremiah 31:2–22, which announces the restoration of Israel. Jeremiah approved Josiah's expansionist policies after 626 B.C. as he annexed the Assyrian province of Samaria. The authentic poems in chapter 30 are probably verses 5–7, 12–17, and 23–24, but in these the element of comfort is small indeed. Jeremiah 31:23–34, which contains Jeremiah's basic thought, is probably the work of a later compiler.

The third section of the book of Jeremiah consists of oracles against foreign nations (Jer. 46–51). Most scholars believe these oracles consist of a few authentic lines by Jeremiah which have been enlarged upon by the Deuteronomic editors.

The fourth section of the book of Jeremiah is chapter 52. It was taken from the book of 2 Kings to serve two purposes: first, to conclude the collection of Jeremiah's work with a section on hope, since the little book of consolation had been attached to the biographical section; second, to serve as an introduction to the book of Lamentations. The description of Jerusalem's collapse would fittingly set the mood for the dirges over the city and its citizens.

Extensive additions were made to the book of Jeremiah by the Deuteronomic editors. Their orientation is noticeable throughout with their characteristic words, phrases, and religious affirmations.

The Historical Situation in Jeremiah

Dating Jeremiah's call to be a prophet determines in large measure where one begins a discussion of the historical background of the book. Scholars have tendered three different dates for the beginning of Jeremiah's work. First, most scholars believe that Jeremiah 1:1–4 is a reliable passage stating explicitly that Jeremiah became a prophet in 626 B.C.[4] This dating means that Jeremiah was at work throughout Josiah's religious and political reformation. Chapter 11 is quoted to show that he supported the imposition of the Deuteronomic Code throughout Judah. Jeremiah 1:13 is quoted to prove that his prophetic vocation began as a result of the Scythian invasion which overran Palestine in that year. The enemy from the north (Jer. 4:6, 5:15, 6:1, 22) was, presumably, those terrifying horsemen. The oracles in Jeremiah 21:11–14 and 22:1–10 show that Jeremiah encouraged Josiah in his efforts to establish justice and charity in the land. Jeremiah said of Josiah:

> *you are as Gilead to me,*
> *as the summit of Lebanon.* (Jer. 22:6a)

Certainly Jeremiah would not have given Jehoahaz, Jehoiakim, Jehoiachin, or Zedekiah such approbation. Jeremiah's frequent denunciations of Jerusalem expressed his disillusionment with the Deuteronomic revolution because it placed emphasis upon cult and sacrifice rather than upon moral responsibility (Jer. 2:1 – 8:3).

[4] See also Jeremiah 25:3.

Another date claimed for Jeremiah's call is early in the reign of Jehoiakim (609–598 B.C.). The arguments set forth for this date claim that the "thirteenth year of Josiah's reign" (Jer. 1:2) is the birthdate of Jeremiah; the enemy from the north were Babylonians, not Scythians; Jeremiah actually opposed the Deuteronomic reforms; no passage can be dated with assurance to the reign of Josiah. What national calamity would force a sensitive man to be a prophet? The death of King Josiah would do that.[5]

A third proposed date for Jeremiah's call is 616 B.C. This date is suggested because if the year 626 B.C. is adopted it requires a silent period in Jeremiah's career following his oracles about the Scythians. Furthermore, if he supported the Deuteronomic reform he was a rather inept prophet who stirred himself to public activity after eighteen years of inaction. By changing the reading of Jeremiah 1:2 from "thirteenth year" to "twenty-third year of Josiah," and by using Jeremiah 25:3 as the original form from which Jeremiah 1:2 was incorrectly copied, one arrives at 616 B.C. as the date of his call.[6]

Most Probable Date for Jeremiah's Call

My discussion of historical background uses the year 626 B.C. as the most probable date for the opening of Jeremiah's career. He was born at Anathoth, about two miles north of Jerusalem. His father was a priest, but nowhere is there a claim that he, too, was one. He was quite young when he began his career; so young that he was reluctant to accept the call (Jer. 1:6–8). After Yahweh had touched his mouth, as Isaiah had been touched, he felt strong enough to be set

> over nations and over kingdoms,
> to pluck up and to break down,
> to destroy and to overthrow,
> to build and to plant. (Jer. 1:10)

Denunciation of the Nature Religions

The first years of Jeremiah's work were devoted to denouncing the nature religions to which the Judeans responded so enthusiastically. Typical of earlier prophets, he used the threat of an invading army as punishment if religious corruption were not overthrown. Whether he had in mind the Scythians, the Babylonians, or the Medes is not

[5] See James Philip Hyatt, "Jeremiah," in George A. Buttrick, ed., *The Interpreter's Bible*, Vol. V (New York: Abingdon Press, 1955), pp. 779–80.
[6] See Norman K. Gottwald, *All the Kingdoms of the Earth* (New York: Harper & Row, 1964), pp. 241–2.

clear. It was enough that the last powerful Assyrian monarch, Asshurbanapal, had died in 633 B.C., and the air of revolt in the empire was acrid with intrigue and rebellion. Political instability in the ancient Near East always meant villages overrun and cities destroyed. As Amos had announced exile for Israel long before Tiglath-pileser III had reestablished the Assyrian empire in 745 B.C., so Jeremiah proclaimed destruction upon Judah long before the Medes and Babylonians had full possession of Assyrian provinces.

There is some evidence that Jeremiah supported Josiah's religious revolution. Chapter 11 narrates that Jeremiah spoke the "words of this covenant," and that may refer to the Deuteronomic Code. He met strenuous opposition to many of its policies even in his home town, where some men tried to kill him (Jer. 11:21–23). Although he saw in Josiah possibilities of a great ruler, he was not fooled by external appearances (Jer. 21:11, 22:1–4, 6). The Deuteronomic Code was sound, but its full application was nearly impossible. There is no reason why the oracles in chapters 5 and 6 should not be assigned to the period of Josiah's rule. Even under that pious king, it is doubtful that justice and truth prevailed in Jerusalem (Jer. 5:1–3). It is equally doubtful that all Canaanite and Assyrian rites were abolished (Jer. 5:7–11). It is likely that his great Temple sermon was preached when the Deuteronomic reform was in full swing (Jer. 7:1–8:3). The words of Jeremiah 13:1–11 were concerned with Jerusalem's pride. That pride was highest when the Temple had been fully returned to the cult of Yahweh and Josiah rode tall in the saddle during his conquests. It is doubtful that such words were necessary after the death of Josiah, when Jehoiakim was a full vassal of Pharaoh Neco. Jeremiah probably accepted the values of love and charity implicit in the Deuteronomic Code, but he had plenty to criticize, and through Josiah's life time he did just that.

The Prophet's Falling-Out with King Jehoiakim

Jehoahaz (609 B.C.) was elevated to kingship following Josiah's death, but Neco rejected the new king's nationalistic policy. After a conference at Riblah in Syria, Neco bound Jehoahaz and sent him, a prisoner, to Egypt (2 Kings 23:31–33). Neco preferred Jehoiakim on the throne, because of his pro-Egyptian attitude. At the coronation of Jehoiakim Jeremiah preached a sermon in the court of the Temple (Jer. 26:1–6, 7:1–8:3). The people were stirred to anger rather than repentance, and they mobbed the prophet. Some noblemen and landowners rescued him from the rioters, permitted him to finish his sermon, and then freed him because they found him guilty of no crime. They drew upon the history of another prophet for a precedent (Jer. 26:16–19). He was freed, but a decree was issued barring him from the Temple (Jer. 36:5).

THE EXILE

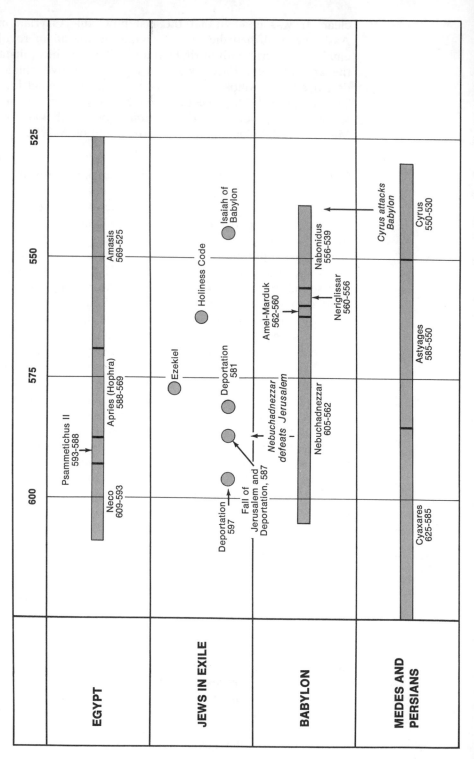

Jehoiakim had guessed wrong. Egypt's power in Palestine and Syria withered away after Neco was defeated at Carchemish in 605 B.C. while supporting the remnants of Assyrian rule. Babylonian control of previously held Egyptian territory was almost automatic as Neco retreated with his battered army to safety along the Nile. Palestine's new overlord was Nebuchadnezzar (605–562 B.C.). Judah's king switched his allegiance to Nebuchadnezzar. After this Jehoiakim and Jeremiah became bitter enemies. Jeremiah accused the king of expanding the royal residence using slave labor and some tricky business deal (Jer. 22:10–17). He spoke libelous words about Jehoiakim to the effect that he would have a burial as royal as an ass's (Jer. 22:18–19).

Babylon's victory at Carchemish had a profound effect upon Jeremiah, and this event may have been the stimulus behind the transcription of his oracles to a scroll. This was the document read to and destroyed by Jehoiakim. Jeremiah counseled total submission to Babylon, and Jehoiakim submitted, but always with an eye to revolt when the moment might present itself. That moment came after three years (2 Kings 24:1). Nebuchadnezzar sent mercenary troops mobilized from Syria, Moab, and Ammon to harass Judah, but Jehoiakim's surprising strength drove off those invaders in 602 B.C., and it was not until 598 B.C. that Nebuchadnezzar turned to punish his western rebel. He attacked Jerusalem in that year. Jehoiakim died while the siege was on and Jehoiachin, an eighteen-year-old, ruled for three months before he surrendered the city. He was deported to Babylon with his palace entourage where he lived in house arrest for thirty-seven years, finally to be released by Amel-Marduk (Evil-Merodach, Jer. 52:31–34). The deportation of artisans, political leaders, military personnel, and priests was a serious blow to the economy of Jerusalem, for this punitive attack seemed directed against Jerusalem itself rather than against the villages and towns of Judah.

Nebuchadnezzar permitted Judah to continue as a vassal nation with Zedekiah as king. Great hunks of land were cut from Judah's possessions especially in the Negeb (Jer. 13:18–19). This land was probably given to the Edomites whose expansion west and north was already in progress. Judah's nationalistic fervor was not quelled by Babylon's punitive action of 598 B.C. By 593 B.C. Hananiah prophesied that Judah would be restored to its former independence with Jehoiachin on the throne again (Jer. 28:1–4). Zedekiah took these pronouncements seriously despite Jeremiah's insistence that they were false (Jer. 28:5–9). In Babylon two prophets agitated the exiles to rebellion, but Jeremiah claimed that Babylon's power

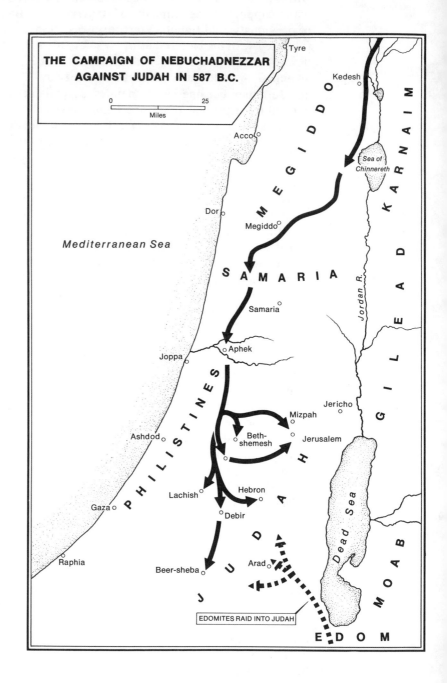

THE CAMPAIGN OF NEBUCHADNEZZAR
AGAINST JUDAH IN 587 B.C.

0   25
Miles

Tyre

Kedesh

MEGIDDO

KARNAIM

Acco

Sea of
Chinnereth

Dor

Megiddo

Mediterranean Sea

SAMARIA

Samaria

Jordan R.

Aphek

Joppa

GILEAD

Jericho

Mizpah

Beth-
shemesh

Jerusalem

PHILISTINES

Ashdod

JUDAH

Dead Sea

Lachish

Hebron

Gaza

Debir

MOAB

Raphia

Beer-sheba

Arad

EDOMITES RAID INTO JUDAH

JUDAH

EDOM

would last seventy years (Jer. 29:21; 25:11–12). He saw no reason for the exiles to look for repatriation before two generations had come and gone. He wrote a letter to this effect to the exiles in Babylon (Jer. 29). Nebuchadnezzar's policy of deportation was designed to so weaken Judean leadership that it could not connive with Egypt any longer, but the revolutionary party in Judah was still strong.

Zedekiah was an indecisive king, and the promises of politicians from other vassal states finally convinced him to revolt. Why not? Nebuchadnezzar was fighting a war against Elam in 595 B.C. (Jer. 49: 34–38), and a revolt in Babylon's home army in 594 B.C. brought civil war. Therefore a conference of leaders of small states was held in Jerusalem, which Jeremiah addressed counseling against their anticipated revolt (Jer. 27:1–7). A new king in Egypt, Psammetichus II (593–588 B.C.), continued Neco's policy of interference in Palestine. Everything seemed prepared for Zedekiah's break with Nebuchadnezzar. He made the tragic move. The Old Testament does not inform us how long it took Nebuchadnezzar to respond to Zedekiah's challenge, but by 588 B.C. Babylonian troops, not mercenaries this time, appeared in Judah. They overran the open country and besieged the fortified cities.

The Siege of Lachish Excavations at Lachish have unearthed bits of pottery with Hebrew script on them. Eighteen of these fragments inscribed with black ink are referred to as the Lachish letters. Three of these letters reported the Babylonian attack from the Judean point of view. Hoshaiah was a soldier at an outpost beyond Lachish, and Ya'osh, his superior, was in the city itself. These letters reveal the desperate condition of Judean defenses. One letter reported that "we give heed to the signals of Lachish . . . we can no longer see the (signals) of Azekah." Azekah had probably capitulated to Babylonian troops. The situation in Jerusalem was reported. There were those "who weaken the hands of the land and the city." This may refer to Jere-

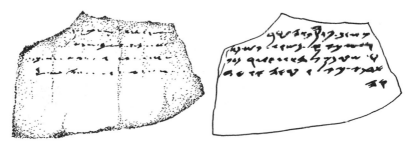

Ostracon IV of the Lachish letters. This is the one reporting that the signals of Azekah could no longer be seen.

miah (Jer. 38:4). A Jewish officer named Kebaryahu "went down to Egypt." The seige of Jerusalem was not so tight, apparently, as to limit escape through the lines if carefully undertaken. No information on Kebaryahu's mission was given, but we can imagine that he went to Egypt to beg for aid and to give intelligence information in preparation for Egypt's attack on Babylon's army (Jer. 37:5).[7]

The siege was tight enough, though, to force a food shortage on the city. To allow the wealthy to escape the duties of feeding their slaves Zedekiah decreed that all slaves should be released (Jer. 34:8–10). When the Babylonian army moved south to meet the pharaoh's attack, the nobility retrieved their former slaves and put them in bondage again (Jer. 34:11–16). This indicates that Egypt's attack was vigorous enough to make Jerusalemites think the war was over, but they were premature. The besieging army returned. This time it stayed until the job was finished. In August of 587 B.C. — the ninth day of the fourth month of Zedekiah's eleventh year — sappers undermined the wall (2 Kings 25:2–3). Zedekiah fled toward Ammon, but he was captured near Jericho.

Jeremiah's Counsel of Surrender

During the siege Jeremiah actively campaigned for surrender to Nebuchadnezzar. His treasonous speech was curtailed by imprisonment. While he was there a cousin, Hanamel, came to him offering to sell a field in Anathoth. Family duty may have demanded the purchase, but Jeremiah used the occasion to proclaim Judah's survival and his family's continued possession of the field (Jer. 32:6–15). This story may seem out of chronological order since the siege was in full swing. Jeremiah may have had some money, however, and Hanamel may have known a merchant who had hoarded food to sell for ready cash. On another occasion, when the siege had been lifted and he had been released from prison, Jeremiah set out for Anathoth to look over his new land. He was apprehended at the Benjamin Gate by a sentry. Accused of desertion, his explanation of visiting his new property fell on unbelieving ears, and he was thrown into a dungeon (Jer. 37:11–15). Zedekiah expected a hopeful word from Jeremiah after this incident, and he took him out of prison for an audience. All Jeremiah could announce was that Zedekiah would be taken prisoner by the king of Babylon.

King Zedekiah ordered Jeremiah released from the dungeon and given a ration of bread daily, but kept under house arrest. Jeremiah's continual pronouncements of the fall and destruction of the city

---

[7] "Lachish," in George A. Buttrick, ed., *The Interpreter's Dictionary of the Bible*, K–Q (New York: Abingdon Press, 1962), pp. 56–7. Hereafter cited as *IDB*.

seriously undermined the defenders' morale. Three men, presumably officials, took him from the court of the guard and put him into an empty cistern. There they hoped he would die of thirst. Ebed-melech, a black slave, appealed to Zedekiah, and the king gave orders to draw him out. The description of the rescue shows that Jeremiah was weak from hunger and thirst, but no amount of threats and punishment could draw from the prophet any words of hope for the royal family and the city (Jer. 38:1–13).

The Fall of Jerusalem to Babylon

The end was horrible. Shops and homes were looted. Government buildings and the Temple were set afire. Able-bodied citizens of reputation were readied for deportation to Babylon. Those who resisted were cut down by swords. Jeremiah was among the prisoners. When his identity became known to the Babylonian guard, Jeremiah was given the option of special treatment on the journey to Babylon or staying as advisor to Gedaliah, Nebuchadnezzar's appointee as governor of the province of Judah. He chose to stay in Judah and became attached to the occupation government at Mizpah, a city which the Babylonians had spared (Jer. 40:1–6). Jeremiah continued his belief in subservience to Babylon while Judah struggled for economic recovery (Jer. 40:7–12). But some patriots saw the occupation government as a breach of trust. A certain Ishmael, who numbered among the nobility, pretended friendship for Gedaliah but then assassinated him as they sat at table (Jer. 41:1–3). He may have hoped to restore rulership to the Davidic family or he may have done his deed in a fit of revenge against the Jews who had collaborated with the conquerors. At any rate, he ran amok taking men, women, and children captives, massacred eighty men who were on their way to Jerusalem to bewail the destruction of the Temple, and started a small civil war (Jer. 41:1–18). Nebuchadnezzar ordered a reprisal raid for Ishmael's senseless behavior. Although the culprit escaped to the Ammonites, the Babylonians took nearly a thousand captives in reprisal (Jer. 52:30).

Jeremiah Is Taken to Egypt

Before the Babylonian punitive force had arrived at Mizpah, Johanan ben Kareah asked Jeremiah whether he and those who had helped him pursue Ishmael should stay in Judah or flee to Egypt. Jeremiah counseled them to remain because the king of Babylon would be merciful toward Johanan's action in trying to avenge Gedaliah's death (Jer. 42:1–17). Johanan was not convinced by the prophet. He took Jeremiah as hostage for safe passage on his flight, and sped away to Egypt (Jer. 43:1–7). The last words of Jeremiah were spoken in Egypt as he prophesied again against the corrupt religious rites practiced by Jews in their adopted land (Jer. 44:11–30).

Jeremiah had given himself to Judah for four decades. He had stood almost alone against the intrigues of small politicians and the on-slaught of giant nations. He seemed to be a traitor, and yet his in-sight from the perspective of history was the correct one. Few in Jerusalem believed that Babylonian power was so great. Why they held this erroneous view is difficult to understand. Perhaps it had to do with Babylon's deportation policies. Whereas the Assyrians had wiped out whole nations by dislocating their populations, the Babylonians preferred to keep national groups on their land in their normal way of life. The Assyrian army was a ruthless vehicle of destruction; the Babylonians showed more restraint and respect for civilian populations. Assyria turned former states into provinces and drained their economies; Babylon prefered a policy of rule by local kings and princes so long as tribute was paid. Assyria insisted on incorporation of its national deities in the cultic rites of a con-quered nation; Babylon held this idea in theory but practiced it negligibly. These seeming weaknesses of the Babylonians, after the traditions of cruelty and gore associated with Assyrian conquest, may have lulled Judean leaders into false evaluation of Babylon's strength. Jeremiah seemed to sense the power that lay untapped beneath the supposed weakness. But he also knew that the Baby-lonians gave a conquered nation certain freedoms and encouraged local economy and self-rule. He was correct in his assessments, but he left unconvinced those who could have learned from him.

Jeremiah's sensitive personality was revealed most clearly in his "Confessions." Through these superb reflections one gets a glimpse into his emotions and unspoken thoughts. He revealed himself also through his dramatic, and often stubborn, behavior. He heard and saw the world about him with a vividness which eludes most men. His imagination, for instance, enabled him to call up word pictures that penetrate the mind's eye.

> *How can I pardon you?*
> > *Your children have forsaken me,*
> > *and have sworn by those who are no gods.*
> *When I fed them to the full,*
> > *they committed adultery*
> > *and trooped to the house of harlots.*
> *They were well-fed lusty stallions,*
> > *each neighing for his neighbor's wife.* (Jer. 5:7–8)

His inner life was just as vividly portrayed.

O Lord, thou hast deceived me,
and I was decieved;
thou art stronger than I,
and thou has prevailed.
I have become a laughingstock all the day;
every one mocks me.
For whenever I speak, I cry out,
I shout, "Violence and destruction!"
For the word of the Lord has become for me
a reproach and derision all day long.
If I say, "I will not mention him,
or speak any more in his name,"
there is in my heart as it were a burning fire
shut up in my bones,
and I am weary with holding it in,
and I cannot. (Jer. 20:7–9)

It was just such sensitivity that dramatized his religious affirmations.

In addition to his sensitivity he proved to be exceedingly bold and courageous. Some might call it stubbornness. But whatever name one gives it, he looked upon himself as "a fortified wall of bronze" against whom the unheeding and disobedient Judeans "shall not prevail" (Jer. 15:20). This attitude was borne out in actual behavior. He was beaten and left to exposure in the stocks (Jer. 20:1–2). A mob rioted against him, but he stood his ground (Jer. 26:7–15). He was put in a dungeon (Jer. 37:16), thrown into a muddy cistern (Jer. 38:6), and as an old man forced to flee to Egypt (Jer. 43:5–7). Through all this he never complained publicly about his treatment. He faced his commission with stoic fortitude.

His sensitivity coupled with physical and intellectual courage produced some of the finest religious expressions in the Old Testament. Jeremiah's beliefs were not put in systematic order, but his conceptions of the nature of God, of the individual, of sin, cult, and expectations of the future, reveal a prodigious mind.

Jeremiah's Concept of the Nature of God   Jeremiah believed, like every faithful Hebrew, that Yahweh was the creator of the world and the sustainer of nature (Jer. 27:5, 5:22). He believed also that Yahweh directed human destiny by guiding the Hebrews into "a plentiful land," and continued to direct history on a larger scale by using a nation from the north to bring His judgment on Jerusalem (Jer. 2:4–7, 4:6, 5:15, 6:1, 22, 13:20). Even

Nebuchadnezzar was Yahweh's servant, not as a worshipper but as one who did the Lord's work even though unknowingly (Jer. 25:9). Despite His power in history and His rigorous demands for justice, Yahweh was as well a God of love. Images of husband and father invoke the mood of filial love, and His faithfulness sprang from His love (Jer. 2:2, 3:19–20, 31:3). Two splendid images typify Jeremiah's appreciation of Yahweh. He was like "a fountain of living water." What an image to use when drought had decimated Judah in Jeremiah's lifetime! (Jer. 2:13, 17:13, 14:1–10). Another image likened Yahweh to a potter, who was sovereign and independent of the material he molded (Jer. 18:1–11). But God's immensity was not fathomable. Creator, sustainer, judge, father, husband, living water, potter; each said something about God which left out that element which frightens and offends a man. Yahweh brought loneliness, pain, dismay (Jer. 15:17–18). He made Jeremiah feel deceived, weak, alienated (Jer. 20:7–10). Jeremiah never assumed that he knew the totality of God.

Jeremiah's View of God and the Individual

Jeremiah expressed special concern for the individual. His intimacy with the unfathomable God revealed that God was concerned for persons. Jeremiah's insights laid the foundation for the "I will put my law within them, and I will write it upon their hearts; and I will be their God, and they shall be my people" (Jer. 31:27–40). Here the inner quality of religious experience is stressed, rather than external cult. Here is fellowship with God rather than the placating of a tempestuous Being. Here is trust in a dependable God rather than the fearing of a capricious tyrant (Jer. 31:35–36). Here is the universality of the sacred rather than a little spot of earth and rock on which a temple was founded (Jer. 31:38–40). Jeremiah introduced belief in the validity of individual religious experience, but he did not abandon Israel's concept of community. He served the state as official prophet for forty years, always believing that *the nation* was chosen for responsibility. The covenant was a contract between God and nation, and although Yahweh had to destroy Israel, he would reestablish his covenant "with the house of Israel." Belief in the nation as a corporate personality did not give way to belief in the individual Israelite as the important social entity until a generation after Jeremiah, but he had planted the seed that later came to bloom.

Jeremiah's Condemnation of Sin

Idolatrous worship struck Jeremiah as ridiculous, but even so it was a tragic sin against Yahweh (Jer. 2:26–27). He pictured the strongest lye soap as powerless to wash away Israel's guilt incurred through nature worship (Jer. 2:20–22). But deepest concern was over sins against persons. If such sins had been committed out of ignorance perhaps Jeremiah would have been less condemnatory, but they were deliberate, planned, and vicious. Wicked men lurked like fowlers, setting traps to catch the innocent. They grew rich from their treachery and deceit (Jer. 5:26–29). But Jeremiah did not see the wicked as only a certain class of men in Judah. All men were wicked because their hearts were deceitful. Sin was written on their hearts with a diamond-studded iron pen (Jer. 17:1, 23:26, 9:4–5). Prophets, whose responsibility was to warn the people of their deceit, were involved in the same wickedness (Jer. 23:14–15). Whether Jeremiah believed that deceit, wickedness, and treachery were inborn or not is unclear, but he certainly saw persons as choosing to do evil rather than good, and capable of goodness if they so chose (Jer. 2:10–12, 13:23). To choose goodness over evil, a man needed to repent. The Hebrew words evoke a mood of action. The word *naham*, for instance, pictured Yahweh as relenting or unrelenting of decisions made or actions taken (Jer. 18:8, 4:28, 15:6). The word *shub* gives the image of a complete about face (Jer. 3:12–14, 4:1–4). Repentance was not a mental process conducted in abstraction, but a complete reversal of a way of life. It meant rejecting old ways and taking on new ways with no regretful afterthoughts.

The Prophet and the Cult

Jeremiah descended from a priestly family, but at no place is there clear evidence that he performed the duties of a priest. It seems rather that he abhorred the priestly vocation, at least the way it was performed in Jerusalem in his lifetime. He held that confidence placed in the benefits of ritual behavior and costly offerings was misplaced (Jer. 6:20). Redundant invocations were no more beneficial than rich sacrifices (Jer. 7:4). Yahweh asked for justice, charity, decency, and a tender heart (Jer. 11:15, 7:5–7, 21–22). Although he despised the ghastly spectacle of animals with slit throats, carcasses burned to carbon, and food piled before the altar, there are several places in the book where his words reflect the imagery of cultic rites. He sang, for example, a lament in the language and meter of the psalms (Jer. 9:17–22). The song originated in Zion, where victories and disasters were commemorated ritually. The dirge over the drought was rendered in antiphonal form, as if Jeremiah had composed the hymn to be sung with leading voices and choir.[8] A hymn promising Judah eventual victory is found at Jeremiah 30: 10–11. A hymn from Jeremiah's pen recalled Israel's past and looked forward to the future, when Zion would issue forth in singing and celebrating (Jer. 31:2–14). These lovely hymns show that Jeremiah was comfortable in the forms of ritual ceremonies. It is really impossible to picture a Hebrew prophet who did not participate in some way in the national cult of Israel.

[8] See p. 306.

Jeremiah's View of the Future

How did the future look to Jeremiah? In Jeremiah's letter to Jewish exiles in Babylon he opposed revolution, preparation for returning to Palestine, and hopes for immediate independence (Jer. 29). He did hold out a promise, however, that after seventy years of Babylonian rule, the Jewish exiles would be able to return to their land. Yahweh had "plans for welfare and not for evil, to give you a future and a hope" (Jer. 29:11). The prediction of a seventy-year rule by Babylon may have been prophecy after the fact inserted by a scribe of the post-exilic period. This explanation seems unlikely since no really significant seventy-year period clearly existed during Babylonian domination of Palestine and Syria. Jeremiah may have meant that Babylonian hegemony would last over the Near East for a relatively long time; perhaps the ideal lifespan, three-score and ten years (Ps. 90:10). He may have had in mind a mythological number that had special significance in the Babylonian view of the cosmos.[9] Whatever the precise meaning of the seventy years, he looked for a return to normal life in Palestine with abundance of crops and decent living (Jer. 31:10–14).

The Meaning of the Purchase of the Field

The story of Jeremiah's purchase of his cousin's field at Anathoth violates all reason (Jer. 32:1–15). Jerusalem was under siege. Jeremiah was in prison. Jerusalem's farm land had been ravaged by Nebuchadnezzar's quartermaster corps. Farmers had been driven off the land. What future could Judah expect under such black skies? But Jeremiah made a special show of signing the deed of purchase. He charged Baruch to seal the deed in an earthenware jar to preserve it for the future. He was confident that "houses and vineyards shall again be bought in this land" (Jer. 32:15).

Jeremiah believed that Yahweh's love of Israel would be the force behind restoration. Israel would not become strong suddenly among the nations and send them crashing to defeat. No heavenly army would appear to thrash Israel's enemies, providing a ring of protection while home and lands were rebuilt. Restoration would come after Babylon's pride had run its course. Then the hearts of Jews would respond to Yahweh who gives strength to persevere in decency in daily business (Jer. 31:2–22).

Only one authentic passage from Jeremiah's hand spoke about a messiah, the "branch of David" (Jer. 23:5–6). This reference is set among some exceedingly caustic condemnations of Judah's kings from Jehoahaz to Zedekiah. Jeremiah claimed that Yahweh would "raise up for David a righteous Branch, and he shall reign as king and deal wisely." This king was no heavenly being. He was

---

[9] See Gottwald, *All the Kingdoms of the Earth*, pp. 265–6.

from the Davidic royal line, but he stood in utter contrast to Judah's recent kings whose foreign and domestic policies had been so wide of the mark set forth in the covenant Josiah had sealed between Yahweh and the people (2 Kings 23:1–3).

Jeremiah said nothing about rebuilding the Temple, reorganizing a priestly caste, or restoring the stately processions to honor Israel's future kings. He considered those things destroyed, and so much the better. The religious attitude took expression, not in sumptuous ritual or pompous patronage of kings, but in each man's love of God and charitable service to his fellows.

Jeremiah stood at the cataclysmic point of Judean history. It is amazing that he was so well-balanced and stable in a world crumbling into dust about him. A man with so sensitive a nature might collapse into hopelessness. But his message held expectations of a change of heart that would bring new life through love of Yahweh and one's neighbor.

The Book of Lamentations

The book of Lamentations recalls how complete was Judah's degradation. It is an extended funeral chant. As literature, dirges have a long and honorable history in the ancient Near East, and practices in the Near East today testify to the agelong custom of publicly mourning tragedy and death. While mourners carry the casket through the narrow streets in complete silence, at home the women chant woeful songs and speak eulogies through several uninterrupted hours.[10] The prototype of the public dirge in the Old Testament was David's lament over the death of Saul (1 Sam. 1:17–27). Such a chant was a spontaneous reaction to a tragic situation. The book of Lamentations, on the other hand, was a conscious effort to create literature. Its conscious literary quality is shown in the acrostic pattern applied to the first four chapters. Each stanza begins its opening word with successive letters of the Hebrew alphabet. Therefore each of the five chapters has twenty-two stanzas. Chapter five is not an acrostic poem, but it still has twenty-two lines showing that it was designed with the acrostic ideal in mind.[11]

Lamentations as a Traditional Funeral Dirge

The traditional funeral lament was created from two themes: praise of the past achievements of the deceased, and a lament for the present death. The book of Lamentations is patterned on that

[10] In some modern Christian Arab villages the death of a distinguished unmarried woman will bring forth, following the dirges, joyful singing accompanied by the village band to symbolize the union of the unbetrothed to Christ in heaven.
[11] One has to read a Hebrew text to notice the acrostic form. Other examples of acrostic poetry are: Psalms 9 and 10 combined, 25, 34.

form. It praises Jerusalem's past glories — she was a great city among the nations with her palaces and strongholds, her feasts and sabbaths, her perfection of beauty and joy of all the earth (Lam. 1:1, 2:1, 5, 6, 15). The city's gold and holy stones, her precious sons, her dainties, her nobility, and her compassionate women, displayed her wealth (Lam. 4:1, 2, 5, 7, 10). But those things had all been destroyed, and the dirge bewailed the loss of those glories.

Literary analysis of the book of Lamentations may be brief. The five chapters divide evenly into five separate poems. One characteristic of the book is the way in which the songs volley back and forth the voices of the speakers. The first poem opens in the third person singular. At Lamentations 1:12 the voice changes to the first person singular. At verse 17 the third person singular appears again only to revert to the first person singular in the next verse so to the end of the chapter. Chapter two is all in the third person. Chapter three opens in the first person, and changes to third person at verse 25. This voice is interrupted by the first person *plural* at verse 40, to which it returns at verse 49. Chapter four opens in the third person, moves to first person plural at verse 17, and returns to its original voice for the last two stanzas. The final chapter is in the first person plural throughout.

Authorship of the Book of Lamentations

Some scholars have tried to find different authors for the various chapters, pointing out that chapters one, two, and four are from the same pen, chapter three another individual's lament, and chapter five by still another poet. The use of two or three voices in each of the poems, except the last, would suggest that if separate authors are to be looked for they would logically follow the patterns separating the several voices. The acrostic form and the unity of theme, however, argue against breaking up the chapters. Some scholars argue that chapter three is different from the other poems because it is a personal lament. The reference to the speaker as "I am the man" surely does not prove that this poem is a personal lament, since the ancients often personalized their cities and nations by the masculine gender (Lam. 3:1). Some scholars believe that chapters two, four, and five were written shortly after the destruction of Jerusalem because they so vividly describe the dreadful scenes, and that chapters one and three were composed much later. These chapters use stereotyped metaphors and phrases.[12] It is more likely that the five poems come from a single poet and that they were written anytime after the fall of Jerusalem and before Cyrus' decree in 538 B.C. that Jews could return to Palestine. Furthermore, since

[12] See Eissfeldt, *The Old Testament: An Introduction,* p. 501

women were the chief mourners, it is possible that the book was the work of a feminine poet. In Babylon the Jews used the book in their grim ceremony commemorating the fall of Jerusalem.[13]

The book of Lamentations is a sincere, poignant, and powerful expression of a people's grief. No other composition of this magnitude and excellence has survived from the literature of the ancient Near East. Its imagery, in which the people's grief is likened to that of a grieving widow (Lam. 1 and 2), a persecuted prophet (Lam. 3), and a precious ornament (Lam. 4) is enough to make its reading a necessity for students of the Old Testament. Although tradition has assigned the composition to Jeremiah, the Hebrew name is only " 'ekah" and the lament does not employ the style or vocabulary of Jeremiah's sorrowing songs (See 2 Chron. 35:25).

Its historical background lies in the years between 581 and 538 B.C., which will be discussed in the section treating Ezekiel.

The religious attitude reflects the prophetic view, that Israel was doomed because the nation broke faith with Yahweh. Prospects for restoration are anticipated sometimes in an unspecified future (Lam. 5:19-22).[14]

The Book of Ezekiel The mystical visions, dramatic action, and extended allegories in the book of Ezekiel provide a diversity of literary types that challenge one's imagination and ingenuity. This book is a complex literary puzzle. The personality of Ezekiel is both fascinating and disturbing. Those who use psychological language tab him a neurotic.[15] Others treat him as an accomplished actor. The changes in personality and message could be interpreted as the work of different persons.

As the book now stands it has four parts:

1. *Chapters 1–24*   Oracles against Judah and Jerusalem;
2. *Chapters 25–32*   Oracles against foreign nations;

[13] Such national reminders are used today. The United States now commemorates Pearl Harbor Day, and the Armenian community in Lebanon annually reminds itself of the massacre of two million Armenians by the Turks in 1903.
[14] See Norman K. Gottwald, *Studies in the Book of Lamentations* (London: S C M Press, 1954), for a treatment of Lamentations. I have drawn upon some of his main emphases.
[15] A. T. Boisen, *Exploration of the Inner World* (New York: Harper & Row, 1962); J. Lindblom, *Prophecy in Ancient Israel* (Philadelphia: Fortress Press, 1963).

3. *Chapters 33–39* Oracles on the restoration of Israel and Judah (except ch. 35, an oracle against Mount Seir);
4. *Chapters 40–48* The new temple.

A Literary Guess

Scholars have been divided widely in their estimates of how much of the book of Ezekiel is the authentic work of the prophet and how much is later additions and editorializing. There is, in fact, such diversity of opinion that no literary analysis will be greeted with wholehearted approval. Estimates have ranged from about one-fifth of the book to practically the total work being from Ezekiel's own hand. The following literary analysis is a workable guess.

Dating the Books of Ezekiel

Ezekiel himself made the first collection of his oracles and memoirs, and dated them. They were oracles against Judah and Jerusalem. The first of these, the vision of Ezekiel's call to be a prophet, occurred on the fifth day of the fourth month of the fifth year after Jehoiachin's exile to Babylon (Ezek. 1:1–3:15). That was July 21, 592 B.C. The last one came to him on the tenth day of an unlisted month of the twenty-fifth year (Ezek. 40:1, that is, 572 B.C.).[16] Another series of dated oracles was against Tyre and Egypt. The opening oracle dates from the first day of an unlisted month of the eleventh year (Ezek. 26:1, that is, 586 B.C.). The last oracle against foreign nations was given in 570 B.C. (Ezek. 29:17). By studying the dates of this series of oracles it can be seen clearly that they do not stand now as they came from Ezekiel. The following examples show this. The date at Ezekiel 26:1 is 586 B.C., while that at Ezekiel 29:1 is 587 B.C. The two oracles against Egypt are reversed (compare Ezek. 32:1 and 32:17). The story of the fugitive's report that Jerusalem had fallen was originally one continuous story, although it is now reported at Ezekiel 24:26 and picked up again at Ezekiel 33:21. These examples prove that the oracles against nations in chapters 25–32 have been inserted in the midst of Ezekiel's original

---

[16] These passages constitute the original dated oracles and actions against Judah and Jerusalem:

5/5/592 B.C.	*1:1–3:15*	Ezekiel's call to be a prophet.
12/5/592 B.C.	*3:16a, Chs. 4 & 5*	Three actions symbolizing Jerusalem's fate.
5/6/591 B.C.	*Chs. 8–11*	Ezekiel's vision of idolatry in Jerusalem.
10/5/590 B.C.	*Ch. 20*	Ezekiel rejects plans for building a temple in exile.
10/10/588 B.C.	*Ch. 24*	Symbolic action and speeches the day the siege began.
5/10/585 B.C.	*33:21–22*	News of Jerusalem's fall reaches Ezekiel.
10/?/572 B.C.	*Chs. 40–48*	Ezekiel's vision of the new Jerusalem.

collection of oracles against Judah and Jerusalem, and in so doing they were put out of chronological order.[17]

Whereas the passages which have introductory dates deal with specific historical events and personal actions, the passages introduced by the phrase "The word of the Lord came to me" deal with general sayings and pronouncements. These have more editorial material than original sayings. At chapter 20 the pattern of dated oracles treating of specific historical conditions and of undated ones treating general sayings is broken. At this point the specific date, tenth day, fifth month, 590 B.C., is given, and yet no detailed narrative follows. Only oracles against sabbath-breaking and high places follows (Ezek. 20:8–44). What was the *specific event* which called forth the precise date? It was probably the day that elders of Israel came to Ezekiel asking for a temple and for other cultic rites while they were in exile. Ezekiel rejected the elders' plan, claiming that observation of rites would constitute sabbath-breaking, and that to build a high place would violate the integrity of the Jerusalem Temple. It is likely that chapters 40–48, the ideal temple, really belong after Ezekiel 20:44. The positive statement at 20:40–44, after an extensive negative argument, introduces a description of Israel's true worship when Yahweh shall return the people to Palestine.

Problematical Authorship of Undated Passages

There still remain many undated passages dotted among the dated ones, and these demand special study to determine if they belong to Ezekiel. Chapters 33–39 have often been treated as additions to Ezekiel's work, but the narrative of Ezekiel's freedom from dumbness indicates that a major change came over him after Jerusalem was destroyed (Ezek. 24:26, 33:21). He was no longer the harsh, bitter prophet. He became instead a pastor, dedicated to guiding his flock. This is the mood of chapters 33–39 (except chapter 35).

In summation: Ezekiel made two separate collections of his dated oracles, one about Judah and Jerusalem and a second against Tyre

---

[17]These were Ezekiel's original dated oracles against foreign nations:

12/10/587 B.C.	29:1–16	Oracle against the Pharaoh.
7/1/586 B.C.	20:20–26	Oracle against Egypt.
1/3/586 B.C.	31:1–18	Oracle against the Pharaoh.
1/?/586 B.C.	Ch. 26	Oracle against Tyre.
15/1/585 B.C.	32:17–32	Funeral dirge over the Pharaoh.
1/12/585 B.C.	32:1–16	Funeral dirge over the Pharaoh.
1/1/570 B.C.	29:17–21	Oracle that Nebuchadnezzar will defeat Egypt.

and Egypt. Ezekiel also uttered some oracles and performed some dramatics, which reached the printed page in autobiographical form. An editor combined these three authentic works with secondary materials, inserting the oracles against foreign nations into the body of the prophet's words against Judah and Jerusalem.[18]

The Historical Situation in Ezekiel

Ezekiel was a casualty of Babylon's war against Judah in 598–597 B.C. He was taken prisoner to Babylon. Being a priest, it is likely that he belonged to the Zadokite priesthood which controlled the Jerusalem Temple (Ezek. 1:2). Ezekiel preferred the Zadokite priests, and showed antagonism toward Levitical priests (Ezek. 40:46, 44:10–16). He received a prophetic call in 592 B.C. which he describes in a fantastic vision of creatures and chariots. The vision was so overwhelming that he fell upon his face, the first of several manifestations of physical response to psychic experience. Upon recovering his senses he knew that he had been ordained to carry Yahweh's message "to the people of Israel, to a nation of rebels" (Ezek. 2:3). The question immediately arises, did "a nation of rebels" mean the Jews in exile or those in Jerusalem? Did leaders of the Jews in Babylon really consider rebellion possible? Is it likely that he had in mind intrigues by Judean nobles while Zedekiah was a vassal of Nebuchadnezzar? This is a serious historical problem, needing a broader perspective before an answer may be forthcoming.

The End of Davidic Rule

The attacks against Jerusalem in 598 and 588 B.C. marked the end of a long historical process. Judah had lived in the shadow of the powerful Assyrian and Babylonian empires since the middle of the 8th century, but the defeat of Jerusalem was a special point in its history. A descendant of David had ruled in Jerusalem for over four hundred years, even though much of that time under vassalage to a foreign power. The destruction of Jerusalem ended the Davidic rule. Both Ark and Temple, those ancient symbols of the cult of Yahweh, were smashed. With those symbols gone it was an uphill pull to keep Yahwism alive even in Judah. How much harder where Jews lived exiled from their homeland!

There were several groups of exiles, and Jews were scattered from the Persian Gulf to the upper Nile River. Some exiles were deportees to Babylon in 597 B.C. Jehoiachin, his family, nobles, artisans,

---

[18]The foregoing depends greatly on Otto Eissfeldt's analysis of Ezekiel in *The Old Testament: An Introduction*, pp. 372–381. See Herbert G. May, "Ezekiel," in Buttrick, ed., *The Interpreter's Bible*, Vol. VI, pp. 45–51, for a substantially different analysis.

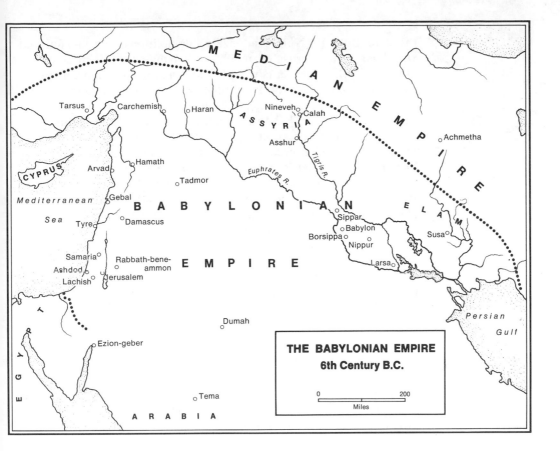

The following are labels on the map:

MEDIAN EMPIRE

Tarsus Carchemish Haran Nineveh Calah Achmetha
ASSYRIA
Asshur

CYPRUS Arvad Hamath
Mediterranean Gebal Tadmor Euphrates R. Tigris R.
Sea Tyre Damascus B A B Y L O N I A N E L A M
Samaria Rabbath-bene- E M P I R E Sippar
Ashdod ammon Borsippa Babylon Susa
Lachish Jerusalem Nippur
Larsa

Dumah Persian
Gulf

EGYPT Ezion-geber

THE BABYLONIAN EMPIRE
6th Century B.C.

0   200
Miles

Tema
A R A B I A

priests, and military leaders were marched overland to Babylon.
There they settled, hoping for Yahweh to return them to Jerusalem
where the Temple functioned and a Davidic king ruled. Jeremiah
ridiculed that hope, and Ezekiel expected the total destruction of
Jerusalem. Those exiles were deprived of traditional religious rites
because the Deuteronomic Code forbade the practice of Yahweh-
worship outside the Temple. Remember that the leaders who came
to Ezekiel asking about constructing a temple and renewing Yahwistic rites in Babylon were from the Israelite tribes long before
deported to Mesopotamia by the Assyrians (Ezek. 20:1). They had
no tradition of the centrality of the Jerusalem Temple.

Vassalage of Judah Jews left in Judah after the deportation of 597 B.C. continued as
vassals to Nebuchadnezzar. If the death of Josiah did not end the
vigor of the Deuteronomic revolution, the attack against Jerusalem
did. Idolatrous worship in the Temple (Ezek. 8:3–18), and instability in government revealed the cracked facade of Josiah's reforms.
Pro-Egyptian and pro-Babylonian parties battled for leadership of

the state. But after Nebuchadnezzar's demolition crews had finished with Lachish and Jerusalem in 587 B.C., no major towns stood intact. Only the lowliest peasants were left to farm the land, and commerce came to a standstill. Normal life halted while the conqueror cruelly "reeducated" the natives to the futility of revolt. Jews who escaped the carnage of war fled to Ammon and Moab. When fighting had ended, they returned hoping to recover their property and wanting to rebuild their shattered lives. Judah was administered as a Babylonian province after it went under as a state. Gedaliah was cited as "governor of the cities of Judah" (Jer. 40:5), but it is more likely that he was the province's financial officer rather than a governor (Jer. 40:5). Reference to vinedressers and plowmen indicates the lowly economic status of the region (2 Kings 25:12). A seal-impression recovered in the excavations at Lachish reading "Belonging to Gedaliah who is over the house" may have been the Gedaliah of Jeremiah 40. The title "over the house" would indicate his position as an officer responsible for financial affairs (cf. 2 Kings 15:5).[19]

The Babylonian Exile

After 586 B.C. exiles in Babylon had no land to look to, and no Temple to sustain their hopes. Thousands of captives trudged into Babylon slowly realizing that their nation had plunged to the depths of degradation. Since Jerusalem had fallen, Marduk and Ishtar of Babylon were stronger than Yahweh. Those who had never traveled beyond Judah saw how grand were Babylon's culture and religious practices as compared with Judah's. Excavations at Babylon by R. Koldewey, a German archaeologist, between 1898 and 1917, revealed the magnificent Ishtar Gate opening onto the Processional Way leading to the temple of the god Marduk. The reliefs of lions, bulls, and dragons carved on the gateway astonished and offended the Jewish deportees. Architectural remains suggest the wealth and pomp associated with official religion in Babylon. How many Jews gave up their belief in Yahweh in favor of Ishtar and Marduk we shall never know, but probably many did.

King Jehoiachin enjoyed the luxuries of Babylon. Taken with the captives of 597 B.C., he was given special privileges. Some clay tablets found in the ruins of Nebuchadnezzar's palace datable between 594 and 569 B.C. reveal the name of Jehoiachin on four of them. They dealt with food distributed to the king. The king's five sons were mentioned as being with him. These tablets confirm the biblical passage reporting how the king received a daily allowance all his life (2 Kings 25:30). It is probable that his private lands in

[19]John Gray, *Archaeology and the Old Testament World,* (New York: Harper Brothers, 1962), p. 181.

A reconstruction in the Berlin Museum of the Ishtar Gate of Babylon during the reign of Nebuchadnezzar. Through this gate the New Year's procession paraded.

Judah supplied him with a regular income, rather than that his income came from Nebuchadnezzar. Part of Gedaliah's job in Judah may have been to oversee cultivation of the king's property.[20] Excavations at Nippur, south of Babylon, have uncovered tablets with many Jewish names on them. These were for the most part business documents in which large firms reported their purchases and receipts. Although these tablets come from nearly a century after the opening of the exile, it is evident that many Jews gave up their own cultural associations in order to get by in a new land. Others among the Jewish deportees built homes, married, raised families, developed communities, and generally conducted life similar to the ways they had before (Jer. 29). They had frequent communication with friends in Palestine, as Ezekiel's prophecies show. Prisoners from Judah were thrown into contact with captives from other regions. Citizens of Philistia, Tyre, and Byblos, Elam, Media, and Persia were in daily contact with Jews, so that either Judean provincialism was more firmly embraced, or else Jews shed

[20] See André Parrot, *Babylon and the Old Testament* (New York: Philosophical Library, 1958), pp. 15–67, 110–11.

their self-consciousness and accepted the cosmopolitan life of Babylon. Clay tablets found in Nebuchadnezzar's palace list the names of persons from all those countries.[21]

Jews in Egypt

Many Jews fled to Egypt. Political leaders who had backed a pro-Egyptian policy, if they were fortunate enough to escape, went to the land of the Nile. Communities of Jews had been settled along the Nile River from the Delta to the island of Elephantine at the first cataract since the 7th century B.C. In these settlements Jews carried on a form of Yahwism, worshipping at temples to Yahu whose consort was Anatyahu, queen of heaven (Jer. 44). Egyptian Jews resisted attempts to reform their religious practices, and it seems doubtful that the steady influx of Judeans significantly changed the Jews already in voluntary exile in Egypt (Jer. 44:16–19).

Ezekiel's Prophecies in Jerusalem and Babylon

Ezekiel became a prophet in Babylon, from where he steadfastly advocated an anti-Egyptian, pro-Babylonian attitude much like Jeremiah's (Ezek. 30:20–26, 29:1–16). Some passages showing his pro-Babylonian stance report conditions existing at the time of his return to Palestine after 592 B.C. A little over a year after his initial vision, Ezekiel probably returned to Jerusalem. This is quite possible, as we know that Jeremiah sent letters by messenger to exiles in Babylon, and a messenger brought news of Jerusalem's fall to Ezekiel (Ezek. 24:26, 33:21). Other evidence accumulates as one looks at specific references. He sat among the elders of Judah after he had been told in his vision to speak to a nation of rebels (Ezek. 8:1, 2:3). He described the profanation of the Temple so vividly that it appears like an eyewitness account (Ezek. 8:5–16). While prophesying in the Temple he had an argument with Pelatiah. Later he saw Pelatiah die while he was prophesying against him (Ezek. 11:1–13). He acted out little dramas while dwelling in the midst of a rebellious house (Ezek. 12:1–16). Before the siege of Jerusalem began he did some pantomimes which would make no sense in the city of Babylon (Ezek. 4:1–3, 9–17, 5:1–12, 12:17–20). He knew the instant that Nebuchadnezzar began the siege of Jerusalem (Ezek. 24:1–2). The death of his wife symbolized the death of the Temple, "the delight of your eyes, and the desire of your soul," and the siege was on at the time she died (Ezek. 24–21).

Later, a messenger reported to Ezekiel while he was in Babylon that Jerusalem had surrendered (Ezek. 33:21–22). The question pops up, how did he get back to Babylon if he had been in Jerusalem during the siege? It is possible that after his wife's death, and it

[21] See Parrot, *Babylon and the Old Testament*, p. 113.

appears that she had not been deported in 597 B.C., he saw no reason for prophesying there. So, when the Babylonian army lifted its siege to meet Egypt's attack, he made the long journey to the Jewish colonies in Babylon.[22]

Oracles Against Tyre The oracles against Tyre are difficult to put into historical perspective, but they are superb poems (Ezek. chs. 26–28, 29:17–21). The book of Ezekiel cites two dates for those oracles. The first cites the year 587 B.C. as the date of Ezekiel's oracle against Tyre when an attack seemed imminent (Ezek. 26:1). The second gives the year 570 B.C., when a siege of Tyre produced no booty worth the cost of the war (Ezek. 29:17). Josephus mentioned a siege beginning in Nebuchadnezzar's seventh year (589 B.C.) which lasted thirteen years. If the siege mentioned by Josephus in *Against Apion* and that in Ezekiel 26:1 were the same, then Ezekiel's proclamation is a bit tardy and its significance nil. Perhaps Nebuchadnezzar was unsuccessful in his war between 598 and 586 B.C., and he launched another attack before 570 B.C. as he undertook his campaign against Egypt in 568 B.C. No satisfactory explanation of these different dates for the siege of Tyre has been given, but the oracles are in themselves superb literature and excellent cultural information.

Tyre was built on a small island a short distance from the shore. A breakwater about thirty feet wide jutted into the sea for nearly 2,500 feet, and it was capable of resisting the fiercest Mediterranean storms. The harbor on the south side of the island was the best on the Phoenician coast. Assyrian monarchs boasted that they had subdued Ushu, the town on the mainland, and Nebuchadnezzar preened himself because he subdued "All the kings of the Hattiland," which included Tyre, in his campaign of 604–601 B.C.[23] It is doubtful, however, that the island fortress was captured before Alexander's conquest in 333 B.C. He did so only by building a causeway from shore to island for his siege weapons and blockading the sea approaches with his navy. Drifting sand has silted-in the strip of water between the island and the coast, so that a large infertile area stretches between the cultivated coast and the modern town of Sur.

Ezekiel's lament over Tyre cited the city's might as a maritime power and its imposition of terror on inhabitants of Syria's mainland (Ezek. 26:17). Such terror originated not from military might but from

---

[22]Jeremiah 34:8–11, 37:3–5, and Ezekiel 30:20–26 give relevant data on that episode. Robert H. Pfeiffer, *Introduction to the Old Testament* (New York: Harper Brothers, 1948), pp. 536–41, gives a cogent argument for this interpretation.
[23]See D. Winton Thomas, *Documents from Old Testament Times* (New York: Harper & Row, 1965), pp. 78–9.

Tyre's reputation as a formidable competitor in trade. The sins for which Tyre was to be punished, according to Ezekiel, were those of pride, of pretending to divine status, and of possessing great wealth and beauty (Ezek. 27:3, 28:2, 6, 28:5, 17). Ezekiel ironically cited Tyre's wisdom as greater than the mythical Daniel's (Ezek. 28:3). The Ugaritic literature referred to Daniel as

> He who judges the case of the widow
> And judicates the cause of the fatherless.

He was probably a god or a legendary king whose reputation for righteousness and wisdom was traditionally appealed to.[24]

Ezekiel's Strange Behavior

Ezekiel's strange antics are matters everyone reading the book of Ezekiel will find fascinating. His familiarity with Babylonian customs, religious rites, and traditional mythology may account for some of his bizarre visions and descriptions. But his use of Babylonian literature cannot fully explain his cataleptic state, his ecstatic trances, his fainting spells, and his muteness (Ezek. 4:4–8, 1:28, 3:22–26, 24:25–27). How will one explain that after Jerusalem had fallen to Babylon his cataleptic states, muteness, and fainting spells did not recur?[25] Making a model of Jerusalem so that he could batter it down, eating a scroll, and shaving his head, burning a third of the hair, distributing a third about the city, and scattering a third to the winds, are rather pecular doings for a grown man (Ezek. 4:1–3, 3:1–3, 5:1–4). Fascinating as Ezekiel's dramatic exhibitions were, this is not the place for treating them. The striking similarity of his behavior to that of modern schizoid personalities is worth noting, but beyond that it is impossible to go in this book.[26]

The Prophet's Changed Role After the Fall of Jerusalem

Ezekiel's fanatical pronouncements of doom gave way to a compassionate attitude after the surrender of Jerusalem (Ezek. 33: 21–22). From that point on he looked upon the exiles as people who needed a leader (Ezek. 34). He became a watchman whose duty

[24] See C. H. Gordon, *The Ancient Near East* (3rd ed. rev.; New York: W. W. Norton Co., 1965), p. 97.

[25] Fainting spells in Ezekiel 43:3 and 44:4 belong to a vision prior to the fall of Jerusalem if most of chapters 40–48 is authentically Ezekiel's and literarily and historically the sequence of chapter 20. That oracle was given in 590 B.C. The date at Ezekiel 40:1 is cast differently from Ezekiel's other dates, and probably was an editorial addition.

[26] For a treatment of Ezekiel from this point of view see Kelvin Van Nuys, "Evaluating the Pathological in Prophetic Experience," *The Journal of Bible and Religion,* XXI, No. 4 (1953), 244–51.

it was to inform individuals of their wickedness but not to judge them for it (Ezek. 33:7–9).

History had dealt harshly with all of the small nations of Syria and Canaan. Many of them were exiled to the factories, mines, shops, and army of Babylon. But there is no record of a people other than Judah preserving its way of life and its faith. Judah treated its traditions with profound respect, at the same moment that it looked expectantly to the future. Prophets had spoken of destruction but they had spoken also of restoration. Ezekiel was one who kept alive the ember of national identity, and trusted Yahweh to bring to pass His promises spoken to the prophets. A small change in the balance of power in the Near East would be enough to spring the hope of restoration in the breasts of the exiles.

Ezekiel's Religious Affirmations

Ezekiel was a pessimist like all of Israel's prophets, but his pessimism was even blacker. Amos and Hosea cheerfully recalled Israel's nomadic days, thinking that then Israel had been loyal to Yahweh. Isaiah thought of the years under David as the ideal ones. For Ezekiel there never was a period in Israel's history when the people were faithful to their God. Israel originated from an abominable marriage: an Amorite father and a Hittite mother gave birth to a hideous child in the land of Canaan (Ezek. 16:1–5). Although Ezekiel's judgments were more accurate historically than he could suspect, he really meant that Israel's origins were about as unwholesome as imagination could make them. Amorite, Hittite, and Canaanite symbolized the nations that threatened Israel's early existence. In Egypt the people never rejected the detestable idols (Ezek. 20:5–9). Under Moses Israel rejected Yahweh's rules of living, preferring their own rebellious ways (Ezek. 20:9–13). Upon entering Canaan they simply accepted the intriguing worship of the local population on high hills and in wooded spots. With this pessimistic historical perspective it is amazing that Ezekiel found anything worth saving in hopes of restoration.

Confidence in Yahweh

Ezekiel's hopefulness originated in his abundant confidence in Yahweh. His trust in Israel's leaders withered with their inept handling of international intrigues, but his trust in Yahweh expanded. To Ezekiel, convinced that Yahweh directed events in history, even the destruction of the Temple was not a violation of Yahweh's character. Yahweh himself called forth the cruel foreigners who would desecrate the Temple (Ezek. 7:20–21). But Yahweh did not lose face when this terrible event happened. God did not expire when the Temple was looted and put to the torch. He turned His face away when the pillage began (Ezek. 7:22). His Splendor, which dwelt in the Temple, left before its destruction. Of its own accord it went to the Temple's threshold (Ezek. 9:3), and from there it was carried on the backs of the cherubim, who now were capable of moving themselves, to the outer court (Ezek. 10:3–5). The cherubim continued their flight out the east gate of the Temple until they brought the Splendor of Yahweh to rest upon the mountain (Mount of Olives) east of the city (Ezek. 10:18–19, 11:22–23). Yahweh's glory did not die in the flames but sat in perpetual grandeur overlooking Jerusalem until the people of Israel would purify themselves and return to build a new and perfect Temple for His Splendor (Ezek. 40–48). Yahweh had not yet become a God without need of an abode, but He could wait in the vicinity of the old Temple until Israel recognized Him again as God.

Yahweh's Transcendence

Ezekiel's understanding of Yahweh widened the gulf between God and man. When Yahweh was conceived as utterly holy a gulf existed, between the holiness of God and the sinfulness of man, which was difficult to bridge. The higher Ezekiel raised Yahweh above the confines of the Temple the more the people became a mob of sinners. Whereas earlier prophets had discriminated between God and man in moral terms, Ezekiel deepened the rift by stressing the cosmic distinction between them. Yahweh's choice of Israel was almost accidental, and unfortunate at that. The history of Israel was a chain of rebellions against God, but Yahweh preserved His name and honor by actually giving bad laws, destroying Jerusalem, and eventually preserving the people from extinction (Ezek. 20:25–26, 42–44). Although earlier prophets believed that the people had a large degree of independence, according to Ezekiel such a belief was fiction. Everything good, bad, and indifferent occurred for the splendor of Yahweh's name. With such a transcendent view of God, it is not surprising that Ezekiel felt messengers had to exist in order to serve as agents to carry God's messages across the chasm of cosmic and moral holiness (Ezek. 9:2, 3, 40:3). As time passed a whole system of angels developed to account for Yahweh's continued contact with corrupt man. God's purity would not permit his direct association with sinners.

Religious Perversion

Ezekiel charged Israel with religious and moral corruptions so gross and so numerous as to be almost unbelievable. If we believe Ezekiel's charges, there were high places and special shrines all over the city of Jerusalem. These, he threatened, would be devastated (Ezek. 6:1–7). He looked back upon the days when Israel practiced child sacrifice, and pronounced merciless judgment on Jerusalem for a rite performed in a less enlightened age (Ezek. 16:20–22). He abhorred the competition foreign gods gave Yahweh in the Temple precincts. The "image of jealousy" may have been a stone slab on which carvings or paintings of mythological tales were inscribed and set against the Temple wall or in a niche (Ezek. 8:3, 5). Several of these slabs from cult centers in northern Mesopotamia dating from the 7th century B.C. have been excavated, suggesting that Assyrian religious practices had returned to plague Yahwists in Jerusalem. Mysterious rites conducted by seventy elders in a dark room amidst clouds of incense surrounded by portraits of serpents, crocodiles, and loathesome beasts appear to have been Egyptian rites with magical features (Ezek. 8:10–12). Manuscripts of the Book of the Dead contemporary with Ezekiel have been found in Egypt. These had illustrated margins with serpents, crocodiles, beetles, baboons, and lions in profusion. The ceremony of "weeping for Tammuz" was practiced in the lower Tigris-Euphrates valley from early days, and was introduced into Syria and Palestine during the 8th century B.C. (Ezek. 8:14–15). Tammuz was a god similar to Canaanite Baal, and women wept before him appealing to his sexual vigor for their own impregnation. Sun worship was conducted by twenty-five men as they stood with backs to Yahweh's altar and faced the rising sun (Ezek. 8:16). The Temple itself was oriented toward the east, so that the rays of the rising sun would shine directly into the Holy of Holies at the autumnal equinox.[27] Disrespect shown the Temple raised Ezekiel's ire, as men in the Temple worshipped the sun instead of Yahweh who made the sun to rise.[28] There is no way to know exactly how widespread these syncretistic cults were, and caution should be used in accepting Ezekiel at face value; yet there is no question that Josiah's religious reform was incomplete and short-lived.

Expectations of Deliverance

It is impossible to be sure when Ezekiel turned from expectations of judgment to the hope of deliverance. Some scholars believe it was only near the end of his career, which they associate with the vision of the restored Temple—that is, 572 B.C.[29] It is likely he carried the hope of deliverance in his mind side by side with his gloomy pronouncements of destruction. This would seem compatible with a man whose schizoid tendencies were resolved only by the fall of Jerusalem. After the fall of the city, his mind dwelt primarily, if not exclusively, upon the restoration of Israel as a people under Yahweh. Several undated pronouncements give clues to Ezekiel's expectations of deliverance. Nebuchadnezzar made punitive raids against Ammon and Moab in 582 B.C., and after 580

[27] See Julian Morgenstern, *Hebrew Union College Annual,* VI (1929), pp. 1–38.
[28] See William F. Albright, *Archaeology and the Religion of Israel,* (Baltimore: The Johns Hopkins Press, 1942), pp. 165–8.
[29] See "Ezekiel," in Buttrick, ed., *The Interpreter's Bible,* Vol. VI, p. 61.

B.C. the small western states had been pacified completely by military domination (Ezek. 25:2–11). The hopefulness of Ezekiel's message in chapters 34, 36, and 37 may have resulted from his expectations that the Babylonian king would begin rebuilding those shattered states. The wisdom of this is clear if one looks at the map on page 329. If Babylon were to control Egypt's meddling in Asian politics, it could use a strong province at the tip of its southwestern holdings. Ezekiel agitated for a rebuilt Jewish state, economically and culturally renewed, as the best defense of Babylon's western provinces. This may be the historical context out of which hopes for restoration were made (Ezek. 36:8–15, 37:22–24). Ezekiel probably saw himself as the leader of such a return to Palestine (Ezek. 29:21).[30]

Yahweh's Vindication Before the Nations

The indivisible relationship between politics and religion in the ancient Near East is illustrated by Ezekiel's agitation for a recovery of Palestine under a semi-free political system. One reason for his concern was that Yahweh's name had suffered grievous harm before all nations of the world. Yahweh's might had been ridiculed because He had permitted His city to fall and His people to be carried into captivity. Babylonians, Phoenicians, Philistines, and practically all nations with whom Israel had dealings, stood on the streets of Babylon taunting "These are the people of Yahweh, and yet they had to go out of his land" (Ezek. 36:20b). Ezekiel imagined that Yahweh was furious with such derision, and that He planned to vindicate Himself before the world (Ezek. 36:21). How would he proceed to recoup His fortunes before all the nations? Punishment was one way, but it had only limited effect. He would show the world by rebuilding the community of Israel in Palestine (Ezek. 36:23). Even though Israel had failed Yahweh before, He would take no chances this time. The restored community, purged of idolatry and moral defection, would be brought under one king (Ezek. 37:15–28). Worship would be permitted only in the perfect temple. The nations of the world would rue their mockery of Yahweh. The bleached bones of two dead nations would be reclothed in living flesh, and all would see the power of Yahweh again (Ezek. 37:1–10).[31]

Ezekiel's theological emphases continued those of earlier Hebrew prophecy. The beauty of language in Isaiah and Jeremiah, however, gave their work a quality lacking in Ezekiel. His grotesque allegories are memorable but they are literarily unattractive. His visions of

[30] See Gottwald, *All the Kingdoms of the Earth*, pp. 327–9.
[31] See Gottwald, *All the Kingdoms of the Earth*, pp. 326–7.

Yahweh in bizarre figures and ornate symbolism alienated the Lord from man. His conception of Israel as corrupt throughout its entire history widened the gap between God and man. Relief from pessimism came only from Ezekiel's conception of a restored community fully chastened and obedient under a divinely ordained king.

It was, perhaps, Ezekiel's appeal to the fantastic and exotic that caught the imagination of folk art. "'Zekiel saw the wheel way ob in the middle of the air" and "Hear 'dem bones" are known to most audiences even though they have never read a line of the book of Ezekiel itself. His work lives on because it was vivid literature in its own day, and because its understanding of the nature of man gives serious men pause for long consideration.

The Holiness Code

Leviticus 17–26 was originally an independent code of cultic regulations. A. Klostermann in 1877 noticed its independence, and named it the Holiness Code. Its independence is shown by the following evidence. It opens with the command to sacrifice animals only "at the door of the tent of meeting" (Lev. 17:1–9). It closes with an offer from Yahweh that the people will be given good fortune and long life if they faithfully observe the laws (Lev. 26:3–45). This was precisely *the form* of the original book of Deuteronomy. Material in the Holiness Code is in some disarray, showing that it was compiled from several smaller units rather than composed by a single hand. Furthermore, several laws were repeated within the code, showing, too, the presence of several small codes.

Possible Link Between Holiness Code and Ezekiel

The evidence is not conclusive, but reading the Holiness Code after Ezekiel shows literary and theological similarities which could mean that one borrowed from the other or that they originated in the same historical setting, about 550 B.C. It is possible that the author of the Holiness Code was inspired by Ezekiel's prophecies to prepare a scroll that would put the essence of his preaching into a legal system. He agreed with Ezekiel's emphasis in making ritual holiness the dominant element in Judaism. He may also have had in mind the attempt to correct errors committed by Ezekiel against traditional legal matters. He refused to accept Ezekiel's cavalier treatment of traditional law. He returned to archaic forms with the literary fiction that they had come from Moses at Sinai (Lev. 17:1). The author of the Holiness Code never heard of a "guilt offering" (Ezek. 40:39, 42:13). He showed his dislike of Ezekiel's distinction between Zadokite priests and Levites (Ezek. 44:9–16) by ignoring the distinction. He cited the traditional festival days in Leviticus 23, Passover and Unleavened Bread, First Fruits, Feast of Weeks, Day of Atonement, Feast of Booths, and the Sabbath, but he was silent about festivals newly introduced by Ezekiel (Ezek. 45:18–25). He silently rejected Ezekiel's concurrence with Deuteronomy that priests in Jerusalem should judge criminal cases (Ezek. 44:24). He was prepared to codify the laws for use in the restored community of Jews in Jerusalem, but he wanted none of Ezekiel's easy treatment of legal and cultic matters which did not stem from long traditions.[32]

The principle religious motif of the Holiness Code was the idea of a new community of Jews whose main duty was to worship in undiluted and ritual purity. If the Jews put their trust in proper cultic practices, then all of life would fall into perspective. A high moral order would prevail. Economic stability would be ensured. Peace would be inevitable because the strength and courage of five Yahwists would be more than a hundred enemy could face (Lev. 26:8). To worship rightly was not necessarily to love each other, but loving each other would be impossible without worshipping rightly.

Although emphasis was upon worship, the ethical precepts in the Holiness Code were permeated with the elevated moral demands of the prophets. Yahweh's holiness was ceremonial but it spilled over into the humanitarian. Religion was the source of one's moral life (Lev. 19:15–18). There lies a religious maxim as great as the one in Deuteronomy "The Lord is our God, the Lord alone" (Deut. 6:4). It is "you shall love your neighbor as yourself: I am the Lord."

The Book of Isaiah of Babylon

The book of Isaiah is clearly divisible into three major sections. Scholars have given the name Deutero-Isaiah to the author of chapters 40–55, but it is more courteous to call him Isaiah of Babylon since that was his home.

After reading Ezekiel and the Holiness Code, the poetry of this great writer lifts one to unparalleled heights of literary excellence and exalted ideas. Several poems have served to beautify aesthetic expressions because of their inherent worth. How often these words are used introducing the prayer of confession in liturgical worship:

Seek the Lord while he may be found,
call upon him while he is near;
let the wicked forsake his way,
and the unrighteous man his thoughts;

---

[32] See Pfeiffer, *Introduction to the Old Testament*, pp. 242–4.

> let him return to the Lord, that he may have mercy on him,
>> and to our God, for he will abundantly pardon.
> For my thoughts are not your thoughts,
>> neither are your ways my ways, says the Lord.
> For as the heavens are higher than the earth,
>> so are my ways higher than your ways
>> and my thoughts than your thoughts. (Isa. 55:6–9)

Almost everyone knows George Frederick Handel's oratorio "Messiah" and can hum the tune to the opening tenor recitative

> *Comfort ye, comfort ye my people,*
> *saith your God. Speak ye*
> *comfortably to Jerusalem, and cry unto her,*
> *that her warfare is accomplished, that*
> *her iniquity is pardoned: for she*
> *has received of the Lord's hand double*
> *for all her sins.* (Isa. 40:1–2 KJV)

Who doesn't thrill to the alto air

> *He will feed his flock like a shepherd,*
> *he shall gather the lambs in his arm,*
> *and carry them in his bosom, and shall*
> *gently lead those that are with young?* (Isa. 4:11 KJV)

One does not readily forget the words and melody of the soprano air

> *How beautiful upon the mountains*
> *are the feet of him that bringeth good*
> *tidings, that publisheth peace.* (Isa. 52:7 KJV)

Those who know Johannes Brahms' "Requiem" emotionally tread the stately rhythms of the chorus "Behold all flesh is as the grass" (Isa. 40:6–8).

An Anthology Not only have these few chapters served artistic ends for many generations, they are in themselves one of the finest anthologies of Hebrew poetry ever collected. This is a collection of about fifty poems, songs, and sayings. It is difficult to take an exact count since a literary unit may have several smaller poems within it. Isaiah 40:1–8, for example, is ideally a unit, but it has three distinct parts to it. The second part begins "a voice cries" (Isa. 40:3) while the third part opens with "a voice says" (Isa. 40:6). In spite of these different formulae, it is best to think of verse 1–8 as a single composition. Although it is likely that all of the poems and songs were composed by one author, there is no single idea binding all of the units together. There is no progressive argument. They are vignettes of thoughts expressed poetically.[33] Nonetheless a uniformity of diction, vocabulary, and mood pervades the poems in chapters 40–55, and chapters 60–62 show these characteristics, too.

There are several types of poems and one narrative description in this anthology. There is, for example, a poem on the majesty of God. (Isa. 40:9–31). This composition is not a psalm in the sense that a psalm praises God's majesty, and yet it described God in all His grandeur. It appears to be a solo rendition, perhaps for synagogue worship, as an affirmation of faith. There is a poem on God's action in history (Isa. 41:1–9). Judgment dispensed at the city gate was the setting for this poem. Nations were called before the bar of the God of history to be judged as Cyrus rang up victory after victory ending the era of Mesopotamian domination over the ancient Near East. A hymn in the style of enthronement psalms sung on the day of the New Year is found at Isaiah 42:10–13. There are songs about Yahweh's special servant (Isa. 42:1–4, 42:5–9, 49:1–6, 50:4–9, 52:13 – 53:12). A prose description of idol-making is a contemptuous account of the technique of the artisan at his craft (Isa. 44:9–20). There is a poetic account of Cyrus' conquests showing that Yahweh stood behind all the Persian's achievements (Isa. 45:1–7). One poem contrasted Yahweh with idols (Isa. 45:18 – 46:13). An oracle against Babylon, in the style of a taunt song, described how the city of Babylon, once so grand, will be reduced to insignificance (Isa. 47:1–15).

The diversity of poetic types in this anthology shows that the author was a man skilled in his craft. His skill in using repetition, onomatopoeia,[34] introductions and conclusions, imperative voice, imaginative words of address (Isa. 47:1b, 5b), contrast, and personification was unrivaled by any contemporary either among He-

---

[33] Contrast with Samuel Sandmel, *The Hebrew Scriptures* (New York: Alfred A. Knopf, 1963), pp. 169–93, who presents all of Second Isaiah as a drama in two acts the theme of which is that the God of Israel is the only God, He is universal, and Israel is the means of working out His plans.
[34] Which translators of the RSV have tried to retain from the Hebrew.

brew poets or elsewhere in the Semitic world. This collection of poems has no author's name. It is odd that literature with such power, grandeur, and skilled diction did not carry the memory of its creator. Its attachment to the Isaiah scroll was fortuitous, but gives no clue to authorship. It is likely that the author had to remain anonymous. He championed Cyrus (Isa. 45:1) as a deliverer of the Jews from their subservience. He was sharply critical of Babylon's policies, and showed inflamatory animosity toward the empire (Isa. 47:1). His contempt for Babylon's gods and religious practices would have brought upon his head the wrath of the Babylonian priesthood (Isa. 46:1, 45:18). He claimed that one day Israel would avenge itself and dominate the empire (Isa. 49:22–26). He probably circulated these poems among the Jewish communities along the Euphrates River, and since they contained seditious material, his identity was withheld even from the Jews themselves.

The Servant Songs Several passages present a special literary problem. These passages have been named the "Servant Songs" because they reveal the work of Yahweh's servant as distinct from Yahweh's own dealings with nations in the rest of the book of Isaiah of Babylon (Isa. 42:1–4, 42:5–9, 49:1–6, 50:4–9, 52:13 – 53:12). These verses have received a tremendous amount of discussion from Old Testament scholars, and there is still no unanimity as to their origins, who the servant was, or which sections from Isaiah of Babylon are truly the Servant Songs. C. C. Torrey, for example, selected also Isaiah 61:1–3, 10–11, 62:1–12, and 63:7–14, as passages that bear the literary and religious marks of Servant Songs. The diversity of interpretation indicates how complex and significant the problems about these passages are.

The Servant Songs have a recognizable similarity of vocabulary, literary style, and subject matter so that they can be detached from their context and put together to form a small unit. This suggests they were inserted into the book of Isaiah of Babylon after it had been completed. The separation of several chapters cannot obscure the fact that Isaiah 42:4 points to the statements in Isaiah 53:1–2. But the distinctive problem is to explain how similarities and differences of the Servant Songs can exist alongside the other compositions of Isaiah of Babylon. The phrase, "taken you by the hand" (Isa. 42:6), referring to the Servant, is used elsewhere in connection with Cyrus (Isa. 45:1). The phrase "I am the Lord" followed by a series of identifying traits is a style found in the Servant Songs and in other poems in the collection (cf. Isa. 42:8 with 43:11, 15, 44:24, 45:5). The conception of Yahweh as the originator of salvation, the vision of a mission, and Gentiles waiting for salvation are topics in both the Servant Songs and the rest of the book. But differences are also pronounced. The Servant Songs are personal, even autobiographical, in quality whereas the rest of Isaiah of Babylon is quite impersonal. The servant is a single person in the Servant Songs whereas in the rest of Isaiah of Babylon "servant" designates the people of Israel (Isa. 41:8, 42:19, 42:10). Missionary work is performed by the servant in the Servant Songs whereas according to other portions of the book Israel passively witnesses God's power as He brings His purposes to pass.

Who was the author of the Servant Songs? Literary analysis indicates that Isaiah of Babylon wrote them. The similarities are real, and the differences resulted from the poems having been composed for different audiences. The Servant Songs perhaps were delivered to his personal disciples.

Another problem arises. Who was the servant? Scholarly opinion has ranged widely on this question. Many claim that the servant is the people of Israel. Some scholars have pointed out that in the Old Testament nations often were personified. There is, therefore, no reason to distinguish the servant in the poems as Israel and the servant in the Servant Songs as personal. They both indicate the nation. But it is almost impossible to associate the distasteful qualities of the servant in the Servant Songs with a collective party (Isa. 50:4–6, 52:14).

Some have identified the Servant Songs with a myth connected with the worship of Tammuz who died and rose again each year. This view proposes that the whole book of Isaiah of Babylon was an imitation of the liturgy used during the Babylonian festival of the New Year. The Servant Songs were efforts to present a messianic figure which combined certain features of the Davidic kingship with those of a myth widely known in the ancient Near East.[35]

Others have claimed the honor for individuals: Moses, Jeremiah, Hezekiah, Jehoiachin, Isaiah of Jerusalem, Zerubbabel, an unnamed martyr of the Exile known to Isaiah of Babylon. Why not the prophet himself? The autobiographical quality of the Servant Songs suggests their use for a small circle of readers. The author seemed to be involved in legal proceedings and suffered persecution (Isa.

[35] See H. H. Rowley, ed., *The Old Testament and Modern Study* (London: Oxford University Press, 1961), 147–51, and Artur Weiser, *The Old Testament: Its Formation and Development*, trans. Dorothea M. Barton (New York: Association Press, 1961), pp. 200–205.

50:5–9). This is not surprising in view of his political activity and writings. He described facing physical punishment and the expected execution with the gallant hope that God would use his death to show the way of salvation to Israelite and Gentile alike. The prophet's followers were amazed at the idea that the death of one man could point the way to salvation. The Servant Songs seem to be the prophet's effort to understand the meaning of his own life. Imminent death brought his reflection to a peak of lyric excellence, and his insight revealed that his faith in Yahweh's final victory in history was his own victory (Isa. 52:13–53:12). After he had passed this insight on to his disciples, they shared it with later generations by inserting the Servant Songs in the collected works of the poet.

However one interprets the Servant Songs, they form a central part of the anthology of Isaiah of Babylon. These poems reveal a sensitive soul working on a theme of magnificent proportions. The tensions of the historical situation in which the Judean exiles found themselves made imperative a radical shift from attitudes and practices long held sacred in Israel, but no longer applicable.

The Historical Situation

Babylon never intended to obliterate Judah's national characteristics as the Assyrian empire had with Galilee and Samaria. Assyria stamped out all evidence of nationality in a province, and relocated whole populations so that families, clans, and villages were separated from one another in the wide reaches of the empire. Babylonians practiced a deportation system only when vassal nations faulted their obligations. Yahwism and its traditional rites might have survived intact had not Zedekiah rebelled against Nebuchadnezzar in 588 B.C. Even when Babylon deported populations, it permitted national groups to relocate together. More productivity was achieved from the deportees' labor under such circumstances. Thus Judeans were settled near the city of Babylon. They built homes, cultivated their own plots of land, married within their group, and governed their communities by their own laws. Jeremiah urged them to seek the welfare of Babylon, and to reject the false patter of prophets who counseled rebellion within the heart of the empire. He believed national identity could be maintained in anticipation of an eventual return to Palestine (Jer. 29:1–28).

Assyria's Fall; The Rise of Nebuchadnezzar

Babylon's triumph over Assyria began in 626 B.C. when Nabopolassar (626–605 B.C.) led a successful revolt against Assyrian armies outside of Babylon. He was crowned king of Babylon that year, and was officially able to conduct negotiations with Cyaxares (625–585 B.C.), the Mede. Together these two men directed campaigns against Assyrian armies in the Mesopotamian valley and in the mountainous regions of Urartu. The Medes and the Babylonians divided the crumbling Assyrian empire between them. Nebuchadnezzar's brilliant career (605–562 B.C.) began when he was eighteen years old with victory over Egyptian and Assyrian armies at Carchemish in 605 B.C. He took the throne upon the death of his father, Nabopolassar. The rout of Assyria and Neco's retreat into Syria and Palestine gave Nebuchadnezzar time to deal with the Medes. He signed a treaty with Cyaxares which gave Babylon the river valley and the Medes the highlands to the north and east. He cruelly smashed revolts in Syria and Palestine, but at home he was a benevolent ruler insofar as that term can be applied to any monarch of the ancient Near East.

Synagogues in Babylon

The young monarch set out to make Babylon the greatest city in the world, and in his long reign he made it that. Wealthy and complex, Babylon and its nearer towns, Nippur, Erech, Ur, and Sippar, submerged the Jews beneath their grandeur. But they were not absorbed. They maintained their distinctive religious beliefs even as they worked shoulder to shoulder with exiles from all parts of the far-flung empire. Their homogeneous community life made imperative religious rites of some kind. The Jerusalem Temple had been gutted with fire, and no regular priesthood maintained sacrifices there, but the need to worship Yahweh had in no wise diminished. Since the exiles who remained loyal Yahwists had accepted the Deuteronomic theory of a central sanctuary they would not sacrifice animals while in Babylon. The three great festivals had been nationalized for a full generation, and could be celebrated only in Jerusalem (Deut. 16:16). The priesthood had been nationalized, too, so that no priest considered himself eligible for official duties while in exile. A substitute for the Temple was found, however. The small neighborhood gatherings that had voluntarily sprung up in Judah when Josiah disallowed any formal worship outside the Temple now became immensely practical. The synagogue may have been the ideal fulfillment of religious needs among the exiles.

As synagogues developed, ancient religious practices had to be drastically modified. As practices changed, so beliefs were adjusted to the new conditions.

The sabbath day became one of the practices that Jews stressed while in exile. This rite was familiar to the Babylonians whose ancestors had observed a day of relaxation, "the day of quieting of the heart," every seven days during certain months. The Babylonian name was *shabbatu,* and its obvious similarity with the Hebrew *sabbath* caused some scholars to believe that the Hebrews had observed the day for the first time while in exile. This was certainly not the case, because a law formulated in the 10th century B.C. demanded rest on the seventh day (Exod. 34:21). The Jews brought observation of the sabbath with them to Babylon, and a certain similarity of practice between Jews and Babylonians expanded the ceremonial significance of the day. Certain liturgical practices conducted in Babylonian temples on the day of rest were borrowed for use in the synagogue. The prohibition of all forms of labor was subordinated to acts of praise to Yahweh. This gave the day a quality of comfort, pleasure, and thanksgiving for Yahweh's continued care of His people even in their adversity.[36]

Forms of Synagogue Worship

Sabbath worship in the synagogue consisted of prayers, readings from the prophets, and interpretation of what had been read by an elder of the community. As the interpretive task became more complex the sermon was created. Ezekiel's "parable of the harlot" (Ezek. 16), for example, is an interpretation of Hebrew history. Ezekiel explained what the Jewish community had to look forward to in another sermon (Ezek. 37). The Hebrew propensity for grand poetry and music furnished the ingredients for singing in the synagogue, and psalmnody became a highly developed art. A hymn with an historical theme was written for congregational chanting, and kept alive anticipation of Yahweh's victory over Babylon (Isa. 42:10–13). A mournful hymn lamented the victor's recognition of the Hebrew's singing ability, and glorified the homeland (Ps. 137).

Although the synagogue served primarily as a gathering place for the community to praise Yahweh, it developed two other functions. One was the administration of justice in the Jewish community. The other was the instruction of the young in the traditional ways of their people. There is no specific evidence that the educational function existed in Babylon, but Jews in 3rd century Palestine understood the synagogue to be a *beth sepher,* a house of the book.[37]

Circumcision

Another rite that developed significantly during the exile was circumcision. Like sabbath observance, this rite originated in dim antiquity. It was practiced among the Egyptians, as a carving from a tomb at Saqqarah dating from 2350–2000 B.C. shows, but not among Assyrians and Babylonians. Circumcision was performed among the Hebrews, either at puberty or at marriage, but at the

---

[36] See "Sabbath," *IDB,* R–Z, pp. 135–41.
[37] "Synagogue," *IDB,* R–Z, pp. 476–91.

Stone carving on the wall of an Egyptian tomb at Saqqarah
(2350–2000 B.C.) depicts the operation of circumcision.

time of the Deuteronomic reform it was probably not considered an essential rite. Deuteronomy does not mention physical circumcision, although it calls for circumcision of the heart (Deut. 10:16, 30:6). Jeremiah called the people of Egypt, Judah, Edom, Ammon, Moab, and Arabia circumcised in the flesh, but not in their hearts (Jer. 9:25–26). Such passages indicate that its religious significance was known, but not held to be crucial. Infant circumcision probably began among the Jews in exile. A passage from the Priestly writer reporting the circumcision of Abraham and his male dependents required the operation on the eighth day of the infant's life (Gen. 17:9–14).

Circumcision served as a mark of distinction. It distinguished a faithful Yahwist from Jews who had given up their faith, as well as marking off Yahwists from Babylonians. It stood as a symbol of those who had been faithful and survived.[38] Circumcision also symbolized the historic ties the exiles had with Israel's heroes, Abraham, Joshua, and Moses, all of whom had stories told about

[38] The tattooed numbers placed on the interior of the Jews' forearms during Hitler's regime in Germany became a symbol of faithfulness to many Jews.

their circumcision (Gen. 17:9–14; Josh. 5:2–9; Exod. 4:24–26, 12:43–49). The ceremony was probably performed in the synagogue.

Distinction Between Clean and Unclean Foods Pure food and forbidden food became matters of serious religious concern during the exile. Although the distinction between clean and unclean foods had long been observed by the Hebrews as matters of self-preservation from the hostile powers of the universe, only during the exile did food laws become central to their religious practices.[39] The pig had been a sacrificial animal for Canaanites, and it was abhorred by Hebrews in Palestine. In Babylon the same animal was venerated, and the Jews there forbade its use. Ancient communities cherished their eating customs, and did not easily tolerate change, but they were made more rigorous by priestly interpretations. The camel, for example, was an animal introduced to the Hebrews after they had begun their settlement in Canaan, and not being among the foods enjoyed by the Hebrew tribes, it was always forbidden (Deut. 14:7). Bedouin Arabs ate the camel from antiquity, and it is still considered a favorite food among desert dwellers of the Near East. But the basic reason for strictures on certain food in the exile was to distinguish the Jewish community from its neighbors.

As these changes took place in the lives of exiled Jews, outside the empire mighty upheavals were in process. Cyrus, tribal chief in the mountains of the Median province of Anshan, revolted against Astyages (585–550 B.C.). The year 553 B.C. marked the rise of non-Semitic control of the ancient Near East, and a period of religious toleration previously unknown. Cyrus' revolt in Anshan initiated a campaign which gave him undisputed control of Persia by 550 B.C. In that year he was crowned king and also drove north to subdue the Median capital of Ecbatana. His military exploits were so successful that he sent his armies eastward to the Indus River. Then he swung west avoiding Babylon's border fortresses by moving over the mountain roads north of them. He camped on the shores of Lake Van only long enough to prepare his campaign against Croesus, king of Lydia, at the western end of Anatolia. These campaigns consumed about three years, and should have given Babylon time to build for the expected assault against her valley holdings.

Nabonidus (556–539 B.C.) was not the man for the crisis, however. He was at odds with the strong priesthood which supported the

---

[39] Contrast the emphasis upon food laws in Deuteronomy 14:3–21 and those in an exilic document, Leviticus 11:1–47.

worship of Babylon's patron god Marduk. He preferred the worship of the moon god Sin. His interests in history prompted him to excavate ruined temples in Babylon, and to revive ancient rites. For reasons historians have not yet discovered, he moved the royal residence to Tema in Arabia and spent eight years there while his son Belsharusur[40] ran the government in Babylon. During his absence the New Year festival involving the king's sexual intercourse with a priestess, symbolic of Marduk's consorting with his queen, was bypassed. The citizens were incensed by this affront to the city's patron god.

Cyrus Takes Babylon

While Nabonidus enjoyed the temperate climate of Arabia's high mountains, Cyrus concluded his campaign against Croesus, won territory in Syria, and began mopping up Babylonian resistance in the Mesopotamian valley. In a pitched battle up river from Babylon Persian archers poured arrows into the enemy's infantry while skillful horsemen attacked the exposed wings of the Babylonian formation. Persian strategy never allowed the Babylonian foot soldier to get close enough for hand to hand combat. The Babylonian army was so shattered that it was unable to regroup for defense of the capital. Cyrus entered Babylon unopposed. There he was hailed as a liberator, and the Cyrus Cylinder reported how the population of Babylon bowed down to him in gratitude. He reinstituted the official ceremonies of Marduk, and he himself daily worshipped him. Persian troops moved about the city unopposed restoring dilapidated buildings and removing the yoke of slavery from minority groups.[41] Jewish expectations of a return to Palestine had risen to feverish pitch by the time Babylon submitted in 538 B.C. In previously captured parts of the Babylonian empire Cyrus had permitted Babylon's captive populations to go free. These expectations were clearly enunciated by Isaiah of Babylon.

The Prophet's View of Cyrus

What was Isaiah of Babylon's attitude toward Cyrus? First, he clearly expected the capitulation of Babylon because Yahweh was using the Persian for His purposes (Isa. 41:1–4). Second, Cyrus was sent on his missions of conquest by Yahweh (Isa. 45:1–7). It is possible that Isaiah of Babylon referred to Cyrus' campaign against Croesus and his conquest of Syria which would date Isaiah 41:1–29 to about 546 B.C. (See Isa. 41:2, 25). References to Kedar and Sela may call to mind Nabonidus as he dwelt isolated from

[40] Daniel 5:2, Belshazzar, erroneously noted as Nebuchadnezzar's son.
[41] See Thomas, *Documents from Old Testament Times*, pp. 92–5, for a translation of the cylinder. Also, Harold Lamb, *Cyrus, the Great* (Garden City, N.Y.: Doubleday & Co., 1960), is an excellent popular treatment of Cyrus' career. Herodotus, Book I gives a vigorous account of the great Persian.

Babylonian politics. These names may be associated with Tema and Petra, major cities on the overland caravan routes, whose citizens will rejoice when Babylonian domination ended (Isa. 42:11). This psalm could be dated also about 546 B.C. Third, Cyrus' policy of releasing subject populations stimulated Isaiah of Babylon to think of him as a servant of Yahweh. His release of the Jews would be "a light to the Gentiles" (Isa. 42:6, 49:6, 62:1–2) so that Cyrus really carried out the Lord's intentions. Fourth, Isaiah of Babylon expected Cyrus to become a Yahwist. His enlightened tolerance for small religious groups was well known before he ever arrived in Babylon. Once he had seen the resistance Yahweh's faithful people had put up to Babylonian idolatry, he himself would embrace the true faith and establish Yahwism as the official religion of the empire (Isa. 44:24–28).

It was a simple matter of deduction that if Cyrus would so favor the Jews, they would become the dominant people of the Near East. Isaiah of Babylon exuberantly anticipated Israel's ascendancy (Isa. 41:15–16). As with a threshing-sledge the nations will be crushed. Egyptians and Arabs will bring their precious wealth to Jerusalem and become wholly subject to restored Israel (Isa. 45:14–17). Kings and queens will bow down to "lick the dust of your feet" (Isa. 49:22–23). But the goal of Israel's ascendancy was not military and political domination, so that Jews could lord it over their former captors. It was only to serve the Persian empire which was an instrument of Yahweh's purposes (Isa. 49:23, 24–26). The Jews should serve to let "all flesh know that I am Yahweh your Savior." All nations would know the extent of Yahweh's power to redeem when Israel had been reestablished as a people under Yahweh in Palestine. There "all nations will come to your light." The herds of south Arabian camels, the gold and frankincense of Sheba, the sheep of north Arabians, and the cargoes of Phoenician ships will be insufficient to glorify Yahweh. Jerusalem will be rebuilt and peace will flourish throughout the Persian empire, so that the city's gates will always be open. The *kabodh* of Yahweh (His splendor) in the restored Temple will be so bright that even the sun will be unnecessary. Righteousness will be practiced by everyone, so that the least person in Jerusalem shall be accounted as important as the head of a clan. Yahweh will be victorious, and Cyrus will be His agent (Isa. 60:1–22).

The great poet's expectations were not fulfilled in history. The Babylonians did not let him live to see the shambles made of a great ideal when the Jews did return to Judah. But that story will have to wait for a subsequent chapter.

The poet's religious convictions were by no means revolutionary. It is clear, however, that the usual prophetic denunciations of Israel and neighboring nations are absent from this anthology. There are splendid descriptions of the manufacture of idols and of their impotence in contrast with Yahweh's creativity (Isa. 44:9–20, 45: 18–25). Yet there is no proclamation of doom upon the mistaken idolaters. An oracle against Babylon is cast in the form of a lament, but its diction is quiet and restrained compared with Jeremiah's and Ezekiel's (Isa. 47:1–15). Israel had been punished enough, and pronouncements of doom were no longer necessary (Isa. 42:22–25, 51:12–14). Comfort rather than retribution was what Israel could expect. It is clear, then, that Isaiah of Babylon's conception of Yahweh was different from the prophets who preceded him.

It will be enough to stress a few characteristics of his beliefs that differ somewhat from earlier prophets.

An Elevated Conception of Yahweh. First, Yahweh and man were so described that they stood in sharp contrast. Like Ezekiel, Isaiah of Babylon had an elevated conception of God. He was totally distinct from His created world, and He had created the world by Himself. He received no help from other gods. The Babylonian Creation Epic told how the earth and heavens were created as the result of conflict between Marduk and Tiamat. The gods Anu, Enlil, and Ea were part of the creative process.[42] But Isaiah of Babylon affirmed that Yahweh was solely responsible.

> *I am Yahweh, who made all things*
> > *who stretched out the heavens alone,*
> > *who spread out the earth.* (Isa. 44:24)

Isaiah of Babylon knew the Babylonian story of creation, and he rejected its claim that Marduk had cut Tiamat in half to create the heavens and the earth. *Yahweh* had cut Rahab (Tiamat), the dragon in half, and established the heavens and the earth (Isa. 51:9). Yahweh's creative act can in no sense be paralleled by anything man does (Isa. 40:12–26). Man in contrast is no stronger or more permanent than grass, and the richest rulers soon wither away like a poorly rooted flower (Isa. 40:6–8, 23–24).

Yahweh as the God of History. Second, Yahweh directs history. His command brought forth Cyrus who trampled all other kings

---

[42] See Thomas, *Documents from Old Testament Times*, pp. 3–16.

underfoot (Isa. 41:2–4, 25). Mankind's efforts, on the other hand, were futile. Devices conceived in wickedness bring ruin upon men suddenly, and no amount of sorcery can predict the future or show ways to extricate man from his blunders (Isa. 47:10–15).

The Dependability of Yahweh. Third, Yahweh stands loyally behind his word and his character. Although man's passing glory fades quickly, Yahweh can always be depended on (Isa. 40:8). Long after the heavens have vanished like smoke, and earth has worn itself out, Yahweh will stand firm in His promises (Isa. 51:4–6). Confidence in Yahweh is not wasted, because like the rain, which cannot go back into the clouds once it has fallen, Yahweh's word never returns to Him without his purposes fulfilled (Isa. 55:10–11). Man, on the contrary, is undependable. Only after passing through the crucible of suffering is he able to approach the loyalty and dependability of Yahweh (Isa. 48:9–11, 49:14–21, 51:12–16). Isaiah of Babylon did not contrast man with God because he thought man was so worthless, but because he understood God to be so exalted. The emphasis was upon Yahweh high and holy, not upon man broken and lowly. Thus, he treated man with more respect than did Ezekiel, at the same time that he found his conception of Yahweh compatible with Ezekiel's.

Yahweh the Savior of the Jews. Isaiah of Babylon, fourthly, put stress upon Yahweh's rescue of His people rather than His destruction of them. Jerusalem lay destroyed, and there was no leadership there to bring the city back to its grandeur (Isa. 51:17–20). Some of the Jews in exile were in a wretched condition (Isa. 42:22–23, 51:13). There was no vitality left in a people who had once defied the armies of the Babylonian empire. What could Yahweh do with a people whose fortunes had sunk so low? He brought comfort. Yahweh recognized that Israel had suffered enough for its disloyalty, and now the past was fully pardoned (Isa. 40:1–2). Although Israel was a nation without provisions, with none of the means to sustain its national life, Yahweh would supply the wine and milk of corporate life to bring Israel again into covenant with Himself (Isa. 55:1–13). But Yahweh's care extended beyond comfort. He was to be the means of Israel's salvation. Although the Jews were bowed down, despairing, hopeless, physically wretched, and forbidden from performing the religious duties that distinguished the people of Yahweh from all others, Yahweh promised them restoration in the homeland.

Yahweh as the Trustee of Israel's Heritage. It was the nature and extent of Yahweh's salvation that distinguished Isaiah of Babylon's religion from previous Old Testament prophets. Israel had understood Yahweh as a God of salvation from its earliest days. Salvation from an Egyptian patrol, from desert famine, from marauding bedouin, from the Canaanites' chariots were tasks the Lord had performed on repeated occasions. In Isaiah of Babylon's fifth distinctive thought, the name Redeemer is applied to Yahweh in a new way. The Hebrew word is *goel*. It is derived from a root whose legal meanings dealt with the purchase of family property when a kinsman had fallen upon hard days and could no longer maintain his land. Jeremiah's purchase of a field from Hanamel is a good illustration of how the word was used in a legal context (Jer. 32: 6–12). Yahweh was the *goel* who paid the price when Israel was destitute. In many places Yahweh was named the "Redeemer, the Holy One of Israel" (Isa. 41:14, 43:14, 47:4, 48:17) which gave to the word *goel* the significance of Yahweh's divinity and purity. There was no necessity on Yahweh's part to pay the purchase price. The whole phrase emphasized the quality of grace which lay in Yahweh's action.

Isaiah of Babylon clearly described the Redeemer's work. Israel would be released from bondage in a mighty repetition of the Exodus from Egypt (Isaiah 43:5–7, 55:12–13, 63:10–14, remembering that Isaiah 63:7–19 was originally part of Isaiah 40–55). Then Israel's enemies would receive Yahweh's wrath (Isa. 41:11–13, 49:25–26). Next, the exiles would return to Palestine to rebuild their shattered land, and roads would be leveled and plainly marked to show the way (Isa. 40:9–11, 43:19–21, 49:8–12). On the Jews' return to Judah Jerusalem would be rebuilt, and the land would become productive again (Isa. 44:26, 45:13, 49:19, 51:3). Finally, the nations would see Yahweh's power and grace and they, too, would turn to Him (Isa. 45:20–23, 51:4–6). But Yahweh's salvation was not only the physical return to Palestine. It was also an inward redemption and spiritual renewal (Isa. 43:25, 44:22, 54:8). Like Ezekiel, Isaiah of Babylon believed that Yahweh's acts of redemption were to exalt His name (Isa. 44:25) and to expose His glory among the nations (Isa. 48:11). Yahweh's great power gave Him the *capacity* to redeem; His great love gave Him the *desire* to redeem.

The Identity of Yahweh's Servant

Paradoxically Yahweh, despite His power, chose an agent to serve Him in a unique way. He used a servant whose externalities made him appear unlikely to be an agent of God. Who this servant was has entered the discussion already (pp. 343–345), and it was concluded that it was the poet himself, although this is only one suggestion among many. Charged with special responsibility in the drama of salvation, he suffered for Israel. Above all he was humble. He was beaten, spat upon, and had his beard pulled, a despicable act in the ancient Near East (Isa. 50:5–6). He was personally unattractive (Isa. 52:14, 53:2). Despite his humility and his uncomely appearance, he was chosen to restore the exiles to influence (Isa. 49:6). In addition, he served as a judge, and he was charged with the dispatch of justice among all people, no matter how small or insignificant that people may have been. Justice over all the earth was his goal (Isa. 42:1–4).[43] Even as he established universal justice, he was charged with reconstituting the covenant with the people of Israel. In these many ways he served as "a light to the Gentiles" (Isa. 42:6). It was probably while he went among Jewish and Gentile exiles in Babylon offering just decisions and legal counsel that he fell afoul of Babylonian law. He was charged with sedition and faced a court of inquiry where witnesses against him were hard to find (Isa. 50:5–9). He believed himself to be innocent, but he was found guilty. He faced physical punishment before his execution (Isa. 53:4–10). His punishment and death served vicariously for Israel because it showed that the highest form of human life was when a man stuck by his ideals so completely that even though death destroyed him his ways lived on in idealized form.

Changes in the Concept of Yahweh: Monotheism

Isaiah of Babylon's religious affirmations were the climax of centuries of changes in the ways Israel thought about Yahweh. His statements show his complete conviction that only Yahweh existed as Lord of the universe. Monotheism of the most exalted type was his sixth contribution to the stream of thought in Israel. Prophets and priests before him had known Yahweh as sole God of Israel and as director of history among all nations, but never had that sublime idea been combined with such purity of language.

His poems about the servant of Yahweh, whose combination of beauty of form and clarity of expression have no rival, affirm that suffering may purify a man. Such suffering was the highest achievement of mankind, and set an example to aliens as well as to his own people. Not until this view of suffering was applied to God Himself in the 1st century A.D. did religious thought rise again to such elevated heights. This poet was the watershed of Israelite religion. For five hundred years beliefs about the nature of God and man had undergone changes and additions until they reached this peak. It would be another five hundred years before the ancient Near East again gave to the western world so majestic an expression.

[43] This passage is equally applicable to Cyrus as to the Suffering Servant. Cf. 45:1 ff.; 49:1–6 could also be applied to Cyrus by simply substituting Cyrus for Israel in 49:3.

The exile was a fertile period in Israel's literary history for the composition of psalms. The substitution of synagogue worship for national ceremonies conducted at a royal shrine gave opportunity for gifted poets to express their feelings outside official religious rites. The synagogue provided incentives for artistic creativity within the forms of worship. Prayers, sermons, and hymns were composed with individualistic traits because the traditional formulas for verbal and dramatic presentation which had existed in the Jerusalem Temple were broken by the events of history. Sensitive priests were able to improvise in the context of a new religious situation.

Psalms 137

Psalms were one of the ways that the Jewish exiles expressed their awe and wonder, fear and anxiety, expectations and hopes in an alien and hostile world. Psalm 137 is the exilic hymn that is typical above all others. Its lyric quality and doleful mood impress the reader with the painful emotions the exiles felt when they arrived in Babylon. With no sanctuary in which to make communal wailings for their wasted homeland, the exiles collected on the banks of the river to mourn their loss. Citizens of Babylon chided them for their backward look, and ordered them to sing their native songs for their mocking entertainment. Jerusalem's desolation will be remembered even though the bitterness of exile is ever so severe. At verse 7 the psalm's real purpose is revealed. It was a curse upon the Edomites and Babylonians for the destruction of Jerusalem. Edomitic mercenaries had harassed Jerusalem in 603 B.C. while Nebuchadnezzar was busy with border revolts elsewhere. They had joined his army in the final assault in 587 B.C. In addition, Edomites were encroaching upon Palestinian land vacated by exiles taken to Babylon, and land once Jewish had now become property of aliens. Bitterness dominated Jewish exiles, who thought mainly of returning to their homes in Palestine to reclaim the land which had been stolen from them. The Babylonian tormentors were probably astounded by the vindictiveness of the conclusion of a song which had begun in such lyric sadness.

Psalm 73

The poet of Psalm 73 considered himself a righteous person, but as he experienced the world, he discovered that the wicked prospered, they had no pangs of conscience, they were physically sound, and they received the adulation of men (Ps. 73:3–11). These wicked persons were probably Jewish exiles who had given up Yahwism, and imitated Babylonian customs so that they got along very well with their captors. This sensitive soul struggled against the temptation to give up his beliefs (Ps. 73:2), and kept the purity of his traditions as well as he could. His weakness of faith was replaced by strength when he went into the sanctuary of God. The term "sanctuary of God" (Ps. 37:17) may mean the Jerusalem Temple, and so most scholars interpret this passage. But the Hebrew word is plural, so that the psalmist recalls going into several sanctuaries of God. The same construction is used at Numbers 18:29 where the word means the holiest *parts* of an offering. The passage in Numbers comes from the exilic Priestly writer. The same word is used in the plural at Psalm 68:35, and this psalm is often assigned to the 10th century B.C. Therefore Psalm 73 was written either before the Temple was built or after it was destroyed. The latter seems more probable. The remainder of the psalm represents the plight of the author as he tries to maintain his beliefs and moral integrity in difficult days. His participation in synagogue worship pulls him through his crisis (Ps. 73:24).

Psalm 74 In Psalm 74 the memory of the Temple's destruction is vivid, and the author recalls the exact manner of its desecration (Ps. 74:3–7). Perhaps he was a priest caught in the Temple when the demolition crews moved in. References to "meeting places of God" (Ps. 74: 8) may mean the houses of worship that sprung up in towns and villages after the centralization of sacrifice and festivals in Jerusalem in 621 B.C. References to the Babylonian Creation myth in verses 13–14 make exilic origins certain. This psalm shows no anticipation of release from bondage, so that it was written before Cyrus had begun his campaigns into Babylon.

Psalm 87 Psalm 87 supplies the opening lines to one of the greatest English hymns. A former sea captain and slave trader, the Reverend John Newton, in a moment of religious exultation following his conversion to Christianity wrote

> *Glorious things of thee are spoken*
> *Zion, city of our God; (Ps. 87:3)*
> *He whose word cannot be broken*
> *Formed thee for His own abode:*
> *On the Rock of Ages founded,*
> *What can shake thy sure repose?*
> *With salvation's walls surrounded,*
> *Thou mayst smile at all thy foes.*

After years of sailing ships loaded with Africans crowded into filthy holds, his release from captivity to the cruelist of all social sins was like the expectation of deliverance the Jewish exile felt as he looked to the Holy City. The words, set to the tune of Franz Joseph Haydn's famous Austrian Hymn, still communicate the mood of confidence which freedom offers.

Psalm 89

Psalm 89 may have been composed when the poet learned that Jehoiachin had been cast into a Babylonian prison by Nebuchadnezzar. Jewish captives were not usually incarcerated by the Babylonian army, but were permitted to live in communities among the citizens of that great city. As Jeremiah informed us (Jer. 29:15–23), however, some Jews were rebellious in exile, and these men were executed. The servant of Yahweh in Isaiah 40–55, 60–61 was probably put to death for fomenting treason. Jehoiachin was thrown into prison sometime during his exile and released by Amel-Marduk (562–560 B.C.), the Evil-Merodach of 2 Kings 25:27, in the first year of the new king's reign. This psalm is a hymn of praise and an oracle on Davidic royalty that turned to a lament (Ps. 89:8–51) when the expectations of a speedy return to Judah were dashed by the turn of fortune against Jehoiachin.

Psalms 102 and 132

Psalms 102 and 132 give little indication of their dates of composition. The emphasis upon Zion as the special abode of Yahweh which has been temporarily abandoned sounds like Ezekiel's conception of Yahweh removing His splendor from the Temple when it was being destroyed. The usage of traditional symbols like ark and footstool (Ps. 132:8, 7) need not make Psalm 132 a hymn of pre-exilic Judah. Both psalms look toward the reestablishment of Yahweh's favorite home.

These examples of hymns composed by exiles help one appreciate the agony of body and soul through which faithful Yahwists went. No amount of reading about the historical and religious facts will substitute for the firsthand recital of those themselves caught in a desperate situation. These psalms uniquely communicate the personal experiences of degradation felt by the exiles.

Restoration of Jerusalem did take place, but it was a more painful experience, with almost insurmountable difficulties, than Ezekiel or Isaiah of Babylon had imagined it would be.

XIII

**Exiles Return
and Rebuild
Jerusalem**

Cyrus issued a decree in 538 B.C. that permitted Jews in exile to
return to Jerusalem. Records for a period of about one hundred and
forty years after this momentous decree are surprisingly scanty,
and those that exist are sometimes more confusing than clarifying.
Documents written by individuals between 538 and 398 B.C. offer
little difficulty in interpretation, but those compiled rather indiscriminately respecting content and style bring on literary headaches.
After literary analysis has provided some workable conclusions,
historical problems diminish, but they do not disappear. Considerable guesswork is required to attain an historical reconstruction of
this "dark period."

The Book of Haggai The book of Haggai contains four prophetic pronouncements each
with its date, after the manner of Ezekiel's autobiographical visions.
The first pronouncement was a response to discussion about building the Temple (Hag. 1:2–11). Some people had counseled against
it. Haggai proclaimed that the Jerusalemites' wretched economic
condition was due precisely to their neglect of the Temple (Hag.

Core Readings

Haggai

Zechariah 1–8

Obadiah

Malachi

Isaiah 34, 35, 56–66 (excluding 60–62, 63:7–19)

Leviticus 1–16

Ezra

Nehemiah

Psalms 19, 33, 44, 51, 91, 150[1]

---

[1] This was a period of abundant psalm writing. The following also came from the post-
exilic age: 23, 24, 27, 30, 31, 38, 42–43, 47, 48, 50, 55, 64, 65, 67, 68, 69, 94, 95,
96, 99, 103, 104, 105, 111, 115, 122, 123, 124, 125, 126, 133, 134, 138, 147.

1:4–6). Yahweh had sent drought because the citizens permitted the house of Yahweh to lie in ruins (Hag. 1:11). The second declaration promised that the rebuilt Temple would be more splendid than the first (Hag. 2:1–9). The declaration was made to Zerubbabel the governor, to Joshua the high priest, and to the "remnant of the people." The third utterance was an answer to a question about holy food. Was holiness contagious? Did meat prepared by priests make other food holy if the meat touched it? Haggai's answer was negative, but uncleanness was contagious (Hag. 2:10–14). A promise that crop-failure will end seems out of place (Hag. 2:15–19). The fourth pronouncement was political. Haggai promised to Zerubbabel the signet ring of rulership after the incumbent power was toppled (Hag. 2:20–23).

Dating Haggai's Oracles

These four oracles were spoken in the second year of the reign of Darius (522–486 B.C.), within a period of three months. The dating of the second oracle is particularly interesting. Haggai made his first appeal for building the Temple on June 1st, 520 B.C. The second oracle was dated on July 21st, 520 B.C.; that means that within seven weeks work on the Temple had commenced. Whether architects' plans had already been prepared is unknown, but Haggai had performed a major task to get the project underway. This chronology may reveal more about his abilities than his little book reports directly.

Solutions to two literary problems increase appreciation of the book. The first is the peculiar way the date in Haggai 1:15 hangs suspended. Does not an oracle belong with this date as with the others? In reading the third oracle, notice that a question about contamination is attached to the problem of crop failure. The Temple had been under construction for three months. Would Haggai still promise crop failure, since Yahweh's word to build the Temple had been followed? No. Since June 24th, 520 B.C. (Hag. 1:15), when the foundation of the Temple had been laid (Hag. 2:18), Yahweh had promised to bless the harvests. It is likely, therefore, that Haggai 2:15–19 should follow Haggai 1:15. "The twenty-fourth day of the ninth month" in Haggai 2:18 is an editor's insertion. Not working carefully, he found an oracle on the twenty-fourth day of the sixth month at Haggai 1:15. The editor used an oracle dated on the twenty-fourth day of the ninth month at 2:10. At 2:20 he had another oracle on the twenty-fourth day of the ninth month. In trying to use three oracles, all given on the twenty-fourth day of the month, he overlooked the fact that the oracle in 2:15–19 came from the sixth month, and should have followed after Haggai 1:15.

The second literary problem is simpler. The first oracle (Hag. 1: 2–11) seems out of order. Verses 5–6 are a parallel to verses 7, 9–11. Therefore, verses 1a, 7, 9–11 constitute the original oracle. Verses 1b–6, 8 were the words of an editorial note about Haggai. That, and the report of Zerubbabel's and Joshua's reaction to Haggai's first oracle (Hag. 1:12–14), were additions made to Haggai's original dated scroll.

The Book of Zechariah

The book of Zechariah divides naturally into two sections, chapters 1–8 and 9–14. Style and content demonstrate that these two parts were not written by the same author nor did they originate under the same historical circumstances. Some of the oracles in chapters 1–8 are dated, so that they may easily be placed in their proper period. Chapters 9–14 will be studied when we turn to apocalyptic writings.

Oracles and Visions in Chapters 1–8

As chapters 1–8 now stand they contain five oracles and visions that deal with problems of the restored Jewish community in Jerusalem. The first oracle calls for general repentance (Zech. 1:1–6). Next, Zechariah reports eight visions or dreams to his listeners (Zech. 1:7 – 6:8). The vision of the horse patrol sees the nations pacified, the Temple rebuilt, and Jerusalem again prosperous (Zech. 1:7–17). Probably in the original vision there were four horses representing the four directions. The vision of the four horns and four smiths depicts punishment upon nations that had destroyed Jerusalem (Zech. 1:18–21). The vision of the tape measure shows Jerusalem glorified (Zech. 2:1–13). The vision of Joshua the high priest shows him newly sanctified for his tasks in the restored Temple (Zech. 3:1–10). The fifth vision, interrupted by the insertion of an oracle (Zech. 4:6b–10a), reports a candelabra and two olive trees, symbolizing Yahweh and his two representatives, Zerubbabel and Joshua (Zech. 4:1–6a, 10b–14). Vision six is of a flying scroll that searches out thieves and liars (Zech. 5:1–4). Vision seven reports a woman sitting in a basket carried to Babylon through the air by storkwomen (Zech. 5:5–11). The final vision shows four chariots drawn by different-colored horses (Zech. 6:1–8). All these visions seem to have the quality of dreams. They show Zechariah's intensity and personal involvement in Jerusalem's crucial predicaments as Ezekiel's visions did.

The third section is an oracle commanding Zechariah to make a golden crown, and to set it upon Zerubbabel the son of Shealtiel, the governor (Zech. 6:9–15). Verse 11 should not read Joshua, the son of Jehozadak, the high priest—the text was tampered with. Zerubbabel was the person credited with messianic qualities, not

Joshua (see Hag. 2:21). Another oracle answers the question about fasting on the anniversary of the day the Temple was destroyed by Babylon's demolition squads (Zech. 7:1–14). A fifth oracle offers seven promises, each one introduced by the formula "thus says the Lord of hosts" (Zech. 8:1–23).

The visions and oracles show that Zechariah 1–8 was a dated work similar to the book Ezekiel produced. Some literary problems in these chapters need attention. *First*, undated oracles have been inserted by someone other than the original author (Zech. 4:8, 6:9, 7:8). The vision of the candelabra and two olive trees, for example, (Zech. 4:1–14), is interrupted by an oracle about Zerubbabel's responsibility for building the Temple (Zech. 4:6b–10a) in an effort to explain the last line of the vision (Zech. 4:14). Another insertion is found in the two sections at Zechariah 7:1 – 8:23. The question about fasting raised at Zechariah 7:3 is not answered until Zechariah 8:18. *Second*, the vision of Joshua's purification is composed of two narratives; one concerns charges brought against Joshua for his disrespect of his professional office (Zech. 3:1–7), the other concerns the messiah, "my servant the Branch" (Zech. 3:8–10). *Third*, the original text at Zechariah 6:11 was tampered with. Here "Zerubbabel son of Shealtiel, the governor" was replaced by the name Joshua. Verses 12–13 show this because Zerubbabel is referrred to as the one who would build the Temple (Zech. 4:6b–10). It is probable that Zerubbabel was altered to Joshua by someone whose nationalistic hopes were unrealized by Zerubbabel's leadership. *Lastly*, the promises in the fifth section are sayings artificially connected by the formula "Thus says the Lord." There is no conclusive evidence for or against Zechariah's authorship of these seven promises.

The Book of Obadiah

The book of Obadiah was composed from two independent poems. The first poem (Obad. 1–14) deals with a threat against Edom. Obadiah took an old oracle against Edom (Obad. 1–4, 8) and added a few lines to make a decisive threat against that people. Then he explains why the threat was made (Obad. 10–14). The Edomites had seized upon Jerusalem's misfortune to heap further insult and injury upon the city. Verse 15b belongs to the concluding threats against Edom, being a proper conclusion to that poem. It is clear that the threats against Edom are traditional materials because Jeremiah 49:7–22 uses practically the same words against Edom. A poem about the day of Yahweh was appended to the oracle against Edom (Obad. 15a, 16–21). These two literary units were joined because of their common subject matter.

Three periods in Israel's history have been suggested for the composition of these poems. One may have been about 850 B.C., when Edom successfully rebelled against Judah's control (2 Kings 8:20–22). A second may have been shortly after the fall of Jerusalem in 587 B.C. The poet condemns Edomites for their support of Babylonian troops, indiscriminate looting, and "bounty-hunting" of fugitives which they returned to the Babylonian army. A third date seems the most likely. This was the period during the 6th and 5th centuries B.C. when Edomites migrated in large numbers into Judah, driven there by an unheaval of Arab tribes in the interior deserts. Unstable Judah was incapable of coping with their seizure of land and trade concessions, and Obadiah uttered a curse upon their heads. The curse proved ineffective. The Edomites were simply the first migrants pushed out of their land by a steady infiltration of north Arabian tribes into Moab and Edom. These tribes were known as Nabateans.[2] Traditional denunciations are used by Obadiah to utter his threat. The vivid memory of Edomitic assistance in destroying Jerusalem burned white-hot in the memory of Jews for centuries. In fact, the further removed from the actual event, the more intense were literary depictions of it.

The Book of Malachi

Malachi is one of the most unusual books in the Old Testament. It has no significant literary problems, but a few additions to the text are noticeable. Verses 2:11b—13a are out of context respecting the covenants in Malachi 2:10–16. Additions at 4:4 and 4:5–6 deal with different matters, so it is probable that they were added independently of each other and subsequent to the publication of the original scroll. Verses 4:5–6 are an effort to identify the messenger mentioned in 3:1.

The book of Malachi is cast in the form of a dialogue. Yahweh speaks, or the prophet as His spokesman does, and the people reply by asking questions. Then Yahweh explains His point. The questions are asked in explicit form, and they reveal what Malachi is upset about.

> *Does Yahweh love Israel?* (Mal. 1:2)
> *How has Yahweh's name been despised?* (Mal. 1:6)
> *How was the altar polluted?* (Mal. 1:7)
> *Why are we faithless in our contracts?* (Mal. 2:10)

[2] See "Nabateans," in George A. Buttrick, ed., *The Interpreter's Dictionary of the Bible,* K–Q (New York: Abingdon Press, 1962), pp. 491–3. Hereafter referred to as *IDB.*

Why doesn't Yahweh accept our sacrifices? (Mal. 2:14)
How have we wearied Yahweh? (Mal. 2:17)
Where is the God of justice? (Mal. 2:17)
How do we return to Yahweh? (Mal. 3:7)
How are we robbing God? (Mal. 3:8)
How have we spoken against Yahweh? (Mal. 3:13)
What good comes from keeping Yahweh's law? (Mal. 3:13)

The book has six sections whose similarity of style show that they are homogeneous. Section one contrasts Yahweh's love for Israel with His hate of Edom (Mal. 1:2–5). Section two criticizes the priests for accepting inferior animals for sacrifice. It augurs a curse if they continue such unlawful practices (Mal. 1:6 — 2:9). Section three condemns Jewish men for divorcing their wives to marry foreigners (Mal. 2:10–16). Section four pronounces a day of judgment on those who doubted divine retribution (Mal. 2:17 — 3:5). Section five explains a plague as Yahweh's punishment for withholding Temple tithes (Mal. 3:6–12). Section six proclaims that the wicked appear to prosper, but a day will come when they shall be destroyed (Mal. 3:13 — 4:3).

This book has no certain date, but the Temple cult is practiced in it, therefore it must have come after Haggai and Zechariah. Reforms that were needed in the cult and in marriage practices were accomplished by Nehemiah, so it came before him. Sometime between 500 and 450 B.C. would be a safe guess. The name "Malachi" does not appear in any lists in Chronicles, Ezra, or Nehemiah. In fact, it is not a proper name at all: it means in Hebrew "my messenger." An anonymous scroll was supplied with an author's name by making the undesignated messenger (Mal. 3:1) the writer of the book. Some equally unknown scribe tried to erase the mistake by stating that Elijah was the messenger who would come before the day of the Lord (Mal. 4:5).

Isaiah of the Restoration

Scholars have debated the unity of Isaiah 56–66, but no sure conclusions have been reached. Few argue any longer that chapters 56–66 were written by the author of chapters 40–55. The last eleven chapters of Isaiah, therefore, are often named Trito or Third Isaiah. Historical allusions give few clues to the origins of these several chapters, but most of them represent the period of Jewish restoration of Jerusalem. Certain literary characteristics in several of these chapters remind one of Isaiah of Babylon, but differences in style and vocabulary are also striking.

Additions to the Isaiah Scroll

Isaiah 56–66 and 34–35 were originally separate poems from many authors collected into fairly uniform units. How they became attached to the Isaiah scroll is problematic. Consider two possibilities. *First*, the original Isaiah scroll consisted of most of chapters 1–39. At some unknown time that material was copied onto a larger-than-usual scroll and, so chapters 40–55, which had some literary similarities, were appended. The same process occurred again, and the anonymous poems in chapters 56–66 were written on the scroll with the two other collections. As time passed all three collections were given the name of Isaiah. *Second*, precisely because of the similarities of style and religion, three originally independent scrolls were combined onto a single one under the name of the great prophet of Jerusalem. It is possible that the school of prophecy originated by Isaiah of Jerusalem in the 8th century B.C. continued through the exile and period of reconstruction. Its greatest contribution to literary and theological history was the preservation of its chief spokesmen on the single Isaiah scroll.

Whatever the history of the preservation of the scrolls, it is necessary to separate the poems in Isaiah 55–66, 34–35 according to style and content. Precision in grouping poems is never perfectly successful, but sorting is necessary. To treat all these chapters as coming from a single author and period would confuse the religious affirmations found there. The chapters form four groups, providing insight not only as literature but also as religious expressions from four periods of post-exilic Israel.

The first group of poems shows a harmony of style and content that suggests they were once a unit of literature. Probably they should be considered part of the anthology of Isaiah of Babylon.

Isaiah 57:14–21 reflects the return to Jerusalem.
Isaiah 60–62 looks upon the reconstruction of Jerusalem, the wealth of nations offered to the city, and the righteousness of its citizens as being about to take place.
Isaiah 66:7–16 likens the rebirth of Jerusalem to a child born without labor.
Isaiah 35 speaks of exiles returning to Jerusalem on broad highways and through gardens that had once been desert.
Isaiah 65:17–25, 66:22–23 sees Jerusalem as the center of a new earth.

This group portrays the mounting hope of Jews in the last years of exile and the beginning of the return to Palestine, about 540–530 B.C.

A second group of poems reflects Yahweh's distress, anger, and punishment. Accusations and laments predominate in these poems.

Isaiah 56:9 – 57:13 contrasts evil and righteous men.

Isaiah 59 cites the gross iniquities which have driven justice away. Yahweh's displeasure at injustice prompts Him to anger and vengeance.

Isaiah 63:7 – 64:12 recalls Yahweh's steadfast love. Israel rebelled but Yahweh's memory of Moses made His repent even though the people's sins were grave.

Isaiah 65:1–16 points out how Yahweh had made Himself available, but the rebellious Israelites turned away.

Isaiah 66:5, 17–21, 24 contrasts those who performed corrupt cultic rites and those who offered clean ones.

This group of poems represents the period when the Temple had been rebuilt but when corruptions began to erode the cult. They were similar to Malachi's complaints, about 500–450 B.C.

A third group of poems are oracles against Edom: Isaiah 34, 63:1–6. These two poems are companions of the two in Obadiah, from the early 5th century B.C.

A fourth group of poems deals with sabbath observance and participation in the cult of the restored community.

Isaiah 56:1–8 tends to equate sabbath keeping with the rites that would bring Yahweh's deliverance. Foreigners and eunuchs were permitted in the cultic community.

Isaiah 58 sees the sabbath day as important but fast days were less significant than righteousness and charity.

These poems probably date from the period during Ezra's reforms and presentation of the law, 398 B.C.

Isaiah 66:1–4 stands alone. It is a strong condemnation of the Temple. It denies special holiness to Zion and the building (Isa. 66:1–2a). It denies spiritual value to sacrifice, cereal offering, and incense. The truly religious man is "he that is humble and contrite in spirit" (Isa. 66:2b). This poem may have come from an unnamed prophet who opposed Haggai and Zechariah when they were agitating for the construction of the Temple, 520 B.C.

Although most of the poems in Isaiah 56–66, 34–35 are not as inspiring in their literary and religious excellence as those of Isaiah of Babylon, they clearly represent several different attitudes toward beliefs and practices in Israel's religion in the post-exilic period. The historical records are so scanty that any materials are useful in helping to inform us on problems of history in post-exilic Israel.

The Priestly Writer

The theory that the Pentateuch was compiled from three narratives of Israel's origins and the book of Deuteronomy (JEDP) has already been set forth.[3] The Priestly source, that theory claims, was written in post-exilic Palestine. The style of the Priestly writer is so distinct that one usually has no trouble in tracing his narration in the Pentateuch. His formal redundancy and prolix language with its many stereotyped phrases sets it off from the simpler styles of the Yahwist and Elohist narrators. The Priestly storyteller recites Israel's origins emphasizing cultic practices rather than history and biography. His narrative divides the history of Israel from Creation to the Conquest into four unequal literary units. The first unit takes in the period from Creation to Noah. P uses Elohim as the name for the deity throughout this section, and Elohim is the supreme ruler of the world, not merely the private god of a small group of people. His sovereign, creative power is specified by his ability to bring order out of a preexistent chaos. Man is the crowning achievement of God in His several creative acts. The list of Adam's descendants is mighty impressive, with their lengths of life as great as nine hundred and sixty-nine years (Gen. 5:27). This first division originally was introduced by the phrase "These are the generations of the heavens and the earth when they were created" (Gen. 2:4a) but it was somehow misplaced.[4]

The Priestly narrative's second unit opens with "These are the generations of Noah" (Gen. 6:9). This division spans the epoch between Noah and Abraham. Noah's righteousness brings him the task of saving his family and a male and female of each type of animal from destruction by a great flood. Noah is man enough for the task. For his labor he is rewarded with a covenant with God, whereby God promises never to efface the earth's surface again if Noah will not eat flesh which still had blood in it (Gen. 9:4).[5]

The third unit covers the lives of the Patriarchs. Here is recorded the Sumerian ancestry of Abraham, his covenant with El Shaddai (one name for God in this division), the origins of circumcision, a

[3]See pp. 116–117.
[4]The passages belonging to P in this first section are: Genesis 1:1–31; 2:1–4a; 5:1–28, 30–32.
[5]Genesis 6:9–22; 7:6, 11, 13–16a, 17a, 18–21, 24; 8:1–2a, 3b–5, 13a, 14–19; 9:1–17, 28–29; 10:1a, 2–7, 20, 22–23, 31–32; 11:10–26.

few details about Isaac, Jacob, and Esau, the seventy Israelites
who went to Egypt, and the death of Jacob. Ths introductory "Now
these are the generations of Terah" ("descendants" in the RSV
Gen. 11:27) illustrates the precise structure of the Priestly writer's
style.[6]

P's fourth unit relates the story of Moses. This unit begins with the
introductory formula slightly revised, "These are the names of the
sons of Israel who came to Egypt . . ." (Exod. 1:1). The bitter
servitude of the sons of the people of Israel brings action from El
Shaddai. He reveals Himself to Moses as Yahweh, and from that
moment on Yahweh takes charge of the people of Israel through
Moses, Aaron, and Miriam. The plagues, the institution of Passover,
the journey to Sinai, and the revelation to Moses of Yahweh's cultic
demands, are the major actions in this section before detailed accounts are related of priestly rituals and equipment, and of how
Israelites should behave since they are people holy to Yahweh.

At Numbers 10:11 the narrative of Israel's trek toward Canaan is
resumed. Upon approaching Canaan spies are sent out, and they
return with a depressing report on Canaan. There is rebellion in
the ranks, Miriam and Aaron die, there is a plague in Moab, the
census of the people is taken, and Moses dies on Mount Nebo
(Deut. 32:49).[7]

**Literary Characteristics
of the Priestly Narrative**

Literary traits of the Priestly narrative are easily identified. It is
quite clear that P assumes the readers of his story know the JE
narrative already. With no preliminary explanation about Moses
and his role in Egyptian-Israelite politics, for instance, nor of any
journey to the sacred mountain, P writes, "God said to Moses, I am
Yahweh" (Exod. 6:2). P's study is monotonous, although in some
places the style rises to the dramatic and colorful. This occurs in
Genesis 1:1 − 2:4a, 17:15−21, ch. 23, but then P is rewriting earlier

[6]Genesis 11:27, 31−32; 12:4b−6a; 13:6, 11b−12a; 16:3, 15−16; 17; 1−27; 19:29;
21:1b, 2b−5, 23:1−20; 25:7−10, 12−17, 19−20. 26c; 26:34−35; 27:46; 28:1−9;
29:24, 28b−29; 30:4a, 9b; 35:6a, 9−13, 15, 22c−29; 36:1−8; 37:1−2a; 41:46; 46:
6−27; 48:3−6; 49:1a, 28c−33; 50:12−13.
[7]The passages belonging to P are: Exodus 1:1−5, 7, 13−14; 2:23b−25; 6:2−30;
7:1−13, 19−20a, 21c−22; 8:5−7, 16b−19; 9:8−12; 11:9−10; 12:1−20, 28, 37a, 40−41,
42b−51; 13:1−2, 20; 14:1−4, 8−9, 15−18, 21ac−23, 26−27a, 28−29, 19; 16:1−3,
6−24, 31−36; 17:1a; 19:1−2a; 24:15−18a; 25:1 − 31:18a; 34:29 − 40:38. All of Leviticus (exclusive of chs. 17−26) and Numbers 1:1 − 10:28 are assigned to P. The
narrative of the journey from Sinai to Mount Nebo in Moab begins at Numbers
10:11. Numbers 10:11−28; 13:1−17a, 21, 25−26a, 32a; 14:1−2, 5−7, 10, 26−30,
34−38; 15:1−41; 16:1a, 2b−11, 16−23, 27a, 35−50; 17:1 − 19:22; 20:1a, 2, 3b−4,
6−13, 22−29; 21:4a, 10−11; 22:1; 25:6 − 31:54; 32:18−19, 28−33; 33:1 − 36:13;
Deuteronomy 1:3; 32:48−52.

sources which were themselves fascinating. P uses a technical vocabulary, and once he has the correct word he repeats it again and again. Some of his favorites are: *assembly, congregation, to create, covenant, generations, possession, inheritance, and testimony.* His prolixity is illustrated by such phrases as "[he] breathed his last and died, and was gathered to his people" (Gen. 25:8, 17; 49:29–33; Num. 20:24, 26) rather than "he died." He repeats phrases in wearisome manner, for example, "The Lord said to Moses, Tell the people of Israel" (Exod. 14:1, 15; 25:2; Lev. 1:2, 4:2). He redundantly identifies the Pharaoh as "the king of Egypt" (Exod. 6:11, 13, 27), and Sarah as "Abram's wife" rather unnecessarily after she is introduced at Genesis 11:31 (Gen. 12:5, 16:3). Canaan and Egypt are always called the "land of Canaan" and the "land of Egypt." Other examples of tiring redundancy are found at Exodus 2:23b–25, where groaning and crying for help while in bondage are piled on top of each other, and at Exodus 12:18–20, where the command to eat only unleavened bread is given five times.

The first three units of P are entitled "These are the generations of . . . ," and the fourth "These are the names of . . ." (Gen. 2:4a, 5:1, 6:9, Exod. 1:1). Subdivisions are also set off by title. The section on the generations of Shem, Ham, and Japheth, for example, is divided under the titles "The sons of Japheth" (Gen. 10:2a), "The sons of Ham" (Gen. 10:6), and "The sons of Shem" (Gen. 10:22). Each subdivision is closed out by the phrase "These are the sons of Japheth (Ham, and Shem), by their families, their languages, their lands, and their nations" (Gen. 10:5, 20, 31).

P's Dependence on Written Sources

P depends upon written sources almost exclusively. Whereas J and E had used mostly oral traditions, as Herman Gunkel so clearly showed,[8] P depended upon non-Israelite written material as well as on JE and other Israelite sources (Exod. 34:29–35). He completely rewrote either a Canaanite or Babylonian source for his Creation story in Genesis 1. He depended upon parts of the Babylonian Gilgamesh Epic for his story of the Flood.

The Priestly writer's division of Israel's origins into four periods was a system of reckoning he acquired from the Babylonians. Each epoch of creation is identified with sabbath observance. The epoch of the flood is known by its prohibition of eating blood (Gen. 9:1–17). The epoch of the patriarchs is typified by circumcision.

[8] Herman Gunkel, *The Legends of Genesis,* trans. W. H. Carruth, 1901 (New York: Schocken Books, 1964).

The last epoch is the one which begins with Moses and in which the Jews live. Its special rite is Passover (Exod. 12:1–20). Into this original narrative based on the four-epoch plan later Priestly writers inserted legal documents which they developed as part of their tendency to heighten ritual as population increased, as economic improvement occurred, and as Priestly influence grew. Insertions are found, for example, in a collection of laws on sacrifices (Lev. 1–7) and on ritual purity (Lev. 11–15).[9]

P's Fascination with Numerology

The Priestly writer was especially intrigued by numerology, and it is likely that this Babylonian science had some influence on his thinking.[10] He gives exaggerated ages to the pre-flood patriarchs, a literary convention practiced in Babylon.[11] He reports that Noah kept a logbook and gave exact measurements of the flood waters and the number of days the flood lasted, exactly one solar year. His report on the census in Numbers 1:46 gives the exact male population of the traveling tribes as 603,550. This figure was probably arrived at by a scheme using the numerical equivalents of a favorite Hebrew phrase. The ancient Hebrews had no numbers, so the letters of their alphabet were assigned numerical value. *Aleph* equaled one, *beth* two, *gimel* three, and so forth. The phrase "the census of the people of Israel" (Exod. 30:12) is the phrase from which the number 603,550 is derived. Transliterated from Hebrew the phrase is *rosh kol benē Yisra'el*. *Rosh kol* equals 551, *benē Yisra'el* equals 603. Multiply 603 by 1,000 and add 551 and total is 603,551, or rounded off, 603,550.[12]

The Priestly School

The Priestly narrator was only one member of a school whose influence upon post-exilic Israel was tremendous. Sometimes it is convenient to think of Ezekiel, with his emphasis upon an ideal temple and his precise style of writing, as the founder of the Priestly school of literature and religion. If Ezekiel was its founder, and for this there is no proof, Ezra may be cited as its most notable student. The Jewish return from Babylon was sparked by a passionate concern that Yahweh be given His due. Temple rites were, according to the Priestly school, the highest duties Jews could perform for

[9] Laws for Nazirites (Numbers 6), purification from ashes of a red heifer (Numbers 19), and inheritance by daughters (Numbers 27:1–11), are other examples of late insertions.
[10] See "Number, Numbering, Numbers," *IDB*, K–Q, pp. 561–7.
[11] The list of Sumerian kings gave incredibly long years to reigns of the ancient kings: Eridu 28,800 years, Alalgar 36,000 years, En-Men-lu-Anna 43,200 years. See James B. Pritchard, *Ancient Near Eastern Texts,* Princeton, N.J.: Princeton University Press, 1955), pp. 265–6. Hereafter referred to as *ANET*.
[12] See Julius A. Bewer, *The Literature of the Old Testament,* rev. Emil G. Kraeling, (3rd ed.; New York: Columbia University Press, 1962), p. 279.

Yahweh. Practically, too, the only rallying point for returnees was about the Temple. The organization of Judah as a Persian province forbade independent political leadership, so that it was priests who served as leaders of rebuilt Jerusalem. It is likely that a theocracy actually served the organizational and communal needs of the returnees in the first one hundred years of Jewish life in post-exilic Judah.

The Priestly school significantly influenced the theoretical aspects of the theocracy. Its account of Israel's origins was written precisely to give authority to many rites only recently established. Furthermore, such materials served nicely as a guide for Priestly instruction to the people on their duties and obligations in the theocracy. P's narrative began with the majestic story of creation in order to show that the sabbath day was built into the very framework of the universe. Since circumcision had become a major rite of Yahwism in exile, Israel's noblest legendary ancestor, Abraham, was credited with origination of the act (Gen. 17). The Jews who returned from captivity needed land. But the cultivable land was occupied by Jews who had not been exiled and by immigrants from Edom, Ammon, and Moab who had taken over vacated property. The story of Abraham's purchase of a burial plot for Sarah (Gen. 23) attempted to give legal claim to the returnees because their ancestor had bought the land from its original owner. Historically the land had become Israel's by right of conquest, but such a claim could not be set forth because Edomites, Ammonites, and Moabites could use that claim themselves. The laws of the Temple were seated in history, too. The Exodus from Egypt was sketched rapidly by P until the children of Israel arrived at Sinai. There he slowed his narration to report in rich detail the construction of the tabernacle and the creation of the priesthood (Exod. 25–29). The narration picked up speed again as the people were numbered (Num. 1–2), and began their invasion of Canaan (Num. 13).

From Ezekiel's day to Ezra's the Priestly school of literature and religion gave direction to the Jewish community and its cultic expressions. Stress on order and organization typified its community life as well as its literature, and two men appeared upon the scene to carry forward those characteristics. Nehemiah and Ezra represent the practical application of the Priestly school's theoretical formulation of the ideal Jewish community.

The Books of Ezra and Nehemiah   The books of Ezra and Nehemiah constitute a literary unit. The complications of these two documents are frustrating at first, but careful analysis enables one to reconstruct post-exilic Judah in a fairly satisfactory way. These two books were originally the conclusion of the work known as Chronicles. It is clear that Ezra was detached from 2 Chronicles subsequent to the composition of the whole work because the last two verses of 2 Chronicles are nearly identical with Ezra 1:1–4. When the books were separated at this point, the opening lines of Ezra were appended to the end of 2 Chronicles.

Chronicles and Ezra–Nehemiah should be studied as a literary unit, but the historical information available in Ezra–Nehemiah is more conveniently handled at this point. To delay treatment of the accounts of post-exilic Israel contained in Ezra–Nehemiah would confuse one further on this shadowy period. Despite a few scholars who would place the Chronicler's compositions before 400, most date the completed work after 350 B.C.[13]

The Chronicler's Sources

The Chronicler[14] had available several sources, and he put them together with harmonizing and expanding touches from his pen. One source for the Chronicler was lists of official persons. There are two lists of returnees from Babylon to Jerusalem (Ezra 2:1–67, Neh. 12:1–26). Another list contains the names of those who promised to divorce their non-Jewish wives (Ezra 10:18–44). Yet another records the men responsible for repairs to certain sections of the wall (Neh. 3:1–32). A short list names Ezra's special assistants (Neh. 8:4–8, 9:1–5). Another list cites the men who agreed to support Nehemiah's reform policies (Neh. 9:38 – 10:27, policies of 10:30–39). Another records heads of families selected to move into Jerusalem from the countryside (Neh. 11:1–35). From the Temple archives the Chronicler retrieved an account of utensils for cultic rites returned from Babylon (Ezra 1:9–11).

Another source for the Chronicler was official records. One is a letter written in Aramaic, the diplomatic language used in Syria and Palestine during the Persian empire, to Artaxerxes (Ezra 4:11–16) and Artaxerxes' reply (Ezra 4:17–22). Another is a letter from Tattenai, governor of the province of Syria, to Darius, questioning rebuilding of the Temple (Ezra 5:7–17). Darius' reply to Tattenai

---

[13]John Bright, *A History of Israel* (Philadelphia: Westminster Press, 1959), pp. 375–86, separates Chronicles–Ezra from Nehemiah. He proposed that Chronicles–Ezra was the original work, written about 400 B.C., and that Nehemiah's memoirs were a secondary addition to the books. This interpretation supports his theory that 428 B.C. was the date of Ezra's return to Jerusalem.

[14]The author of Chronicles and Ezra–Nehemiah is usually called the Chronicler, and that will be our term even though analysis of Ezra–Nehemiah alone is being done.

is also given (Ezra 6:6–12). A record of Cyrus' decree permitting the Jews to rebuild the Temple is used (Ezra 6:3–5). Artaxerxes' commission to Ezra to establish in Judah the law of God and the law of the king is cited (Ezra 7:12–26).

The Memoirs of Nehemiah

A third source in the hands of the Chronicler were the memoirs of Nehemiah and Ezra. These memoirs are, of course, the most reliable history. But the Chronicler does not use them accurately, and the job of reconstructing them must be the first task of the literary critic. Nehemiah preceded Ezra in returning to Jerusalem, as will be shown later, and so his memoirs are reported first. Nehemiah's memoirs report his anguish at hearing about the destitute condition of Jews in Palestine. He appeals to King Artaxerxes for permission to go to Jerusalem, which is granted. Upon arrival he inspects the city walls, and in the face of opposition begins their repair (Neh. 1:1–2:20). Nehemiah tells how Sanballat's opposition led to a plot to attack Jerusalem, but when Nehemiah heard of it he armed his masons and stone cutters and they continued to build. While the wall was being finished Nehemiah turned his attention to monetary and land reforms. But Sanballat persisted in his attack against Nehemiah, and plotted to assassinate him. The plot failed. The wall was finished in fifty-two days, at which time Nehemiah appointed his brother Hanani governor of the city. Then he enrolled the people in a genealogical book after the fashion of one he had found listing those who came to Jerusalem in 537 B.C. (Neh. 4:1–7:73).

Nehemiah reports the dedication ceremonies at the time the wall was completed (Neh. 12:31–43). His narrative concludes as he reported returning to Susa for a while, then coming again to Jerusalem and finding Tobiah the Ammonite living in one of the Temple rooms. He drives him out and cleans the room. He adjusts complaints of the Levites, forbids trading on the sabbath, and tries to eliminate non-Jewish officials from positions of leadership in Jerusalem. He offers his memoirs as a sacrifice to Yahweh (Neh. 13:1–31).

Ezra

Ezra's own words are found at 7:10, 8:15–9:5.[15] He states his qualifications as a jurist and reports how he gathered men to accompany him to Jerusalem. They camped for three days at Ahava, fasted, divided the gold and silver cultic utensils among the travelers, and set out for Palestine. They escaped attack from bandits.

---

[15] Nehemiah 8–9 may have been part of Ezra's memoirs but those two chapters have been fully rewritten by the Chronicler.

Upon arrival in Jerusalem Ezra was appalled at the lax religious conditions and he set about to correct them.

The Chronicler also used the prophetic writings of Haggai and Zechariah. These are the only documents, except for official decrees and letters, which give any firsthand information of the rebuilding of the Temple (Ezra 5:1–2, 3:1–9).

The Chronicler encrusts his sources with his own accounts of Temple ritual (Ezra 3:10–13), the extravagance of the sacrifices (Ezra 6:16–22), and the lengthy prayers offered by his heroes (Ezra 9:6–15, Neh. 9:6–37). His reference to the heavy rain sounds authentic (Ezra 10:9). It was in the ninth month, based on a calendar whose New Year's Day was in the spring, that is December, and it usually rains heavily and gets cold at that time of year in Jerusalem. Chronological dislocations, historical inaccuracies, and religious biases show that the Chronicler did not use his source material with the accuracy modern historians require, but even with these deficiencies he left a treatment of post-exilic Judaism valuable to historians of that era.

Placing the Accounts   It seems likely that Nehemiah 8–9 is out of place, and should follow Ezra 8:36. Look at the evidence for this. The first fact to notice is the dating. The events reported in Nehemiah 8–9 took place in the seventh month between the first and the twenty-fourth days (Neh. 8:2, 13, 18, 9:1). Since no year was mentioned it is necessary to use the last date cited: the first month in the twentieth year of Artaxerxes' reign (Neh. 2:1). The city wall was completed on the twenty-fifth day of the sixth month, that is June 25th, 444 B.C., but the dedication of the wall did not take place until after the events recorded in Nehemiah 8–9. It is hard to understand why the dedication of the wall was delayed for a full month. Furthermore, scholars are almost unanimous in recognizing Nehemiah's name as an editor's addition at Nehemiah 8:9.

Ezra arrived in Jerusalem on the first day of the fifth month of the seventh year of Artaxerxes (Ezra 7:7–9). Divorce proceedings are precisely noted as taking place between the twentieth day of the ninth month through the first day of the first month in the seventh year of Artaxerxes (Ezra 10:9, 16, 17). This means that Ezra did nothing for nearly five months, if we follow the present arrangement of Ezra's activities (Ezra 7:10 – 10:43, Neh. 8:1 – 9:37). This is incredible. Ezra's commission was to act for the Persian king to enforce "the law of your God and the law of the king" (Ezra 7:26).

Furthermore, Ezra 9:1 says "after these things had been done," indicating that something more important took place than just delivering the sacred utensils and offering a sacrifice (Ezra 8:33–36). The rightful place for the story of the reading of the law (Neh. 8–9) belongs immediately after Ezra 8:36. In this arrangement the divorce measures in Ezra 9–10 tie onto Nehemiah 8–9, where the law is made fully known but is not happily received by the "peoples of the land" (Ezra 9:1–2).

Nehemiah 9:38 introduces a story of how several leaders, headed by Nehemiah the governor, vowed to keep the law. It is apparent that what they pledged themselves to was the Deuteronomic Code, "God's law which was given by Moses" (Neh. 10:29). Since Ezra's name does not appear in the list of pledges, it is clear he had nothing to do with that covenant (Neh. 10:1–29). But it is also clear that the cultic exactions found in Nehemiah 10:31–39 are related to those carried out by Nehemiah in chapter 13. The conclusion is that what follows Nehemiah 8–9 no more belongs to it than does what precedes it.

The Proper Sequence in Ezra–Nehemiah

To read Ezra and Nehemiah chronologically, then one should proceed as follows: Ezra 1–6, the account of Jewish returnees who rebuilt the walls and the Temple between 537 and 516 B.C.; there is a hiatus between 516 and 444 B.C.; then pick up Nehemiah 1–7, which is Nehemiah's report of building Jerusalem's wall in the face of local opposition; at Nehemiah 9:38 – 13:31 one reads about laws enacted to make the Temple financially sound, and the repopulation of Jerusalem with families from outlying districts — Nehemiah returns to Susa for an undetermined time, but comes back to Jerusalem to continue as governor; Ezra 7:1 – 8:36 tells how Ezra goes to Jerusalem as agent of King Artaxerxes, to return sacred utensils to the Temple, and to teach a new law to the Jews in Judah; Nehemiah 8:1 – 9:37 reports the ceremony associated with reading the new law; finally, Ezra 9–10 tells how negatively the new law is received by the "peoples of the land," Ezra's great disappointment, and how he tries to force reform upon a reluctant population.

The Chronicler's Faults as an Historian

The Chronicler used his sources with a freedom not acceptable to critical historians. He was guided by a religious purpose rather than the reporting of events as they occurred. He was a careless worker in other respects, too. Ezra 6:2 reports that Cyrus' decree was recorded on a scroll. All official Persian documents were written on clay tablets, so far as archaeologists have been able to determine.[16]

[16] See Pritchard, *ANET*, pp. 265–317.

Again, Ezra 1:2–4 reports Cyrus' decree that Jews were permitted to return to Jerusalem to build a temple, and that voluntary gifts were to be the sources of funds for the reconstruction. But compare that decree with the one cited at Ezra 6:3–5, where explicit mention of sacrifices is made, minimum specifications are listed, the cost is covered by the Persian treasury, and the Temple utensils are decreed to be returned. Ezra 5:13–16 reports that Sheshbazzar, governor of Judah, began to rebuild the Temple in 538 B.C. Haggai reports, however, that Zerubbabel and Joshua undertook construction of the Temple in 520 B.C. (Hag. 1:1–2). Ezra 1:1–2 reports the same thing, contradicting Ezra 5:13–16. The conflict between Zerubbabel and the "people of the land" was over the construction of the Temple, according to Ezra 4:1–5. But Ezra 4:6–23, the official letter written by Bishlam, Mithredath, and Tabeel to Artaxerxes, complains that the Jews were rebuilding the wall and planning rebellion.

The number of documents for a study of about a hundred and fifty years of biblical history is few. Furthermore, some of these writings, especially Obadiah, Malachi, and Isaiah of the Restoration have few historical allusions in them. Those that are historically based were used by the Chronicler with small regard for chronology. Archaeologists have provided the most reliable sources for the period between 538 and 398 B.C., so that a reconstruction of the biblical literature and the use of non-biblical materials provide a fairly clear account of happenings during those important years.

An Historical Reconstruction: The Persian Empire

Persian political control had been established in Syria and Palestine before Babylon fell to Cyrus the Great in 538 B.C. Babylonian provinces were converted into Persian satrapies, and there was a difference between domestic and imperial administration. Whereas Babylonian provinces had been administered by an official who was military commander as well as political governor, Persian provinces were ruled by two men. The political governor, or satrap, had responsibility for purely civil affairs. He designated lesser officials to handle financial and legal matters in small cities, but he governed from a large city located conveniently for his subordinates. The military commanders were completely independent of the governors and were personally loyal to the king alone. This reduced the number of satraps who had the capability of revolting. At the beginning of the empire the Persian kings encouraged their subjects to continue their own ways of life. They were permitted to use their own languages so that there were several official languages in the Empire. Aramaic served that purpose in Syria and Palestine. Local religious traditions were permitted, even encouraged, to flourish, and the

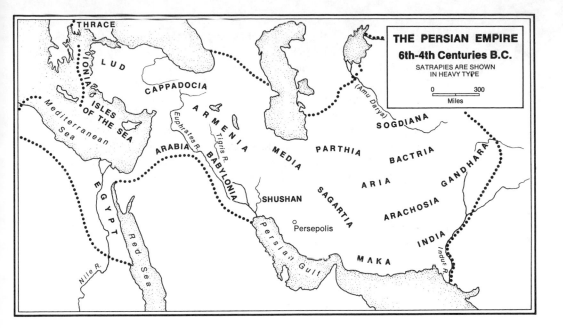

THE PERSIAN EMPIRE
6th-4th Centuries B.C.
SATRAPIES ARE SHOWN
IN HEAVY TYPE

0   300
Miles

early Persian rulers decreed that temples be constructed for the worship of national gods. This explains why Isaiah of Babylon looked upon Cyrus as the servant of Yahweh. It also explains why the Jews were permitted to return to Jerusalem. Nehemiah and Ezra were Persianized Jews who accepted the rule of Persia and fostered Jewish religion with no expectations of independence. But this was probably not the case with Jewish political and religious leaders at the beginning of the Persian empire.

The Return to Jerusalem

The course of events among the Jews may have happened something like the following. In 537 B.C. some Jewish exiles formed a party under Sheshbazzar who was given the title of governor of Jerusalem. Jerusalem was one of the small units in the great satrapy of "Beyond the River," with Damascus as its chief city. "Beyond the River" referred to territory west and south of the Euphrates. Sheshbazzar was referred to as "the prince of Judah," and some scholars have tried to identify him with Shenazzar, a son of exiled King Jehoiachin (Ezra 1:8, 1 Chron. 3:18). This is not likely, since Sheshbazzar is the Hebrew rendering of the Babylonian name Shamashaplausur.[17] The Chronicler exaggerated a bit by calling Sheshbazzar a prince. Sheshbazzar was supposed to undertake the

---

[17]See Martin Noth, *The History of Israel* (2d ed.; New York: Harper & Row, 1960), p. 309, n. 1.

construction of the Temple, but apparently he began the work only to find it impossible (Ezra 5:16). Several reasons may be offered for his failure. *First*, he may have had insufficient funds: Ezra 6:4 does not specify the amount available, and costs may have been much larger than Cyrus thought necessary. *Second*, there was vigorous opposition to the project (Ezra 4:4–5). *Third*, the technical staff was not available in Judah, and no reference to artisans and stone masons is made in the lists of returnees (Ezra 2:1–63). Priests, Levites, singers, and temple servants there are a plenty, but no one knew how to cut stone and erect a building.

The Reconstruction of the Jerusalem Wall

Opposition to the returnees who settled in Jerusalem was so strong despite their official papers that the only way they had of protecting themselves from the local population, from harassment by soldiers sent from Bishlam, Methredath, and Tabeel, and from marauding bands of Edomites and bedouin was to reconstruct Jerusalem's wall. This is the charge made against them in Ezra 4:7–16.[18] The constant antagonism of the local population, Jewish and non-Jewish, is one of the major themes in the books of Ezra and Nehemiah. To survive, the official community needed a wall around the city. This wall was probably poorly constructed, and built upon the foundations of the wall destroyed by the Babylonians, but it was enough to give protection. Why would the Chronicler use an official letter such as Ezra 4:4–16 and not narrate anything about the construction of Jerusalem's walls until Nehemiah arrived on the scene? Because the writer was an apologist for the Temple, and he could not conceive of anything more important. Therefore, the Temple, in his mind, was built before the wall. The improbability of this is clear from the simple fact that if numerous gold and silver utensils were returned for use in the Temple, raiding the Temple would have been simple for bedouin, Edomites, and local bands of thiefs if there had been no fortifications.

The wall was probably completed by 520 B.C., in the face of severe local opposition. Within the span of seventeen years residents had managed to build some nice homes. They were sufficiently imposing so that Haggai criticized citizens who lived in houses paneled in wood while the Temple lay in ruins (Hag. 1:4). But on the whole the residents of Jerusalem probably lived on a low social and economic level. Sheshbazzar and his associates had failed to fulfill their commission to rebuild the Temple.

[18]See Obadiah, Isaiah 63:1–6, 34.

A new party of returnees provided the incentive for starting work on the Temple again. Zerubbabel was appointed governor and Joshua high priest (Ezra 3:8, Hag. 1:1). They came from Babylon with a fresh contingent of workers. Haggai and Zechariah were already in Jerusalem, and as soon as feasible they began agitating for work to start on the Temple. Perhaps part of the stimulation was the appointment of Zerubbabel, a grandson of King Jehoiachin, as governor. Having a descendant of the Davidic family in charge of political affairs in Jerusalem may have encouraged the Jews to hope that survival was possible in the face of obdurate hostility from people on all sides.

Another reason for renewed appeals for building the Temple was the empire's political situation. Cambyses (530–522 B.C.) had died without leaving a male heir to the Persian throne. The kingship fell upon Darius, the son of Hystaspes, another side of the Achaemenid family than that which had had reared kings Cyrus and Cambyses. Darius was plagued by uprisings all over the empire. It took him more than a year to put out these political brushfires. The revolts had repercussions in Judea. Haggai and Zechariah acted like typical nationalistic prophets, proclaiming that Zerubbabel would be Yahweh's servant and that the crown of the Davidic household would be set upon his head (Hag. 2:20–23, Zech. 6:9–14, reading Zerubbabel for Joshua).

Whether or not Zerubbabel was impressed with the prophets' promises for him we do not know. He did order construction commenced on the Temple, and in four years it was completed, on December 3rd, 516 B.C. (Ezra 6:15). Passover was celebrated in March, and the returned exiles had to perform special rites of purification, because of their pollution from contact with the "peoples of the land," (that is, the people who resided in Palestine), before they could participate in Passover (Ezra 6:21). The Chronicler did his best to show that the trouble in building the Temple was caused by the "people of the land." They did not want the building, and they were not permitted to work on it (Ezra 3:3, 6:6, 13–15). But Haggai, whose record ought to be trusted, made it clear that both the "people of the land" (Hag. 2:4) and the "remnant of the people" (Hag. 2:2)—the returnees from Babylon—worked together on rebuilding the Temple.

The most interesting oracles for historical reconstruction were those in Haggai and Zechariah which proclaimed the overthrow of the

Persian throne and the making of a new Davidic crown (Hag. 2:20–23, Zech. 6:9–14). These two oracles had a familiar and ominous sound. They blared forth the call to Jewish nationalism. But the only answer was a portentous silence; a silence that lasted from 516 to 444 B.C. There are no biblical records on events in Judah between those dates. Few archaeological facts fit perfectly into that silent niche. It is worth asking a few questions, even though final answers are unlikely to be forthcoming. Did Judah continue to develop quietly and without incident during those years? Was this the period when the theocracy became influential and commentary upon the Torah was the chief literary work? Did the Priestly school formulate its narrative and legal codes during those decades? Most scholars answer these questions affirmatively. But other questions are more realistic. Did Zerubbabel rebel? Was the wall, so laboriously and crudely built, torn down? Did Joshua the high priest succeed Zerubbabel as chief political officer as well as religious leader?[19] The silence of the sources, the loss of Zerubbabel as an important name in the records, and the statement of conditions in the book of Nehemiah brings tentatively the answer "yes" to the last three questions.

Nehemiah, Governor of Judea

Jerusalem's tortuous reconstruction, which began in 537 B.C., had to be started all over again in 444 B.C. Nehemiah was the person in charge this time. The Chronicler placed Ezra before Nehemiah, but critical evaluation of the sources will not allow his chronology to stand. It seems incredible that two men of such stature should work in little Jerusalem without mentioning one another in their memoirs. Most scholars agree that Nehemiah's name is a gloss at Nehemiah 8:9. According to Ezra 7:7, the seventh year of Artaxerxes (465–424 B.C.) was the year that Ezra returned to Palestine. That was 458 B.C. According to Nehemiah 2:1, in the twentieth year of Artaxerxes, or 444 B.C., Nehemiah became governor in Jerusalem. Some scholars suggest that it was simply a confusion between Artaxerxes I and Artaxerxes II (404–358 B.C.). It is perfectly clear why the Chronicler put Ezra first. He knew that Nehemiah was inseparably associated with rebuilding Jerusalem's wall. Ezra was not associated with any building program, but his interest in cultic procedures and legal codes associate him with the Temple. The Chronicler could not conceive of his favorite people, the returnees from Babylon, building a wall before they did the most sacred work of all, building the Temple. Therefore, it was convenient to put Ezra in conjunction with the narrative of Temple building, to wipe out all references, except one (Ezra 4:12), to wall-building before Nehemiah, and to put Ezra chronologically first.

[19] See the editorial gloss at Zechariah 6:11.

THE RESTORATION OF JEWS IN JERUSALEM

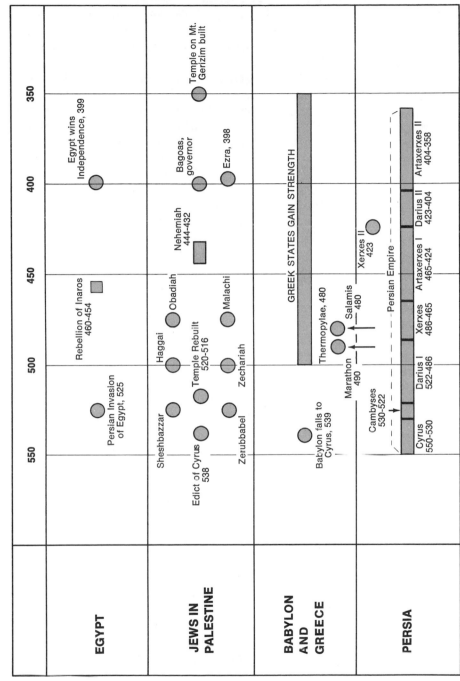

But sober historiography concludes that Nehemiah returned to Jerusalem in 444 B.C. to repair the walls of Jerusalem, and to reorganize political and social life so that the southern end of the satrapy of Samaria would be a little more productive. Nehemiah's information about Jerusalem came from men who had recently left Judah. Nehemiah asks about "the Jews that survived, who had escaped exile" (Neh. 1:2). Could Nehemiah have referred to the exile of 587 B.C.? It hardly seems credible. He probably had in mind the exile connected with Zerubbabel's efforts to become king after 516 B.C. Nehemiah is asking, then, about the conditions of life for second generation Jews after the Persian retaliation around 516 B.C. (Neh. 1:1–3). It seems impossible that Jerusalem existed with a Temple and nicely furnished houses from 537 to 444 B.C. without a wall. Nehemiah's task was to rebuild Jerusalem as the chief city on the southernmost edge of Persia's empire. He rebuilt the walls in the face of Sanballat's opposition. Sanballat was satrap of Samaria, and his opposition to Nehemiah's commission was practical. Megabyzos, satrap of the province of Beyond the River with headquarters at Damascus, had rebelled about 450 B.C., and Sanballat's satrapy was suspect, too. Being close to Egypt it could easily be led into revolt. Artaxerxes' primary qualification for a governor of Jerusalem was that he be a Jew *personally loyal* to him. Sanballat did not think Jerusalem needed walls, being less than fifty miles from Samaria. But Judah, not Samaria, was the more strategic location for a strong city, since Egypt was in a perpetual state of rebellion against Persia. Strength in Judah was necessary if Egypt was to be held.

Archaeological evidence from Lachish tends to support this interpretation of Nehemiah's walls and the reasons for constructing them. Excavations at Tell ed-Duweir have shown that the site lay abandoned from 587 to about 450 B.C. Sometime shortly after 450 B.C. a large residence was constructed on the site. Rooms surrounded an open court in the style of Mesopotamian homes, a house plan rare in Palestine. Columns graced the four sides of the court and supported the second floor with its overhanging balcony. Houses built on this plan were for government officials, and it is likely that a Persian governor lived there in the years that witnessed Egypt's struggle to free itself from Persian control.[20] The ruins of a large warehouse dated to the 5th century B.C. were found south of Gaza, the frontier area between Persian Palestine and Egypt, and this building was probably the supply depot for Persian soldiers who

[20] See Olga Tufnell, *Lachish III, The Iron Age, Text* (London: Oxford University Press, 1953), Plate 120.

served in Egypt.[21] Excavations in Jerusalem uncovered a wall dating from post-exilic days. It was probably Nehemiah's wall. It was built near the top of the ridge upon which ancient Jerusalem was built, and the walls of Davidic Jerusalem were far down the slope. This comparison shows how much the city had contracted in area since the Babylonian and Persian destructions. This wall encompassed the Temple area. The necessity of building quickly and cheaply is sufficient explanation for the placement of the wall near the top of the ridge rather than further down where military strategy would have demanded.[22] These archaeological facts show that Persia supported a major buildup of military operations in southern Palestine and a revival of the economy during the mid-fifth century B.C.

Papyrus excavated from the island of Elephantine in the Nile River contains a letter from the Jewish leaders at Elephantine to Temple authorities in Jerusalem describing how the Egyptians had destroyed their temple in 410 B.C. The letter reported their appeal to Bagoas, the Persian governor of Judea, for permission to rebuild their temple. The letter mentioned the two sons of Sanballat by name. This information confirms the record in the book of Nehemiah that Sanballat and Nehemiah were contemporaries. It also mentions the name of the priest Johanan (Ezra 10:6) who was in office in 407 B.C., at the end of the reign of Darius II (423–404 B.C.). He was the grandson of Eliashib ("son of . . ." often means grandson), who had been a leader under Nehemiah's rule (Ezra 10:6, Neh. 12:22). That Ezra had personal contact with Johanan, who was the grandson of Eliashib, is more evidence for dating Ezra's return to Jerusalem during the reign of Artaxerxes II (404–358 B.C.).[23]

Nehemiah's story of favors from the Persian king is the only record from that period which reports how political jobs were handed out (Neh. 1:1 – 2:8). His political acumen was shown by his discretion in having an official letter showing Artaxerxes' special permission to lumber in the king's preserve, since timber was scarce in Jerusalem (Neh. 2:7–8).[24] Nehemiah's shrewdness was demonstrated also by his ability to keep his plans to himself. Upon arrival

[21] See Noth, *The History of Israel* (2d. ed.), p. 318.

[22] See Kathleen M. Kenyon, "Excavations in Jerusalem, 1962," *Palestine Exploration Quarterly* (January–June 1963), p. 15.

[23] See D. Winton Thomas, *Documents from Old Testament Times* (New York: Harper & Row, 1965), pp. 260-9.

[24] Such an official letter also indicates that a governorship of Jerusalem and Judea was a new office since the days of Zerubbabel. This is additional evidence to show that some significant event had eliminated the office of Judean governor for about seventy years.

The first cataract on the Nile River where the island of Elephantine, with its Jewish community and temple to Yahu, was located between 600 and 400 B.C.

in Jerusalem he made no public announcement of his intentions, but waited three days to inspect the ruins of the wall. He made his inspection at night accompanied only by his advisors from Susa. Only after full plans had been laid did he announce his intentions to the citizens. After that it was necessary to move rapidly. Opposition from Sanballat, Tobiah, and Geshem came almost immediately (Neh. 2:19–20).

Opposition to the Jerusalem Wall

Why did the governor of the province of Samaria oppose rebuilding Jerusalem? For one reason, he would lose a certain tax revenue when Jerusalem and Judah became an independent province. Another is that a wall about Jerusalem would indicate the ascendancy of that city over Samaria in official Persian policy. But the two persons who joined Sanballat in opposing Nehemiah's plan are the most interesting. Tobiah the Ammonite and Geshem the Arab represent areas of the Persian empire which might have been anticipating rebellion (Neh. 2:19). Perhaps the three men had been planning a revolt which a loyal, fortified city in the midst of their territory would effectively block. Nehemiah 4:7–8 indicates that Sanballat retained a personal army. Furthermore, it is doubtful that Persian troops would be used against a man whose authority was given him directly from Susa. The inclusion of the word "Ashdodites" has often been interpreted as an editorial addition, but enough ancient manuscripts support that reading to speak for its originality (Neh. 4:7). If it is original, it adds evidence that a widespread coalition had formed pretty quickly against Nehemiah. Of course it is possible that the memory of a punitive Persian campaign against Zerubbabel two generations earlier still frightened those leaders. They may have interpreted Nehemiah's actions as another foolhardy effort to establish independence. This interpretation is supported by Nehemiah 4:10–12, where some Jews themselves express fear of carrying out Nehemiah's plans.

The completion of the wall was achieved in fifty-two days (Neh. 6:15). It may not have been the finest wall, as Tobiah's taunt indicates, but it was sufficient to deter any attack from Nehemiah's enemies (Neh. 4:3). When success on the wall was assured, Nehemiah set about some social and economic manipulation. His first action was to proclaim cancellation of all debts and mortgages on land. Apparently a drought had contributed to extensive mortgaging of land in order to buy seed, and perhaps even daily food (Neh. 5:3); perhaps a naive expectation on the part of returnees also augmented the condition. Nehemiah's proclamation was not the generous reform it might seem to be at first. Many of those who were exiled to Babylon had come from the landed class. Their land lay unused until landless peasants settled on it. Without deeds to the property the peasants nonetheless came to hold title simply by farming the land. Many exiles returned after 537 B.C. to find their land no longer available, although they had been led to expect full restitution of property rights. They had to borrow in order to buy other property. Those who had once been peasants had now become landholders, and they exacted mortgages in the same manner previous generations of gentry had from them. Nehemiah's financial program was intended, then, to benefit the returnees who had been unable to recover their financial positions. He was an aristocrat acting for the benefit of those who had been and still claimed to be aristocrats. It is hard to understand why the "nobles and the officials" (Neh. 5:7) who had risen to that status only recently agreed so readily with Nehemiah's demands (Neh. 5:12) unless they feared even more drastic action by the governor who had complete backing by Artaxerxes I. This action, too, shows that imperial Persia was acting in its self-interest, and not as a reforming agent in its Judean province.

Nehemiah's Governing of Jerusalem After the wall had been completed and mortgages and interest payments cancelled in order to benefit the old-line aristocrats, Nehemiah appointed his brother Hanani governor of the city but kept for himself the chief office as governor of the province of Judea (Neh. 7:2–4). He successfully avoided Sanballat's plot to assassinate him

(Neh. 6:1–14). He restored normal operations in the Temple by decreeing a Temple tax. This stimulated employment in two ways. Levites had returned from Babylon but found themselves unemployed since the Temple had not been under official patronage since 516 B.C. Nehemiah's Temple tax assured resumption of official services and employment for a certain number of priests. Others of the Levites became tax collectors, roaming through the towns and villages gathering the tithes (Neh. 10:37–39).

One economic problem was the small population in Jerusalem. In order to augment the population a lottery was instituted which arbitrarily selected one family in ten from the villages of Judea to move into the city. Those who volunteered to move into Jerusalem were given special consideration (Neh. 11:1–2). The increase of Jerusalem's population by bringing in villagers caused another problem: most of the new city dwellers had not been in the exile, so they had no tradition of observing the sabbath as a day of rest as had the recent returnees. Therefore the returnees pledged themselves to do no business with those uninformed residents, hoping that they would learn by example (Neh. 10:31). In all these things Nehemiah took the lead. He was an unusual governor for the Near East because he took no cut from taxes nor did he extort land from the citizens for his own personal income. His memoirs report that for twelve years he took no salary, and he paid for his official household from his own income. Apparently he was a eunuch, since at no time does he mention a wife, and the position of "cupbearer," which was Nehemiah's title in Persia, was usually filled by an emasculated person.[25]

After twelve years in Jerusalem Nehemiah returned to Susa to report personally on what he had accomplished for Artaxerxes (Neh. 13:6). He couldn't stay away from his favorite city, however. He probably heard rumors that as soon as he had left, the powerful Tobiah family of Ammon had started to undermine his work. He came back to Jerusalem unexpectedly, to find Tobiah comfortably living in the Temple, ready to spread his influence over Eliashib, the high priest, and ultimately to gain control of the Temple's institutions (Neh. 13:4–9). Nehemiah found, too, that the Levites had been deprived of their income from the Temple services, so that they neglected the official rites. He corrected that graft, and established a system in the treasury whereby four men representing different aspects of the Temple checked on one another in the collection and

---

[25] George A. Buttrick, ed., *The Interpreter's Bible*, Vol. III (New York: Abingdon Press, 1955), p. 671.

distribution of Temple funds (Neh. 13:10–14). The efforts to inaugurate sabbath observance unofficially had not succeeded, so he personally imposed a business curfew at sundown on the sabbath, closed the city's gates, and threatened to confiscate any merchandise sold outside the walls on that day (Neh. 13:15–22). The practice of rejecting marriage with any family which had not returned from Babylon had not worked well. But Nehemiah persisted in this social experiment so vigorously that he personally abused some persons who had not followed his directives. He cursed some, beat others, and even pulled out the hair of a few (Neh. 13:23–27). Nehemiah's efforts to make Jerusalem a city utterly loyal to Persia succeeded. Whether or not he was so successful in making it an enclave of Jews who followed the social customs and religious practices of those who had returned from Babylon is not so clear. So long as his dynamic personality was felt, and probably feared, in Jerusalem, his policies prospered. When he absented himself they lapsed. It is clear that they lapsed badly when he was no longer governor, because Ezra eventually appeared on the scene to initiate reforms in policies already inaugurated by Nehemiah.

Ezra in Jerusalem Exactly when Ezra appeared in Jerusalem is a matter of considerable debate. The text as it now stands reads "the seventh year of Artaxerxes" (Ezra 7:7). Sufficient discussion has already been given as to why the Chronicler put Ezra's career before Nehemiah's (pp. 374–376). The seventh year of Artaxerxes I was 458 B.C. But it seems unlikely that this was the date of Ezra's journey to Jerusalem. It is unlikely that Ezra did not teach the law in Jerusalem until thirteen years after his arrival (Neh. 2:1, 8:1–8). Another date suggested in 428 B.C. This suggestion rests upon the belief that the text of Ezra 7:7–8 is corrupted. It should read, according to this theory, the "thirty-seventh year of the king." This argument states that the three Hebrew words that give "the thirty-seventh year" each begins with the letter *shin*. It was easy enough for a scribe to lose one of those words when he copied the text. Thus, Ezra did his work while Nehemiah was in his second term as governor.[26] A look at the Hebrew text, however, shows that the three Hebrew words did not all begin with *shin*. The first word begins with *beth*. Transliterated the phrase would be *bishanath sheba'* as it now stands. If it had been "the thirty-seventh year" it would be *bishanath sheloshim sheba'*. This shows that only two words began with "sh," and it seems unlikely that a scribe would make the mistake so easily as some modern scholars think.

[26]See Bright, *A History of Israel,* pp. 375–86 and Noth, *The History of Israel* (2d ed.), p. 331.

The best date for Ezra's appearance in Jerusalem is 398 B.C., that is, in the seventh year of Artaxerxes II (404–358 B.C.). This is the simplest solution, taking into account the Chronicler's desire to see the priest placed before the civil authority as well as his careless use of sources.

Ezra's Position and Duties in Jerusalem

Ezra was a priest of the Zadokite order, as distinguished from the Levites. He had the official title of "a scribe of the law of the God of heaven," which the Chronicler has made over into his own terminology (Ezra 7:21, 7:6). His official title was a special term applied to certain officers of the empire whose duties include serving as commissioner of religion.[27] It is clear from official Persian records that Ezra went to Jerusalem not only as a scribe to teach Jewish religion, but as an official of Artaxerxes II (Neh. 8:26). There is no information on how Ezra received such a distinguished post from the king, but there is no question that his mission was political just as Nehemiah's was.

The Chronicler stresses that side of Ezra's duties which deal with his religious office. Papyrus recently discovered in Egypt shows that Persian rule continued in Egypt until about 399 B.C., contrary to some scholars' opinions that it ended in 404 B.C. As the Persians lost their hold on Egypt it was necessary for them to strengthen their hand in Palestine. This was done to prevent revolt and to deter attack against their border by a rejuvenated Egypt.[28] This was probably one reason for sending Ezra to Jerusalem. He was the one person who Artaxerxes II felt could bring the necessary order.

Ezra Institutes the New Law in Jerusalem

When he left Babylon with a band of returnees, Ezra took some of the Temple's cultic utensils with him. He also received gifts from the king and offerings from fellow Jews. He was authorized to draw from the treasury of the satrapy of "Beyond the River" a prescribed amount of material for beautification of the Temple. His trip was uneventful, although he had taken precautions to distribute the Temple's vessels among the caravan so as not to lose all of them in case of attack by bandits (Ezra 8:24–30). Ezra's memoirs record that his first task was to institute the new law. No account of the precise contents of the new law is given, but scholarly opinion holds that it was the new code that the Priestly school had put together.[29] A public ceremony was held on July 1st, 398 B.C. in which Ezra read the law in the square before the Water Gate (Ezra 7:8, Neh. 8:2).

[27] See Noth, *The History of Israel* (2d ed.), p. 332.
[28] See Otto Eissfeldt, *The Old Testament: An Introduction*, trans. Peter R. Ackroyd (New York: Harper & Row, 1965), pp. 555.
[29] Remember that Nehemiah 8–9 follows Ezra 8:36.

This location indicates the law was not solely cultic, or else it would have been recited in the Temple precincts. On the second day of the ceremony the heads of clans gathered to be further instructed in the law. They learned that the Feast of Booths should be celebrated the same way that Jews in exile observed it. On July 24th, 398 B.C. a day of penitence and fasting was observed in which Jews agreed to separate themselves from foreigners. Their acceptance of the new law was one way by which they showed their separation from non-Jews (Neh. 9:1-3).

Resistance to Ezra's Divorce Decrees

After Ezra had obtained a small following in Jerusalem, he proceeded to enforce legislation which decreed that Jews who wished to associate with the community of returned exiles under the new law would divorce their wives. All returnees were ordered to appear in Jerusalem on September 20th, 398 B.C. or else have their property confiscated and be excommunicated from the congregation of the returnees (Ezra 10:7-8). This assembly was held in the court of the Temple, showing that it was a sacred occasion in contrast to the one in the square before the Water Gate when the new law was read (Ezra 10:9). It was a particularly memorable occasion because it rained heavily, it was cold, most unusual in Jerusalem at that season, and the people generally revolted against Ezra's demands (Ezra 10:9-15). It was an unfortunate day for Ezra and his program. The heavy rain made it impossible to conduct the assembly as Ezra had planned. He had hoped to obtain a community consensus that divorces would be gotten from all native Palestinian women. But the assembly preferred that the matter be negotiated by representatives of the people and done individually (Ezra 10:14). Obviously most of the men loved their wives and desired to be in the religious community too, and they tried to have both in the face of official opposition. Ezra had the support of only four men and the will of the assembly carried against Ezra. On October 1st, 398 B.C. they began examination of each case of improper marriage. This court of appeals lasted until January 1st, 397 B.C. The Chronicler gave a list of those whose cases were decided in favor of divorce. Eighteen priests, ten Levites, and eighty-four citizens had to divorce their alien women. A total of one hundred and two men from a population of several thousands does not seem a terribly large number to cause such a great amount of discussion. It is obvious, then, that the Chronicler purposely omitted the more important work that Ezra did as an official of Artaxerxes II.

Ezra's Main Work

Some Old Testament scholars are convinced that Ezra's primary work was reforming Judea's religious and moral practices.[30] In

[30] See especially Bright, *A History of Israel*, p. 378.

this they believe he was completely successful. He may have been successful in beautifying the Temple, but on this matter there is no information (Ezra 7:27). Regarding his measures on divorce the text shows that the Chronicler had a hard task selecting material that proved Ezra's success. He seemed to have come up against formidable opposition just as had Nehemiah. Then, as now, it was difficult to get obedience to legislation that went against custom and personal loyalties. It is obvious, too, that there were capable poets and religious leaders who opposed Ezra's reform. Isaiah 56:1–8 is a poem which may have been directly opposed to such separatists policies. It claimed that all who observed the sabbath, foreigners and eunuchs included, belonged to the community of Yahweh. Isaiah 58 also deplored dependence upon fast days when anger rather than penitence was the result. Yahweh's true fast was to free the oppressed, to share food with the hungry, to clothe the naked, and to enjoy the benefits of the sabbath in serving Yahweh through a neighborly attitude.

A close reading of the books of Ezra and Nehemiah, and archaeological evidence, show that Ezra's religious achievements were less significant than his political ones.

The restored Jewish community in Jerusalem was not homogeneous. It harbored political and religious factions that threatened stable Persian rule. Ezra accomplished political results, though, that gave significant directions to future generations of Palestinian Jews. His chief accomplishment was the achievement of some autonomy. Archaeology has provided the evidence for this conclusion. Coins with the inscription YHD (Judah) have been found with their official values stamped on them. Excavations in other parts of the ancient Persian empire have revealed coins minted in other provinces. Permission to mint coins may have been a recognition that the Jewish province was loyal. The earliest coin with a Hebrew inscription was discovered at Hebron. This, and other coins, copied the Greek type, with images of human heads and animals on them. This is a bit surprising in view of prohibitions against image-making in Exodus 20:4 and Deuteronomy 5:8. In fact, the permission for Judeans to mint coins but with the imprint of secular themes on them may have been a form of cultural control, so that autonomy was never complete.[31] Stamped jar handles also indicate some political and economic independence. The Hebrew words for Judah and Jerusalem were impressed on wet clay jar handles, indicating their special use for

[31] See D. Winton Thomas, *Documents from Old Testament Times* (New York: Harper & Row, 1965), pp. 231–5.

official tax purposes. Other ceramic ware shows importation into Judah of much Greek pottery. The amount of Greek pottery found in excavations dating from the Persian period suggests that a vital trade with the Greek islands and mainland was carried on in Persian satrapies despite the enmity between Persians and Greeks which culminated in the wars at Marathon, Thermopylae, and Salamis between 490 and 480 B.C.[32]

Cultural Conditions

Cultural achievements of this period were surprisingly numerous in view of the unsettled conditions of Palestine, the poverty of the economy, and Persian political domination. Persia's political genius was its willingness to permit subject peoples to develop their own cultures so long as they were loyal to the king at Susa. The Priestly writer, some fine poetry in Isaiah 56–66, the large number of excellent psalms, and the growth of a rich Temple liturgy, as the Chronicler reports, were all admirable literary accomplishments.

The Canonization of Scripture

The pinnacle of accomplishment, however, was the origination of the concept that certain literature was sacred. During this period the Pentateuch acquired the rank of holiness. Its basic documents had been in process of development for centuries, but never before had they been regarded as the authoritative rule for the behavior of the whole community. What had once been beautiful narratives about Yahweh's dealings with Israel, repeated by uncounted numbers of Israelites since the United Monarchy, now became the official documents of a religious state. The legal documents attached to the narratives by editorial additions became definitive laws for the regulation of personal and communal ethics. Large numbers of scribes, probably from the Zadokite priesthood, interpreted those ancient laws for application in a radically different society. Customs and requirements that had been developed in synagogues in Babylon had to be squared with those of the revived Temple. Scribes looked to the ancient laws and rites for wisdom, and came forward with interpretations which became additional precepts binding upon the community. The basic structure of Judaism was formed during the Persian period. It is a structure which exists in Judaism even in the modern world.

The Collecting and Annotation of Ancient Literature

After the Pentateuch became the rule of the Jewish community, that is, became canonized, scribal attention was turned to the great prophets. Recent prophets, like Haggai and Zechariah, had left their marks, but the truly great ones like Amos, Hosea, Isaiah, and Jere-

[32] See Noth, *The History of Israel* (2d ed.), p. 344.

miah were especially heeded. Scribes began the laborious process of collecting and editing their oracles. As was the case with the Pentateuch, much rewriting, explanatory commentary, and coupling with unauthentic works took place. Those prophets had announced the punishment of Yahweh's people, and their proclamations had come true. What other reliable truths were among the sayings of the prophets? The process of making scrolls which brought together the ancient literature achieved a remarkable degree of effectiveness in this age. Since the temper of the learned men was to look to the wisdom of ancients for directions on how to become great once again, all kinds of archaic material was accumulated. There is no way to know what process was used for sifting poor from great literature, since the rejected literature did not survive, but it is probably correct to assess the scribes' work as one of the most brilliant achievements of literary history.

Exclusivity of the Returning Exiles

One of the saddest things about the Jewish community at Jerusalem during the Persian period was its animosity toward people other than returned exiles. Relations between returnees and the "people of the land," and between returnees and Samaritans, marred prophetic expectations of a grand recovery of the people of Yahweh. The "people of the land" were those persons who had not been deported by Nebuchadnezzar's army to Babylon. They remained in Judah scratching a living from an abused soil or trading enough to eke a few shekels from a smashed economy. They slowly coaxed the soil into productivity again and revived a semblance of their former crafts and trades. The returnees, therefore, dealt with people who had risen from despair to self-reliance.

Enmity developed between returnees and the people of the land. According to Ezra 3:3 returnees feared the people of the land because they interfered with efforts to rebuild the Temple. The text is almost certainly corrupt. "For fear was upon them because of the peoples of the land" was inserted in order to push the animosity between returnees and local Jews back to the first efforts to begin worship in Jerusalem again. Also, that clause interfers with the sense of the text which read originally "They set the altar in its place, and they offered burnt offerings. . . ." As the text now reads, it implies the altar was built because returnees feared the local residents. Such has never been the reason for the construction of an altar.[33] Furthermore, Haggai 1:12 shows clearly that the people of the land were directly involved in the first full-scale effort to re-

[33] See W. O. E. Oesterley, *A History of Israel,* Vol. II (London: Oxford University Press, 1932), p. 149.

build the Temple. The account in Ezra 4:1–3, reciting how certain adversaries approached Zerubbabel about helping to build the Temple, sounds like the Chronicler's own words. He tries to explain the animosity between the people of the land and the remnant of the people as a conflict over the reconstruction of the Temple. Conflicts of interests between the two groups were economic and social, not religious. Such conflicts were normal, it would seem, since the Jews deported to Babylon had been Judah's wealthiest citizens — priests, government officials, and military commanders. Furthermore, social animosities between the two groups were based upon the exiles' convictions that they had suffered terrible tragedies while the people of the land had gotten off lightly. The historic fact is that the Jews who remained in Judah probably were the harder hit. They had a right to be proud of their achievements. The returnees brought with them royal patronage in money and political support (Ezra 6: 1–5); the people of the land had achieved their economic and social status by hard work alone. No doubt these animosities slowed down the redevelopment of Jerusalem and Judah, but the conflicts being economic and social, were susceptible to settlement with time.

Enmity Between Jews and Samaritans

The more tragic animosity occurred between the returnees and the Samaritans. The root of this split was religious, and did not take place until Nehemiah returned as governor. Samaritans were descendants, in part, of those persons who had been permitted to stay on the land after the Assyrian army had deported thousands of Israelites in 722 B.C. The population of Samaria had been augmented by importations from distant Assyrian provinces (2 Kings 17:24–34). As time passed the newcomers took on religious traits borrowed from their Israelite neighbors. Yahweh was the God of the land, therefore His rites were proper and useful. There is no historical evidence that the populations of Samaria and Judea originally hated each other. There had been wars between Israel and Judah, but when Samaria fell Jerusalem was still looked upon as the proper place for the worship of Yahweh. Samaritans continued to worship in Jerusalem even after it was destroyed (Jer. 41:5). Only in the post-exilic period did enmity develop between Samaritans and Jews.

The first cause of the rupture was Sanballat's opposition to Nehemiah's reconstruction of the walls of Jerusalem. Considerable numbers of wealthy Jews also opposed Nehemiah's work (Neh. 2:16, 4:12). Both Sanballat and local Jews probably feared that such action was the first sign of rebellion and subsequent Persian retaliation. But Nehemiah stimulated another kind of animosity. He wanted to segregate the people according to their places of origin, Babylon or Palestine. The returned exiles looked upon the people of the land as half-heathen because they had married other than Israelite women (Neh. 13:1–3, Ezra 10:2, 10–11). The returnees also despised Jews who traded with the local population on the sabbath (Neh. 10:31). Hatred for the people of the land became so great that Ezra called them by the names of people feared and despised by ancient Israel: Canaanites, Hittites, Perizzites, Jebusites, and so forth (Ezra 9:1). The returnees were designated as "the holy race" (Ezra 9:2), the "remnant of the people" (Hag. 1:2), or just "the remnant" (Ezra 9:8, 15). They had been guided home by Yahweh and so stood, like the people under Moses, in special relationship to Him (Neh. 9:9–25). The local population compared unfavorably in their religion as well as in their social and economic practices.

Perhaps Nehemiah's own personality aggravated the religious and social disruption between the two groups. The Tobiah family was prominent in Ammon, and continued as the chief clan in that area well into the 3rd century B.C. (Neh. 2:19). So long as Tobiah was associated with Sanballat and Geshem in opposition to Nehemiah, he could be controlled by royal edict. But when he moved into Jerusalem on Nehemiah's absence, it was too direct a challenge to the governor's authority (Neh. 13:4–9). Nehemiah drove him out. At this point biblical history does not continue its information on the Jewish-Samaritan rupture. Post-exilic literature records no open split up to the time of Ezra. But the seeds of dissension had been sown. Tobiah may have fled to the sons of Sanballat, Delaiah and Shelemaiah,[34] where his injured pride was aggravated by the hatred Sanballat had had for Nehemiah. When Nehemiah banished Jehoiada, Eliashib's grandson, for marrying Sanballat's daughter, an attempt to consolidate power in the two households, the rift between Nehemiah and Sanballat was probably irreparable. Ezra naturally continued Nehemiah's animosity toward the Samaritans. It is likely that when the Samaritans saw rewards from lucrative Temple taxes dwindling they withdrew completely to Samaria, built their own temple on Mount Gerizim, and declared themselves the true inheritors of the blessings of Moses.[35] The date of the construction of the Gerizim temple is unknown, but it was destroyed about 128 B.C. A sound guess is that it was built some time shortly after 350 B.C. Excavations on Mount Gerizim reveal considerable rebuilding of the site between 330 and 250 B.C.[36]

[34] See Thomas, *Documents from Old Testament Times*, pp. 264–5.
[35] A small community of Samaritans exists today at Nablus. It is an independent, conservative group who observes Passover by ritual slaying of a sheep, strictly enforces sabbath observance, and marries only among its own. Technology in these people's land has seriously modified their ability to isolate themselves.
[36] See G. Ernest Wright, *Shechem: The Biography of a Biblical City* (New York: McGraw-Hill Book Co., 1965), pp. 170–81.

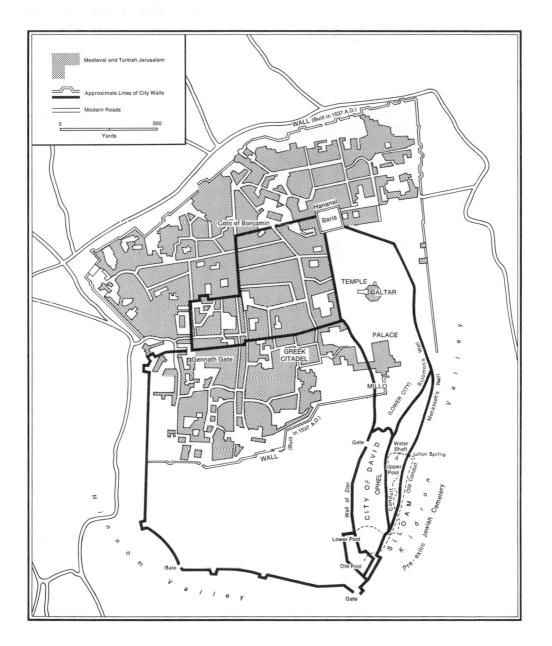

OLD TESTAMENT JERUSALEM

The history of post-exilic Israel from about 538 to 350 B.C. is difficult to recover due to inadequate and sharply falsified records. But
there is enough material so that a fairly clear portrayal is possible.
Religious material was more accurately preserved, since religion
dominated the writers' concerns.

**Religious
Affirmations**

Religious affirmations of the post-exilic writers reveal many different
particular beliefs rather than commonly accepted general convictions. Rapidly changing social and political conditions did not permit the Jewish community to integrate its affirmations. Therefore,
it is necessary to comment on the beliefs and practices recorded
in the several documents.

**Haggai
and Zechariah**

Haggai and Zechariah were the heirs of Ezekiel. Like their greater
predecessor, they called for humility before God, high moral practices, and the belief that the Jews were Yahweh's unique people.
They saw the Temple as central in the creation of a new society.
Without it Yahweh could not work His will in the world. Zechariah
was especially aware that greater prophets had preceded him, and
he drew upon them for style and inspiration (Zech. 1:4, 7:7, 12). He
held the belief that Yahweh's revelation was given to the early
prophets, and that in his time prophets were intended to interpret
the work of the former revelation. Furthermore, revelation came
only through visions and angels. No longer did the prophet carry
the authority of "Thus says Yahweh." This indicates that Zechariah
believed Yahweh was too holy, too transcendent, too remote to
communicate directly even to His favorite spokesmen. Haggai and
Zechariah both looked forward to a messianic age. The messiah
would be a descendant of David. In due time Yahweh would once
again reinstate the royal family (Hag. 2:20–23, Zech. 5:9–14).
The messianic age was thought to be political, local, and just about
to arrive.

**Obadiah
and Malachi**

Obadiah reiterates the ancient and negative theme of the day of the
Lord. Malachi, on the other hand, expresses a profoundly humble
spirit before Yahweh. His many questions show a manly effort to
comprehend God's mysterious ways. Having qualities of the quest-
ing temperament admired today, Malachi wanted to know answers
to precisely formulated questions. His opening question is one that
plagued his contemporaries, as it does the man of faith in every age,
"Does God love Judah?" (Mal. 1:2). Next to that question in perennial interest was "Where is God's justice?" (Mal. 2:17). These
questions became, in the hands of another Hebrew thinker, the
basis for the greatest poem the Hebrews ever produced, the book
of Job.

The collection of poems in Isaiah 56–66, 34–35 provides different religious opinions. One poet despises Jewish separatism (Isa. 56: 1–8, 58:1–14). Another pictures Yahweh as primarily concerned with stamping out wickedness (Isa. 59). Still another looks to Yahweh as a gracious God who looks for the afflicted, the brokenhearted, the prisoner, and the mourners in order to save them (Isa. 60–62). Another thinks nature's abundant flowering and harmonious integration with men's affairs are sure signs of Yahweh's care for man (Isa. 35).

The Priestly school provided the most consistent religious views of the post-exilic age. Like Ezekiel and Isaiah of Babylon, and in concord with other post-exilic thinkers, the Priestly school had an exalted view of Yahweh. He was the only God. Influenced by Isaiah of Babylon's stately rhythms about Yahweh's sovereignty (Isa. 40:12–31) and by Babylonian accounts of their gods' creative activities, the Priestly writer produced a creation song in which the act of creation was accomplished by a single, august, Being.[37] In other Hebrew narratives the tales of Yahweh's appearance to men were purged of their folksy simplicity and endowed with traits of a transcendent God. Furthermore, Yahweh was depicted as ultimately powerful because He needed only to speak a word for His will to become physical fact. God was also orderly. His eight creative acts in Genesis 1:1 – 2:4 (light, firmament, seas, land and vegetation, heavenly lights, birds, fish, animals and man) reflect the traditional eight-day Babylonian week compressed into the Hebrews' six days of work and one of rest.

With all of His transcendance, stately demeanor, creativity, and orderly habits, God was still a Being who thought and acted like a man. He rested from His labors on the seventh day, as man must. He made man in His image. He prescribed that Aaron wear bells on his robe so that He would know when to absent Himself from the Holy of Holies when Aaron went in to do his priestly duties (Exod. 28:33). God's philanthropy was not unlike that of a great king. He saved Noah from certain death. He provided manna in the Sinai desert (Exod. 16:1–3, 6–24, 31–35). He gave the Israelites a land. But above all God was like a high priest. He loved the detail of ritual and gloried in the smoke and incense of sacrificial rites (Exod. 25–31). He was interested in the continuous function of the priesthood more than He was in the nation as a whole. If the priesthood was intact and operative His revelation was assured. Religion was chiefly a matter of correct actions in worship, and guilty persons

---

[37] See Pritchard, *ANET*, pp. 60–72.

were those improperly prepared for worship as well as those who committed crimes against society. Even natural bodily functions such as sexual intercourse, childbirth, skin eruptions, and burying the dead were unclean, and there were special rites to purify the defiled worshipper.

The Day of Atonement

Of course, God was a forgiving God. The Day of Atonement was the chief ritual elaborated by the Priestly tradition to express God's forgiveness. Two ceremonies were integrated into a single ritual (Lev. 16). One was the sacrifice of a bull, which served to atone for the high priest's sinfulness. On one day of the year the high priest was permitted to enter the most sacred place on earth to Jews, the Holy of Holies. There he sprinkled the bull's blood upon the "mercy seat" (Lev. 6:14). The second ritual was the goat for Azazel, the rugged desert regions (Lev. 16:20–22). In this rite the religious community furnished two goats, one to be blessed for Yahweh, sacrificed, and its blood splashed on the mercy seat to atone for the sins of the people. The other goat was brought to the high priest who placed his hands on the goat's head, thus placing all the conscious and unconscious faults of the Israelites upon the animal. The goat was then led into the desert where the people's sins were left. The goat wandered or was killed by wild animals. The man who led the goat into the desert became corrupted in the act, and had to bathe thoroughly and wash his garments before being readmitted to the community.

Many ancient religions practiced rites like these. In Babylon the New Year festival was enlivened by the beheading of a sheep whose corpse was rubbed against the temple of Nebo to destroy the impurities of the temple. Then two men carried head and body to the Euphrates and threw them in. Then they had to hide in the desert until the New Year feast was over. How like the ceremony of the goat for Azazel![38]

Yahweh and his Holy Race

The Priestly writer's understanding of man's relationship to Yahweh grew from previous Israelite traditions. Amos, for example, had taken Israel's national God and elevated Him to universality. Isaiah of Babylon had so exalted that universal Being that mankind was no more than grass used for burning, or a worm easily crushed (Isa. 40:6–8, 41:14). The Priestly writer had to reduce the universal God once again to a racial one, and to elevate Israel to the status of a

[38] See Roland de Vaux, *Ancient Israel: Its Life and Institutions*, trans. John McHugh, (New York: McGraw-Hill Book Co., 1961), pp. 507–10.

sacred society. He may have been offended, too, by Isaiah of Babylon's belief that Israel's mission was to humble itself in order to bring redemption to the Gentiles. In order to make Israel a special people with certain privileges, he traced all generations from Abraham back to Adam, Yahweh Elohim's original man (Gen. 2:4, 5:1, 6:9, 10:1, 11:10, 11:27, 25:12, 25:19). But the relationship of God's holy race to Himself was more than racial, it was also religious (Ezra 9:2). God had established covenants with His people from ancient days: with Adam (Gen. 1:28–30), with Noah (Gen. 9:1–17), with Abraham (Gen. 17), with Moses (Exod. 6:1–9), and now again with the returnees.

Attitudinal Problems of the Returnees

Because a few persons in the new Israel believed that God had blessed them in particular, they acquired property with small regard for the way in which they did it. They gouged borrowers with high interest, took mortgages and foreclosed, and claimed property long since passed into the hands of the people of the land. The great reforming prophets had fought this same problem but with little success. The Priestly writer tried to solve the problem by idealistic legislation. He conceived of the land as belonging to Yahweh. He created the year of jubilee, when at the end of seven sabbath years (every fiftieth year) all slaves would be freed and all land returned to its original owners. He believed that in this way tremendous estates would be broken up, and deprived and displaced persons given equal opportunity again (Lev. 25). Of course, such an idealistic law was never put into practice.

A Special Land With New Laws

If God was creator and ruler of all the earth and He had a special people, they must be given a land of their own. Such a concept had long before motivated the Yahwist storyteller to relate how Israel conquered Canaan. But now the same theme had to be proclaimed again. The Priestly writer believed that Yahweh had given Canaan to the Jews as an everlasting possession, and Abraham had purchased his rights to the land (Gen. 17:7–8, ch. 23). Therefore there was no story of conquest in the P narrative. Yahweh simply assigned the land to the tribes (Num. 34–36). In such legal fashion did the Priestly writer believe that Judea should be given to those exiles from Babylon.

A people on a special land had to have laws, therefore a new code was put together. The Priestly school took the material compiled in the Holiness Code (Lev. 17–26), and around this nucleus wove a vast array of cultic and social laws that would suit the special circumstances of a special people devoted to a special God. It is unlikely that all the legal requirements for worship were fulfilled, and impossible that all the social ones were operative, but the ideal may be admired even though recognized as impractical.

Ezra was a practical spokesman for the Priestly point of view. He probably never tried to impose the minuscule detail of the Priestly Code on the community under his governance, but he sympathized with the intent. He attempted to create of the new Israel a special and pure people. His efforts at segregating all allegedly non-Jewish citizens from the community met with severe opposition, but still he persisted. One reason for the struggle of Nehemiah and Ezra against foreign elements was the desire to preserve the Hebrew language (Neh. 13:24). Since Hebrew was the language of sacred writings, that is, of the Mosaic traditions, then its corruption was a violation of God's laws. In this effort they were loyal to the law of God.

In addition, Nehemiah and Ezra strove to apply the ideals of the earlier prophets. How often Amos, Hosea, Isaiah, and Jeremiah had criticized their fellow Israelites for falling prey to the beguiling and corrupting appeal of Canaanite religions! These two officials saw the same problem in intensely practical concerns. They knew that the only way to build a distinctive community was to isolate it in its early stages of growth. This they did, but they suffered the effects of separatism. They became proud, rigid, scornful of others, and impossible to deal with in business. But they preserved the community. Their hardheaded approach enabled Israel to maintain itself as a religious community for another five hundred years.

Finally, Nehemiah and Ezra were profoundly aware of God's providence. The sense of personal relationship with God which motivated those two men is admirable. Each gave up official and lucrative positions in Babylon to take charge of a frontier outpost. Each did so because he understood that his motivations originated in God's will. Narrow, restrictive, harsh, or whatever one calls them, they still served what they believed was the highest cause to which they could put their hand.

Psalms in Post-Exilic Israel

Post-exilic Israel was a creative age. Some interpreters have regarded the separatism and legalism of the restored community as signs of poverty of spirit and lack of creativity. But a study of the psalms written for use in the Temple, for use by the community at large, and for use by individuals, reveals that creative genius went into them. A few psalms selected for study represent the types under which most of the psalms from this period could be classified.

Psalm 19 Psalm 19 represents one type of hymn sung in the synagogues of Judah. This psalm was created from two distinctive compositions. The first part may have been an ancient Canaanite hymn extolling the sun (Ps. 19:1–6). This was taken over by the Hebrew psalmist to exult Yahweh's creative power. Put next to this is the psalmist's own exaltation of Yahweh's Torah (Ps. 19:7–14). It is to him as marvelous a creation as the natural world. *God's revelation in nature and in Torah* are two motifs stressed in post-exilic psalmnody. A marginal note at some time was slipped into the text of the scroll (Ps. 19:3). Some scribe in copying this psalm did not like the viewpoint that claimed the heavens spoke for Yahweh. He made his complaint in a marginal gloss saying that nature has no voice, no words, no speech. He meant to say Yahweh alone speaks, and through the Torah.

Psalm 33 Psalm 33 is a masterfully symmetrical hymn. It is typical of the individual *songs of thanksgiving* sung by townsman and villager alike as they went about their essential chores. The opening (Ps. 33:1–3) and closing stanzas (Ps. 33:20–22) enclose a hymn extolling Yahweh's actions in creation, like that of the Priestly writer in Genesis 1:1 – 2:4, and in history, like that in the poems of Isaiah of Babylon. Notice as well the twenty-two lines of the psalm which equal the number of letters in the Hebrew alphabet. This alphabetic order carries spiritual significance as a symbol of completeness. The psalm's stress upon "the eye of Yahweh" in a time of famine and death may indicate that the psalm was especially appropriate for the Jewish farmer as he looked forward to the rainy season (Ps. 33:18). The creative word of Yahweh and the selection of Israel for special privileges displays Priestly religion (Ps. 33:6, 12).

Psalm 44 Psalm 44 divides into three parts using the traditional form of the conventional *community lament* (cf. Lamentations). There is first the glorification of Israel's past (Ps. 44:1–8), then a chant concerning the distress which came upon Israel (Ps. 44:9–16), and finally, an assurance that Yahweh is still faithful, with a plea for His deliverance (Ps. 44:17–26). A military catastrophe had struck Israel at a time subsequent to the exile (Ps. 44:11, 14, 16). This lament came after Persian armies had crushed Judah's uprising under Zerubbabel, an event deduced from obscure biblical and non-biblical sources. The lament was chanted by a gifted poet with the heart of a convinced and stalwart Yahwist (Ps. 44:18–22).[39]

Psalm 51 The plaintiveness of Psalm 51 unfolds a *personal lament* different from the community lament of Psalm 44. The psalmist's religious

[39] See pp. 376–380.

experiences are interior and personal. His sin is a hideous fact to him, but his confidence in eventual forgiveness gives him joy (Ps. 51:3–12). Depth of feeling and superior artistry in this psalm is revealed in the way its intensely personal quality has been universalized. Christian worship for generations has taken one stanza of this powerful psalm to introduce penitents to the act of general confession in the liturgy.

> Create in me a clean heart, O God;
> > and renew a right spirit within me.
> Cast me not away from thy presence;
> > and take not thy holy spirit from me.
> Restore unto me the joy of thy salvation;
> > and uphold me with thy free spirit. (Ps. 51:6–9, KJV)

The author of this psalm repudiates lavish ritual and sacrifice in the Temple (Ps. 51:16). He was a spokesman for that small but staunch group who looked upon the revival of Temple worship as a reinstatement of the causes of Yahweh's punishment of Israel by enemy attacks (cf. Isa. 56:1–8, 58:1–14). The appendix at verses 18 and 19 shows that some scribe did not accept the psalmist's rejection of ostentatious worship, and he countered with a little poem on God's delight in altar, offerings, and sacrifice.

Psalm 91 Psalm 91 is a *ritual chant* designed to combat a plague. In an age when people believed demons were the causes of pestilence and disease such liturgical protections from curses were normal. The psalm does not suggest that Yahweh had sent the "deadly pestilence," a way of thinking typical of pre-exilic Israel. This psalm shows that Yahweh and some evil, unnamed power were pitted against each other. The psalmist has taken sactuary in the Temple because of its holiness. There the demonic powers cannot attack him (Ps. 91:1–2). The plague is particularly virulent because the night terror and the noonday waster have combined forces to rack Israel with disease (Ps. 91:5–6). Early Christian writers quoted this chant when they narrated how Jesus was tempted by the devil on the parapet of the Temple. They, too, saw the psalm as a trial between the divine and the demonic (cf. Matt. 4:5–6, Luke 4:9–11).

Psalm 150 Psalm 150 is particularly appropriate for closing the Jewish hymn book. With Psalm 1, which extols the man who follows Torah, it puts a binding around the psalmbook. To follow Torah and to praise God sum up the duties man owes his Creator and himself. Psalm

150 answers four questions about worshipping God. It tells where Yahweh should be praised (Ps. 150:1), why He should be praised (Ps. 150:2), how He should be praised (Ps. 150:3–5), and who should praise Him (Ps. 150:6).

XIV

**Prudence,
Speculation, and
Love**

Some of the choicest passages in all the Old Testament are found in the writings called Wisdom. How often Job 28 has been read for the scripture lesson at Baccalaureate services!

Surely there is a mine for silver,
and a place for gold which they refine.

. . .

But where shall wisdom be found?
And where is the place of understanding? (Job 28:1, 12)

One of the poems most quoted to brides in Bible-reading families of earlier generations was Proverbs 31:10–31, opening with the words "A good wife who can find?" Familiar lines have been set to music for the highbrow's taste as well as for the teenage set.[1]

For everything there is a season,
and a time for every matter under heaven:

Core Readings

Proverbs 1–9, 25–29

Job

Ecclesiastes

Song of Solomon

Ruth

Jonah

Psalms 1, 15, 34, 37, 73, 127[2]

---

[1] See Miklos Arozsa, "To Everything There Is a Season," Breitkoff and Hartel, Weisbaden, Germany, No. 3702, and "Turn, Turn, Turn (To Everything There Is a Season)," The Byrds, Columbia Record No. 4–43424.

[2] Psalms 32, 36, 41, 49, 88, 107, 112, 119, and 128 can be read with great profit.

> *a time to be born, and a time to die;*
> *a time to plant, and time to pluck up what is planted;*

> . . .

> *a time to weep, and a time to laugh;*
> *a time to mourn, and a time to dance;* (Eccl. 3:1–4)

Wisdom literature appealed to persons of diverse religious interests in Old Testament times just as it still does. Its authors were very different from those who composed the Law and the books of the Prophets. Both as literature and as religion it is so different that some general remarks should be recorded about Wisdom before proceeding to analysis of individual books.

Near Eastern Wisdom

Wisdom writers in the Old Testament borrowed extensively from other cultures in the ancient Near East. Canaanites, Edomites, and Arabs had traditions of wisdom which were assimilated by the Hebrews (Jer. 49:7, Obad. 8, Job 1:1).[3] Some of the aphorisms in the book of Proverbs have their origins in the literature of Canaan, going back as far as the Late Bronze Age (1500–1200 B.C.). The style of an ancient Canaanite proverb matches that of the Old Testament. Compare

> *Like the feeling of a wild cow for her calf,*
> *Like the feeling of a wild ewe for her lamb,*
> *So [was] the feeling of Anath for Baal.*

and

> *As vinegar to the teeth*
> *and as smoke to the eyes*
> *So is the sluggard to those who send him.* (Prov. 10:26)

---

[3] Wisdom in the Quran has a quality similar to that in the Old Testament. Luqman, a relative of Job according to Islamic tradition, was quoted by Muhammad: "Give thanks to Allah. He that gives thanks to Him has much to gain. . . ." "My son, Allah will bring all things to light, be they as small as a grain of mustard seed, be they hidden inside a rock, or in heaven or earth." "My son, . . . endure with fortitude whatever befalls you. . . . Do not treat men with scorn nor walk proudly on the earth: Allah does not love the arrogant and the vainglorious. Rather let your gait be modest and your voice low: the harshest of voices is the braying of the ass." Reprinted by permission of the publisher from *The Koran*, trans. N. J. Dawood (Baltimore: Penguin Books, 1956), Sura 31, pp. 185–7.

Compare subject matter of a Canaanite proverb:

> *If ants are smitten,*
> *They do not accept quietly,*
> *but they bite the hand of the man who smites them.*

with two from the Old Testament:

> *Go to the ant, O sluggard;*
> *Consider her ways and be wise.* (Prov. 6:6)

> *The ants are a people not strong,*
> *Yet they provide their food in the summer.* (Prov. 30:25)

The belief among Hebrew sages that Wisdom was God's first act of creation was learned from Canaanite wisdom literature. The Baal epic reports how El brought forth Wisdom even before he had conquered the primordial dragon (Tehom) and established his home. In like manner Yahweh created Wisdom

> *. . . at the beginning of his work,*
> *the first of his acts of old.*
> *Ages ago I was set up,*
> *at the first, before the beginning of the earth.*
> *When there were no depths [t^{e}homath] I*
> *was brought forth.*
> *when there were no springs abounding with water.* (Prov. 8:22–24)

The book of Proverbs carries several direct borrowings from Old Canaanite wisdom. Compare Proverbs 6:11 with

> *And poverty will come upon thee like a vagabond,*
> *and want like a beggar;*

Proverbs 18:18 with

> *The lot puts an end to law suits*
> *And decides between the mighty.*[4]

[4]See William F. Albright, "Canaanite-Phoenician Sources of Hebrew Wisdom," in Martin Noth and D. Winton Thomas, eds., *Wisdom in Israel and in the Ancient Near East,* (Leiden, Netherlands: E. J. Brill, 1960), pp. 5–10. Reprinted by permission of the publisher.

Israel's borrowings from Egyptian wisdom were greater than its borrowing from Canaan. From the Pyramid Age (2600–2175 B.C) came the instruction of a certain Ptah-hotep, a counselor to Pharaoh Izezi, which sounds much like the book of Proverbs.

> *Then he said to his son:*
> *Let not your heart be puffed-up because of thy*
> *knowledge; be not confident because thou*
> *art a wise man.*
> *Good speech is more hidden than the emerald,*
> *but it may be found with maidservants*
> *at the grindstones. . . .*
> *If thou art one of those sitting at the table*
> *of one greater than yourself, take what he*
> *may give, when it is set before thy nose.*
> *If thou desirest to make friendship last in*
> *a home to which thou hast access as*
> *master, as a brother, or as a friend, into*
> *any place where thou mightest enter, beware*
> *of approaching the women. It does not go well*
> *with the place where that is done.*[5]

The Instruction for King Meri-Ka-re formulated by his father King Khety II (c. 2150–2080 B.C.) was foundational to Hebrew proverbs.

> *Calm the weeper and oppress not the widow.*
> *Do not oust a man from the property of his father.*
> *Beware of punishing wrongfully.*
> *Punish with caution by beatings—so shall*
> *this country be peaceful—except [for] the rebel*
> *when his plans have been discovered, for*
> *God knows the treacherous of heart, and God requiteth*
> *his sins in blood.*
> *Eternal is the existence yonder. He who makes light*
> *of it is a fool.*[6]

The Hebrew sages took over the Instruction of Amen-em-Opet almost intact. This Egyptian document dates between 1000–600

---

[5] James B. Pritchard, ed., *Ancient Near Eastern Texts Relating to the Old Testament* (rev. ed.; Princeton: N.J.: Princeton University Press, 1955), pp. 412–13. Reprinted by permission of Princeton University Press.
[6] D. Winton Thomas, *Documents from Old Testament Times* (New York: Harper & Row, 1965), p. 160. Copyright © 1958 by Thomas Nelson & Sons, Ltd. (British Publishers). Reprinted by permission of Harper & Row, Publishers.

B.C., and subject matter, organization, and mood show that Proverbs 22:17–24:22 came from it.[7] Another Egyptian book of proverbs dating from about the 5th century B.C. is a collection of nearly 550 sayings and precepts stressing practical morality. Many of these can be compared with biblical proverbs.

If a woman is at peace with her husband,
*   it is the will of God.* (See Prov. 19:14)

Better to have a statue for a son than a fool. (See Prov. 17:21)

Do not go to your brother if you are in trouble;
*   go to your friend.* (See Prov. 27:10)

There is no wise man who comes to grief;
*   there is no fool who finds reward.* (See Prov. 12:21)

He who shakes the stone—it will fall upon
*   his foot.* (See Prov. 26:27)[8]

Mesopotamia, too, offered its literary harvest to the sages of the Old Testament. That region of the world produced proverbs of the type already cited from ancient Egyptian sources, but it also generated wisdom of a pessimistic mood in the style of Job and Ecclesiastes.[9] In a long poem given the title "I will Praise the Lord of Wisdom" a righteous man bemoaned the day he was smitten by a disease. He believed that gods and men had turned against him, although he insisted his piety was exemplary. In his illness no one, neither gods nor man, came to help him. Still he was confident that he would be vindicated. In a dream he saw Marduk restraining the evil forces and giving life to those in the grave.[10] A humorous piece of wisdom named "A Pessimistic Dialogue Between Master and Servant" relates how a master decides to do something but immediately reverses his decision. In each instance the servant expresses his agreement with both actions, giving equally cogent reasons for doing the opposite.

[7] Excellent translations are available in Thomas, *Documents from Old Testament Times,* pp. 172–91, and in Pritchard, *ANET,* pp. 421–4.
[8] From R. B. Y. Scott, "Proverbs" and "Ecclesiastes," in *The Anchor Bible,* Vol. 18. (Garden City, N.Y.: Doubleday & Co., 1966), p. XLV. Copyright © 1965 by Doubleday & Co., Inc. Reprinted by permission of the publisher.
[9] See "The Words of Ahikar," in Thomas, *Documents from Old Testament Times,* pp. 270–5 for an excellent translation of Assyrian proverbs. The narrative of Ahikar has found its way in modified form into Aesop's fables, the Arabian Nights, the Quran, as well as the Old Testament.
[10] See Pritchard, *ANET,* pp, 434–7.

> *Servant obey me.*
> *Yes, my lord, yes.*
> *I will do something helpful for my country.*
> *Do it, my lord, do it. The man who does something*
> > *helpful for his country, his helpful deed is placed*
> > *in the bowl of Marduk.*
>
> *No, servant, I will not do something helpful for*
> > *my country.*
>
> *Do it not, my lord, do it not. Climb the mounds*
> > *of ancient ruins and walk about: look at*
> > *the skulls of late and early men; who among*
> > *them is an evildoer, who a public benefactor?*[11]

This little dialogue shows throughout how ambiguous decent behavior is, and how omnipresent the element of death.

"A Dialogue about Human Misery," also called "The Babylonian Theodicy," approximates the biblical Job both in style and content. In it a man who suffers a disease tries to reconcile his experience of suffering with belief in godly justice. The sufferer cites his case in one stanza, followed by his comforting friend who represents the standard view of justice; that is, suffering is due to sin. This poem dates from about 1400–1000 B.C.[12]

Wisdom appealed to people widely spread throughout the ancient Near East. It furnished a cultural quality which crossed political lines and religious expression. The polytheist and the monotheist could use the same wisdom sayings, and with only slight adjustments fit them into their own religious contexts. Old Testament priests and prophets may have rejected alien forms of worship and beliefs, but the Israelite sage welcomed wisdom from Canaan, Egypt, and Mesopotamia.

Wisdom in Ancient Israel

Priests and prophets were concerned with official religious life in Israel. They often found themselves in opposition to one another because they emphasized dissonant aspects of religious experience. There was little conflict, however, between Israel's wisdom writers and the official functionaries of religion. Sages constituted a "third

---

[11]James B. Pritchard, ed., *Ancient Near Eastern Texts Relating to the Old Testament* (rev. ed.; Princeton, N.J.: Princeton University Press, 1955), p. 438. Reprinted by permission of Princeton University Press.

[12]See the translation and arrangement in Thomas, *Documents from Old Testament Times*, pp. 97–103.

agency" in Israel whose concentrations were different from priests' and prophets'. Sages laid little stress upon revelation. Wisdom was sometimes personified as a woman who had been created at the beginning of God's work, but the concept of God's revelation of His will in historical events eluded the Hebrew sages (Prov. 8:1, 22). Truth and righteousness were humanly discoverable elements within mundane affairs. Sages claimed that moral responsibility was based on common sense rather than on Yahweh's revelation. Israel's sages may be likened to modern observers of human affairs whose moral decisions rest upon intelligent appraisal of the evidence they have collected. They conducted schools for the youth of their society, where they spoke about natural phenomena, social behavior, and personal ethics.

The Sages' Cities, and The Wise Kings

Apparently sages lived in special communities in some such fashion as did priests and prophets. The town of Kiriath-sepher may have been such a sages' city (Josh. 15:16). In Hebrew *Kiriath* means village and *sepher* means book, so that Kiriath-sepher may be called "village of the book" or "booktown." After the Israelites changed the name to Debir (Judg. 1:11), they still retained the meaning of the original name. A *d^ebir* was an oracle or wisdom saying. Some kings, too, had reputations for being wise men. Solomon was gifted in the natural and social sciences (1 Kings 4:33, 3:16–28), and Ahab made a proverb to answer Benhadad's demand for search and seizure in Samaria. He said "Let not him that girds on his armor boast himself as he that puts it off" (1 Kings 20:11). Hezekiah was enarmored with the wisdom of his age. He commissioned wise men under royal patronage to collect proverbs, and to produce a book of them (Prov. 25:1).

Two types of wisdom predominate in the Old Testament. The first enunciated practical, didactic, and optimistic proverbs (the book of Proverbs). The second criticized conventional beliefs and practices. This wisdom was speculative and pessemistic: a challenge to the commonplace (The books of Job and Ecclesiastes).

The Book of Proverbs

The book of Proverbs is a collection of sayings, each collection having its own literary style, form, and ethical emphases. Five literary units form the book of Proverbs.

The first part is composed of ten discourses, seven poems of various lengths, and four selections of brief maxims (chs. 1–9). Each of the discourses is introduced by the address "Hear, my son."

The second part is a collection of proverbs attributed to Solomon. These sayings are unorganized as to subject matter. Each one is two lines long (10:1 – 22:16).

Part three corresponds in some of its sayings with The Instruction of Amen-em-Opet. The little "sayings of the wise" at 24:23–34 is a kind of appendix to the larger collection (22:17 – 24:22).

Part four is a second collection attributed to Solomon and gathered under Hezekiah's patronage. These sayings are of the same order, style, and subject matter as the earlier Solomonic collection (chs. 25–29).

The fifth part is a miscellaneous assortment. "The Dialogue of a Sceptic" may be a good title for 30:1–9. Various warnings and numerical sayings make up 30:10–33. The wise words of a queen are preserved in 31:1–9. A song about the ideal wife is an acrostic poem whose alphabetical arrangement is perfectly preserved Prov. 31:10–31.

The book of Proverbs was probably collected about 400 B.C., although many individual sayings are much older.

Religious Attitudes in Proverbs

Learning proverbs was part of a young man's education, just as was learning to handle weapons, to manage an estate, and to deal skillfully in business. Wise sayings provided subject matter for students gathered about sages. Monotonous in the manner that prescribed school work often is, the instructor spoke the first line, for instance, "A wise son makes a glad father," and students responded in chorus, "but a foolish son is a sorrow to his mother" (Prov. 10:1). Although the collections attributed to Solomon are rather dull, others seem to have been hammered out of the school of practical living and in the exchange of sages sharply debating the utilitarian value of one action over another.

The Secular Emphasis of Proverbs

Two emphases are discernible in the book of Proverbs. The first might be called *the secular emphasis*. Teachers with this point of view observed human affairs with a kind of scientific exactitude, and made witty, caustic, or descriptive comments about success and failure in the venture of living. To these men success came through hard work, intelligent observation, knowledge of a skill, and decent behavior. Man gained his goals through his own effort (Prov. 19:4, 17:8, 10:15, 22:7). Work and intelligence brought wealth (Prov.

24:3). The world being what it is, a man's riches might be taken from him overnight (Prov. 23:4–5, 27:23–24), but every effort should be bent toward saving something. Pleasures of the body were acceptable when enjoyed in moderation. A man could have oil and perfume (Prov. 27:9), a little wine (Prov. 31:6–7), marriage and a family (Prov. 5:5–20) even though a nagging wife might come of a marriage

(Prov. 17:1, 21:9, 19). If one avoided harlots (Prov. 5:9–10), drunkenness (Prov. 23:20–21, 29–35), and laziness (Prov. 6:6–11), he would be more likely to prosper and enjoy life. This view of life was unheroic. By the exercise of skill, a practical morality, an enlightened self-interest, a man could attain all that this life had to offer. God's place in man's affairs was distant and impersonal. God was the creator of the world (Prov. 3:19–20), and He also directed the mind, words, and steps of a man. But this was recognition of a state of affairs rather than a confession of faith. Practically, though, man was unable to get any true knowledge of God (Prov. 30:2–4).

The Ethical-Religious Emphasis in Proverbs

The second emphasis points out *the close relationship between religion and ethics*. Although critical of ritual and sacrifice, the sages represented in this section advocated an ethical ideal based upon piety. Although God was incomprehensible to these religious wise men, they overcame that barrier by personifying wisdom and imagining it as God's agent (Prov. 8:22–31). In that way they succeeded in identifying moral behavior and religious beliefs with wisdom. The truly wise man was the pious man (Prov. 9:10–11). One's behavior was judged and rewarded strictly according to God's standards. God knew even the hidden thoughts of a man (Prov. 5:21–23), and these were judged as surely as were his external deeds (Prov. 24:12). The doctrine of strict retribution for one's behavior was rigorously applied to individuals by this pietistic emphasis. Wealth and length of years were the rewards of a pious life (Prov. 3:16, 8:18) while poverty was sure to follow from impiety (Prov. 28:14, 18–20).

Whether the emphasis was secular or godly the ethical standard in the book of Proverbs is exemplary. Goodness is motivated by personal interest, but the motivation in no way reduces the quality of behavior. The ethics of Proverbs are directed toward the individual's welfare rather than the community's, so that an individual might acquire restraint in speech, self-discipline, kindness to the poor, patience, generosity, modesty, and trustworthiness.[13]

[13] Robert H. Pfeiffer, *Introduction to the Old Testament* (New York: Harper & Brothers, 1948), pp. 645–59 has a particularly insightful commentary on Proverbs.

The Book of Job   Practically everyone has heard of the patience of Job. Common speech as well as religious training have accustomed people to associate Job with unusual degrees both of suffering and of patience. But how accurate is the phrase "the patience of Job?" What is popularly supposed about the book does not match what is actually in it. *It is a collection of poems dealing with the meaning of life.*

What is the meaning of life? A modern playwright, Archibald MacLeish, gives his answer in a play apparently fashioned on the original story of Job. He calls it *JB*. A circus tent is the setting; the platform of a sideshow is prominently shown. Churchly vestments lie discarded at one side of the stage, and bare electric light bulbs give dim illumination to a dreary scene after the public has gone. The opening lines discuss heaven and earth in the context of a drama. Through eleven scenes the playwright traces a negative appraisal of man's possibilities after his hopes had burned so brightly. The play, avowing that no objective good exists in the world, ends with the words

> *Blow on the coal of the heart.*
> *The candles in churches are out.*
> *The lights have gone out in the sky.*
> *Blow on the coal of the heart*
> *And we'll see by and by . . .*
> > *We'll see where we are.*
> *The wit won't burn and the wet soul smoulders.*
> *Blow on the coal of the heart and we'll know . . .*

> *We'll know . . .*[14]

What is the meaning of life? This question so agitated an unnamed poet that he wrote one of the world's greatest poems in an effort to clarify, if not answer, the question. He wanted to know, in a world such as this, if he could put his faith in God.

Intentions of   People have discussed the intention of the author of Job ever since
the Book of Job   the book was written, I suppose, but no proposal has met with universal acceptance. Some interpreters believe the book of Job is a treatise on the question "Why do the righteous suffer?" There is no

---

[14] Archibald MacLeish, *JB* (Boston: Houghton Mifflin Co., 1958), p. 153. Reprinted by permission of the publisher.

doubt that this problem is a significant part of the book as it now stands. Others claim the principal theme to be that suffering comes to certain men in order to test their righteousness. That seems to be the motif of the prose portions (1–2, 42:7–17). Still others insist that the book of Job advocates suffering as a means of strengthening a man's faith. This is the main point in Elihu's speeches (32–37). Some readers have understood the book of Job to say that suffering is an experience intended to prepare a person for a future happiness. In many respects this is the point made by Eliphaz, Bildad, and Zophar. Some have held that the author wrote the book in order to refute the orthodox theological view of his day, namely, the belief that there is a divine retributive force exacting justice in the world. The belief that a good man prospers and an evil man suffers was orthodox doctrine in post-exilic Judaism. The author of the book of Job enters the debate over this belief, and demolishes its presuppositions.

The basic question lies deeper than any of the traditional explanations offered so far. What is the meaning of life? is the secular version of the theological question "What is the nature of God and what is His relationship to man?" Job, like other profound literary artists of history, asks this eternally contemporary question.

Before one can fully appreciate Job's treatment of this question, however, one must get to the bottom of the literary problems that surround this masterpiece of literature and religion.

Clarifying the Form

The book of Job is composed of five parts. Part one, chapters 1–2, is a narrative about Job from the land of Uz, reporting how that righteous and wealthy man is the object of a game between Elohim and Satan. His ten children have all been killed in a terrible windstorm. His body is afflicted with sores. In his sorrow and pain three friends come to commiserate with him.

The Form of Jobian Dialogue

Part two, chapters 3–31, is poetry. It opens with Job cursing the day of his birth and questioning the meaning of life in the face of his misery. Eliphaz replies with an affirmation of the doctrine of divine retribution upon individuals. Job speaks again, claiming his complaint is justified by his physical anguish. Bildad then speaks to Job and calls his talk nothing but a big wind. Job replies to Bildad that no man is just before God. Zophar then takes up the conversation and accuses Job of babbling. Job answers Zophar in a sarcastic tone about how wise his three friends are. A speech by Job, followed by a friend's speech three times repeated, is the form of the Jobian dialogue. This is completed in three cycles.

Part three, chapters 32–37, is a single poem by Elihu, who is angered both by Job's justification of his position and by the three friends who have failed to convince Job of his unrighteousness.

Part four, 38:1 – 42:6, is Yahweh's poetic declaration of His power and superiority over the natural world in contrast to the weakness of Job. At the end of this section Job acknowledges his despicable condition.

Part five, 42:7–17, is a narrative in which Yahweh rebukes Eliphaz and his two friends for not having spoken correctly about Him. Job prays for his friends, his fortune is restored, ten children are born to him, and he lives to be an old man.

Literary Problems
of Job

Several problems concern the composition of the book of Job. *First,* the opening and concluding narratives were originally one story which are dismembered by the intrusion of the poetic sections.

Second, inconsistencies between the narrative parts and Job's dialogue with the three "friends" are evident. In the narrative Job is composed and patient in the face of his affliction. In the dialogues he complains bitterly about his condition, and blames God for such injustice. It is a surprise to find in the closing narrative that the "friends" rather than Job are rebuked for not having spoken the truth. The dialogues show that Job has entirely negated the argument that virtue is always rewarded and evil always punished, yet in the closing narrative he is rewarded with riches, children, and long life in an artificial way. The names for God in the narratives are Yahweh and Elohim. In the dialogues they are El, Eloah, Elohim, and Shaddai. The mood of the narratives represents the attitude of an impersonal storyteller; in the dialogues the anguish of a man in torment prevails.

Third, some of the text of the dialogues has been violated purposefully. Chapters 24–27 in their present form confuse the reader by putting the words of Zophar in Job's mouth, and by confusing one of Bildad's speeches with Job's. Furthermore, the literary form of the dialogues, in which Job's speech is followed by his friends' speech repeated in a cycle of three recurrences, shows tampering. Tampering with the text was done to rob strength from Job's argument against belief in divine retribution. The following reconstruction reinstates the original literary form and also connects the thoughts in the text with the person who uttered them.

Job speaks	23:1–24:17, 25
Bildad speaks	25:1–6, 26:5–14
Job speaks	26:1–4, 27:1–12
Zophar speaks	24:18–24, 27:13–23
Job speaks	29:1–31:40.[15]

Fourth, chapter 28 has been inserted into the text.

Fifth, Elihu's speech in chapters 32–37 is an addition to the book of Job. This material adds nothing to the dialogue, and is an imitation of the arguments already rendered against Job. Elihu adds only the belief that suffering may be beneficial because of its disciplinary quality.

Sixth, it is possible that the speeches by Yahweh are also additions to the scroll of Job (Job 38:1–41:34). This idea has been debated vigorously by scholars. Those who argue for the Jobian originality of these chapters claim that vocabulary and style have close likenesses with the dialogues. They claim, too, that no poet of the stature of the dialogues' author would leave his work suspended, as is done, if the scroll ended at Job 31:40. The dialogues portray a man who speaks with only half knowledge. The purpose of Yahweh's speeches is to show him the full truth. Those who argue against their originality claim the dialogues tell the story of a single man overcome by adversity, rather than dealing with the universal problem of mankind's relationship to God. These critics also point out that Job and his "friends" have already admitted God's sovereignty over the world and that chapters 38–41 are therefore redundant. They say, too, that the editor added these poems because Job's rebellious spirit needed to be condemned once and for all. The editor thoughtlessly overlooked the fact that Job's repentance at 42:1–6 was contradicted by Yahweh's approval of the hero at 42:7–17. These literary problems do not diminish the excellence of the book if they are understood as being additions to an original, brilliant work which in ancient Israel, as it does in the modern age, evoked conflicting interpretations and opinions.

The author's brilliance is shown not only in the grandeur of the problem he handles but also in the style he employs. There are some vignettes of poetry as finely wrought as a pen engraving. The absolute equality brought to all men by death is neatly displayed in

[15] See Samuel Terrien, "Job," in George A. Buttrick, ed., *The Interpreter's Bible*, Vol. III (New York: Abingdon Press, 1955), p. 888.

Job 3:11–19. The terror a man feels at having seen a ghostly apparition is displayed in Job 4:12–20. Job 24:4–12 etches the sorrowful plight of the landless outcast whose plight is the same in all ages.

> They thrust the poor off the road;
> > the poor of the earth all hide themselves.
> Behold, like wild asses in the desert
> > they go forth to their toil,
> seeking prey in the wilderness
> > as food for their children.
> They gather their fodder in the field
> > and they glean the vineyard of the wicked man.
> They lie all night naked, without clothing,
> > and have no covering in the cold.
> They are wet with the rain of the mountains,
> > and cling to the rock for want of shelter.
> They go about naked, without clothing;
> > hungry, they carry the sheaves;
> Among the olive rows of the wicked they make oil;
> > they tread the wine presses but suffer thirst.
> From out of the city the dying groan,
> > and the soul of the wounded cries for help;
> > yet God pays no attention to their prayer.

Job's vocabulary overflows in richness which does not come through in the English translation. At Job 4:10–11, for example, there are five different Hebrew words for lion. It is necessary to attach adjectives to them in the English in order to give their meaning. Four words for darkness with shades of meaning take a variety of adjectives and nouns to render into English (10:21–22). Job's style is intensely personal and packed with emotion. Chapter 13 is a splendid example. Rich contrasts invigorate his style (9:1–11). He is a master of metaphor and simile.

> My days are swifter than a runner;
> > they flee away, they see no good.
> They go by like skiffs of reed,
> > like an eagle swooping on the prey. (9:25–26)

> His confidence breaks in sunder,
> > and his trust is a spider's web. (8:14)

Didst thou not pour me out like milk
and curdle me like cheese?
They didst clothe me with skin and flesh,
and knit me together with bones and sinew. (10:10–11)

There are some individual chapters of unsurpassed merit. The description of animals in Job 39 stands as one of the finest pieces of zoology from ancient literature. The code of a Hebrew gentleman in chapter 31 represents the ethical values admired by the sages. The symmetry of Job's artistry is noticeable in individual poems as well as the symmetrical arrangement of the dialogue. Eliphaz's long discourse, for example, in Job 4:2 – 5:27 has a balance that illuminates the superb ability of the poet. It has four parts. Part one deals with the doctrine of theodicy (4:2–11). It is composed of two sections, each made up of stanzas of three lines followed by two lines (4:2–6 and 4:7–11). Part two discusses the problem of suffering (4:12–21). It also has two sections, each made up of stanzas of two lines followed by three lines (4:12–16 and 4:17–21). Part three is about obstinacy (5:1–7). It is a stanza with seven lines. Part four reports on man's duty on earth (5:8–27). This part has two sections, each dividing into three stanzas of three lines each terminated by a fourth single-line verse.[16]

The original beauty of the lyrical quality of Job and its impact upon the hearer cannot be fully appreciated by English readers. It was chanted, as was all Hebrew poetry, and its combination of thought and sound probably enraptured its original hearers. Only an approximation of its quality can be made by English readers, but this can be increased by oral recitation with different voices speaking for the several protagonists.

The Historical Situation in Job

The post-exilic world was the life situation for the book of Job as it was for the book of Proverbs. Just when in the post-exilic age it came into being scholars are not agreed. The author of the dialogues may have drawn upon Jeremiah 20:14–18 ("Cursed be the day on which I was born"), so that the dialogue section would have been written not before the early 6th century B.C. The opening and closing narrative is from a folk tale whose style is similar to stories in Genesis and Judges. It is earlier than Ezekiel, at any rate, because Ezekiel knew a story of a pious Job (Ezek. 14:14). There is no sure way of deciding upon the date of the Elihu and the Yahweh speeches.

[16] See "Job," in Buttrick, ed., *The Interpreter's Bible*, Vol. III, pp. 894–6.

The dialogue section was created by a person who knew international wisdom literature when it had fully influenced Hebrew thought. The Edomitic background is recognizable in the hero's origins. He is from the land of Uz in north Arabia. The use of Eloah, the Edomitic word for God, thirty-five times in the dialogues argues, along with reference to Tema and Sheba (Job 6:19), for Edomitic influence on the author.

Egypt had its influence on Job, too. The author knew of the Egyptian skiff of reeds (Job 9:26) and the watch at the tomb over an Egyptian corpse (Job 21:32). He knew the Egyptian "Dispute over Suicide," a dialogue between a man, who is weary of life, and his soul.

> *To whom shall I speak today?*
> *Hearts are rapacious,*
> *no man has a heart upon which one can rely.*
> *To whom shall I speak today?*
> *There are no righteous men.*
> *The land is left over to workers of iniquity. . . .*
> *To whom shall I speak today?*
> *I am laden with misery*
> *through lack of an intimate.*[17]

Compare this with Job 24:1–3. Death's attraction for Job is more typically Egyptian than Hebraic.

> *Death is in my sight today*
> *Like the smell of myrrh,*
> *Like sitting under an awning on a windy day.*
> *Death is in my sight today*
> *Like the scent of lotus flowers*
> *Like sitting on the bank of drunkenness.*
> *Death is in my sight today*
> *Like a well-trodden way,*
> *As when a man returns home from an expedition.*[18]

Compare this with the longing for death in Job 10:18–22.

[17] Thomas, *Documents from Old Testament Times*, p. 165. Copyright © 1958 by Thomas Nelson & Sons, Ltd. (British Publishers). Reprinted by permission of Harper & Row, Publishers.
[18] Thomas, *Documents from Old Testament Times*, p. 165. Copyright © 1958 by Thomas Nelson & Sons, Ltd. (British publishers). Reprinted by permission of Harper & Row, Publishers.

The view of human nature found in the dialogues of Job approaches that of The Babylonian Theodicy.

> *I have looked around society, but the evidence is contrary.*
> *The gods do not impede the way of a devil.*
>
> *A father drags a boat along the canal*
> *while his firstborn lies in bed.*
>
> *The firstborn son pursues his way like a lion;*
> *The second son is happy to be a mule driver.*
>
> *The heir stalks along the road like a bully;*
> *The younger son will give food to the destitute.*
> *How have I profited that I have bowed down to my god?*
>
> *I have to bow beneath the base fellow that meets me;*
> *The dregs of humanity, like the rich and opulent, treat me*
> *with contempt.*[19]

The author of the dialogues of the book of Job was a man comfortably capable of handling the international wisdom literature of his age.

Religious Attitudes in Job

The ending of the book of Job is an enigma. Why would a man whose vigorous defense of his righteousness suddenly wilt into a self-despising creature? There is a contrast too great to be acceptable as the book now stands between the man who quarrels with God (Job 3–27, 29–31), and a man groveling in dust and ashes (Job 42:1–6). Literary criticism has clarified the composite origin of the book, and enables one to make sense of the conflicting religious beliefs.

The narrative of prosperous, prolific, and pious Job was a folk tale happily retold for the sake of its general interest and didactic qualities. Its view of God and man coincided with those of the Deuteronomists.

The Job of the dialogue is an entirely different person. This man reacts angrily to a world which he feels he does not understand. But

[19]Thomas, *Documents from Old Testament Times*, p. 101. Copyright © 1958 by Thomas Nelson & Sons, Ltd. (British publishers). Reprinted by permission of Harper & Row, Publishers.

such a person must have had an experience of life, before he was wracked by suffering, when he believed he understood. At one time he must have known a God of justice and mercy, a God whom he could trust like a friend. That God loved Job and protected him. He certainly was not the God who played games with Satan to see if His friend could withstand the grief of his children's deaths and the tortures of an infected body. But for some reason, (and this portion of the dialogue has been taken away and the narrative substituted in its place), that friendly, trustful relationship has ended. Now God appears to Job as incalculable, untrustworthy, unloving, and unlovable. The dialogue concerns the relationship of God to Job. Which is the true relationship: that of man as suffering creature under God, or of man loved and as a fellow creator with God?

The Greatness of Job's Poetry

Job is a great poet, for one reason, because he is able to elevate his particular experience to the level of the universal. He speaks for the whole of mankind. He faces the facts of life. He sees that good people are actually suppressed while the wicked prosper and triumph. He counters the pious affirmation that the present order of life is as it should be and that God's government of the world is just. As a single observer on the scene he is unable to provide a satisfactory explanation of what he sees about him, but he is unafraid to raise doubts and ask questions. The poet reports with objective clarity and emotional vigor how his tortured soul sees the world. He sees suffering, and he wonders if it is deserved. He sees punishment, and he doubts its divine wisdom. He is fully aware of the doctrine of divine retribution, but he goes to the heart of the matter by asking, what is the nature of God and man's relationship to Him?

Later Attempts to Counter Job's Pessimism

Elihu's Counter-Argument. Two attempts were made by subsequent authors to offset Job's general pessimism about God's justice and man's place in God's scheme. The first is the speech by Elihu. In an inferior style, Elihu tries to counter Job's insight by arguing that suffering is a disciplinary experience. This argument shows that he, like some modern interpreters, does not understand the subtlety of Job's use of the problem of suffering to discuss the nature of God and man. The second is a masterful effort to present another point of view. This is Yahweh's speech and Job's reaction (Job 38: 1 – 40:14, 42:1–6).[20] In this magnificient speech, every bit the equal in style with Job's dialogue, the author tries to put Job in his place.

---

[20] It is usually agreed by literary critics that not all the stanzas were original. The sections on Behemoth and Leviathan, often called hippopotamus and crocodile incorrectly (Job 40:15 – 41:34), were late additions.

This author sees man as an integral part of nature. He has no right to question God because he is simply a small part of God's grand design of heavens and earth, sea and sky, animals and birds. What is man, or any individual man, in contrast to the fantastic, creative work of God?

Yahweh's Humbling of Job. The author of the Yahweh speech takes up Job's argument and reprimands him for it. He begins with Job's admission that God would crush Job in a windstorm (Job 9: 16–17). God spoke out of the whirlwind (Job 38:1) and in this way He tried to prove that man must be silent and humbly accept what the Almighty does to him. After all, He who has the greater strength has the right to use it as He pleases (Job 40:7–14). So, if you, Job, cannot do something better than God, then do not criticize. The poet makes Job admit the merit of this in 42:1–2. At the end of this argument Job is bowed and defeated, ready to admit that he belongs no higher on the scale of God's creation than the animals, and he repents in dust and ashes (Job 40:3–5, 42:3–6). This author reiterates one of the prevailing views of man found in the Old Testament. This viewpoint claims that man is part of God's work in nature, but not distinct from it. This idea is expressed categorically, for example, in Genesis 2 and 3 and in Psalm 104. In these passages man is seen as part and parcel of nature.

The View of Man as God's Unique Creation. Still another view is expressed in the Old Testament. This view holds that man is a unique creature, the crowning act of God's creation. The question in Genesis 1:1 – 2:4 is the same, for example, as that asked in Psalm 8, "What is man that thou art mindful of him?" The answer comes back:

> *Thou hast made him little less than God,*
> > *and dost crown him with glory and honor.*
> *Thou has given him dominion over the works of*
> > *thy hands;*
> > *thou hast put all things under his feet,*
> *all sheep and oxen,*
> > *and also the beasts of the field,*
> *the birds of the air, and the fish of the sea,*
> > *what passes along the paths of the sea.*

Most of Old Testament literature can be posited with either of these two views of the nature of man. Man is either *one with nature,* or he is *above it* because he lies so close to its creator.

Job finds both positions too simple, and therefore unsatisfactory. On the one hand he agrees that man is inferior to God (9:1–12, 12:7–12); on the other he never brings himself to accept this station fully. He believes there is in man some quality that makes him quarrel with God, to assert his independence, to claim an individual integrity (7:17–21, 10:1–17, 13:1–28). He struggles to perceive God's nature and His relationship to man without bowing before either of the dominant views of his day. Job is torn in misery between seeing man as humble, content, and acceptive of his place in the world, and as proud, questioning, and eager to debate the issues of life with the Almighty Himself. He is a man living his life in ambiguity.[21]

Job handles the wonderfully complex problems of man's life with penetration and skill. He is disturbed by glibly offered characterizations of man as immersed in nature or superior to angels, and he grapples with other controversial matters. He grasps the immensity of the problem of evil. The prophet Amos had introduced into Hebrew beliefs a startlingly new concept. He claimed Yahweh was completely just in punishing Israel for its breach of covenant. Amos explained that God's sending famine and enemies across the land and striking whole cities with plagues, resulted from His righteousness, not from capriciousness. If God was righteous, He demanded a like character from His covenanted people. The Deuteronomists carried the idea of a just God one step further, affirming that if a man were good then a righteous God must reward him with the good things of life as well as punish him for his failures. This point of view is argued by Job's three "friends." Eliphaz insists that no innocent man ever suffered (4:7). Job must have concealed a secret sin. Impatience lies behind his bad temper (5:2). After all, God is only reproving Job (5:17). Bildad accuses Job of pride, and this, coupled with the probability that his children had sinned, causes his suffering (8:2, 4). If Job will confess his errors to God, restitution will follow inevitably (8:20–22). Zophar claims Job had committed sins that deserved even greater punishment (11:6). Job is simply stupid to deny his guilt (11:12).

Job hears these three expressions of orthodoxy and rejects them. He does not claim that man is good. On the contrary, he is convinced that humans are basically evil (4:17–21, 15:14–16, 25:4–6). Job's observations of human conduct have sufficiently convinced him of that. He knows man's deceit (31:5–8), adultery (31:9–12),

---

[21] See Duncan Black MacDonald, *The Hebrew Literary Genius* (Princeton, N.J.: Princeton University Press, 1933), for additional discussion along these lines.

greed (31:24–28), and inhumane treatment of the unfortunate (24: 2–4). Life consists of pain and suffering because of man's basically evil nature. *But,* and the "but" is the crux of the issue, is the awful suffering he endures justifiable in view of these facts? Is the hand of God heavier upon man than the situation merits?

Job's View of God

To these questions Job gives no easy answers. He rejects the homey God that his three "friends" press upon him. He avoids the personal name of the Hebrews' God, Yahweh, and uses only the transcendent terms El, Elohim, Eloah, and Shaddai. Rather than either the God who had made man a little lower than Himself or who provided for his well being as He did the birds of the air and the animals, Job sees a God having nothing in common with man (9:10–11). Man's noblest efforts are utterly meaningless to God (9:14–20). God is a cosmic and creative force but blind to human struggle and striving (9:32–35, 10:4–7). His unlimited power builds and tears down, but in it all there is neither rhyme nor reason (12:13–25). His holiness is indisputable, but it is cosmic holiness not moral holiness (21:15–26). God is creator: wise, holy, powerful, and impersonal. Man cannot know about His goodness. Job, unable to see goodness in God, raises the point that perhaps God is not good, and therefore is not perfect.

This was the position most repugnant to the author of the Yahweh speeches (38:1 – 40:14, 42:1–6). Since he could neither tolerate Job's argument nor destroy that masterpiece, he affixed his own argument that man does not know about God's goodness because of his own sinful plight. Man, seen in the magnificence of God's power, is only an infinitisimal part of God's grand scheme. He advocated acceptance of this inferior position with unquestioning humility.

Job's Courage Before the Imponderable

The wonderfully challenging part of Job's thought is his willingness to stand before a terrifying force asserting his own convictions. His "friends" counsel him to silence and acceptance (Job 13:11–12), but he wishes to argue his case before God (Job 13:3, 13–22). Job has the temerity to say that even though God were to strike him dead, he would defend his integrity before the Almighty. Job has asserted his position, and he will not be put down until that awful Power has listened to his case (Job 27:1–6). This is the thrilling quality in the tone of Job's speech. It is the wisdom of a learned man. He fully admits man's feeble position in the world, but he also defends man's right to be heard before the terrible Unknown of the universe. In Job is the amazing comprehension that man is not much, but he is independent, and intelligent enough to make his claims for freedom in a world of ambiguity.

The grandeur of the book of Job lies not solely in the magnificence of the hero, but also in the vitality of the debate that it calls forth among its readers. The challenge of greatness was recognized in the post-exilic world just as it is today by those patient enough to work through the subtleties and complexities of this finest of religious poems.

The Book of Ecclesiastes English literature and everyday speech are indebted to Ecclesiastes. How many phrases have been taken from this book to become a part of our speech!

There is nothing new under the sun. (1:9)

He who increases knowledge increases sorrow. (1:18)

A living dog is better than a dead lion. (9:4)

The race is not to the swift, nor the battle to the strong. (9:11)

Cast your bread upon the waters,
for you will find it after many days. (11:1)

It is a charming book. It is neither great literature in style and content, nor great religion, yet it has an attractiveness that draws today's critical minds to it in a way which few other Old Testament books do.

Literary Analysis Ecclesiastes defies precise literary analysis, even though its literary problems are obvious. The structure of the book has been explained in four different ways. One explanation is that the book is a literary unit, with its own coherence except for the addition of the introduction (1:1) and the conclusion (12:9–14). This viewpoint sees no contradictions or inconsistencies in the book. A second explanation complicates the analysis by suggesting that the book was written in three stages. The earliest stage was an anonymous tract written by a Jew in Palestine under the influence of Greek philosophy. A sage intrigued by the ideas added, in the second stage, some "wise sayings" which soften the pessimism of the original author.[22]

---

[22] These are 4:5, 9–12, 6:7, 9a, 7:1a, 4–6, 7–12, 19, 8:1, 9:17–18, 10:1–3, 8–11, 12–15, 18–19, 12:11–12.

The third stage was handled by a pious scribe who, offended by the skepticism of the work, tried to make the ideas palatable by neutralizing their taste. He added his bland diet to the concoction.[23] A third explanation of Ecclesiastes' literary problems recognizes the inconsistencies and contradictions and explains them as simply the wit and personality of the original author.

The book may call to mind a country store with men sitting around a cracker barrel, while one of them, wise, sagacious, and full of human experience, regales the others with his sharp tongue and acid comments on affairs, uttering bold and heretical statements. He keeps his hearers fascinated, for what everyone else calls black, he calls white, and what everyone else calls good, he calls bad. Just as they are about to conclude that he is a heretic par excellence, he suddenly arises, says good night, and announces that he must go home to get a good night's sleep in order to be in church bright and early the next morning.[24]

The Best View of Ecclesiastes

A fourth and best explanation sees the book as a collection of independent maxims, aphorisms, and wisdom sayings, each treating a topic from its own angle. Trying to find a unity is a hopeless task, and finding the mind of a single clever personality is equally futile. The first misinterpretation of the book was made when some pious soul added the words at Ecclesiastes 12:11–14. To visualize a learned skeptic sitting before a fire expressing his thoughts in these aphorisms may be permissible, but trying to trace a single argument or even a witty conversation through the book surpasses credence. One notices many different styles: first person reminiscences (1:13–18), exhortations to a second, younger person (5:1–8), sentiments of a general nature (1:1–11), and separate wisdom sayings like those in Proverbs (9:17 – 10:20). Pious additions to the text are readily observable.[25]

Reference to *Koheleth* as Ecclesiastes' Author

The title of the book presents an interesting problem. Some scribe tried to convince his contemporaries that Solomon had written the book (1:1). No scholar accepts this as historical fact. The English title derives from the Septuagint version which translates the Hebrew *koheleth* as "The Preacher." The word *koheleth* comes from *kahal,* a community or assembly. *Koheleth* means, then, the one who calls together or addresses an assembly. It is obvious that this title is inapplicable to the book of Ecclesiastes, since it deals with

---

[23] These are 2:26, 3:14b, 17, 5:1–6, 7:18b, 26b, 29, 8:2a, 3, 5, 6a, 11–13, 11:9b, 12:1a, 13–14. "Ecclesiastes," in George A. Buttrick, ed., *The Interpreter's Bible,* Vol. V, p. 8.

[24] Samuel Sandmel, *The Hebrew Scriptures* (New York: Alfred A. Knopf, 1963), p. 269.

[25] These are 2:26, 3:14, 17, 7:18b, 26b, 29, 8:2b, 5, 11–13, 11:9b, 12:1a, 8–14.

reflections directed to an individual and a small group of persons. Even with this error, it is still convenient to speak of the author as *Koheleth*.

The Historical Situation in Ecclesiastes

Arguments for the composition of Ecclesiastes in the late post-exilic period are unassailable. Some scholars have found pronounced influence of the philosophy of Epicurus' (341–270 B.C.) on *Koheleth*. Epicurus taught that pleasure was the goal of the good life and that man's wisdom and culture should be directed to that objective. The absence of pain, rather than joy or debauchery, was the simplest way to achieve man's desire. In seeking pleasure, self-control, prudence, wisdom, and frugality were the surest means. He condemned belief in the supernatural interference in the affairs of men. Other scholars have noted the strong Aramaic elements in the book. It has, in both vocabulary and syntax, a pronounced Aramaic character. It has been proposed that it was originally a Hebrew translation of an Aramaic book. The saying "Woe to you, O land, when your king is a child" (Eccl. 10:16) has been thought by some to allude to Egypt when Ptolemy V Epiphanes (203–181 B.C.) became king at five years of age. Others have concluded that its "tired philosophy" could represent a time only at the last stages of Old Testament development. Since there are no references to historical events in the book of Ecclesiastes it is probably best to place its origins some time between 400 and 200 B.C.

Religious Thought in Ecclesiastes

Koheleth's thought seems to coincide with the modern temper, which asserts with Bertrand Russell that "it is undesirable to believe a proposition when there is no ground whatsoever for supposing it is true." Although some of the older generation have thought that "the book has . . . the smell of the tomb about it,"[26] most of the younger generation appreciate it because its author was unafraid to face the difficulties of belief in God, admitting that life without roses could still be a fairly decent affair. Such minds are essential in every age because they keep a sense of balance while one chops away at the really significant questions about man's meaning and destiny. They also perform a service by shocking away easy complacencies and patterns that comfort the mind but anesthetize inquiry. They inject into cocksure minds a healthy dose of critical acumen, so that the world appears as it really is instead of the way one might like it to be. *Koheleth*, like most of the wisdom writers, warned his readers about the assurances of out-dated religion and the comfort of familiar cultic patterns.

[26] H. Wheeler Robinson, *Inspiration and Revelation in the Old Testament* (London: Oxford University Press, 1946), p. 258.

How did *Koheleth* look at the world? Certain of his observations informed him that the world was a vain thing. It existed, to be sure, but without fundamental significance. He noticed that nature never seems to get anywhere (1:5–7). His efforts in cooperating with nature ended in frustration (2:4–6). He saw nothing in nature that drew from him a sense of wonder, awe, and appreciation, unlike the psalmist (Ps. 19, 104). His personal life told him, too, that the world was vain. He had an ingrained desire to explain events and experiences (1:17) in terms of a wider meaning, but he could only conclude that

> *The more you know the more you suffer;*
> *the more you understand, the more you ache.*[27]

He experimented with many forms of human enterprise, and in this *Koheleth* showed great resilience. He became a sage in hopes of discovering life's secrets (1:13–18). He pursued physical pleasure expecting to find satisfaction (2:1–3). He applied himself to work. This too was "vanity and a striving after wind" (2:4–8). He became a wealthy man only to be disillusioned (2:9–11). He tried to despair of life, like a modern nihilist, but even this was unrewarding (2:22–23). He discovered after all these excursions into meanings for life that his only enjoyments came from his friends, his frugal pleasures, and his daily toil (2:24). But even friendship was a purely utilitarian thing, because in the event of hardship or reversals of fortune, it would be wise to have a few (11:1–9).

Koheleth's experience with society added to his suspicions that life was futile. He saw that injustice prevailed in high places (3:16, 5:8–9, 7:15–16), envy and greed were the mainsprings of productivity, and wealth, so often proclaimed as the benefactor of man and provider of happiness, proved to be elusive and ephemeral (4:1–4, 5:13–17). There was no trustworthy pattern to life, and chance really permitted whatever happened to a man (9:11–12). Finally, death was the principal human experience that deprived life of meaning. Wisdom was better than folly and light superior to darkness, but in the final tally neither counted for anything because death closed all books (2:13–17). No reward comes to anyone or anything in death. Human life, like the animals', ends in complete nothingness (3:19–22). After all, either life or death, what does anything matter? All is vanity.

[27]James Moffatt, *A New Translation of the Bible* (New York: Harper & Brothers, 1922), Ecclesiastes 1:18.

| The "Kindly Agnostic's" View of God | The "gentle cynic" pondered life and found it vain and unstable. When he thought of God he found an equally baffling problem. In his less dour moods he admitted that life offered a few joys in eating and drinking and working. These came as gifts from God (5:18–20). But the very joys acquired in these simple necessities were proof that God made a mockery of human life (6:1–3). Despite God's gifts of simple pleasures He was in no sense personal or loving (3:10–15). He had established the cycles of the seasons. He had created man so that he yearned after the beautiful and the permanent. He had dropped man flat, though, doomed to hopelessness. What king of a God was He who could be so cruel? He made life go on ceaselessly (9:7–10), but He ruled from a distant sphere (5:2). He was not righteous (5:4–6). He was not concerned with man's affairs (9:2–5). Things happen as they are determined to happen, not by God, but by the nature of things (10:5–11). God was inscrutable. "As you do not know how the spirit comes to the bones in the womb of a woman with child, so you do not know the work of God who makes everything" (11:5). *Koheleth* was a kindly agnostic. |

The "Kindly Agnostic's" View of God *(side heading)*

The Values of the "Gentle Cynic"

What values did life hold for a man who found no permanence in human achievements and no confidence in God? There were four things that assuaged the bitterness of such a philosophy. *First,* though life itself was fleeting, a wise man took what it offered without bitter complaint (11:7–9a). In this respect *Koheleth* and Job differed greatly. *Second,* wisdom is better than foolishness. Although wisdom gives no lasting benefit, it furnishes a man a little light in a gloomy world (2:13–14). Wisdom gives a man some comfort and provides him a little advantage over fools in preserving his inheritance and in making money (7:11–13). It may help in time of crisis, but no one should think that wisdom has a lasting value (9:15). Pleasure is the *third* thing that man may value. This was, of course, like Epicurus' view of pleasure, a controlled and frugal pleasure (2:24, 8:15, 9:7–10). *Fourth,* one's work was of value. When nothing else counted, one's toil gave some small satisfaction (3:22, 5:18, 9:10).

Ecclesiastes in the Bible

How did such a book get into the Old Testament? Its mood is so pessimistic compared with the rest of Hebrew literature that some explanation is necessary. Job's bitterness is at least countered by the orthodoxy of Elihu and the Yahweh speeches. It is doubtful that the few pious additions to Ecclesiastes were by themselves sufficient to justify its inclusion in the canon. It was probably an exceptionally popular book. There is no safer way to counter an unorthodox opinion than to modify it just enough to include it within orthodoxy. The book's superior literary qualities also made it attractive. It avoided clichés, so that men who were irritated by official religion could read this book with pleasure. The temper of the late post-exilic period had been broadened by contact with the Greek world, and doors to new ideas had been opened to intelligent persons. The scroll also had the backing of sages who were the influential "third force" in Israel's world of thought. Uncowed by priests or prophets, sages spoke up to win Ecclesiastes a place. Of course, the scribe who inserted the opening lines did much to get the book received. Its reputation as a product of Solomon's wisdom probably convinced the conservative theologians. They believed that if the great Solomon had written such things they must be valuable.

The Song of Solomon

How could a book which not once mentions the name Yahweh get into the Old Testament? It was difficult for the cynicism of Ecclesiastes to be accepted. How much more difficult for the Song of Songs to be considered sacred!

Explanations of the Origins of the Song

This book has almost as many interpretations as it has readers. It is probable that one of the earliest interpretations secured it a place in the canon. It was looked upon as an allegory of Yahweh's love for Israel. Yahweh was the bridegroom, Israel the bride. Modern scholarship does not accept the Solomonic authorship of the book, so that other explanations of its origins have been sought.

The Song as Drama. Some scholars have thought that the Song of Songs (a better name than the Song of Solomon) was originally a drama. Two characters were the actors: Solomon disguised as a shepherd and a Shulammite maid. Some interpreters added a third actor to the drama in the figure of a male lover who contested with Solomon for the love of the maid. Unfortunately for the belief that the book was a drama, there are too many loopholes. First, drama was alien to Jewish tastes. Second, drama calls for dialogue, not monologue. Third, characters in a drama need precise identity, and the speakers in the Song of Songs are not named.

The Song as Part of the Wedding Ceremony. Others have seen the book as a collection of Palestinian wedding songs after the style of wedding songs found among Syrian Arabs today. They were rustic, traditional compositions sung during the week of the wedding. The bride and groom's pavilion is thought to be described in

Song of Songs 3:6–11. The groom sings his song to the bride (4:1–7), and she replies with hers (5:10–16). The ladies in waiting then sing their song to the bride (7:1–5). Some critics find this explanation improbable because such secular lyrics would never have gotten by the censors of sacred literature.

The Song as Jewish Liturgy. Another theory, held vigorously by those who accept it, is that the Song of Songs was originally part of a liturgical ceremony at a Jewish festival. This, so the proponents claim, is the only satisfactory explanation of how it was canonized. The Hebrews celebrated the New Year like all other people of the ancient Near East. During that festival priests chanted the myths which dealt with creation. The Song of Songs is a survival of a part of the myth which extolled lovemaking. The absence of Yahweh's name in the book is explained by the fact that the festivals of Unleavened Bread and of Booths were Yahwistic in nature, so that He was understood as the God who was invoked.[28]

The Song as a Collection of Love Songs. The simplest explanation of literary origins is that it is a collection of songs of various sorts connected by the theme of love. The study of literary forms in the Old Testament has shown that literary types tended to be grouped together. Therefore, the rustic love songs of a group of humble people were gathered together by someone entranced by their beauty and simplicity. The vocabulary and syntax of the songs are unique in all the Old Testament, which would argue decisively against the liturgical theory of the origins of the book.[29] Language and form would have to be in a universal idiom for cultic use. The collection includes songs chanted at wedding feasts (3:6–11, 4:1–8, 5:10–16, 7:1–5), songs expressing love between man and woman (1:2–17, 6:1–10), and those expressing the raptures and heartaches of being in love (2:1–17, 3:1–5). To interpret the Song of Songs as a drama, or as part of a liturgical ceremony, or as a full recitation of a week-long wedding feast, is unnecessary when the simplest explanation is that the book is a collection of songs on the theme of love.

It is unnecessary to discuss the historical setting of these poems since they could be sung almost anywhere anytime in the Near East.

[28]See "The Song of Songs," in Buttrick, ed., *The Interpreter's Bible*, Vol. V, 92–6.
[29]"The Song of Songs," in Buttrick, ed., *The Interpreter's Bible*, Vol. V, p. 92.

The voice of the swallow speaks, saying,
"The land is bright. What of thy way?"
Prithee, do not, O bird scold me.
I have found my brother [an Egyptian term for lover] in his bed
And my heart is pleased even more.
We have said [to one another],
"I shall not go far away
While my hand is in thy hand,
I shall stroll about
Being with thee in every beautiful place."
He has made me the chief of his lovely women
Lest he should wound my heart.[30]

Compare this Egyptian poem of the 12th century B.C. with Song of Songs 2:12–15. Modern Arabic poetry shows simplicity of form and content similar to both ancient Egyptian and Hebrew love songs.

Her body is silk like water
With the curves of water,
Pure and restful as water.

To be with her in the night!
Her hair, the wings of night;
And her hands the pole stars of night.

God said: Let there be eyes,
And lo! the dew of her eyes,
The dark wine of her eyes.[31]

Compare this poem with Song of Songs 7:6–9.

Unless one interprets this book as an allegory of God's love for Israel, or as cultic drama, there is only one religious emphasis. It does look upon sensual lovemaking as a desirable human experience, and in this way it shows a basic admiration for the human body. The poems really affirm the essential beauty of this world and of men and women who love well and strongly. No sneaky,

---

[30] Thomas, *Documents from Old Testament Times*, p. 189. Copyright © 1958 by Thomas Nelson & Songs, Ltd. (British Publishers). Reprinted by permission of Harper & Row, Publishers.
[31] E. Powys Mathers, *Sung to Shahryar: Poems from the Book of the Thousand Nights and One Night* (New York: Casanova Society, 1925), p. 73.

guilt feelings are attached to those who love in passion. The world is good as it is.

The Book of Jonah

This little story was created out of basic mythological and legendary elements. The myth was the story told worldwide of a great fish swallowing a man and vomiting him out upon the shore. One legend deals with Jonah's resistance to preaching repentance to Nineveh (chs. 1 and 3). Another tells of Jonah's anger at Yahweh for his leniency toward sinners (ch. 4). These ancient tales were combined into a single narrative which forms a suspenseful short story. The plot tells of a man who tries to flee from Yahweh's commission to preach repentance to Nineveh. The setting is the historical period of the Assyrian empire, with all its associations of conquest and terror. The main characters are Jonah and God, in conflict with one another. The sailors and the king of Nineveh appear briefly in the narrative. Suspense is achieved by reporting the antics of a great fish and by having a Jew walk down the streets of Nineveh.

The psalm in chapter 2 was added to the book subsequent to the original composition. The narrative continues smoothly if the psalm is taken away.

A prophet by the name of Jonah (2 Kings 14:25) lived during the reign of Jeroboam II (768–746 B.C.), but that these stories were connected with him is doubtful. The author fixed upon a prophet's name, and designed his tale to bring home a moral lesson to post-exilic Israel. There is no doubt that the story originated then, because only the dimmest memories of its sinfulness were still alive.

The moral of the story carries an attitude of universalism and tolerance that would have been inconceivable before the Exile. Its fundamental intention is to show that Yahweh cares as much for sinful Nineveh as he does for good Jews like Jonah. One can imagine the author writing his short story precisely to counter the exclusiveness of the Jewish community in Jerusalem stressed by Nehemiah and Ezra.

The Book of Ruth

Another short story, which in plot, setting, characters, and suspense shows the masterful ability of its author, was the book of Ruth. The charming recital of agrarian life made it particularly appropriate for reading at the Feast of Weeks—the celebration of the annual wheat harvest. The story of faithful Ruth, who follows her mother-in-law from Moab to Judah, who offers herself to Boaz, who marries him, and who gives birth to an ancestor of King David, is as familiar as any story of the ancient Near East. Its setting is the period of the Judges in Israel, and its placement in the Old Testament between the books of Judges and Samuel is due to its historical background.

The Characters of Ruth

The main characters of this little novel are Naomi and Ruth, and neither would be a complete personage without the other. Naomi is a woman of such strength and beauty that her widowed daughter-in-law leaves her native land to take up residency in a hostile country to be with her. Naomi looks after her daughter-in-law's welfare. She sees to it that she meets a kinsman who will provide for the two widows. Ruth is an obedient and dependable daughter. She supplies what Naomi can no longer supply, her body, for the continuation of the family name. Boaz is described as a righteous, kindly, and law-abiding man. He knows his duty as a kinsman of Naomi, but he deals fairly with all concerned with the marriage and property transaction (4:1–6). It is difficult to know whether the names in the story are proper names or were meant as symbolic types. Mahlon (1:5) means "weakness," Chilion (1:5) means "consumption," Orpah (1:14) means "unfaithful," and Ruth means "faithful." Naomi's name means "the pleasant one." These names are not found elsewhere in the Old Testament.

A Literary Problem in Ruth

The material at Ruth 4:17–22 presents an interesting literary problem. Why Ruth's son is named Obed when he was adopted by Naomi is not clear. In other Old Testament passages dealing with the naming of a person, the name has something to do with his relationships or with an unusual happening. Obed simply means "servant" or "slave," for which the story does not prepare us. Isaac, for example, was given his name because Sarah laughed (Gen. 18:9–15). Isaac means "laughter."[32] In the case of Obed, it is probably a name substituted for the one in the original text, which may have been *ben-Na'om* or "son of pleasantness."[33] The name Obed is derived from 1 Chronicles 2:11–15. This shows that the addition of the genealogy of King David to the original story was done by some scribe who was delighted with this lovely account of a Bethlehemite family and believed it must have had something to do with David. This interpretation should eliminate any idea that David was part Moabite.

The book of Ruth originated in post-exilic Israel under circumstances identical with those of Jonah. The efforts to use archaic

[32] See Genesis 39:31–35 for several other examples.
[33] See Otto Eissfeldt, *The Old Testament: An Introduction*, trans. Peter R. Ackroyd (New York: Harper & Row, 1965), p. 479.

conditions and customs should not blind one to its anti-separatist tone. The opening line "In the days when the judges ruled," the situation in Moab, the ceremony of the threshing floor (3:6–13), and the rite of the sandal (4:7–12) are literary devices to take the reader back in time in his imagination, not in historical fact.

The author of this book understands Yahweh as a God who gives rewards to righteous and faithful people. As in the folk tale of Job, those who have suffered hardships, famine, death of loved ones, hunger, and hostility, will be rewarded if they continue to trust Yahweh. The acceptive attitude toward a citizen of Moab represented in this short story shows that its author was opposed to the separatism that characterized official Judaism in the days of Nehemiah and Ezra.

The wisdom of Israel's sages in the book of Proverbs, the critical appraisal of orthodoxy in the book of Job, the gentle skepticism of *Koheleth,* the appreciation of life and love in the Song of Songs, and the universalism in Jonah and Ruth, all speak for a point of view significantly different from what came from prophets and priests from Amos through Ezra. There is a warmth and humaneness about these writings that draw the reader gently to them. It is to the eternal credit of the learned men who authorized the canon of the Old Testament that they preserved these lovely books for the enjoyment of all who came after.

Psalms in the Wisdom Tradition

Didactic themes, wise sayings, and personal petitions typify those psalms related to the wisdom tradition.

Psalm 1

The first psalm in the book is a simple didactic hymn. It has the characteristic formula used by the sage as he instructed the young: "Blessed is the man who. . . ." The sage contrasts the wise man, who was equated with a person who observed Torah (Ps. 1:1–3), with the evil man, who did not know the way of the righteous (Ps. 1:4–6). The word "blessed" could better be translated "Happy is the man," as is done in Proverbs (Prov. 3:13, 8:34, 28:14). Notice that Psalm 1 is more prosy than poetic in its style. This has led some commentators to conclude that the psalm was written especially as an introduction to the entire collection of psalms. If so, it tells us two things about the book as a whole. First, it shows that the compilation was done by scribes influenced by the wisdom movement. Second, it shows that the collection was done in the late post-exilic period, when wisdom had been assimilated into Judaism to such an extent that it was equated with Torah. Regardless of these possibilities Psalm 1 was composed after Ezra, since "the congregation of the righteous" (Ps. 1:5) is the ideal community from which all sinners are excluded.

Psalm 15 Psalm 15 is another didactic psalm instructing the young who will one day worship in the Temple. A question is posed to the students and they respond with the ten rules for those who may worship at the Temple (Ps. 15:1). These are typical admonitions for young children, and they deal solely with social relationships. The demands of ritual purity are passed over, and seriously antisocial sins, such as, murder, theft, and adultery, are not mentioned. Rules of behavior such as the ten listed in Psalm 15 originated out of the ancient custom of seeking an oracle from the priest which would offer the inquirer guidance in a course of action.[34] The prophets so influenced such instruction in Israel that oracles were taken out of the realm of pure divination and were given moral dimensions. Thus in the post-exilic age, giving moral instruction to the young fell to the priests. These "ten rules of piety" are preparation for the deeply personal experience of appearing morally clean as well as ritually clean within the Temple.

Psalms 34 and 37 Wise sayings entered psalmnody under the influence of the wisdom movement. Psalms 34 and 37 use wisdom sayings, have an acrostic pattern, and contrast the righteous with the wicked. Psalm 34 has two divisions. Verses 1–10 report the personal experience of the poet who has been set free from fears and troubles. Although the poet uses metaphors which display an immanent view of God (Ps. 34:8 "O taste and see"), he was also influenced by late Jewish thought which conceived of Yahweh as too far removed from man's life to act directly in his affairs. Therefore, heavenly messengers had to be employed to do His bidding.[35] "The young lions" in verse 10 should probably be read "the unfaithful ones" (*kaphrim* for *k^{e}phirim*), although "the young lions" could be understood metaphorically as aggressive and proud young men.[36] Psalm 34:11–22 is instruction in the good life in the style of wisdom sayings.

Note especially the title of this psalm. The psalm is identified with an incident in David's life when he pretended to be mad (1 Sam. 21:10–15). The editor mixed up the story of David's pretended madness before Achish of Gath with the one when Abraham lived with Abimelech, king of Gerar (Gen. 20–21). This little fact sup-

---

[34] See 1 Samuel 23:2, 4, 10, 12 for examples of this procedure used by King David.
[35] Psalm 34:7; "messenger" is a better translation than "angel."
[36] See "Psalms," in Buttrick, ed., *The Interpreter's Bible*, Vol. IV, p. 178.

plies some notion of the carelessness of some Jewish scribes in the late post-exilic period.

Psalm 37 was written at the same time that some men were questioning the Deuteronomic doctrine of divine retribution and reward. The opening two verses show that this author believes implicitly in the doctrine that righteousness is rewarded with long life and prosperity (Ps. 37:3, 11). Psalm 37 might be a direct rebuttal of Ecclesiastes. Like the author of that book, the poet of the psalm is an old man (Ps. 37:25). He uses the style of wisdom sayings to refute the pessimism of *Koheleth*.

Psalm 73   Personal petition was a third type of psalm influenced by wisdom. Psalm 73 is in contrast with those already studied. In six short stanzas it searches the same ground as Job. This poet had believed in a God of rewards and punishments, but he loses that belief when he looks at the world as it really is. He sees the prosperity, sleek bodies, and untroubled lives of the wicked. His beliefs flee before these facts, and he envies the wicked. When he compares his spiritual life with their external success, he is ready to join them. But he considers once again his own personal integrity, and tries to visualize his life without virtue. This vision drives him to the sanctuary of God (Ps. 73:15–17). There he goes through a rigorous self-analysis which makes him admit that he had blamed God for the sins of the world (Ps. 73:21–22), but he now realizes that his conclusions were wrong. He does not expect prosperity and ease for having returned in faithfulness to God. He expects only the personal confidence that comes from knowing that he has not sold his soul to evil (Ps. 73:26–28).

Psalm 127   Psalm 127 is not easily classified with any of the preceding types, yet it has the didactic quality of Psalm 1 and the moral emphases of wisdom psalms like Psalms 34 and 37. Its stress on secular pursuits makes it different from them, however. Human enterprises, such as building a house, tilling the soil, and raising children are vain experiences without taking God into account. The tone of this psalm reminds one of the hearty frontier families in America who left schools, churches, and towns in order to settle the virgin land. But how often those families read the Bible and respected belief in God even though formal religious practices were considered unessential.

The psalmist knew well that building a house was an enterprise fraught with danger. Evil spirits, earthquake, fire, and heavy hail could destroy the house unless Yahweh was consulted. What use is there in protecting a city from invasion when pestilence, famine, or treachery can destroy it from within (Ps. 127:1)? It is vain to toil from dawn to dusk on the land and to think that the laborer gives it fertility. Sons are a precious heritage, and they afford a father pleasure and defend him in court (Ps. 127:5). In these experiences the wise man seeks his fundamental aid from God. How interesting that a modern novelist should use this ancient psalm as thematic material in fiction.

Except the Lord Joyce Cary, an English novelist, used the first phrase (King James Version) of this psalm for the title of a novel. *Except the Lord*[37] is the story of Chester Nimmo, who grew up in England's West Country during the Victorian Age. In one sense it is a success story, because the narrator is Chester Nimmo himself, who in old age, after having risen to be Prime Minister of England, is writing his memoirs. In another sense it is a story of crime and tragedy, because of what happens to the lives of those about Chester Nimmo as he rises from one position of power to another.[38]

Chester, his brother and his sisters, are children of a poor farmer whose pietism brought Christian love to the family but kept them in poverty because of Mr. Nimmo's honesty and contempt of money. The gruelling labor of the farm, which racked the body and killed the spirit, leaves its mark upon Chester. When he grows to young manhood he becomes a labor organizer among the farm workers of the West Country, and later on the docks. After a disastrous experience with the cruel methods of professional labor leaders, he is converted to Christianity, having previously renounced his father's faith, and he becomes an evangelistic preacher. His popularity and leadership eventually lead him into control of Britain's Labor Party.

The title of the novel affirms that the author's major theme depends upon that of Psalm 127, that man by his own efforts struggles for success in vain. In the truly significant events of life — creating a home, defending a nation, working in one's vocation, and raising children — a man must depend upon God, Who constitutes the enduring foundation of achievement.

[37] New York: Harper & Brothers, 1953.
[38] Chester Nimmo's life is told from the point of view of Nimmo's wife in Cary's *Prisoner of Grace* (New York: Harper & Brothers, 1952), and from that of Nimmo's wife's lover in *Not Honour More* (New York: Harper & Brothers, 1955).

Wisdom was the most popular form of scholarship in post-exilic Israel. It had a long and honorable heritage which borrowed willingly from folk learning, priestly knowledge, and prophetic oracles. It utilized those resources in new ways, organizing them into maxims for daily behavior, using them for critical analysis of accepted doctrines, and as appeals for breadth of understanding, and to appeal for acceptance of alien ways that might prove useful in making life in post-exilic Judah meaningful. Although the collection and arrangement of knowledge was one of the sage's main jobs, he also applied learning to practical affairs. He was the person who kept a balance between piety and reason in a way that gave strength and vitality to Israel's religious traditions. Others, such as the authors of the books of Jonah and Ruth, expressed a breadth of understanding and tolerance of others through engaging short stories that have made them cousins of the wisdom tradition.

XV

The Close
of the Old
Testament Age

The literature of the close of the Old Testament age is exceedingly varied, covering a period of about 370 years (c. 300 B.C.–70A.D.). The *Apocrypha* rightly belongs with study of the Old Testament, but the literature from Qumran is less easily assignable.

Core Readings

1 Chronicles 10–22
2 Chronicles 34–36
Zechariah 9–14
Joel
Isaiah 24–27
Daniel
Esther
Psalms 46, 39, and 71, 56 and 129, 98 and 148[1]
From *The Apocrypha*[2]
    1 Maccabees 1–5
    Susanna
    Tobit
    Sirach 1–11
From *Qumran*[3] documents
    The Community Rule
    Hymns 1, 2, 3, 4, 5
    Commentary on Hosea, Micah, Nahum, Habakkuk[4]

[1] The following psalms also belong to the close of the Old Testament age: 40, 52, 57, 58, 59, 62, 100, 130, 135, 136, 141, 142, 143, 145, 146.
[2] Two editions of the Apocrypha are: Bruce M. Metzger, ed., *The Apocrypha* (Oxford Annotated Apocrypha; New York: Oxford University Press, 1965); Edgar J. Goodspeed, trans., *The Apocrypha* (New York: Modern Library Paperback, 1959).
[3] The discovery of ruins near Wadi Qumran on the northwest shore of the Dead Sea has supplied the name for the people who produced the Dead Sea Scrolls.
[4] These readings correspond to titles in G. Vermes, *The Dead Sea Scrolls in English* (Baltimore: Penguin Books, 1962). Another edition is Theodor H. Gaster, *The Dead Sea Scriptures* (revised and enlarged; Garden City, N.Y.: Doubleday & Co., 1964).

The Books of Chronicles

The books of Chronicles are valued primarily for information filtered through them on the 100 years from Ezra (398 B.C.) to the end of the 4th century B.C. The Chronicler used the history of Israel found in the books of Genesis through Kings as his chief source, copying many sections word for word. From other sections he eliminated much about Israel, and added stories about the kings of Judah. He also eliminated sections unfavorable to David and Solomon.

Reasons for the Writing of Chronicles

The Chronicler put pen to paper for several reasons. First, he was updating the history of Israel which had ended with the destruction of Jerusalem and exile to Babylon, at the same time he was trying to teach a religious lesson using the vehicle of history. Second, he was offering explanation for the strictness of Temple worship: i.e., that Greek culture was a threat to its purity. Third, he was defending the uniqueness of the Temple cult against the claims of the Samaritans that they were the true successors of the Yahwist tradition.[5]

He wrote his history of the Jews about 325–300 B.C., when Alexander the Great had conquered Palestine and the Samaritan conflict had first become a serious issue. The author's deliberate confusion of the careers of Nehemiah and Ezra "proves" that several generations had passed: no one alive knew the correct sequence in which those men had lived.

Late Post-Exilic Prophecy

Zechariah 9–14 was compiled from prophetic oracles, laments, allegories, and apocalyse. Prophetic oracles are at 9:1–12, 9:13–17, 10:1–2, 10:3–12, 13:7–9. These oracles declare destruction upon an enemy, judgment upon Judah's leaders, and Judah's victory over its enemies. Historical allusions in these oracles are few, so that dating them is tentative. Zechariah 9:1–12 is an oracle against cities in Syria, Phoenicia, and Philistia. The reference to Tyre's defensive preparations and its destruction puts it in the year when Alexander the Great spent seven months besieging that city (Zech. 9:3). He was successful only after he built a causeway from the mainland to the island city, closed off the sea traffic with his navy, and stormed the city walls. This oracle looks upon Alexander as a benefactor who will secure peace and prosperity for Jerusalem (Zech. 9:9–12).

---

[5] See Martin Noth, *The History of Israel* (2d ed.; New York: Harper & Row, 1960), p. 356.

Another oracle was uttered subsequent to the foregoing, pronouncing doom upon the sons of Greece (Zech. 9:13–17). Peace did not materialize from Alexander's conquest of Palestine. At his death his generals fought each other for his empire, and Palestine felt the rough heels of Ptolemy and Seleucus as they marched back and forth across that land. This oracle denounces their bloody wars and proclaims victory for Judah through God's intervention (Zech. 9:16–17). Still another oracle continues the judgment against Ptolemaic and Seleucid kings who ground innocent Judah under their war machines (Zech. 10:3–12). Reference to Assyria masks the real culprit: the Seleucid empire, master of the territory once held by Assyria. The oracle against the shepherd judges some Jewish leader who ruled badly (Zech. 13:7–9). It was probably against John Hyrcanus (128–104 B.C.), whose rule as high priest and king was supported by mercenary troops, not by the people.

The Book of Joel

Prophetic proclamation is also found in the book of Joel. This fascinating little book reports how terrifying swarming locusts were. Farmers watched utterly helpless while the insects ate every green leaf in sight. Even the bark of trees was stripped off (Joel 1:7). Joel thinks of this destruction as *the day of the Lord* (Joel 1:15, 2:1). The prophet calls upon all responsible people across the land to repent in a day of general fasting. The day of mourning completed (Joel 2:12–17), the prophet announces that the turning point has come. Zion can once again rejoice. Yahweh has spared some of the crops (Joel 2:18–29).

The mood and tone change drastically at Joel 2:30. Some scholars argue that a secondary author wrote a commentary upon the original prophetic liturgy. Perhaps that interpretation is unnecessary. Rather, after the plague of locusts had run its course, Joel wrote down the liturgy he had composed for the day of national mourning. In doing so he added the material between Joel 2:30 and 3:21. This section, however, hovers between prophetic recitation and apocalyptic imagery. The cosmic dimensions of his imagery (Joel 2:30–31, 3:15), the full salvation of those who worship Yahweh irrespective of their moral stature (Joel 2:32), the destruction of alien nations at Yahweh's hand (Joel 3:1–3, 11–12), and the extravagance of Jerusalem's prosperity (Joel 3:17–18), represent apocalyptic motifs rather than classical prophetic images. Joel seems to have stood astride both the prophetic and apocalyptic traditions.

Apocalyptic

The prophetic movement clung to life in the post-exilic age, feeding on the Temple cult. It spawned a grotesque progeny. This child was named apocalyptic: in the Old Testament Zechariah 12–14,

Daniel, and Isaiah 24–27.[6] Conceived in prophecy, and given birth by historical circumstances, it was nurtured on foreign religious beliefs. The word *apocalypse* comes from two Greek words, *apo* plus *kalyptein*. *Kalyptein* means "to cover over," and *apo* is the preposition "from." The word means, then, "to take the cover from" or "to reveal." Apocalypse is a type of writing purporting to reveal the future.

Characteristics of Apocalyptic Literature

It has several other characteristics by which one can identify it. 1. Apocalyptic literature is usually anonymous, or if it carries the name of an author, it is a false name. The Book of Enoch, for example, is supposedly the revelations of Enoch who never died (Gen. 5:21–24). 2. Apocalyptic literature uses animal imagery and bizarre figures, and a little experience with Daniel and Isaiah 24–27 shows one how distinctive these are from the prophets'. 3. Sometimes history is narrated in the future tense so as to disguise real persons and events (Dan. 11). 4. One of the most distinctive features of apocalyptic is its use of extravagant contrasts (Isa. 24:4–7 and 25:6–9). Using such contrasts it draws word pictures of memorable quality. Its literary appeal lies chiefly along these lines. 5. Apocalyptic writers use history unimaginatively and rigidly, with periods of time cited in exact number (Dan. 9:24–27, 12:7). 6. Astrology, a Zoroastrian cousin, got woven into apocalyptic symbolism.

Zoroastrian Influence

Zoroastrian influence on Jewish apocalyptic gives it a dualistic concept of the world. This is not the simple dualism of mind and body, spirit and flesh that one so readily thinks of. It means a *cosmic* or *radical dualism,* in which men understand the world to be a battleground between two principles: the good creative principle named Ormazd (Ahura-Mazda), and the evil principle named Ahriman (Angra-Mainyu). These two gods battle for control of the world. Dualism of this sort was alien to Hebrew religion before its contact with the Persians. When David ordered a census in Israel, as reported in 2 Samuel 24:1, Yahweh was the inciter of that evil act. In the Chronicler's report of the same event, Satan was the one who caused David to sin (1 Chron. 21:1). In Job, Satan is one of Yahweh's agents (Job 1:6 ff). In apocalyptic literature, Satan is imagined as another Power. In Isaiah 24:21, for example, Yahweh and the "host of heaven" are in cosmic conflict.

Another concept in Zoroastrian thought is the *ultimate destruction of evil by fire.* Fiery streams of molten metal will scorch the earth

[6]Two examples of nonbiblical apocalyptic books are the *Book of Enoch,* and the *Apocalypse of Baruch* in the Pseudepigrapha. The Pseudepigrapha is a collection of books written between 200 B.C. and 200 A.D.

and consume sinners. Fire will come upon the whole world with a mighty rumbling, and the whole earth and all men, all cities and rivers, and even the sea, will be devoured by this heavenly fire (cf. Dan. 7:10).

The *division of world history into epochs* also characterizes Zoroastrian thought. There are 12,000 years of existence in all, and these are divided by quarters. Zarathustra appears at the end of 9,000 years, and impregnates the virgin Hvov, who miraculously gives birth to Shaoshyant, the savior of the world. After this event the world moves on gradually for 3,000 years to perfection. When this point is reached, the end of the world will have arrived, and the dead will be raised for judgment.

Influence of Persian Belief in Resurrection

The doctrine of *resurrection of the body* had only slight impact upon Old Testament thought.[7] Two verses in the Old Testament are all that show the influence of Persian belief in resurrection. Daniel 12:2 reflects the doctrine of the dead raised to be judged, and Isaiah 26:19 sends forth the assurance

> *Thy dead shall live, their bodies shall rise.*
> > *O dwellers in the dust, awake and sing for joy!*
> *For thy dew is a dew of light,*
> > *and on the land of the shades thou wilt let it fall.*

The belief in resurrection of the body became a full doctrine among the Pharisees of New Testament fame, however. A radically transcendent view of God, crossed with a pessimistic view of man, joined to a doctrine of divine judgment, bears belief in resurrection. These four elements of Zoroastrian religion cast a heavy shadow upon Old Testament apocalyptic.

Zechariah and Isaiah

Zechariah 12–14 (exclusive of 13:7–9) is apocalyptic. It draws word pictures that violate normal human experience, such as continuous daylight, streams flowing from Jerusalem to the Persian Gulf, and universal plague on all Jerusalem's enemies (Zech. 14: 6–12). It is free, however, of bizarre symbols and numerology. Its author looks forward to a day when the good people and the

---

[7] Some interpreters have tried to find a doctrine of resurrection in Job 19:25–26, but the Hebrew text is so corrupted at that point that no positive statement based on it can be made. Psalm 73:24 unwisely has also been interpreted as a passage showing belief in resurrection.

bad people will be pitted against each other. A representative of the Davidic family will serve as Yahweh's agent in bringing victory to the good people, and in purifying them from contamination of idols and prophets' lies (Zech. 14:1-3). Zechariah 14 describes the last siege of Jerusalem in an atmosphere of supernatural horror.

Isaiah 24-27 speaks apocalyptic language more plainly than does Zechariah 12-14. The destruction at Yahweh's hands is of cosmic dimensions (Isa. 24:4). Whereas the prophets spoke about the destruction of a particular people, these passages rehearse the pageant of universal doom. Yahweh's victory will be complete when He imprisons the heavenly hosts (Isa. 24:21-22). Extravagant contrasts are drawn between the day of Yahweh and the final age (Isa. 25:6-9 and 24:4-13). Reference to a single nation is most unusual in the context of apocalyptic writing, and many scholars change the word "Moab" to "enemy" (Isa. 25:10). Such a change involves only a small adjustment of Hebrew letters. These three chapters are a collection of post-exilic psalms, poems, and apocalypses which formed a booklet. This booklet was inserted into the Isaiah scroll sometime in the Maccabean period.[8]

The Book of Daniel

The book of Daniel is the largest apocalypse in the Old Testament. Apocalyptic elements in Daniel are anonymity, complex and extravagant animal symbolism (Dan. 7:1-8), narration of past events in the future tense (Dan. 11), numerology (Dan. 8:14, 12:11-12), and sharp contrasts between good Jews and bad Chaldeans (Dan. 1). The book of Daniel can be one of the most confusing books of the Old Testament, but with suitable explanation it provides a treasure of information of Jewish history and religion at the close of the Old Testament age.

The story of Daniel opens in Babylon, where Daniel and his three companions have risen to responsible positions in Nebuchadnezzar's administration. Because of Daniel's wisdom in dream-interpretation, he is awarded a high post in the government. He requests instead that his three friends, Shadrach, Meshach, and Abednego, govern the province of Babylon in his place. Nebuchadnezzar's image was erected on the plain of Babylon, but even though royal orders demanded that the three bow down to it, they refuse. They are cast into a fire, but escape unharmed.

Daniel, as a court counselor, interprets the mysterious writing "Mene, Mene, Tekel, and Parsin" for Belshazzar. Daniel, too,

[8] See Artur Weiser, *The Old Testament: Its Formation and Develpment,* trans. Dorothea M. Barton (New York: Association Press, 1961), p. 192.

goes through a trial after the manner of his three friends, and is thrown to the lions. Yahweh's intervention saves him. After that, Daniel has visions of four beasts and another about "one that was ancient of days" (Dan. 7:9). The beasts are kings of the four empires which eventually gave way before the kingdom of the Jews. In another vision from the capital at Susa, Daniel sees a ram with horns of unequal length. A male goat with a single horn comes from the west and broke the ram's horns. After a while the single horn of the male goat breaks into four smaller ones. The smallest soon grows to huge size, and attacks the sacrifices in the sanctuary. The mystery of these visions is cleared up when the angel Gabriel interprets them for Daniel.

Daniel then contemplates Jeremiah's prophecy concerning the seventy years (Jer. 25:11–12, 29:10), and learns from Yahweh that they mean seventy weeks of years or 490 years. Daniel has a final vision of a man clothed in linen[9] who tells him about three Persian kings to be followed by a Greek king whose realm shall be broken into four parts. Then a king of the north and a king of the south shall be continually at war. Michael will succor Daniel's people, and all whose names were "written in the book" shall be saved. The dead will rise from their graves. Daniel is commissioned to keep this information secret "until the end of the time" (Dan. 12:4). Daniel then learns that the end of the time be "a time, two times, and half a time" (Dan. 12:7), that is, three and a half years.

Literary Problems of Daniel

Written in Two Languages. What literary problems need resolution before comprehension of this confusing recital can be achieved? *First,* the book of Daniel was written both in Hebrew and in Aramaic.[10] Why was the book written that way? Some scholars believe the section now in Aramaic was accidentally lost, and was filled in by an Aramaic translation of the original Hebrew book. Others believe the book was originally in Aramaic, and the sections in Hebrew were translations of the original. Some believe that chapters 1–6 were older than chapters 7–12, that they originally formed an Aramaic book, and that only the opening story was written in Hebrew when it was added to the book of visions composed now of chapters 7–12. Others believe, and probably correctly, that this form is a literary device employed consciously by the author.[11]

[9] See Ezekiel 9:2, 40:3.
[10] Hebrew at 1:1 – 2:4a, Aramaic at 2:4b – 7:28, Hebrew at 8:1 – 12:13.
[11] See Otto Eissfeldt, *The Old Testament: An Introduction,* trans. Peter R. Ackroyd (New York: Harper & Row, 1965), pp. 516, 527–8, and Cyrus H. Gordon, *The Ancient Near East* (3d ed. rev.; New York: W. W. Norton & Co., 1965), p. 290.

Deals With Two Historical Periods. Second, it is clear that the contents of the book divide naturally between chapters 1–6 and 7–12. The first part deals with affairs of Jews in Babylon. The second part deals with Jews under Greek rule. What sources were at the author's disposal when he improvised his story? For the first part there were legends of Jews stationed in official places in the Persian empire. The histories of Nehemiah and Ezra confirm the basic accuracy of reports that Jews like Shadrach, Meshach, Abednego, and Daniel did rise to positions of public trust. The details of their stories are, of course, legend. The stories of Nebuchadnezzar's self-image (Dan. 3), his madness (Dan. 4), and Belshazzar's fear at the writing on the wall (Dan. 5), are free compositions based upon the Babylonian "Verse Account of Nabonidus."[12]

The legendary figure of Daniel is more of a mystery. A pious Daniel is mentioned in Ezekiel 14:14 along with Noah and Job, but piety does not describe the Daniel of these legends. The Dan'el of the Ras Shamra texts, who appears as a protector of widows and orphans, seems not to fit the character of the biblical Daniel.[13] Daniel the sage in Ezekiel 28:3 is the closest approximation, yet not enough is shown of his character in that passage to make an identification. It is likely that Jews of the Babylonian exile knew about a man named Daniel and his three companions who rose to positions of responsibility under Persian rule. Their historical existence is suggested by the presence of their names among exiles returned to Palestine.[14] Legend has overlaid their historical personalities so that it is impossible to identify them as real people.

The second part of the book of Daniel also draws upon traditional material. The fourth beast (Dan. 7:19–20) is based upon a mythological monster with whom Baal of the Ugaritic texts had to battle (Dan. 7:19–20).[15] The figure of the Ancient of Days, whose garments are white as snow and whose hair is woolly white, is also drawn from the imagery of the Phoenician god El, who had gray hair and beard. The author also uses written materials which reported the conflicts between the Ptolemies and Seleucids, from which he generalizes his accounts in chapter 11. Jewish tradition is used: the expectation that the ruler of world powers will perish at the gates of Jerusalem (Dan. 11:45). This is not historical, how-

---

[12] See James B. Pritchard, *Ancient Near Eastern Texts Related to the Old Testament* (rev. ed.; Princeton, N.J.: Princeton University Press, 1955), pp. 312–15.
[13] *Ibid.,* pp. 149–55 and A. F. Rainey, "The Kingdom of Ugarit," *The Biblical Archaeologist,* Vol. XXVIII, No. 4 (1965), p. 115.
[14] See Nehemiah 8:4, 10:2, 24, cf. Daniel 1:6.
[15] See Pritchard, *ANET,* pp. 129–42.

ever, since Antiochus IV, to whom Daniel 11:20–45 refers, actually died in a campaign against the Parthians at the eastern end of his empire.

Unified by an Unnamed Author.   Third, some unnamed Jew used the two groups of material to form a balanced series of tales. The three visions in part one are balanced by three visions in part two. Both in the part about Babylon (Dan. 1–6), and in the part about Greece (Dan. 7–12), the author affirms that perseverance in the face of persecution brings its rewards. In both parts the ultimate cause of Jewish victory is the presence of Yahweh. The use of the Hebrew-Aramaic-Hebrew sequence is part of the author's efforts at form and symmetry. The author may have had the books of Ezra and Nehemiah as his literary models, since they use the same sequence. They, of course, do so not for literary effect, but because some of their source material was in Aramaic. The author of Daniel may have misunderstood this and tried to stylize his book on the supposed artistry of Nehemiah and Ezra.

Varying Accuracy of Historical Material.   Fourth, as the author describes the events he knows about his historical accuracy increases. His information about the course of Babylonian and Persian empires is faulty. There was no invasion of Palestine by Nebuchadnezzar in the third year of Jehoiakim, 605 B.C. (Dan. 1:1). Belshazzar was not Nebuchadnezzar's son (Dan. 5:2); he was Nabonidus' son, and never was king of Babylon. Cyrus the Persian, not Darius the Mede, succeeded Babylon's last king (Dan. 5:30–31). Darius was not the son of Xerxes (Ahasuerus), nor was Cyrus his successor (Dan. 9:1, 6:28, 10:1). The author knew of only four Persian kings, Darius, Cyrus, Xerxes, and Artaxerxes (Dan. 11:2), whereas historically there were nine Persian kings. His description of the Greek empire's separation into four sections, of the wars between the "king of the north" (Seleucids) and the "king of the south" (Ptolemies), and the intervention of the "Kittim" (Rome), is quite accurate.[16] He probably wrote his book some time between 168 and 163 B.C., since the prediction at Daniel 11:29 is actually a report of the return of Antiochus IV (175–163 B.C.) from his unsuccessful attack against Ptolemy VI (181–146 B.C.). It is a prediction after the fact. At Daniel 11:40–45 the prediction of the death of Antiochus IV is made, but it does not accord with historical fact, as noted above.[17]

---

[16] Kittim was identified with Cyprus, deriving from the city-state of Kition (Latin: Citium) on the site of modern Larnaka. Citium was a major Roman naval base during the end of the Old Testament Age.

[17] See Eissfeldt, *The Old Testament: An Introduction*, p. 520.

The Book of Esther   The book of Esther is an historical novelette. Characterization is clear. Who can forget the heroic and beautiful Esther? Mordecai is believable as a pious and capable Jew. Haman ranks as one of the villains in literature whose fate is more terrible than his evil. The figure of King Ahasuerus is drawn so that he stands indistinct but essential to the narrative. The plot is developed with deft certainty. Esther and Mordecai rise from nothingness to influence in the Persian court. As their fortunes rise so, too, do those of the Jews. What is going to happen to Esther, and how her success or failure will determine the fate of the Jews, loads the narrative with suspense.

The uses of this little novel are clear. It "proved" that Jews need not remain in a servile condition. It also seated the new feast of Purim in a distant, if fictional, past so as to give it authority. Haman had determined by lot (Hebrew "pur") the appropriate day for the annihilation of the Jews (3:7). The day of extermination became a day of joy, for on that day the Jew's enemies were massacred (9:18–32). There is no historical verification of such an event. It is likely that an ancient Persian festival was incorporated into Jewish practice, and that the book of Esther is a learned effort to authenticate the celebration. Perhaps the festival was the Jewish exiles' version of the Babylonian New Year. It does seem more than coincidental that the names of the characters can so easily be matched with gods and goddesses active in that festival. Mordecai sounds suspiciously like Marduk, and Esther like Ishtar. Vashti may originally have symbolized Mashti, and Haman symbolized Human — Elamite goddess and god who were defeated by Marduk.

Facts have been radically misused, which is perfectly permissible in historical novels. Mordecai was an exile of the deportation of 598 B.C. (2:5). Therefore at the beginning of the reign of Xerxes (486–465 B.C.) he would have been at least one hundred and twelve years old. History has been foreshortened because the novelist thought that Xerxes (Ahasuerus) was a close successor to Nebuchadnezzar. There are no Persian records that a Jewish girl was ever a Persian queen. A royal decree permitting Jews to annihilate their Persian overlords is incredible. That a gallows was erected seventy-five feet high seems to be modest exaggeration, to say the least (5:14).[18]

When the author wrote his novel, he was looking back upon distant history. He glories in degradation and massacre of one's enemies,

[18] A cubit was about 18 inches.

attitudes in Jewish history reflecting the Maccabean period. That the people of Palestine would accept a festival whose origins were based upon the massacre of their enemies speaks strongly for a period when Jews were persecuted. This condition prevailed when Antiochus IV prohibited the basic rites of Judaism in Palestine, and when John Hyrcanus (135–104 B.C.) oppressed his own people by using mercenaries.

The Latest Psalms

Psalms of the late post-exilic period are not particularly creative. By this age the spark had died to smoking embers, and little light remained. Hymns selected for study represent four types of composition: apocalyptic; personal lament; revenge; and festival hymns.

Apocalyptic Psalms: Psalm 46

The first type is *apocalyptic*. Psalm 46 carries the themes, imagery, and mood of apocalypse. The psalmist accepts one sure fact in this transient world: God. Mountains quake. The face of the earth is changed. Nations rise and fall (Ps. 46:6). After God has wrought desolation upon the earth, then wars will cease and a universal peace will ensue with Yahweh universally exalted.

Personal Laments: Psalm 39

Psalms 39 and 71 typify *personal laments* due to sickness and old age. The author of Psalm 39 has suffered a severe physical illness. Like Job, he does not understand why such a blow should fall upon him. He keeps his complaining thoughts to himself, but his disease grows worse (Ps. 39:1–3). Apparently he has enemies who gloat over his suffering, but he vows to keep his anguish under control so that their delight in his illness will not be satisfied. Finally his anguish overflows into words, and he tries to examine the relationship of his faith in Yahweh to his wretched condition. He has to admit that man's stance in the face of adversity is puny (Ps. 39:4–6). Because of his weakness in adversity he appeals to Yahweh who alone can provide explanation for his condition and remove the evil from him. Indeed, it is evil in him, he finds, that has brought on his personal calamity (Ps. 39:8). His final plea is that Yahweh will give him a few pleasant days before he passes into oblivion (Ps. 39:12–13).

Psalm 71

The author of Psalm 71 is an old man (Ps. 7:9). His life has been punctuated with one crisis after another. Unjust and cruel men have persecuted him (Ps. 71:4, 13). Many hardships have fallen on his shoulders (Ps. 71:20). All, he believes, has been sent by Yahweh as a test of his faithfulness. His attitude is much like that of Job's "three friends." He never once blames God for his troubles. Nor does he consider that his sufferings come because of his own faults. All his problems come from some alien source. These two laments represent a sample of the prevailing religious mood of the Maccabean period: evil was brought upon Yahweh's faithful by wicked men. The fault never lay within the sufferer.

Psalms of Revenge: 56 and 129

Psalms 56 and 129 represent the theme of *revenge* upon one's enemies. The psalmists' enemies probably are Greek cultural officers, who foist Hellenistic manners upon Jews and Hellenized Jews who work even harder at the task of modernizing Judeans than do the Seleucid officials themselves. The author appeals to Yahweh to avenge his enemies. The psalmist believes that if the people fulfill vows before God, probably of a ritual nature, He will liquidate the foe.

Festival Hymns: Psalms 98 and 148

Psalms 98 and 148 are examples of lovely *festival hymns,* whose beauty matches that of the fine liturgical psalms of early periods. They demonstrate that post-exilic Yahwism had not become a religion solely concerned with personal feeling and mopping up one's enemies. The mood of objective praise of God is found in these hymns. There is no historical information to support the belief that they were written as celebration hymns for the dedication of the cleansed altar in 164 B.C., but their sense of gladness for victories won by Yahweh could easily place them as hymns for Hanukkah. As Yahweh was enthroned at the New Year's festival in Israel's earlier days, so here too, He is elevated in a glad ceremony of praise. In Psalm 148 the poet expresses his belief in a three-storied universe, the common belief of the ancients. There is the earth (Ps. 148:7). There are heavens above (Ps. 148:1). There are the deeps below the earth (Ps. 148:7). The inhabitants of these segments of the world are called upon to praise God. The great psalmists praised Yahweh using the imagery of the natural world. This was true of early and later psalmists alike, such as in Psalm 104 and Psalms 98 and 148. It seems to be true that the finest literary achievements are those psalms where nature imagery predominates.

The psalms at the close of the Old Testament age were modest literary and religious achievements in comparison with those from earlier periods. They do reveal, though, the affirmations of the religions in the chaotic period under study. Primarily concerned with personal problems, revenge against enemies, and apocalyptic visions, only rarely does the grace and grandeur of praise to Yahweh flow forth.

The Apocrypha   The word "apocrypha" meant originally something that was hidden or secret. As a literary term it refers to "hidden books," of which there are fifteen, written between 200 B.C. and A.D., whose authors remain mostly anonymous.[19]

History (1 Esdras and 1 Maccabees), moralistic novels (Tobit and Judith), folk stories (Susanna and Bel and the Dragon), wisdom (Sirach and Wisdom of Solomon), devotional literature (Prayer of Manasseh, Prayer of Azariah, Baruch, and the Song of the Three Young Men), a letter (Letter of Jeremiah), and Apocalyptic (2 Esdras) are all found in the Apocrypha. Prophecy is not found in the collection.

The book of 1 Maccabees relates the burdens under which the Jews labored, their staunch defense under Judas Maccabeus, and the establishment of the Hasmonean dynasty (175–103 B.C.). Although the book is generally reliable as history, one must be wary of the exaggerated numbers given for troops in battle. The term "Maccabeus" was a nickname for Judas (1 Macc. 2:4), which probably meant "the hammerer." The name "Hasmonean" refers to descendants of Mattathias Hasmon, whose murder of Jewish and Syrian officials sparked a rebellion against the Seleucid empire under Antiochus IV (175–163 B.C.).

The story of Susanna is a gem of detective fiction. Plot, suspense, conflict, and character study are well presented. It is the story of how Susanna (Lily) is charged with adultery and a brave youth named Daniel ("God judges") defends her. Read the story to see how Susanna fares.

The book of Tobit takes its name from its hero. Its theme is the eventual reward of the righteous whose piety keeps them true to God and free of contamination from aliens. It is a well-wrought story of family life. Tobit's blindness is cured by Tobias' ministrations, and Sarah's misfortune at the hands of the demon Asmodaeus is overcome by pious trust. Much of the narrative depends upon non-Jewish literary sources, which deal extensively with demons

[19]For introductory treatments of the Apocrypha see "Apocrypha," in George A. Buttrick, ed., *The Interpreter's Dictionary of the Bible*, A–D (New York: Abingdon Press, 1962), pp. 161–6. Hereafter referred to as *IDB*. and W. W. Sloan, *Between the Testaments* (Paterson, N.J.: Littlefield, Adams & Co., 1964). Critical works are: Robert H. Pfeiffer, *History of New Testament Times With An Introduction to the Apocrypha* (New York: Harper & Brothers, 1949); Eissfeldt, *The Old Testament: An Introduction*: pp. 571–603; R. H. Charles, ed., *The Apocrypha and Pseudepigrapha* (London: Oxford University Press, 1913).

and angels. Folk stories from Persia to Germany have carried the basic plot through hundreds of generations.

The wisdom of Jesus the son of Sirach is also known by the name Ecclesiasticus. It is the work of a Jew, who lectured to an academy of young men in Jerusalem about 180 B.C., and eventually committed to writing his own teachings (Sirach 51:23). His work is important because it is one link between the style of wisdom found in Proverbs and the newer form of learning typified by the Pharisees of the New Testament.

Literature from Qumran

The Discovery of the Scrolls

One of the greatest archaeological discoveries in the past fifty years was not made by an archaeologist but by an Arab shepherd boy. In the summer of 1947 Muhammed ed-Diib was chasing a goat which had climbed among the caves in the rough cliffs bordering the Dead Sea. Muhammed threw a rock into the opening of a cave hoping to scare his goat. His rock hit neither goat nor earth. The sound of breaking pottery frightened the boy so that he abandoned his search for his animal. Later, with a companion, he returned to investigate the cause of that peculiar sound. There Muhammed and his friend found the jars in which the now world-famous Dead Sea Scrolls were stored. The story of how the Scrolls came into the hands of scholars is almost a "cops-and-robbers" story.

Apparently Muhammed took some of the scrolls from their containers. He kept them for a while, but then he was probably informed that a certain Kando, a dealer in antiquities in Bethlehem, would give him some money for them.[20] Kando knew immediately that a treasure had been unearthed, but he did not betray his knowledge to the bedouin boy. For a price never reported, he got possession of some scrolls. Tension, which eventually led to war, was increasing among British, Zionists, and Arabs in Palestine, but Kando and a friend known only as George set out on a private archaeological expedition to the caves above the Dead Sea. What they found has never been revealed, but later Kando took five scrolls to the Syrian Convent of St. Mark in Jerusalem. The Metropolitan of the St. Mark's Convent peddled the scrolls through the Hebrew University, the American School of Oriental Research, and the Ecole Biblique, to see if some one would give him cash. When Professor E. L. Sukenik of Hebrew University heard about the scrolls, he made a trip to Bethlehem and obtained three from Kando. When John C. Trever at the American School of Oriental Research in Jerusalem

[20] The man's full name is Khalil Iskander Shahin.

Cave at Qumran where clay jars with scrolls in them were discovered.

saw the Metropolitan's scrolls, he photographed their contents, and urged the Metropolitan to get them out of Palestine. The conflict between Zionists and Arabs was about to erupt into full-scale war. It was not until November, 1948, that G. Lankester Harding, Chief of the Bureau of Antiquities for the British Mandate in Palestine, heard of the scrolls. He ordered a full-scale archaeological expedition to the site of the original find. In 1954 Professor Yigael Yadin of Hebrew University, Jerusalem, bought five scrolls for $250,000.[21]

In the meantime scrolls, or at least fragments, were appearing in several places. In Jericho and Bethlehem Joseph Saad, secretary of the Palestine Archaeological Museum, undertook negotiations with authorization from Harding to pay up to 1,000 pounds (nearly $3,000) for an undamaged scroll. The natives were reluctant to appear with their contraband finds because the law sharply punished

[21] See "The Dead Sea Scrolls," *IDB*, A–D, p. 791.

illegal possession of antiquities. It was finally got across to them that law or no law the Americans, French, and British scholars wanted those scrolls. When bedouins who worked on the archaeological expeditions learned how precious even small fragments were, and learned that scholars paid cash, they began to mutilate whole scrolls in order to increase their revenue. When scholars became aware of this the price of fragments went down and the price of undamaged scrolls went up. Eventually seven scrolls were recovered almost complete. They are the Damascus Document, the Manual of Discipline, the Habakkuk Commentary, the War of the Sons of Light and the Sons of Darkness, the Isaiah Scroll, the Thanksgiving Psalms, and the Lamech Scroll (now called the Genesis Apocryphon). An eighth full-length scroll surfaced more recently among the antiquities of Palestine. It has been named the Temple Scroll.[22]

Fragments by the thousands have been recovered from several caves along the western edge of the Dead Sea. Every book of the Old Testament except Esther is represented among the small pieces of parchment and papyrus sifted from the soil of the caves. These thousands of fragments are collected in the scrollery of the Palestine Archaeological Museum in Jerusalem, where an international team of scholars is engaged in fitting pieces together. Large tables in the scrollery leave only aisles for the scholars to move about. The tables are covered with the fragments, under glass. Each scholar has been assigned a particular task in reconstructing books of the Old Testament or compositions of the Qumran Community. As the jigsaw puzzle takes shape the men move about the room going from table to table looking for the piece that will fit the pattern. Both the edges of the pieces and the writing on them are clues to where each fragment belongs. The writing is often so faint that magnifying glasses are essential to spot the less decipherable passages. Imagine the excitement when a piece is discovered that fits a growing page! When a full sheet has been pieced together the celebration is large and genuine. A full sheet is placed between glass, sealed permanently, and filed so as to be ready when the scholar gets to the task of photographing. These photographs with translation, notes, and interpretation, are published as soon as the busy schedules of the international team permits. Of course, the original glass-encased papyrus is available on the grounds of the museum for any qualified scholar in the world to study. Because of the public interest in the so-called Dead Sea Scrolls a traveling display has been offered in Europe and America to which thousands of fascinated visitors have been attracted.

[22] Yigael Yadin, "The Temple Scroll," *The Biblical Archaeologist,* XXX, No. 4 (1967), pp. 135–9.

The literary value of the Dead Sea Scrolls has been immense since they have contributed so much to study of the Old Testament. Those scrolls, scraps, and fragments which reproduce the text of Old Testament books have been used to correct the text. The basic text is the Massoretic. This version dates from the 9th century A.D., when Jewish scholars settled upon a definitive edition. The Septuagint version, however, differs from the Massoretic text at many places. Since it is a Greek translation from Old Testament scrolls far older than the Massoretic text (between the 3rd century B.C. and 2nd century A.D.), it has been judged more accurate at many points. Jerome's translation of the Old Testament, the Vulgate, was done in the late 4th century A.D. These three versions, in addition to Targumim,[23] and Peshitta,[24] make up most of the textual materials among which scholars compare passages in order to get the most accurate text. With the discovery of the Dead Sea Scrolls the oldest Hebrew editions of Old Testament books are now available for comparison.[25]

The Writings of the Qumran Community

The Scrolls have also supplied important historical and religious information about a group of separatist Jews whose influence may have been negligible upon Judaism but which influenced to some extent the early Christian Church and the New Testament.

The Community Rule

The document called the Community Rule has eleven well-preserved columns.[26] The Community Rule was probably composed about the end of the 2nd century B.C., and therefore represents one of the first literary accomplishments of the Qumran Community. Written for the Community's leaders, it reproduced drafts from rituals, a sermon on truth and falsehood, rules on initiation into the community, the system of organization and discipline, a penal code, and a poem on the Teacher's duties and the sacred seasons celebrated by the Community. Although nothing similar to this document has been known from ancient Hebrew sources, it has a companion in the Christian document called *the Didache,* written, perhaps, in the 2nd century A.D.

The Hymns

Psalms of the Qumran Community are often listed under the title *Hodayoth,* the Hebrew word for Thanksgivings. There are eighteen columns on the Hymn Scroll. The bottom of the scroll has badly

---

[23] Aramaic translation of Old Testament texts with sermonic commentary.
[24] Syriac translation of the Old Testament.
[25] See p. 11 for an example of how the text of 1 Samuel has been improved.
[26] It was first published under the title "The Manual of Discipline." See Millar Burrows, *The Dead Sea Scrolls* (New York: Viking Press, 1955).

deteriorated so that although each hymn was originally marked off by a blank space in the column it is now impossible to know where psalms that extend into the destroyed part of the scroll end and a new one begins. Where it is clear that a hymn begins it usually opens with the words "I give thanks unto Thee, O Lord." A few other hymns begin with "Blessed art Thou." The creative element in these hymns is pretty slim. They are mostly adaptations of Old Testament passages with a large amount of personal interpretation of the quotations thrown in. Nonetheless they carry a mood of mystical exaltation that is typical of the devout religionist. There is emphasis upon the sense of personal isolation, the eventual movement toward God, the rebirth into spiritual power, the struggle for communion with the divine, and the sense of secret mission to be revealed only at the end of days. These hymns provide one with the religious mood of the community in which they were written, much as do the Old Testament psalms.

Some scholars have explained the paucity of fresh themes in these hymns as being due to their use primarily at one season of the year or on one special occasion. It may be as well that the literary imagination of these devout men was limited by their narrow experience in a confined village in a monotonous physical environment.

Biblical Interpretation   Members of the Qumran Community searched the Old Testament prophets for predictions about their own times. They believed that they stood at the end of an old age and on the threshold of a new. They rather clumsily, or adroitly as interpretations differ, combined apocalyptic and prophetic forms to make the prophets read as they wished them to. They saw ancient words and actions as directly applicable to events in their own days.

Most of the interpretations were of a secretive nature, and modern scholars disagree radically over the historical events to which the the commentary has reference. Close attention has been given to the commentary on Nahum, because it refers to an historical event described by Josephus.[27] It deals with a Jewish uprising against Alexander Janneus (103–76 B.C.) because of his cruelty. Josephus reports that the Jews sent a delegation to Demetrius, king of the Seleucid empire, and asked his help in ridding the Jews of their king. Demetrius sent an army of 3,000 cavalry and 40,000 infantry against Alexander's 26,000 mixed mercenaries and Jewish regulars. Alexander was defeated near Shechem, and he fled east of the

[27] See *Antiquities of the Jews*, Bk. XIII, 14:1–2.

Jordan Valley. The date of this battle was 88 B.C. Therefore, the composition of the Nahum commentary, and likely all the others, was after this event.

The Habakkuk commentary is also particularly interesting because some scholars have proposed that in the notes on Habakkuk 2:15 a Teacher of Righteousness, like the figure of Jesus of Nazareth, was persecuted but appeared again among the Community on the Day of Atonement. It has been suggested that this was a prototype of the Christian belief in suffering, death, and resurrection for its Teacher. This is an area which has received extensive scholarly attention, but for which no final answer has been given.

The literary value of the Dead Sea Scrolls for study of the Old Testament has been immense. Even more significant, perhaps, has been the analysis of names and terms contained in the Scrolls for gaining a better understanding of the New Testament. But that study will have to wait for reading the literature of the New Testament.[28]

The Historical Situation

The close of the Old Testament age was a fascinatingly complex period. The Old Testament itself supplies slight information on those years, so that historical reconstruction must depend upon the reports in 1 Maccabees and in Josephus' *Antiquities* and *Wars of the Jews*. Archaeological discoveries aid considerably in supplying cultural details.

The Coming of The Greeks

Alexander defeated Darius III at the Battle of Issus in 333 B.C. This was truly a significant year for Old Testament history as it was for the history of the western world. From this date forward the cultural focus of the ancient Near East was to be directed more and more to the west. Alexander's conquest of the oriental world carried western culture into the east, but his victories for the first time offered the luxuries and ancient learning of the orient to the curiosity of Greeks and Romans. From Issus Alexander moved rapidly down the Palestinian coast.[29] Within two years he had taken Egypt. He returned through Palestine, marched through northern

---

[28] See John Marco Allegro, "The Untold Story of the Dead Sea Scrolls," *Harper's Magazine* (August 1966), pp. 46–54, for discussion on deciphering names and handling puns. In the same article Dr. Allegro charges that certain scholars have deliberately held back publication of the Scrolls because the information in them contradicts their theological beliefs. That is a serious and nearly libelous charge. The excellence of the article is marred by that irresponsible section.

[29] His siege of Tyre may have been reported in Zechariah 9:1–12.

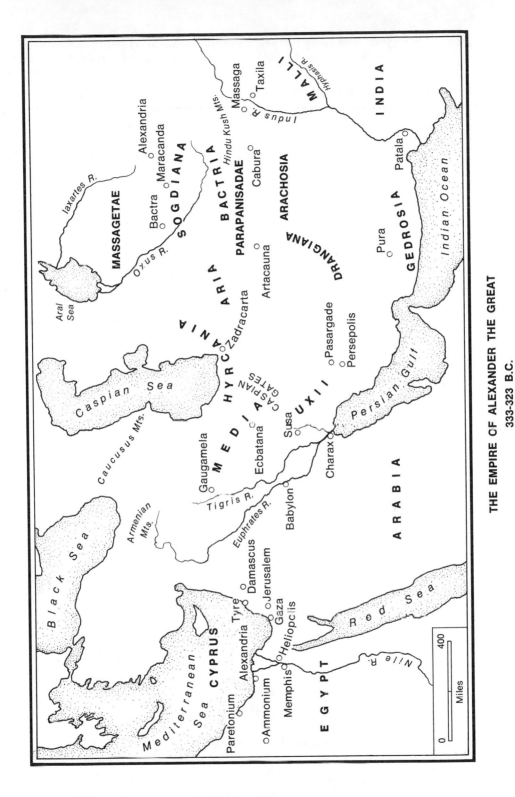

THE EMPIRE OF ALEXANDER THE GREAT
333-323 B.C.

Syria, and forced Persia into final, disastrous battle at Gaugamela. For the first time a western power dominated the civilized world.

Alexander's death in 323 B.C. splintered his vast empire into fragments. It was divided among his four greatest generals: Ptolemy in Egypt; Seleucus in Syria, Anatolia, and the Mesopotamian valley; Lysimmachus in Thrace; and Cassander in Macedon and Greece. Only Ptolemy and Seleucus were directly involved in Jewish affairs at the close of the Old Testament age.

Palestine, as usual, came in for more than its share of turmoil and destruction, due to its critical position in straddling the overland trade routes. Alexandria became Ptolemy's capital, and he dominated the Nile valley, the north coast of Africa westward to Cyrenaica, and Palestine with both sea and land forces. The Jewish community at Jerusalem probably went about its business with few changes, although the influence of Greek culture was extensive. Alexander had founded Greek colonies at choice locations throughout Palestine. Centers for garrison troops, these colonies also disseminated Greek culture. From them agricultural products were collected for distribution to large cities. The local economy was stimulated, and great buildings were constructed at Sebaste (Samaria), Philadelphia (Rabbah), Ptolemais (Acre), and Scythopolis (Bethshan). Archaeological excavations at these places have revealed how extensive were Greek and, later, Roman engineering operations. Trade with these vigorous cities influenced life at Jerusalem, the heart of Judaism.

Peaceful cultural assimilation did not last long in Palestine. The Seleucid empire rose under the leadership of Antiochus III (223–187 B.C.) to end in 198 B.C. the Ptolemaic dynasty's hundred-year rule of Palestine. Jews in Jerusalem welcomed their new rulers. Josephus reports that they captured the Ptolemaic garrison in the city and opened the gates to the Seleucid army. Because of this friendly assistance Jerusalem was awarded several tax benefits, a return of all exiles who wished to be repatriated there, and a subsidy for rebuilding the city, since Jerusalem had suffered greatly in the Ptolemaic-Seleucid wars. Decrees reaffirming Alexander's previous generous subsidy of Temple cultus made the religious leaders of Jerusalem all the more grateful to Antiochus III. Except for the hatred between Jew and Samaritan, Palestine was again peaceful, and Jews rejoiced in their relative independence.

The Hasmonean Period

Such fortune dwindled when Seleucus IV (187–175 B.C.) began to rule in Antioch, the Seleucid capital on the Orontes River. He

Extensive trading and building enterprises under Hellenistic stimulation in Palestine were continued by the Romans. This is a Roman temple at Gerasa (modern Jerash).

introduced forced Hellenization on subject peoples. His dozen years did not seriously disturb the Jews, but when Antiochus IV seized the throne, he immediately ordered a program of Hellenization of all provinces. Religious and civil conflict erupted in Jerusalem.

Hellenization in Palestine

The conflict in Jerusalem had two dimensions. *First*, there was conflict over the cultural character of Jerusalem. Should it be essentially a traditionalist city where ancient Jewish customs prevailed, or should it be a city modeled on Hellenistic lines like Philadelphia, Scythopolis, and Ptolemais? Competition for trade told the merchants that it had to be Hellenized. Conservative landholders struggled to retain established customs. One priestly group tried to incorporate Greek athletics in the Temple area by encouraging young men to wear Greek hats, throw the discus, and wrestle (2 Macc. 4:12–17). All Greek games were participated in completely nude. Civil strife broke out over these disputes.

Second, priests who favored Hellenization vied with one another for the highly lucrative position of high priest. Under Seleucus IV

A street of Roman Gerasa where Hellenistic economic programs had developed a flourishing city.

a Jew named Onias was high priest. He was apparently congenial toward Greek ways but was able to serve the more conservative Jews, too. But when Antiochus IV seized power in Antioch, a certain Jason waited upon the king and secured Onias' removal and his own appointment as high priest. He promised rich gifts and active support of the king's cultural program in Jerusalem (2 Macc. 4:7–11). Three years later another priest named Menelaus bribed the king with richer gifts, and he was made high priest (2 Macc. 4:23–29).

Antiochus IV and Jerusalem

In 169 B.C. Antiochus IV attacked Egypt, and it was rumored Antiochus had been killed. Jason foolishly acted upon that rumor, and attacked Jerusalem in order to rout Menelaus and retrieve his post as high priest. Because of this civil war Antiochus attacked Jerusalem, massacred indiscriminately Jews on both sides, and put Menelaus back in the chief spot in the Temple (2 Macc. 5:1–14). In this way Antiochus IV became personally involved in the civil and religious strife that rent Jerusalem.

Antiochus IV was hard pressed to defend his borders. Defense meant money. In a moment of desperation and poor judgment Antiochus plundered the Jerusalem Temple (1 Macc. 1:20–23). This act produced a smoldering contempt and rising hatred for the king.

Antiochus' second campaign against Egypt proved successful until he received notice from the Roman Senate to get out of Egypt for good. In his humiliation he once again attacked Jerusalem. This time he sacked the city, tore down houses, destroyed the wall, killed women and children, took many slaves, and drove off all the flocks and herds (1 Macc. 1:29–35). He also built a fortification on the site of the ancient city of David, just south of the Temple, where he garrisoned a large contingent of troops. This spot was called the Citadel.

Excavations in Jerusalem have confirmed the existence of a strongly fortified city-within-a-city during the Hasmonean period. In the 1920's Macalister and Duncan uncovered, on the eastern slope of Mount Ophel, foundations of a massive tower which they named David's Tower. Archaeological work in 1961 clearly showed that the tower was no earlier than the lst century A.D., and that a massive wall under it from the 2nd century B.C. was probably part of Antiochus' Citadel. On the western side of Mount Ophel a large gateway datable to Hasmonean times was found by Crowfoot in 1927–28. These explorations show that the Seleucid Citadel was in an area that had a plentiful supply of water from the Gihon Spring, and connected with roads from the south by which caravans could keep the garrison fully equipped.[30]

Antiochus' actions in Jerusalem caused the population's resentment to boil over. Hoping to contain their wrath, which he thought was fired by Jerusalem's religious faction, he issued a decree forbidding Jews to perform circumcision or sacrifice, or to observe sabbath (1 Macc. 1:41–64). He ordered all sacred books destroyed. He went further. He ordered built in the Temple an altar to Zeus on which pigs were sacrificed; Jews were forced to eat the meat. Such forced "acculturation" met with retaliation.

The Revolt of Mattathias Hasmon

Not long after the altar to Zeus was erected, December, 167 B.C., Mattathias Hasmon, a priest in the village of Modein, murdered a Jew who sacrificed a pig in his village. He also killed the Seleucid officer who had forced the Jew to perform that sacrilegious act. These murders signaled open revolt among conservative Jews in villages throughout Palestine. Mattathias' fame spread, and like-minded Jews joined him in the hills to defend the faith. The guerrillas attacked and smashed pagan cult centers. They forcibly circum-

---

[30] See Kathleen M. Kenyon, "Excavations in Jerusalem, 1962," *Palestine Exploration Quarterly* (January–June 1963), and J. Simons, *Jerusalem in the Old Testament* (Leiden, Netherlands: E. J. Brill, 1952).

cised children whose parents had observed Antiochus' decree. They struck at supply caravans and armed themselves with Greek weapons. Pious by Jewish standards, the guerrillas observed the sabbath even during war. On one occasion a Greek army caught some of Mattathias' followers on a sabbath. They massacred about a thousand including women and children, but the men did not lift a weapon or move farther than the Law prescribed (1 Macc. 2:29–48). Because of this show of piety the Hasidim, "pious ones," were attracted to the Hasmonean cause.

The Guerrillas of Judas Maccabeus

Upon Mattathias' death shortly after he instigated the revolt, Judas, his third son, took command of the growing resistance movement. Under his leadership guerrilla fighting was improved, and even large scale war was planned against the Seleucids. It is no wonder that he was nicknamed "the hammerer," which is probably the meaning of "Maccabeus" (1 Macc. 2:4). Judas' boldness and imagination drew thousands after him, and he carried the war offensively against the Seleucids. Antiochus IV sent one general after another to quell the rebellion, but their overconfidence or ineffectiveness in the hills of Judah lost them battle after battle. Apollonius, Seron, Ptolemy, Nicanor, and Gorgias each tried his hand against the wily and courageous Judas, but each took defeat from the clever Jew. By the end of the summer of 165 B.C. Judas controlled all the major military sites in Judea except the Citadel in Jerusalem. A Greek garrison still kept control of the city from that point. Judas besieged the Citadel and established defensive strongholds about it so that it was rendered ineffective. Its formidable walls, on a naturally defensible position, made the fort impossible to capture.

Success of the Revolt

In December of 164 B.C., just three years after the desecration of the altar, the success of the Maccabean revolt was officially celebrated. The Temple area was purified, a new altar was erected, and for eight days a gala ceremony of military victory and religious obligations was observed. After that the Temple area was fortified to protect it from the Citadel's garrison. A major fortification at Beth-zur was also constructed in order to defend the southern approach to Jerusalem. That was the only route over which the Seleucid generals had had any success (1 Macc. 4:52–60).

The Deaths of Antiochus IV and Judas Maccabeus

In the spring of 163 B.C. Antiochus IV died while campaigning against the Parthians. The death of this infamous king, who had presumed to call himself Epiphanes, *manifestation of God*, seemed to many Jews like direct intervention from the Almighty. They believed that their name for him, Epimanes, *the mad one*, more

Jerusalem, with the Dome of the Rock in foreground. This is the
site of the Jewish Temple purified by Judas Maccabeus.

accurately described that Seleucid monarch. Judas began a series of
campaigns in an effort to capture territory while the Seleucid political structure was shaky. He extended the borders of Judah by
attacking Greek garrisons in Galilee and in Transjordan. He sent
an army into territory held by the Nabateans, successors of the
Edomites. Judas himself mounted a campaign against Ashdod. The
Maccabean rebellion had turned from a religious revolt to a political one. From that time on Judas lost the support of the Hasidim,
the pious religionists, and he stood alone in his struggle for political
independence. He was killed in a battle against a large Seleucid
army, and many of his faithful companions were captured and executed (1 Macc. 9:1–22). The Maccabean rebels were again reduced
to guerrilla fighters. Jonathan, Judas' youngest brother, was elected
their leader.

**Intrigue Among Judas'
Successors;
John Hyrcanus**

When the Seleucid state was torn by internal intrigue, Jonathan
backed Alexander Balas, who claimed to be the son of Antiochus IV,
against Demetrius, Antiochus' successor. Alexander appointed
Jonathan high priest and king of Jerusalem. Thus, Jonathan was the
first Israelite in history to hold the position of high priest and king.
Further intrigue among the Seleucids led to Jonathan's death.
Simon, another brother of Judas Maccabeus, was made king and
high priest when Jonathan was assassinated. He dated his official
records from the year of his accession to the high priesthood, sent
embassies to Rome and Sparta, built the walls of Jerusalem, and

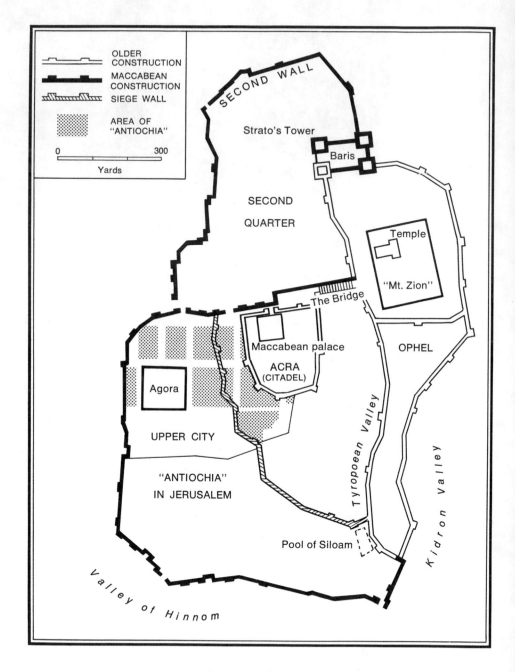

MACCABEAN JERUSALEM

captured Joppa, giving the Jews a port on the Mediterranean Sea. He expanded the borders of Judea, so that he brought large tracts of fertile agricultural territory under his control.

But the political disease that infected the Seleucids spread to the Jews. In 134 B.C. Simon was murdered by his son-in-law Ptolemy, who killed for good measure the king's sons Mattathias and Judas. A third son, John, escaped Ptolemy's assassins and became king in place of Simon. John took the throne-name Hyrcanus I. Although he ruled successfully for thirty years (134–104 B.C.), John Hyrcanus had his share of trouble from the Seleucids; on one occasion a Seleucid army put Jerusalem under siege. John Hyrcanus was hated by the sect of Pharisees in Judea, but was friendly with the Sadducees, the official Temple priests. Probably at the Sadducees' instigation he attacked the Samaritans and destroyed their temple on Mount Gerizim. The land and taxes from that fruitful region were his special attraction, however. He died a natural death after having ruled 31 troubled years.

The Reign of Alexander Janneus

Aristobulus I became king and high priest in 104 B.C. He was assassinated within a year, and his brother Alexander Janneus (104–78 B.C.) succeeded him. Although Janneus was a competent king, waging war and capturing territory so that all Palestine came under his domination, he was hated by the Pharisees. To them he was a bloodthirsty, drunken, immoral scoundrel. When he officiated one year at the Feast of Booths they hurled insults at him and followed these soon with oranges and other fruits. For this insult he ordered hundreds of Pharisees executed. Janneus' widow, Alexandra became queen on his death and ruled for nine years of unusual peace, wooing the Pharisees from their implacable hatred of Janneus.

Roman Troops Enter Jerusalem; The End of Old Testament Times

When Alexandra died, Aristobulus II (69–63 B.C.) fought his older brother Hyrcanus II for the throne. Hyrcanus looked for help to the Nabateans in Petra. Antipater, a wealthy Idumean merchant whose father had governed the region known anciently as Edom, for the Nabatean king Aretas, backed Hyrcanus. Aristobulus had the support of the aristocratic families of Jerusalem and Judea, but both Hyrcanus and Aristobulus appealed to Rome. Pompey had assumed control over the defunct Seleucid empire, and from his headquarters at Damascus he heard their stories. Aristobulus occupied the fortress Alexandrium overlooking the central Jordan Valley (modern *Karn Sartabe*), and Pompey looked upon this as a hostile act. He sent his troops against Aristobulus. Aristobulus gave up Alexandrium and withdrew to Jerusalem. Although Aristobulus

GREEK DOMINANCE IN PALESTINE

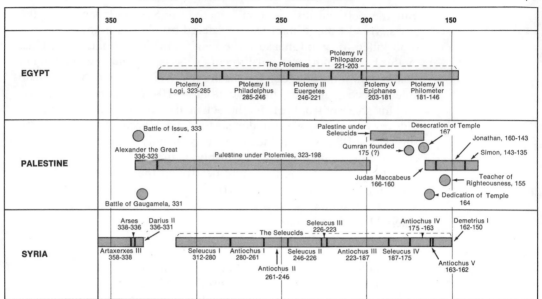

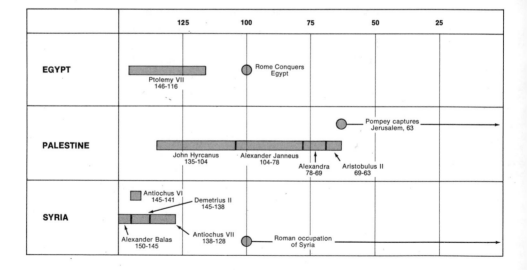

sued for peace by offering huge gifts, Pompey took him prisoner and advanced on the city. The followers of Hyrcanus opened the city's gates to the Romans, but Aristobulus' followers barricaded themselves in the Temple area. Roman troops laid siege to the Temple for three months. Finally, battering rams breached the walls. While priests were performing their rites at the altar Roman soldiers cut them down. The Romans massacred twelve thousand Jews who had resisted them. Pompey himself went into the Holy of Holies to see what riches he could confiscate. He was astonished to find nothing there. Placing a Roman garrison in the city, he took Aristobulus and his family as captives of war to Rome where they were paraded through the streets in one of Pompey's victory celebrations. Hyrcanus II continued as high priest and ethnarch. The end of the Hasmonean dynasty came the year Rome took charge in Palestine, 63 B.C. This properly closes the Old Testament age, too.[31]

Religious Affirmations

There is wide-ranging diversity of religious affirmation in the literature of the close of the Old Testament age. The piety of the Qumran community, for instance, is at odds with that found in the book of Daniel. The religious motivations of Judas Maccabeus and his brothers contrast sharply with those of Sirach.

The Chronicler

The Chronicler's God punishes all who fail the observation of His cult. Belief that Yahweh reveals Himself through the events of history is subordinated to the belief that Yahweh finds pleasure in people extravagantly performing cultic rites. Yahweh's control over historical process is seen to be limited to a few interventions from time to time (2 Chron. 13:13–20, 14:8–14). The Chronicler does not interpret specific events as coming from Yahweh's hand, but he looks over Israel's history and there discerns that the nation's life exists by dispensation of a moral order originally ordained by Yahweh. Like the far off God of Job and Ecclesiastes, the Chronicler's God has set the moral order going and tinkered with it just enough to keep it working. Temple cult is seen as the lubrication which keeps the cosmic engine frictionless. So long as it operates the world will not sputter and stop. If the oil pump breaks down— that is, if the cult ceases to function—then holiness and purity, the reasons for human existence, will corrode. Anyone responsible for the breakdown of cult can expect divine retributive justice. Animal sacrifice so purifies human behavior in God's sight that so long as it continues the Jewish community will be acceptable to God.

[31]See "Hasmoneans," *IDB*, E–J, pp. 529–535 for a superior summary of Hasmonean rulers from Simon to Aristobulus II. See also Noth, *The History of Israel*, 2d ed., pp. 346–401, for the period from Alexander the Great to Pompey's Jerusalem victory.

The Romans brought their massive architectural techniques to
Palestine with them. These are columns of a temple at Baalbek,
Lebanon.

The Chronicler was a dramatist of sorts. The cult was a drama enacted regularly, and as a participant in the drama he tried to write
a narrative with a dramatic quality. In ranging from Adam to Ezra
he describes Israel's glorious and tragic past so that its dramatic
quality reveals God still proclaiming His living word in Torah and
cult. The glorous prophetic word purified the nation sufficiently so
that the people survived the tragedy of political annihilation. God
did not permit the nation to die, and although its political life had
not been revived, the community's cultic vitality, patterned on the
style of that greatest liturgist, David the King, binds it together into
a worshiping society.[32]

[32] See "Chronicles," in George A. Buttrick, ed., *The Interpreter's Bible* (New York:
Abingdon Press, 1955), Vol. 3, pp. 341–8 for a perceptive introduction to this work.
See also W. F. Stinespring, "Eschatology in Chronicles," *Journal of Biblical Litera-
ture*, LXXX, Pt. III (1961), pp. 209–19, and Robert North, S.J., "Theology of the
Chronicler," *Journal of Biblical Literature*, LXXXII, Pt. IV (1963), pp. 369–81.

The religion of the prophets Zechariah and Joel add little to the thought of earlier spokesmen for Yahweh. Judgment falls upon Israel's enemies (Zech. 9:1–12). Joel believes that God works His will through nature (the plague of locusts) so that His moral purposes become clear. The plague is held to be a sign of God's displeasure, and when it terminates God declares His beneficence. Both personal and national repentance will touch God's tenderer emotions, inducing Him to send benefits. Joel believes *the day of the Lord* will be a time when judgment will fall upon Gentiles in a universal and final climax to history. Amos had first used the term to designate a day of judgment on Israel alone. In the book of Joel it is a day of judgment upon all nations, accompanied by the outpouring of God's spirit upon faithful Israel. It will flow upon young and old, men and women, owners and slaves equally (Joel 2:28–29). When God's spirit overflows in that fashion the whole world will be changed. It was such a belief that the first Christians had, when Joel was quoted to authenticate their belief that the new age of spiritual outflow had arrived (Acts 2:14–21). Joel contributes to Old Testament religion by placing a balanced emphasis upon the interior and the exterior elements of religious experience. God's revelation occurs in plagues of locust, but He also demands repentance. The rites of external worship are held essential, but individual faith is essential, too.

Several generalizations may be made about the religious affirmations of apocalypticism. 1. Revelations occurred in trances and visions. Whether trances and visions were actual spiritual insights among apocalyptists or not is debatable. The revelations of Yahweh reported by Isaiah and Ezekiel have the quality of personal experience, but apocalyptic visions appear more as literary creations than as reports of firsthand inner experiences. Allegory served apocalyptic writers more readily than did intense spiritual experience.

2. Apocalyptic literature carries a strong sense of *theistic determinism*. This phrase means that everything that occurs in the world, whether it be a new astronomical phenomenon, a plague of locusts, or the rise and fall of kings, is determined beforehand by God. Events occur because a perfect, schematic timetable working with computer-like precision, has been established by God. Ordinary men, of course, cannot foretell the foreordained events, but God had prepared a few obedient and righteous persons to know His secret timetable. The apocalyptists believed themselves commissioned by God to unfold divine secrets to a few other specially chosen persons. The esoteric visions of beasts, numbers, and

heavenly portents could only be understood by those selected for the privilege.

3. Apocalyptists believed their contemporary world had passed into an irrecoverable state. Men were so hopelessly corrupt that repentance would no longer cleanse. The total cosmos had become infected by the diseases of disobedience and disloyalty so that even the heavenly planets and the earth had to be destroyed to make way for the new age (Isa. 24:4, 21–23). The end of *time* had come, and the visionary stood on the threshold of the eschatological age (Dan. 12:2–3).[33]

4. The apocalyptists believed that in the midst of catastrophe a messianic leader would arise to lead the faithful through their hours of strife and tribulation.[34] Israel had entertained a messianic concept since the days of the monarchy, but by the time we are discussing that concept had changed considerably. David was an anointed king, and all kings of Judah had been considered special appointments of Yahweh. One post-exilic conception of messiah was that Elijah would return to teach Israel the true way before the great and terrible day of the Lord (Mal. 4:5). Others thought of messiah as a teacher and healer who would bring consolation to those who were ill and abused in Israel (Isa. 61:1–3). In Daniel the idea of a preexistent, superhuman figure (Dan. 7:9–14) is presented as the one chosen and anointed to perform God's task in introducing and conducting the eschatological age.

5. Jerusalem will eventually become the center of a new world (Zech. 14:16). But first the fertility of the earth will decline. Plaintive voices will ask for a little wine to quench their thirst. Earthquakes will shake the earth so that everyone will enter his house, shut the door, and stay hidden, while blood runs deep and the dead are not buried (Isa. 24:8–13, 21–23, 26:20–21). All of Israel's foes will be crushed by God's might alone (Ps. 72), and Jerusalem will assume its durable place among the cities of the new age.

6. A spirit of universalism runs through apocalyptic thought. The righteous will pass through terrible times along with the ungodly, although in the end the righteous will survive while the ungodly will be destroyed. Sometimes this universalism is expressed as a general destruction which will obliterate everything and everybody. Only in

---

[33] *eschatos* means "last"; therefore *eschatology* means the study of or knowledge about the last things — or ultimate destiny and purpose.
[34] *Messiah* means someone anointed for special responsibilities.

the resurrection to judgment will the just be privileged and the evil cast into oblivion. Even decent Gentiles will be able to participate in the good things achieved in the new age (Isa. 25:6–9). This point of view was delivered to the writers of the New Testament.

Purim

Esther is one of the two books in the Old Testament that never uses the words Yahweh or God.[35] It makes religious affirmations only to the extent that it became the explanation of the festival of Purim. Purim did not have its origins in a religious situation, nor was it celebrated to honor Yahweh or to commemorate some event in the history of Israel. It did not have any cultic rites associated with it. Neither did it originate among the Jewish people themselves. It was a foreign festival which, when it was assimilated into late Judaism, proved to be purely secular in character. It was taken into Jewish life by a segment of oriental Jews who had lost almost all of their Yahwistic religious traits. The intensity of religious devotion expressed by devout Palestinian Jews could not permit such a secular holiday to remain unsanctified. Therefore, the reading of the book of Esther was transferred to the synagogues where it was given some religious respectability. But Purim continued basically as a social spree. Gifts were exchanged. A day of fasting was followed by a day of feasting. Regardless of religious convictions men went to the synagogue to hear the book of Esther read. When the parts about Haman were recited, the congregation in good fun interrupted the rabbi to curse the villain. Everybody had a good time during that levity in the house of prayer. After the synagogue service banquets and amusements not usually permitted in Judaism were encouraged. Excesses and debauchery were overlooked for a short time. The book of Esther serves solely a social function, but its place in Old Testament scripture is assured because of the popularity of the feast of Purim.[36]

Apocrypha

Religious beliefs and practices represented in the Apocrypha need some examination. The author of 1 Maccabees wrote a straightforward book whose religious message is clear. He was devoted to Judaism both in its religious and national aspirations. He rejected the inclusion of foreign religions and social institutions in Jewish life because he did not distinguish between religious beliefs and national identity. He was a religio-national patriot. He was clear-eyed respecting faith and its rewards. He probably appreciated Daniel's aid in strengthening the will of Jews to resist Hellenistic encroachments, but he saw all rewards for patience and loyalty to God as

---

[35] The other is Song of Songs.
[36] See Roland de Vaux, *Ancient Israel, Its Life and Institutions* (New York: McGraw-Hill Book Company, Inc., 1961), pp. 514–17.

terrestial. There was no resurrection as a pious prize for his heroes' fight for survival. The reason Jews suffered for their beliefs was because the heathen were wicked. He did not believe that the restrictions and penalties placed upon Jews by Antiochus IV and his successors were God's way of punishing Israel for its sins. The author of 1 Maccabees was interested in what Judas Maccabeus did, not how God used him. He did not see God as One to intervene in the affairs of men. Nowhere did God step in to set things right. When the Jews beat the Greeks, it was their victory. When they lost, it was their misfortune. Behind the lives of Jews, however, stood Yahweh, and obedience to him was to live according to the Law and to keep the Temple services going.

The Festival of Hanukkah

The chief religious rite described in 1 Maccabees is the festival of Hanukkah (1 Macc. 4:36–59). Antiochus IV profaned the Temple by constructing an altar to Zeus there and sacrificing swine on it. After three years of desecration Judas Maccabeus recaptured the Temple and reconstituted Jewish ritual. The festival is called "Hanukkah," which means "renewal." Josephus refers to the season as the feast of Lights by reason of the chief rite. Lamps were lighted in each home, and people paraded through the streets with branches and palm fronds. The feast lasted for eight days. This Jewish festival is one for which there is ample historical evidence. Judas ordered the proper services reconstituted exactly three years after the Temple's desecration. The twenty-fifth day of the ninth month was chosen for the celebration.[37] Alien influences are found in Hanukkah just as in the case of Purim. In the Seleucid empire the twenty-fifth of each month was celebrated as a reminder of the king's birthday. Hellenized Jews who practiced this secular rite may have influenced the selection of that particular day. The carrying of branches and palm fronds may have been borrowed from the Greek feast of Dionysus which Hellenized Jews also engaged in. Therefore, like all religious rites, even Hanukkah, founded so strictly upon an historical event, could not escape borrowing from neighboring cults.

The Books of Susanna and Tobit; The Book of Sirach

Susanna and Tobit typify the pious and quiet Jew of the late postexilic age. Susanna is a faithful wife unjustly accused of adultery. Her steadfast trust in God and the wisdom of a brilliant young lawyer combine to acquit her of false charges. In the book of Tobit,

---

[37]Notice that 1 Maccabees 1:54 claims the 15th day of Chislev as the day of desecration of the altar. 1 Maccabees 4:52 claims that the new altar was dedicated on the 25th day of Chislev, three years later "on the very day that the Gentiles had profaned it." 1 Maccabees 1:54 is probably a scribal error.

models of Jewish piety and morality serve the author's ends. The heroes all trust implicitly in God and are reverent toward His name. By their patience during suffering, respect for parents, charity toward the poor, and pure dispositions, the few characters in this novel prove their obedience to the Law.[38] The wisdom of Sirach makes the same religious affirmations as does the book of Proverbs. There is more respect for legal piety and ritual forms in the life of a righteous person than is shown in the book of Proverbs. It is truly amazing that Sirach, who was so widely travelled, effectively resisted the influences of Hellenization. This sage throws his weight on the side of Judaism typical of that defended by Judas Maccabeus.

Religious Convictions of the Qumran Community

Religious affirmations among the disciples of the Qumran community were distinctive. The separated themselves from the normal associations of life in order to keep from ritual and personal defilement. In doing this they formed a settlement of like-minded individuals who were committed to a "new covenant." This "new covenant" was established because the disciples understood themselves to be the faithful remnant, who served God by preserving His holy ways and keeping themselves unspotted by the world. They believed themselves to be not only the remnant of loyal Jews, but the only ones who would survive the devastation of the last days. The scriptures had foretold, according to their beliefs, all the events occuring in their days, and the Teacher of Righteousness was a person capable of unravelling the mysteries of Torah. The "new covenant" committed them to perfect obedience to Torah and to ritual purity.

The Religious Routine at Qumran

These convictions bound them into a tightly knit band who held their goods and took their meals in common. They were presided over by a council of twelve men and three priests. They lived by a penal code so strict that only a physically and emotionally inert person could survive its rigors. Lying was punished by six months of penance. Insulting a companion brought penance for a year and exclusion (whatever that meant). Sleeping during an assembly meant thirty days of penance. Spitting on the floor during assembly demanded thirty days penance.

Most of the hours not consumed by essential chores were spent in religious ceremonials. Purification with water was a central feature of the devotional life. The number of large cisterns archaeologists

[38]See Weiser, *The Old Testament: Its Formation and Development*, p. 398.

have discovered, as well as the many references in the scrolls to ritual bathing, show how significant this act was. They also sent their offerings to the Jerusalem Temple. Although they despised the Temple priesthood, so long as a ritually clean person carried their gifts from Qumran to the Temple, and did not offer them on the sabbath, they believed their sacrifices were honored by God. So long as sacrifice could not be performed in the community itself, public prayer atoned for sins. Circumcision was performed on the young. Festivals such as the Feast of Weeks were celebrated. They observed a special festival of their own known as the Renewal of the Covenant. A sacred meal was one of their holiest ceremonies. The careful treatment of the bones of the sacrificial animals shows how sacred that meal was. The meal was eaten by the members of the community in a carefully prescribed ritual after an assembly, although the scrolls do not report how often the meal was celebrated. This has been of particular interest to New Testament scholars because of some likenesses with the Lord's Supper. It has stronger identification, however, with the apocalyptic meal reported in Isaiah 25:6–9.

Qumran an Apocalyptic Community

Other beliefs of the sect at Qumran were typical of apocalypticism. *First,* their view of the world was radically dualistic. They believed there were two spirits in the universe, one of truth and one of error. A paragraph in the Community Rule shows this dualism clearly.

He has created man to govern the world, and has appointed for him two spirits in which to walk until the time of His visitation: the spirits of truth and falsehood. Those born of truth spring from a fountain of light, but those born of falsehood spring from a source of darkness. All the children of righteousness are ruled by the Prince of Light and walk in the ways of light; but all the children of falsehood are ruled by an Angel of Darkness and walk in the ways of darkness.[39]

The War Rule described the cataclysmic battle between the Sons of Light and the Sons of Darkness.

Second, they believed that salvation came through special knowledge. Special people with a special covenant had special ways of being saved. Each member of the community had knowledge which he brought to the community of God where it was purified in the truth of God's precepts. Their interpretation of the Scriptures was

[39] G. Vermes, *The Dead Sea Scrolls in English* (Baltimore: Penguin Books, 1962), pp. 75–6. Reprinted by permission of the publisher.

proof of their special knowledge. The Teacher of Righteousness was specially blessed with insight, and hence all within the community benefited by his knowledge. No one on the outside knew the secret things he did. Although the group used the same Old Testament as did scribes elsewhere in Judaism, it claimed a particular insight which revealed the final truths of this age and clear visions of the next.

Third, they had a developed angelology. Belial was the personification of evil, while Michael, Gabriel, Raphael, and Sariel protected the battlements of the faithful.

Fourth, belief in divine election enabled them to look upon themselves as chosen by God from the beginning. This aspect of theistic determinism gave to individuals as well as to the community a sense of special destiny.

Fifth, the community boasted that two messiahs would execute justice in the time to come. There was a messiah of Israel who had kingly qualities. There was a messiah of Aaron with priestly qualities. Such a dual designation recalls the double leadership in post-exilic Jerusalem, when Zerubbabel was civil governor and Joshua was high priest (Hag. 1:1–2). Although some scholars have tried to identify the Teacher of Righteousness as a messiah, the information is too scanty to make such identification clear. If any messianic figure of Old Testament scripture was in the minds of the Qumran disciples, it was probably "the suffering servant" of Isaiah of Babylon. The age of the messiah was still future, although at one time the sectaries believed the messianic age would begin forty years after the death of the Teacher. This number had to be allegorized as time passed and the new age did not commence. They expected a conversion of Jews and Gentiles as the new age approached, but those who did not change their ways and join the elected community, both Jew and Gentile, would be ruled over by the Angel of Darkness. In the gigantic struggle between good and evil all such unbelievers would be wiped from the earth. At last the world would be regenerated, and the community would become the true glory of Adam.

Within late post-exilic Judaism several groups splintered off the solid bodies in Jerusalem. Most famous among these splinter groups were the Hasidim, the Samaritans, the Zealots, the Essenes, the Sicarii, and the Christians. Each of these groups formed itself as a protest against the main parties attached to the Jerusalem Temple.

Only two of these protestant groups have continued in any significant way to maintain themselves with a lengthy history — Hasidism and Christianity both survived the Hellenistic-Roman age. All the others have expired. Hasidism became the sect of Pharisees which bequeathed a brilliant tradition to Rabbinic Judaism. Christianity has passed its original insights on through the Church.

General Bibliography

I. Literary

Bentzen, Aage, *Introduction to the Old Testament.* Copenhagen: G.E.C. Gadd, 1952. This book's format will surprise American readers. Excellent insights are given on the influence of oral tradition upon the written Old Testament.

Bewer, Julius A., *The Literature of the Old Testament* (3d ed.), revised by Emil G. Kraeling. New York: Columbia University Press, 1962. A simple, clear description of the literary development of the Old Testament. Easy to use and fully reliable.

Eissfeldt, Otto, *The Old Testament: An Introduction,* trans. Peter R. Ackroyd. New York: Harper & Row, 1965. A superior treatment of the literary growth of the Old Testament beginning with the pre-literary stage. A second part deals with the sources of the historical, legal, prophetic, and poetic books. A third analyzes each book of the Old Testament while the fourth treats the Apocrypha and Pseudapigrapha. The final part discusses the complexities of textual criticism.

Pfeiffer, Robert H., *Introduction to the Old Testament.* New York: Harper & Brothers, 1948. A literary analysis of the Old Testament beginning with the Pentateuch. In turn the historical, the poetical, and the prophetic books are treated. Introduces one to the complex study of how the books of the Old Testament were put together.

Sellin, Ernst, *Introduction to the Old Testament,* completely revised and rewritten by Georg Fohrer, trans. David E. Green. New York: Abingdon Press, 1968. A book first published in 1910, which goes through ten editions, is completely rewritten (in 1965), and finally is translated into English, has a special quality. A scholar's book, this is written so simply that neophytes to Old Testament study can benefit equally. Part One tells about the formation of the historical and legal books. Analysis of the creation of the poetic, wisdom, and prophetic-apocalyptic books follows. The concluding part treats the compilation of the Old Testament.

Weiser, Artur, *The Old Testament: Its Formation and Development,* trans. Dorothea M. Barton. New York: Association Press, 1961. German scholarship has produced a superior book which is delightfully readable. All interested in literary problems of Old Testament lore will find this book clear, concise, and capable.

II. Historical

Aharoni, Yohanan and Michael Avi-Yonah, *The Macmillan Bible Atlas.* New York: The Macmillan Co., 1968. The most comprehensive Bible atlas yet published for the general reader. It has lovely maps clarifying the unfolding of Israel's history. Its diagrams showing movements of people, armies, and conquests clarify historical situations.

Bright, John, *A History of Israel.* Philadelphia: Westminster Press, 1959. The people of the Old Testament are placed in the context of the ancient

Near East while retaining an historical integrity of their own. The author is sometimes reluctant to be critical of Old Testament conceptions of history. It is a readable volume.

May, Herbert G., ed., *Oxford Bible Atlas*. London: Oxford University Press, 1962. An atlas is essential to historical study of the Old Testament people, and this volume is superior. Its maps are multicolored, complete in detail, and well indexed. *Paperback* edition available.

Noth, Martin, *The History of Israel* (2d ed.). New York: Harper & Row, 1960. This book was written by this generation's greatest historian of Israel. It treats Old Testament traditions critically, proposing reasonable solutions to historical problems raised by literary criticism. Essential to anyone putting the literature and history of the Old Testament together.

Orlinski, Harry M., *Ancient Israel* (2d ed.). Ithaca, N.Y.: Cornell University Press, 1960. Gives a rapid survey of Israel's major historical periods and movements. It is usually reliable, except that the reader must be aware that the prophets were not the last of Israel's great religious traditions. *Paperback.*

Rowley, Harold H., *From Joseph to Joshua: Biblical Traditions in the Light of Archaeology*. London: Oxford University Press, 1950. Although much that Professor Rowley reports on Israel's history based on archaeology needs revision in the light of recent excavations and interpretations, this is an intensely interesting book. Some readers will find his immense work on footnotes disconcerting, but diligent readers will not doubt his ability to use sources.

Wright, George E. and Floyd V. Filson, eds., *The Westminster Historical Atlas to the Bible*. Philadelphia: Westminster Press, 1945. This older volume, oversize and sometimes difficult to handle, is still useful. Its text gives a fine historical survey of the Old Testament people, and complements the maps.

III. Religious

Albright, William F., *Archaeology and the Religion of Israel*. Baltimore: The Johns Hopkins' Press, 1942. The valuable information in this book makes the difficulty of reading insignificant. It interprets archaeological material so as to cast a beam of light upon Israel's religious beliefs and practices. Comparisons and contrasts with other peoples' religions put Israel in a cosmopolitan context.

———, *From the Stone Age to Christianity; Monotheism and the Historical Process* (2d ed.). Garden City, N.Y.: Doubleday & Co. (Anchor Books), 1957. This volume is an expression of the author's belief that Israel's monotheism is traceable to Moses. He shows that cultural borrowing by Israel was less extensive than previous writers had supposed. Many parts of this book will raise questions for discussion. *Paperback.*

Alt, Albrecht, *Essays on Old Testament History and Religion*, trans. R. A. Wilson. Garden City, N.Y.: Doubleday & Co., (Anchor Books), 1968. A series of essays gathered in one volume which brings the distinguished scholarship of Professor Alt to the popular level. Essays on Hebrew law and the religion of Israel's patriarchs are particularly insightful. *Paperback.*

Burrows, Millar, *An Outline of Biblical Theology*. Philadelphia: Westminster Press, 1946. A systematic treatment in simple style of theological ideas, such as the nature of God, the universe, man, the covenanted people, religious practices, and moral ideals. One of the best introductions to biblical religion.

Eichrodt, Walther, *Theology of the Old Testament* (Vols. I, II), trans. J. A. Baker. Philadelphia: Westminster Press, 1961 and 1967. A complete treatment of religious affirmations as interpreted by a fine German scholar. Not easy reading, but these volumes will give one material for deep penetration of the Old Testament.

Gelin, Albert, *The Religion of Israel,* trans. J. R. Foster. New York: Hawthorne Books, 1959. A simplified treatment of the major ideas of Old Testament religion. *Paperback.*

Irwin, William A., *The Old Testament: Keystone of Human Culture.* New York: A. Schuman, 1952. Lectures originally given at the University of Chicago. This volume is essential for adding a dimension of understanding to the Old Testament that comes only from integration of many separate investigations. Not strictly a literary, or an historical, or a religious approach, it weaves all three together into a comprehensive system.

Köhler, Ludwig, *Old Testament Theology.* Philadelphia: Westminster Press, 1957. The concepts of the Old Testament, God, man, salvation, and so forth, arranged in a convenient form and garnished with careful scholarship.

Leslie, Elmer A., *Old Testament Religion in the Light of Its Canaanite Background.* New York: Abingdon Press, 1936. The title is a sufficient description of the book. It was one of the earliest efforts to show in the light of archaeological discoveries how the Israelites had used and rejected Canaanite religious forms. Still valuable.

Pfeiffer, Robert H., *Religion in the Old Testament: The History of a Spiritual Triumph,* ed. Charles Conrad Forman. New York: Harper & Brothers, 1961. The editor, after Professor Pfeiffer's death, used his notes to put together this volume. It has the deficiencies of such an effort, but nonetheless is a superior treatment in simple manner of Israelite beliefs and practices. Literary-critical methods are used to the fullest, and conclusions are consistent with what that discipline has revealed about Old Testament ideas.

Ringgren, Helmer, *Israelite Religion,* trans. David E. Green. Philadelphia: Fortress Press, 1966. A systematic study of the growth of religious beliefs and practices. Opening with an exposition of the pre-Davidic period, it treats the developments in the monarchy, and concludes with the period of the Exile. A readable book.

Rowley, Harold H., *The Faith of Israel: Aspects of Old Testament Thought.* Philadelphia: Westminster Press, 1957. With his customary erudition and thoroughness with footnotes, the author treats of seven topics: Revelation, God, Man, Community, the Good Life, Death, and the Day of the Lord. Excellent treatment of these few ideas.

Smith, William Robertson, *The Religion of the Semites; the Fundamental Institutions.* New York: Meridian Books, 1956. This book was published first in 1889. Using his vast knowledge of religion among the Arabs, the author applied many of his observations to beliefs and practices reported in the Old Testament. It is a truly monumental book even though some of his conclusions may be doubtful. *Paperback.*

Vriezen, Theodorus C., *An Outline of Old Testament Theology,* trans. S. Neuijen. Newton, Mass.: C. T. Branford Co., 1958. The first part treats the methodology of biblical theology, with an emphasis on the Church's use of the Old Testament. Part Two launches discussions on God and man and their relationship, with special attention to the meaning of that relationship to ethics. Primarily for those who wish an advanced discussion of Old Testament theology.

Wallis, Louis, *The Bible and Modern Belief; A Constructive Approach to the Present Religious Upheaval.* Durham, N.C.: Duke University Press, 1949. A sociological study of the Bible. It is a good corrective to many of the theological perspectives which try to draw conclusions based on purely rational principles. This volume stresses the humanistic elements of biblical religion.

IV. Psalms

Barth, Christoph F., *Introduction to the Psalms,* trans. R. A. Wilson. New York: Charles Scribner's Sons, 1966. A brief description of origins, authors, purposes, and kinds of psalms.

Buttenwieser, Moses, *The Psalms Chronologically Treated with a New Translation.* Chicago: University of Chicago Press, 1938. An effort to treat each psalm according to its origins in the history of Israel.

Buttrick, George A., ed., "Psalms," *The Interpreter's Dictionary of the Bible,* K–Q. New York: Abingdon Press, 1962. J. Hempel has written a concise article clarifying poetic forms, describing types, and discussing the religion of the psalms.

Buttrick, George A., ed., *The Interpreter's Bible* (Vol. IV). New York: Abingdon Press, 1955. A good introduction and exposition of the psalms by William R. Taylor and W. Stewart McCullough. These scholars are inclined to place most of the psalms in the post-exilic period.

Crim, Keith R., *The Royal Psalms.* Richmond, Va.: John Knox Press, 1962. After a discussion of kingship in Israel, an exposition of the psalms concerned with the kings of Israel is given (Psalms 2, 18, 20, 21, 45, 72, 89, 101, 110, 144).

Dahood, Mitchell, S. J., Psalms I, 1–50, *The Anchor Bible.* Garden City, N. Y.: Doubleday & Co., 1966.

————, Psalms II, 51–100, *The Anchor Bible.* Garden City, N.Y.: Doubleday & Co., 1968. Using Canaanite, Babylonian, and Egyptian psalm-types, the author has shown how the Israelite psalmists used and modified the hymns of their cultural neighbors. The translations vitally suggest the religious sensitivity of the psalms.

Gunn, George S., *Singers of Israel: The Book of Psalms.* London: Lutherworth Press, 1963. A simple treatment of the psalms according to their purposes, plan, substance, and use in ancient Israel.

Guthrie, Harvey H., Jr., *Israel's Sacred Songs: A Study of Dominant Themes.* New York: Seabury Press, 1966. A fine handling of the major themes of the psalms, such as God as Overlord, Cosmic King, Saviour, and Source of Wisdom.

Leslie, Elmer A., *The Psalms: Translated and Interpreted in the Light of Hebrew Life and Worship.* New York: Abingdon Press, 1949. After a discussion of the vigor of Israel's worship, the psalms are interpreted topically. Some examples are: psalms of the New Year festival, the Hebrew year, the nature of God, liturgies of the Temple, the King, thanksgivings. This large volume is one of the best introductions to the book of Psalms.

Mowinckel, Sigmund, *The Psalms in Israel's Worship* (2 vols.), trans.

and rev. D. R. Ap-Thomas. London: Oxford University Press, 1963. Accurate dating of each psalm is impossible, but more of them belong to pre-exilic Israel than scholars have usually admitted. This is one theme of these outstanding volumes. Another is that the official cult of Israel's Temple gave impetus to most of the psalms. Psalms are bracketed according to types.

Weiser, Artur, *The Psalms: A Commentary,* trans. Herbert Hartwell. Philadelphia: Westminster Press, 1962. After introductory matters such as origins, authorship, collection, and canonization of the book of Psalms, each psalm is translated and discussed. Sometimes the obvious is treated at length, otherwise it is a good introductory volume.

Westermann, Claus, *The Praise of God in the Psalms,* trans. Keith R. Crim. Richmond, Va.: John Knox Press, 1965. The influence of Babylonian and Egyptian hymns is treated as important in the final structuring of Israel's psalms of praise and thanksgiving.

V. Other References   Baly, Denis, *The Geography of the Bible.* New York: Harper & Brothers, 1957. A useful volume relating significant biblical events to the terrain of Palestine. The author lived in Palestine for years, and is a keen student of both the Bible and "the land."

Buttrick, George A., ed., *The Interpreter's Dictionary of the Bible* (4 vols.). New York: Abingdon Press, 1962. One of the most useful works on biblical lore in print. In four volumes the core material for a comprehensive knowledge of the Bible is given by leading scholars. All place names and proper names are described. Lengthy articles are offered on related topics, such as Palestine, the Dead Sea Scrolls, archaeology, textual criticism, and so forth.

Davis, John D., *The Westminster Dictionary of the Bible,* revised and rewritten by Henry S. Gehman. Philadelphia: Westminster Press, 1944. A handy, one-volume dictionary, but outdated. For an example of conservative scholarship, however, it is outstanding.

Fleming, James, *Personalities of the Old Testament.* New York: Charles Scribner's Sons, 1939. A study of some of the characters of the Old Testament with something of a romantic tinge to it. A useful volume to read as companion to more critical treatments of Old Testament figures. It does have some neat insights.

Gray, John, *Archaeology and the Old Testament World.* New York: Harper & Row, 1962. One of the best books interpreting archaeological evidence in such a way that the Old Testament lives in the perspective of the ancient Near East. After brief discussions of the three major areas, influencing the Hebrews (Mesopotamia, Egypt, and Canaan), an interpretation of Israel's history is offered using the aid of recent discoveries. *Paperback.*

Kenyon, Kathleen M., *Archaeology in the Holy Land.* New York: Frederick A. Praeger, Inc., 1960. A dependable treatment of Palestine's archaeological unfolding from prehistoric times to the period of late Judaism. Although some effort is made to relate findings to the Old Testament, that aspect of Palestinian archaeology is not stressed. Readers will find it a well-written interpretation of complex data. *Paperback.*

Miller, Madeleine S. and J. Lane Miller, *Harper's Bible Dictionary.* New York: Harper & Brothers, 1958. Probably the best single-volume dictionary for a beginning reader of the Old Testament.

Pedersen, Johannes, *Israel: Its Life and Culture* (4th ed., 4 vols.), trans.

A. Moller. London: Oxford University Press, 1959. A sociological and psychological study of the Old Testament indispensable to the serious reader of the Old Testament. It provides insights into the world of the Old Testament gathered by a superb scholar.

Pritchard, James B., *Ancient Near Eastern Texts Relating to the Old Testament* (2d ed.). Princeton N.J.: Princeton University Press, 1955. This book must be used to be appreciated. Its wealth of information on life in the ancient Near East helps to put the Old Testament into proper context. References to corollary Old Testament passages in the margins makes the book useful to beginners and scholars alike.

Thomas, D. Winton, *Documents From Old Testament Times.* New York: Harper & Row, 1965. (British publisher: Thomas Nelson & Sons, Ltd., Sunbury-on-Thames, Middlesex.) This book does for the new reader of the Old Testament what Pritchard's *Ancient Near Eastern Texts* does for scholars. It is a handy volume giving historical, mythological, and legal texts that relate directly to the Old Testament. It is based on the latest archaeological interpretations, and has some excellent commentary and notes. *Paperback.*

Bibliography By Chapters

Chapter I

Auerbach, Erich, *Mimesis: The Representation of Reality in Western Literature,* trans. W. Trask. New York: Doubleday & Co. (Anchor Books), 1957. The treatment of contrasts between Homer and an Old Testament author are handled in this fine book as well as the continuing influences of biblical themes and plots upon subsequent masterpieces in Western literature.

Beebe, H. Keith, "Biblical Adventures in an American Novel," *The Journal of Bible and Religion,* XXVII, No. 2 (1959), P. 133. This article shows how Saul Bellow uses biblical allusions, themes, and events in his novel *The Adventures of Augie March.*

_____, "Biblical Motifs in *All the King's Men,*" *The Journal of Bible and Religion,* XXX, No. 2 (1962), p. 123. How Robert Penn Warren's uses of biblical references give certain thematic directions to the novel.

Horowitz, Edward, *How the Hebrew Language Grew.* New York: Jewish Education Committee Press, 1960. A simple treatment of the Hebrew language. For those who are reading the Old Testament for the first time this book will offer many helpful facts about the language of the men who wrote the Old Testament.

Chapter II

Albright, William F., *The Archaeology of Palestine* (rev. ed.). Baltimore: Penguin Books, Inc., 1960. This handy volume by one of the great Palestinian archaeologists introduces the reader to the art and science of archaeology. It has outstanding chapters on the people and daily life of ancient Palestine. Its style is not altogether pleasing, but careful work will reward the diligent. *Paperback.*

Burrows, Millard, *What Mean These Stones?* New York: Meridian Books, 1957. This carefully prepared book is an excellent topical introduction to the culture of ancient Palestine as revealed through archaeology. Some of its topics are: topography, houses, fortifications, weapons and tools, and economic life. It is an excellent companion to the Old Testament. *Paperback.*

Buttrick, George A., ed., "Palestine," *Interpreter's Dictionary of the*

Bible, K–Q, pp. 621–46. New York: Abingdon Press, 1962. Excellent short treatments of climate, geography, and geology of Palestine.

Campbell, Edward F., Jr. and David Noel Freedman, eds., *The Biblical Archaeologist Reader* (Vol. II). New York: Doubleday and Co., 1964. This volume treats the cities and nations neighboring ancient Israel and the major excavated cities of Palestine and the Roman Empire related to the Bible. These articles combine scholarly excellence and simple presentation for outstanding interpretations of biblical material. *Paperback.*

Gordon, Cyrus H., *The Ancient Near East* (3d ed. rev.). New York: W. W. Norton & Co., 1965. A book that interprets the biblical text as historically accurate at almost every stage. The author seeks to relate Homeric Greece and the Old Testament's United Monarchy in a cultural continuum. Quite controversial among qualified scholars. *Paperback.*

Pritchard, James B., *Gibeon Where the Sun Stood Still*. Princeton N.J.: Princeton University Press, 1962. A simplified story of the excavations at El Jib, the site of biblical Gibeon. The author has unfolded a charming account of how the citizens of that city lived. Although criticized by some archaeologists for omissions and questionable interpretations, it serves as a good introduction to methods and accomplishments in biblical archaeology.

Thomas, D. Winton, ed., *Archaeology and Old Testament Study*. Oxford, England: the Clarendon Press, 1967. A volume clarifying for general readers the impact of archaeological discoveries on the study of the Old Testament. The contributions are made by some of England's foremost archaeologists and biblical scholars yet the articles carry, on the whole, nontechnical interpretations of results of excavations. Excellently indexed, it should serve the purposes of general readers of the Old Testament for a long time.

Wright, George Ernest, *Biblical Archaeology* (new and rev. ed.). Philadelphia: Westminster Press, 1962. A handy reference volume for complete information on what archaeology has done in clarifying biblical lore. It carries the reader from prehistoric Palestine through the first Christian century. *Paperback* abridged version available.

———, *Shechem: The Biography of a Biblical City*. New York: McGraw-Hill Book Co., 1965. A popular treatment of the Drew University–McCormick Theological Seminary excavations at Tell Balata. The report indicates the relevance of archaeological findings for an understanding of Old Testament narratives involving Shechem.

Wright, George Ernest and David Noel Freedman, eds., *The Biblical Archaeologist Reader*. New York: Doubleday & Co (Anchor Books), 1961. Short articles on topics which have been clarified by recent archaeological interpretations. Sample topics are: "Sodom and Gomorrah," "What Were the Cherubim?" "The Significance of the Temple in the Near East." *Paperback.*

Chapter III   Barr, James, *The Semantics of Biblical Language*. London: Oxford University Press, 1961. This book will help a reader understand the psychology of biblical language. The differences between Hebraic and Greek ways of thinking, this volume suggests, arise because of the different structures of the languages rather than because of an inherent mental difference.

Chase, Mary Ellen, *The Bible and the Common Reader.* New York: The Macmillan Co., 1958. A discussion of the growth of biblical literature with some suggestive ways for appreciating the subtleties of Hebrew literary form.

Childs, Brevard S., *Memory and Tradition in Israel.* London: S C M Press, 1962. A good although in some places complex discussion of the psychology of Hebrew memory and its importance to the Israelite cult and history.

Nielsen, Edward, *Oral Tradition.* London: S C M Press, 1954. A cogent argument for the vitality and accuracy of Semitic traditions transmitted orally.

Vansina, Jan, *Oral Tradition: A Study in Historical Methodology,* trans. H. M. Wright. Chicago: Aldine Publishing Co., 1965. A general discussion by one of the greatest authorities of primitive cultures of how the living traditions of simple people are carried orally.

READINGS FROM THE GENERAL BIBLIOGRAPHY:

Bewer, Julius A., *The Literature of the Old Testament,* pp. 1–22.

Bright, John, *A History of Israel,* pp. 128–60.

Eissfeldt, Otto, *The Old Testament: An Introduction,* pp. 57–128.

Noth, Martin, *The History of Israel,* pp. 85–163.

Ringgren, Helmer, *Israelite Religion,* pp. 41–54.

Weiser, Artur, *The Old Testament: Its Formation and Development,* pp. 11–53.

Chapter IV   Gordon, Cyrus H., *The World of the Old Testament* (2d ed. rev.). Garden City, N.Y.: Doubleday & Co., Inc., 1958. In an effort to put the Old Testament into its historical and cultural background, the author calls upon the results of archaeological excavations. In many instances he treats as historical Old Testament materials that are probably legendary. May be used, but with caution.

Hertzberg, Hans Wilhelm, *I and II Samuel: A Commentary,* trans. J. S. Bowden. Philadelphia: Westminster Press, 1964. A detailed treatment of the literary and historical character of 1 and 2 Samuel. Many helpful insights are offered on the historical and cultural settings for the Yahwist religion during the United Monarchy.

Rainey, A. F., "The Kingdom of Ugarit," *The Biblical Archaeologist,* XXVIII, No. 4 (1965), pp. 112–17. A valuable introduction to the study of Canaanite social and political influences upon Israel.

Yadin, Yigael, *The Art of Warfare in Biblical Lands in the Light of Arcaeological Discoveries* (2 vols.). New York: McGraw-Hill Book Co., 1963. Beautifully illustrated, this treatment of defensive and offensive armaments, military tactics, and specific battles supplements one's reading about these matters in the Old Testament.

READINGS FROM THE GENERAL BIBLIOGRAPHY

Albright, William F., *Archaeology and the Religion of Israel,* pp. 95–129.

Bewer, Julius A., *The Literature of the Old Testament,* pp. 25–32.

Bright, John, *A History of Israel*, pp. 161–219.

Eichrodt, Walther, *Theology of the Old Testament*, pp. 98–176.

Eissfeldt, Otto, *The Old Testament: An Introduction*, pp. 268–81.

Gray John, *Archaeology and the Old Testament World*, pp. 129–45.

Kenyon, Kathleen M., *Archaeology in the Holy Land*, pp. 221–59.

Noth, Martin, *The History of Israel*, pp. 164–215.

Pfeiffer, Robert H., *Introduction to the Old Testament*, pp. 338–73.

_____, *Religion in the Old Testament*, pp. 58–116.

Ringgren, Helmer, *Israelite Religion*, Ch. II.

Vriezen, Theodorus C., *An Outline of Old Testament Theology*, Ch. IX.

Weiser, Artur, *The Old Testament: Its Formation and Development*, pp. 157–82.

Chapter V
Gerstenberger, Erhard, "Covenant and Commandment," *Journal of Biblical Literature*, LXXXIV, Part I (1965), pp. 38–51. A well-documented article arguing that treaty arrangements among ancient Near Eastern rulers were not the bases for Old Testament commandments.

Gurney, O. R., *The Hittites*. London: Penguin Books. 1952, pp. 88–103. A general survey of Hittite history and culture. The chapter on Hittite law is especially helpful for interpretation of Old Testament law. *Paperback*.

Meek, Theophile J., *Hebrew Origins*. New York: Harper & Brothers, 1960. A volume treating the origins of the Hebrew people, their law, their God, their priesthood, prophecy, and monotheism. The section on law (pp. 49–81), is helpful but not altogether dependable. *Paperback*.

Mendenhall, George E., *Law and Covenant in Israel and the Ancient Near East*. Pittsburgh: The Biblical Colloquium, 1955. A study of treaty formation in the ancient world and its impact upon the literary forms of legal traditions.

Smith, J. M. Powis, *The Origin and History of Hebrew Law*. Chicago: University of Chicago Press, 1931. A survey of Israelite legal traditions. It is somewhat outdated, but is still a good general introduction.

READINGS FROM THE GENERAL BIBLIOGRAPHY

Alt, Albrecht, *Essays on Old Testament History and Religion*, pp. 101–71.

Bewer, Julius A., *The Literature of the Old Testament*, pp. 33–46.

Buttrick, George A., ed., "Law in the Old Testament," *Interpreter's Dictionary of the Bible*, J–O, pp. 77–89.

Eichrodt, Walther, *Theology of the Old Testament*, pp. 36–97.

Eissfeldt, Otto, *The Old Testament: An Introduction*, pp. 212–19.

Pedersen, Johannes, *Israel: Its Life and Culture* (Vols. I–II), pp. 263–310.

Pritchard, James B., *Ancient Near Eastern Texts*, pp. 159–97.

Chapter VI
Good, Edwin M., *Irony in the Old Testament*. Philadelphia: Westminster Press, 1965. This study of irony in several parts of the Old Testament is a distinct addition to the literary analysis of the Old Testament. The chapter on irony in Israel's mythological tales (pp. 81–114) is particularly helpful.

Gunkel, Herman, *The Legends of Genesis,* trans. W. H. Carruth. New York: Schocken Books, 1964. One of the best treatments of the literary structure of Genesis. Although first published in 1901, its usefulness has not diminished. *Paperback.*

Sandmel, Samuel, *The Hebrew Scriptures.* New York: Alfred A. Knopf, 1963. A simple treatment of literature and religion in the Old Testament focusing upon some of the eminent passages. Pages 319–419 deal with the narratives in the Pentateuch.

Speiser, E. A., "Genesis," *The Anchor Bible.* Garden City, N.Y.: Doubleday & Co., Inc., 1964. A new translation of Genesis. The introduction and notes show the superior scholarship of the translator.

Wright, G. Ernest, ed., *The Bible and the Ancient Near East.* London: Routledge and Kegan Paul, 1961. A collection of essays by students and associates of William F. Albright which deals with the specific scholarly tasks of Old Testament study. The article by John Bright, "Modern Study of Old Testament Literature" (pp. 13–31), applies to the material in Chapter VI.

READINGS FROM THE GENERAL BIBLIOGRAPHY

Bewer, Jullus A., *The Literature of the Old Testament,* pp. 65–88, 273–92.

Eissfeldt, Otto, *The Old Testament: An Introduction,* pp. 155–212.

Pfeiffer, Robert H., *Introduction to the Old Testament,* pp. 129–337.

Pritchard, James B., *Ancient Near East Texts,* pp. 42–119.

Weiser, Artur, *The Old Testament: Its Formation and Development,* pp. 70–142.

Wright, George E. and Floyd V. Filson, eds., *The Westminster Historical Atlas to the Bible,* pp. 15–46.

Chapter VII
Baly, Denis, *The Geography of the Bible.* New York: Harper & Brothers, 1957. A clear, simple treatment of Palestine by a person who spent many years living in that land. A unique combination of personal experience and scholarly knowledge.

Campbell, Edward F., Jr., "The Amarna Letters and the Amarna Period," *The Biblical Archaeologist,* XXIII, No. 1 (1960). A good study of how the Amarna letters supply information about the 14th century B.C., when Canaan was invaded by alien tribes.

Gordon, Cyrus H., *The Ancient Near East* (see Bibliography, Ch. II), pp. 15–167. This author gives an interpretation of Israel's origins radically different from those of most critical scholars.

Meek, Theophile J., *Hebrew Origins* (see Bibliography, Ch. V), pp. 1–48. A sturdy defense of a complex history of Israel's infiltration into Canaan.

Mendenhall, George E., "The Hebrew Conquest of Canaan," *The Biblical Archaeologist,* XXV, No. 3 (1962). A refutation of the generally accepted belief that Israel originated as desert tribes and attacked Canaan from the east. A provocative theory of Israel's origins from within Canaan as a social, not an ethnic, movement.

READINGS FROM THE GENERAL BIBLIOGRAPHY

Bright, John, *A History of Israel,* pp. 39–160.

Kenyon, Kathleen M., *Archaeology in the Holy Land,* pp. 162–239.

Noth, Martin, *The History of Israel,* pp. 53–163.

Orlinski, Harry, *Ancient Israel,* pp. 1–66.

Weiser, Artur, *The Old Testament: Its Formation and Development,* pp. 143–82.

Wright, George Ernest, *Biblical Archaeology,* pp. 40–119.

Chapter VIII Buttrick, George A., ed., *The Interpreter's Bible* (Vol. I). New York: Abingdon Press, 1952. "The History of the Religion of Israel" by James Muilenburg is one of the best short studies of the topic available in English. It treats the topic chronologically, pp. 292–348. "The Faith of Israel" by George Ernest Wright discusses the task of biblical theology. It treats in brief and excellent fashion the nature of Israel's God, the world, man, and forms of worship, pp. 349–89.

de Vaux, Roland, O.P., *Ancient Israel: It's Life and Institutions,* trans. John McHugh. New York: McGraw-Hill Book Co., 1961. A significant book describing Israel's family, civil, military, and religious institutions. Indispensable for a serious student of the Old Testament.

Meek, Theophile J., *Hebrew Origins* (see Bibliography, Ch. V), pp. 83–118.

Rowley, H. H., *The Rediscovery of the Old Testament.* Philadelphia: Westminster Press, 1956. A collection of essays on some of Israel's major religious themes: the meaning of history, monotheism, prophecy, the revelation of God, and the destiny of man. The essays are not organized on any central theme.

READINGS FROM THE GENERAL BIBLIOGRAPHY

Albright, William F., *From the Stone Age to Christianity,* pp. 200–272.

Bright, John, *A History of Israel,* pp. 78–94, 128–60.

Pedersen, Johannes, *Israel: Its Life and Culture* (Vols. III–IV), pp. 198–465.

Pfeiffer, Robert H., *Religion in the Old Testament,* pp. 12–116.

Chapter IX Albright, William F., *The Archaeology of Palestine* (see Bibliography, Ch. II), pp. 110–45.

Chadwick, Nora, *Poetry and Prophecy.* New York: Cambridge University Press, 1942. A study of modern poets and prophets in primitive cultures which helps clarify the function of prophecy in the Old Testament.

de Vaux, Roland, "The Excavations at Tell el Far'ah and the Site of Ancient Tirzah," *Palestine Exploration Quarterly* (1956–1957), pp. 125–40. Archaeological work helps to understand the confusing period of Israel's history when the capital was transferred from Tirzah to Samaria.

———, *Ancient Israel: It's Life and Institutions* (see Bibliography, Ch. VIII), pp. 65–212.

Mazar, Benjamin, "The Aramaean Empire and Its Relations with Israel," *The Biblical Archaeologist,* XXV, No. 4 (1962). A helpful study of how the Aramaean empire impacted upon Israel's religious and political life.

Patai, Raphael, "The Goddess Asherah," *Journal of Near Eastern Studies,* Vol. XXIV, Nos. 1 and 2 (January–April 1965). A thorough treatment of how the Palestinian goddess Asherah influenced Israelite beliefs and practices.

Yadin, Yigael, *The Art of Warfare in Biblical Lands* (see Bibliography, Ch. IV), pp. 291–375.

READINGS FROM THE GENERAL BIBLIOGRAPHY

Albright, William F., *Archaeology and the Religion of Israel*, pp. 130–75.

Bewer, Julius A., *The Literature of the Old Testament*, pp. 229–45.

Bright, John, *A History of Israel*, pp. 209–320.

Kenyon, Kathleen M., *Archaeology in the Holy Land*, pp. 260–81.

Noth, Martin, *The History of Israel*, pp. 253–358.

Pedersen, Johannes, *Israel: Its Life and Culture* (Vols. III–IV).

Pfeiffer, Robert H., *Introduction to the Old Testament*, pp. 374–410.

Pritchard, James B., *Ancient Near Eastern Texts*, pp. 263–4, 275–91.

Thomas, D. Winton, *Documents from Old Testament Times*, pp. 46–94, 201–38.

Weiser, Artur, *The Old Testament: Its Formation and Development*, pp. 170–82.

Wright, George Ernest, *Biblical Archaeology*, pp. 146–98.

Chapter X   Anderson, B. W. and W. Harrelson, eds., *Israel's Prophetic Heritage*. New York: Harper & Brothers, 1962. A collection of essays dealing with special problems in prophetic literature. Chapters VI, VII, and IX are applicable to the prophets during Israel's crisis and prophetic challenge.

Buber, Martin, *The Prophetic Faith*, trans. Carlyle Witton-Davies. New York: The Macmillan Co., 1949. A study of the prophets' understanding of Yahwistic religion by one of Judaism's greatest modern theologians.

Buttrick, George A., ed., *The Interpreter's Bible* (Vols. I, V, VI). New York: Abingdon Press, 1952, 1956. "The Prophetic Literature" by Hughell E. W. Fosbroke in Vol. I, pp. 201–11, is a superior introduction to the subject of prophecy. He deals with the problem of ecstacy, the form of prophetic speech, and the meaning of prophetic prediction. His "The Book of Amos, Introduction" in Vol. VI, pp. 763–76, is also an excellent study of the first writing prophet. John Mauchline has a challenging study of the book of Hosea in the same volume, and Rolland E. Wolfe, "The Book of Micah, Introduction," handles that prophet with clarity and discretion. "The Book of Isaiah, Chapter 1–30, Introduction" by R. B. Y. Scott in Vol. V, offers a good beginning on Isaiah of Jerusalem.

Buttrick, George A., ed., *The Interpreter's Dictionary of the Bible*, I–Q, pp. 897–900. New York: Abingdon Press, 1962. B. Davie Napier has a good introduction to the prophets with the emphasis that the writing prophets did not participate in ecstacy.

Gottwald, Norman K., *All the Kingdoms of the Earth*, pp. 94–217. New York: Harper & Row, 1964. A study of Israel's prophets in relation to the historical conditions of the ancient Near East. It is an interesting and almost indispensable book on the historic events in which the prophets participated.

Haldar, Alfred, *Associations of Cult Prophets Among the Ancient Semites,* trans. H. S. Harvey. Uppsala, Sweden: Almquist and Wiksells, 1945. A study of the guilds of prophets as they participated in the official religious rites of the Semitic world. Information culled from Mesopotamian and Canaanite sources clarifies Old Testament prophetic life.

Heaton, E. W., *The Old Testament Prophets.* Baltimore: Penguin Books, 1958. This book carries the theme that the prophetic tradition is the key to the doors of Old Testament religion. The historical situation is sketched when the author considers the unparalleled contribution prophecy has made to subsequent forms of belief and practice. *Paperback.*

Hyatt, James P., *Prophetic Religion.* New York: Abingdon Press, 1947. Discussion of the major religious affirmations of the great prophets. Still useful although changes in methods dealing with the prophets have made some of the author's conclusions questionable.

Meek, Theophile J., *Hebrew Origins* (see Bibliography, Ch. V), pp. 148–83.

Mowinckel, Sigmund, *Prophecy and Tradition,* Oslo, Norway: I. Kommisjon hos J. Dybwad, 1946. This study argues that original prophetic sayings were fragmentary, carried in Israel's memory by oral tradition as well as in writing. These oral and written gems were treated by successive generations of traditionists who adapted the original oracles to the needs of the times.

Scott, R. B. Y., *The Relevance of the Prophets* (rev. ed.). New York: The Macmillan Co., 1968. One of the best general introductions to the life, work, and beliefs of the prophets. *Paperback.*

Von Rad, Gerhard, *Old Testament Theology* (Vol. II, *The Theology of Israel's Prophetic Traditions*), trans. D. M. G. Stalker. New York: Harper & Row, 1965. After considering the oral tradition, the prophets' call to prophecy, and Israel's ideas about time and history, the author deals with the prophets from the classical age through the post-exilic period. The prophets dealt with "sacred history" and placed their messages at a point in time related to that of God's previous actions in Israel's past.

Westermann, Claus, *Basic Forms of Prophetic Speech,* trans. Hugh Clayton White. Philadelphia: Westminster Press, 1967. The prophet was a messenger of God. As such he used the basic form of sending messages employed by officials in the ancient Near East. This book includes a close study of the judgment speeches against individuals as well as against Israel and other nations.

READINGS FROM THE GENERAL BIBLIOGRAPHY

Albright, William F., *Archaeology and the Religion of Israel,* pp. 130–75.

Bewer, Julius A., *The Literature of the Old Testament,* pp. 89–174.

Eissfeldt, Otto, *The Old Testament: An Introduction,* pp. 303–29, 384–91, 395–401, 406–12.

Gray, John, *Archaeology and the Old Testament World,* pp. 154–79.

James, Fleming, *Personalities of the Old Testament,* pp. 211–81.

Pfeiffer, Robert H., *Introduction to the Old Testament,* pp. 415–51, 566–72, 577–83, 589–93.

———, *Religion in the Old Testament,* pp. 117–60.

Weiser, Artur, *The Old Testament: Its Formation and Development,* pp. 183–96, 232–7, 241–6, 252–5.

Chapter XI   Buttrick, George A., ed., *The Interpreter's Bible,* Vols. II, VI. New York: Abingdon Press, 1953, 1956. George Ernest Wright in Vol. II, pp. 311–30, presents a helpful introduction to the book of Deuteronomy clarifying structure, style, and theology admirably. Volume VI contains good introductions to the books of Zephaniah (pp. 1007–13), Nahum (pp. 953–956), and Habakkuk (pp. 973–9).

Frankfort, Henri, *Kingship and the Gods,* pp. 101–42, 231–48, 313–33. Chicago: University of Chicago Press, 1948. This is one of the great books on the ancient Near East. The author contrasts the theory of kingship in various cultures of the biblical world, and shows the distinctive character of the king's relationship to God in Israelite political thought.

Gaster, Theodor H., *Thespis: Ritual, Myth, and Drama in the Ancient Near East,* pp. 23–106. New York: Harper & Row, 1961. This is a brilliant treatment of the importance of myth and ritual in the communities of the ancient world. Rites of mortification, purgation, invigoration, and jubilation gave seasonally renewed expectations of life to the ancients. *Paperback.*

Gottwald, Norman K., *All the Kingdoms of the Earth* (see Bibliography, Ch. X), pp. 219–38.

Meek, Theophile J., *Hebrew Origins* (see Bibliography, Ch. V), pp. 49–81.

Oesterley, W. O. E., and Theodore H. Robinson, *Hebrew Religion: Its Origin and Development,* pp. 247–68. London: Society for Preservation of Christian Knowledge, 1952. The theory that Israelite religion followed the developmental pattern of religions the world over is pursued in this book. These authors reveal the remnants of animism, totemism, and polytheism in the Old Testament. The sections on Israel's religion in the period of the monarchies and the exile is especially helpful.

Robinson, Theodore H., *A History of Israel* (Vol. I), pp. 411–28. Oxford, England: Clarendon Press, 1932. A standard history of Israel, the section on King Josiah's reformation sees the situation clearly.

Smith, J. M. Powis, *The Origin and History of Hebrew Law* (see Bibliography, Ch. V), pp. 39–69 on the Code of Deuteronomy.

Voegelin, Eric, *Israel and Revelation,* pp. 353–79. Baton Rouge: Louisiana State University Press, 1956. The discussion of the Deuteronomic Reformation and the formation of the myth of Mosaic authorship of the new code is a splendid interpretation and description of the conditions of Josiah's reign.

Von Rad, Gerhard, *Studies in Deuteronomy,* trans. David Stalker. London: S C M Press, 1953. A brief treatment by a great Old Testament scholar of the sacred traditions which lie behind the book of Deuteronomy, the origins, and the purposes of the book.

READINGS FROM THE GENERAL BIBLIOGRAPHY

Bewer, Julius A., *The Literature of the Old Testament,* pp. 125–52, 229–45.

Bright, John, *A History of Israel,* pp. 288–319.

Eissfeldt, Otto, *The Old Testament: An Introduction,* pp. 219–32, 413–25.

Noth, Martin, *The History of Israel,* pp. 253–99.

Pfeiffer, Robert H., *Introduction to the Old Testament,* pp. 178–87, 228–38, 594–601.

Weiser, Artur, *The Old Testament: Its Formation and Development,* pp. 125–234, 252–66.

Chapter XII   Bright, John, *"Jeremiah," The Anchor Bible.* Garden City, N.Y.: Double-day & Co., 1965. A new translation and introduction incorporating linguistic and archaeological information in such a way as to give the period and personality of Jeremiah new life.

Buttrick, George A., ed., *The Interpreter's Bible* (Vols. V, VI). New York: Abingdon Press, 1956. James Philip Hyatt has a good introduction to the book of Jeremiah (Vol. V, pp. 777–93), Theophile J. Meek to the book of Lamentations (Vol. VI, pp. 3–6), Herbert G. May to the book of Ezekiel (Vol. VI, pp. 41–66), and James Muilenberg to Isaiah 40–66 (Vol. V, pp. 381–419).

Finegan, Jack, *Light from the Ancient Past,* pp. 164–208. Princeton, N.J.: Princeton University Press, 1947. An archaeological introduction to the ancient Near East; the section on the culture of the exilic period is particularly useful.

Gottwald, Norman K., *All the Kingdoms of the Earth* (see Bibliography, Ch. X), pp. 239–348.

_____, *Studies in the Book of Lamentations.* London: S C M Press, 1954. The freshest treatment of Lamentations available. Thorough literary and theological analyses so that the historical context of the book is perfectly clear.

Parrot, André, *Babylon and the Old Testament.* New York: Philosophical Library, 1958. An excellent short treatment of archaeological contributions to understanding Babylon and the Jews in exile.

Rowley, H. H., ed., *The Old Treatment and Modern Study.* London: Oxford University Press, 1961. A Trends in Old Testament study with articles on archaeology, the Pentateuch, the historical books, psalms, wisdom literature, and so forth. The article on prophetic literature (pp. 115–61) is especially good in connection with this chapter. *Paperback.*

READINGS FROM THE GENERAL BIBLIOGRAPHY

Albright, William F., *Archaeology and the Religion of Israel,* pp. 130–75.

Bewer, Julius A., *The Literature of the Old Testament,* pp. 214–28.

Bright, John, *A History of Israel,* pp. 321–40.

Eissfeldt, Otto, *The Old Testament: An Introduction,* pp. 330–40, 346–81, 233–6.

Gray, John, *Archaeology and the Old Testament World,* pp. 180–98.

Noth, Martin, *The History of Israel,* pp. 289–99.

Pfeiffer, Robert H., *Introduction to the Old Testament,* pp. 531–41.

_____, *Religion in the Old Testament,* pp. 175–8.

Thomas, D. Winton, *Documents from Old Testament Times,* pp. 84–117.

Chapter XIII   de Vaux, Roland, *Ancient Israel: Its Life and Institutions* (see Bibliography, Ch. VIII), pp. 387–405, 475–8, 507–9, 358–71.

Gordon, Cyrus H., *The Ancient Near East* (see Bibliography, Ch. II), pp. 264–303.

Myers, Jacob M., "Ezra" and "Nehemiah," *The Anchor Bible*. Garden City, N.Y.: Doubleday & Co., 1965. A recent and reliable effort to reevaluate the literary, historical, and religious problems connected with the times of Ezra and Nehemiah. The translation is less important than the introduction which sets the Jews in Persian history, rearranges the literary sources, and evaluates the achievements of these post-exilic leaders.

Oesterley, W. O. E., and Theodore H. Robinson, *Hebrew Religion* (see Bibliography, Ch. XI), pp. 312–39.

Wright, G. Ernest and David Noel Freedman, eds., *The Biblical Archaeologist Reader* (see Bibliography, Ch. II), pp. 128–250.

READINGS FROM THE GENERAL BIBLIOGRAPHY

Bewer, Julius A., *The Literature of the Old Testament*, pp. 229–320.

Bright, John, *A History of Israel*, pp. 341–86.

Eissfeldt, Otto, *The Old Testament: An Introduction*, pp. 341–5, 426–33, 441–2, 401–2.

Gray, John, *Archaeology and the Old Testament World*, pp. 180–98.

Noth, Martin, *The History of Israel*, pp. 300–344.

Pfeiffer, Robert H., *Introduction to the Old Testament*, pp. 188–209, 584–5, 602–6, 612–15.

―――――, *Religion in the Old Testament*, pp. 175–90.

Thomas, D. Winton, *Documents from Old Testament Times*, pp. 231–78.

Weiser, Artur, *The Old Testament: Its Formation and Development*, pp. 135–42, 205–7, 247–8, 267–71, 275–7, 317–22.

Chapter XIV   Buttrick, George A., ed., *The Interpreter's Bible* (Vols. III, V). New York: Abingdon Press, 1954, 1956. In Vol. III Samuel Terrien has written one of the best short introductions to the book of Job. He shows the author's participation in the universal wisdom movement, reconstructs many confused passages, and gives a critical evaluation of the religious content. Superior! In Vol. V Theophile J. Meek summarizes the scholarly treatments of the Song of Songs, opting for use of the poems in a cultic celebration. Worth one's diligent study.

Gordis, Robert, *Koheleth: The Man and His World*. New York: Jewish Theological Seminary of America, 1954. A sound treatment of the book of Ecclesiastes which should be compared with the R. B. Y. Scott study (see below).

Jastrow, Morris, *The Gentle Cynic*. Philadelphia: J. B. Lippincott, 1919. Although an old commentary on Ecclesiastes, it states clearly and simply the problems of accurate interpretation of this enigmatic book.

Mathers, E. Powys, *Sung to Shahryar: Poems from the Book of the Thousand and One Night*, pp. 55–108. New York: Casanova Society, 1925. These Arabic poems may be used as companions to the love songs in the Song of Songs.

McDonald, Duncan Black, *The Hebrew Literary Genius*. Princeton, N.J.: Princeton University Press, 1933. A treatment of legends, history, and wisdom writings in the Old Testament that is not usually cited by Old Testament scholars. Whether one agrees with his conclusions or not, the essays are stimulating. The one on Job is particularly valuable.

Noth, Martin, and D. Winton Thomas, *Wisdom in Israel and in the Ancient Near East*. Leiden, Netherlands: E. J. Brill, 1960. A helpful treatment of wisdom as its universal character affected the sages of the Old Testament.

Pope, Marvin, "Job," *The Anchor Bible*. Garden City, N.Y.: Doubleday & Co., 1965. The introduction surveys several interpretations of the book of Job and gives the author's own. The translation and notes are superior.

Rowley, H. H., ed., *The Old Testament and Modern Study* (see Bibliography, Ch. XII), pp. 210–37. An excellent introduction to wisdom literature in the Old Testament. The major literary problems are treated especially well and the religious spirit behind wisdom is clarified.

Scott, R. B. Y., "Proverbs" and "Ecclesiastes," *The Anchor Bible*. Garden City, N.Y.: Doubleday & Co., 1965. One of the best short studies in English of wisdom in the ancient Near East. Wisdom writers were a "third force" in Israel, distinct from prophets and priests. Interpretations of Proverbs and Ecclesiastes are capable and convincing.

Waterman, Leroy, *The Song of Songs*. Ann Arbor: University of Michigan Press, 1948. After citing the history of criticism, the author treats the recensions of these love poems. He argues for their use in seasonal sequences. A translation with notes is given.

Whybray, R. N., *Wisdom in Proverbs*. London: S C M Press, 1965. Only the first nine chapters of the book of Proverbs are studied. However, after showing the Egyptian prototype of wisdom with its concepts of order, God, man, and authority, the author shows how wisdom developed in Israel.

READINGS FROM THE GENERAL BIBLIOGRAPHY

Bewer, Julius A., *Literature of the Old Testament*, pp. 321–412.

Eissfeldt, Otto, *The Old Testament: An Introduction*, pp. 403–6, 454–99.

Pfeiffer, Robert H., *Introduction to the Old Testament*, pp. 586–8, 645–719, 724–31.

Weiser, Artur, *The Old Testament: Its Formation and Development*, pp. 249–251, 287–304, 307–309.

Chapter XV

Allegro, John, *The Dead Sea Scrolls: A Reappraisal*. Baltimore: Penguin Books, 1964. A convenient summary of the fantastic scrolls found near the Dead Sea. Fine photographs illumine the life of the Qumran sect. Interpretations of John the Baptist, Jesus, and the Church garnish the treatment of this Jewish splinter group.

Black, Matthew, *The Scrolls and Christian Origins*. London: Thomas Nelson and Sons, Ltd., 1961. The Jewish background of the New Testament is revealed as a result of studies in the Dead Sea Scrolls. Not easy reading, this book will reward the diligent and perceptive reader.

Burrows, Millar, *The Dead Sea Scrolls*. New York: Viking Press, 1955. The first reliable and complete study of the scrolls with translations of most of the material from five documents. How the texts help scholars in literary criticism, historical interpretations, and theological understanding is made clear.

———, *More Light on the Dead Sea Scrolls*. New York: Viking Press, 1958. Continuation of the earlier book with discussion of the results of study of the scrolls for Old Testament interpretation and Christian origins. The sect's origins, beliefs, and rites are treated with translations of newer discoveries.

Charles, R. H., *Eschatology*. New York: Schocken Books, 1963. A reprint of one of the greatest works on the chief literary and theological movement of the close of the Old Testament age. Indispensable for this period of Jewish history. *Paperback.*

Cross, Frank Moore, Jr., *The Ancient Library of Qumran and Modern Biblical Studies*. Garden City, N.Y.: Doubleday & Co., 1961. The title gives the content of the book. Treating the origins, leadership, and literature of the community of Qumran, the author shows the implications for Old Testament and New Testament studies. *Paperback.*

Driver, G. R., *The Judaean Scrolls: The Problem and a Solution*. New York: Schocken Books, 1965. A great Old Testament scholar reports on the discoveries of new scrolls and fragments, the parties in Judaism of the lst century B.C., the historical background, and the importance of the scrolls to Old Testament study.

Gaster, Theodor H., *The Dead Sea Scriptures* (rev. ed.). Garden City, N.Y.: Doubleday & Co., 1964. Although the title honors the Qumran writings more than they deserve, the introduction, translations, and notes are a major contribution to study of the Dead Sea Scrolls. *Paperback.*

Gordon, Cyrus H., *The Ancient Near East* (see Bibliography, Ch. II), pp. 275–303.

Milik, J. L., *Ten Years of Discovery in the Wilderness of Judaea*, trans. J. Strugnell. London: S C M Press, 1963. The story of discovery, the Qumran library, the identification with the Essenes, the organization and teachings of the sect are told. Evaluation of importance of the scrolls is given. *Paperback.*

Roth, Cecil, *The Dead Sea Scrolls: A New Historical Approach*. New York: W. W. Norton & Co., 1965. An argument that the Qumran community was associated with the Zealotic group barricaded at Masada. The Teacher of Righteousness is identified as a leader of the bandits who held Masada against Jewish and Roman peace-keeping operations. *Paperback.*

Russell, D. S., *The Method and Message of Jewish Apocalyptic.* Philadelphia: Westminster Press, 1964. One of the fullest modern treatments of the nature of apocalyptic and its meaning in the context of Jewish life.

Sloan, W. W., *Between the Testaments*. Paterson, N.J.: Littlefield and Adams Co., 1964. A book summarizing the literature not found in the Old and New Testaments, but important for appreciating the relationship of the two scriptures. *Paperback.*

Vermes, G., *The Dead Sea Scrolls in English*. Baltimore: Penguin Books, 1962. A translation of the scrolls with an excellent introduction interpreting the nature of the community, its beliefs and practices, and the historical circumstances. Recommended highly!

Wilson, Edmund, *The Scrolls from the Dead Sea*. New York: Oxford University Press, 1955. A poorly named book, since the scrolls were not taken from the Dead Sea itself, it is the effort of a distinguished essayist and literary critic to assess the impact of the scrolls before qualified scholars had done their tasks. Excellently written, as one would expect, it is highly entertaining in the light of sober research.

Babylon (*Cont.*)

397; conquest of Hebrews, 119, 192, 198, 282, 315–17; destruction of Jerusalem, 119, 192–3, 198, 221, 267, 282, 303, 316–17, 362–3, 383; deities, 153, 164–5; Jews in, 242–3, 279, 282–3, 293, 300, 303, 305, 308, 318, 322, 325, 328–35, 447; laws, 104, 108.; literature, 165, 369, 409, 420, 447; writing, 201

"Babylonian Theodicy," 409, 420

Balaam, 39, 211, 219

Balas, Alexander, 465

Baruch, 33, 304, 307–8, 322

Bathsheba, 72

Bedouin, 22, 61, 71, 96, 113, 125, 138, 142, 147, 163, 166, 191, 239, 349, 354, 378

Beerlaharoi, 128, 154

Beersheba, 21, 27, 116, 133, 156, 166, 208, 226, 240, 288

Behemoth, 421 (n. 20)

Beisan. *See* Bethshan

Belshazzar, 445, 447–8

Benhadad, 179, 183–8, 214, 410

Benjamin, 239

Benjamin (tribe), 44, 132, 137, 146

ben Zakkai, Rabbi, 14

Bethel, 26, 116, 132, 137, 141, 145, 147, 154, 156, 166, 176, 208, 214, 222, 226, 229, 240–41, 283, 288

Bethhoron, 75, 175–6

Bethlehem, 60, 144, 434, 453–4

Bethshan, 21, 24, 27, 29, 86, 142, 177–8, 187, (Scythopolis), 460–61

Bethzur, 144, 464

Bible, The: A New Translation (Moffatt), 12

Bildad, 414–16, 423

Bit-Adini, 182

Bit-Khalupe, 182

Blacks in Old Testament, 317. *See also* Ethiopia, Shabako

Bloch, Ernest, 4, 275 (n. 6)

Boaz, 433–4

Book of the Dead, Egyptian, 337

Booths, Feast of (*Succoth*), 291, 293, 301, 340, 398, 431, 467

Brahms, Johannes, 341

Buttenwieser, Moses, 93

Byblos, 18, 84, 94, 211, 255, 331

Cain, 10

Calebites, 142, 144, 146, 160

Canaan, Canaanites, 38–9, 112–13, 237, 248, 280, 282, 300, 335, 349, 354, 369, 394, 399, concepts of god, 49, 51, 337; integration with Israelites, 76, 89, 92, 106, 181, 211, 230–31; laws, 97, 102, 106, 109; myths, 163–7, 253; period of independent states, 57; entry of Israelites, 114, 116–17, 125–6, 130–51, 240, 276, 290, 300, 368; literature, 405–7; Philistines enter, 39, 43, 46, 57, 114, 142, 228, 265; poetry, 15, 47, 51, 93–5;

prophets, 219; raids on Israel, 43, 45; under Israelite control, 62–9, 71; under Solomon, 76; religion, 82, 89, 161–2, 264, 291, 400–401

Canaan (son of Noah), 35

Canonization of texts, 13–14, 391

Caravan Routes, 20–23

Carchemish, 193, 250, 254, 285, 313, 346

Carmel, Mt., 26, 28, 74, 212

Cary, Joyce, 438

Casemate wall, 175, 183

Casuistic laws, 101, 278

Ceramics, Israelite, 198–200

Chaldea, Chaldeans, 132, 255, 296, 445

Chemosh, 91

Cherubim, 84

Chinnereth, Sea of, 21, 23–4, 145, 187

Christianity, Christians, 456, 458, 471, 477–8

Chronicler, The, 372–80, 387–91, 393, 441, 469–70

Circumcision, 155–6, 347–9, 367, 369, 371, 463–4, 476

Codes of Law, Bilalama, 104; covenant, 101–2, 108–9; Decalogue, 99–100; Deuteronomy 275–81; Hammurabi, 98, 104–5, 108–9; Hittite, 104; Holiness, 339–40; Lipit-Ishtar, 104; Middle Assyrian, 104–5; Ritual Decalogue, 100–1; Ur-Nammu, 104–5

Complete Bible, The: An American Translation (Smith and Goodspeed), 12

Covenants, 64, 107–9, 133, 135–7, 141–2, 156–7, 159, 220, 222, 262, 265–6, 275, 277, 284, 289, 311, 320, 375, 423, 475–6

Covenant Code, 96, 98 (n. 1)–104, 106, 108–9, 115, 266, 277–8, 281, 290

Croesus, 349–50

Cyaxares, 192, 285, 345–6

Cyrus, 324, 342–3, 349–51, 355 (n. 43), 357, 359, 373, 375–9, 448

Dagon, 84, 91

Dahood, Mitchell, 51

Damascus, 21–2, 57, 69, 145, 169, 178, 182–3, 185–9, 210, 214, 221–4, 227, 229, 232–3, 242, 245–8, 254, 377, 382, 467

Dan (town), 27, 132, 147, 208

Dan (tribe), 44, 132, 146, 160–1

Daniel, 334, 445–7, 473

Darius I, 360, 372, 448

David, 10, 16, 35, 45, 50, 81–96, 128, 132, 147, 158, 160, 168–9, 173, 178, 200, 210, 217, 223–4, 227, 262, 275, 284, 290–91, 322, 328, 335, 396, 433–4, 443, 463, 471; ascendancy, 54–6, 59–62; unites kingdoms, 63–4; ruler of United Monarchy, 64–71; poet and musician, 39–41, 47, 93, 323, 470; elements of success, 71; and Uriah, 82, 212; and laws, 105–6

Day of the Lord (Day of Yahweh), 226–7, 270–71, 273–4, 471

Dead Sea, 23–4, 29, 37, 75, 145, 223, 453, 455

Dead Sea Scrolls, 11–12, 298, 453–6, 458
Debir, 144, 205, 410
Deborah, 43, 48, 212, 241
Deborah, Song of, 43, 48–9
Decalogue (Ten Commandments), 83, 96, 99–101
Delilah, 131
Demetrius, 457, 465
Deutero-Isaiah. *See* Isaiah of Babylon
Deuteronomic Code, 277–8, 309, 375
Deuteronomists ("D"), 56, 117, 130, 156, 279–83, 286–93, 295, 298, 300, 305, 309–11, 348, 367, 420, 423
De Vaux, Roland, 62, 180, 182
Dies Irae (Thomas of Celano), 270–71. *See also* Day of the Lord
Dirges, 39–41, 47, 50, 63, 323–4
"Dispute over Suicide" (Egyptian), 419
Divination, 81, 87
Dome of the Rock, 91
Douay Version, (Bible), 13

East of Eden (Steinbeck), 2
Ebal, Mt., 144, 156, 276
Ecclesiastes (*Koheleth*), 7, 424–30, 437, 469
Edom, Edomites, 16, 19, 22, 39, 47, 50, 57, 60, 65, 69, 73–4, 91, 95, 106, 125, 128, 134, 142, 145, 193, 223–5, 227–8, 232, 245, 251–2, 255, 313, 348, 356, 362–3, 366, 371, 378, 405, 465, 467
Egypt, Egyptians (ancient), 6, 11, 39–40, 57, 79, 92, 128, 211, 228, 234, 237, 242, 265, 269, 273–4, 286, 288, 290, 302, 311–17, 319, 327–8, 338, 346–8, 354, 369, 382–3, 388, 458, 460, 462–3, architecture, 206; art, 198, 207; concepts of god, 49–50; conquered by Assyria, 272; Israelites in, 113–14, 120, 122–6, 132–3, 135–6, 138–44, 239–40, 273, 308, 332, 368; literature, 201–2, 225, 407, 419, 432; Tanite (21st) Dynasty, 73, 79; and Solomon, 73, 76–9; at end of United Hebrew Monarchy, 175–9, 190–93, 224, 248–52, 254–7
Eichhorn, Johann, 115
Eichrodt, Walther, 8
Eissfeldt, Otto, 118
Ekron, 254–56
Elam, 191, 242, 253, 257, 315, 331, 449
Elephantine Island, 273, 332
Eli, 79, 212, 283
Elihu, 414–16, 418, 421, 429
Elijah, 14, 169–70, 184, 207, 211–15, 219, 234, 364, 372
Elijah (Mendelssohn), 4
Eliphaz, 414–15, 418, 423
Elisha, 14, 57, 169–70, 213–15, 233
Elohim, 49, 94, 97, 112, 116, 120, 124, 156, 216, 239–40, 367, 414–15, 424
Elohist writer ("E"), 116–30, 153, 156, 158, 238–41, 282, 289 (n. 18), 367–9
Endor, witch of, 56

Enkidu, 165
Enoch, 443
En-Rogel Spring, 72, 90
Ephod, 81–2, 87
Ephraim (tribe), 44–5 (n. 11), 136, 146, 234
Epicurus, 427, 429
Esau, 35–6, 113, 125, 133, 368
Esdraelon, Plain of, 233
Eshbaal. *See* Ishbosheth
Essenes, 477
Esther, 153, 449
Ethiopia, Ethiopians, 7, 77, 228, 242, 261, 265, 274, 308
Et-Tell (Ai), excavations, 16–17
Euphrates River, 20–21, 114, 164, 182, 192, 211, 239, 291, 343, 377, 398
Eve, 84
Evil-Merodach. *See* Amel-Marduk
Except the Lord (Cary), 438
Exodus, the, 39, 122–4, 126, 142–3, 237, 262, 264, 283, 371
Ezekiel, 151, 302, 325–9, 332–40, 347, 352–4, 358–9, 370–71, 396–7, 418, 471
Ezion-geber, 22, 74–8, 176
Ezra, 366, 370–75, 377, 380, 387–90, 394, 400, 433, 435–6, 441, 447, 470

Far'ah. *See* Tell el Far'ah, Wadi Far'ah
Faulkner, William, 2
Faust (Goethe), 271
Fertility rites, 82, 84, 161–3, 222, 237, 305, 337

Gabriel, 446, 477
Gad (tribe), 146, 160
Galilee, 26–7, 233, 248, 284, 345, 465
Garden of Eden, 84
Gath, 40, 61, 224
Gaza, 21, 222, 224–5, 248, 254, 382
Gedaliah, 308, 317, 330–31
Gerar, 120, 140, 179, 240, 436
Gerizim, Mt., 28, 144, 151, 156, 276, 394
Gezer, 73, 75, 175–76
Gibeon, 18, 38, 62–3, 90, 137, 141, 175–6
Gideon, 130–31, 161
Gihon spring, 63–4, 72, 90, 217, 463
Gilboa, Mt., 42, 61, 65
Gilead, 43, 57, 145, 188, 224, 309
Gilgal, 38, 53, 57, 89, 137, 156, 222, 226, 230
Gilgamesh, 165, 369
Goethe, Johann Wolfgang von, 271
Goliath, 55
Gomer, 229–31, 235–6
Goodspeed, Edgar J., 12
Goshen, 142
Gottwald, Norman K., 245 (n. 20)
Graf, Karl H., 115–16
Greece, Greeks, 391, 425, 430, 441–3, 446–8, 451, 458–62, 464–5, 474
Gunkel, Hermann, 118–20, 369

Michael, 446, 477
Michal, 54, 61–2, 64, 83, 107
Michelangelo, 2, 4
Midas, 250
Midian, Midianites, 126, 133, 157–8, 239
Middle Assyrian Code, 104–5
Millo, The, 74–5
Milton, John, 1, 34
Miriam, 40, 368
Mitanni, 140
Mizpah, 54, 89, 141, 175–6, 317
Moab, Moabites, 1, 16, 20, 36, 38, 47, 50, 57,
    65, 69, 75, 91, 106, 134, 145, 166, 178, 180,
    184, 188, 193, 213, 222, 228, 238, 243, 251–2,
    255, 313, 330, 337, 348, 363, 368, 371, 433–5,
    445
Moffatt, James, 8–9, 12
"Molten Sea," the, 86–7
Monotheism, 155, 158–60, 289, 355, 409
Mordecai, 153, 449
Moriah, Mt., 154, 239
Moses, 35, 38, 47–8, 83, 96, 98–9 (n. 6),
    101–3, 105, 108, 111–15, 118, 122–4, 126,
    128, 130, 133, 136–7, 139, 143–6, 155–60,
    238–40, 262, 275–7, 280, 287–9, 293,
    335, 339, 344, 348, 366, 368–70, 375, 394
Moses (Michelangelo), 2–4
Moses, Song of, 50, 280
Mot, Canaanite god, 95, 163
Mowinckel, Sigmund, 93
MT. *See* Massoretic Bible
Musil, Alois, 37

Nabonidus, 349–50, 447–8
Nabopolassar, 192–3, 285, 345–6
Naboth, 169
Nahr Ibrahim, 152
Nahum, 293–6, 298
Naomi, 434
Naphtali (tribe), 44–5, 146
Nathan, 72, 82, 100 (n. 7), 212
Nazirites, 11–12, 131, 212, 222, 226
Nebuchadnezzar, 193, 198, 305, 313, 315–17,
    320, 322, 327 (n. 17)–333, 337, 345–6, 358,
    392, 445, 447–9
Neco II, Pharaoh, 192–3, 285–6, 299, 306, 311,
    313, 315, 346
Negeb, 21, 61, 112, 132–3, 142–3, 254, 313
Nehemiah, 371–5, 377–8, 380–7, 390, 393–4,
    400, 433, 435, 441, 447
Newton, Rev. John, 357
Nile River, 20, 164, 239, 264, 272, 313, 328,
    332
Nineveh, 190–91, 257, 271, 273, 294–6, 298,
    433
Noah, 10, 35, 367, 397, 399, 447
Nob, 69, 88
Numerology, 444–5

Obadiah, 362–3, 376
Obed-Edom, 84, 88
Ode to a Nightingale (Keats), 1
"Odysseus' Scar" (Auerbach), 4
Odyssey (Homer), 4
Omri, Omrides, 16–17, 170–71, 178–86, 205,
    212
Ophir, 77
Oral tradition, 32–4, 96, 119, 131, 168, 220
Ormazd (Ahura-Mazda), 443
Orontes River, 51, 193, 286, 460

Paradise Lost (Milton), 2
Parallelism in Hebrew poetry, 40–42, 50
    (n. 17), 51
Passover, 135, 147, 151, 155, 279, 291–3, 301,
    339, 369, 379, 394 (n. 35)
Pekah, 229, 232–3, 245–6, 248
Pentateuch, 103, 111–12, 114–21, 130, 132, 140,
    367, 391–2
Peoples of the Sea. *See* Philistines
Persia, Persians, 6, 206, 331, 342, 349, 371,
    374–7, 379–88, 390–92, 444, 446–9, 453
Pfeiffer, Robert H., 8, 118
Pharisees, 453, 467, 478
Philistia, 28, 69, 91, 189, 227, 242, 250, 331,
    441
Philistines, 41, 82, 87, 109, 120, 131, 135,
    224–5, 232–3, 240, 245, 281, 283, 338,
    alliance with David, 55, 61, 63, 71; capture
    of Ark, 91, 268; conflict with David, 45, 47,
    60, 65, 71; invasion of Canaan, 39, 43, 46,
    57, 114, 142, 228, 265; rebellion against
    Assyria, 250–51; war with Saul, 55, 57, 65;
    and Yahweh, 7, 50, 261
Philo, 120
Phoenicia, Phoenicians, 28, 67, 71, and
    Solomon, 72–5, 77–8; 173, 180, 182, 201,
    207, 211–13, 225, 227, 243, 256, 333, 338,
    351, 441, 447, 460
Pompey, 467, 469
"Preacher, The." *See* Ecclesiastes, *Koheleth*
Priestly Code, 400
Priestly writer, the ("P"), 116–18, 121–30,
    155–6, 158, 239–41, 289 (n. 18), 348, 357,
    367–71, 398–9
Pritchard, James B., 104
Prophecy, modern, 57–8, 213
Prophetic party, 64, 69, 79, 169
Prophets, 81–2, 92, 169–70, 174, 211–15,
    219–69, guild, 223, 263; 270–74, 287, 290,
    296, 304–23, 326–8, 332–9, 352–5, 359–67,
    391, 409, 441, 471
Proverbs, 41, 410–12
Psalms, 15, 41, 51, 92–5, 215–18, 268–9,
    297–302, 321, 350, 356–8, 391, 400–403,
    422, 435–9, 450–51, 456–7
Psammetichus I, Pharaoh, 191–2, 273
Psammetichus II, Pharaoh, 315

Song of Songs, 430–33, 435, 473 (n. 35)
Steinbeck, John, 2
Succoth (town), 77, 125, 186–7
Succoth. See Booths, Feast of
Sukenik, E. L., 453
Susanna, 452, 474
Synagogue, 293, 346–7, 357, 391
Syria, Syrians (ancient), 7, 15, 65, 69, 71, 73,
    78, 87, 91, 95, 112, 140–41, 170, 178–9,
    182–3, 185–6, 191, 193, 211, 213, 228, 233,
    239, 243, 248, 285–6, 311, 313, 322, 333, 335,
    337, 346, 350, 372, 376, 441, 452, 460
Syria, Syrians (modern), 15, 92, 430

Taanach, 18, 27, 176
Talmud, 33
Tammuz, 337, 344
Tappuah, 232, 234
Targumim, 12, 456
Tarshish, 78, 188 (n. 24)
Taunt songs, 36, 242, 253
Tekoa, 223
Tel Aviv, 29
Tell el Far'ah, 178, 180–81
Tell Elful, 59
Tells, 16–19
Temple of Jerusalem, 50, 55, 72, 74–5, 79, 81,
    83–7, 89, 91, 95, 115, 171–2, 176, 191–2, 203,
    206, 208–10, 217–18, 262, 268, 275–6, 278–9,
    283–4, 289, 291–3, 297–302, 304, 311, 317,
    323, 327–30, 336–7, 356–7, 359–62, 365,
    372–3, 376, 378–9, 383, 436, 441, 461–4,
    469, 474
Ten Commandments. *See* Decalogue
Teraphim, 84
Third Isaiah. *See* Isaiah of the Restoration
Thomas of Celano, 270
Tiamat, Akkadian deity, 164, 352
Tiglath-pileser III, 189–90, 207, 210, 225,
    229–30, 232–4, 245, 247–8, 251, 311
Tigris-Euphrates Valley, 193, 228, 255, 293,
    337
Tigris River, 20, 164, 239
Tirzah, 27, 175–6, 178–83, 205, 232
Tobiah the Ammonite, 373, 384–6, 394
Tobit, 452, 474
Torah, 11, 13–14, 102–3, 105, 290–91, 380,
    401, 435, 470, 475
Torrey, C. C., 343
Transjordan, 17, 19, 23, 141, 233, 248, 465
Trever, John C., 453
Trito-Isaiah. *See* Isaiah of the Restoration
Tyre, 26, 28, 74–5, 77–8, 85, 182, 184, 193,
    212, 228, 243, 327, 331, 333–4, 346, 441,
    458 (n. 29)

Ugarit, 15, 21, 92, 163. *See also* Ras Shamra
Ugaritic texts, 15, 92–5, 163, 334, 447
United Hebrew Monarchy, 6, 34, 38, 46,
    beginnings, 53–61; Davidic rule, 64–71; laws,

96–110; religion, 79–95; under Solomon, 72–9
Ur, 104, 132, 346
Uriah, 82, 100 (n. 7), 212
Urim and Thummim (oracles), 13, 87
Ur-Nammu Code, 104–5
Uzziah, 223–4, 244, 259

Vulgate Bible, 3–4, 12, 456

Wadi Far'ah, 24, 26–7, 178, 187
Warren, Robert Penn, 2
Wars of the Jews (Josephus), 458
Wars of Yahweh, Book of, 33
Wellhausen, Julius, 116–21
Wen-Amon, 211
Winckler, Hugo, 104
Wisdom writing, 404–10, 426, 435, 439,
    453
Witter, Pastor, 115, 117

Xerxes (Ahasuerus), 448–9

Yadin, Yigael, 454
Yahweh, Yahwism, 39, 44, 46–7, 54, 154,
    229–30, 237–8, 243–4, 259–60, 271–6, 306,
    364, 366, 392–3, 396, 401, 403, 410, 415–16,
    418, 421–4, 429–31, 433, 435–6, 438, 443,
    450–51, 471–4, Ark, 37, 55, 81–4, 86–92, 106,
    133–4, 157, 268, 277, 290, 328; Canaanite
    parallels, 51, 161–3; ceremonies of worship,
    79–92, 274, 292–3; consecration of Israelite
    chiefs, 70, 131, 217–18; cult, 220, 270, 299;
    end of Yahwism as state religion, 303;
    Hebrew images of, 48–52, 91–2, 96, 158–60,
    210–11, 220, 228, 235–6, 260–62, 264–9, 294,
    296–8, 301–2, 319–22, 335–6, 338–40, 343,
    345, 351–5, 398–9, 469; judgments on Israel,
    222, 225–8, 230, 245, 255, 319, 402; as leader
    of Hebrews, 131–3, 135, 139, 144, 151, 168,
    172, 222, 224, 230–31, 234, 252, 276, 282,
    284, 286–91, 295; name, 112, 115–29; and
    patriotism, 82, 92–3, 171–2, 275; in
    post-United Monarchy Palestine, 208–13,
    215–18, 220, 222, 224
Yahwist writer ("J"), 92, 116–30, 153, 156,
    158, 228, 239–41, 282, 286, 289 (n. 18), 367–9
Yamm, Canaanite god, 95, 163–4

Zadok, 54, 70, 90, 283
Zadokite priests, 328, 339, 388, 391
Zarathustra, 444
Zealots, 477
Zebulun (tribe), 44, 145–6
Zechariah, 232–3 (n. 11), 361–2, 364, 366, 374,
    379, 391, 396, 441, 471
Zedekiah, 193, 198, 214, 306–7, 309, 313,
    315–16, 322, 328, 345